AQA Science
Biology

Teacher's Book

GCSE

Geoff Carr

Ruth Miller

Bev Cox

Niva Miles

Editor

Lawrie Ryan

Nelson Thornes

Published in 2011 by:
Nelson Thornes Ltd
Delta Place
27 Bath Road
CHELTENHAM
GL53 7TH
United Kingdom

13 14 15 16 / 10 9 8 7 6 5 4

A catalogue record for this book is available from the British Library

ISBN 978 1 4085 0827 5

Cover photograph: Bloom Works Inc./Alamy

Page make-up by Tech-Set Ltd, Gateshead

Printed in China by 1010 Printing International Ltd

GCSE Biology — Contents

Welcome to AQA Biology!

AQA GCSE Science is written and reviewed by experienced teachers. This book is structured around the Student Book and offers guidance, advice, support for differentiation and lots of practical teaching ideas to give you what you need to teach the AQA specifications.

Learning objectives

These tell you what your students should know by the end of the lessons and relate to the learning objectives in the corresponding Student Book topic, although extra detail is provided for teachers.

Learning outcomes

These tell you what your students should be able to do to demonstrate that they have achieved against the learning objectives. These are differentiated where appropriate to provide suitable expectations for all your students. Higher Tier outcomes are labelled.

Specification link-up: Biology B1.1

These open every spread so you can see the AQA specification references covered in your lessons, at a glance.

Lesson structure

This provides you with guidance and ideas for tackling topics in your lessons. There are short and long starter and plenary activities so you can decide how you structure your lesson. Explicit **support** and **extension** guidance is given for some starters and plenaries.

Support

These help you to give extra support to students who need it during the main part of your lesson.

Extend

These provide ideas for how to extend the learning for students aiming for higher grades.

Further teaching suggestions

These provide you with ideas for how you might extend the lesson or offer alternative activities. These may also include extra activities or suggestions for homework.

Summary answers

All answers to questions within the Student Book are found in the Teacher's Book.

Practical support

For every practical in the Student Book you will find this corresponding feature, which gives you a list of the equipment you will need to provide, safety references and additional teaching notes. There are also additional practicals given that are not found in the Student Book.

The following features are found in the Student Book, but you may find additional guidance to support them in the Teacher's Book:

 Did you know ...?

 How Science Works

 Maths skills

Activity

How Science Works

There is a chapter dedicated to 'How Science Works' in the Student Book as well as embedded throughout topics and end of chapter questions. The teacher notes within this book give you detailed guidance on how to integrate 'How Science Works' into your teaching.

End of chapter pages

And at the end of each chapter you will find Summary answers and Practice answers. You will also find:

Kerboodle resources

Kerboodle is our online service that holds all of the electronic resources for the series. All of the resources that support the chapter that are provided on Kerboodle are listed in these boxes.

Where you see **k** in the Student Book, you will know that there is an electronic resource on Kerboodle to support that aspect.

Just log on to www.kerboodle.com to find out more.

Practical suggestions

These list the suggested practicals that you need to be aware of. Support for these practicals can be found on Kerboodle, or are covered within the practical support section of the Teacher Book. The **k** indicates that there is a practical in Kerboodle. The ⚙ indicates that there is a 'How Science Works' worksheet in Kerboodle. The 📖 indicates that the practical is covered in this Teacher's Book.

Study tip

These give advice on what students need to remember and highlight common errors.

H1

How does science work?

Learning objectives

Students should learn:

- that observations are often the starting point for an investigation
- that a hypothesis is a proposal intended to explain certain facts or observations
- that a prediction is an intelligent guess, based on some knowledge
- that an experiment is a way of testing your prediction
- that a conclusion is when you decide whether or not your prediction was correct.

Learning outcomes

Students should be able to:

- make first-hand observations
- distinguish between a hypothesis and a prediction
- explain the purpose of an experiment
- show how results can help to decide whether a prediction was correct.

Specification link-up: How Science Works

'How Science Works' is treated here as a separate chapter. It offers the opportunity to teach the 'thinking behind the doing' as a discrete set of procedural skills. However, it is of course an integral part of the way students will learn about science, and those skills should be nurtured throughout the course.

It is anticipated that sections of this chapter will be taught as the opportunity presents itself during the teaching programme. The chapter should also be referred back to at appropriate times when these skills are required and in preparation for the Controlled Assessment ISAs.

The thinking behind the doing

Science attempts to explain the world in which we live. It provides technologies that have had a great impact on our society and the environment. Scientists try to explain phenomena and solve problems using evidence. The data to be used as evidence must be repeatable, reproducible and valid, as only then can appropriate conclusions be made.

A scientifically literate citizen should, amongst other things, be equipped to question, and engage in debate on, the evidence used in decision-making.

The repeatability and the reproducibility of evidence refers to how much we trust the data. The validity of evidence depends on these as well as whether the research answers the question. If the data is not repeatable or reproducible the research cannot be valid.

To ensure repeatability, reproducibility and validity in evidence, scientists consider a range of ideas which relate to:

- how we observe the world
- designing investigations so that patterns and relationships between variables may be identified
- making measurements by selecting and using instruments effectively
- presenting and representing data
- identifying patterns, relationships and making suitable conclusions.

These ideas inform decisions and are central to science education. They constitute the 'thinking behind the doing' that is a necessary complement to the subject content of biology, chemistry and physics.

Lesson structure

Starters

Key words – Create a quiz looking at the meaning of key words used in this lesson: knowledge, observation, prediction and experiment. Support students by making this activity into a card sort. Extend students by asking them to put the key words into a context, i.e. the television remote control idea. *(5 minutes)*

Good science – Collect newspaper articles and news items from the television to illustrate good and poor uses of science. There are some excellent television programmes illustrating good and poor science. *(10 minutes)*

Main

- Students should begin to appreciate the 'thinking behind the doing' developed during KS3. It would be useful to illustrate this by a simple demonstration (e.g. *Elodea* bubbling oxygen) and posing questions that build into a flow diagram of the steps involved in a whole investigation. This could lead into recap questions to ascertain each individual student's progress. Emphasis should be placed on an understanding of the following terms: hypothesis, independent, dependent and control variables, and reproducibility.

- It is expected that students will be familiar with:
  - the need to work safely
  - making a prediction
  - controls
  - the need for repetition of some results
  - tabulating and analysing results
  - making appropriate conclusions
  - suggesting how they might improve methods.

Support

- When carrying out the 'Coconut seeds' activity, students could be given the headings in the form of a flow chart, with an 'either/or' option at each stage.

Extend

- Students could be allowed to use the internet to find out more about how coconut seeds are dispersed along the coast and between islands in the tropics.

- Revealing to the students that they use scientific thinking to solve problems during their everyday life can make their work in science more relevant. Use everyday situations to illustrate this and discuss in groups or as a class.

  For example: 'How can I clear the car windscreen when it "mists" up in the winter? It only seems to happen when we get into the car [observation]. The windscreen is probably cold, and I know we breathe out moist air [knowledge].'

  'I can use observations and knowledge to make a prediction that switching on the hot air fan next to the windscreen will clear the "mist". I can test my prediction and see what the results are. I can check again the next day to see whether I get the same results [repeatability].'

- Students should now be asked to complete the 'Coconut seeds' activity.

Summary answers

1 knowledge, observation, prediction, experiment, conclusion

Plenaries

Misconceptions – Produce a list of statements about practical work (similar to the ones listed below), some of which are true and others false. Support students by getting them to simply write 'true' or 'false' by each statement. Extend students by asking them to write down why the false statements are untrue. *(5 minutes)*

Poor science – Using the internet, organise a competition for who can bring in the poorest example of science used to sell products – shampoo adverts are very good examples! *(10 minutes)*

How Science Works

H1 How does science work? (k)

Learning objectives
- What is meant by 'How Science Works'?
- What is a hypothesis?
- What is a prediction and why should you make one?
- How can you investigate a problem scientifically?

This first chapter looks at 'How Science Works'. It is an important part of your GCSE because the ideas introduced here will crop up throughout your course. You will be expected to collect scientific **evidence** and to understand how we use evidence. These concepts will be assessed as the major part of your internal school assessment.

You will take one or more 45-minute tests. These tests are based on data you have collected previously plus data supplied for you in the test. They are called Investigative Skills Assignments (ISA). The ideas in 'How Science Works' will also be assessed in your examinations.

How science works for us

Science works for us all day, every day. You do not need to know how a mobile phone works to enjoy sending text messages. But, think about how you started to use your mobile phone or your television remote control. Did you work through pages of instructions? Probably not!

You knew that pressing the buttons would change something on the screen (**knowledge**). You played around with the buttons, to see what would happen (**observation**). You had a guess based on your knowledge and observations at what you thought might be happening (**prediction**) and then tested your idea (**experiment**).

Perhaps 'How Science Works' should really be called 'How Scientists Work'.

Science moves forward by slow, steady steps. When a genius such as Einstein comes along, it takes a giant leap. Those small steps build on knowledge and experience that we already have.

The steps don't always lead in a straight line, starting with an observation and ending with a conclusion. More often than not you find yourself going round in circles, but each time you go around the loop you gain more knowledge and so can make better predictions.

⊙⊙ **links**
You can find out more about your ISA by looking at H10 The ISA at the end of this chapter.

Each small step is important in its own right. It builds on the body of knowledge that we have, but observation is usually the starting point. In 1796, Edward Jenner observed that people who worked with cows did not catch smallpox but did catch a very similar disease called cowpox. This observation led him to develop a system of inoculating people with cowpox to prevent them from catching smallpox. Jenner called this process vaccination, from the Latin word for cow, *vacca*.

Figure 1 Albert Einstein was a genius, but he worked through scientific problems in the same way as you will in your GCSE

Activity

Coconut seeds

Once you have got the idea of holidays out of your mind, look at the photograph in Figure 2 with your scientific brain.

Work in groups to *observe* the beach and the plants growing on it. Then you can start to think about why the plants can grow (*knowledge*) so close to the beach.

One idea could be that the seeds can float for a long while in the sea, without taking in any water.

You can use the following headings to discuss your investigation. One person should be writing your ideas down, so that you can discuss them with the rest of your class.

- What prediction can you make about the mass of the coconut seed and the time it spends in the sea water?
- How could you test your prediction?
- What would you have to control?
- Write a plan for your investigation.
- How could you make sure your results were repeatable?

Figure 2 Tropical beach

Summary questions

1 Copy and complete this paragraph using the following words:
   experiment   knowledge   conclusion   prediction   observation
   You have learned before that a cup of tea loses energy if it is left standing. This is a piece of .... You make an .... that dark-coloured cups will cool faster. So you make a .... that if you have a black cup, this will cool fastest of all. You carry out an .... to get some results, and from these you make a ....

?? Did you know ... ?

The Greeks were arguably the first true scientists. They challenged traditional myths about life. They put forward ideas that they knew would be challenged. They were keen to argue the point and come to a reasoned conclusion.

Other cultures relied on long-established myths and argument was seen as heresy.

Key points

- Observations are often the starting point for an investigation.
- A hypothesis is a proposal intended to explain certain facts or observations.
- A prediction is an intelligent guess, based on some knowledge.
- An experiment is a way of testing your prediction.

2

3

Further teaching suggestions

Common misconceptions

Some common misconceptions that can be dealt with here and throughout the course are:
- the purpose of controls – some students believe that it is about making accurate measurements of the independent variable.
- the purpose of preliminary work – some believe that it is the first set of results.

Some students also think that:
- the table of results is constructed after the practical work – students should be encouraged to produce the table before carrying out their work and to complete it during their work
- anomalies are identified after the analysis – they should preferably be identified during the practical work or at the latest before any calculation of a mean
- they should automatically extrapolate the graph to its origin
- lines of best fit must be straight lines
- you repeat readings to make sure your investigation is a fair test.

H2

Fundamental ideas about how science works

Learning objectives

Students should learn:

- to distinguish between opinion based on scientific evidence and non-scientific ideas
- the importance of continuous and categoric variables
- what is meant by valid evidence
- the difference between repeatability and reproducibility
- to look for links between the independent and dependent variables.

Learning outcomes

Students should be able to:

- identify when an opinion does not have the support of valid and reproducible science
- recognise measurements as continuous, or categoric
- suggest how an investigation might demonstrate its validity
- distinguish between repeatability and reproducibility
- state whether variables are linked, and if so, in what way.

Support

- When looking at the 'cress grown under different light conditions' practical, a list of possible variables could be made from which to select the most appropriate type of variable. This could be done as a card sort or as a table.

Extend

- Discussion could range into the ethics of drug provision and the increased importance of having scientifically based opinions. It might develop into an appreciation of the limits of science in terms of ethical delivery of drugs. Decisions of this nature are not always as clear cut as scientists might want them to be. Some experts estimated the number of accidental deaths in the UK caused by prescribed medical drugs at 20 000 per year.

Specification link-up: Controlled Assessment B4.3

Demonstrate an understanding of the need to acquire high quality data, by:

- appreciating that, unless certain variables are controlled, the results may not be valid [B4.3.2 a)]
- identifying when repeats are needed in order to improve reproducibility. [B4.3.2 b)]

Lesson structure

Starters

Crazy science – Show a video clip of one of the science shows that are aimed at entertainment rather than education or an advert that proclaims a scientific opinion. This should lead into a discussion of how important it is to form opinions based on sound scientific evidence. *(5 minutes)*

Types of variable – Produce a list of observable or measurable variables, e.g. colour, temperature, time, type of material. Ask students to sort them into two types: these can then be revealed as being either categoric or continuous. Support students by giving them a full definition of categoric and continuous variables. Extend students by asking them to add other examples of their own to the lists. *(10 minutes)*

Main

- Discuss some examples of adverts that make 'scientific' claims about products.
- From a light-hearted look at entertainment science, bring the thalidomide example into contrast and discuss how tragic situations can be created by forming opinions that are not supported by valid science. Search for video clips about thalidomide at www.britishpathe.com.
- Show some cress seedlings grown in different light levels. Review some of the terminology highlighted as key words in the Student Book. Discuss, in small groups, the different ways in which the independent and dependent variables could be measured, identifying these in terms of continuous and categoric measurements.
- Discuss the usefulness in terms of forming opinions of each of the proposed measurements.
- Consider that this might be a commercial proposition and the students might be advising an investor in a company growing cress.
- Discuss how they could organise the investigation to demonstrate its validity and repeatability and reproducibility to a potential investor.
- Discuss what sort of relationship there might be between the variables.

Plenaries

Evidence for opinions – Bring together the main features of scientific evidence that would allow sound scientific opinions to be formed from an investigation. *(5 minutes)*

Analyse conclusions – Use an example of a poorly structured investigation and allow the students to critically analyse any conclusions drawn, e.g. data from an investigation into different forms of insulation, using calorimeters and cooling curves. Support students by telling them the mistakes that had been made in the design and ask them to say why this would make the conclusion invalid. Extend students by allowing them to first identify the mistakes in the design. *(10 minutes)*

Practical support

Cress grown under different light conditions

Equipment and materials required

Petri dishes growing cress to show differences in height and colour. There should be enough for small group work.

Details

Students should look at the differences between cress grown under different light conditions and highlight the variables. They should examine the different ways in which the independent and dependent variables could be measured, identifying these in terms of continuous and categoric measurements.

How Science Works

H2 Fundamental ideas about how science works

Learning objectives

- How do you spot when an opinion is not based on good science?
- What is the importance of continuous and categoric variables?
- What does it mean to say that evidence is valid?
- What is the difference between a result being repeatable and a result being reproducible?
- How can two sets of data be linked?

Study tip

Read a newspaper article or watch the news on TV. Ask yourself whether any research presented is valid. Ask yourself whether you can trust that person's opinion and why.

Science is too important for us to get it wrong

Sometimes it is easy to spot when people try to use science poorly. Sometimes it can be funny. You might have seen adverts claiming to give your hair 'body' or sprays that give your feet 'lift'!

On the other hand, poor scientific practice can cost lives.

Some years ago a company sold the drug thalidomide to people as a sleeping pill. Research was carried out on animals to see if it was safe. The research did not include work on pregnant animals. The **opinion** of the people in charge was that the animal research showed the drug could be used safely with humans.

Then the drug was also found to help ease morning sickness in pregnant women. Unfortunately, doctors prescribed it to many women, resulting in thousands of babies being born with deformed limbs. It was far from safe.

These are very difficult decisions to make. You need to be absolutely certain of what the science is telling you.

a Why was the opinion of the people in charge of developing thalidomide based on poor science?

Deciding on what to measure: variables

Variables are physical, chemical or biological quantities or characteristics.

In an investigation, you normally choose one thing to change or vary. This is called the **independent variable**.

When you change the independent variable, it may cause something else to change. This is called the **dependent variable**.

A **control variable** is one that is kept the same and is not changed during the investigation.

You need to know about two different types of these variables:

- A **categoric variable** is one that is best described by a label (usually a word). The 'colour of eyes' is a categoric variable, e.g. blue or brown eyes.
- A **continuous variable** is one that we measure, so its value could be any number. Temperature (as measured by a thermometer or temperature sensor) is a continuous variable, e.g. 37.6 °C, 45.2 °C. Continuous variables can have values (called quantities) that can be found by making measurements (e.g. light intensity, flow rate, etc.).

b Imagine you were growing seedlings in different volumes of water. Would it be better to say that some were tall and some were short, or some were taller than others, or to measure the heights of all the seedlings?

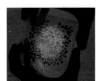

Figure 1 Cress seedlings growing in a Petri dish

Making your evidence repeatable, reproducible and valid

When you are designing an investigation you must make sure that other people can get the same results as you. This makes the evidence you collect **reproducible**.

A measurement is **repeatable** if the original experimenter repeats the investigation using the same method and equipment and obtains the same results.

A measurement is reproducible if the investigation is repeated by another person, or by using different equipment or techniques, and the same results are obtained.

You must also make sure you are measuring the actual thing you want to measure. If you don't, your data can't be used to answer your original question. This seems very obvious but it is not always quite so easy. You need to make sure that you have controlled as many other variables as you can, so that no one can say that your investigation is not **valid**. A measurement is valid if it measures what it is supposed to measure with an appropriate level of performance.

c State one way in which you can show that your results are repeatable.

How might an independent variable be linked to a dependent variable?

Looking for a link between your independent and dependent variables is very important. The pattern of your graph or bar chart can often help you to see if there is a link.

But beware! There may not be a link! If your results seem to show that there is no link, don't be afraid to say so. Look at Figure 2.

The points on the top graph show a clear pattern, but the bottom graph shows random scatter.

Study tip

When designing your investigation you should always try to measure continuous data whenever you can. This is not always possible, so then you have to use a label (categoric variable). You might still be able to put the variables in an order so that you can spot a pattern. For example, you could describe flow rate as 'fast flowing', 'steady flow' or 'slow flowing'.

Figure 2 Which graph shows that there might be a link between x and y?

?? Did you know ... ?

Aristotle, a brilliant Greek scientist, once proclaimed that men had more teeth than women! Do you think that his data collection was reproducible?

Key points

- Be on the lookout for non-scientific opinions.
- Continuous data give more information than other types of data.
- Check that evidence is reproducible and valid.

Summary questions

1 Copy and complete this paragraph using the following words:
continuous   independent   categoric   dependent
Stefan wanted to find out which was the strongest supermarket plastic carrier bag. He tested five different bags by adding weight to them until they broke. The type of bag he used was the .... variable and the weight that it took to break it was the .... variable. The 'type of bag' is called a .... variable and the 'weight needed to break' it was a .... variable.

2 A researcher claimed that the metal tungsten 'alters the growth of leukaemia cells' in laboratory tests. A newspaper wrote that they would 'wait until other scientists had reviewed the research before giving their opinion'. Why is this a good idea?

Answers to in-text questions

a The original animal investigation did not include pregnant animals and was not carried out on human tissue. Therefore, it was not valid when the opinion was formed that it could be given to pregnant women.

b Measure the heights of all the seedlings. Continuous measurements (variables) are more powerful.

c If the experiment can be repeated to obtain the same results.

Summary answers

1 independent, dependent, categoric, continuous

2 The investigation can be shown to be reproducible if other scientists can repeat their investigations and get the same findings. Because it is reproducible, opinions formed from it are more useful.

H3

Starting an investigation

Learning objectives

Students should learn:

- how scientific knowledge can be used to observe the world around them
- how good observations can be used to make hypotheses
- how hypotheses can generate predictions that can be tested.

Learning outcomes

Students should be able to:

- state that observation can be the starting point for an investigation
- state that observation can generate hypotheses
- describe how hypotheses can generate predictions and investigations.

Support

- Assist students in the fieldwork activity by getting them to record the density of the grass at different distances from a footpath or from the goal line on a football pitch.

Extend

- Extend students by getting them to formulate a hypothesis, e.g. the further from the footpath/goal line, the greater the density of the grass.

Specification link-up: Controlled Assessment B4.2 & B4.3

Develop hypotheses and plan practical ways to test them, by:

- being able to develop a hypothesis *[B4.1.1 a)]*
- being able to test hypotheses. *[B4.1.1 b)]*

Make observations, by:

- carrying out practical work and research, and using the data collected to develop hypotheses. *[B4.3.1]*

Lesson structure

Starters

Demo observation – Begin the lesson with a demonstration – as simple as lighting a match or more involved such as a bell ringing in a bell jar, with air gradually being withdrawn. Students should be asked, in silence, and without further prompting, to write down their observations. These should be collated and questions should be derived from those observations. *(5 minutes)*

Linking observation to knowledge – Discuss with students any unusual events they saw on the way to school. If possible, take them into the school grounds to look and listen to events. Try to link their observations to their scientific knowledge. They are more likely to notice events that they can offer some scientific explanation for. Support students by prompting with some directed questions. Extend students by getting them to start to ask questions about those observations. *(10 minutes)*

Main

- If in the laboratory, allow students to participate in a 'scientific happening' of your choice, e.g. trying to ignite different foods. Preferably use something that they have not met before, but which they will have some knowledge of. As an alternative, if possible take students onto the school field, where there will be many opportunities to observe plants (ideally the school pond), and questions should be asked around where certain plants/animals are to be found and their adaptations.

- If students need some help at this point, they should read through the section on 'observations' in the Student Book. Then answer in-text questions **a** and **b**.

- In groups, they should discuss possible explanations for one agreed observation. Encourage a degree of lateral thinking. You might need to pose the questions for some groups, e.g., why do some foods ignite easily and others do not? or why does grass grow when it is cut, but other plants are killed? Ask the group to select which of their explanations is the most likely, based on their own knowledge of science.

- Work these explanations into a hypothesis.

- Individually, each student should try in-text question **c**. Gather in ideas and hypotheses.

- Students, working in groups, can now turn this into a prediction.

- They could suggest ways in which their prediction could be tested. Identify independent, dependent and control variables and the need to make sure that they are measuring what they intend to measure.

- Go over in-text question **d** as a class. For a touch of humour towards the end, you might get students to think about which variable you might be measuring.

Plenaries

Poster – Ask students to design, but not make, a poster that links 'Observation + knowledge → hypothesis → prediction → investigation.' *(5 minutes)*

Discussion on evolution – The story of evolution could be used at many points in this chapter but is particularly useful here. Briefly, evolution is of course closely related to the work of Charles Darwin (1809–82). It was not a term that he used while gathering observations from around the world. The term 'evolution' had been used long before Darwin. Lamarck (1744–1829) used the term 'progression' in the way in which we would use evolution. His example of giraffes stretching their necks to reach the more succulent shoots and thus passing on these characteristics is very familiar. He also explained progression by an upward striving of organisms to higher levels of complexity. Darwin's grandfather, Erasmus, used the term 'evolution'. Malthus laid the foundation for the theory of evolution by natural selection by his observations and mathematical calculations that the supply of food could never keep up with the demand for food, and so some organisms prospered while others struggled. This theory, linked to Darwin's observations, led to The theory of evolution by natural selection (1859). Those members of a species with an innate advantage would survive to pass on those characteristics, whilst others would perish. A. R. Wallace had also thought of the idea independently. Also independently, the Moravian monk Mendel proposed units of inheritance, which he called 'factors' (1865). In 1869, Miescher, a Swiss scientist, observed what he called nuclein, because he found the substance inside the nucleus of cells from the pus in bandages! Chromosomes were first observed in 1888 and by the turn of the century were thought to be involved in inheritance. Morgan, in the early years of the century, experimented with fruit flies. He zapped them with radiation, put them in centrifuges, and heated them up and cooled them down, trying to induce mutations. By the 1940s it was widely agreed that genes existed on chromosomes. By 1953, the structure of DNA was revealed. Now we know most of the structure of the DNA of humans and other organisms. Support students by listing the important points on a 'timeline' for them. Extend students by discussing whether evolution is a fact or a theory. It is possible to view it as a theory which is well established or as a fact that can be explained by theories. *(10 minutes)*

How Science Works

H3 — Starting an investigation

Learning objectives

- How can you use your scientific knowledge to observe the world around you?
- How can you use your observations to make a hypothesis?
- How can you make predictions and start to design an investigation?

Figure 1 Plant showing positive phototropism

?? Did you know ... ?

Some biologists think that we still have about one hundred millions species of insects to discover – plenty to go for then! Of course, observing one is the easy part – knowing that it is undiscovered is the difficult bit!

Observation

As humans we are sensitive to the world around us. We can use our many senses to detect what is happening. As scientists we use observations to ask questions. We can only ask useful questions if we know something about the observed event. We will not have all of the answers, but we know enough to start asking relevant questions.

If we observe that the weather has been hot today, we would not ask whether it was due to global warming. If the weather was hotter than normal for several years, we could ask that question. We know that global warming takes many years to show its effect.

When you are designing an investigation you have to observe carefully which variables are likely to have an effect.

> **a** Would it be reasonable to ask whether the plant in Figure 1 is 'growing towards the glass'? Explain your answer.

A farmer noticed that her corn was much smaller at the edge of the field than in the middle (observation). She noticed that the trees were quite large on that side of the field. She came up with the following ideas that might explain why this is happening:

- The trees at the edge of the field were blocking out the light.
- The trees were taking too many nutrients out of the soil.
- The leaves from the tree had covered the young corn plants in the spring.
- The trees had taken too much water out of the soil.
- The seeds at the edge of the field were genetically small plants.
- The drill had planted fewer seeds on that side of the field.
- The fertiliser spray had not reached the side of the field.
- The wind had been too strong over winter and had moved the roots of the plants.
- The plants at the edge of the field had a disease.

> **b** Discuss each of these ideas and use your knowledge of science to decide which four are the most likely to have caused the poor growth of the corn.

Observations, backed up by really creative thinking and good scientific knowledge, can lead to a hypothesis.

Testing scientific ideas

Scientists always try to think of ways to explain how things work or why they behave in the way that they do.

After their observations, they use their understanding of science to come up with an idea that could explain what is going on. This idea is sometimes called a hypothesis. They use this idea to make a prediction. A prediction is like a guess, but it is not just a wild guess – it is based on previous understanding.

A scientist will say, 'If it works the way I think it does, I should be able to change **this** (the independent variable) and **that** will happen (the dependent variable).'

Predictions are what make science so powerful. They mean that we can work out rules that tell us what will happen in the future. For example, electricians can predict how much current will flow through a wire when an electric cooker is connected. Knowing this, they can choose the right thickness of cable to use.

Knowledge of energy transfer could lead to an idea that the insides of chips cook by energy being conducted from the outside. You might predict that small, thinly sliced chips will cook faster than large, fat chips.

> **c** Look at the photograph of a frog in Figure 2. Note down anything you find interesting. Use your knowledge and some creative thought to suggest a hypothesis based on your observations.

Not all predictions are correct. If scientists find that the prediction doesn't work, it's back to the drawing board! They either amend their original idea or think of a completely new one.

Figure 2 A frog

Starting to design a valid investigation

observation **+** knowledge ⟹ hypothesis ⟹ prediction ⟹ investigation

We can test a prediction by carrying out an **investigation**. You, as the scientist, predict that there is a relationship between two variables.

The independent variable is one that is selected and changed by you, the investigator. The dependent variable is measured for each change in your independent variable. Then all other variables become control variables, kept constant so that your investigation is a fair test.

If your measurements are going to be accepted by other people, they must be valid. Part of this is making sure that you are really measuring the effect of changing your chosen variable. For example, if other variables aren't controlled properly, they might be affecting the data collected.

> **d** Look at Figure 3. When investigating his heart rate before and after exercise, Darren got his girlfriend to measure his pulse. Would Darren's investigation be valid? Explain your answer.

Figure 3 Measuring a pulse

Summary questions

1 Copy and complete this paragraph using the following words:
controlled   dependent   independent   knowledge   prediction   hypothesis
An observation linked with scientific .... can be used to make a .... A .... links an .... variable to a .... variable. All other variables need to be ....

2 What is the difference between a prediction and a guess?

3 Imagine you were testing how an enzyme affects the rate of reaction. The reaction might cause the solution to get hot.
 a How could you monitor the temperature?
 b What other control variables can you think of that might affect the results?

Key points

- Observation is often the starting point for an investigation.
- Testing predictions can lead to new scientific understanding.
- You must design investigations that produce valid results if you are to be believed.

6 — 7

Answers to in-text questions

a No, because we know that the glass is unlikely to be sensed by the plant, but light is.

b The trees at the edge of the field were blocking out the light.
 The trees were taking too many nutrients out of the soil.
 The trees had taken too much water out of the soil.
 The fertiliser spray had not reached the side of the field.

c E.g. observation: the frog is green and so is the leaf.
 Hypothesis: the frog moves around until its skin is roughly the same colour as its surroundings.

d No, because his heart rate might increase because his hand is being held by his girlfriend and not just because of exercise. The results are not valid.

Summary answers

1 knowledge, hypothesis, prediction, independent, dependent, controlled

2 A prediction is based on knowledge or observation, a guess is not.

3 **a** By using a thermometer or temperature sensor to check the temperature during the reaction.

 b Examples include the volume of the solutions, the degree of mixing or stirring, or the type of container.

H4

Planning an investigation

Learning objectives

Students should learn:

- how to design a fair test
- how to set up a survey
- how to set up a control group or control experiment
- how to reduce risks in hazardous situations.

Learning outcomes

Students should be able to:

- identify variables that need to be controlled in an investigation
- design a survey
- design a fair test and understand the use of control variables and control groups
- identify potential hazards and take action to minimise risk.

Specification link-up: Controlled Assessment B4.2 & B4.3

Assess and manage risks when carrying out practical work, by:

- identifying some possible hazards in practical situations *[B4.2.1 b)]*
- suggesting ways of managing risks. *[B4.2.1 b)]*

Demonstrate an understanding of the need to acquire high quality data, by:

- appreciating that, unless certain variables are controlled, the results may not be valid. *[B4.3.2 a)]*

Lesson structure

Starters

Risk assessment – Give students a picture sheet illustrating a situation showing a number of hazards. Ask the students to spot the hazard and write down what could be done to minimise the risk. The situation illustrated could be one in the school laboratory, or it could be outside the school environment, e.g. in the road, in a factory or on a farm. *(5 minutes)*

Head start – Start, for example, with a video clip of a 100 m race. (Search for 'marathon' or 'race' at www.video.google.com or www.bbc.co.uk). This has to be a fair test. How is this achieved? Then show the mass start of the London marathon and ask if this is a fair test. Support students by asking why there is no official world record for a marathon. (Instead they have world best times.) This could lead to a discussion of how difficult it is to control all of the variables in the field. Extend students by going on to discuss why athletes can break the 100 m world record and this may not be recognised because of a helping wind. *(10 minutes)*

Main

- Move into group discussion of in-text question **a**.
- Start group discussions on how and why we need to produce survey data. Use a topical issue here. It might be appropriate to see how it should *not* be done by using a vox pop clip from a news programme.
- Students will be familiar with the idea of a placebo, but possibly not with how it is used to set up a control group. This might need explanation.
- Consider the case of whether it is possible to tell the difference in taste if the milk is put in before or after the tea. R. A. Fisher tested this using a double-blind taste test, and went on to devise 'Statistical Methods for Research Workers'.
- Use the school or college laboratory rules to review safety procedures.
- Ask students to carry out a risk assessment on the 'burning food' experiment.

Plenaries

Prize giving! – Award a prize to the group achieving (a) the most accurate result; (b) the most precise results. Let the groups try to explain their success. *(5 minutes)*

Survey – Ask students to imagine they have been asked to conduct a survey to find out whether or not people prefer a particular brand of toothpaste. They should produce a questionnaire that lists the questions that you could ask people on the street. Support students by supplying them with a list of questions, some of which would be relevant, others irrelevant. Ask students to tick which questions would be the most appropriate. Extend students by asking them to suggest how many people should be chosen and on what basis they should be selected. *(10 minutes)*

Support

- Show students the 'burning food' experiment and ask them to write down as many hazards that they can think of. If necessary, give them a list of about ten different hazards, some of which are relevant and some not, and ask them to tick the ones that they think apply here.

Extend

- Show students a complex experiment. Ask them to list as many other variables as possible that should be controlled.

Practical support

Risk assessment on burning food

Equipment and materials required

Boiling tube, boiling tube holder and stand, measuring cylinder, water, thermometer, mounted needle, safety equipment, eye protection.

Details

Students could burn a crisp held on the end of a mounted needle to heat a small quantity of water in a boiling tube and measure the temperature rise.

Before doing so, they should identify any possible hazards and then write down ways in which they could minimise any risk. After carrying out the experiment, they should discuss whether or not their plans for risk reduction were sufficient.

Safety: Take care with food allergies – do not use peanuts.

Note: Teachers should check the CLEAPSS Laboratory Handbook on the CLEAPSS website or CD for more ideas and further safety information. Put 'peanuts' into the search box.

How Science Works

H4 Planning an investigation

Learning objectives

- How do you design a fair test?
- How do you set up a survey?
- How do you set up a control group or control experiment?
- How do you reduce risks in hazardous situations?

Study tip

If you are asked about why it is important to keep control variables constant, you need to give a detailed explanation. Don't just answer, 'To make it a fair test.'

When you are asked to write a plan for your investigation, make sure that you give all the details. Ask yourself, 'Would someone else be able to follow my written plan and use it to do the investigation?'

Fair testing

A fair test is one in which only the independent variable affects the dependent variable. All other variables (called control variables) should be kept the same. If the test is not fair, the results of your investigation will not be valid.

Sometimes it is very difficult to keep control variables the same. However, at least you can monitor them, so that you know whether they have changed or not.

Figure 1 Corn being examined

a Imagine you were testing how close together you could plant corn to get the most cobs. You would plant five different plots, with different numbers of plants in each plot. List some of the variables that you could not control.

Surveys

Not all scientific investigations involve deliberately changing the independent variable.

Imagine you were investigating the effect of diet on diabetes. You might conduct a survey. You would have to choose people of the same age and same family history to test. The larger the sample size you test, the better your results will be.

Control group

Control groups are used in investigations to try to make sure that you are measuring the variable that you intend to measure. When investigating the effects of a new drug, the control group will be given a **placebo**. This is a 'pretend' drug that actually has no effect on the patient at all. The control group think they are taking a drug but the placebo does not contain the drug. This way you can control the variable of 'thinking that the drug is working' and separate out the effect of the actual drug.

Usually neither the patient nor the doctor knows until after the trials have been completed which of the patients were given the placebo. This is known as a **double-blind trial**.

Risks and hazards

One of the first things you must do is to think about any potential hazards and then assess the risk.

Everything you do in life presents a hazard. What you have to do is to identify the hazard and then decide the degree of risk that it gives. If the risk is very high, you must do something to reduce it.

For example, if you decide to go out in the pouring rain, lightning is a possible hazard. However, you decide that the risk is so small that you will ignore it and go out anyway.

If you decide to cross a busy road, the cars travelling along it at high speed represent a hazard. You decide to reduce the risk by crossing at a pedestrian crossing.

Figure 2 The hazard is the busy road. We reduce the risk by using a pedestrian crossing.

Activity

Burning foods

Imagine you were testing crisps to see how much energy they give out when burned.

- What are the **hazards** that are present?
- What could you do to reduce the **risk** from these hazards?

Study tip

Before you start your practical work you must make sure that it is safe. What are the likely hazards? How could you reduce the risk caused by these hazards? This is known as a **risk assessment**. You may well be asked questions like this on your ISA paper.

Key points

- Care must be taken to ensure fair testing – as far as is possible.
- Control variables must be kept the same during an investigation.
- Surveys are often used when it is impossible to carry out an experiment in which the independent variable is changed.
- Control groups allow you to make a comparison.
- A risk assessment must be made when planning a practical investigation.

Summary questions

1 Copy and complete this paragraph using the following words:
investigation hazards assessment risks

Before you carry out any practical ...., you need to carry out a risk .... You can do this by looking for any potential .... and making sure that the .... are as small as possible.

2 Explain the difference between a control group and a control variable.

3 Briefly describe how you would go about setting up a fair test in a laboratory investigation. Give your answer as general advice.

Further teaching suggestions

Which?

Look at some recent *Which?* reports on consumer goods. Discuss issues such as:

- Was the size of the sample surveyed sufficient?
- Could the people who were surveyed have been biased?
- Could the people conducting the survey have been biased?

Answers to in-text questions

a Any variables associated with the weather, the soil, the genetic variability of the seeds, and human error in planting.

Summary answers

1 investigation, assessment, hazards, risks

2 In an experiment to determine the effect of changing a single variable, a **control** is often set up in which the independent variable is not changed, thus enabling a comparison to be made. If the investigation is of the survey type (q.v.), a control group is usually established to serve the same purpose.

3 Control all the variables that might affect the dependent variable, apart from the independent variable whose values you select.

H5

Designing an investigation

Learning objectives

Students should learn:

- how to choose the best values for the variables
- how to decide on a suitable range
- how to decide on a suitable interval
- how to ensure accuracy and precision.

Learning outcomes

Students should be able to:

- use trial runs to establish the best values for the variables
- use trial runs to establish a suitable range for the independent variable
- use trial runs to establish a suitable interval for the independent variable
- design a fair test that will yield valid and repeatable results.

Support

- In the 'holly leaf' experiment (see Starter activity), students may find it easier if they are given a series of drawings of holly leaves with different numbers of prickles.

Extend

- The 'holly leaf' experiment can be extended to a discussion about the wide variation of results that occur when dealing with living material.

Specification link-up: Controlled Assessment B4.1 & B4.3

Develop hypotheses and plan practical ways to test them, by:

- using appropriate technology *[B4.1.1 c)]*

Demonstrate an understanding of the need to acquire high quality data, by:

- appreciating that, unless certain variables are controlled, the results may not be valid *[B4.3.2 a)]*
- identifying when repeats are needed in order to improve reproducibility *[B4.3.2 b)]*
- recognising the value of further readings to establish repeatability and accuracy *[B4.3.2 c)]*
- considering the resolution of the measuring device *[B4.3.2 d)]*
- considering the precision of the measured data where precision is indicated by the degree of scatter from the mean *[B4.3.2 e)]*
- identifying the range of the measured data. *[B4.3.2 f)]*

Lesson structure

Starters

Interval – Give students a graph of enzyme activity that shows a peak, but where the interval on the *x*-axis is very large, so that it is difficult to judge the exact position of the peak. Ask students to suggest what other values should be tested in order to ascertain the peak more accurately. *(5 minutes)*

Preliminary work – Give students two samples of holly leaves: one from low down on the tree (lots of prickles) and one from much higher up the tree (much smoother leaves). Tell them that the main experiment would be to collect data to show how the number of prickles changes with the height up the tree. Support students by giving them a number of leaves from different heights and ask them to arrange them in order of height. Extend students by asking them to suggest a suitable interval for the heights up the tree to be tested. *(10 minutes)*

Main

- Discuss the results of the preliminary work on holly leaves.
- Carry out the main investigation on holly leaves. Allow students to compare the results of different groups. Compile a table of pooled results and discuss the possible reasons for any differences.
- Discuss the benefits of repeating results.
- It is important that students appreciate the difference between accuracy and precision. Get students to plot their results on a large class graph, and then draw a line of best fit. Discuss the amount of scatter, and how far away the points are from the best-fit line (this is an indication of the **precision** of the individual measurements). Then discuss how far away from the 'true value' (the teacher's result?) the graph is. Accurate readings will be taken by those who use their equipment most carefully.

Plenaries

Prize giving! – Award a prize to the group achieving (a) the most accurate result; (b) the most precise results. Let the groups try to explain their success. *(5 minutes)*

Out of range – Ask students to predict from the class graph what the number of prickles might be at a height that was not tested. Support students by asking them why the pattern shown by the graph would not extend indefinitely. Extend students by asking them to discuss why precision is not usually very great in biological investigations such as this. *(10 minutes)*

Further teaching suggestions

Repeatability

- Using the data from the experiment, consider the range of their repeat measurements and judge repeatability. Find the maximum range for the whole class – who got the highest reading and who got the lowest? Can we explain why?

Graphs and charts

- The 'holly leaf' experiment can be expanded – discuss whether the results should be plotted on a line graph or a bar chart.

How Science Works

H5 — Designing an investigation

Learning objectives

- How do you make sure that you choose the best values for your variables?
- How do you decide on a suitable range?
- How do you decide on a suitable interval?
- How do you ensure accuracy and precision?

Choosing values of a variable

Trial runs will tell you a lot about how your early thoughts are going to work out.

Do you have the correct conditions?

A photosynthesis investigation that produces tiny amounts of oxygen might not have enough light, pondweed or carbon dioxide. Alternatively, the temperature might not be high enough.

Have you chosen a sensible range?

Range means the maximum and minimum values of the independent or dependent variables. It is important to choose a suitable range for the independent variable, otherwise you may not be able to see any change in the dependent variable.

For example, if the results are all very similar, you might not have chosen a wide enough range of light intensities.

Have you got enough readings that are close together?

The gap between the readings is known as the interval.

For example, you might alter the light intensity by moving a lamp to different distances from the pondweed. A set of 11 readings equally spaced over a distance of 1 metre would give an interval of 10 centimetres.

If the results are very different from each other, you might not see a pattern if you have large gaps between readings over the important part of the range.

Accuracy

Accurate measurements are very close to the **true value**.

Your investigation should provide data that is accurate enough to answer your original question.

However, it is not always possible to know what that the true value is.

How do you get accurate data?

- You can repeat your measurements and your mean is more likely to be accurate.
- Try repeating your measurements with a different instrument and see whether you get the same readings.
- Use high-quality instruments that measure accurately.
- The more carefully you use the measuring instruments, the more accuracy you will get.

Precision, resolution, repeatability and reproducibility

A **precise** measurement is one in which there is very little spread about the mean value.

If your repeated measurements are closely grouped together, you have precision. Your measurements must be made with an instrument that has a suitable **resolution**. Resolution of a measuring instrument is the smallest change in the quantity being measured (input) that gives a perceptible change in the reading.

It's no use measuring the time for a fast reaction to finish using the seconds hand on a clock! If there are big differences within sets of repeat readings, you will not be able to make a valid conclusion. You won't be able to trust your data!

How do you get precise data?

- You have to use measuring instruments with sufficiently small scale divisions.
- You have to repeat your tests as often as necessary.
- You have to repeat your tests in exactly the same way each time.

If you repeat your investigation using the same method and equipment and obtain the same results, your results are said to be **repeatable**.

If someone else repeats your investigation in the same way, or if you repeat it by using different equipment or techniques, and the same results are obtained, it is said to be **reproducible**.

You may be asked to compare your results with those of others in your group, or with data from other scientists. Research like this is a good way of checking your results.

A word of caution!

Precision depends only on the extent of random errors – it gives no indication of how close results are to the true value. Just because your results show precision does not mean they are accurate.

a Draw a thermometer scale reading 49.5 °C, showing four results that are both accurate and precise.

Summary questions

1 Copy and complete this paragraph using the following words:

   range   repeat   conditions   readings

   Trial runs give you a good idea of whether you have the correct .... to collect any data; whether you have chosen the correct .... for the independent variable, whether you have enough ...., and whether you need to do .... readings.

2 Use an example to explain how a set of repeat measurements could be accurate, but not precise.

3 Explain the difference between a set of results that are reproducible and a set of results that are repeatable.

Study tip

You must know the difference between accurate and precise results.

Imagine measuring the temperature after a set time when a fuel is used to heat a fixed volume of water. Two students repeated this experiment, four times each. Their results are marked on the thermometer scales below:

- A precise set of repeat readings will be grouped closely together.
- An accurate set of repeat readings will have a mean (average) close to the true value.

Precise
(but not accurate)

Accurate
(but not precise)

Key points

- You can use a trial run to make sure that you choose the best values for your variables.
- The range states the maximum and minimum values of a variable.
- The interval is the gap between the values of a variable.
- Careful use of the correct equipment can improve accuracy and precision.
- You should try to reproduce your results carefully.

Answers to in-text questions

a Diagram of thermometer showing the true value with four readings tightly-grouped around 49.5 °C.

Summary answers

1 conditions, range, readings, repeat

2 Any example that demonstrates understanding of the two terms, e.g. 'I measured the pH of the distilled water as 7.5, 6.8, 7.2, 5.5 and 8.2. The average of my results is 7.0. I know that the pH of pure water should be 7.0. My results were accurate but not precise.'

3 **Repeatable:** a measurement is repeatable if the original experimenter repeats the investigation using the same method and equipment and obtains the same results.

   Reproducible: a measurement is reproducible if the investigation is repeated by another person, or by using different equipment or techniques, and the same results are obtained.

H6

Making measurements

Learning objectives

Students should learn:

- that they can expect results to vary
- that instruments vary in their accuracy
- that instruments vary in their resolution
- the difference between systematic errors and random errors
- that human error can affect results, and what to do with anomalies.

Learning outcomes

Students should be able to:

- distinguish between results that vary and anomalies
- explain that instruments vary in their accuracy and resolution
- explain that anomalies should be discarded or repeated before calculating a mean.

Support

- Students will need support when interpreting data and identifying evidence for systematic and random errors. For systematic errors, they should look to see whether the measured values are always larger or smaller than the calculated values. For random errors, they should look to see whether there is any scatter around the mean.

Extend

- Demonstrate a different experiment in which there is a built-in systematic error, e.g. measuring the effect of temperature on the rate of an exothermic reaction.

Specification link-up: Controlled Assessment B4.5

Review methodology to assess fitness for purpose, by:

- identifying causes of variation in data *[B4.5.2 a)]*
- recognising and identifying the cause of random errors. When a data set contains random errors, repeating the readings and calculating a new mean can reduce their effect *[B4.5.2 b)]*
- recognising and identifying the cause of anomalous results *[B4.5.2 c)]*
- recognising and identifying the cause of systematic errors. *[B4.5.2 d)]*

Lesson structure

Starters

Demonstration – Demonstrate different ways of measuring the width of the laboratory. Use a 30 cm rule, a metre rule, a tape and a laser/sonic measure. Discuss the relative merits of using each of these devices for different purposes. Discuss the details of the measuring instrument – its percentage accuracy, its useful range and its resolution. *(5 minutes)*

Human reaction time – Allow students to test their reaction times using a computer program (e.g. www.bbc.co.uk. Search for 'Sheep Dash'.) and then by dropping and catching a ruler, using a stopwatch. Discuss the advantages and disadvantages of each method. Support students by explaining that the human reaction time is normally about 0.2 s. Extend students on the 'dropping the ruler' method by getting them to explain whether it would be better for the same person to drop the ruler and operate the watch, or whether it would be better to use two different people. *(10 minutes)*

Main

- In small groups, plan the most accurate way to measure a person's height. Students can have any equipment they need. They will need to think about what a person's height includes, e.g. hair flat or not, shoes on or off. They might suggest a board placed horizontally on the head, using a spirit level, removing the person being measured and then using the laser/sonic measure placed on the ground.

- Stress that we do not have a true answer. We do not know the person's true height. We trust the instrument and the technique that is most likely to give us the most accurate result – the one nearest the true value.

- Demonstrate an experiment in which there is a built-in systematic error, e.g. weighing some chemicals using a filter paper without using the tare, or measuring radioactivity without taking background radiation into account.

- Point out the difference between this type of systematic error and random errors. Also, how you might tell from results which type of error it is. You can still have a high degree of precision with systematic errors.

- Complete in-text questions **a** and **b** individually.

- Encourage students to identify anomalies whilst carrying out the investigation, so that they have an opportunity to check and replace them.

Plenaries

Human v. computer – Class discussion of data logging compared to humans when collecting data. Stress the importance of data logging in gathering data over extended or very short periods of time. *(5 minutes)*

Checklist – Ask students to draw up a checklist for an investigation so that every possible source of error is considered. Support students by giving them a list of possible sources of error that includes a mixture of relevant and irrelevant suggestions. Ask them to tick the ones that they think are relevant. Extend students by asking them to suggest what they could do to minimise the effect of any errors. *(10 minutes)*

Further teaching suggestions

Data logging

- Data logging provides a good opportunity to exemplify changes in dependent variables.

  Use data logging to illustrate how detailed measurements taken frequently can show variation in results that would not have been seen by other methods.

  Data logging can increase the accuracy of readings that can be taken where it might not otherwise be possible to take readings accurately.

For example:

- Compare two students taking their hand temperatures – one with a thermometer, one with a logger.
- Set the logger to record room temperatures until the next lesson.
- Compare measurements using a tape measure with those of a distance sensor linked to a computer. Draw attention to the ability to measure distances as you move the sensor.

How Science Works

H6 Making measurements

Learning objectives

- Why do results always vary?
- How do you choose instruments that will give you accurate results?
- What do we mean by the resolution of an instrument?
- What is the difference between a systematic error and a random error?
- How does human error affect results and what do you do with anomalies?

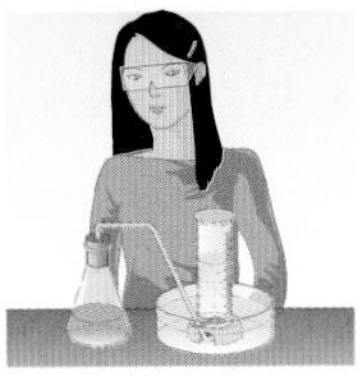

Figure 1 Student testing the rate at which oxygen is produced using an enzyme

Using instruments

Try measuring the temperature of a beaker of water using a digital thermometer. Do you always get the same result? Probably not! So can we say that any measurement is absolutely correct?

In any experiment there will be doubts about actual measurements.

a Look at Figure 1. Suppose, like this student, you tested the rate at which oxygen was produced using an enzyme. It is unlikely that you would get two readings exactly the same. Discuss all the possible reasons why.

When you choose an instrument you need to know that it will give you the accuracy that you want. You need to be confident that it is giving a true reading.

If you have used an electric water bath, would you trust the temperature on the dial? How do you know it is the true temperature? You could use a very expensive thermometer to calibrate your water bath. The expensive thermometer is more likely to show the true temperature. But can you really be sure it is accurate?

You also need to be able to use an instrument properly.

b In Figure 1 the student is reading the amount of gas in the measuring cylinder. Why is the student unlikely to get a true measurement?

Instruments that measure the same thing can have different sensitivities. The **resolution** of an instrument refers to the smallest change in a value that can be detected. This is one factor that determines the precision of your measurements.

Choosing the wrong scale can cause you to miss important data or make silly conclusions. We would not measure the weight of a prescription drug in kilograms, we would use milligrams.

c Match the following scales to their best use:

Used to measure	Resolution of scale
Size of a cell	millimetres
Human height	metres
Length of a running race to test fitness	micrometres
Growth of seedlings	centimetres

Errors

Even when an instrument is used correctly, the results can still show differences.

Results may differ because of **random error**. This is most likely to be due to a poor measurement being made. It could be due to not carrying out the method consistently.

If you repeat your measurements several times and then calculate a mean, you will reduce the effect of random errors.

12

Making measurements

The **error** might be a **systematic error**. This means that the method was carried out consistently but an error was being repeated. A systematic error will make your readings be spread about some value other than the true value. This is because your results will differ from the true value by a consistent amount each time a measurement is made.

No number of repeats can do anything about systematic errors. If you think that you have a systematic error, you need to repeat using a different set of equipment or a different technique. Then compare your results and spot the difference!

A **zero error** is one kind of systematic error. Suppose that you were trying to measure the length of your desk with a metre rule, but you hadn't noticed that someone had sawn off half a centimetre from the end of the ruler. It wouldn't matter how many times you repeated the measurement, you would never get any nearer to the true value.

Look at the table. It shows the two sets of data that were taken from the investigation that Sara did. She tested five different volumes of enzyme.

Sara's investigation into the volumes of enzymes

Amount of enzyme used (cm^3)	1	2	3	4	5
Oxygen produced (cm^3)	3.2	8.9	9.5	12.7	75.9
Volume of oxygen expected (cm^3)	3.1	6.4	9.7	12.5	76.1
Calculated oxygen production (cm^3)	4.2	8.4	12.5	16.6	20.7

d Discuss whether there is any evidence of random error in these results.
e Discuss whether there is any evidence of systematic error in these results.

Anomalies

Anomalous results are clearly out of line. They are not those that are due to the natural variation you get from any measurement. These should be looked at carefully. There might be a very interesting reason why they are so different. You should always look for anomalous results and discard them before you calculate a mean, if necessary.

- If anomalies can be identified while you are doing an investigation, it is best to repeat that part of the investigation.
- If you find anomalies after you have finished collecting data for an investigation, they must be discarded.

Summary questions

1 Copy and complete this paragraph using the following words:

accurate discarded random resolution systematic use variation

There will always be some .... in results. You should always choose the best instruments that you can in order to get the most .... results. You must know how to .... the instrument properly. The .... of an instrument refers to the smallest change that can be detected. There are two types of error – .... and .... Anomalies due to random error should be ....

2 What kind of error will most likely occur in the following situations?
  a Asking everyone in the class to measure the length of the bench.
  b Using a ruler that has a piece missing from the zero end.

Study tip

If you are asked what may have caused an error, never answer simply '**human error**' – you won't get any marks for this.

You need to say what the experimenter may have done to cause the error, or give more detail, e.g. 'Human reaction time might have caused an error in the timing when using a stopwatch.'

Did you know ... ?

Sir Alexander Fleming had grown bacteria on agar plates. He noticed an anomaly. There was some mould growing on one of the plates and around it there were no bacteria. He decided to investigate further and grew more of the mould. Only because Fleming checked out his anomaly did it lead to the discovery of penicillin.

Key points

- Results will nearly always vary.
- Better quality instruments give more accurate results.
- The resolution of an instrument refers to the smallest change that it can detect.
- Human error can produce random and/or systematic errors.
- We examine anomalies; they might give us some interesting ideas. If they are due to a random error, we repeat the measurements. If there is no time to repeat them, we discard them.

13

Answers to in-text questions

a Variability of living materials, conditions (e.g. light availability, temperature) may change.

b Random error.

c

Used to measure	Resolution of scale
Size of a cell	micrometres
Human height	centimetres
Length of a running race to test fitness	metres
Growth of seedlings	millimetres

d Difficult to tell as no repeats done. Value for 5 cm^3 may be due to a random error, but may just be an anomaly.

e There is no evidence of a systematic error, although this does not mean that there is not one.

Summary answers

1 variation, accurate, use, resolution, random, systematic, discarded

2 **a** Random.
b Systematic.

H7

Presenting data

Learning objectives

Students should learn:

- what is meant by the range and the mean of a set of data
- how to use tables of data
- how to display data.

Learning outcomes

Students should be able to:

- express accurately the range and mean of a set of data
- distinguish between the uses of bar charts and line graphs
- draw line graphs accurately.

Specification link-up: Controlled Assessment B4.4

Show an understanding of the value of means, by:

- appreciating when it is appropriate to calculate a mean *[B4.4.1 a)]*
- calculating the mean of a set of at least three results. *[B4.4.1 b)]*

Demonstrate an understanding of how data may be displayed, by:

- drawing tables *[B4.4.2 a)]*
- drawing charts and graphs *[B4.4.2 b)]*
- choosing the most appropriate form of presentation. *[B4.4.2 c)]*

Lesson structure

Starters

Newspapers – Choose data from the press – particularly useful are market trends where they do not use the origin (0,0). This exaggerates changes. This could relate to the use of data logging, which can exaggerate normal variation into major trends. *(5 minutes)*

Spreadsheet – Prepare some data from a typical investigation that the students may have recently completed. Use all of the many ways of presenting the data in a spreadsheet program to display it. Allow students to discuss and reach conclusions as to which is the best method. Support students by presenting data as either a line graph or a simple bar chart, so that they can make the link between continuous data and line graphs and between categoric data and bar charts. Extend students by showing graphs and charts that have non-linear scales or false origins. *(10 minutes)*

Main

- Choose an appropriate topic to either demonstrate or allow small groups to gather data, e.g. cooling of water against time; using food labels to determine saturated fat content of different foods; force applied and degree of bending in rules; investigate the period of a pendulum. Choose any topic that will allow rapid gathering of data. Be aware that some data will lead to a bar chart; this might be more appropriate to groups struggling to draw line graphs.

- Students should be told what their task is and should therefore know how to construct an appropriate table. This should be done individually prior to collecting the data. Refer to the first paragraph under 'Tables' in the Student Book.

- Start a group discussion on the best form of table.

- Carry out data gathering, putting data directly into the table. Refer to the second paragraph under 'Tables' in the Student Book.

- Individuals produce their own graphs. Refer to the section 'Displaying your results' in the Student Book.

- Graphs could be exchanged and marked by others in the group, using the criteria in the section mentioned above.

Plenaries

Which type of graph? – Give students different headings from a variety of tables and ask them how best to show the results graphically. This could be done as a whole class, with individuals showing answers as the teacher reveals each table heading. Each student can draw a large letter 'L' (for line graph) on one side of a sheet of paper and 'B' (for bar chart) on the other, ready to show their answers. *(5 minutes)*

Key words – Students should be given key words to prepare posters for the laboratory. Key words should be taken from the summary questions in the first six sections. Support students by giving them a poster in two sections – one containing the key word, the other the definition. Students should then match the pairs together correctly. Extend students by getting them to write their own definitions. *(10 minutes)*

Support

- Some students struggle with plotting graphs. They should start with bar charts and move on to line graphs.

Extend

- Students could be asked to handle two dependent variables in the table and graph, e.g. cooling and weight loss of a beaker of water with time, with repeat readings included.

- They could also be given more difficult contexts that are more likely to produce anomalies. They could, for example, be given a context that produces both random and systematic errors.

Further teaching suggestions

ICT link-up

● Students could use a set of data within spreadsheet software to present the data as pie charts, line graphs, bar charts, etc. Allow them to decide on the most appropriate form. Care needs to be given to 'smoothing', which does not always produce a line of best fit.

How Science Works

H7 Presenting data

Learning objectives

● How do you calculate the mean from a set of data?

● How do you use tables of results?

● What is the range of the data?

● How do you display your data?

Figure 1 Petri dish with discs showing growth inhibition of bacteria

For this section you will be working with data from this investigation:

Mel spread some bacteria onto a dish containing nutrient jelly. She also placed some discs onto the jelly. The discs contained different concentrations of an antibiotic. The dish was sealed and then left for a couple of days.

Then she measured the diameter of the clear part around each disc. The clear part is where the bacteria have not been able to grow. The bacteria grew all over the rest of the dish.

Tables

Tables are really good for getting your results down quickly and clearly. You should design your table **before** you start your investigation.

Your table should be constructed to fit in all the data to be collected. It should be fully labelled, including units.

You may want to have extra columns for repeats, calculations of means or calculated values.

Checking for anomalies

While filling in your table of results you should be constantly looking for anomalies.

● Check to see whether any reading in a set of repeat readings is significantly different from the others.

● Check to see whether the pattern you are getting as you change the independent variable is what you expected.

Remember, a result that looks anomalous should be checked out to see if it really is a poor reading.

Planning your table

Mel had decided on the values for her independent variable. We always put these in the first column of a table. The dependent variable goes in the second column. Mel will find its values as she carries out the investigation.

So she could plan a table like this:

Concentration of antibiotic (μg/ml)	Size of clear zone (mm)
4	
8	
16	
32	
64	

Or like this:

Concentration of antibiotic (μg/ml)	4	8	16	32	64
Size of clear zone (mm)					

All she had to do in the investigation was to write the correct numbers in the second column to complete the top table.

Mel's results are shown in the alternative format in the table below:

Concentration of antibiotic (μg/ml)	4	8	16	32	64
Size of clear zone (mm)	4	16	22	26	28

The range of the data

Pick out the maximum and the minimum values and you have the range of a variable. You should always quote these two numbers when asked for a range. For example, the range of the dependent variable is between 4 mm (the lowest value) and 28 mm (the highest value) – and don't forget to include the units!

a What is the range for the independent variable and for the dependent variable in Mel's set of data?

Maths skills

The mean of the data

Often you have to find the mean of each repeated set of measurements. The first thing you should do is to look for any anomalous results. If you find any, miss these out of the calculation. Then add together the remaining measurements and divide by how many there are.

For example:

● Mel takes four readings, 15 mm, 18 mm, 29 mm, 15 mm

● 29 mm is an anomalous result and so is missed out. So 15 + 18 + 15 = 48

● 48 divided by three (the number of valid results) = **16 mm**

The repeat values and mean can be recorded as shown below:

Concentration of antibiotic (μg/ml)	Size of clear zone (mm)			
	First test	Second test	Third test	Mean
8	15	18	15	16

Displaying your results

Bar charts

If one of your variables is categoric, you should use a bar chart.

Line graphs

If you have a continuous independent and a continuous dependent variable, a line graph should be used. Plot the points as small 'plus' signs (+).

Summary questions

1 Copy and complete this paragraph using the following words:

categoric   continuous   mean   range

The maximum and minimum values show the .... of the data. The sum of the values in a set of repeat readings divided by the total number of these repeat values gives the .... Bar charts are used when you have a .... independent variable and a continuous dependent variable. Line graphs are used when you have .... independent and dependent variables.

2 Draw a graph of Mel's results from the top of this page.

Study tip

When you make a table for your results, remember to include:

● headings, including the units

● a title.

When you draw a line graph or bar chart, remember to:

● use a sensible scale that is easy to work out

● use as much of the graph paper as possible; your data should occupy at least a third of each axis

● label both axes

● draw a line of best fit if it is a line graph

● label each bar if it is a bar chart.

Study tip

Marks are often dropped in the ISA by candidates plotting points incorrectly. Also use a **line of best fit** where appropriate – don't just join the points 'dot-to-dot'!

Key points

● The range states the maximum and the minimum values.

● The mean is the sum of the values divided by how many values there are.

● Tables are best used during an investigation to record results.

● Bar charts are used when you have a categoric variable.

● Line graphs are used to display data that are continuous.

14 / 15

Answers to in-text questions

a Independent variable (concentration) range is 4–64 μg/ml. Dependent variable (size of clear zone) is 4–28 mm.

Summary answers

1 range, mean, categoric, continuous

2 Graph should be a line graph, concentration on the *x*-axis and size of clear zone on the *y*-axis.

H8 Using data to draw conclusions

Learning objectives

Students should learn:
- how to use charts and graphs to identify patterns
- how to identify relationships within data
- how to draw valid conclusions from relationships
- how to evaluate the repeatability of an investigation.

Learning outcomes

Students should be able to:
- draw a line of best fit when appropriate
- identify different relationships between variables from graphs
- draw conclusions from data
- evaluate the repeatability and validity of an investigation.

Support

- Provide students with a flow diagram of the procedure used to draw conclusions, so that they can see the process as they are going through it.

Extend

- Students could take the original investigation and then design out some of the flaws, producing an investigation with improved validity and repeatability.
- Summary question 2 could be examined in some detail and the work researched on the internet.

Specification link-up: Controlled Assessment B4.5 & B4.6

Identify patterns in data, by:
- Describing the relationship between two variables and deciding whether the relationship is causal or by association. [B4.5.3 a)]

Draw conclusions using scientific ideas and evidence, by:
- writing a conclusion, based on evidence that relates correctly to known facts [B4.5.4 a)]
- using secondary sources [B4.5.4 b)]
- identifying extra evidence that is required for a conclusion to be made [B4.5.4 c)]
- evaluating methods of data collection. [B4.5.4 d)]

Review hypotheses in the light of outcomes, by:
- considering whether or not any hypothesis made is supported by the evidence. [B4.6.1a)]

Lesson structure

Starters

Conclusions – Prepare a number of tables of results, some of which show that as *x* increases *y* increases, some that show that as *x* increases *y* decreases, and some where there is no relationship between *x* and *y*. Ask students what conclusion they can draw from each set of results. *(5 minutes)*

Starter graphs – Prepare a series of graphs that illustrate the various types of relationship in the specification. Each graph should have fully labelled axes. Students, in groups, should agree to statements that describe the patterns in the graphs. Support students by giving them graphs that illustrate simple linear relationships. Extend students by giving them more complex graphs with curved lines, and encourage them to use terms such as 'directly proportional' and 'inversely proportional'. Gather feedback from groups and discuss. *(10 minutes)*

Main

- Using the graphs from the previous lesson, students should be taught how to produce lines of best fit. Students could work individually with help from Figures 1 and 2 in the Student Book.
- They should identify the pattern in their graph.
- They now need to consider the repeatability and validity of their results. They may need their understanding of reliability and validity reinforced. Questions can be posed to reinforce their understanding of both terms. If the investigation was not carefully controlled, it is likely to be invalid, thus posing many opportunities for discussion. There is also an opportunity to reinforce other ideas such as random and systematic errors.
- A brief demonstration of a test, e.g. finding the energy transfer when burning crisps of different mass, could be used. Students should observe the teacher and make notes as the tests are carried out. They should be as critical as they can be, and in small groups discuss their individual findings. One or two students could be recording the results and two more plotting the graph, as the teacher does the tests. A spreadsheet could be used to immediately turn the results into graphs.
- Return to the original prediction. Look at the graph of the results. Ask how much confidence the group has in the results.
- Review the links that are possible between two sets of data. Ask them to decide which one their tests might support.
- Now the word 'conclusion' should be introduced and a conclusion made … if possible! It is sometimes useful to reach a conclusion that is 'subject to … e.g. the repeatability being demonstrated'.

Plenaries

Flow diagram – When pulling the lesson together, it will be important to emphasise the process involved – graph → line of best fit → pattern → question the repeatability and validity → consider the links that are possible → make a conclusion → summarise evaluation. This could be illustrated with a flow diagram generated by a directed class discussion. *(5 minutes)*

Evaluating – Students could review the method used in the experiment of burning crisps. Support students by asking them to identify where errors could have been made. Extend students by asking them to suggest improvements that could be made to minimise these errors. *(10 minutes)*

Further teaching suggestions

Case studies

- Students should be able to transfer these skills to examine the work of scientists and to become critical of the work of others. Collecting scientific findings from the press and subjecting them to the same critical appraisal is an important exercise. They could be encouraged to collect these or could be given photocopies of topical issues suitable for such appraisal.

How Science Works

H8 — Using data to draw conclusions

Learning objectives

- How do you best use charts and graphs to identify patterns?
- What are the possible relationships you can identify from charts and graphs?
- How do you draw conclusions from relationships?
- How can you decide whether your conclusions are valid?

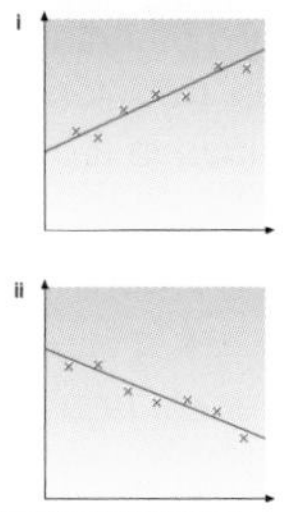

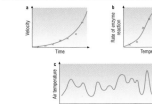

Figure 1 Graphs showing linear relationships

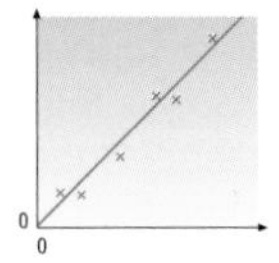

Figure 2 Graph showing a directly proportional relationship

Figure 3 a Graph showing predictable results **b** Graph showing complex results **c** Graph showing very complex results

Identifying patterns and relationships

Now that you have a bar chart or a line graph of your results you can begin to look for patterns. You must have an open mind at this point.

First, there could still be some anomalous results. You might not have picked these out earlier. How do you spot an anomaly? It must be a significant distance away from the pattern, not just within normal variation. If you do have any anomalous results plotted on your graph, circle these and ignore them when drawing the **line of best fit**.

Now look at your graph. Is there a pattern that you can see? When you have decided, draw a line of best fit that shows this pattern.

A line of best fit is a kind of visual averaging process. You should draw the line so that it leaves as many points slightly above the line as there are points below. In other words it is a line that steers a middle course through the field of points.

The vast majority of results that you get from continuous data require a line of best fit.

Remember, a line of best fit can be a straight line or it can be a curve – you have to decide from your results.

You need to consider whether your graph shows a **linear relationship**. This simply means, can you be confident about drawing a straight line of best fit on your graph? If the answer is yes – is this line positive or negative?

a Say whether graphs **i** and **ii** in Figure 1 show a positive or a negative linear relationship.

Look at the graph in Figure 2. It shows a positive linear relationship. It also goes through the origin (0,0). We call this a **directly proportional** relationship.

Your results might also show a curved line of best fit. These can be predictable, complex or very complex! Look at Figure 3 below.

Drawing conclusions

If there is a pattern to be seen (for example as one variable gets bigger the other also gets bigger), it may be that:

- changing one has caused the other to change
- the two are related, but one is not necessarily the cause of the other.

Your conclusion must go no further than the evidence that you have.

Activity

Looking at relationships

Some people think that watching too much television can cause an increase in violence.

The table shows the number of television sets in the UK for four different years, and the number of murders committed in those years.

Year	Number of televisions (millions)	Number of murders
1970	15	310
1980	25	500
1990	42	550
2000	60	750

Plot a graph to show the relationship. Do you think this proves that watching television causes violence? Explain your answer.

Poor science can often happen if a wrong decision is made here. Newspapers have said that living near electricity substations can cause cancer. All that scientists would say is that there is possibly an association.

Evaluation

You will often be asked to evaluate either the method of the investigation or the conclusion that has been reached. Ask yourself: Could the method have been improved? Is the conclusion that has been reached a valid one?

Summary questions

1 Copy and complete this paragraph using the following words:
   anomalous   complex   directly   negative   positive
   Lines of best fit can be used to identify .... results. Linear relationships can be .... or .... If a straight line goes through the origin of a graph, the relationship is .... proportional. Often a line of best fit is a curve which can be predictable or ....

2 Nasma knew about the possible link between cancer and living near to electricity substations. She found a quote from a National Grid Company survey of substations:
   Measurements of the magnetic field were taken at 0.5 metres above ground level within 1 metre of fences and revealed 1.9 microteslas. After 5 metres this dropped to the normal levels measured in any house.
   Discuss the type of experiment and the data you would expect to see to support a conclusion that it is safe to build houses over 5 metres from an electricity substation.

Study tip

When you read scientific claims, think carefully about the evidence that should be there to back up the claim.

Key points

- Drawing lines of best fit helps us to study the relationship between variables.
- The possible relationships are linear, positive and negative, directly proportional, predictable and complex curves.
- Conclusions must go no further than the data available.
- The reproducibility of data can be checked by looking at other similar work done by others, perhaps on the internet. It can also be checked by using a different method or by others checking your method.

Answers to in-text questions

a Graph **i** – positive linear.
   Graph **ii** – negative linear.

Summary answers

1 anomalous, positive, negative, directly, complex

2 Survey of substations; measure magnetic field drop; measure 'microteslas' at different distances from substation; also in houses well away from substations; repeat all readings several times; fieldwork; check accuracy of measuring instruments.

H9

Scientific evidence and society

Learning objectives

Students should learn:

- that science must be presented in a way that takes into account the reproducibility and the validity of the evidence
- that science should be presented without bias from the experimenter
- that evidence must be checked to appreciate whether there is any political influence
- that the status of the experimenter can influence the weight attached to a scientific report.

Learning outcomes

Students should be able to:

- make judgements about the reproducibility and the validity of scientific evidence
- identify when scientific evidence might have been influenced by bias or political influence
- judge scientific evidence on its merits, taking into account the weight given to it by the status of the experimenter.

Support

- Groups could prepare posters that use scientific data to present their case for or against any of the developments discussed.

Extend

- Arrange a class debate and nominate individuals to speak for or against any of the developments discussed.

Specification link-up: Controlled Assessment B4.5

Distinguish between a fact and an opinion, by:

- recognising that an opinion might be influenced by factors other than scientific fact [B4.5.1 a)]
- identifying scientific evidence that supports an opinion. [B4.5.1 b)]

Lesson structure

Starters

Ask a scientist – It is necessary at this point to make a seamless join between work that has mostly been derived from student investigations and work generated by scientists. Students must be able to use their critical skills derived in familiar contexts and apply them to second-hand data. One way to achieve this would be to bring in newspaper cuttings on a topic of current scientific interest. They should be aware that some newspaper reporters will 'cherry-pick' sections of reports to support sensational claims that will make good headlines. Students could be supported by highlighting key words in the article. To extend students, ask them to produce a 'wish-list' of questions they would like to put to the scientists who conducted the research and to the newspaper reporter. *(5 minutes)*

Researching scientific evidence – With access to the internet, students could be given a topic to research. They should use a search engine and identify the sources of information from, say, the first six webpages. They could then discuss the relative merits of these sources in terms of potential for bias. *(10 minutes)*

Main

- The following points are best made using topics that are of immediate importance to your students. The examples used are only illustrative. Some forward planning is required to ensure that there is a plentiful supply of newspaper articles, both local and national, to support the lesson. These could be displayed and/or retained in a portfolio for reference.

- Working in pairs, students should answer in-text question **a**. They should write a few sentences about the headline and what it means to them.

- Use the next section to illustrate the possibility of bias in reporting science. Again use small group discussions, followed by whole class Plenary.

- If you have access to the internet for the whole class, it is worth pursuing the issue of mobile phone masts in relation to their political significance. Pose the question: 'What would happen to the economy of this country if it was discovered that mobile phone masts were dangerous?' Would different people come together to suppress that information? Should they be allowed to suppress scientific evidence? Stress that there is no such evidence, yet people have that fear. Why do they have that fear? Should scientists have the task of reducing that fear to proper proportions? There is much to discuss. Students can work in small groups or individually.

Plenaries

Contentious issues – Make a list of contentious issues on which scientists might be able to make a contribution to the debate. Examples might include the siting of wind farms or sewage works, the building of new motorways, the introduction of new drugs, etc. *(5 minutes)*

Group report – Groups could report their findings on the research they have carried out on the internet into mobile phone masts to the class. Support students by allowing them to present their findings by posters. Extend students by asking individuals to give a one-minute talk to the rest of the class. *(10 minutes)*

Further teaching suggestions

Role play

- Students could role-play a public enquiry. They could be given roles and asked to prepare a case for homework. The data should be available to them, so that they all know the arguments before preparing their case. Possible link here with the English department. This activity could be allocated as a homework exercise.

Local visit

- Students might be able to attend a local public enquiry or even the local town council as it discusses local issues with a scientific context or considers the report of a local issue.

The limitations of science

Examples could be given of the following issues:

- We are still finding out about things and developing our scientific knowledge (e.g. the use of the hadron collider).
- There are some questions that we cannot yet answer, maybe because we do not have enough valid evidence (e.g. are mobile phones completely safe to use?).
- There are some questions that science cannot answer at all (e.g. Why was the universe created?).

How Science Works

H9 Scientific evidence and society

Learning objectives

- How can science encourage people to trust its research?
- How might bias affect people's judgement of science?
- Can politics influence judgements about science?
- Do you have to be a professor to be believed?

Now you have reached a conclusion about a piece of scientific research. So what is next? If it is pure research, your fellow scientists will want to look at it very carefully. If it affects the lives of ordinary people, society will also want to examine it closely.

You can help your cause by giving a balanced account of what you have found out. It is much the same as any argument you might have. If you make ridiculous claims, nobody will believe anything you have to say.

Be open and honest. If you only tell part of the story, someone will want to know why! Equally, if somebody is only telling you part of the truth, you cannot be confident about anything they say.

> **a** A disinfectant claims that it kills 99.9% of germs on surfaces that you come in contact with every day. What is missing? Is it important?

You must be on the lookout for people who might be biased when presenting scientific evidence. Some scientists are paid by companies to do research. When you are told that a certain product is harmless, just check out who is telling you.

> **b** Bottles of perfume spray contain this advice: 'This finished product has not been tested on animals.' Why might you mistrust this statement?

Suppose you wanted to know about how to slim. Who would you be more likely to believe? Would it be a scientist working for 'Slim Kwik', or an independent scientist? Sometimes the differences are not quite so obvious.

?? Did you know … ?

A scientist who rejected the idea of a causal link between smoking and lung cancer was later found to be being paid by a tobacco company.

Study tip

If you are asked about bias in scientific evidence, there are two types:

- the measuring instruments may have introduced a bias because they were not calibrated correctly
- the scientists themselves may have a biased opinion (e.g. if they are paid by a company to promote their product).

We also have to be very careful in reaching judgements according to who is presenting scientific evidence to us. For example, if the evidence might provoke public or political problems, it might be played down.

Equally, others might want to exaggerate the findings. They might make more of the results than the evidence suggests. Take as an example the data available on animal research. Animal liberation followers may well present the *same* evidence completely differently to pharmaceutical companies wishing to develop new drugs.

> **c** Check out some websites on smoking and lung cancer. Do a balanced review looking at tobacco manufacturers as well as anti-smoking lobbies such as ASH. You might also check out government websites.

The status of the experimenter may place more weight on evidence. Suppose a lawyer wants to convince a jury enquiry that a particular piece of scientific evidence is valid. The lawyer will choose the most eminent scientist in that field who is likely to support them. Cot deaths are a particularly difficult problem for the police. If the medical evidence suggests that the baby might have been murdered, the prosecution and the defence get the most eminent scientists to argue the validity of the evidence. Who does the jury believe?

EXPERT WITNESS IN COT DEATH COURT CASE MISLED THE JURY

A child abuse expert was struck off as a doctor today for giving seriously misleading evidence in a court case. The court case led to a woman being wrongly convicted of murdering her two children. *Full report – Page 6*

The limitations of science

Science can help us in many ways but it cannot supply all the answers. We are still finding out about things and developing our scientific knowledge. For example, the Hubble telescope has helped us to revise our ideas about the beginnings of the universe.

There are some questions that we cannot answer, maybe because we do not have enough reproducible, repeatable and valid evidence. For example, research into the causes of cancer still needs much work to be done to provide data.

There are some questions that science cannot answer at all. These tend to be questions where beliefs, opinions and ethics are important. For example, science can suggest what the universe was like when it was first formed, but cannot answer the question of why it was formed.

Summary questions

1 Copy and complete this paragraph using the following words:
status balanced bias political
Evidence from scientific investigations should be given in a ………… way. It must be checked for any ………… from the experimenter. Evidence can be given too little or too much weight if it is of ………… significance. The ………… of the experimenter is likely to influence people in their judgement of the evidence.

2 Collect some newspaper articles to show how scientific evidence is used. Discuss in groups whether these articles are honest and fair representations of the science. Consider whether they carry any bias.

3 This is the opening paragraph from a review of GM foods.
The UK government has been promoting … a review of the science of GM, led by Sir David King (the Government's Chief Scientific Adviser) working with Professor Howard Dalton (the Chief Scientific Adviser to the Secretary of State for the Environment, Food and Rural Affairs), with independent advice from the Food Standards Agency.
Discuss this paragraph and decide which parts of it make you want to believe the evidence they might give. Next, consider which parts make you mistrust any conclusions they might reach.

?? Did you know … ?

Science can often lead to the development of new materials or techniques. Sometimes these cause a problem for society where hard choices have to be made.

Scientists can give us the answers to many questions, but not to every question. Scientists have a contribution to make to a debate, but so do others such as environmentalists, economists and politicians.

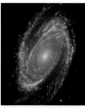

Figure 1 The Hubble space telescope can look deep into space and tell us things about the Universe's beginning from the formations of early galaxies

Key points

- Scientific evidence must be presented in a balanced way that points out clearly how valid the evidence is.
- The evidence must not contain any bias from the experimenter.
- The evidence must be checked to appreciate whether there has been any political influence.
- The status of the experimenter can influence the weight placed on the evidence.

Answers to in-text questions

a E.g. what are the 0.1% of bacteria that are not killed?; how dangerous are they?; how quickly do they reproduce?; are they more likely to reproduce in the absence of other competitor bacteria?; what are the surfaces that we come in contact with?; what evidence is there?; who did the research?

b It might not be safe for humans to use. The constituents of the perfume might have been tested on animals before being made into the final product.

c Identification of any political bias; this could be from companies and individuals as well as governments.

Summary answers

1 balanced, bias, political, status

2 Identification of any bias in the reports.

3 They should be independent. They should have the necessary skills as a scientist. They should not be capable of being influenced politically.

H10

The ISA

Learning objectives

Students should learn:
- how to write a plan
- how to make a risk assessment
- how to make a hypothesis
- how to reach a conclusion.

Learning outcomes

Students should be able to:
- structure a plan for an investigation so as to include key points such as the range and interval of the independent variable
- identify potential hazards in practical work
- show how the results of an experiment can confirm or refute a hypothesis
- reach a valid conclusion from the results of an investigation.

Specification link-up: Controlled Assessment B4.5 & B4.6

Distinguish between a fact and an opinion, by:
- recognising that an opinion might be influenced by factors other than scientific fact [B4.5.1 a)]
- identifying scientific evidence that supports an opinion. [B4.5.1 b)]

Review hypotheses in the light of outcomes, by:
- considering whether or not any hypothesis made is supported by the evidence [B4.6.1a)]
- developing scientific ideas as a result of observations and measurements. [B4.6.1b)]

Lesson structure

Starters

Structure of an investigation – Use an interactive whiteboard or sticky labels that show the different stages of an investigation and ask students to arrange them in the correct order. *(5 minutes)*

Predictions and hypotheses – Make a table containing one column of hypotheses and another column of predictions. Students should match the prediction to the correct hypothesis. *(10 minutes)*

Main

These activities may be spread over more than one lesson:
- Use a specimen ISA to guide students through the different stages that will be required.
- Start by outlining the problem that is to be investigated. Set a context for the investigation. Ask the students the best way to test it, to develop a hypothesis and discuss.
- Research one or two (depending on the investigation) possible methods that can be used to carry out an experiment to test the hypothesis. Get them to practise making brief notes, similar to the notes they will be able to make for the real ISA.
- Review any possible hazards. Discuss how any risk associated with these hazards could be reduced.
- Discuss the control variables that should be kept constant in order to make it a fair test.
- Students should decide the range and interval of the values of the independent variable, and whether or not repeats will be needed.
- Allow the students to carry out a rough trial with the equipment in order to establish suitable values for these.
- Students should now be able to write a structured plan for the investigation.
- Ask students to design a blank table ready for the results. This should contain space to record all the measurements that will be taken during the experiment. Stress the need to include proper headings and units.
- Students carry out the investigation, recording their results.
- Draw a chart or graph of the results.
- Analyse the results and discuss any conclusion that could be reached. Make sure the students refer back to the hypothesis when making their conclusion.

Plenaries

Graph or bar chart – Give students a list of titles of different investigations and ask them to decide whether the results should be plotted on a bar chart or on a line graph. *(5 minutes)*

Comparing results – Groups should report their findings to others and compare results. Support students by making a table of pooled results. Extend students by asking individuals to give a one-minute talk to the rest of the class explaining why they think their results are or are not repeatable and reproducible. *(10 minutes)*

Support

- Groups could prepare posters that show a flow diagram for the different stages of an ISA investigation.
- Students can be provided with a plan if their plan is unworkable, unsafe or unmanageable. An example plan will be provided by the AQA. Students should not lose any marks if their plan is unworkable for a good reason (i.e. lack of equipment). However, if their plan is dangerous or unworkable this must be reflected in their mark.

Extend

- Give students a hypothesis and ask them to make a prediction based on it.

Further teaching suggestions

Writing a plan
- Give students a plan of an investigation that contains a number of errors, e.g. control variables not kept constant, or unsuitable range or interval of the independent variable, and ask them to spot and explain the mistakes.

How Science Works

H10 The ISA

Learning objectives
- How do you write a plan?
- How do you make a risk assessment?
- What is a hypothesis?
- How do you arrive at a conclusion?

There are several different stages to the ISA (Investigate Skills Assignment) that you will complete for your Controlled Assessment. This will make up 25% of your GCSE marks.

Stage 1

Your teacher will tell you the problem that you are going to investigate, and you will have to develop your own hypothesis. They will also set the problem in a context – in other words, where in real life your investigation could be useful. You should have a discussion about it, and talk about different ways in which you might solve the problem. Your teacher should show you the equipment that you can use, and you should research one or two possible methods for carrying out an experiment to test the hypothesis. You should also research the context and do a risk assessment for your practical work. You will be allowed to make one side of notes on this research, which you can take into the written part of the ISA.

Figure 1 Doing practical work allows you to develop the skills needed to do well in the ISA

You should be allowed to handle the equipment and you may be allowed to carry out a preliminary experiment.

Make sure that you understand what you have to do – now is the time to ask questions if you are not sure.

Study tip

When you are making a blank table or drawing a graph or bar chart, make sure that you use full headings, e.g.
- the length of the leaf, **not** just 'length'
- the time taken for the reaction, **not** just 'time'
- the height from which the ball was dropped, **not** just 'height'
and don't forget to include any units.

How Science Works

Section 1 of the ISA

At the end of this stage, you will answer Section 1 of the ISA. You will need to:
- develop a hypothesis
- identify one or more variables that you need to control
- describe how you would carry out the main experiment
- identify possible hazards and say what you would do to reduce any risk
- make a blank table ready for your results.

a What features should you include in your written plan?
b What should you include in your blank table?

Stage 2

This is where you carry out the experiment and get some results. Don't worry too much about spending a long time getting fantastically accurate results – it is more important to get some results that you can analyse.

After you have got results, you will have to compare your results with those of others. You will also have to draw a graph or a bar chart.

c How do you decide whether you should draw a bar chart or a line graph?

Stage 3

This is where you answer Section 2 of the ISA. Section 2 of the ISA is all about your own results, so make sure that you look at your table and graph when you are answering this section. To get the best marks you will need to quote some data from your results.

How Science Works

Section 2 of the ISA

In this section you will need to:
- say what you were trying to find out
- compare your results with those of others, saying whether you think they are similar or different
- analyse data that is given in the paper. This data will be in the same topic area as your investigation
- use ideas from your own investigation to answer questions about this data
- write a conclusion
- compare your conclusion with the hypothesis you have tested.

You may need to change or even reject your hypothesis in response to your findings.

Study tip

When you are comparing your conclusion with the hypothesis, make sure that you also talk about the **extent** to which your results support the hypothesis. Which of these answers do you think would score the most marks?
- My results support the hypothesis.
- In my results, as x got bigger, y got bigger, as stated in the hypothesis.
- In my results, as x got bigger, y got bigger, as stated in the hypothesis, but unlike the hypothesis, y stopped increasing after a while.

Key points
- When you are writing the plan make sure that you include details about:
  – the range and interval of the independent variable
  – the control variables
  – the number of repeats.
- Try to put down at least two possible hazards, and say how you are going to minimise the risk from them.
- Look carefully at the hypothesis that you are given – this should give you a good clue about how to do the experiment.
- Always refer back to the hypothesis when you are writing your conclusion.

Summary questions

1 Copy and complete the paragraph using the words below:
control independent dependent
When writing a plan, you need to state the variable that you are deliberately going to change, called the .... variable. You also need to say what you expect will change because of this; this is called the .... variable. You must also say what .... variables you will keep constant in order to make it a fair test.

Answers to in-text questions

a Control variables, interval and range of the independent variable. Identify possible hazards and how to reduce any risk.

b Columns for quantities that are going to be measured, including complete headings and units.

c A bar chart if one of the variables is categoric, a line graph if both variables are continuous.

Summary answers

1 independent, dependent, control

Summary answers

1 Could be some differences which would be fine, e.g. hypothesis; prediction; design; safety; controls; method; table; results; repeat; graph; conclusion; improve.

2 a Scientific opinion is based on repeatable, reproducible and valid evidence. An opinion might not be.

b Continuous variable because it is more powerful than an ordered or a categoric variable.

3 a A hypothesis is an idea that fits an observation and the scientific knowledge that is available.

b Increasing the concentrations of sulphur dioxide reduces the growth rate of lichens.

c A prediction can be tested.

d The hypothesis could be supported or refuted or it might cause you to change your hypothesis.

e The theory on which you based the hypothesis might have to be changed.

4 a When all variables but the one being used as the independent are kept constant.

b Important variables are constantly changing, e.g. weather.

c You would set up the investigation so that all of the changing variables affected the plants in the same way.

d You could run trials to see: if you have the correct conditions; if you have the correct range; if you have the correct interval readings; if you need to repeat your readings.

5 E.g. were the readings taken at the exact times stated? Could the bubbles be accurately counted? Were the bubbles all the same size? Were the correct concentrations measured accurately? Was the time given to allow the yeast to start respiring rapidly?

6 a Take the highest and the lowest.

b the sum of all the readings divided by the number of readings

c when you have an ordered or categoric independent variable and a continuous dependent variable

d when you have a continuous independent variable and a continuous dependent variable

7 a Examine to see if it is an error; if so, repeat it. If identified from the graph, it should be ignored. Be aware that it could lead to something really interesting and to a new hypothesis.

b Identify a pattern.

c That it does not go further than the data, the repeatability, reproducibility and the validity allow.

d By repeating results, by getting others to repeat your results and by checking other equivalent data.

8 a The science is more likely to be accepted.

b They might be biased because of who is funding the research or because they are employed by a biased organisation. There might be political influences, the public might be too alarmed by any conclusions.

9 a For many scientific developments there is a practical outcome which can be used – a technological development. Many technological developments allow further progress in science.

b Society – all of us should have an opinion.

10 a That stomata are vey small holes on the surface of leaves.

Summary questions

1 a Put these words into order. They should be in the order that you might use them in an investigation.
design; prediction; conclusion; method; repeat; controls; graph; results; table; improve; safety; hypothesis

2 a How would you tell the difference between an opinion that was scientific and a biased or prejudiced opinion?

b Suppose you were describing the height of plants for some fieldwork. What type of variable would you choose and why?

3 You might have observed that lichens do not grow where there is air pollution. You ask the question why. You use some theory to answer the question.

a Explain what you understand by the term 'hypothesis'.

b Sulfur dioxide in the air forms acids that attack the lichens. This is a hypothesis. Develop this into a prediction.

c Explain why a prediction is more useful than a hypothesis.

d Suppose you have tested your prediction and have some data. What might this do for your hypothesis?

e Suppose the data does not support the hypothesis. What should you do to the theory that gave you the hypothesis?

4 a What do you understand by a 'fair test'?

b Explain why setting up a fair test in fieldwork is difficult.

c Describe how you can make your results valid in fieldwork.

d Suppose you were carrying out an investigation into how pulse rates vary with exercise. You would need to carry out a trial. Describe what a trial would tell you about how to plan your method.

5 Suppose you were watching a friend carry out an investigation measuring the carbon dioxide produced by yeast cells. You have to mark your friend on how accurately she is making her measurements. Make a list of points that you would be looking for.

6 a How do you decide on the range of a set of data?

b How do you calculate the mean?

c When should you use a bar chart?

d When should you use a line graph?

7 a What should happen to anomalous results?

b What does a line of best fit allow you to do?

c When making a conclusion, what must you take into consideration?

d How can you check on the repeatability and reproducibility of your results?

---

b The size of the stomata affected the rate of diffusion of carbon dioxide.

c The smaller the stomata, the greater the rate of diffusion of carbon dioxide.

d Diameter of the hole.

e Volume of carbon dioxide diffusing per hour.

f 2 mm–22.7 mm

g To ensure that temperature changes did not affect the rate of diffusion.

h Yes, because it was a practical solution to a difficult problem, *or* no, it did not represent the actual sizes of stomata.

i Repeat readings should have been taken; compare results with those of other groups and compare results with those from secondary sources e.g. research on the internet.

j Yes, because there are differences between the readings that form a pattern. However, without repeat readings it is not certain that readings of less than 6.0 mm might not show any real differences.

k Suitable line graph with diameter of the hole on the x axis and volume on the y axis; points plotted correctly and a line of best fit drawn through the points.

l Directly proportional with a positive correlation.

m That increased size of the hole increases the rate of diffusion of CO_2 per hour.

n No.

a Why is it important when reporting science to 'tell the truth, the whole truth and nothing but the truth'?

b Why might some people be tempted not to be completely fair when reporting their opinions on scientific data?

a 'Science can advance technology and technology can advance science.' What do you think is meant by this statement?

b Who should answer the questions that start with 'Should we … '?

Look at the electron micrograph image below. Stomata are very small holes in the leaves of plants. They allow carbon dioxide to diffuse into the leaf cells for photosynthesis. The size of the hole is controlled by guard cells. It was suggested that the size of the hole might affect the rate at which carbon dioxide diffused through the hole.

Stomata are very small holes (when fully open they are 10–20 μm in diameter). The question was:

Are small holes better than large holes? This would seem reasonable as plants have very small stomata. The hypothesis was that small holes would allow more carbon dioxide to pass through than large holes.

It was decided to use much larger holes than the stomata because it would be easier to get accurate measurements. The investigation was carried out and the results were as follows.

Diameter of hole (mm)	Volume of CO_2 diffusing per hour (cm³)
22.7	0.24
12.1	0.10
6.0	0.06
3.2	0.04
2.0	0.02

a What was the observation on which this investigation was based?

b What was the original hypothesis?

c What was the likely prediction?

d What was the independent variable?

e What was the dependent variable?

f What is the range for the diameter of the hole?

g Why was the temperature kept the same during the investigation?

h Was this a sensible range of size of holes to use? Explain your answer.

i How could the investigation be made more repeatable and reproducible?

j Was the sensitivity of the instrument measuring volumes of CO_2 satisfactory? Provide some evidence for your answer from the data in the table.

k Draw a graph of the results in the table above.

l Describe the pattern in these results.

m What conclusion can you make?

n Does your conclusion support the prediction?

23

Commentary

Changes to How Science Works

Although HSW has remained largely unchanged, there have been some additions in this specification, particularly with regard to the Controlled Assessment Unit (ISA).

These include a requirement for candidates to:

● identify potential hazards and devise a plan to minimise risk

● understand the term 'hypothesis'

● test and/or make a prediction

● write a plan for an investigation, having been shown the basic technique to be used. Candidates should be able to decide upon issues such as the range and interval of the independent variable, the control variables and the number of repeats.

B1 1.1

Diet and exercise

Learning objectives

Students should learn:

- that a healthy diet contains the right balance of the different foods you need and provides the right amount of energy
- that the metabolic rate is the rate at which the chemical reactions in the body are carried out
- that the less exercise you take, the less food you need; people who exercise regularly are usually fitter than those who take little exercise.

Learning outcomes

Most students should be able to:

- describe the constituents of a healthy diet
- define metabolic rate and explain how it can vary according to the amount of activity carried out and the proportion of muscle to fat in the body
- describe the relationships between food intake, exercise and fitness.

Some students should also be able to:

- explain all the interactions between food intake, exercise, fitness, metabolic rate, gender, genetic factors, etc., which affect body mass.

Study tip

Students need to be able to define metabolic rate. They often confuse it with breathing and heart rate.

Support

- Demonstrate how foods can contain the same amount of energy but have different masses. Choose three different foods, each with the same energy content but very different masses. Have the samples hidden and get the students to pick a substance, and then show how much of it would contain the specific amount of energy.

Extend

- Ask students to think of ways we could manufacture artificial extra-high energy foods in the future.

Specification link-up: Biology B1.1

- A healthy diet contains the right balance of the different foods … *[B1.1.1 a)]*
- The rate at which all the chemical reactions in the cells … *[B1.1.1 c)]*
- Evaluate information about the effects of food on health. *[B1.1]*

   Controlled Assessment: B4.3 Collect primary and secondary data *[B4.3.2 a) b) c)]*; B4.5 Analyse and interpret primary and secondary data. *[B4.5.2 a) b) c) d)]*

Lesson structure

Starters

Do you have a healthy diet? – Ask each student to write out what they ate the previous day. Then assign the items to the correct food groups. Compare with the other students in small groups. Which food groups were eaten? Were any missing? Students could be supported by giving them the names of the seven food groups. Extend students by asking them to comment on whether their diet fulfilled the recommendations for a healthy diet. *(5 minutes)*

Sorting out food groups – Prepare six A4 sheets, each with the name of a major food group written in large letters on it and make a separate list of foods of all types. Give one A4 sheet to each of the first six students who come in through the door. As the other students enter, assign them a food from your list ('you are a tomato', 'you are a pint of milk,' etc.), making sure you have all food types covered. Ask the students to move to the food group that they feel they belong to, adding that they may well be able to fit into two groups. Go through a group at a time finding out which food groups are where and discussing any anomalies. *(10 minutes)*

Main

- **Measuring energy in foods** – This practical is based on a burning food experiment. It provides plenty of scope for the introduction of concepts covered in How science works. The accuracy of the measurements, the quantities of food used, the control of variables and evaluation of the results can all be discussed.

- **The 'How much energy do I use when …?'** Practical is based on the fact that 10 J of energy is required to raise a 1 kg mass a distance of 1 m. Ask students to raise a 100 g mass up into the air for 1 m and then tell them they have done 1 J of work. You can vary this with different masses depending on availability.

Plenaries

Matching diets to people – Write 'Energy intake (in kJ)' down on one side of the board, and different occupations, genders and ages down the other side. Students are asked to match the energy intake with age, gender and occupation. Students could be supported by using occupations and gender only. Students could be extended by including teenagers, a pregnant woman, a person training for a marathon, a senior citizen, etc. *(5 minutes)*

Role playing exercise – Ask students to take the roles of nutritional advisors and people with different energy needs, such as a pregnant woman, top athlete, body builder, etc. *(10 minutes)*

Answers to in-text questions

a For energy and to build new cells.

b Because a pregnant woman has to provide energy for a growing baby as well as herself.

c Athletes have a lot of muscle tissue and muscle tissue burns up a lot of energy.

Practical support

Measuring energy in food

Equipment and materials required

Each group will need: 25 cm³ measuring cylinder, boiling tubes/test tubes, mounted needles or 20 cm lengths of wire, a Bunsen burner, a test tube rack, a heatproof mat, a metal-jawed clamp, a thermometer, a range of foods cut into cubes or small pieces (exclude peanuts due to allergic reactions).

Details

A measured volume of cold water is put in each test tube and a thermometer used to record the initial temperature. A piece of food is chosen and placed on the end of a 20 cm length of wire, or a mounted needle, and ignited. As soon as it is alight, it is held as close as possible under the test tube of water. When it has finished burning, record the highest temperature reached in the water in the test tube. Suitable foods for testing are bite-sized shredded wheat, corn snacks such as 'Wotsits' and dry bread. If using sweets, beware of falling hot sugar, and fatty foods have a tendency to spit.

Students can work in groups or individually, and results pooled. It is advisable to avoid using nuts due to allergies.

Safety: See CLEAPSS Laboratory Handbook/CD-ROM section 9.4.2.

How much energy do I use when ...?

Equipment and materials required

A supply of weights ranging from 100 g to 1 kg would be useful, together with a metre rule. Access to a staircase, a measuring tape and scales to weigh the student volunteers are needed for the main experiment.

Details

This practical is based on the fact that 10 J of energy is required to raise a 1 kg mass a distance of 1 m. Ask students to raise a 100 g mass up into the air for 1 m and then tell them they have done 1 J of work. You can vary this with different masses depending on availability.

Safety: Care is needed with the handling of weights and when running up and down stairs. Do not encourage competition and be aware of student sensitivities.

Keeping healthy

B1 1.1 Diet and exercise

Learning objectives

- What does a healthy diet contain?
- Why can some people eat lots of food without getting fat?
- How does an athlete's diet differ from yours?

Did you know ...?

Whether you prefer sushi, dahl, or roast chicken, you need to eat a varied diet that includes everything you need to keep your body healthy.

What makes a healthy diet?

A balanced diet contains the correct amounts of:

- carbohydrates
- proteins
- fats
- vitamins
- minerals
- fibre
- water.

Your body uses carbohydrates, proteins and fats to release the energy you need to live and to build new cells. You need small amounts of vitamins and minerals for your body to work healthily. Without them you will suffer deficiency diseases. If you don't have a balanced diet then you will end up malnourished.

Figure 1 A balanced diet provides everything you need to survive, including plenty of energy

Fortunately, in countries like the UK, most of us take in all the minerals and vitamins we need from the food we eat. However, our diet can easily be unbalanced in terms of the amount of energy we take in. If we take in too much energy we put on weight. If we don't take in enough we become underweight.

It isn't always easy to get it right because different people need different amounts of energy. Even if you eat a lot, you can still lack vitamins and minerals if you don't eat the right food.

a Why do you need to eat food?

How much energy do you need?

The amount of energy you need to live depends on lots of different things. Some of these things you can change and some you can't.

Males need to take in more energy than a female of the same age – unless she is pregnant.

If you are a teenager, you will need more energy than if you are in your 70s.

b Why does a pregnant woman need more energy than a woman who isn't pregnant?

Your food supplies energy to your muscles as they work. So the amount of exercise you do affects the amount of energy you need. If you do very little exercise, then you don't need as much food. The more you exercise the more food you need to take in.

Figure 2 Athletes have a great deal of muscle tissue so they have to eat a lot of food to supply the energy they need

People who exercise regularly are usually much fitter than people who take little exercise. They make bigger muscles – up to 40% of their body mass. Muscle tissue transfers much more energy than fat. But exercise doesn't always mean time spent training or 'working out' in the gym. Walking to school, running around the house looking after small children or doing a physically active job all count as exercise too.

c Why do athletes need to eat more food than the average person?

The temperature where you live affects how much energy you need as well. In warmer countries you need to eat less food. This is because you use less energy keeping your body temperature at a steady level.

The metabolic rate

Think of a friend who is very similar in age, gender and size to you. Despite these similarities, you may need quite different amounts of energy in your diet. This is because the rate of chemical reactions in your cells (the **metabolic rate**) varies from person to person.

Men generally have a higher metabolic rate than women. The proportion of muscle to fat in your body affects your metabolic rate. Men often have a higher proportion of muscle to fat than women. You can change the proportion of muscle to fat in your body by exercising. This will build up more muscle.

Your metabolic rate is also affected by the amount of activity you do. Exercise increases your metabolic rate for a time even after you stop exercising.

Scientists think that your basic metabolic rate may be affected by genetic factors you inherit from your parents. This is an example of how **inherited** factors can affect our health.

Figure 3 If you work somewhere really cold your metabolic rate will go up to keep you warm. You will need lots of fat in your diet to supply the energy you need.

Did you know ...?

Between 60–75% of your daily energy needs are used up in the basic reactions needed to keep you alive. About 10% is needed to digest your food – and only the final 15–30% is affected by your physical activity!

Study tip

'Metabolic rate' refers to the chemical reactions which take place in cells.

Key points

- Most people eat a varied diet, which includes everything needed to keep the body healthy.
- Different people need different amounts of energy.
- The metabolic rate varies from person to person.
- The more exercise you take, the more food you need.

Summary questions

1 What is 'a balanced diet'?

2 a Why do you need more energy in your diet when you are 18 than when you are 80?
   b Why does a top athlete need more energy in their diet than you do? Where does the energy in the diet come from?

3 a What is the 'metabolic rate'?
   b Explain why some people put on weight more easily than others.

Further teaching suggestions

Investigating fitness equipment

- Ask students to investigate the different types of fitness equipment available at their local gym, from articles in magazines or on the internet. Ask them to evaluate these against the exercise they get from PE periods in school and ordinary activities. Why do they think these machines have been devised and who benefits from them?

A sudden release of energy

- Carry out internet research on explosions in food factories.

Energy practical

- Extend the 'How much energy do I use when ...' practical by calculating the energy used/work done when carrying out activities such as climbing stairs or stepping up on to an object. The mass of the student should be measured and the height of the object or staircase determined. If several volunteers are used, the work done can be calculated and then this value can be used to work out the quantity of sugar they would need to eat to replace the energy. [100 g of sugar contains 1630 kJ of energy, so not much!]

Summary answers

1 A diet which contains the right amount of carbohydrates, proteins, fats, vitamins, minerals, fibre and water and the right amount of energy.

2 a Generally, teenagers use more energy than the very elderly because they are more active and to build new cells as they are still growing.

   b A top athlete probably has more muscle, which uses a lot of energy. The energy comes from proteins, fats and carbohydrates.

3 a The rate at which all the chemical reactions in the cells of the body are carried out.

   b Some people have a slower metabolic rate, some take less exercise, some eat more and do not use up all the energy they take in as food so they store the excess as fat.

B1 1.2

Weight problems

Learning objectives

Students should learn:

- that arthritis, diabetes, high blood pressure and heart disease are more common in overweight people than in thinner people
- that exercise as part of a healthy lifestyle reduces the chance of developing serious health conditions.

Learning outcomes

Most students should be able to:

- describe the problems associated with excess food in the diet and how these may be overcome by modifying the diet
- describe how health problems can be reduced by regular exercise
- state some claims made by slimming programmes or products.

Some students should also be able to:

- evaluate, when supplied with relevant information, the claims made by different slimming programmes.

Support

- Students can be given a set of pictures and descriptions of fictitious characters and asked to match the characters with their correct BMI category.

Extend

- Speculate on societal factors that might correlate with body mass index. Students can look at the recommended exercise levels associated with various slimming regimes.
- The use of Wii Fit programs has increased. Students could discuss if they are a substitute for 'real' exercise?
- The 'comparison of foods' activity can be extended by making a more detailed comparison of the different types of fat (saturated and unsaturated), different types of carbohydrate, the use of different sweeteners, etc. It may also be of interest to consider some of these products in a diabetic diet.

Specification link-up: Biology B1.1

- A healthy diet contains the right balance of the different foods … *[B1.1.1 a)]*
- A person loses mass when the energy content of the food … *[B1.1.1 b)]*
- People who exercise regularly are usually healthier than people who take little exercise. *[B1.1.1 e)]*
- Analyse and evaluate claims made by slimming programmes, and slimming products. *[B1.1]*

  Controlled Assessment: B4.5 Analyse and interpret primary and secondary data. *[B4.5.1 a) b)]*

Lesson structure
Starters

Punishment of luxury? – Imagine being invited to a fabulous party where there are unlimited quantities of excellent quality food. Ask students for all their favourites – they are all there, all free and in abundance! How will you know when you have had enough? What if the feast went on for weeks or months? Or a lifetime? How would you know when to stop? In pairs, discuss what makes people decide when they have had enough to eat. What advice would you give to someone at the big party? *(5 minutes)*

The food groups beetle game – This is a version of the traditional beetle game which can be used to recap the 'Diet and exercise' lesson. Students are supplied with an outline of a beetle with no legs but the letters C, P, F, V, M and Fi (C 5 carbohydrate, P 5 proteins, F 5 fats, V 5 vitamins, M 5 minerals, Fi 5 fibre) around the thorax. Call out names of different foods and ask the students to put them into the right group by labelling one of the 'legs' with the name of the food. To support students, give them images of food and restrict them to one food group per image. To extend students, try to use foods that fit into more than one group. The winning student is the one that completes their beetle first. *(10 minutes)*

Main

- Discuss with the students what is meant by the term 'obesity'. Distinguish between being overweight, moderately obese and clinically obese, introducing BMI values. Search the internet for 'obesity statistics' about various groups of people (different age groups, different ethnic groups, different countries). Students can discuss these statistics and consider the problems associated with the condition.
- A practical experiment on BMI can be suggested (optional – see 'Practical support').
- Remind students that some athletes with highly developed musculature have high BMIs and although very fit would fall into the obese category. This will encourage students to be aware of the limitations of formulae.
- This could lead into another practical investigation on 'Are "slimming", "low fat" or "diet" foods worth buying if you want to lose weight?' (see 'Practical support'). How Science Works concepts could be introduced here as this is a useful exercise in evaluation. Students should be encouraged to work out fat content per gram and energy content per gram, in order to make their investigation valid.

Plenaries

'What advice would you give Homer Simpson on how and why to lose weight?' – Search the internet for an image or cartoon clip of Homer Simpson, or Peter Griffin of *Family Guy*. Use either as a stimulus and award a doughnut as a prize for the best advice! *(5 minutes)*

The science behind the slimming diet – Compare different slimming programmes/techniques, e.g. WeightWatchers, Atkins diet, glycaemic index. Support students by asking them to suggest what each diet is based on (e.g. GI is carbohydrate control, Atkins based on eating fat and protein, etc.). Students could be extended by being asked to explain/discuss and evaluate the scientific basis of each. *(10 minutes)*

Answers to in-text questions

a Arthritis, diabetes, high blood pressure, heart disease plus any other correct answers such as breathlessness.

b Reduce your food (energy) intake, increase your exercise (energy output) or both.

Practical support

Measurement of BMI

Equipment and materials required

Scales to measure mass in kilograms, measuring tapes to measure height in metres, or sheets of data for fictitious characters. The actual BMI formula is not difficult to use, but a BMI calculator can be found at www.bbc.co.uk. Search the internet for 'BMI calculators' to find graphs and normal ranges. There are also graphs for displaying the data and turning the BMI into a descriptor.

Details

Students can measure their own mass (kg) and height (m) and use the formula to calculate their own BMI.

Be aware that weight problems are widespread and this is a potentially sensitive topic. It might be wise to warn students in advance in order to prevent nasty comments. The actual activity should be optional.

Alternatively, a sheet of data for fictitious characters with heights and body masses could be supplied. If a set of fictitious characters is used, then you can ask the students to do the calculations and classify them into the correct categories. Those that come in the 'obese' and 'overweight' groups could then be recommended a slimming programme.

Are 'slimming', 'low fat' or 'diet' foods worth buying if you want to lose weight?

Equipment and materials required

A selection of foods – different brands of yogurt or cereal bars – make sure they have the information on fat and energy content etc. Include both normal and 'low fat' or 'diet' varieties of similar products.

Details

A comparison of such foods with 'normal' brands can be made by checking their fat and energy content and other constituents from their labels. This would work quite well with different brands of yogurt or cereal bars. Things to remember are differences in size, differences in mass and differences in contents as well as differences in price. Students could be encouraged to suggest/bring in their own yogurt/cereal bar for a general class comparison.

Students should be encouraged to work out fat content per gram and energy content per gram, in order to make their investigation reliable. Remind students that they are not allowed to eat in the laboratory.

Keeping healthy

B1 1.2 — Weight problems

Weight problems

Learning objectives

- What health problems are linked to being overweight?
- Why is it unhealthy to be too thin?
- Why are people who do exercise usually healthier than those who do not?

Figure 1 In spite of some of the media hype, most people are not obese – but the amount of weight people carry varies a great deal!

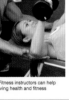
Figure 2 Fitness instructors can help with improving health and fitness

Obesity

If you take in more energy than you use, the excess is stored as fat. You need some body fat to cushion your internal organs. Your fat also acts as an energy store for when you don't feel like eating. But if someone eats a lot more food than they need, this is a form of malnourishment. Over time they could become **overweight** or even **obese**.

Carrying too much weight is often inconvenient and uncomfortable. Obesity can also lead to serious health problems such as arthritis, type 2 diabetes (high blood sugar levels which are hard to control), high blood pressure and heart disease. Obese people are more likely to die at an earlier age than non-obese people.

a What health problems are linked to obesity?

Losing weight

Many people want to be thinner. This might be for their health or just to look better. You gain fat by taking in more energy than you need. You lose **mass** when the energy content of your food is less than the energy you use in your daily life. There are three main ways you can lose mass.

- You can reduce the amount of energy you take in by cutting back the amount of food you eat. In particular, you can cut down on energy-rich foods like biscuits, crisps and chips.
- You can increase the amount of energy you use by doing more exercise.
- The best way to lose weight is to do both – reduce your energy intake and exercise more!

Scientists talk about 'mass', but most people talk about losing weight. Many people find it easier to lose weight by attending slimming groups. At these weekly meetings they get lots of advice and support from other slimmers. All slimming programmes involve eating fewer energy-rich foods and/or taking more exercise.

Exercise can make you healthier by helping to control your weight. It increases the amount of energy used by your body and increases the proportion of muscle to fat. It can make your heart healthier too. However, you need to take care. If you suddenly start taking vigorous exercise, you can cause other health problems.

Fitness instructors can measure the proportion of your body that is made up of fat. They can advise on the right food to eat and the exercise you need to become thinner, fitter, or both.

Different slimming programmes approach weight loss in different ways. Many simply give advice on healthy living. They advise lots of fruit and vegetables, avoiding too much fat or too many calories and plenty of exercise. Some are more extreme and suggest that you cut out almost all of the fat or the carbohydrates from your diet.

b What must you do to lose weight?

How Science Works

You can find lots of slimming products in the supermarket. Used in the right way, they can help you to lose weight. Some people claim that 'slimming teas' or 'herbal pills' will enable you to eat what you like and still lose weight.

- What sort of evidence would you look for to decide which approaches to losing weight work best?

Figure 3 Slimming products can help you lose weight, but only if you control the total amount of energy you take in

Lack of food

In some parts of the world many people are underweight and malnourished because there is not enough food to eat. Civil wars, droughts and pests can all destroy local crops.

Deficiency diseases, due to lack of mineral ions and vitamins, are common in both children and adults when they never have enough food. Deficiency diseases can also occur if you do not have a balanced diet.

Summary questions

1 Copy and complete using the words below:

energy fat less more obese

If you take in more .... than you use, the excess is stored as .... If you eat too much over a long period of time, you will eventually become .... To lose weight you need to eat .... and exercise ....

2 Why do people who are very thin, and some people who are obese, suffer from deficiency diseases?

3 One slimming programme controls your food intake. Another controls your food intake but also has an exercise programme. Which do you think would be the most effective? Explain your answer.

Did you know ...?

The number of obese and overweight people is growing. The WHO (World Health Organisation) says over 1 billion adults worldwide are now overweight or obese.

Study tip

The word 'malnourished' can be used to describe people who do not have a balanced diet. They may have too little food or too much food, or take in the wrong combination of foods.

Key points

- If you take in more energy than you use, you will store the excess as fat.
- Obese people have more health problems than others.
- People who do not have enough to eat can develop serious health problems.
- Exercise helps reduce weight and maintain health.

26 / 27

Further teaching suggestions

Nutrition and dietary benefits

- Ask students how they could persuade their local doctor that they needed to employ a nutritionist or a dietician in their practice.

Weight discussion

- Start a discussion on role models and the pressure to be thin. Is the ideal body shape the same throughout the World? Some pictures of people of different shapes and sizes from around the world could help here. In order not to be sexist in a mixed school, include men and women, especially as men can suffer from weight problems as well.

Understanding obesity

- Write a letter of advice to a person who suffers from either obesity or anorexia, being supportive as well as helpful.

Summary answers

1 energy, fat, obese, less, more

2 People who are very thin do not take in enough food to get all the nutrients (vitamins, minerals, etc.) they need. Some people who are obese eat a lot of junk/fast food which is very low in minerals and vitamins, high in salt, fat, etc. So both can suffer from deficiency diseases.

3 The programme which combines controlled food intake and exercise. Taking in less energy and using up more energy will be most effective. It builds muscle which uses more energy.

B1 1.3 Inheritance, exercise and health

Learning objectives

Students should learn:

- that inherited factors, such as cholesterol level, can affect our health
- that there are two types of cholesterol
- that a diet high in saturated fats can upset the balance between good and bad forms of cholesterol in the blood and increase the risk of disease of the heart and blood vessels
- that people who exercise regularly are usually healthier than those who take little exercise.

Learning outcomes

Most students should be able to:

- explain what cholesterol is
- describe the effects of high levels of 'bad' cholesterol in the blood
- explain the benefits of regular exercise on health.

Some students should also be able to:

- evaluate information on the effects of exercise on our health
- explain the importance of the balance of the different types of cholesterol in the blood and how this is affected by diet.

Support

- Students could be given cards with the key words and their definitions and asked to match them correctly.
- Students could be given menus from different restaurants and asked to choose the healthy options, explaining their reasons.

Extend

- Students could research the structure of cholesterol and distinguish between 'good' and 'bad' cholesterol.
- Students could find out how much of different types of exercise may be needed to 'work off' items of fast food. For example, how much fast walking is needed for a blueberry muffin?

Specification link-up: Biology B1.1

- Inherited factors also affect our health; for example, cholesterol level. *[B1.1.1 d)]*
- People who exercise regularly are usually healthier than people who take little exercise. *[B1.1.1 e)]*
- Evaluate information about the effect of lifestyle on development of disease. *[B1.1]*
  Controlled Assessment: B4.5 Analyse and interpret primary and secondary data. *[B4.5.4 b)]*

Lesson structure

Starters

A diet of fast food for a month – Start a discussion of the film documentary *Super Size Me*, where a reporter, Morgan Spurlock, ate nothing but fast food for a month. *(5 minutes)*

Fast food as a way of life … – To support students you could bring in a fast food meal, such as pizza or burger and chips and show it to the class. Ask: 'What is in it? What problems might you get if you ate lots of these in the short term? What happens if it becomes a way of life (i.e. long term)?' To extend students, you could ask 'Why is fast food so popular?' Discuss and make a list of how and why eating habits have changed in the past 30 years. *(10 minutes)*

Main

- Practical on testing for fats in burger and chips or test any other fast foods, such as crisps, pizza, etc. The students could bring in some small samples of their own.
- An alternative to the emulsion test is to wipe pieces of fatty food on to greaseproof paper. A translucent mark is left if there is fat present. This might be quicker and less messy to do than the emulsion test if large numbers of food items are to be tested.
- As an extension, some 'low fat' alternatives, such as burgers made from Quorn, could be tested and compared with normal burgers. As these tests are not quantitative, only qualitative comparisons can be made.
- 'Good to eat Fred the Red' – This is an interactive food and nutrition programme to download from the Science Year CD website (www.sycd.co.uk), from Manchester United Football Club or on the Science Year CDs. If computers are available, the students can work through it themselves, or it can be projected, or accessed as homework.
- Look at the graph in the Student Book (Figure 3) to emphasise the effect of exercise on the risk of death and link with the benefits of exercise in keeping cholesterol levels low. This could lead to a discussion on different levels of exercise and the need to link diet and exercise in a healthy lifestyle. Students can draw conclusions from these data.

Plenaries

Explain the terms – Write or tack up key words from this topic on the board and pick/invite two students to come to the front and explain one each. They remove the word they have explained, if they are judged to have been successful in explaining it to the rest of the class. They can then choose the next pair and the key words to be explained. If stuck, a student can choose someone to help them. *(5 minutes)*

Why don't Inuits have high cholesterol levels? – Inuit tribesmen (show pictures) traditionally eat large amounts of fat in the form of seal and whale blubber. They do not have high average cholesterol readings. Support students by asking: 'Why might this be? What factors of their lifestyle, genetics and living conditions could account for this? Is it inherited?' Extend students by asking them to write down recommendations to an Inuit who is giving up the traditional lifestyle for a sedentary life. *(10 minutes)*

Practical support

Testing for fats in burger and chips
Equipment and materials required
Each group will need: a pestle and mortar, filter papers and filter funnels or greaseproof paper, test tubes and test tube rack, ethanol, fatty foods to test.

Details
Grind up portions of the foods to be tested with a little water in a pestle and mortar. Allow to settle, decant off some of the liquid and filter it into a small test tube. Add the filtrate to half a small test tube of ethanol and shake vigorously (caution with eyes and naked flames). If there is fat present, a creamy emulsion is obtained. Demonstrate what an emulsion looks like by shaking up some cooking oil in a gas jar three-quarters full of water (or, on a smaller scale in a test tube and then each group could do their own).

Safety: Wear eye protection and no naked flames. CLEAPSS Hazcard 40A Ethanol – highly flammable/harmful.

B1 1.3 — Inheritance, exercise and health

Learning objectives
- How can inherited factors affect your health?
- Why does your cholesterol level matter?
- Does exercise make you healthier?

links
For information on metabolic rate, look back at B1 1.1 Diet and exercise.

Inheriting health
Inherited factors from your parents affect your appearance, such as the colour of your eyes. They also have a big effect on your health. They affect your metabolic rate, which affects how easily you lose and gain mass. Being overweight has a bad effect on your health. Inherited factors affect the proportion of muscle to fat in your body. They also affect your risk of heart disease, partly because they influence the levels of cholesterol in your blood.

Figure 1 Lots of things affect your health – your diet, how much exercise you take and what you inherit from your parents

Controlling cholesterol
The way your body balances cholesterol is an example of how an inherited factor can affect your health. You need cholesterol for your cell membranes and to make vital hormones. There are two forms of cholesterol carried around your body in your blood. One form is healthy but the other can cause health problems. If the balance of your cholesterol levels is wrong, your risk of getting heart disease increases.

a Why do you need cholesterol in your body?

The way your liver deals with the fat in your diet and makes the different types of cholesterol is inherited from your parents. For most people, eating a balanced diet means your liver can keep the balance of cholesterol right.

Eating lots of high-fat food means you are likely to have raised levels of harmful cholesterol and an increased risk of heart disease. But 1 in every 500 people inherit factors which mean they will have high levels of harmful cholesterol and an increased risk of heart disease whatever they eat. This is an example of how an inherited factor can affect your health.

Did you know ...?
The maximum healthy blood cholestrol is given as 6 mmol/l, 5 mmol/l and 4 mmol/l on different medical websites.
Scientists don't always agree!

Figure 2 Next time you eat a burger and fries, think about all the fat you are taking in. Will your body be able to deal with it, or are your blood cholesterol levels about to go up?

Exercise and health
Scientists have collected lots of evidence about exercise and health. It shows that people who exercise regularly are generally healthier than people who don't do much exercise. The graph in Figure 3 shows the results of an American study published in the journal *Circulation*. 6213 men were studied. The least active men were 4.5 times more likely to die early than the fittest, most active men.

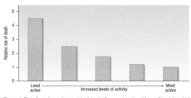
Figure 3 The effect of exercise on risk of death (Source: Jonathan Myers, *Circulation*, 2003)

These are some of the scientific explanations why exercise helps to keep you healthy.
- You are less likely to be overweight if you exercise regularly. This is partly because you will be using more energy.
- You will have more muscle tissue, which will increase your metabolic rate. If you can control your weight, you are less likely to be affected by problems such as arthritis, diabetes and high blood pressure.
- Your cholesterol levels are affected by exercise. Regular exercise lowers your blood cholesterol levels. It also helps the balance of the different types of cholesterol. When you exercise, your good cholesterol level goes up and the harmful cholesterol level goes down. This lowers your risk of heart disease and other health problems.

b How could you change your cholesterol levels?

Summary questions
1 Copy and complete using the words below:
heart   metabolic   inherited   cholesterol   balance
There are .... factors such as your .... rate that can affect your health. The way your liver makes .... is inherited and if the .... of cholesterol is wrong it can increase your risk of .... disease.
2 Why are people who exercise regularly usually healthier than people who take little exercise?
3 Using the data in Figure 3, which group of people do you think are most at risk of death? Why do you think this might be? What could they do to reduce the risk?

Key points
- Inherited factors affect our health. These include our metabolic rate and cholesterol level.
- People who exercise regularly are usually healthier than people who take little exercise.

Further teaching suggestions

Fat around the heart
- Search the internet for 'video heart surgery' to show the layers of fat around the heart.

Nutritional data on school meals
- Ask the school kitchen for nutritional data on the fat content of some sample school meals. This might need to be negotiated first! Alternatively, it could be useful to invite the person in charge of your school canteen in for a discussion about the nutritional guidelines they work to in producing school meals. Ask what they think about Jamie Oliver's suggestions for altering the school meals menus.

The structure of saturated and unsaturated fats
- Moly-models could be used to demonstrate the differences in the structure of saturated and unsaturated fats. Compare fats and oils from plant and animal sources and what they are used for.

Healthier fast food?
- Ask students to collect literature from fast-food restaurants explaining how they have made their food healthier and discuss whether this is true.

Answers to in-text questions
a To make the membranes of your body cells and maintain normal hormone production, e.g. your sex hormones.

b By exercising and reducing the amount of fat in your diet.

Summary answers
1 inherited, metabolic, cholesterol, balance, heart
2 They are less likely to be overweight and will have more muscle so will burn more energy. This controls their weight and means that they are less likely to get arthritis, diabetes and high blood pressure. It also reduces cholesterol levels which reduces the risk of heart disease.
3 People who are least active are most at risk of dying. Unfit people have the most health problems and so any careful improvement in activity levels will be of benefit and they will lose weight.

B1 1.4

Pathogens and disease

Learning objectives

Students should learn:

- what pathogens are
- how pathogens cause infectious diseases
- how Semmelweis tried to control the spread of infectious disease caused by microorganisms.

Learning outcomes

Most students should be able to:

- define the term 'pathogen'
- explain how pathogens cause disease
- describe the contribution made by Semmelweiss to the control of the spread of infection in hospitals.

Some students should also be able to:

- explain the process by which Semmelweiss came to his conclusions
- explain why Semmelweis' ideas were not immediately accepted.

Answers to in-text questions

a Pathogens/microorganisms/bacteria and viruses.

b Viruses are smaller than bacteria.

c Pathogens reproduce rapidly inside your body; they damage your cells; they produce toxins that make you feel ill. Your body reacts to pathogens and the damage they cause/toxins they make, which also makes you feel ill.

Support

- Use a 'pairs' cards activity with the key words from the spread which could be played like the game 'Fish', where a player holding one card of a group asks others if they have the matching cards. Players collect groups of cards that are linked.

Extend

- Students could research the life and times of Semmelweis. How did his work rank alongside the contributions made by Lister and Pasteur?
- Some Fungi and Protoctista are also pathogenic, causing diseases such as athlete's foot and ringworm (Fungi) and malaria (Protoctista); students could investigate how these diseases are spread. Are they infectious?

Specification link-up: Biology B1.1

- Microorganisms that cause infectious disease are called pathogens. [B1.1.2 a)]
- Bacteria and viruses may reproduce rapidly inside the body and may produce poisons (toxins) that make us feel ill. Viruses damage the cells in which they reproduce. [B1.1.2 b)]
- Relate the contribution of Semmelweis in controlling infection to solving modern problems with the spread of infection in hospitals. [B1.1.2]
- Semmelweis recognised the importance of hand washing in the prevention of spreading some infectious diseases. By insisting that doctors washed their hands before examining patients, he greatly reduced the number of deaths from infectious diseases in his hospital. [B1.1.2 f)]

Controlled Assessment: B4.3 Collect primary and secondary data. [B4.3.2 a), b)]

Lesson structure

Starters

Bush tucker challenge – eat some bacteria! – Provide some small pieces of blue cheese, yogurt and 'helpful bacteria' culture drinks for the students to sample (under hygienic conditions in the food technology room and check for allergies). Alternatively, just allow students to inspect and smell the foods. Discuss the usefulness of bacteria, illustrating that not all bacteria are 'baddies'. (5 minutes)

Diseases we've had in our group – Give each small group of students a sheet of A3 paper and get them to write on the names of any diseases they have had. To support students, ask them to sort out which diseases were infectious and which were not. Which bench had the most? To extend students, ask 'What were they caused by? What medication, if any, did they take when they were ill?' [Note: some sensitivity is needed here about things students do not wish to discuss.] This could be extended to 'My family'. (10 minutes)

Main

- **Microorganisms and disease** – search image banks on the internet for 'bacteria and virus' and use them to show the differences between bacteria and viruses. There are some very good images of different bacteria and viruses (good electron microscope pictures available) and such a presentation could include references to size: what can be seen with the naked eye, with a microscope and with the electron microscope. Include some examples of other pathogenic microorganisms, such as fungi and protists.

- Experiment to show the benefits of washing hands (see 'Practical support'). Alternatively, this could be set up as a demonstration. Discuss the ideas of Semmelweis and why his recommendations were not immediately adopted by fellow doctors in hospitals. Discuss which aspects of 'How Science Works' can be applied to the work of Semmelweis.

- Experiment to demonstrate the presence of microorganisms in the air (see 'Practical support') – this experiment is similar to one carried out by Louis Pasteur. It can be done as a demonstration and set up a few days before the lesson. 'How Science Works' concepts can be introduced here. For example, the experiment illustrates the need for controls, replication of results for reliability and evaluation of the method used.

Plenaries

Do you know the key words? Wordsearch and crossword – To support students, give them a wordsearch using the key words in the spread. To extend students, ask the students to write definitions of the key words and use them as clues to construct a crossword. This could begin in the lesson and students could write more clues for homework. (5 minutes)

How can I make you understand? – Semmelweis was not the only person to struggle to get his ideas accepted. Discuss other examples, such as the theory of evolution or whether the Earth is round or flat, with students and get them to think about how people are persuaded to accept new theories. How do you convince other scientists? How do you convince the general public? Discuss how the acceptance of new theories has changed over time. (10 minutes)

Practical support

Was Semmelweis right?

Equipment and materials required
Sterile agar plates, adhesive tape, incubator at 25 °C.

Details
The benefits of washing hands can be demonstrated by touching the surface of a sterile agar plate with unwashed fingers, replacing the lid and securing the plate in the usual way. Wash hands thoroughly, dry them and then touch the surface of a similar sterile agar plate, replacing the lid and securing it as before. Label both plates. Incubate at 25 °C and observe what grows.

Safety: Sterile techniques should be used; agar plates should on no account be sealed all the way round the lid during incubation, incubated at a higher temperature or opened and should be disposed of safely following CLEAPSS advice. See CLEAPSS Handbook section 15.2.14.

Microorganisms in air demonstration

Equipment and materials required
Nutrient broth, three test tubes, distilled water, water bath, 250 cm³ glass beaker, tripod and gauze, Bunsen burner, heatproof mat, cotton wool, pressure cooker/autoclave, straight glass tube, S-shaped glass tube, test tube rack.

Details
Make up some nutrient broth in a test tube (using a broth tablet and 10 cm³ of distilled water). Boil the broth to sterilise it and then pour half of it into each of two test tubes. One test tube should then have a cotton wool plug through which a straight piece of glass tubing is inserted so that it does not reach the top of the liquid. The other test tube should also have a cotton wool plug, but the piece of glass tubing is longer, bent into an S-shape and inserted so that there is a straight piece going through the cotton wool and the S-shape arranged outside. Both test tubes should then be sterilised by heating them in a pressure cooker for 15 minutes and allowed to cool (or boiled in a water bath over a Bunsen burner for about a minute – care needed). Look at the tubes and their contents at intervals over the next few days. Ask: 'Which tube goes cloudy first? Why?' Discuss what is happening in both sets of apparatus.

Safety: Eye protection should be worn. Sterile techniques should be used; the contents of the tubes should be disposed of safely.

B1 1.4   Pathogens and disease

Learning objectives
- What are pathogens?
- How do pathogens cause disease?
- How did Ignaz Semmelweis change the way we look at disease?

Infectious diseases are found all over the world, in every country. Some diseases are fairly mild ones, such as the common cold and tonsilitis. Other diseases are known killers, such as tetanus, influenza and HIV/Aids.

An infectious disease is caused by a microorganism entering and attacking your body. People can pass these microorganisms from one person to another. This is what we mean by infectious.

Figure 1 Many bacteria are very useful but some, like these *E. coli*, can cause disease

Microorganisms which cause disease are called pathogens. Common pathogens are bacteria and viruses.

a What causes infectious diseases?

The differences between bacteria and viruses

Bacteria are single-celled living organisms that are much smaller than animal and plant cells.

Although some bacteria cause disease, many are harmless and some are really useful to us. We use them to make food like yoghurt and cheese, to treat sewage and to make medicines.

Viruses are even smaller than bacteria. They usually have regular shapes. Viruses cause diseases in every type of living organism from people to bacteria.

Figure 2 These tobacco mosaic viruses cause disease in plants

b How do viruses differ from bacteria?

How pathogens cause disease 🄺

Once bacteria and viruses are inside your body they reproduce rapidly. This is how they make you ill. Bacteria simply split in two – they often produce toxins (poisons) which affect your body. Sometimes they directly damage your cells. Viruses take over the cells of your body as they reproduce, damaging and destroying the cells. They very rarely produce toxins.

Common disease symptoms are a high temperature, headaches and rashes. These are caused by the damage and toxins produced by the pathogens. The symptoms also appear as a result of the way your body responds to the damage and toxins.

You catch an infectious disease when you pick up a pathogen from someone else who is infected with the disease.

c How do pathogens make you feel ill?

📖 **links**

For more information on bacteria that are resistant to antibiotics, see B1 1.8 Changing pathogens.

😃 **How Science Works**

The work of Ignaz Semmelweis

Ignaz Philipp Semmelweis was a doctor in the mid-1850s. At the time, many women in hospital died from childbed fever a few days after giving birth. However, no one knew what caused it.

Semmelweis noticed something about his medical students. They went straight from dissecting a dead body to delivering a baby without washing their hands. He wondered if they were carrying the cause of disease from the corpses to their patients.

Then another doctor cut himself while working on a body. He died from symptoms which were identical to childbed fever. Semmelweis was sure that the fever was caused by something that could be passed on – some kind of infectious agent.

He insisted that his medical students wash their hands before delivering babies. Immediately, fewer mothers died from the fever.

Getting his ideas accepted

Semmelweis talked to other doctors. He thought his evidence would prove to them that childbed fever was spread by doctors. But his ideas were mocked.

Many doctors thought that childbed fever was God's punishment to women. No one had ever seen bacteria or viruses. So it was hard to believe that disease was caused by something invisible passed from person to person. Doctors didn't like the idea that they might have been spreading disease. They were being told that their actions had killed patients instead of curing them.

In hospitals today, bacteria such as MRSA, which are resistant to antibiotics, are causing lots of problems. Getting doctors, nurses and visitors to wash their hands more often is part of the answer – just as it was in Semmelweis's time!

❓ **Did you know …?**

Semmelweis couldn't bear to think of the thousands of women who died because other doctors ignored his findings. By the 1860s he suffered a major breakdown and in 1865, aged only 47, he died – from an infection picked up from a patient during an operation.

Figure 3 Ignaz Semmelweis – his battle to get medical staff to wash their hands to prevent infections is still going on today

---

Summary questions

1 Copy and complete using the words below:

toxins viruses microorganisms reproduce pathogens damage symptoms bacteria

The _____ which cause infectious diseases are known as _____ . Once _____ and _____ get inside your body they _____ rapidly. They _____ your tissues and may produce _____ which cause the _____ of disease.

2 Give five examples of things we now know we can do to reduce the spread of pathogens to lower the risk of disease, e.g. hand-washing in hospitals.

3 Write a letter to Ignaz Semmelweis to a friend explaining how he formed his ideas and the struggle to get them accepted.

Key points

- Infectious diseases are caused by microorganisms called pathogens, such as bacteria and viruses.
- Bacteria and viruses reproduce rapidly inside your body. Bacteria can produce toxins which make you feel ill.
- Viruses damage your cells as they reproduce. This can also make you feel ill.
- Semmelweis recognised the importance of hand-washing in preventing the spread of infectious diseases in hospital.

Further teaching suggestions

Bacterial colonies
- Some sterile agar plates, which have previously been exposed to the air around the laboratory partially sealed, and incubated, can be fully sealed and examined for signs of bacterial colonies and compared with the results of the broth experiment.

The fate of microbes
- Watch a clip from *The Simpsons* episode 'Marge in chains' from the video 'Crime and Punishment', showing microbes getting into various characters and the immune system attacking them, followed by a discussion.

Biohazard warning symbol
- Introduce the biohazard warning symbol.

Summary answers

1 microorganisms, pathogens, viruses, bacteria, reproduce, damage, toxins, symptoms

2 Any sensible suggestions should be accepted, such as: wiping work surfaces, cleaning toilets, using tissues to blow nose, washing hands before handling food, etc.

3 Students should show in their letter the main points made in the relevant spread including an appreciation of why the new ideas met resistance.

B1 1.5

Defence mechanisms

Learning objectives

Students should learn:

- how pathogens get into the body and are spread from person to person
- that the body has different ways of preventing the entry of pathogens
- that white blood cells help to defend the body against pathogens that do gain entry.

Learning outcomes

Most students should be able to:

- explain the ways in which infectious diseases are spread
- describe the ways in which the body prevents the entry of pathogens
- describe the functions of the white blood cells within the body.

Some students should also be able to:

- explain in detail the role of the white blood cells.

Specification link-up: Biology B1.1

- The body has different ways of protecting itself against pathogens. *[B1.1.2 c)]*
- White blood cells help to defend against pathogens by:
  - ingesting pathogens
  - producing antibodies which destroy particular bacteria or viruses
  - producing antitoxins, which counteract the toxins released by the pathogens. *[B1.1.2 d)]*

Lesson structure

Starters

How does it get in? – Give the students a picture of four doors labelled 'Droplets', 'Direct contact', 'Food and drink' and 'Breaks in the skin' and a list of diseases underneath (flu, TB, impetigo, herpes, salmonellosis, Aids, hepatitis). Ask the students to join the disease with the way it enters the body, leaving undone any they do not know and completing these as the lesson proceeds. Check and discuss. (*5 minutes*)

Gaining entry – Show a picture of the human body and write up a list of the possible ways in which pathogens can get into the body. To support students give them red (not sure at all), green (entirely sure) and amber (partly sure) cards. Ask them to hold these up in response to questions about how certain organisms get into the body. Pick one student each time to explain their response. To extend students, use the same cards and questions but ask students to explain how the organisms are prevented from entering the body, i.e. what the defence strategy is. (*10 minutes*)

Main

The lesson suggestions here concentrate on students gaining an understanding of the ways in which the blood is involved in defending the body against pathogens. The activities vary in length; a shorter one could be paired with a longer one, e.g. show a video clip and play the dice game.

- Introduce a brief practical where students look at the two types of white blood cells (see 'Practical support').
- Search the internet for 'sneeze video' to show a clip of a sneeze in slow motion and/or video footage.
- Before the lesson, make a video to demonstrate clotting using a digital video camera. Show a finger being pricked with a sterile lancet, a drop of blood being forced out and then the tip of a needle being drawn through the blood until it starts to pick up threads of fibrin. These can very soon be drawn out from the blood. All materials used should be disposed of hygienically and safely. This should not be done during the lesson.
- Play a dice game in pairs. One student is allocated a bacterial disease. The student must state which way the disease is going to try to get into the body (the other student must check to see if this is appropriate). The first student must throw a six before entry can be gained. Once inside, they start to produce toxins, one for every point on the dice. They take turns with their opponent, who represents a defending white blood cell producing antitoxins. When the opponent throws the dice, the points represent antitoxins, which counteract the toxins produced by the bacterium. A running score should be kept until the white blood cell throws a six, which represents an antibody and kills the bacterium to win the game. If the running score of toxins reaches 10, the white cell dies and the bacterium wins.
- The game can be continued by playing against more partners. If, as a white cell, you have produced an antibody against a specific bacterium before, you can kill the bacterium with any even number, not just a six.

Support

- Students could be provided with a series of pictures showing a bacterium being engulfed by a white blood cell and asked to put them in order.

Extend

- Students should be capable of extending the concept map, putting in further links and connections.

Plenaries

Fill in the missing concepts – Students to complete a preprepared concept map, which has the connections made and labelled already; they fill in the concepts. (*5 minutes*)

Overcrowded refugee camp – Pin up or project a picture of an overcrowded refugee camp. To support students, ask them to identify as many ways as they can in which the people shown are in danger from infectious diseases (e.g. lack of fresh water, contaminated food and drink, close proximity to people with diseases, raw sewage, etc.). Extend students by asking them to list the infectious diseases that could occur in such a situation and how they would spread in the crowded conditions. (*10 minutes*)

Practical support

Investigating white blood cells
Equipment and materials required
Microscopes and prepared slides of blood smears.

Details

Introduce students to the two types of white blood cells and their functions. Project images of these, including scanning electron microscope pictures. Set up microscopes and prepared slides of blood smears for students to look at. Get them to count the numbers of each type of white blood cell they can see in a field of view and compare with the numbers of red blood cells.

Keeping healthy

B1 1.5 — Defence mechanisms

Learning objectives
- How does your body stop pathogens getting in?
- How do white blood cells protect us from disease?

There are a number of ways in which pathogens spread from one person to another. The more pathogens that get into your body, the more likely it is that you will get an infectious disease.

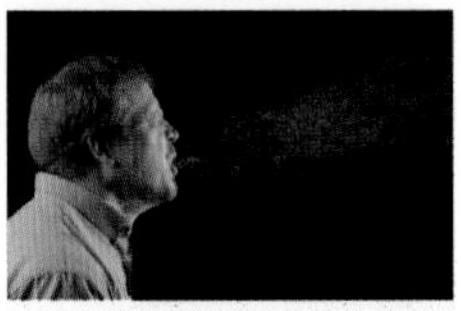

Figure 1 Droplets carrying millions of pathogens fly out of your mouth and nose at up to 100 miles an hour when you sneeze

Droplet infection: When you cough, sneeze or talk you expel tiny droplets full of pathogens from your breathing system. Other people breathe in the droplets, along with the pathogens they contain. So they pick up the infection, e.g. flu (influenza), tuberculosis or the common cold.

Direct contact: Some diseases are spread by direct contact of the skin, e.g. impetigo and some sexually transmitted diseases like genital herpes.

Contaminated food and drink: Eating raw or undercooked food, or drinking water containing sewage can spread disease, e.g. diarrhoea or salmonellosis. You get these by taking large numbers of microorganisms straight into your gut.

Through a break in your skin: Pathogens can enter your body through cuts, scratches and needle punctures, e.g. HIV/Aids or hepatitis.

When people live in crowded conditions, with no sewage treatment, infectious diseases can spread very rapidly.

a What are the four main ways in which infectious diseases are spread?

Preventing microbes getting into your body

Each day you come across millions of disease-causing microorganisms. Fortunately your body has several ways of stopping these pathogens getting inside.

Your skin covers your body and acts as a barrier. It prevents bacteria and viruses from reaching the tissues beneath that can be infected.

If you damage or cut your skin you bleed. Your blood quickly forms a clot which dries into a scab. The scab forms a seal over the cut, stopping pathogens getting in through the wound.

Your breathing system could be a weak link in your body defences. Every time you breathe you draw air full of pathogens inside your body. However, your breathing system produces sticky liquid, called mucus. This mucus covers the lining of your lungs and tubes. It traps the pathogens. The mucus is then moved out of your body or swallowed down into your gut. Then the acid in your stomach destroys the microorganisms. In the same way, the stomach acid destroys most of the pathogens you take in through your mouth.

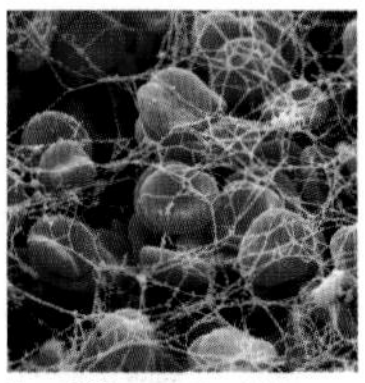

Figure 2 When you get a cut, the platelets in your blood set up a chain of events to form a clot that dries to a scab. This stops pathogens from getting into your body. It also stops you bleeding to death!

b What are the three main ways in which your body prevents pathogens from getting in?

How white blood cells protect you from disease

In spite of your body's defence mechanisms, some pathogens still get inside your body. Once there, they will meet your second line of defence – the white blood cells of your immune system.

The white blood cells help to defend your body against pathogens in several ways.

Table 1 Ways in which your white blood cells destroy pathogens and protect you against disease

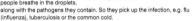

Role of white blood cell	How it protects you against disease
Ingesting microorganisms 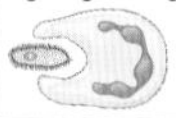	Some white blood cells ingest (take in) pathogens, destroying them so they can't make you ill.
Producing antibodies 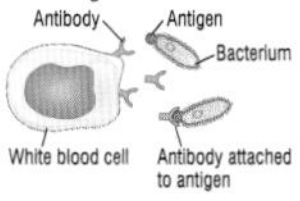 — Antibody, Antigen, Bacterium, White blood cell, Antibody attached to antigen	Some white blood cells produce special chemicals called **antibodies**. These target particular bacteria or viruses and destroy them. You need a unique antibody for each type of pathogen. Once your white blood cells have produced antibodies once against a particular pathogen, they can be made very quickly if that pathogen gets into the body again.
Producing antitoxins 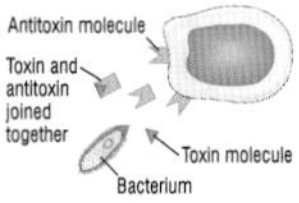 — Antitoxin molecule, Toxin and antitoxin joined together, Toxin molecule, Bacterium	Some white blood cells produce antitoxins. These counteract (cancel out) the toxins (poisons) released by pathogens.

Summary questions

1. Explain how diseases are spread by:
   a droplet infection   c contaminated food and drink
   b direct contact   d through a cut in the skin.
2. Certain diseases mean you cannot fight infections very well. Explain why the following symptoms would make you less able to cope with pathogens.
   a Your blood won't clot properly.
   b The number of white cells in your blood falls.
3. Here are three common things we do. Explain carefully how each one helps to prevent the spread of disease.
   a Washing your hands before preparing a salad.
   b Throwing away tissues after you have blown your nose.
   c Making sure that sewage does not get into drinking water.
4. Explain in detail how the white blood cells in your body work.

Key points
- Your body has several methods of defending itself against the entry of pathogens using the skin, the mucus of the breathing system and the clotting of the blood.
- Your white blood cells help to defend you against pathogens by ingesting them, making antibodies and making antitoxins.

Further teaching suggestions

Blood clotting and haemophilia
- Link the blood-clotting video to haemophilia and discuss clotting times. This can be extended further with reference to the use of blood-thinning drugs such as warfarin.

Blood clotting and practical applications
- Also link blood clotting to the self-sealing fuel tanks on fighter aircraft and some racing cars.

Preservatives and bacteria
- Discuss the preservation of foods, such as onions, in vinegar and draw parallels with the destruction of bacteria by the stomach acids.

Investigating how infectious diseases enter the body
- 'How did you get in?' Put a list of diseases/infections on the board. Students are to break into small groups and come up with as many ways as possible for each particular infective agent to get into the body. Share with the rest of the class on completion.

White cell animation
- Stop motion animation of a model white cell engulfing a bacterium can be made using 'Digital Blue' or similar cameras in conjunction with Windows MovieMaker.

Answers to in-text questions

a Droplet infection; direct contact; contaminated food and drink; through a break in the skin.

b Skin acts as a barrier; breathing organs produce mucus to trap pathogens or acid in stomach kills pathogens; blood uses platelets to produce clots to seal wounds.

Summary answers

1. **a** When we cough, sneeze or talk, droplets full of pathogens pass into the air to be breathed in by someone else.
   b Pathogens on skin passed to someone else's skin on contact.
   c Pathogens taken in on food or in drink.
   d Pathogens can get through the barrier of the skin to the tissue underneath.

2. **a** Pathogens cannot be stopped from getting into cuts.
   b You have not got enough white blood cells to ingest pathogens or to produce antibodies/antitoxins, so pathogens are not destroyed.

3. **a** Prevents pathogens getting from your hands to the food.
   b Removes pathogens from where they might come into contact with other people or get on your hands.
   c Prevents pathogens from the gut being taken in with drinking water.

4. Explanation to include the ingestion of microorganisms, the production of antibodies and antitoxins.

B1 1.6

Using drugs to treat disease

Learning objectives

Students should learn:

- that medicines, such as painkillers, relieve symptoms but do not kill pathogens
- that antibiotics help to cure bacterial diseases by killing infective bacteria inside the body
- that antibiotics cannot kill viral pathogens which live and reproduce inside cells.

Learning outcomes

Most students should be able to:

- explain what is meant by the term 'medicine' and describe how some relieve symptoms but do not kill pathogens
- describe how antibiotics can be used to treat bacterial infections
- explain why antibiotics are not used to treat diseases caused by viruses.

Some students should also be able to:

- explain the difficulty of developing antiviral drugs.

Study tip

Remember: antibiotics are drugs that kill bacteria. Antibodies are produced by white blood cells to kill bacteria. Students often confuse antibodies, antitoxins and antibiotics so make sure that you know the differences.

Support

- Students could be shown pictures of people with various complaints and asked to decide which medicines they should be given.

Extend

- Encourage students to find out why we need new antibiotics to keep us ahead in the battle with pathogens. This should lead them to gain some knowledge of mutations in preparation for later topics.

Specification link-up: Biology B1.1

- Some medicines, including painkillers, help to relieve … *[B1.1.2 g)]*
- Antibiotics, including penicillin, are medicines that help … *[B1.1.2 h)]*
- Explain how the treatment of disease has changed as … *[B1.1.2]*

  Controlled Assessment: B4.1 Plan practical ways to develop and test candidates' own scientific ideas. *[B4.1.1a) b)]*; B4.2 Assess and manage risks when carrying out practical work *[B4.2.1 a) b)]*; B4.3 Collect primary and secondary data *[B4.3.2 a) e) f)]*; B4.5 Analyse and interpret primary and secondary data. *[B4.5.4 a)]*

Lesson structure

Starters

Horrible history! – Read a description of someone dying of an infection in the past, before the days of penicillin. For example, Lord Caernarvon dying from an infected mosquito bite following the discovery of Tutankhamen's tomb. Ask: 'Was the curse really an ancient biological hazard warning?' Discuss. *(5 minutes)*

What medicine do I need? – Either pretend to feel unwell yourself or pick someone from the class, wrap them up in a scarf and give them a hot water bottle. Produce a bottle of over-the-counter cough medicine, a box of aspirins or paracetamol, some throat sweets and a bottle of prescription antibiotics. To support students, discuss what should be given to the 'patient' and why. To extend students, allow them to question the 'patient' (as in a consultation at the doctor's), before making any decision as to what medicine should be given. They should offer an explanation to the 'patient'. *(10 minutes)*

Main

There are several important issues in this spread and some interesting ideas for practical work.

- If the first starter activity is not used, then ask the students what they understand by the term 'medicine' and compile a list of suggested medicines and their uses on the board. Distinguish between those that relieve symptoms, such as painkillers, and those that kill pathogens, such as antibiotics. Discuss the use of antibiotics and why they are effective in destroying bacteria but not effective against viruses.

- Search the internet to find pictures of Alexander Fleming, the discovery of penicillin and his work.

- Set up an experiment to show the sensitivity of bacteria to antibiotics (see 'Practical support'). It can be shown as a demonstration or carried out by the students in groups. Predictions can be made. This involves the introduction of many 'How Science Works' concepts. [Note: There are restrictions on the use of bacteria in schools, so guidelines would need to be consulted and all suitable precautions taken if this is to be used as a class experiment.]

Plenaries

Quick quiz – Support students by asking them to make a list of the key terms on the board and another list of the definitions and ask students to come up and match a key term with its definition. Extent students by getting them to use either the list of key terms or the list of definitions and, working in teams, ask them to supply the correct key term or definition. *(5 minutes)*

Should antibiotics be used for … ? – Provide a list of statements about the use of antibiotics and ask students to say whether or not each is a good idea, with reasons to back up their decision. Statements could include:
'Chickens raised in barns are given antibiotics in their food.'
'If you have a cold you should go to the doctor for some antibiotics.'
'In some countries, antibiotics can be bought over the counter.'
'Milking cows may have tubes of antibiotics placed in their udders.'
'Some chopping boards have antibiotics/antibacterial substances built into them.'
(10 minutes)

Practical/demonstration support

 Experiment to show the sensitivity of bacteria to antibiotics

Equipment and materials required
Agar plates, a suitable bacterium, such as *Bacillus subtilis* (several antibiotics; or different concentrations of one antibiotic could be used), Oxoid multidiscs (available from suppliers).

Details
This can be shown as a demonstration or carried out by the students in groups.

Agar plates are inoculated with a suitable bacterium, such as *Bacillus subtilis*, have antibiotic-impregnated discs placed on them and are incubated for 24 hours. The antibiotics diffuse from the discs into the agar and inhibit the growth of bacteria around them, resulting in clear zones in the agar. The diameter of these clear zones can be measured.

Safety: If this is to be carried out by the students, then all the usual precautions need to be taken. The agar plates could be set up for them and sealed after incubation, but if facilities allow it, it is more instructive if they do it themselves following all the safety measures involved with the handling of sterile equipment and bacteria. (Teacher should be trained in aseptic techniques.) More information available from the CLEAPSS Handbook Section 15.2.

B1 1.6 — Using drugs to treat disease

Learning objectives
- What is a medicine?
- How do medicines work?
- Why can't we use antibiotics to treat diseases caused by viruses?

When you have an infectious disease, you generally take medicines which contain useful drugs. Often the medicine doesn't affect the pathogen that is causing the problems. It just eases the symptoms and makes you feel better.

Drugs like aspirin and paracetamol are very useful as painkillers. When you have a cold they will help relieve your headache and sore throat. On the other hand, they will have no effect on the viruses which have entered your tissues and made you feel ill.

Many of the medicines you can buy at a chemist's or supermarket are like this. They relieve your symptoms but do not kill the pathogens. They do not cure you any faster. You have to wait for your immune system to overcome the pathogens.

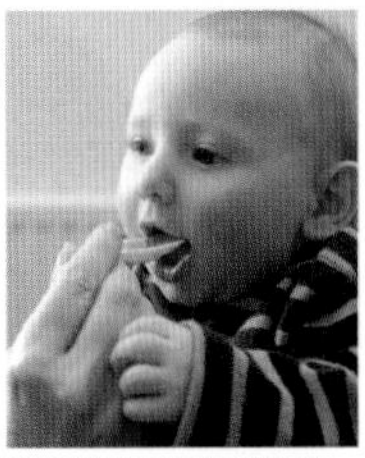

Figure 1 Taking paracetamol will make this child feel better, but she will not actually get well any faster as a result

a Why don't medicines like aspirin actually cure your illness?

Antibiotics [k]

Drugs that make us feel better are useful but what we really need are drugs that can cure us. We use antiseptics and disinfectants to kill bacteria outside the body. But they are far too poisonous to use inside your body. They would kill you and your pathogens at the same time!

The drugs that have really changed the way we treat infectious diseases are **antibiotics**. These are medicines that can work inside your body to kill the bacteria that cause diseases.

b What is an antibiotic?

How antibiotics work [k]

Figure 2 Penicillin was the first antibiotic. Now we have many different ones which kill different types of bacterium. Scientists are always on the look out for new antibiotics to keep us ahead in the battle against pathogens.

Antibiotics like penicillin work by killing the bacteria that cause disease while they are inside your body. They damage the bacterial cells without harming your own cells. They have had an enormous effect on our society. We can now cure bacterial diseases that killed millions of people in the past.

Unfortunately antibiotics are not the complete answer to the problem of infectious diseases. They have no effect on diseases caused by viruses.

The problem with viral pathogens is that they reproduce inside the cells of your body. It is extremely difficult to develop drugs that kill the viruses without damaging the cells and tissues of your body at the same time.

c How do antibiotics work?

Discovering penicillin

Alexander Fleming was a scientist who studied bacteria and wanted to find ways of killing them. In 1928, he was growing lots of bacteria on agar plates. Alexander was rather careless, and his lab was quite untidy. He often left the lids off his plates for a long time and forgot about experiments he had set up!

After one holiday, Fleming saw that lots of his culture plates had mould growing on them. He noticed a clear ring in the jelly around some of the spots of mould. Something had killed the bacteria covering the jelly.

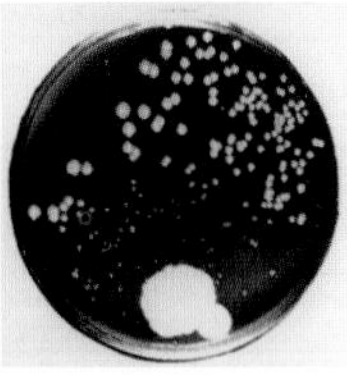

Fleming saw how important this was. He called the mould 'penicillin'. He worked hard to extract a juice from the mould. But he couldn't get much penicillin and he couldn't make it survive, even in a fridge. So Fleming couldn't prove it would actually kill bacteria and make people better. By 1934 he gave up on penicillin and went on to do different work.

About 10 years after penicillin was first discovered, Ernst Chain and Howard Florey set about trying to use it on people. They gave some penicillin they extracted to Albert Alexander, who was dying of a blood infection. The effect was amazing and Albert recovered. But then the penicillin ran out. Florey and Chain even tried to collect unused penicillin from Albert's urine, but it was no good. The infection came back and sadly Albert died.

They kept working and eventually they managed to make penicillin on an industrial scale. The process was able to produce enough penicillin to supply the demands of the Second World War. We have used it as a medicine ever since.

d Who was the first person to discover penicillin?

Figure 3 Alexander Fleming was on the lookout for something that would kill bacteria. As a result of him noticing the effect of this mould on his cultures, millions of lives have been saved around the world.

Summary questions

1 What is the main difference between drugs such as paracetamol and drugs such as penicillin?

2 **a** How did Alexander Fleming discover penicillin?
   b Why was it so difficult to make a medicine out of penicillin?
   c Who developed the industrial process which made it possible to mass-produce penicillin?

3 Explain why it is so much more difficult to develop medicines against viruses than it has been to develop antibacterial drugs.

Study tip
Remember:
- Antibiotics are drugs which kill bacteria.
- Antibodies are produced by white blood cells to kill bacteria.

Key points
- Some medicines relieve the symptoms of disease but do not kill the pathogens which cause it.
- Antibiotics cure bacterial diseases by killing the bacteria inside your body.
- Antibiotics do not destroy viruses because viruses reproduce inside the cells. It is difficult to develop drugs that can destroy viruses without damaging your body cells.

Further teaching suggestions

Aspirin – more than just a painkiller
- Remind students that aspirin has a role to play in the treatment of heart and other diseases as well as being a painkiller. It is also an anti-inflammatory which can be tolerated well by people with arthritis and other muscle conditions.

Old remedies, did they work?
- Ask: 'Is there any truth in old wives' tales and ancient remedies for healing?' Show a piece of mouldy bread in a sealed plastic bag, a jar of honey, a bottle of vinegar, a soldering iron (for cauterising), some wood ash and some cobwebs. Discuss the scientific background to these remedies and consider what was available to people before there were antibiotics.

Allergies to antibiotics
- 'What about people who are allergic to penicillin?' Introduce the idea that there are different antibiotics, perhaps mentioning narrow-spectrum and broad-spectrum antibiotics. Ask students if they have been prescribed antibiotics other than penicillin.

Answers to in-text questions

a Because they do not kill the pathogens that are making you ill.

b A drug that kills pathogenic bacteria in your body.

c They damage bacterial cells without damaging human cells.

d Alexander Fleming.

Summary answers

1 Paracetamol relieves symptoms/makes you feel better, whereas antibiotics kill the bacteria and actually make you better.

2 **a** He noticed a clear area around mould growing on bacterial plates.
   b It was difficult to get much penicillin out of the mould and it does not keep easily.
   c Florey and Chain.

3 Viral pathogens reproduce inside your cells, so it is very difficult to develop a drug that destroys them without destroying your cells as well.

B1 1.7

Growing and investigating bacteria

Learning objectives

Students should learn:

- to grow an uncontaminated culture of bacteria in the lab
- why we need uncontaminated cultures
- why we incubate bacteria at no more than 25 °C in schools.

Learning outcomes

Most students should be able to:

- successfully grow an uncontaminated culture of bacteria at below 25 °C
- explain why it is important to maintain sterile conditions
- describe the different conditions used to grow cultures in schools and industry.

Some students should also be able to:

- explain why cultures are incubated at a temperature below 25 °C in a school laboratory but industry uses higher temperatures.

Answers to in-text questions

a A nutrient-rich medium used to culture microorganisms such as fungi and bacteria.
b To prevent contamination by microbes already on the equipment.

Support

- Show a picture of a wound and an infected wound. Ask students what should be done with a wound to stop it from becoming infected. Draw out that there are bacteria all around us and that they will grow where conditions are right. Discuss the potential for blood poisoning and gangrene and the consequences.

Extend

- Show a photo of a child in an isolation tent. Get the students to give reasons why the child might be in there, what apparatus must be attached to the tent and why. What would happen if it were perforated, and how the necessities of living are catered for.

Specification link-up: Biology B1.1

- Uncontaminated cultures of microorganisms are required for ... *[B1.1.2 m]*
- In school and college laboratories, cultures should be incubated at ... *[B1.1.2 n]*
- In industrial conditions higher temperatures can produce more rapid growth. *[B1.1.2 o]*

  Controlled Assessment: B4.2 Assess and manage risks when carrying out practical work. *[B4.2.1 a) b)]*

Lesson structure

Starters

Growing pure cultures – Show the students an agar plate that has been exposed to the air and then incubated. Ask them what this shows and what each colony represents. Draw out from them that we can only see the bacteria because there are such large numbers forming a colony. Ask for suggestions as to how they would set about obtaining a pure culture of one of the microorganisms on the plate. How could they stop other bacteria growing? Introduce the term 'aseptic' and discuss the techniques involved with growing pure cultures. *(5 minutes)*

What do we need to know in order to grow bacteria? – Support students by asking them what are the ideal growing conditions for living organisms and discuss whether these are the same for bacteria. Extend students by asking them for suggestions about where bacteria can be found (e.g. in air, on food, in soil, in hot springs, inside organisms) and then ask the students what would be the ideal growing conditions for the bacteria in each situation. This should draw out that the ideal conditions can vary according to the situation and introduce the idea that bacteria can be dormant until the conditions are right for them. *(10 minutes)*

Main

- The preparation of a pure (uncontaminated) culture of a microorganism is described in the Student Book and here (see 'Practical support'), with a series of steps to follow. This practical could be carried out by the students using a non-pathogenic bacterium such as *Bacillus subtilis*.

- As suggested in the Student Book, the cultures set up in the previous practical or pre-inoculated plates can be used to investigate the action of disinfectants and antibiotics on bacteria. The investigation of the sensitivity of bacteria to different antibiotics was described in the previous spread. A similar technique can be used to investigate the action of different antiseptics or different concentrations of the same antiseptic on bacteria. It would be helpful to the students for the techniques involved in inoculating an agar plate to be demonstrated to them before they carry out the activity for themselves. The need for sterile conditions and the use of aseptic techniques can be reinforced. Make sure that the students understand all the safety precautions and that they follow the instructions for the safe disposal of their agar plates.

- In addition to the experiment above, the action of antiseptics on bacteria could be investigated (see 'Practical support') and the results compared with those of the experiment described in the previous spread (B1.1.6).

Plenaries

The twit got it wrong! – Get students to imagine a scenario where improper techniques used in a lab led to unfortunate consequences. Have them write a 'tweet' of 140 characters or less on the subject and choose one or more students to read out their account. *(5 minutes)*

Summary time – To support students, prepare a series of cards with the steps of the procedure for growing a pure culture on them and ask students to place them in the correct order. Extend students by asking them to construct their own flow chart for the procedure. This will review the lesson and summarise the main points. For both groups, check the results and reinforce the points by use of questioning and getting students to vocalise their understanding. *(10 minutes)*

Practical support

Growing uncontaminated cultures

Equipment and materials required
Sterile Petri dishes, inoculating loops, Bunsen burners, cultures of suitable bacteria, adhesive tape.

Details
The Petri dishes must be sterilised before using them to grow microorganisms. The nutrient agar, which will provide their food, must also be sterilised. This kills off any unwanted microorganisms. Heat can be used to sterilise glass dishes. A special oven called an autoclave is often used. It sterilises by using steam at high pressure. Plastic Petri dishes are often bought already sterilised. UV light or gamma radiation is used to kill the bacteria. The next step is to inoculate the sterile agar with the microorganisms you want to grow.

Once the plates are inoculated, lids should be fixed with tape in three places. Do not seal all the way round. The sealed Petri dishes need to be incubated (kept warm) for several days so the microorganisms can grow. In school and college laboratories the maximum temperature at which cultures are incubated is 25 °C. Turning the dishes upside down during incubation stops condensation forming on the agar.

Investigating the action of disinfectants, antibiotics and antiseptics on bacteria

Equipment and materials required
Pre-inoculated agar plates; cork borers; discs impregnated with antibiotics, disinfectants or antiseptics as required; sterile forceps; Bunsen burners.

Details
Either use the cultures you set up yourself or use pre-inoculated agar. Agar plates are inoculated with a harmless bacterium and have wells cut into them by removing cylinders of agar with a cork borer. Solutions of the antimicrobial substances being tested could be placed in the wells and the plates incubated. Although it is common practice for plates to be inverted during incubation, these plates will contain liquid, so they should be incubated right-side-up. The relative effects can be judged by the diameter of the clear areas around the wells – an area of clear jelly indicates that the bacteria have been killed. (See CLEAPSS Handbook/CD ROM Section 15.2).

Safety: Precautions should be taken when handling and disposing of bacterial cultures and plates.

Keeping healthy

Growing and investigating bacteria

B1 1.7 Growing and investigating bacteria

Learning objectives
● How can we grow an uncontaminated culture of bacteria in the lab?
● Why do we need uncontaminated cultures?
● Why do we incubate bacteria at no more than 25 °C in schools and colleges?

To find out more about microorganisms we need to culture them. This means we grow very large numbers of them so that we can see all of the bacteria (the colony) as a whole. Many microorganisms can be grown in the laboratory. This helps us to learn more about them. We can find out what nutrients they need to grow and investigate which chemicals are best at killing them. Bacteria are the most commonly cultured microorganisms.

Growing microorganisms in the lab

To culture (grow) microorganisms you must provide them with everything they need. This means giving them a liquid or gel containing nutrients – a culture medium. It contains carbohydrate as an energy source along with various minerals and sometimes other chemicals. Most microorganisms also need warmth and oxygen to grow.

You usually provide the nutrients in agar jelly. Hot agar containing all the nutrients your bacteria will need is poured into a Petri dish. It is then left to cool and set before you add the microorganisms.

You must take great care when you are culturing microorganisms. The bacteria you want to grow may be harmless. However, there is always the risk that a mutation (a change in the DNA) will take place and produce a new and dangerous pathogen.

You also want to keep the pure strains of bacteria you are culturing free from any other microorganisms. Such contamination might come from your skin, the soil or the water around you. Investigations need uncontaminated cultures of microorganism. Whenever you are culturing microorganisms you must carry out strict health and safety procedures to protect yourself and others.

a What is agar jelly?

??? Did you know …?
You are surrounded by disease-causing bacteria all the time. If you cultured bacteria at 37°C – human body temperature – there would be a very high risk of growing some dangerous pathogens.

Figure 1 Culturing microorganisms like bacteria makes it possible for us to observe them and see how different chemicals affect them

Figure 2 When working with the most dangerous pathogens, scientists need to be very careful. Sensible safety precautions are needed when working with microorganisms.

Growing useful organisms

You can prepare an uncontaminated culture of microorganisms in the laboratory by following a number of steps.

The Petri dishes on which you will grow your microorganisms must be sterilised before using them. The nutrient agar, which will provide their food, must also be sterilised. This kills off any unwanted microorganisms. You can use heat to sterilise glass dishes. A special oven called an autoclave is often used. It sterilises by using steam at high pressure. Plastic Petri dishes are often bought ready-sterilised. UV light or gamma radiation is used to kill the bacteria.

b Why must everything be sterilised before you start a culture?

The next step is to inoculate the sterile agar with the microorganisms you want to grow.

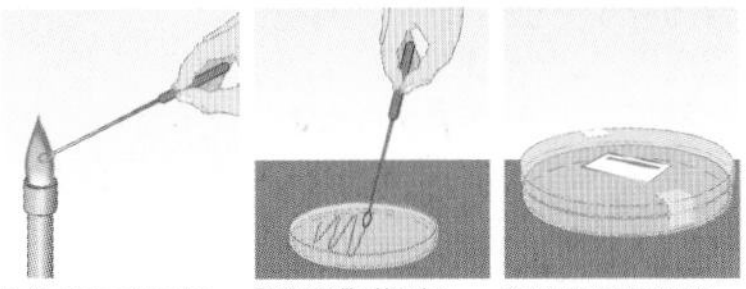

Sterilise the inoculating loop used to transfer microorganisms to the agar by heating it until it is red hot in the flame of a Bunsen and then letting it cool. Do not put the loop down or blow on it as it cools.

Dip the sterilised loop in a suspension of the bacteria you want to grow and use it to make zigzag streaks across the surface of the agar. Replace the lid on the dish as quickly as possible to avoid contamination.

Seal the lid of the Petri dish with adhesive tape to prevent microorganisms from the air contaminating the culture – or microbes from the culture escaping. Do not seal all the way around the edge so oxygen can get into the dish and harmful anaerobic bacteria do not grow.

Figure 3 Culturing microorganisms safely in the laboratory

Once you have inoculated your plates, the sealed Petri dishes need to be incubated (kept warm) for several days so the microorganisms can grow. In school and college laboratories the maximum temperature at which cultures are incubated is 25 °C. This greatly reduces the likelihood that you will grow pathogens that might be harmful to people. In industrial conditions, bacterial cultures are often grown at higher temperatures, which allow the microorganisms to grow more rapidly.

Practical

Investigating the action of disinfectants and antibiotics

You can use cultures set up yourself or pre-inoculated agar to investigate the effect of disinfectants and antibiotics on the growth of bacteria. An area of clear jelly indicates that the bacteria have been killed or cannot grow.
● What are the safety issues in this investigation and how will you manage any risks?

Summary questions
1 Why do we culture microorganisms in the laboratory?
2 Why don't we culture bacteria at 37°C in the school lab?
3 When you set up a culture of bacteria in a Petri dish (see Figure 3) you give the bacteria everything they need to grow as fast as possible. However these ideal conditions do not last forever. What might limit the growth of the bacteria in a culture on a Petri dish?

Study tip
Make sure you understand why we sterilise. We boil solutions and heat-treat apparatus in an autoclave to **kill bacteria** already in them. This is sterilising.

Key points
● An uncontaminated culture of microorganisms can be grown using sterilised Petri dishes and agar. You sterilise the inoculating loop before use and seal the lid of the Petri dish to prevent unwanted microorganisms getting in. The culture is left at about 25°C for a few days.
● Uncontaminated cultures are needed so we can investigate the effect of chemicals such as disinfectants and antibiotics on microorganisms.
● Cultures should be incubated at a maximum temperature of 25°C in schools and colleges to reduce the likelihood of harmful pathogens growing.

36

37

Further teaching suggestions

More practicals
● Once students are familiar with the techniques, they could try isolating bacteria from live yogurts. The usual precautions and safety regulations should be followed.

Using a culture broth
● Pure cultures of bacteria do not always have to be grown on agar plates. It could be useful to set up a broth culture as a demonstration. Students could compare the conditions, e.g. food sources, aeration, etc.

Useful commercial bacteria
● Ask students to compile a list of useful bacteria that might need to be produced as pure cultures for commercial use, e.g. in the food industry (yoghurt, cheese).

Keeping clean
● Give the students time to look at a more detailed coverage of aseptic techniques such as that found at www.biotopics.co.uk. Search for 'microbiological techniques – the basics'. Get them to make a note of key words from the text.

Summary answers

1 To find out more about them. To find out which nutrients they need to grow and to investigate what will affect them and stop them growing.

2 This is the human body temperature so any bacteria which grow at that temperature would be likely to be able to infect people and cause harm.

3 Using up the available food and oxygen, build up of waste products such as carbon dioxide and other toxins.

B1 1.8 | Changing pathogens

Learning objectives

Students should learn:

- that bacteria and viruses can mutate causing new strains to appear
- that new strains of bacteria and viruses may be resistant to antibiotics
- that resistant strains of pathogens survive as a result of natural selection
- that overuse of antibiotics should be avoided in order to prevent more resistant strains of bacteria arising.

Learning outcomes

Most students should be able to:

- describe how mutations of bacteria and viruses can give rise to resistant strains
- describe how natural selection causes the populations of resistant strains to increase
- describe how new strains of pathogens can spread rapidly causing epidemics and pandemics.

Some students should also be able to:

- explain in detail how bacteria become increasingly resistant to antibiotics **[HT only]**
- evaluate the problems of preventing the spread of a new disease such as a mutated form of bird flu.

Support

- Students could make a poster with reasons why it is important to finish a course of antibiotics.
- Students could write a list of precautions that could be taken to avoid the spread of the flu virus during an epidemic.

Extend

- MRSA is not the only problem or cause of infection in hospitals. Students could research the incidence of other infections, such as *Clostridium difficile*, which can spread in a hospital environment.

Specification link-up: Biology B1.1

- Many strains of bacteria, including MRSA, have … *[B1.1.2 i)]*
- Mutations of pathogens produce new strains … *[B1.1.2 j)]*
- Antibiotics kill individual pathogens of the nonresistant strain … *[B1.1.2 j)]* **[HT only]**
- Explain how the treatment of disease has changed as a result of … *[B1.1.2]*
- Evaluate the consequences of mutations of bacteria … *[B1.1.2]*

Lesson structure

Starters

Let's get it clear! – This is a good opportunity to remind students of which diseases are caused by bacteria and which by viruses. To support students, ask them to draw up a list of ailments on the board and ask students to put a 'B' by those caused by bacteria and 'V' for those caused by a virus. To extend students, include some ailments such as athlete's foot, ringworm and malaria, which are caused by other organisms and, as well as asking students to identify the cause of the ailment, ask them to suggest which ones can be prevented by vaccination and why. *(5 minutes)*

Finish your medicine! – In discussion with the students, build up a flow chart of what happens when you are prescribed a course of antibiotics and how you should take them. What are the consequences of not finishing the course? What are the dangers of taking antibiotics too frequently? If appropriate, you could mention the effects that antibiotics have on the gut flora and the possible consequences. *(10 minutes)*

Main

It is important that students understand how antibiotic resistance arises and how mutations occur. It would be possible to combine two or more of these suggestions if time permits.

- What is a mutation and how does it occur? Prepare a PowerPoint presentation or a video on mutations and how they occur. Provide students with a worksheet which they can complete as the presentation proceeds. It could be worth pointing out that mutations occur under natural circumstances all the time, but that the mutation rate in microorganisms appears to be greater as they reproduce more rapidly than other organisms.

- A presentation on antibiotic resistance could follow the suggestion made above. Link in with the practical work suggested in the Main lesson notes in this book on spread B1 1.7 Growing and investigating bacteria'on the sensitivity of bacteria to different antibiotics.

- Provide groups of students with reference material on the MRSA story, such as suitable websites, newspaper and magazine articles, and information given to hospitals, and suggest that they write a script for a radio or TV programme about MRSA. The emphasis is to be on the facts rather than on sensational reporting.

- Initiate a general discussion on the difference between the two terms 'pandemic' and 'epidemic' with examples. Using the information in the Student Book, students could draw up a list of how diseases spread from country to country. Alongside each method of spread, suggestions for a control could be made. Finally, the students could decide on how they personally would recommend precautions that they and their families could take to avoid exposure to the disease and thus survive.

Plenaries

Can you catch flu from …? – To support students, collect information from them about the different types of influenza virus they have heard of or read about. Discuss with them why it is rare for the strain of the virus that causes the disease in animals to cause the disease in humans. This reinforces the idea that a *change* or *mutation* is needed before humans are affected. Extend students by discussing why bird flu spreads so quickly in Asia and why Asia is a likely source of mutated viruses which might cause a pandemic. *(5 minutes)*

Get your flu jab! – Ask students why it is important that people aged 65 and over should be vaccinated against influenza every year. Who else qualifies for the flu jab? Why? Should it be given to everyone? If time permits, include a discussion about who was offered swine flu jabs and why there were different age restrictions. *(10 minutes)*

Further teaching suggestions

Survival poster
- Students could design a poster setting out how people can avoid/reduce their chances of catching flu or other infectious diseases. The poster could be displayed in schools, surgeries and public places.

Research previous flu pandemics
- Students may find it interesting to find out more about major outbreaks of influenza. Some of their grandparents might remember the outbreak in the 1950s. History websites could provide information on the rapidity with which the disease spread and how long it lasted. An interesting comparison could be made between the times involved previously, e.g. Spanish flu after the First World War, and the predicted timescales for any future outbreaks.

Swine flu – did you get it?
- This could be incorporated in the previous suggestion. Students could discuss whether they thought that the public were properly informed and that all the precautions taken were necessary.

Antiviral medicines and vaccines
- Initiate a class discussion on the use of antiviral medicines to bridge the gap between the outbreak of the disease and the development of a suitable vaccine. Why does it take so long for the vaccine to be developed? How do antiviral medicines work?

Keeping healthy

B1 1.8   Changing pathogens

Learning objectives
- What is antibiotic resistance?
- How can we prevent antibiotic resistance developing? [H]
- Why is mutation in bacteria and viruses such a problem?

If you are given an antibiotic and use it properly, the bacteria that have made you ill are killed off. However some bacteria develop resistance to antibiotics. They have a natural mutation (change in the genetic material) that means they are not affected by the antibiotic. These mutations happen by chance and they produce new strains of bacteria by **natural selection**.

More types of bacteria are becoming resistant to more antibiotics. Diseases caused by bacteria are becoming more difficult to treat. Over the years antibiotics have been overused and used when they are not really needed. This increases the rate at which antibiotic resistant strains have developed.

Antibiotic-resistant bacteria

Normally an antibiotic kills the bacteria of a non-resistant strain. However individual resistant bacteria survive and reproduce, so the population of **resistant** bacteria increases.

Antibiotics are no longer used to treat non-serious infections such as mild throat infections, which are often caused by viruses. Hopefully this will slow down the rate of development of resistant strains.

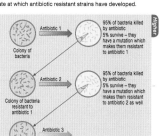

Figure 1 Bacteria can develop resistance to many different antibiotics in a process of natural selection as this simple model shows

To prevent more resistant strains of bacteria appearing it is important not to overuse antibiotics. It's best to only use them when you really need them. Antibiotics don't affect viruses so people should not demand antibiotics to treat an illness which the doctor thinks is viral.

Some antibiotics treat very specific bacteria. Others treat many different types of bacteria. The right type of antibiotic must be used to treat each bacterial infection to prevent further antibiotic resistance developing. It is also important that people finish their course of medicine every time.

a Why is it important not to use antibiotics too frequently?

Study tip
Washing hands removes the pathogens on them, but it may not kill the pathogens.

The MRSA story

Hospitals use a lot of antibiotics to treat infections. As a result of natural selection, some of the bacteria in hospitals are resistant to many antibiotics. This is what has happened with MRSA (the bacterium methicillin-resistant *Staphylococcus aureus*).

As doctors and nurses move from patient to patient, these antibiotic-resistant bacteria are spread easily. MRSA alone now contributes to around 1000 deaths every year in UK hospitals.

There are a number of simple steps which can reduce the spread of microorganisms such as MRSA. We have known some of them since the time of Semmelweis, but they sometimes get forgotten!
- Antibiotics should only be used when they are really needed.
- Specific bacteria should be treated with specific antibiotics.
- Medical staff should wash their hands with soap and water or alcohol gel between patients. They should wear disposable clothing or clothing that is regularly sterilised.
- Visitors should wash their hands as they enter and leave the hospital.
- Patients infected with antibiotic-resistant bacteria should be looked after in isolation from other patients.
- Hospitals should be kept clean – there should be high standards of hygiene.

b Is MRSA a bacterium or a virus?

Mutation and pandemics

Another problem caused by the mutation of pathogens is that new forms of diseases can appear. These new strains can spread quickly and cause widespread illness because no one is immune to them and there is no effective treatment. For example the flu virus mutates easily. Every year there are new strains of the virus that your immune system doesn't recognise. There is no effective treatment against viruses at all. The existing flu vaccine is not effective against new strains of the virus, and it takes time to develop a new vaccine.

There may be a flu **epidemic** (in one country) or even a **pandemic** (across several countries). In 1918–19, a new strain of flu virus killed over 40 million people around the world.

With modern international travel, a new strain of pathogen can spread very quickly. In 2009 there was a pandemic of a new strain of flu, known as swine flu, which spread very fast. Internationally, countries worked to stop it spreading and the death toll was kept relatively low.

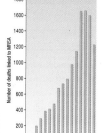

Figure 2 Data that show how the number of deaths in which MRSA played a part from 1993 (Source: National Statistics Office)

links
For more information on the work of Semmelweis, look back at B1 1.4 Pathogens and disease.

Summary questions

1 Copy and complete using the words below:
   antibiotics bacterium (virus) better disease mutation mutate resistant virus (bacterium)
   If bacteria change or .... they may become .... to .... This means the medicine no longer makes you .... A .... in a .... or .... can also lead to a new form of ....

2 Make a flow chart to show how bacteria develop resistance to antibiotics.

3 Use Figure 2 to help you answer these questions.
   a How could you explain the increase in deaths linked to MRSA?
   b How could you explain the fall in deaths linked to MRSA, which still continues?

Key points
- Many types of bacterium have developed antibiotic resistance as a result of natural selection. To prevent the problem getting worse we must not overuse antibiotics.
- If bacteria or viruses mutate, new strains of the pathogen can appear causing disease.
- New strains of disease which spread rapidly can cause epidemics and pandemics. Antibiotics and vaccinations may not be effective against the new strain.

38   39

Study tip

Washing hands removes the pathogens on them, it may not kill the pathogens.

It is worth reminding students that some resistant bacteria are not killed by the alcohol gels and hand washing is still needed.

Answers to in-text questions

a To prevent more antibiotic-resistant strains appearing.

b Bacterium.

Summary answers

1 mutate, resistant, antibiotics, better, mutation, virus (bacterium), bacterium (virus), disease

2 Students should show clear understanding of the different stages involved in the development of antibiotic resistance. Colony of bacteria treated with antibiotic 1 → 5% have mutation and survive → the surviving bacteria are treated with antibiotic 2 → 5% have a mutation and are resistant to antibiotic 1 and 2 → etc.

3 **a** Increased use of antibiotics leading to more resistant bacteria, lower hygiene standards in hospitals, people failing to wash their hands between patients, visitors, etc. Any other sensible point.

   b Could be an improvement in cleanliness in hospital, people being more careful about hand washing, introduction and use of alcohol gels for visitors and staff in hospitals, any sensible points.

B1 1.9

Immunity

Learning objectives

Students should learn:

- how the immune system works
- how vaccination can protect you against bacterial and viral diseases.

Learning outcomes

Most students should be able to:

- describe how the immune system responds to pathogens in the body
- explain how vaccines work
- list some of the advantages and disadvantages of being vaccinated against a particular disease.

Some students should also be able to:

- evaluate the advantages and disadvantages of being vaccinated against a particular disease.

Support

- Students can be given sheets with key words in one column with an empty box next to each one. Write the definitions in another column with a letter in a box next to each one. Students can match the words with the definitions and put the letter corresponding to the correct definition in the box next to each word.

Extend

- What are the consequences of totally eradicating infectious diseases such as smallpox? Discuss this in relation to a possible terrorist attack involving the release of diseases into highly populated areas.
- Students could be given more raw data to analyse, making predictions and extrapolating trend lines.

Specification link-up: Biology B1.1

- People can be immunised against a disease by … *[B1.1.2 l)]*
- Explain how the treatment of disease has changed as … *[B1.1.2]*
- The immune system of the body produces specific … *[B1.1.2 e)]*

    Controlled Assessment: B4.5 Analyse and interpret primary and secondary data. *[B4.5.1 a) b)]*

Lesson structure

Starters

Jabs: who has had them? – Discuss the vaccinations the students have had. Has anyone had special vaccinations in order to visit certain countries? Discuss what might be in the injections. *(5 minutes)*

The work of Edward Jenner – Get the students to locate a webpage about Edward Jenner and vaccination. After a short study of this, ask the students a series of questions to see how much information they have managed to discover. Support students by keeping the questions straightforward and factual (e.g. dates, places, names of people involved and procedure). Extend students by asking them why his work was so remarkable and if it would be allowed today. *(10 minutes)*

Main

- Introduce the key words connected to vaccination: antigen, immunity, immunisation and vaccination. Distinguish 'antigen' from similar words like 'antibody, antibiotic and antitoxin', by establishing clear definitions (use for revision cards). Draw out the links between the words, building up the connections in the context of defence against disease.
- Link with a presentation on what happens when you have your jabs and the importance of the second dose and the boosters. This can be illustrated by using a graph. Why do we need to keep up with tetanus jabs?
- Using the section in the Student Book, discuss the risks associated with vaccination and the controversies surrounding the vaccine debate. How Science Works concepts could be introduced here. Students should be able to distinguish between a fact and an opinion and drawing conclusions using scientific evidence.
- Using a computer, design a poster or a leaflet persuading parents to have their children vaccinated.
- Use graphs to show how many people used to die of infectious/contagious diseases in the past. Information can be obtained from the internet (try BBC, Wellcome Museum, etc. – either for statistics for individual diseases such as cholera and TB, or for more general information). As a practical exercise to emphasise and visualise the numbers involved, use grains of rice, one for each person who dies. By weighing and calculation, you can work out how many grains per gram and therefore how heavy the piles of rice for each year should be.
- It could be interesting to compare deaths from diseases such as TB in different countries, or to compare the decline in deaths from diseases such as smallpox with the increase in deaths from Aids, pointing out that there are always some infectious diseases about!

Plenaries

Why do we need booster doses of vaccines? – If not already done, show a graph of what happens after a single dose of vaccine, followed by a second dose. Discuss in relation to different diseases, such as polio, diphtheria and some of the less well-known ones, such as yellow fever and cholera. *(5 minutes)*

Key words challenge – Return to the key words on the board and support students by asking them to give definitions for each one. Extend students by asking them to make a sentence containing any two of the words. This can be a competition. *(10 minutes)*

Further teaching suggestions

Making a display

- Extend the 'grains of rice' idea from the main section to make a display around the school highlighting how many people in the world die from preventable diseases now. This can be done for different countries, for deaths from specific diseases or as part of a wider campaign to draw attention to poverty in developing countries (campaigns such as 'Make Poverty History').

Investigating causes of death

- If students are interested in the past, there are websites that

give details of the causes of death in different parts of the country: data collected from records of death certificates. (See www.statistics.gov.uk.) They could also research parish registers. The history of the Great Plague of 1665, its spread to Eyam in Derbyshire and the consequences are well documented and accessible via the internet.

Lady Mary Wortley Montagu

- As a follow-up to the work of Edward Jenner, students could find out about the work of Lady Mary Wortley Montagu.

Keeping healthy

Immunity

B1 1.9	**Immunity**

Learning objectives

- How does your immune system work?
- How does vaccination protect you against disease?

Figure 1 No one likes having a vaccination very much – but they save millions of lives!

Every cell has unique proteins on its surface called antigens. The antigens on the microorganisms that get into your body are different to the ones on your own cells. Your immune system recognises they are different.

Your white blood cells then make antibodies which join up with the antigens. This destroys the pathogens.

Your white blood cells 'remember' the right antibody needed to tackle a particular pathogen. If you meet that pathogen again, they can make the same antibody very quickly. So you become immune to that disease.

The first time you meet a new pathogen you get ill. That's because there is a delay while your body sorts out the right antibody needed. The next time, you completely destroy the invaders before they have time to make you feel unwell.

a What is an antigen?

Vaccination

Some pathogens can make you seriously ill very quickly. In fact you can die before your body manages to make the right antibodies. Fortunately, you can be protected against many of these serious diseases by immunisation (also known as vaccination).

Immunisation involves giving you a vaccine. A vaccine is usually made of a dead or weakened form of the disease-causing microorganism. It works by triggering your body's natural immune response to invading pathogens.

A small amount of dead or inactive pathogen is introduced into your body. This gives your white blood cells the chance to develop the right antibodies against the pathogen without you getting ill.

Then, if you meet the live pathogens, your white blood cells can respond rapidly. They can make the right antibodies just as if you had already had the disease, so you are protected against it.

b What is an antibody?

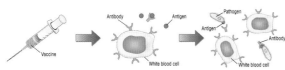

Small amounts of dead or inactive pathogen are put into your body, often by injection.

The antigens in the vaccine stimulate your white blood cells into making antibodies. The antibodies destroy the antigens without any risk of you getting the disease.

You are immune to future infections by the pathogen. That's because your body can respond rapidly and make the correct antibody as if you had already had the disease.

Figure 2 This is how vaccines protect you against dangerous infectious diseases

We use vaccines to protect us against both bacterial diseases (e.g. tetanus and diphtheria) and viral diseases (e.g. polio, measles and mumps). For example, the MMR vaccine protects against measles, mumps and rubella. Vaccines have saved millions of lives around the world. If a large proportion of the population is immune to a disease, the spread of the pathogen is very much reduced. One disease – smallpox – has been completely wiped out by vaccinations. Doctors hope polio will also disappear in the next few years.

c Give an example of one bacterial and one viral disease which you can be immunised against.

How Science Works

The vaccine debate 🔑

No medicine is completely risk free. Very rarely, a child will react badly to a vaccine with tragic results. Making the decision to have your baby immunised can be difficult.

Society needs as many people as possible to be immunised against as many diseases as possible. This keeps the pool of infection in the population very low. On the other hand, you know there is a remote chance that something may go wrong with a vaccination.

Because vaccines are so successful, we rarely see the terrible diseases they protect us against. A hundred years ago nearly 50% of all deaths of children and young people were caused by infectious diseases. The development of antibiotics and vaccines means that now only 0.5% of all deaths in the same age group are due to infectious disease. Many children were also left permanently damaged by serious infections. Parents today are often aware of the very small risks from vaccination – but sometimes forget about the terrible dangers of the diseases we vaccinate against.

If you are a parent it can be difficult to find unbiased advice to help you make a decision. The media highlight scare stories which make good headlines. The pharmaceutical companies want to sell vaccines. Doctors and health visitors can weigh up all the information, but they have vaccination targets set by the government.

Summary questions

1 Copy and complete using the words below:

antibodies pathogen immunised dead immune inactive white

People can be .... against a disease by introducing small quantities of .... or .... forms of a .... into your body. They stimulate the .... blood cells to produce .... to destroy the pathogen. This makes you .... to the disease in future.

2 Explain carefully, using diagrams if they help you:
 a how the immune system of your body works
 b how vaccines use your natural immune system to protect you against serious diseases.

3 Explain why vaccines can be used against both bacterial and viral diseases but antibiotics only work against bacteria.

Study tip

High levels of antibodies do not stay in your blood forever – immunity is the ability of your white blood cells to produce the right antibodies quickly if you are reinfected by a disease.

links

For more information on antibiotics, look back at B1 1.8 Changing pathogens.

Key points

- Your white blood cells produce antibodies to destroy the pathogens. Then your body will respond rapidly to future infections by the same pathogen, by making the correct antibody. You become immune to the disease.

- You can be immunised against a disease by introducing small amounts of dead or inactive pathogens into your body.

- We can use vaccinations to protect against both bacterial and viral pathogens.

40 · 41

Answers to in-text questions

a A unique protein on the surface of a cell that identifies it.

b A chemical (protein) made by the white blood cells that target specific antigens.

c Bacterial: tetanus, diphtheria or any other sensible choice. Viral: measles, mumps, rubella, polio or any other sensible choice.

Summary answers

1 immunised, dead/inactive, inactive/dead, pathogen, white, antibodies, immune

2 **a** Every cell has unique proteins on its surface called 'antigens'. Your immune system recognises that the antigens on the microorganisms that get into your system are different from the ones on your own cells. Your white blood cells then make antibodies to destroy the antigens/pathogens. Once your white blood cells have learnt the right antibody needed to tackle a particular pathogen, they can make that antibody very quickly if the pathogen gets into your system again, and so you are immune to that disease.

 b A small quantity of dead or inactive pathogen is introduced into your body. This gives your white blood cells the chance to develop the right antibodies against the pathogen without you getting ill. Then if you meet the live pathogens, your body can respond rapidly, making the right antibodies just as if you had already had the disease.

3 Vaccines can be made using inactive viruses or bacteria so can stimulate antibody production against either type of pathogen thereby developing immunity. Viruses reproduce inside body cells so antibiotics cannot kill them without killing the cells of the body at the same time.

B1 1.10

How do we deal with disease?

Learning objectives

Students should learn:

- the advantages and disadvantages of being vaccinated
- how the treatment of disease has changed over time.

Learning outcomes

Most students should be able to:

- describe the advantages and disadvantages of being vaccinated against certain diseases
- understand that the treatment of disease has changed over time.

Some students should also be able to:

- describe how scientists are investigating the development of new medicines for the future.

Specification link-up: Biology B1.1

- Evaluate the advantages and disadvantages of being vaccinated against a particular disease. [B1.1.2]
- Explain how the treatment of disease has changed as a result of increased understanding of the action of antibiotics and immunity. [B1.1.2]
- The development of antibiotic-resistant strains of bacteria necessitates the development of new antibiotics. [B1.1.2 k)]

Lesson structure

Starters

Plus and minus – Get the students to make a simple table with a plus sign heading above one column and a minus above the next. Show them a syringe and tell them that they have to think of themselves as parents and write down some reasons why they might have their children vaccinated against diseases, putting them in the plus column and some reasons why they might not want them to be vaccinated into the other column. To support students, provide a set of prompt cards. *(5 minutes)*

The bad old days – Split students into small groups and ask each group to imagine they were living in a time when there were no vaccinations. How might they have treated diseases? What was the effect on child mortality rates? After 5 minutes, pool the collective ideas. *(10 minutes)*

Main

- Exposition – Have the students read, either silently or out loud in sections, the text from the Student Book regarding whooping cough and the controversy surrounding it. Hold a discussion on the issue and then get the students to complete summary notes of the major points. Support students by providing a prompts sheet.

- Direct students to study Figure 1, which shows the effect of the whooping cough scare on both uptake of the vaccine and the number of cases of the disease. Ask them to break the graph into appropriate time segments and comment on what is happening in each one. Share these among the class once completed. Students could be supported by giving them guidance on the different time segments.

- Following some discussion with students, compile a list of questions that a parent might ask before they bring their child for a normal vaccination. Use these questions to design a webpage for parents, as suggested in the Student Book. Students can supply answers to the questions, combining scientific facts with reassurance.

- Show, or read out, an article on a scientific or medical topic (preferably one that glosses over the true facts or is scaremongering!) from a popular newspaper. Invite the students to comment on how accurate they think it is and whether it could have been improved. Working in groups, students could design a presentation making the case for responsible reporting of scientific and medical topics in the media. The whooping cough topic should be included, but the presentation could also include references to other topics, such as climate change or the side-effects of other medicines or treatments.

Support

- Give the students a simple 'True' or 'False' exercise based on the content covered in the lesson.

Extend

- Students could research the difference between broad-spectrum and narrow-spectrum antibiotics.
- **Global Pertussis Initiative**. Students could be given the abstract from the paper *Prevention of pertussis: recommendations derived from the second Global Pertussis Initiative Roundtable meeting* (use a search engine to find this). Students could read this and summarise it in student-friendly language.

Plenaries

True or false? – Give the students a simple true or false exercise based on the content covered in the lesson. Alternatively have them devise one for themselves. *(5 minutes)*

Role play exercise – Direct students to read and discuss the whooping cough story in the Student Book. Then ask one student to play Dr John Wilson, one to play a worried parent seeking compensation, one to play someone from the medical authority insisting that the dangers of whooping cough outweigh any danger from the vaccine and one to play Lord Stuart-Smith. The rest of the class should offer their classmates their help. To support students, provide them with a script. To extend students, direct them to script their own. *(10 minutes)*

Further teaching suggestions

Making sure the drugs are safe
- Discuss the ways in which new drugs are tested. Why does it take so long? Is it right to use animals? Would you volunteer to be part of a drug trial?

Measles, mumps and rubella – what are the risks?
- Find out what the symptoms and effects are. Why can they be life-threatening? This activity can be extended to other infectious diseases for which we have vaccinations, such as diphtheria and polio.

Searching for new drugs
- Students could discuss other possible sources of new drugs. Are there more drugs to be extracted from plants? What effect do you think that rainforest destruction has had on the search for new drugs from plants? Research the development of new drugs and the problems of testing.

How much will it cost?
- The development of new antibiotics and other drugs costs money. Discuss the finances of the drugs industry and how the costs of development are recovered.

Writing a letter to a newspaper
- Ask the students to put themselves in the place of a parent who has lost a child to whooping cough and write a letter to a newspaper urging other parents to make use of the vaccination programme, providing clear reasons.

Creating an advert
- Having gone through the section on Medicines for the future in the Student Book, ask the students to make an advert for a future medicine derived from one of the sources mentioned. This could take the form of a drawing, a sound file, a PowerPoint slide, a song, etc.

Computer simulations
- With students, create computer simulations to model the effect of: balanced and unbalanced diets and exercise; the growth of bacterial colonies in varying conditions; action of the immune system and the effect of antibiotics and vaccines.

B1 1.10 How do we deal with disease?

Learning objectives
- What are the advantages and disadvantages of being vaccinated?
- How has the treatment of disease changed over time?

The whooping cough story

In the 1970s, Dr John Wilson, a UK specialist in treating children, published a report suggesting that the pertussis (whooping cough) vaccine might cause brain damage in some children. The report was based on his study of a small group of 36 patients.

The media publicised the story and parents began to panic. The number of children being vaccinated against whooping cough fell from over 80% to around 30%. This was too low to protect the population from the virus.

People were so worried about the vaccine that they forgot that whooping cough itself can cause brain damage and death. In Scotland about 100 000 children suffered from whooping cough between 1977 and 1991. About 75 of them died. A similar pattern was seen across the whole of the UK.

An investigation into the original research discovered that it had serious flaws. Identical twin girls who were included in the study, and later died of a rare genetic disorder, had never actually had the whooping cough vaccine. It was a small study and only 12 of the children investigated had shown any symptoms close to the time of their whooping cough vaccination. Their parents were involved in claims for compensation from the vaccine manufacturers.

Figure 1 Graph showing the effect of the whooping cough scare on both uptake of the vaccine and the number of cases of the disease (Source: Open University)

No medical treatment (including vaccinations) is completely safe, but when the claims for compensation came to court, the whole study was questioned. After hearing all the evidence, the judge decided that the risks of whooping cough were far worse than any possible damage caused by the vaccine itself.

However, this judgement on the study got much less media coverage than the original scare story. Parents still felt there was 'no smoke without fire'. It was 20 years before vaccination levels, and the levels of whooping cough, returned to the levels before the scare. The number of people having vaccinations now is over 90%, and deaths from whooping cough are almost unknown in the UK.

Activity

Design a webpage for parents that answers the sort of questions they might ask about their child having the normal vaccines. Make it user-friendly, i.e. the sort of thing a health worker could use to help reassure worried parents.

OR

Produce a PowerPoint presentation on the importance of responsible media reporting of science and medicine, using the whooping cough case as one of your main examples.

Medicines for the future

Overuse of antibiotics has lead to spreading antibiotic resistance in many different bacteria. In recent years doctors have found strains of bacteria that are resistant to even the strongest antibiotics. When that happens, there is nothing more that antibiotics can do for a patient and he or she may well die.

The development of antibiotic resistant strains of bacteria means scientists are constantly looking for new antibiotics. It isn't easy to find chemicals which kill bacteria without damaging human cells.

Penicillin and several other antibiotics are made by moulds. Scientists are collecting soil samples from all over the world to try and find another mould to produce a new antibiotic that will kill antibiotic-resistant bacteria such as MRSA.

Crocodiles have teeth full of rotting meat. They live in dirty water and fight a lot. But scientists noticed that although crocodiles often give each other terrible bites, the bites do not become infected. They have extracted a chemical known as 'crocodillin' from crocodile blood and it seems to be a powerful antibiotic. Now the race is on to try and turn these amazing chemicals into antibiotics we can use.

Fish such as this plaice are covered with a slime which helps to protect them from damage and infection. Scientists have analysed this slime and found it contains proteins which have antibiotic properties. The proteins have been isolated from the slime and they still kill bacteria. So maybe fish will provide us with an antibiotic for the future.

Honey has been used since the time of the Ancient Egyptians to help heal wounds. Scientists in Germany and Australia have found that certain types of honey have antibiotic properties. They kill many bacteria, including MRSA. Doctors are using manuka honey dressings more and more to treat infected wounds.

Figure 2 Where will the next antibiotic be found?

Activity

Produce a poster on antibiotic resistance in bacteria and the search for new antibiotics. Make sure you explain how antibiotic resistance has developed and why we need more antibiotics. Use the ideas given here and, if possible, look for more examples of possible sources of new antibiotics.

Summary questions

1 Give one advantage and one disadvantage of being vaccinated.
2 List three examples of bad science from the story of the whooping cough vaccine and explain why the story should never have been published.

Key points
- Vaccination protects individuals and society from the effects of a disease.
- The treatment of disease has changed as our understanding of how antibiotics and immunity has increased.

Summary answers

1 **Advantage:** protected against potentially serious disease.
Disadvantage: small chance of adverse reaction to the vaccine.

2 Bad science examples: Very small sample size, not all sample had actually had the vaccination, only a third of the group developed symptoms anywhere near the time of their vaccinations, financial gains were involved, no proper peer evaluation and repetition of findings.

The papers should not have published without checking the reproducibility and validity of the study. The potential impact of the study should have been considered first before publication to minimise both the drop in levels of vaccination below that needed to maintain herd immunity and illness and death among children who developed the disease.

Summary answers

1 a A diet that contains the right amount of carbohydrates, proteins, fats, vitamins, minerals, fibre and water, and energy.

b Lots of muscles so high metabolic rate. They use lots of energy which comes from food.

2 a Points to include: a realistic picture of healthy weight, sensible dieting to include a balanced diet, include exercise to increase metabolic rate and build up muscle, resist food like chocolate and eat fruit etc. instead.

b Sensible eating, plenty of protein to help build up muscle, complex carbohydrates such as pasta etc. to give stamina, balancing exercise with diet.

3 a Inherited factors, the way your liver makes cholesterol, the level of fat in your diet, the amount of exercise taken.

b Reduce the fat in your diet, take more exercise (take statins).

c Any sensible example e.g. the metabolic rate (which affects obesity, which in turn affects their likelihood of developing problems such as type 2 diabetes).

4 Once inside the body they reproduce rapidly. Bacteria simply split in two. They often produce toxins and sometimes directly damage cells. Viruses take over the cells to reproduce, damaging and destroying them and very rarely produce toxins. The diseases are caused by the cell damage and toxins produced by the pathogens, and also by the way your body responds to that.

5 Spread: droplet infection, direct, contaminated food and drink, through cuts. Ways of reducing spread of diseases – any sensible points, e.g. using tissues and throwing them away, washing hands, hand in front of mouth when coughing, etc.

6 a They have developed resistance to vancomycin through a process of natural selection. They are then spread from patient to patient by contact between patients, on the hands of doctors and nurses, or on the objects around in a hospital.

b Use antibiotics carefully – only when they are needed – and make sure people always finish the course.

7 a Use sterile Petri dish and agar.
Sterilise the inoculating loop by heating it to red hot in the flame of a Bunsen and then let it cool. Do not put the loop down as it cools.
Innoculate agar with zigzag streaks of bacteria using sterile loop. Replace the lid on the dish quickly to avoid contamination.
Secure the lid with adhesive tape but do not seal.
Label the culture and incubate at no warmer than 25 °C.

b Include points such as: Inoculate agar plates with bacteria – ideally from school floor.
Add circles of filter paper soaked with different strengths of the disinfectant and incubate at no higher than 25 °C. Look for areas of clear agar around the disinfectant soaked disk. Recommend lowest concentration that destroys the bacteria.

Summary questions

1 a Define the term 'balanced diet'.

b A top athlete needs to eat a lot of food each day. This includes protein and carbohydrate. Explain how they can eat so much without putting on weight.

2 Two young people have written to a lifestyle magazine problem page for advice about their diet and lifestyle. Produce an 'answer page' for the next edition of the magazine.

a Melanie: I'm 16 and I worry about my weight a lot. I'm not really overweight but I want to be thinner. I've tried to diet but I just feel so tired when I do – and then I buy chocolate bars on the way home from school when my friends can't see me! What can I do?

b Jaz: I'm nearly 17 and I've grown so fast in the last year that I look like a stick! So my clothes look pretty silly. I'm also really good at football, but I don't seem as strong as I was and my legs get really tired by the end of a match. I want to build up a bit more muscle and stamina – but I don't just want to eat so much I end up getting really heavy. What can I do about it?

3 a What factors affect the cholesterol levels in your blood?

b What can you do to help reduce your blood cholesterol levels?

c Cholesterol is one inherited factor which affects your health. Give one other example of an inherited factor which affects your health and explain how it does this.

4 How do tiny organisms like bacteria and viruses make a person ill?

5 There is going to be a campaign to try and stop the spread of colds in Year 7 of your school. There is going to be a poster and a simple PowerPoint presentation. Make a list of all the important things that the Year 7 children need to know about how diseases are spread. Also cover how the spread of infectious diseases from one person to another can be reduced.

6 a Vancomycin is an antibiotic which doctors used for patients infected with MRSA and other antibiotic-resistant bacteria. Now they are finding some infections are resistant to vancomycin. Explain how this may have happened. [H]

b What can we do to prevent the problem of antibiotic resistance getting worse? [H]

7 a How would you set up a culture of bacteria in a school lab?

b Describe how you would test to find out the right strength of disinfectant to use to wash the school floors.

Kerboodle resources

Resources available for this chapter on Kerboodle are:
- Chapter map: Keeping healthy
- Maths skills: BMI calculator (B1 1.1)
- Support: Health on the line (B1 1.1)
- Video: Making predictions (B1 1.4)
- Extension: Shape matters (B1 1.5)
- Bump up your grade: Doctor, doctor (B1 1.6)
- Support: What's what? (B1 1.6)
- How Science Works: Does the concentration of a disinfectant change its effectiveness at killing bacteria? (B1 1.7)
- Practical: Growing microorganisms (B1 1.7)
- WebQuest: The chickenpox vaccine (B1 1.9)
- Animation: Immunity due to vaccination (B1 1.9)
- Interactive activity: Preventing disease
- Revision podcast: Healthy diets and exercise
- Test yourself: Keeping healthy
- On your marks: Keeping healthy
- Practice questions: Keeping healthy
- Answers to practice questions: Keeping healthy

Practice questions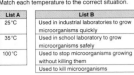

It is possible to grow microorganisms in the laboratory.
List A shows some temperatures.
List B shows situations for which these temperatures might be suitable.
Match each temperature to the correct situation.

List A	List B
25°C	Used in industrial laboratories to grow microorganisms quickly
35°C	Used in school laboratory to grow microorganisms safely
100°C	Used to stop microorganisms growing without killing them
	Used to kill microorganisms (3)

In this question you will be assessed on using good English, organising information clearly and using specialist terms where appropriate.

We need a balanced diet to keep us healthy. Explain the ways in which an unbalanced diet can affect the body. (6)

A person's metabolic rate varies with the amount of activity they do.

a Metabolic rate is ....
  Choose one answer.
  the breathing rate
  the rate of chemical reactions in cells
  the heart rate (1)

b Suggest **one** other factor which can change a person's metabolic rate. (1)

Polio is a disease caused by a virus. In the UK, children are given polio vaccine to protect them against the disease.

a Choose the correct words from each list to complete the sentences below.
  i It is difficult to kill the polio virus inside the body because the virus .... (1)
    is not affected by drugs   lives inside cells
    produces antitoxins
  ii The vaccine contains an .... form of the polio virus. (1)
    active   infective   inactive
  iii The vaccine stimulates the white blood cells to produce .... which destroy the virus. (1)
    antibiotics   antibodies   drugs

b The graph shows the number of cases of polio in the UK between 1948 and 1968.

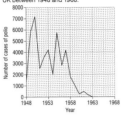

i In which year was the number of cases of polio highest? (1)
ii Polio vaccination was first used in the UK in 1955. How many years did it take for the number of cases of polio to fall to zero? (1)
iii There have been no cases of polio in the UK for many years. But children are still vaccinated against the disease.
    Suggest **one** reason for this. (1)
    AQA, 2006

5 Controlling infections in hospitals has become much more difficult in recent years.

a Suggest **two** reasons why MRSA is causing problems in many hospitals. (2)

b The pioneer in methods of treating infections in hospitals was Ignaz Semmelweis. He observed that women whose babies were delivered by doctors in hospital had a death rate of 18% from infections caught in the hospital. Women whose babies were delivered by midwives in the hospital had a death rate of 2%. He observed that doctors often came straight from examining dead bodies to the delivery ward.
  i In a controlled experiment, Semmelweis made doctors wash their hands in chloride of lime solution before delivering the babies. The death rate fell to about 2% – down to the same level as the death rate in mothers whose babies were delivered by midwives.
    Explain why the death rate fell. (1)
  ii Explain how Semmelweis's results could be used to reduce the spread of MRSA in a modern hospital. (2)
    AQA, 2005

45

Practical suggestions

Practicals	AQA	k	📖	⚙
Investigate the effectiveness of various antibiotic discs in killing bacteria.	✓	✓		
Growing microorganisms in Petri dishes to demonstrate sterile technique & growing pure cultures.	✓	✓	✓	
The use of pre-inoculated agar in Petri dishes to evaluate the effect of disinfectants & antibiotic	✓	✓	✓	✓
Computer simulations to model the effect of: balanced & unbalanced diets and exercise; the growth of bacterial colonies in varying conditions; action of the immune system and the effect of antibiotics and vaccines.	✓		✓	

Practice answers

1 25°C – Used in school laboratory to grow microorganisms safely, 35°C – Used in industrial laboratories to grow microorganisms quickly, 100°C – Used to kill microorganisms
(3 marks)

---

2 Marks awarded for this answer will be determined by the Quality of Written Communication (QWC) as well as the standard of the scientific response.

There is a clear, balanced and detailed description referring to both overeating and deficiency. The answer shows almost faultless spelling, punctuation and grammar. It is coherent and in an organised, logical sequence. It contains a range of appropriate or relevant specialist terms used accurately.
(5–6 marks)

There is some description of a range of the ways in which the diet can be unbalanced and the effects. There are some errors in spelling, punctuation and grammar. The answer has some structure and organisation. The use of specialist terms has been attempted, but not always accurately. *(3–4 marks)*

There is a brief description of at least two ways in which the diet can be unbalanced, which has little clarity and detail. The spelling, punctuation and grammar are very weak. The answer is poorly organised with almost no specialist terms and/or their use demonstrating a general lack of understanding of their meaning. *(1–2 marks)*

No relevant content. *(0 marks)*

Examples of biology points made in the response:
- balanced diet contains all the correct nutrients in the correct amounts
- balanced diet has the correct amount of energy
- too much energy leads to mass/weight increase
- e.g. eating too much fat
- if activity increases use of energy increases
- too little energy leads to decrease in mass/weight
- can lead to anorexia/described symptom
- lack of vitamins/named vitamin can lead to deficiency disease/correctly named
- too much carbohydrate/sugar/overweight can lead to type 2 diabetes
- lack of a mineral ion/named ion can lead to deficiency disease/correctly named
- obesity linked to, e.g. heart disease/arthritis/high blood pressure etc.

3 a the rate of chemical reactions in cells *(1 mark)*
  b Any **one** from:
  - the proportion of fat to muscle
  - inherited factors
  - other sensible suggestion, other than activity *(1 mark)*

4 a i lives inside cells *(1 mark)*
    ii inactive *(1 mark)*
    iii antibodies *(1 mark)*
  b i 1950 *(1 mark)*
    ii 8 (years) *(1 mark)*
    iii Any **one** from: e.g.
    - disease could be reintroduced (from abroad)
    - disease would spread if it came back
    - protection on holiday abroad
    - high proportion of immune people needed to prevent epidemic *(1 mark)*

5 a Any **two** from:
  - resistant to (most) antibiotics
  - contagious or easily passed on or reference to open wounds
  - patients ill therefore less able to combat disease
    (2 marks)

  b i Using chloride of lime to wash their hands killed any bacteria the doctors may have picked up from corpses. Allow diseases/germs/infection/disinfectants as alternative terms. *(1 mark)*
    ii people should wash hands after contact with patient so bacteria/pathogen/MRSA are not transferred to other patients *(2 marks)*

B1 2.1

Responding to change

Learning objectives

Students should learn:

- that the nervous system enables humans to react to their surroundings by means of cells called receptors
- that there are receptors that are sensitive to touch, light, sound, changes in position, chemicals, pressure, pain and temperature
- that information from these receptors passes along cells (neurons) in nerves to the brain, where the response is coordinated.

Learning outcomes

Most students should be able to:

- identify the sense organs involved in responding to light, sound, changes of position, chemicals, touch, pressure and temperature in humans
- describe how the nervous system works
- describe the difference between the functions of a sensory and a motor neuron.

Some students should also be able to:

- explain the importance of the coordination of impulses by the brain in our responses to changes in the environment.

Support

- Provide cards with the separate parts of a nervous pathway, such as 'receptor' and 'sensory neuron' etc. on them and ask students to place them in the correct order in the pathway.

Extend

- Show a picture of a poison arrow frog. Get the students to discuss the use of these in tropical hunting and ask them to speculate about the mechanisms which may be at work when the paralysing dart acts.

Specification link-up: Biology B1.2

- The nervous system enables humans to react to their … *[B1.2.1 a)]*
- Cells called receptors detect stimuli (changes in the environment) … *[B1.2.1 b)]*
- Light receptor cells, like most animal cells, have a … *[B1.2.1 c)]*
- Information from receptors passes along cells … *[B1.2.1 d)]*

Controlled Assessment: B4.1 Plan practical ways to develop and test candidates' own scientific ideas *[B4.1.1 a) b)]*; B4.3 Collect primary and secondary data *[B4.3.2 a) b) c) d)]*; B4.4 Select and process primary and secondary data *[B4.4.1 a) b)]* and B4.5 Analyse and interpret primary and secondary data. *[B4.5.2 a) b) c) d)]*

Lesson structure

Starters

'Be aware!' – Get the class to sit in silence for 30 seconds exactly, asking them to focus on what sensations their skin is giving them. Discuss this. Spend another 30 seconds with eyes shut and silent, focusing on background sounds. How many can they identify? Spend another 30 seconds silently focusing on one spot or point in the room and keeping their eyes still. Discuss the experience. Round off by talking over how we are aware of our surroundings (via our senses). *(5 minutes)*

Circus of activities – Place 'feely' bags around the room involving senses and containing mystery objects, e.g. a sniff test with different essences in film containers, guess the sound on an MP3 player, mystery object photos or objects under a microscope, identifying mystery fruit (care with hygiene). Students could be supported by confining the mystery objects to one sense, e.g. smells, or by restricting the variety of objects for each test. Students could be extended by timing them and allocating points for correct answers. They could also be asked to comment on the amount of information needed to make a correct decision. *(10 minutes)*

Main

The main part of the lesson could be a practical session involving the testing of sensitivity using the following:

- Practical on identifying the density of nerve endings by investigating the sensitivity of different areas of the skin (see 'Practical support'). 'How Science Works' concepts can be introduced here, such as the accuracy of the measurements, the calculation of means, precision and the control of variables. If class results are collated, some indication of the variability can be discussed.

- Try an active learning exercise. Get five of the students to stand in a line, holding on to the cuffs of each others shirts or jumpers. Attach labels to each saying 'receptor', 'sensory neuron', 'coordinator', 'motor neuron', and 'effector'. Create a scenario, e.g. getting stung by a nettle. Get each volunteer to state what it is doing, e.g. the receptor is being stung and creating the impulse and passing it on to the sensory neuron (by tugging its cuff gently), the sensory neuron passes it on to the coordinator which passes it on to the motor neuron which passes it on to the effector. In this case, the effector is the muscles controlling the voice and says, 'Ow!' Repeat with other scenarios, e.g. smelling onions and crying, being cold and shivering, etc.

Plenaries

Does the colour smell right? – A variation of the 'feely' bags could involve the conflicting information from odd combinations of colour and smell, e.g. pink food smelling of peppermint, blue food smelling of strawberry. This could trigger a discussion of how senses are used and that information comes from more than one sense organ. *(5 minutes)*

What is the significance of the results? – What do the results of the experiments tell us? Is it touch, pressure or pain receptors that are being stimulated? Support students by discussing their results and encouraging them to write clear statements as conclusions. Extend students by asking them how this type of experiment could be modified for other receptors such as hot or cold receptors. Suggest that student's link up the density of the receptors to the areas tested. *(10 minutes)*

Practical support

Identifying of the density of nerve endings

Equipment and materials required

Small pieces of blunt wire (unbent paper clip, blunt tapestry needles) mounted in pieces of cork; if two wires are used they should be about 1 cm apart.

Details

Students could be asked to design an investigation to measure the sensitivity of the skin or can do the practical described here.

Working in pairs, one student is blindfolded or told to look in a different direction, while another student touches them on the back of the hand with either one or two pieces of blunt wire about 1 cm apart mounted in a cork. The blindfolded student has to say whether it was one point or two points that touched them. In addition to the back of the hand, other areas of the body, such as the upper arm or the back of the leg, could be investigated. In this way, a comparison could be made about the sensitivity of different areas of the body.

Safety: The wires should be blunt, not sharp, and students reminded not to exert pressure.

[Reproduction of student textbook pages 46–47: "Coordination and control — B1 2.1 Responding to change", covering the nervous system, receptors, neurons, sensory and motor neurons, with Figures 1–3 and Summary questions.]

Further teaching suggestions

How fast is a nerve impulse?

- If you stub your toe, there is a very short interval of time between the action of stubbing and the sensation of pain. Discuss this and suggest to students that they try to work out how the time interval between being touched on the toe and feeling the sensation of touch can be measured. Can this measurement be used to work out how fast the nerve impulse is transmitted? Hint: How might measuring the length of the leg help the calculation?

A receptors experiment

- Students could devise a simple experiment to investigate the density of hot and cold receptors in the skin. This exercise could be used to introduce HSW concept of planning a practical.

Study tip

Students do need to understand the difference between nerve and neuron. A clear definition of each could be made into a revision card. It could be helpful to students to have a good understanding of the different types of neuron and know that nerves can contain either sensory or motor neurons or a mixture of both.

Answers to in-text questions

a Coordination and control; awareness of surroundings.

b i Ears. ii Skin. iii Nose.

c A neuron is a single nerve cell; a nerve is a lot of neurons bundled together.

d A sensory neuron carries impulses from sensory receptors to the CNS; a motor neuron carries impulses from the CNS to the effector organs.

Summary answers

1. nervous, electrical, environment, receptors, neurons, CNS

2. Table showing receptors for light, sound, position, smell (could also have temperature, pain, pressure) with student example of a stimulus for each one.

3. Light from the chocolate is detected by the sensory receptors in the eyes, an impulse travels along the sensory neuron to the brain, information is processed in the brain and an impulse is sent along a motor neuron to the muscles of the arm and hand so you pick up the chocolate and put it in your mouth. Give credit if students add anything further, e.g. sensory impulses from mouth/nose to brain with information about taste, smell of chocolate, touch sensors send impulses about presence of chocolate, motor impulses to muscles for chewing, etc.

B1 2.2

Reflex actions

Learning objectives

Students should learn:

- that reflex actions are automatic and rapid responses to stimuli
- that simple reflex actions involve receptors, sensory neurons, motor neurons and relay neurons, together with synapses and effectors
- that reflex actions take care of basic functions, such as breathing, and help to avoid danger or harm to the body.

Learning outcomes

Most students should be able to:

- explain what is meant by the term 'reflex action'
- describe the roles of receptors; sensory, relay and motor neurons; synapses and effectors in a reflex action
- explain why reflex actions are so important.

Some students should also be able to:

- analyse a specific reflex action in terms of stimulus → receptor → coordinator → effector → response
- explain in detail how a synapse works.

Support

- Students could be given cards with the words needed to complete Question 1 of the Summary Questions on them and asked to place them in the correct places on a large copy of the passage.
- Alternatively, provide some volunteer students with A4 sheets on which the names of parts of the reflex pathway have been printed. The students should then arrange themselves in the correct order. They could be timed as a challenge. Using a lightning-shaped zap, ask the students to talk through their bit of the process as the impulse (zap) gets passed to them.

Extend

- Students could investigate the work of Pavlov and his dogs in the context of the reflex action.

Specification link-up: Biology B1.2

- Information from receptors passes along cells … *[B1.2.1 d)]*
- Candidates should understand the role of receptors … *[B1.2.1 e)]*

  Controlled Assessment: B4.3 Collect primary and secondary data *[B4.3.2 a) b) c) d)]*; B4.4 Select and process primary and secondary data *[B4.4.1 a) b)]* and B4.5 Analyse and interpret primary and secondary data. *[B4.5.2 a) b) c) d)]*

Lesson structure

Starters

Bang goes the theory! – (Background music: 'The Reflex' by Duran Duran.) While the class are quietly settled on a task at the start of the lesson, such as writing the title and date into their books, make a sudden very loud noise. Slapping two dissection boards together will do, or turn the volume right up on a piece of loud music. Ask the students what happened to their bodies and then start to draw out their theories on why and how they responded. *(5 minutes)*

'Get a grip' – Show a photo of a baby gripping its mother's finger. Ask the class to write down what is happening, why and how it is happening. Support students by encouraging them to describe the function of the reflex, i.e. to hold on to the mother so as not to get lost. Extend students by encouraging them to speculate as to how this reflex has arisen and what the process might entail. *(10 minutes)*

Main

- Organise the stick-drop test for measuring reaction time (see 'Practical support'). This is a reaction, not a reflex, but most reflexes are too fast to measure in class. 'How Science Works' concepts can be introduced here: the accuracy of the measurements, the calculation of means, precision and the control of variables. If class results are collated, some indication of the variability can be discussed.

- Further work with the stick-drop test – Do reaction times alter with age, time of day or intake of caffeine? Results can be tabulated and class results compared. Boys can be compared with girls and distribution curves drawn.

- Try testing the knee jerk reflex (see 'Practical support'). Ask for a volunteer, or select a suitable student, from the class and demonstrate the knee jerk reflex on them. If appropriate, allow students to work in pairs and try it out on each other (caution needed here!). Discuss what is happening. NB The knee jerk reflex has to be so fast that it does not have a relay neuron.

- Can we alter reflex actions? – This activity can be included in a lesson if the Plenary 'The override button' is not used. Encourage students to think of situations where it is possible to alter the automatic response (not dropping a hot object, deliberately breathing more slowly, etc.). Are there some reflex actions over which we have no control? Discuss the situations and build up a list.

Plenaries

'The override button' – Can we learn to alter our reflex actions? Support students by showing them a photo of a strongman competition endurance event such as a truck pull. Ask them whether there is pain involved and ask what is going on inside the contestants to get them to keep going. *(5 minutes)*

Response timer exercise – There are many interactive response timer exercises on the internet, such as the BBC sheep tranquilising game at www.gamingdelight.com. (search under 'sheep reaction') which is great fun and can provide a motivating discussion piece for the end of a lesson as well as proving that you get better with practice. *(10 minutes)*

Practical support

The stick-drop test

Equipment and materials required
A metre rule, access to computers for the interactive reaction timers. It could be helpful to have preprinted sheets on which to record reaction times, so that it is easy for students to gather class results.

Details
Working in pairs, one student holds a metre rule vertically at the zero end, between the thumb and forefinger of another student, so that the 50 cm mark is level with the top of the forefinger. Without warning, the first student drops the rule and the second student attempts to catch it between the thumb and forefinger, noting the distance on the ruler just above the forefinger. Repeat several times, so that a mean can be calculated. Then change around so that everyone gets a turn. Write a report of the experiment.

Testing the knee jerk reflex (practical or demonstration)

Equipment and materials required
Ruler.

Details
Get students to work in pairs and try it out the knee jerk reaction on each other (caution needed here!). One student should sit on a chair with one leg loosely crossed over the other at the knee. The other student gives a gentle tap with the edge of a ruler just below the knee cap of the crossed leg. Discuss what is happening. N.B. The knee jerk reflex has to be so fast that it does not have a relay neuron.

Safety: The tap with the ruler does need to be gentle and not vigorous.

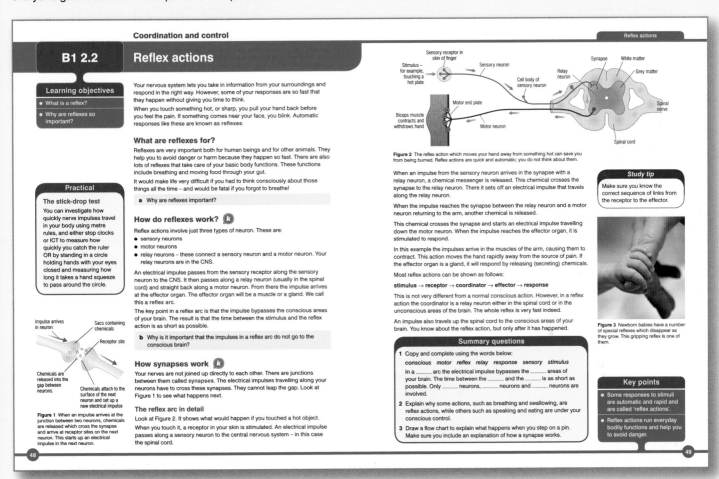

Reproduced student textbook pages 48–49, B1 2.2 "Reflex actions", including Figure 1, Figure 2, Figure 3, Study tip, Summary questions and Key points.

Further teaching suggestions

Eye reflexes
- Working in pairs, the alteration in pupil size when the eyes are opened in bright light can be easily observed by students. Discuss the value of this reflex in protecting the eyes. The relay neuron for this reflex is on the surface of the brain.

Summary of the reflexes and activities of the lesson
- What do tests such as the stick-drop test tell us? Ask students to identify the parts of the body involved. What senses are being used? Can we train ourselves to react more quickly? Does practice make perfect? Can students relate the results to some of the computer games that depend on quick reactions?

Answers to in-text questions

a Reflexes protect the body by avoiding danger or damage, to control bodily functions without the need for conscious thought, e.g. breathing.

b They need to be very quick to avoid danger, so the shorter the distance they have to travel, the quicker you will react.

Summary answers

1 reflex, conscious, stimulus, response, sensory, relay, motor

2 Reflex actions that need to operate automatically, even when you are asleep, cannot rely on conscious thought processes, unlike speaking and eating, which we need to be able to choose when to do them.

3 Stimulus → receptor → sensory neuron → synapse → chemical message → relay neuron → synapse → chemical message → motor neuron → muscles in leg lift the foot.

B1 2.3

Hormones and the menstrual cycle

Learning objectives

Students should learn:

- that many processes within the body are coordinated by chemical substances called hormones
- that the menstrual cycle is controlled by several hormones secreted by the pituitary gland and the ovaries
- the function of FSH (follicle stimulating hormone).

Learning outcomes

Most students should be able to:

- state that hormones coordinate processes in the body
- name the hormones that control the menstrual cycle and state where each is produced
- describe the functions of each hormone and relate each hormone to the different phases of the cycle.

Some students should also be able to:

- explain the relationships between the different hormones and how they interact in the cycle.

Specification link-up: Biology B1.2

- Many processes within the body are coordinated by … [B1.2.2 b)]
- Hormones regulate the functions of many organs and cells … [B1.2.2 c)]
- Several hormones are involved in the menstrual cycle of a woman … [B1.2.2 d)]

Lesson structure

Starters

Jobs for the hormones – Get the students to make a list of the changes that bodies undergo during puberty. Discuss this and draw out any knowledge that they have on the sex hormones and the roles they perform. *(5 minutes)*

What I know so far – Divide the students into small groups. Give each group an A3 sheet of paper. Have them put the word 'period' in large letters in the centre then for three minutes write down anything they know about periods – what age girls are when they start, when they stop, what their function is, etc. Share the findings with the rest of the group. Support students by providing a prompt sheet of questions to think about if necessary. *(10 minutes)*

Main

This lesson does have to focus on the menstrual cycle, so the following suggestions describe some ways in which the information can be put across.

- Before explaining the menstrual cycle, it could be beneficial to discuss the properties of hormones, where they are produced and how they are transported around the body. Project a diagram of the human torso to illustrate the positions of the endocrine glands and the sites of actions of the hormones.

- You can show a PowerPoint presentation introducing the vocabulary and linking the actions of the hormones. A series of PowerPoint diagrams to illustrate the stages could be prepared. Firstly, show the pituitary gland and the female reproductive system; secondly, show secretion of FSH from the pituitary affecting the ovaries in two ways ('stimulation of oestrogen production' and 'stimulation of egg development'); thirdly, show oestrogen production linked to the uterus, labelled 'developing lining' and two links back to the pituitary gland, one labelled 'negative feedback – inhibits FSH production' and the other labelled 'stimulates LH production'; lastly, link from pituitary to ovaries labelled 'ovulation triggered'.

- The PowerPoint diagrams can be used in conjunction with a human torso model if available, so that the location of the pituitary gland and the female reproductive systems can be seen easily. This reinforces some of the properties of hormones, as the students could be asked to consider how the hormones get from one place to another.

- Show a video of ovulation if available. The series *The Human Body* (BBC) shows ovulation *in situ* in detail.

- Explaining Figure 2 in the Student Book using a series of PowerPoint diagrams could be helpful. Make a point of getting the students to understand when conception is likely to occur.

Plenaries

True or false? – Present the students with a series of statements about the hormones and the cycle, some of which are true and others not. Check answers at end. This offers an opportunity to make clear any points about the cycle that students do not understand. *(5 minutes)*

Crossword clues – Get the students to suggest some key words from the spread. Write them on the board and ask them to come up with crossword clues for each one. Collect the best ones and get a volunteer to take them home and produce a crossword as a starter for the next lesson (there are many free crossword compilers available on the internet). Extend students by suggesting they come up with cryptic or clever clues. Support students by providing prompts and examples if necessary. *(10 minutes)*

Support

- Give students broken sentences to sequence, describing the role of the hormones in the menstrual cycle.

Extend

- Students could find out about the male hormones that are equivalent to FSH, LH and oestrogen. They could compare the production of eggs with the production of sperm.

Further teaching suggestions

Mammalian ovaries
- Students could look at slides under the microscope, or projected slides, of mammalian ovaries to show follicles at various stages of development.

Preserved ovaries
- They could look at preserved specimens of ovaries if available (possibly from hens).

Class discussions
- Start a class discussion on mammals: 'Do other mammals have an equivalent of the menstrual cycle? Compare the monthly cycle of human females with the breeding seasons of other mammals.'
- Start a class discussion by asking 'Do males have hormones equivalent to FSH, LH and oestrogen?'

More information on ovulation and conception
- There are some very good pre-birth websites (some have a distinct pro-life angle) with information about ovulation and conception (try www.mumsnet.com).
- View and discuss 'Window on Life' (*Sunday Times* free CDs) for more general information and animations.

Coordination and control

B1 2.3   Hormones and the menstrual cycle

Learning objectives
- How is the menstrual cycle controlled?
- When is a woman most likely to conceive?

Hormones are chemical substances that coordinate many processes within your body. Special **glands** make and release (secrete) these hormones into your body. Then the hormones are carried around your body to their target organs in the bloodstream. Hormones regulate the functions of many organs and cells. They can act very quickly, but often their effects are quite slow and long lasting.

A woman's menstrual cycle is a good example of control by hormones. Hormones are made in a woman's pituitary gland and her ovaries control her menstrual cycle. The levels of the different hormones rise and fall in a regular pattern. This affects the way her body works.

What is the menstrual cycle?

The average length of the menstrual cycle is about 28 days. Each month the lining of the womb thickens ready to support a developing baby. At the same time an egg starts maturing in the ovary.

About 14 days after the egg starts maturing it is released from the ovary. This is known as **ovulation**. The lining of the womb stays thick for several days after the egg has been released.

If the egg is fertilised by a sperm, then pregnancy may take place. The lining of the womb provides protection and food for the developing embryo. If the egg is not fertilised, the lining of the womb and the dead egg are shed from the body. This is the monthly bleed or **period**.

All of these changes are brought about by hormones. These are made and released by the **pituitary gland** (a pea-sized gland in the brain) and the ovaries.

a What controls the menstrual cycle?
b Why does the lining of the womb build up each month?

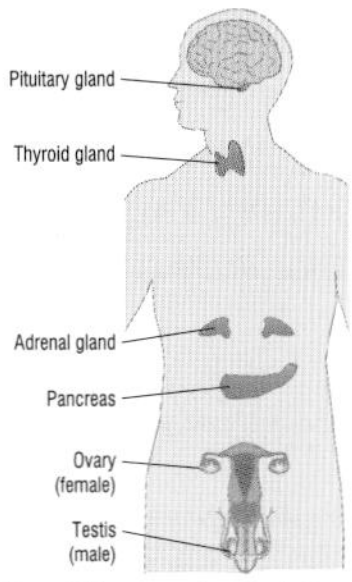

How the menstrual cycle works

Once a month, a surge of hormones from the pituitary gland in the brain starts eggs maturing in the ovaries. The hormones also stimulate the ovaries to produce the female sex hormone **oestrogen**.

- Follicle stimulating hormone (FSH) is secreted by the pituitary gland. It makes eggs mature in the ovaries. FSH also stimulates the ovaries to produce oestrogen.
- Oestrogen is made and secreted by the ovaries. It stimulates the lining of the womb to build up ready for pregnancy. It inhibits (slows down) the production of more FSH.
- Other hormones involved in the menstrual cycle are luteinising hormone (LH) and **progesterone**.

The hormones produced by the pituitary gland and the ovary act together to control what happens in the menstrual cycle. As the oestrogen levels rise they inhibit the production of FSH and encourage the production of LH by the pituitary gland. When LH levels reach a peak in the middle of the cycle, they stimulate the release of a mature egg.

Figure 1 Hormones act as chemical messages. They are made in glands in one part of the body but have an effect somewhere else.

(Figure 1 labels: Pituitary gland, Thyroid gland, Adrenal gland, Pancreas, Ovary (female), Testis (male))

?? Did you know ...?
A baby girl is born with ovaries full of immature eggs, but they do nothing until she has gone through the changes of puberty.

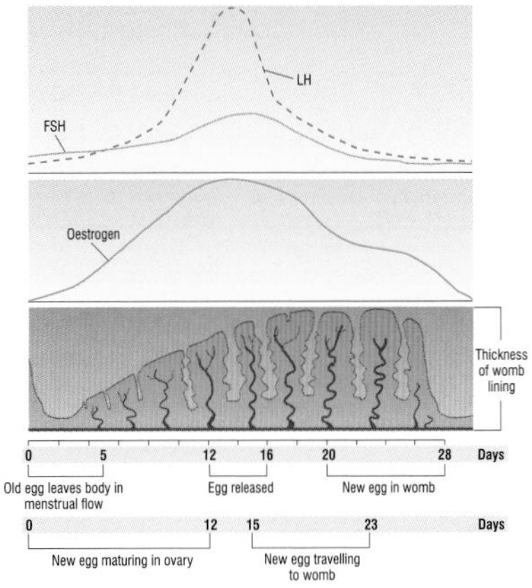

Figure 2 The changing levels of the female sex hormones control the different stages of the menstrual cycle

(Figure 2 labels: LH, FSH, Oestrogen, Thickness of womb lining, Days 0 5 12 16 20 28, Old egg leaves body in menstrual flow, Egg released, New egg in womb; Days 0 12 15 23, New egg maturing in ovary, New egg travelling to womb)

Study tip
Be clear on the difference between FSH and oestrogen.
FSH
- causes eggs to mature
- stimulates the ovary to produce oestrogen.

Oestrogen
- causes the lining of the uterus to develop
- inhibits FSH production
- stimulates the release of a mature egg.

Study tip
Make sure you know the difference between eggs maturing and eggs being released.

Summary questions

1 Copy and complete using the words below:
   28   hormones   FSH   menstrual   oestrogen   ovary
   During the .... cycle a mature egg is released from the .... about every .... days. The cycle is controlled by several .... including .... and ....

2 Look at Figure 2 above:
   a Explain what happens to FSH.
   b On which days is the female having a menstrual period?
   c Which hormone controls the build-up of the lining of the womb?

3 Produce a poster to explain the events of the menstrual cycle to women who are hoping to start a family. You will need to explain the graphs at the top of this page and show when a woman is most likely to get pregnant. Remember sperm can live for up to three days inside the woman's body.

Key points
- Hormones control the release of an egg from the ovary and the build-up of the lining of the womb in the menstrual cycle.
- Some of the hormones involved are FSH from the pituitary gland and oestrogen from the ovary.

?? Did you know ...?

It might be interesting to get the students to calculate roughly how many of the eggs a baby girl is born with actually develop and are released between puberty and when ovulation ceases at the menopause.

Study tip

Students can be confused by the development of an immature egg while it is in the ovary and the release of the egg. If the events are linked to the hormones involved, then it can become clearer.

Answers to in-text questions

a Hormones made in the pituitary gland in the brain and in the ovary.
b So that it would be ready to support the developing embryo if an egg was fertilised.

Summary answers

1 menstrual, ovary, 28, hormones, FSH, oestrogen
2 a Levels rise in the first part of the cycle which stimulates the eggs to mature in the ovary and stimulates the ovary to produce more oestrogen.
  b Days 0–5.
  c Oestrogen.
3 Give credit for a clear poster, which contains good, accurate biology and demonstrates understanding of the relationship between ovulation, sexual intercourse and fertilisation of the ovum.

B1 2.4

The artificial control of fertility

Learning objectives

Students should learn:

- how oral contraceptives work
- how FSH can be used as a 'fertility drug'.

Learning outcomes

Most students should be able to:

- explain how oral contraceptives inhibit FSH production and prevent pregnancy
- describe how treatment with FSH can help a woman produce mature eggs if her own FSH production is too low
- describe how FSH is used in IVF treatments.

Some students should also be able to:

- evaluate the issues arising from the use of hormones to control fertility artificially.

Support

- The students could make a poster showing the stages of a course of IVF treatment.

Extend

- Mature eggs from a woman undergoing fertility treatment can be stored. Students could investigate the exact conditions needed for storage. Why are such conditions necessary? Is there any chance of deterioration if the eggs are kept in storage for long periods of time?
- In the early days of contraceptive pill manufacture, before careful air filtering, the male workers began to develop breasts as a result of being exposed to oestrogen. Students could research the effects of female hormones on males.

Specification link-up: Biology B1.2

- The uses of hormones in controlling fertility include:
  Giving oral contraceptives that contain hormones to inhibit FSH production so that no eggs mature
  - oral contraceptives may contain oestrogen and …
  - the first birth-control pills contained large amounts …
  - progesterone-only pills lead to fewer side effects
  - birth-control pills now contain a much lower dose of …
  Giving FSH and LH in a 'fertility drug' to a woman whose own level of FSH is too low to stimulate eggs to mature, for example in In Vitro Fertilisation (IVF) treatment
  - IVF involves giving a mother FSH and LH to … [B1.2.2 e)]
- Evaluate the benefits of, and the problems that may arise from, the use of hormones to control fertility, including In Vitro Fertilisation (IVF). [B1.2]

Lesson structure

Starters

'To have or not to have …' – Ask the students to imagine a young couple (get them to give them names) and to come up with a list of reasons why the couple might not want to start a family yet. Read out and share these. *(5 minutes)*

Babyless blues – Get the students to empathise with families that want to have children but for some reason cannot do so. They could write a letter to their unborn children telling them of all the lovely things they would like to do with them if only they had the chance. Differentiation – extension students should be able to empathise without aid. You may need to support other students by providing them with a list of things that they enjoy in life and dropping them into gaps in a preformed letter. *(10 minutes)*

Main

This lesson needs to focus on the two main issues: the use of oral contraceptives and the use of FSH as a 'fertility drug'. Both these issues will trigger discussions, so allow time for questions and for students to express their own opinions.

- Ask students to reflect on the question, 'What do I know about contraception and hormones in the menstrual cycle?' The students could be encouraged to write down a list of facts of what they think they know and remember about contraception and the hormones in the menstrual cycle.
- The students should be able to discuss exactly what the pill does and its effect on the secretion of other hormones involved in the cycle.
- The discussion could be extended to include the consequences of failing to take the pill regularly. What happens if the level of artificial hormones drops suddenly?
- Show a video of IVF treatment. You can use the free download IVF orientation video from the San Diego Fertility Center.
- Discuss the advantages and disadvantages of using hormones to control fertility. Ensure that students are encouraged to evaluate the relative importance of different points raised (See 'How Science Works' box in the Student Book).

Plenaries

Injections and patches – The hormones used in contraceptive pills can be given as injections or as patches that stick to the skin. Discuss the advantages and disadvantages of the use of these alternatives. *(5 minutes)*

Keep taking the tablets – Direct the students to write an advice label to go with packets of contraceptive pills, telling how they work and giving relevant instructions and warnings. You may need to support some students by providing a cloze passage label with a set of words to choose from. Students could be shown an advice label from a packet of prescription drugs or the warning labels on packets of painkillers. *(10 minutes)*

Further teaching suggestions

Alternatives to the contraceptive pill
- The contraceptive pill is not the only way to avoid pregnancy. It is not suitable for everyone and there may be medical reasons why it is not appropriate to prescribe it. Ask students to build up a list of other methods of contraception and discuss the advantages and disadvantages. This could lead to some discussion on sexually transmitted diseases and the incidence of HIV/Aids.

How would a contraceptive pill for males work?
- There has been some research on this, but students could be encouraged to work out what would need to happen and consider possible advantages and disadvantages compared with the female pill, e.g. Are men more likely to forget to take a pill?

What happens to the spare embryos?
- Students could carry out a web search for information on this topic. Use websites of newspapers, TV channels and the British Fertility Society (it is now the HFEA) to find stories and topics to discuss.

Louise Brown – the first 'test tube' baby
- Louise Brown was the first baby to be born as a result of IVF in 1978. Tell the students the story and ask them to write a short paragraph about how it might feel to be the first person to be born as the result of a new treatment. Select some students to read their accounts.

Coordination and control

B1 2.4 — The artificial control of fertility

Learning objectives
- How can hormones be used to stop pregnancy?
- How can hormones help to solve the problems of infertility?

Contraceptive chemicals

In the 21st century it is possible to choose when to have children – and when not to have them. One of the most important and widely used ways of controlling fertility is to use **oral contraceptives** (the contraceptive pill).

The pill contains female hormones, particularly oestrogen. The hormones affect women's ovaries, preventing the release of any eggs. The pill inhibits the production of FSH so no eggs mature in the ovaries. Without mature eggs, women can't get pregnant.

Anyone who uses the pill as a contraceptive has to take it very regularly. If they forget to take it, the artificial hormone levels drop. Then their body's own hormones can take over very quickly. This can lead to the unexpected release of an egg – and an unexpected baby.

a What is a contraceptive?

The first birth control pills contained very large amounts of oestrogen. They caused serious side effects such as high blood pressure and headaches in some women. Modern contraceptive pills contain much lower doses of oestrogen along with some progesterone. They cause fewer side effects. Some contraceptive pills only contain progesterone. These cause even fewer side effects. However, they are not quite as good at preventing pregnancy because they don't stop the eggs from maturing.

b What is the difference between the mixed pill and the progesterone-only pill?

Fertility treatments

In the UK as many as one couple in six have problems having a family when they want one. There are many possible reasons for this infertility. It may be linked to a lack of female hormones. Some women want children but do not make enough FSH to stimulate the eggs in their ovaries. Fortunately, artificial FSH can be used as a fertility drug. It stimulates the eggs in the ovary to mature and also triggers oestrogen production.

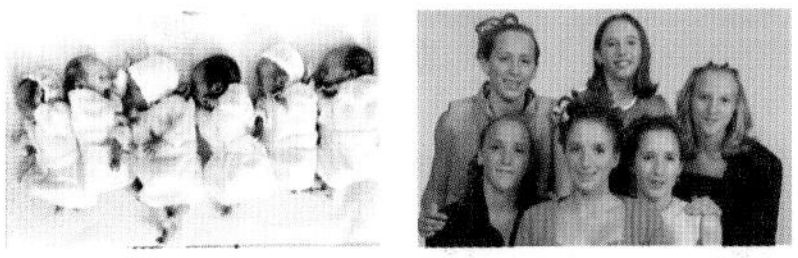

Figure 1 The contraceptive pill contains a mixture of hormones which effectively trick the body into thinking it is already pregnant, so no more eggs are released

Study tip
FSH and LH are used in IVF to stimulate the eggs to mature.

Did you know ... ?
In the early days of using fertility drugs there were big problems with the doses used. In 1971 an Italian doctor removed 15 four-month-old fetuses (ten girls and five boys) from the womb of a 35-year-old woman after treatment with fertility drugs. Not one of them survived.

Figure 2 Most people who take fertility drugs end up with one or two babies. But in 1983 the Walton family from Liverpool had six baby girls who all survived

Fertility drugs are also used in **IVF** (*in vitro* fertilisation). Conception usually takes place in the fallopian tube. This is the tube between the ovary and the uterus that the egg travels along. If the fallopian tubes are damaged, the eggs cannot reach the uterus so women cannot get pregnant naturally.

Fortunately doctors can now help. They collect eggs from the ovary of the mother and fertilise them with sperm from the father outside the body. The fertilised eggs develop into tiny embryos. The embryos are inserted into the uterus (womb) of the mother. In this way they bypass the faulty tubes.

During IVF the woman is given FSH to make sure as many eggs as possible mature in her ovaries. LH is also given at the end of the cycle to make sure all the mature eggs are released. IVF is expensive and not always successful.

How Science Works

The advantages and disadvantages of fertility treatment

The use of hormones to control fertility has been a major scientific breakthrough. But like most things, there are advantages and disadvantages! Here are some points to think about:

In the developed world, using the pill has helped make families much smaller than they used to be. There is less poverty because with fewer children being born there are fewer mouths to feed and more money to go round.

The pill has also helped to control population growth in countries such as China, where they find it difficult to feed all their people. In many other countries of the developing world the pill is not available because of a lack of money, education and doctors.

The pill can cause health problems so a doctor always oversees its use.

The use of fertility drugs can also have some health risks for the mother and it can be expensive for society and parents. A large multiple birth can be tragic for the parents if some or all of the babies die. It also costs hospitals a lot of money to keep very small premature babies alive.

Controlling fertility artificially also raises many ethical issues for society and individuals. For example, some religious groups think that preventing conception is denying life and ban the use of the pill.

The mature eggs produced by a woman using fertility drugs may be collected and stored, or fertilised and stored, until she wants to get pregnant later. But what happens if the woman dies, or does not want the eggs or embryos any more?

- What, in your opinion, are the main advantages and disadvantages of using artificial hormones to control female fertility?

1. Fertility drugs are used to make lots of eggs mature at the same time for collection.
2. The eggs are collected and placed in a special solution in a Petri dish.
3. A sample of semen is collected and the sperm and eggs are mixed in the Petri dish.
4. The eggs are checked to make sure they have been fertilised and the early embryos are developing properly.
5. When the fertilised eggs have formed tiny balls of cells, 1 or 2 of the tiny embryos are placed in the uterus of the mother. Then, if all goes well, at least one baby will grow and develop successfully.

Figure 3 New reproductive technology using hormones and IVF has helped thousands of infertile couples to have babies

Key points
- Hormones can be used to control fertility.
- Oral contraceptives contain hormones, which stop FSH production so no eggs mature.
- FSH can be used as a fertility drug for women, to stimulate eggs to mature in their ovaries. These eggs may be used in IVF treatments.

Summary questions

1. Explain the meaning of the following terms: oral contraceptive, fallopian tube, fertility drug, *in vitro* fertilisation.
2. Explain how artificial female hormones can be used to:
   a prevent unwanted pregnancies
   b help people overcome infertility.

52

Answers to in-text questions

a Something that reduces the risk of you getting pregnant (conceiving).

b The mixed pill contains oestrogen and progesterone, which prevents ovulation, inhibits FSH secretion, stops the build up of lining of the uterus, etc. The progesterone-only pill doesn't stop ovulation, it is not quite as effective but it has fewer side effects.

Summary answers

1. Oral contraceptive: a pill taken by mouth that reduces the risk of pregnancy.

   Fallopian tube: the tube between the ovary and the uterus that the egg travels along (where conception usually takes place).

   Fertility drug: a drug which stimulates the ovaries to produce ripe eggs.

   In vitro fertilisation: in humans this means combining the egg and sperm in a Petri dish, so fertilisation takes place outside the body.

2. **a** The hormones in contraceptive pills can be used to prevent the release of eggs, stop the build up of the lining of the uterus, etc., so that pregnancy cannot take place.

   b Fertility drugs can be used to stimulate the production of eggs in the ovary so that infertile couples can become pregnant, either naturally, once the eggs have been produced or using IVF.

B1 2.5

Controlling conditions

Learning objectives

Students should learn:

- that the nervous system and hormones help us to control conditions inside the body
- that internal conditions, such as temperature, blood sugar levels and the balance of water and ions, are controlled
- why it is important to control the internal environment.

Learning outcomes

Most students should be able to:

- describe how the temperature, blood sugar levels and balance of water and ions are controlled
- explain why it is important to control the internal environment.

Some students should also be able to:

- explain the effects of extremes of temperature on the human body.

Answers to in-text questions

a Homeostasis is important because cells of the body need a constant environment in which to work properly.
b The kidneys control the balance of water and mineral ions in the blood.
c 37 °C.
d It would go up.

Support

- Students could be given a preprinted copy of Summary question 1 and slips with the words on to fill in the gaps.
- Alternatively, put key terms from the Student Book spread on the board (suggest 'internal environment', 'homeostasis', 'ions', 'hormone', 'enzymes' and 'pancreas'). Read out definitions or descriptions of what the words mean. These words are wiped out when the students recognise them. This has the advantage of identifying difficult concepts and giving students the opportunity to get things right.

Extend

- Students could research hypothermia and heat stroke and produce a poster for each one.

Specification link-up: Biology B1.2

- Internal conditions which are controlled include:
  - the water content of the body – water leaves the body via the lungs when we breathe out and via the skin when we sweat, and excess water is lost via the kidneys in the urine
  - the ion content of the body – ions are lost via the skin when we sweat and excess ions are lost via the kidneys in the urine
  - temperature – to maintain the temperature at which the enzymes work best
  - blood sugar levels – to provide the cells with a constant supply of energy. [B1.2.2 a)]

Controlled Assessment: B4.3 Collect primary and secondary data [B4.3.2 a) b) c) d)]; B4.4 Select and process primary and secondary data [B4.4.1 a) b)] and B4.5 Analyse and interpret primary and secondary data. [B4.5.2 a) b) c) d)]

Lesson structure

Starters

What's in a word? – Put up the word 'homeostasis'. Break it into 'homeo' and 'stasis'. Ask what the words 'static' and 'stationary' mean. Explain that 'stasis' means 'standing still'. The 'homeo' means being 'like' or 'similar'. Link this to 'homeopathy', linking the '-pathy' part to 'pathology/pathogen/pathologist' – relating to diseases. 'Homeo' can then be linked with '-pathy' and explain the theory in homeopathy that very dilute substances which cause symptoms similar to a disease will cure it. *(5 minutes)*

Marathon man – Show a picture of a marathon runner. Show the students two test tubes filled with red liquid. Tell them it is a marathon runner's blood. Have one tube labelled 'start' and the other labelled 'finish'. Get them to write down a list of similarities and differences between the two tubes, based on thinking about what will change and what will stay the same in the runner's internal environment. Support students by providing them with a list to choose from. Extend students by encouraging them to research some numerical levels for norms of these substances. Discuss and share findings on completion of the exercise. *(10 minutes)*

Main

Each of the following suggestions could occupy the main part of the lesson, but the first two could be put together if time permitted. The control of blood sugar does highlight the differences between the nervous system and hormone action.

- Try measuring the body temperature of the class using forehead thermometers if available (see 'Practical support'). Some of the concepts in 'How Science Works' can be introduced into this activity: the accuracy of the measurements; the mean and range of a set of data; how the data can be displayed.
- Students could carry out a practical activity to investigate the change in body temperature (skin temperature) with an increase in exercise (see 'Practical support'). Again, class results could be collated: the differences are relevant here. A discussion about why the changes occur would be relevant.
- Finally you could look at the control of blood sugar levels. In this suggested activity, a comparison can be made between the action of hormones and the nervous system. Introduce with a discussion of the 'sugar rush' from eating several jelly babies (or other sweets) in a row.

Plenaries

Mix it! – Hold a competition with a small prize for students who can make the most words out of the word 'homeostasis'. It may be best to get any obvious words which may cause amusement out of the way as examples. *(5 minutes)*

Ins and outs – Support students by providing them with a table with three columns. Title the central column 'substance' and the outer two 'in' and 'out'. For each of water, ions and sugar, ask the students to fill in the relevant 'in' and 'out' boxes with information as to the processes involved. Extend students by getting them to make up their own table rather than being given one. Get them to add extra columns for 'consequences if the level gets too low' and 'consequences if the level gets too high.' *(10 minutes)*

Practical support

Measuring body temperature using forehead thermometers

Equipment and materials required

Forehead thermometers (or clinical thermometers if forehead thermometers not available).

Details

Follow the manufacturer's instructions given with the thermometers and standardise the time of exposure for each student. It is possible to obtain a mean value and also interesting to plot the variation, so that students understand that there is not a 'fixed' body temperature.

Safety: If clinical thermometers are used, they should be disinfected before and after use.

Measuring changes in body temperature during exercise using forehead thermometers

Equipment and materials required

Forehead thermometers.

Details

Students can record skin temperature before undergoing a period of exercise (such as running on the spot) for a set period of time (1–3 minutes). Skin temperature after the exercise should be recorded. The skin temperature should be measured in the same position each time.

Safety: Avoid competition between students.

Coordination and control

Controlling conditions

B1 2.5 Controlling conditions

Learning objectives

- How are conditions inside your body controlled?
- Why is it so important to control your internal environment?

The conditions inside your body are known as its internal environment. Your organs cannot work properly if this keeps changing. Many of the processes which go on inside your body aim to keep everything as constant as possible. This balancing act is called homeostasis.

It involves your nervous system, your hormone systems and many of your body organs.

a Why is homeostasis important?

Controlling water and ions

Water can move in and out of your body cells. How much it moves depends on the concentration of mineral ions (such as salt) and the amount of water in your body. If too much water moves into or out of your cells, they can be damaged or destroyed.

You take water and minerals into your body as you eat and drink. You lose water as you breathe out, and also in your sweat. You lose salt in your sweat as well. You also lose water and salt in your urine, which is made in your kidneys.

Your kidneys can change the amount of salt and water lost in your urine, depending on your body conditions. They help to control the balance of water and mineral ions in your body. The concentration of the urine produced by your kidneys is controlled by both nerves and hormones.

So, for example, imagine drinking a lot of water all in one go. Your kidneys will remove the extra water from your blood and you will produce lots of very pale urine.

b What do your kidneys control?

Controlling temperature

It is vital that your deep core body temperature is kept at 37 °C. At this temperature your enzymes work best. At only a few degrees above or below normal body temperature the reactions in your cells stop and you will die.

Your body controls your temperature in several ways. For example, you can sweat to cool down and shiver to warm up. Your nervous system is very important in coordinating the way your body responds to changes in temperature.

Once your body temperature drops below 35 °C you are at risk of dying from hypothermia. Several hundred old people die from the effects of cold each year. So do a number of young people who get lost on mountains or try to walk home in the snow after a night out.

If your body temperature goes above about 40–42 °C your enzymes and cells don't work properly. This means that you may die of heat stroke or heat exhaustion.

c What is the ideal body temperature?

Figure 1 Everything you do affects your internal environment

Study tip

Sweating causes the body to cool. Energy from the body is used to evaporate the water in sweat.

Figure 2 You can change your behaviour to help control your temperature, for example by adding extra clothing or turning up the heating when it's really cold

Controlling blood sugar

When you digest a meal, lots of sugar (glucose) passes into your blood. Left alone, your blood glucose levels would keep changing. The levels would be very high straight after a meal, but very low again a few hours later. This would cause chaos in your body.

However, the concentration of glucose in your blood is kept constant by hormones made in your pancreas. This means your body cells are provided with the constant supply of energy that they need.

d What would happen to your blood sugar level if you ate a packet of sweets?

Figure 3 Sweets like this are almost all sugar. When you eat them your body has to deal with the effect on your blood.

Summary questions

1 Copy and complete using the words below:

body constant homeostasis hormones internal nervous

Conditions in the .... environment of your .... must be kept .... This is called .... The control is given by both your .... and your .... system.

2 Why is it important to control:
a water levels in the body
b the body temperature
c sugar (glucose) levels in the blood?

3 **a** Look at the marathon runners in Figure 1. List the ways in which the running is affecting their:
i water balance
ii ion balance
iii temperature.
b It is much harder to run a marathon in a costume than in running clothes. Explain why this is.

links

For more information about the control of blood sugar, see B3 3.7 *Controlling blood glucose*.

Key points

- Humans need to maintain a constant internal environment, controlling levels of water, ions and blood sugar, as well as temperature.
- Homeostasis is the result of the coordination of your nervous system, your hormones and your body organs.

Further teaching suggestions

Water balance

- Write on board 'hot day', 'running a marathon' and 'lazy day at home'. Ask students to suggest how their fluid intake and urine output would vary under these different circumstances and why.

More on blood sugar levels

- As a follow-up to the suggestion on the control of blood sugar levels activity, the process of what happens to the sugar can be presented or volunteered by the students to build up a flow chart, so that the way in which the jelly babies affect the production of a hormone in the pancreas can be shown.

Measuring sweat

- Students could use lint or cotton wool to measure the amount of sweat produced during exercise. More 'How Science Works' concepts can be introduced here, e.g. the relationship between different variables.

Summary answers

1 internal, body, constant, homeostasis, nervous, hormones

2 **a** To stop too much water moving in or out of cells, damaging and destroying them.
b Because the enzymes work best at 37 °C.
c Because blood sugar that is too high or too low causes problems in the body.

3 **a** **i** Losing water through sweating.
ii Losing salt through sweating.
iii Temperature going up with exercising.

b Sweating cools you down and helps to keep the body temperature down – a costume makes you sweat more (as you get hotter), which means you lose more water – but also makes it harder for sweat to evaporate (so you don't cool so effectively). Also, a costume is heavy so it's harder work to run.

B1 2.6

Hormones and the control of plant growth

Learning objectives

Students should learn:

- that plants are sensitive to light, moisture and gravity
- that plants produce hormones to coordinate and control growth
- that plant growth hormones are used in agriculture and horticulture as weed killers and rooting hormones.

Learning outcomes

Most students should be able to:

- understand that plants respond to changes in their environment
- describe how plants respond to light, moisture and gravity
- describe how plant hormones can be used in agriculture and horticulture.

Some students should also be able to:

- explain how plant responses are due to uneven distribution of hormones causing unequal growth rates.

Answers to in-text questions

a Auxin.

Support

- Provide students with blank (unlabelled) diagrams of the bean seedlings from the Student Book and ask them to write captions in their own words to explain what is happening.

Extend

- Use the internet to research specific plant hormones such as gibberellins, cytokines, ethylene, abscisic acid, etc.

Specification link-up: Biology B1.2

- Plants are sensitive to light, moisture and gravity … *[B1.2.3 a)]*
- Plants produce hormones to coordinate and control … *[B1.2.3 b)]*
- The responses of plant roots and shoots to light … *[B1.2.3 c)]*

  Controlled Assessment: B4.3 Collect primary and secondary data *[B4.3.2 a) b)]*; B4.4 Select and process primary and secondary data *[B4.4.2 c)]*; B4.5 Analyse and interpret primary data. *[B4.5.4 a)]*

Lesson structure

Starters

Which way is up? – Take a dozen or so tennis balls. Place them in a deep tray. Gather the students around and say that the balls represent seeds. Mark each one on the top with a felt pen. State that the mark represents where the shoot comes out when it germinates. Ask the students whether, when seeds fall from the parent plant, they will all land on the soil the right way up. Mix up the tray of balls to imitate this. Get students to indicate all the different ways the felt pen marks are now pointing. Hand around some broad bean seeds (ensure they do not have toxic seed dressing on) and observe that this is the case in real life. Explain that during this lesson you will find out how come they all finish up growing in the same direction. *(5 minutes)*

Australian gardening – Support students by drawing a circle on the board. Tell them that this represents the Earth. Get volunteer students to come and draw some plants growing on it in a variety of places, including the poles, UK and Australia, including their roots. Establish that the roots grow towards gravity (towards the centre of the Earth) and the shoots grow away from gravity. Ask what else the roots might grow towards and what else the shoots might grow towards. Extend students by encouraging them to postulate mechanisms for how this can come about. *(10 minutes)*

Main

The following experiments need to be left for some time before the results can be recorded, so will need one lesson session to set up and some time in a later lesson to assess the results. Alternatively, they could be set up ahead of the lesson and shown as demonstrations.

- Practical experiment to investigate the effects of light on the growth of seedlings (see 'Practical support'). Get the students to discuss the results and draw conclusions about the effect of light on the seedlings. The results could be recorded by taking photographs of the pots.

- As an alternative, the experiment described in the Student Book can be set up. Cress seedlings growing on filter paper in a Petri dish can be placed under a lightproof box with a hole cut in one side, so that the seedlings are illuminated from one side only.

Plenaries

Day of the Triffids – Remind students of the book and the mini series featuring Eddie Izzard. Show a still from a search engine or a clip. Discuss what features the triffids would have to have to successfully hunt down humans. Discuss other plant movements such as daisies (their flowers close at night), Venus flytraps, sensitive mimosa, etc. *(5 minutes)*

Hormone uses – Support students by creating a jumbled sentence either on paper or using an internet tool such as Hot Potatoes. Students can unravel it and copy it down or link the sections with lines if printed. An example might be 'used Hormones be to help as can to grow can work roots and cuttings weedkillers' becomes 'Hormones can be used to help cuttings to grow roots and can work as weedkillers.' Extend students by getting them into groups to create their own jumbled sentences and then set them for other groups to sort out. *(10 minutes)*

Practical support

The effect of light on the growth of seedlings

Equipment and materials required (per group of students)

Three pots of young pea seedlings, 10–12 seedlings per pot; labels; suitable places for the pots to be placed, e.g. a cupboard etc.

Details

Working in groups, provide each with three pots of very young pea seedlings (the plumules should only just project above the surface of the compost). Get the students to label their pots, one should be placed in a position where it is exposed to light all around it, another should be placed in a cupboard with no light and the third should be placed in a box where it is exposed to light on one side only. The pots should be left for 7–10 days, but students should check to see that the pots do not dry out. When the seedlings have grown up, the pots should be inspected for differences (a movement sensor could be used) and the results recorded (perhaps by taking photographs of the pots). Get the students to discuss the results and draw conclusions about the effect of light on the seedlings.

Encourage the students to consider: What was the appearance of the seedlings in the different pots? Were there differences in colour?

Coordination and control

B1 2.6

Hormones and the control of plant growth

Learning objectives

- What stimuli do plants respond to?
- How do plants respond to their environment?
- Why do farmers and gardeners use plant hormones?

It is easy to see how animals, such as ourselves, take in information about the surroundings and then react to it. But plants also need to be coordinated. They are sensitive to light, water and gravity.

Plants are sensitive **k**

When seeds are spread they may fall any way up in the soil. It is very important that when the seed starts to grow (germinate) the roots grow downwards into the soil. Then they can anchor the seedling and keep it stable. They can also take up the water and minerals needed for healthy growth.

At the same time the shoots need to grow upwards towards the light so they can photosynthesise as much as possible.

Plant roots are sensitive to gravity and water. The roots grow towards moisture and in the direction of the force of gravity. **Plant shoots** are sensitive to gravity and light. The shoots grow towards light and against the force of gravity. This means that whichever way up the seed lands, the plant always grows the right way up!

Plant responses **k**

Plant responses happen as a result of plant hormones which coordinate and control growth. These responses are easy to see in young seedlings, but they also happen in adult plants. For example, the stems of a houseplant left on a windowsill will soon bend towards the light. The response of a plant to light is known as phototropism. The response of a plant to gravity is called gravitropism (also known as geotropism).

The responses of plant roots and shoots to light, gravity and moisture are controlled by a hormone called auxin. The response happens because of an uneven distribution of this hormone in the growing shoot or root. This causes an unequal growth rate. As a result the root or shoot bends in the right direction.

Phototropism can clearly be seen when a young shoot responds to light from one side only. The shoot will bend so it is growing towards the light. Auxin moves from the side of the shoot where the light is falling to the unlit side of the shoot. The cells on that side respond to the hormone by growing more – and so the shoot bends towards the light. Once light falls evenly on the shoot, the levels of auxin will be equal on all sides and so the shoot grows straight again.

Gravitropisms can be seen in roots and shoots. Auxin has different effects on root and shoot cells. High levels of auxin make shoot cells grow more but inhibit growth of root cells. This is why roots and shoots respond differently to gravity.

a What is the name of the plant hormone which controls phototropism and gravitropism?

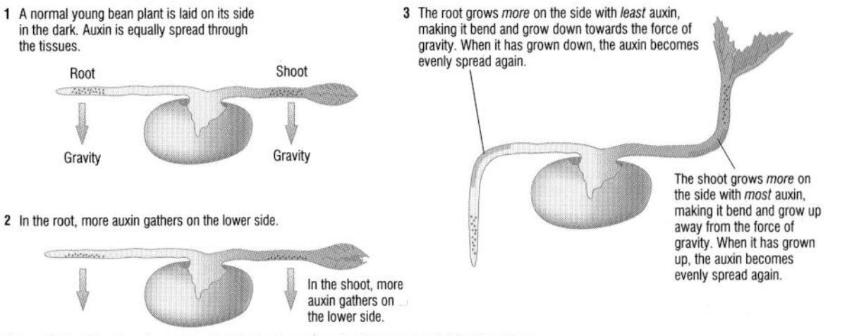

Figure 1 Seedlings like this radish show you clearly how plant shoots respond to light – they grow towards it

Did you know … ?

The first scientists to show the way the shoot of a plant responds to light from one direction were Charles Darwin and his son Francis.

Practical

The effect of light on the growth of seedlings

You can investigate the effect of one-sided light on the growth of seedlings using a simple box with a hole cut in it and cress seedling growing in a Petri dish.

1 A normal young bean plant is laid on its side in the dark. Auxin is equally spread through the tissues.

Root — Shoot

Gravity — Gravity

2 In the root, more auxin gathers on the lower side.

In the shoot, more auxin gathers on the lower side.

3 The root grows *more* on the side with *least* auxin, making it bend and grow down towards the force of gravity. When it has grown down, the auxin becomes evenly spread again.

The shoot grows *more* on the side with *most* auxin, making it bend and grow up away from the force of gravity. When it has grown up, the auxin becomes evenly spread again.

Figure 2 Gravitropism (or geotropism) in shoots and roots. The uneven distribution of the hormone auxin causes unequal growth rates so the roots grow down and the shoots grow up.

Using plant hormones **k**

Plant hormones can be used to manage plants grown in the garden or home. Farmers also use them to grow better crops.

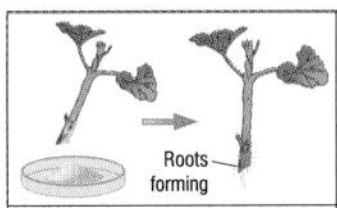 Roots forming	Gardeners and horticulturists rely on taking cuttings to produce lots of identical plants. Plant growth hormones are used as rooting powder. A little placed on the end of a cutting stimulates the growth of new roots and helps the cutting to grow into a new plant.
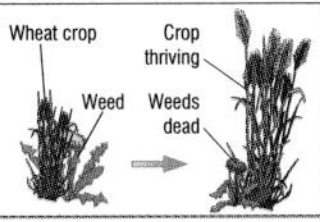 Wheat crop / Crop thriving / Weed / Weeds dead	You can use high doses of plant hormones as weed killers. Most weeds are broad-leaved plants which absorb a lot of hormone weed killer. This makes them go into rapid, uncontrolled growth which kills them. Narrow-leaved plants such as grasses and cereal are not affected, so the crop or lawn keeps growing well.

Figure 3 Some human uses of plant hormones

Summary questions

1 Copy and complete using the words below:

hormone auxin gravitropism light sensitive moisture

Plants are .... to ...., which is called phototropism. They respond to gravity which is .... Plants are also sensitive to .... These responses are coordinated by the plant .... called ....

2 Why are the responses of shoots and roots so important in the life of plants?

3 Explain carefully, using diagrams, how a plant shoot responds to light shining at it from one side only.

Key points

- Plants are sensitive to light, moisture and gravity.
- Plant responses are brought about by plant hormones.
- The responses of roots and shoots to stimuli such as light and gravity are the result of the unequal distribution of plant hormones.
- We can use plant growth hormones as weed killers and as rooting hormones on cuttings.

56

Further teaching suggestions

The effect of gravity on the growth of germinating seedlings

- Use a number of germinating broad bean seeds (5 to 6 with the seed just visible), a sheet of cork and some pins. Ask the students to fix the seeds to the cork in different positions using the pins. Place all the sheets of cork in a large tank with a little water at the bottom, cover with a dark cloth or cardboard to exclude the light and leave for about a week. Then get the students to record the positions of the roots and shoots of the beans and draw conclusions about the effect of gravity.

Demonstrate the effect of a selective weedkiller

- The use of plant hormones as weedkillers can be demonstrated by placing two sections of weedy turf into seed trays and watering one with a selective (hormone) weedkiller and the other with water. Students could record their observations using a movement senors over a period of time, noting which plants were affected by the weedkiller and which were not.

Detecting the stimulus

- A demonstration could be set up, using maize or oat seedlings, to show where the light stimulus is detected and where the response occurs. Grow maize seedlings on moist filter paper in Petri dishes until they are 10 mm long then cover the tips of half of them with aluminium foil caps, leaving the rest uncovered. Place in a box with a slit in one side to allow light in. Leave for several days and record the differences between the two sets of seedlings.

Summary answers

1 sensitive, light, gravitropism, moisture, hormone, auxin

2 To make sure that whichever way up a seed lands, the roots grow down into the soil to anchor the plant and take water and minerals from the soil, and the shoots grow upwards towards the light so they can photosynthesise. This continues to make sure the plant grows to obtain the maximum light.

3 Suitable well-labelled diagram showing movement of auxin away from light and then faster growth on the side of the shoot away from the light until shoot is growing directly towards the light source. Plants responses are relatively slow, which indicates that they are brought about by hormones.

B1 2.7

Using hormones

Learning objectives

Students should learn:
- that there are benefits and problems associated with the use of hormones to control human fertility
- that plant hormones are used to produce our food.

Learning outcomes

Most students should be able to:
- describe the benefits associated with the use of hormones to control human fertility
- describe the problems associated with the use of these hormones
- describe how plant hormones are involved in food production.

Some students should also be able to:
- evaluate the use of hormones in controlling fertility and in the production of food.

Answers to in-text questions
a FSH.
b A chemical based on plant hormones which strips the leaves off trees at high doses.

Support
- Students could produce a poster summarising the benefits of organic farming.

Extend
- Students could perform an internet search to find information on the herbicide Agent Orange. Produce a summary press report covering the Rainbow herbicides, Operation Ranch Hand and the birth deformities which have resulted from its use. Present this when time allows.

Specification link-up: Biology B1.2
- The uses of hormones in controlling fertility include … [B1.2.2 e)]
- Plant growth hormones are used in agriculture and horticulture as weed killers and as rooting hormones. [B1.2.3 d)]
- Evaluate the use of plant hormones in horticulture as weed killers and to encourage the rooting of plant cuttings. [B1.2]

  Controlled Assessment: B4.3 Collect primary data [B4.3.2 a)]; B4.4 Select and process primary and secondary data [B4.4.2 c)]; B4.5 Analyse and interpret primary and secondary data. [B4.5.4 a)]

Lesson structure

Starters

Dear old mum – Draw or project the numbers from 16 to 66 onto the board. Explain that these are ages from the age of consent to the oldest known mother. Ask the students to choose a range of ages they would consider to be acceptable for IVF treatment. If they rule out any age ranges they should be able to explain why they have done this. Be aware of any individuals for whom this may be a personal issue. *(5 minutes)*

Spray away! – Support students by showing them a photograph of an organic garden and the Soil Association sign. Ask what sort of activities organic gardeners could carry out to control weeds without the use of herbicides. Draw out some reasons why they might prefer not to use them in the first place. Extend students by giving them a set of cards with reasons for using herbicides and reasons for not doing so. Get them to place the cards in order of the ones they most agree with, or think are most important, to those they disagree with, or think are not important. They must be prepared to publicly justify their placements. *(10 minutes)*

Main

- Using the information in the Student Book and their own ideas, students could write a two–three-minute report for the school radio entitled 'Older mothers – should science help?' Students could work in groups, discuss the format of the report and make a presentation to the rest of the class.

- If the demonstration of the effects of a selective weedkiller described previously was not used, it would be appropriate here. The investigation could be set up by the students and extended by using different types of weedkiller or different concentrations of the same weedkiller.

- A rooting powder, containing a rooting hormone, can be used to encourage the formation of roots on cuttings from plants. This investigation requires one lesson session to set up and the cuttings need to be left for several weeks – longer if woody tissue is used. Set up some cuttings treated with the rooting powder and some without treatment as controls. The effects of the rooting powder can be assessed by measuring the root formation on the treated cuttings and on the controls.

- Ask students to prepare short speeches either in favour of or against the motion 'Synthetic plant hormones should be banned'. See the 'Is it worth it?' activity in the Student Book. Allow some time for research on the internet and combine it with the Plenary on Agent Orange. At a convenient time, arrange a debate.

Plenaries

Orphaned at 3 – Give the students a printed sheet of news coverage following the death in 2009 at the age of 69 of Maria Del Carmen Bousada de Lara who became the world's oldest mother at 66. Students are to give their views about the ethics of the situation. *(5 minutes)*

Orange hangover – Read the text section on Agent Orange. Support students by making a list of the animals that might be harmed if the jungle was stripped of its leaves and describe how this would harm them. Extend students by getting them to find more information from the internet about Agent Orange and discuss the general effect on wildlife and the surrounding communities. *(10 minutes)*

Practical support

The effect of weedkillers on the growth of plants

Equipment and materials required
Sections of weedy turf; seed trays; selective weedkiller made up according to manufacturer's instructions.

Details
The sections of weedy turf should be the same size and placed in the seed trays and then kept in the same conditions of light and temperature. They should be treated according to the instructions supplied with the weedkiller. Students can record changes in the plant species over a period of time. This can be set up as a demonstration or groups of students can set up their own investigation. The results can be recorded photographically or more quantitatively by estimating the numbers of weed species present in the treated and untreated sections.

Safety: Take care when handling weedkiller. Wash hands after experiment.

Using a rooting powder

Equipment and materials required
Cuttings of hardy perennials or small shrubs; rooting powder; compost; small plant pots.

Details
Cuttings of hardy perennials or small shrubs with soft stems and green leaves can be used. Sections of stem about 10 cm long, cut just below a leaf joint, and with the lower leaves removed, are dipped into rooting powder (follow the instructions provided) and then planted into damp compost. As a control, prepare some cuttings in the same way but do not dip into the rooting powder before planting in damp compost. All the pots should be kept moist.

Safety: Take care when handling rooting powder. Wash hands after experiment.

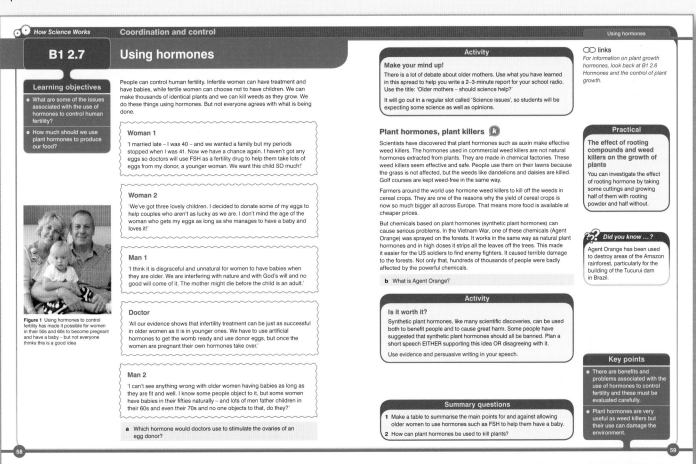

How Science Works — Coordination and control

B1 2.7 — Using hormones

Learning objectives
- What are some of the issues associated with the use of hormones to control human fertility?
- How much should we use plant hormones to produce our food?

People can control human fertility. Infertile women can have treatment and have babies, while fertile women can choose not to have children. We can make thousands of identical plants and we can kill weeds as they grow. We do these things using hormones. But not everyone agrees with what is being done.

Woman 1
'I married late – I was 40 – and we wanted a family but my periods stopped when I was 41. Now we have a chance again. I haven't got any eggs so doctors will use FSH as a fertility drug to help them take lots of eggs from my donor, a younger woman. We want this child SO much!'

Woman 2
'We've got three lovely children. I decided to donate some of my eggs to help couples who aren't as lucky as we are. I don't mind the age of the woman who gets my eggs as long as she manages to have a baby and loves it!'

Man 1
'I think it is disgraceful and unnatural for women to have babies when they are older. We are interfering with nature and with God's will and no good will come of it. The mother might die before the child is an adult.'

Doctor
'All our evidence shows that infertility treatment can be just as successful in older women as it is in younger ones. We have to use artificial hormones to get the womb ready and use donor eggs, but once the women are pregnant their own hormones take over.'

Man 2
'I can't see anything wrong with older women having babies as long as they are fit and well. I know some people object to it, but some women have babies in their fifties naturally – and lots of men father children in their 60s and even their 70s and no one objects to that, do they?'

Figure 1 Using hormones to control fertility has made it possible for women in their 50s and 60s to become pregnant and have a baby – but not everyone thinks this is a good idea

a Which hormone would doctors use to stimulate the ovaries of an egg donor?

Activity
Make your mind up!
There is a lot of debate about older mothers. Use what you have learned in this spread to help you write a 2–3-minute report for your school radio. Use the title: 'Older mothers – should science help?'

It will go out in a regular slot called 'Science issues', so students will be expecting some science as well as opinions.

Plant hormones, plant killers
Scientists have discovered that plant hormones such as auxin make effective weed killers. The hormones used in commercial weed killers are not natural hormones extracted from plants. They are made in chemical factories. These weed killers seem effective and safe. People use them on their lawns because the grass is not affected, but the weeds like dandelions and daisies are killed. Golf courses are kept weed-free in the same way.

Farmers around the world use hormone weed killers to kill off the weeds in cereal crops. They are one of the reasons why the yield of cereal crops is now so much bigger all across Europe. That means more food is available at cheaper prices.

But chemicals based on plant hormones (synthetic plant hormones) can cause serious problems. In the Vietnam War, one of these chemicals (Agent Orange) was sprayed on the forests. It works in the same way as natural plant hormones and in high doses it strips all the leaves off the trees. This made it easier for the US soldiers to find enemy fighters. It caused terrible damage to the forests. Not only that, hundreds of thousands of people were badly affected by the powerful chemicals.

b What is Agent Orange?

Activity
Is it worth it?
Synthetic plant hormones, like many scientific discoveries, can be used both to benefit people and to cause great harm. Some people have suggested that synthetic plant hormones should all be banned. Plan a short speech EITHER supporting this idea OR disagreeing with it.

Use evidence and persuasive writing in your speech.

Summary questions
1 Make a table to summarise the main points for and against allowing older women to use hormones such as FSH to help them have a baby.
2 How can plant hormones be used to kill plants?

links
For information on plant growth hormones, look back at B1 2.6 Hormones and the control of plant growth.

Practical
The effect of rooting compounds and weed killers on the growth of plants
You can investigate the effect of rooting hormone by taking some cuttings and growing half of them with rooting powder and half without.

Did you know ...?
Agent Orange has been used to destroy areas of the Amazon rainforest, particularly for the building of the Tucuruí dam in Brazil.

Key points
- There are benefits and problems associated with the use of hormones to control fertility and these must be evaluated carefully.
- Plant hormones are very useful as weed killers but their use can damage the environment.

Further teaching suggestions

The use of plant hormones in micropropagation
- This topic could be researched and the practical investigation carried out.

The effect of the use of weedkillers on the production of cereal crops
- Students could research the increase in yield and discuss whether that increase means cheaper food at the price of environmental damage from the weedkillers.

Is organic food better for you?
- Continue the discussion begun in the Starter. This could form the basis of a debate – more research could be carried out. The debate could be extended to the use of hormones in the rearing of cattle and increased milk production.

Summary answers

1 Credit for any thoughtful points.

For: allows people to become mothers if they find a partner late in life; people have a right to have a baby when they want one; if someone loses their child they might want to have another; the mother will be financially secure and have had a good career before she has a child; if you go to all that trouble, the baby will be very much wanted.

Against: the mother will be old while the child is still young; the mother may die before the child is an adult; the mother is more likely to have serious illnesses than a younger mother; the mother may not be able to keep up with an energetic child.

2 They can be used to cause excessive growth that kills plants. They are absorbed more by broadleaved plants that are often weeds rather than by cereals. Hormones can also be used to cause leaf fall, which kills plants as well.

Summary answers

1 **a** F **b** C **c** D **d** B **e** A **f** E

2 **a** It enables you to react to your surroundings and to coordinate your behaviour.

  b **i** Eye
   ii Ear
   iii Skin
   iv Skin

  c Diagram of reflex arc. The explanation needs to include the following points: reference to three types of neuron: a sensory neuron; a motor neuron; a relay neuron. The relay neuron is found in the CNS, often in the spinal cord. An electrical impulse passes from the sensory receptor, along the sensory neuron to the CNS. It then passes to a relay neuron and straight back along a motor neuron to the effector organ (usually a muscle in a reflex). This is known as the 'reflex arc'. The junction between one neuron and the next is known as a 'synapse'. The time between the stimulus and the reflex action is as short as is possible. It allows you to react to danger without thinking about it.

3 **a** It is the monthly cycle of fertility in women. The average length of the menstrual cycle is about 28 days. Each month the lining of the womb thickens ready to support a developing baby, and at the same time an egg starts maturing in the ovary. About 14 days after the egg starts maturing, it is released from the ovary. This is known as 'ovulation'. The lining of the womb stays thick for several days after the egg has been released before it is shed as the monthly 'period'.

  b **i** FSH is made by the pituitary gland; it stimulates the maturation of eggs in the ovaries and stimulates the ovaries to produce oestrogen.
   ii Oestrogen is made in the ovary and stimulates the lining of the womb to build up ready for pregnancy. It inhibits FSH production.

4 **a** Hormones are chemicals that control the processes of the body. Hormones are released from glands into the blood. Some hormones act quickly, but many act more slowly. All are slower than nervous control.
Nervous control can be very fast, especially reflexes. It involves the transmission of electrical impulses along neurons. Transmission from one neuron to the next involves chemical substances.

  b A synapse is the junction between two neurons. They are important because they are where neurons meet and the impulses pass from one neuron to another via a chemical (neurotransmitter).

  c Oral contraceptives (the contraceptive pill) contain hormones, including oestrogen, which act on the ovary preventing the release of any eggs. The production of FSH is inhibited so that no eggs mature in the ovaries. If there are no mature eggs, then you cannot get pregnant. If a woman does not make enough FSH to stimulate eggs to mature, she may be given FSH as a 'fertility' drug. As well as stimulating the development of eggs, FSH triggers oestrogen production.

5 **a** A = more, B = less, C = the same or less.

  b Sweating/evaporation.

  c From food (and respiration).

6 To begin with, the body would sweat to try to cool down. As the water shortage becomes apparent, the level of sweating would drop. The amount of water lost in urine would be reduced to maintain internal levels of water. You would feel thirsty and need to get a drink. Reduced sweating would allow body temperature to rise slightly.

Coordination and control: B1 2.1–B1 2.7

Summary questions k

1 This question is about animal responses. Match up the following parts of sentences:

a	Many processes in the body …	A	… effector organs.
b	The nervous system allows you …	B	… secreted by glands.
c	The cells which are sensitive to light …	C	… to react to your surroundings and coordinate your behaviour.
d	Hormones are chemical substances …	D	… are found in the eyes.
e	Muscles and glands are known as …	E	… are known as nerves.
f	Bundles of neurons …	F	… are controlled by hormones.

2 **a** What is the job of your nervous system?
  b Where in your body would you find nervous receptors which respond to:
   i light
   ii sound
   iii heat
   iv touch?
  c Draw and label a simple diagram of a reflex arc. Explain carefully how a reflex arc works and why it allows you to respond quickly to danger.

3 **a** What is the menstrual cycle?
  b What is the role of the following hormones in the menstrual cycle:
   i FSH
   ii oestrogen?

4 **a** Explain carefully the difference between nervous and hormone control of your body.
  b What are synapses and why are they important in your nervous system?
  c How can hormones be used to control the fertility of a woman?

5 The table shows four ways in which water leaves your body, and the amounts lost on a cool day:

Source of water loss	Cool day (water loss in cm³)	Hot day (loss in cm³)
Breath	400	The same
Skin	500	A
Urine	1500	B
Faeces	150	C

  a On a hot day, would the amount of water lost in A, B and C be less, the same or more than the amount of water lost on a cool day?
  b Name the process by which we lose water from the skin.
  c On a cool day the body gained 2550 cm³ of water. 1750 cm³ came directly from drinking. Where did the rest come from?

6 It is very important to keep the conditions inside the body stable. Taking part in school sports on a hot day without a drink for the afternoon would be difficult for your body. Explain how your body would keep the internal environment as stable as possible.

7 **a** What is gravitropism (geotropism)?
  b Explain carefully how the following respond to gravity, including the part played by plant hormones. Diagrams may help in your explanations.
   i a root
   ii a shoot

8 You are provided with some very young single shoots. Devise an experiment which would demonstrate that shoots grow towards the light.

---

7 **a** The response of a plant root or shoot to gravity.

  b **i** A plant root responds positively to gravity, it grows down towards the force of the gravity. Auxin gathers on the side of the root nearest to the pull of gravity. The root grows more on the side with low auxin levels, this causes the root to bend and grow downwards towards gravity (a diagram will help with the explanation).
   ii Shoots respond by growing away from the force of gravity. For example if a shoot is horizontal, auxin accumulates at the lower surface of the shoot. The cells of the shoot grow rapidly in response to high levels of auxin. This means the lower side of the shoot grows faster than the upper side, so the shoot bends upwards away from the force of gravity.

8 Credit for well thought out investigation – needs to include unilateral light. Methods will vary – look for awareness of need for large sample of seedlings, controlling variables, etc.

Practical suggestions

Practicals	AQA	k	📖	⚙
Investigation into candidates' reaction times – measuring reaction times using metre rules, stop clocks or ICT.	✓		✓	
Using forehead thermometers before and after exercise.	✓		✓	

Practice questions

A dog responds to stimuli.

a Link the receptor descriptions to the correct part of the animal by choosing the correct letter (A, B, C or D).

i Contains receptors to detect chemicals (1)

ii Contains receptors to detect light (1)

iii Contains receptors to detect movement of the head and sound. (1)

b The skin of a human contains receptors which are sensitive to touch.

i Give **one** other stimulus which is detected by human skin. (1)

ii Suggest why there are many touch receptors in a person's fingertips. (1)

a When a person touches a hot surface they move their hand away quickly.

Choose the correct word to complete the sentence.

This is called a .... action. (1)

learned   reflex   thoughtful

b What is the importance of this type of action? (1)

This picture shows a Venus flytrap.

a The Venus flytrap catches flies for food. When a fly lands on the leaf the trap closes.

Choose the correct word to complete the sentence.

The shutting of the trap is called a .... (1)

detector   stimulus   response

b Suggest **one** receptor the Venus flytrap has to detect the fly. (1)

4 Hormones are important chemicals which help to control conditions inside living organisms.

a List A shows three hormones

List B shows where some hormones are produced.

Match each hormone with where it is produced.

List A	List B
Hormone	Where produced
auxin	pituitary gland
oestrogen	kidney
FSH	plant stems and roots
	ovary

(3)

b Choose the correct answer to complete each of the following sentences.

i The hormone which causes eggs to mature is .... (1)

auxin   oestrogen   FSH

ii The hormone which causes growth of the uterus(womb) lining is .... (1)

auxin   oestrogen   FSH

5 When light is shone in a person's eyes they blink. When a plant is placed near a lamp the stem bends towards the light.

a Choose the correct answer to complete each of the following sentences.

i The response of the eye to bright light is called a .... action. (1)

learned   reflex   stimulated

ii The response of the plant to light is called .... (1)

gravitropism   hydrotropism   phototropism

b *In this question you will be assessed on using good English, organising information clearly and using specialist terms where appropriate.*

Plants respond to light and gravity. Describe how plant hormones control the growth of roots and shoots. (6)

61

Practicals	AQA		📖	⚙
Demonstrating the speed of transmission along nerves by candidates standing in a semicircle and holding hands and squeezing with eyes closed.	✓		✓	
Design an investigation to measure the sensitivity of the skin.	✓		✓	
Demonstrating the knee jerk reaction.	✓		✓	
Investigation to measure the amount of sweat produced during exercise.	✓		✓	
Investigate: – the effect of light on the growth of seedlings – the effect of gravity on growth in germinating seedlings – the effect of water on the growth of seedlings – using a motion sensor to measure the growth of plants and seedlings – the effect of rooting compounds and weed killers on the growth of plants.	✓	✓	✓	✓

Practice answers

1 a i A   ii C   iii B   *(3 marks)*

b i temperature/pressure/pain   *(1 mark)*

ii idea of increased sensitivity (for a particular task e.g. to feel a pencil when writing)   *(1 mark)*

2 a reflex   *(1 mark)*

b prevents damage/harm OR prevents skin burning   *(1 mark)*

3 a response   *(1 mark)*

b any one of: touch/pressure/chemical   *(1 mark)*

4 a Auxin links to plant stems and roots, oestrogen links to ovary, FSH links to pituitary gland.   *(3 marks)*

b i FSH   ii oestrogen   *(2 marks)*

5 a i reflex   ii phototropism   *(2 marks)*

b There is a clear and detailed scientific description of phototropism and geotropism and how auxin controls growth of both the root and shoot. The answer is coherent and in a logical sequence. It contains a range of appropriate or relevant specialist terms used accurately. The answer shows very few errors in spelling, punctuation and grammar.   *(5–6 marks)*

There is some description of how hormones cause the root and shoot to bend. The answer has some structure and the use of specialist terms has been attempted, but not always accurately. There may be some errors in spelling, punctuation and grammar.   *(3–4 marks)*

There is a brief description of how hormones control growth in either the root or shoot which has little clarity and detail. The answer is poorly constructed with an absence of specialist terms or their use demonstrates a lack of understanding of their meaning. The spelling, punctuation and grammar are weak.   *(1–2 marks)*

No relevant content.   *(0 marks)*

Examples of biology points made in the response:
- Correct use of phototropism
- Correct use of gravitropism (allow geotropism)
- Auxin produced in root/shoot
- More hormone/auxin on lower side of root
- More hormone/auxin on lower/dark side of shoot
- Hormone inhibits growth of root cells
- Hormone stimulates growth of shoot/stem cells
- Longer cells on one side
- Causes root/shoot to bend
- Roots grow towards gravity
- Shoots grow towards light.

Kerboodle resources

Resources available for this chapter on Kerboodle are:
- Chapter map: Coordination and control
- Animation: Reflex action (B1 2.2)
- Bump up your grade: Reflexes in action (B1 2.2)
- Support: What's that for? (B1 2.3)
- Bump up your grade: The artificial control of fertility (B1 2.4)
- Extension: What to do with the rest (B1 2.4)
- WebQuest: Saviour siblings (B1 2.4)
- Support: The ups and downs of life (B1 2.6)
- How Science Works: Does light affect the germination of seedlings? (B1 2.6)
- Practical: Plant growth hormones (2.7)
- Interactive activity: Coordination and control
- Revision podcast: Coordination and control
- Test yourself: Coordination and control
- On your marks: Coordination and control
- Practice questions: Coordination and control
- Answers to practice questions: Coordination and control

B1 3.1

Developing new medicines

Learning objectives

Students should learn:

- that new medical treatments and drugs need to be extensively tested and trialled before being used
- the possible consequences if drugs are not tested thoroughly.

Learning outcomes

Most students should be able to:

- describe and explain the reasons for testing new drugs
- explain the dangers of using drugs that have not been thoroughly tested.

Some students should also be able to:

- explain the main stages in testing drugs
- explain the flaws in the original development of thalidomide.

Support

- Make sets of cards, each with a sentence on regarding the process of drug testing. Students, working in small groups, are to put them into the correct order. This could be a competition to see which group can do it in the shortest time. (If you have the sets made up in different colours, then they are easier to sort out. Keep in separate bags.)
- Lead a session with students on 'Household safety in handling drugs and medicines.' Concentrate on things like: taking the whole prescribed course; keeping medicines away from children; taking care with the right dose and times at which medicines are taken; and discarding out-of-date drugs.

Extend

- Encourage students to explore the medical issues involved, such as the dilemma that doctors have in prescribing expensive treatments in the light of their budgets. Ask: 'Who gets them? Does it depend on age? Does it depend on your postcode?'

Specification link-up: Biology B1.3

- Scientists are continually developing new drugs. *[B1.3.1 a)]*
- When new medical drugs are devised, they have to be … *[B1.3.1 b)]*
- Thalidomide is a drug that was developed as … *[B1.3.1 d)]*

Controlled Assessment: B4.5 Analyse and interpret primary and secondary data. *[B4.5.4 d)]*

Lesson structure

Starters

A good medicine? – Discuss what would and, more importantly, would not make a good medicine. This provides an opportunity to examine what we expect implicitly from a medicine and make it explicit. *(5 minutes)*

'New drug, anybody?' – Show students a pill or medicine bottle and tell them it is a brand new medicine. Give the students a series of statements, adapted to their ability, that describe a sequence of events that would have to happen before a drug is put on the market. Get them to put the statements into a sensible order and then discuss them. This can be extended by asking students to write down, unsupported, what they think happens from the initial idea or discovery, up to the time it is obtainable from the chemist. Build up a sequence on the board from the ideas that the class come up with. *(10 minutes)*

Main

- Build up a more complete picture of the drug thalidomide by extending the information given in the Student Book. A video, or projected pictures, and a commentary could be used. More information about the development of the drug, the consequences of its use as a treatment for morning sickness during pregnancy, and the current possibilities of its use as a treatment for autoimmune diseases and Aids can be obtained from the internet. There are several websites providing information, e.g. www.britishpathe.com.

- Produce a PowerPoint presentation on good medicines and the stages of drug testing. Produce worksheets to accompany the presentation and allow opportunities for the students to discuss points and complete their sheets as you progress through the presentation. You might include consideration of the number of people involved in research and testing, the timescale and the sample size of any trials carried out, and the purpose of a control group using a placebo in double-blind trials, thereby including important elements of 'How Science Works'.

- Following the drug testing presentation, remind students that drugs are tested on healthy volunteers and point out that there are risks attached. Ask: 'Would you volunteer for drug testing?'; 'If so, under what circumstances?' If you would not, give your reasons and suggest other ways in which drugs should be trialled and tested'. This discussion can start in groups and then widen to include the whole class.

Plenaries

What do the words mean? – Write the words 'safe', 'effective', 'stable', 'incorporated' and 'excreted' on the board and discuss with the class how these words can be defined in terms of drugs. Students can be supported by giving them a list of meanings to choose from, or the activity can be extended by asking students to supply the definitions or be given an opportunity to extend the list for themselves. *(5 minutes)*

Should drugs be cheaper? – There has been a great deal of controversy about the cost of drugs and the availability of some new treatments for patients. The costs of development have to be recovered, but is it right that diseases for which there are drugs available are not treated because the costs are too high? Should the drugs to treat HIV and Aids be made available more cheaply in developing countries? Discuss. *(10 minutes)*

Answers to in-text questions

a Effective, safe, stable, successfully absorbed and excreted from our bodies.

b To help stop morning sickness.

Further teaching suggestions

Testing drugs on animals
- Discuss the problems associated with the testing of drugs on animals. Look at the activities of animal rights' supporters and try to get across the difference between antivivisectionist groups and those people concerned with animal welfare (often confused). Are people justified in making the protests they do? How would drugs be tested if animals were not used?

Who to target?
- Another aspect of the finances could be the basis of a class discussion. Who would you target if you wanted to maximise your profits? Are there any groups of the population who have lots of drug needs, but which there would be little point in targeting? What could be done to address this problem?

Feelings about thalidomide
- Provide each student with an A4 sheet divided into four sections: one section for the feelings of the doctor who prescribed thalidomide, one for the feelings of the person who was affected, one for the feelings of the parent and one for the feelings of the drug company. When completed, this could be discussed in class or used in a role play exercise.

Understanding placebos
- Find out what the term 'placebo' means and suggest why some people are given a placebo when new drugs are being trialled ('How Science Works').

Medicine and drugs

B1 3.1 Developing new medicines

Learning objectives
- What are the stages in testing and trialling a new drug?
- Why is testing new drugs so important?

Figure 1 The development of a new medicine takes millions of pounds, involves many people and lots of equipment

Study tip
Make sure you are clear that a medical drug is tested to establish:
- its effectiveness
- its toxicity
- the most appropriate dose.

We are developing new medicines all the time, as scientists and doctors try to find ways of curing more diseases. We test new medicines in the laboratory. Every new medical treatment has to be extensively tested and trialled before it is used. This process makes sure that it works well and is as safe as possible.

A good medicine is:
- **Effective** – it must prevent or cure a disease or at least make you feel better.
- **Safe** – the drug must not be too toxic (poisonous) or have unacceptable side effects.
- **Stable** – you must be able to use the medicine under normal conditions and store it for some time.
- **Successfully taken into and removed from your body** – it must reach its target and be cleared from your system once it has done its work.

Developing and testing a new drug
When scientists research a new medicine they have to make sure all these conditions are met. It can take up to 12 years to bring a new medicine into your doctor's surgery. It can also cost a lot of money; up to about £350 million!

Researchers target a disease and make lots of possible new drugs. These are tested in the laboratory to find out if they are toxic and if they seem to do their job. They are tested on cells, tissues and even whole organs. Many chemicals fail at this stage.

The small numbers of chemicals which pass the earlier tests are now tested on animals. This is done to find out how they work in a whole living organism. It also gives information about possible doses and side effects. The tissues and animals are used as models to predict how the drugs may behave in humans.

Drugs that pass animal testing will be tested on human volunteers in clinical trials. First very low doses are given to healthy people to check for side effects. Then it is tried on a small number of patients to see if it treats the disease. If it seems to be safe and effective, bigger clinical trials take place to find the optimum dose for the drug.

If the medicine passes all the legal tests it is licensed so your doctor can prescribe it. Its safety will be monitored for as long as it is used.

a What are the important properties of a good new medicine?

Double-blind trials
In human trials, scientists use a **double-blind trial** to see just how effective the new medicine is. Some patients with the target disease agree to take part in the trials. They are either given a **placebo** that does not contain the drug or the new medicine. Neither the doctor nor the patients know who has received the real drug and who has received the placebo until the trial is complete. The patients' health is monitored carefully.

Study tip
Remember, the cells, tissues and animals act as models to predict how the drug may behave in humans.

Often the placebo will contain a different drug that is already used to treat the disease. That is so the patient is not deprived of treatment by taking part in the trial.

Why do we test new medicines so thoroughly?
Thalidomide is a medicine which was developed in the 1950s as a sleeping pill. This was before there were agreed standards for testing new medicines. In particular, tests on pregnant animals, which we now know to be essential, were not carried out.

Then it was discovered that thalidomide stopped morning sickness during pregnancy. Because thalidomide seemed very safe for adults, it was assumed to be safe for unborn children. Doctors gave it to pregnant women to relieve their sickness.

Tragically, thalidomide was **not** safe for developing fetuses. It affected the fetuses of many women who took the drug in the early stages of pregnancy. They went on to give birth to babies with severe limb deformities.

The thalidomide tragedy led to a new law being passed. It set standards for the testing of all new medicines. Since the Medicines Act 1968, new medicines must be tested on animals to see if they have an effect on developing fetuses.

There is another twist in the thalidomide story. Doctors discovered it can treat leprosy. They started to use the drug against leprosy in the developing world but again children were born with abnormalities. Its use for leprosy has now been banned by the World Health Organisation (WHO).

However doctors are finding more uses for the drug. It can treat some autoimmune diseases (where the body attacks its own cells) and even some cancers. It is now used very carefully and never given to anyone who is or might become pregnant.

b Why was thalidomide prescribed to pregnant women?

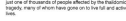

Figure 2 This woman has limb deformities because her mother took thalidomide during her pregnancy. She was just one of thousands of people affected by the thalidomide tragedy, many of whom have gone on to live full and active lives.

Summary questions
1 Copy and complete the words below:
effective trialled safe medicine stable tested
Every new .... has to be extensively .... and .... before you can use it to make sure that it works well. A good medicine can be taken into and removed from your body, and it is ...., ... and ....
2 **a** Testing a new medicine costs a lot of money and can take up to 12 years. Make a flow chart to show the main stages in testing new drugs.
b Why is an active drug often used as the control in a clinical trial instead of a sugar pill placebo which does nothing?
3 **a** What were the flaws in the original development of thalidomide?
b Why do you think that the World Health Organisation has stopped the use of thalidomide to treat leprosy but the drug is still being used in the developed world to treat certain rare conditions?

Key points
- When we develop new medicines they have to be tested and trialled extensively before we can use them.
- Drugs are tested to see if they work well. We also make sure they are not too toxic and have no unacceptable side effects.
- Thalidomide was developed as a sleeping pill and was found to prevent morning sickness in early pregnancy. It had not been fully tested and it caused birth defects.

62 / 63

Summary answers

1 medicine, tested (trialled), trialled (tested), safe, effective, stable (last three in any order).

2 **a** Flow chart to show the main stages in the process.

b If there is already a drug which works reasonably well against a disease, it would be unethical not to give that to a patient. It also allows us to compare how good the new drug is compared to existing drugs. It can only be done if there is already an active drug available.

3 **a** There was a lower standard of testing in those days. Extensive testing on pregnant animals was not carried out. It wasn't developed as a drug for morning sickness, but it turned out to have a beneficial effect and it was assumed that it would be safe.

b When treating leprosy it was still causing complications for patients that were pregnant. Thalidomide is still used for rare diseases for which there is no other effective treatment. Its use in those countries is carefully controlled and it is never given to pregnant women.

B1 3.2

How effective are medicines?

Learning objectives

Students should learn:

- that statins are drugs that lower cholesterol levels in the blood
- that lower blood cholesterol levels reduce the risk of cardiovascular disease
- that the effectiveness of medicines can only be determined in proper double-blind trials.

Learning outcomes

Most students should be able to:

- describe the use of statins in lowering blood cholesterol levels
- evaluate the effect of statins in the treatment of cardiovascular disease
- evaluate the claims made about the effects of prescribed and non-prescribed medicines on health.

Some students should also be able to:

- explain in detail how and why double-blind tests are used.

Support

- Ask students simple questions about the graph in Figure 1 – for example, which statin worked best? Which statin gave the poorest results or was least effective? etc. Alternatively, supply the answers which then have to be matched with the questions.

Extend

- Ask students to find out as much as they can about statins. What are they? Where are they found naturally?

Specification link-up: Biology B1.3

- Candidates should be aware of the use of statins in lowering the risk of heart and circulatory diseases. *[B1.3.1 c)]*
- Evaluate the effect of statins in cardiovascular disease. *[B1.3]*
- Evaluate claims made about the effect of prescribed and non-prescribed drugs on health. *[B1.3]*

Lesson structure

Starters

Good and bad cholesterol – Show a clip from *Futurama* season 3, episode 4 'Parasites Lost' where Dr Zoidberg, while in a miniaturised submarine inside the bloodstream, scraped cholesterol from a heart valve, spread it on a cracker and ate it. He comments, 'It's good cholesterol but it spreads like bad cholesterol.' Discuss the role of cholesterol in heart disease. *(5 minutes)*

The heart of the problem – Show the students a diagram of the heart, or an actual one. Draw out by questioning that it is mostly made of muscle. Ask what muscle must be supplied with in order to work? [Draw out oxygen and food (glucose).] Ask how this can be supplied? [Draw out through the blood and that there must be a good supply of oxygenated blood to the heart.] Show a picture of or the actual coronary artery. State that this is where the blood comes to the heart muscle. Ask what would happen if a lump of fat blocked the coronary artery? Link the outcome [heart attack] to cholesterol in the diet. Students could be supported by prompting but expect some students to be able to deduce much more by themselves. *(10 minutes)*

Main

- Students should look at the graph in the Student Book (Figure 1) and answer the following questions. The height of the bars shows the extent to which they were effective in reducing the levels of the 'bad' cholesterol. The different colours of the bars show the concentrations of the statins in the trial.

  Questions

  1. Which statin was trialled at four different concentrations? [Statin 1]
  2. Which two statins were only trialled at 20 and 40 mg doses? [Statin 3 and Statin 5]
  3. Which concentration was not tried for Statin 2? [80 mg]
  4. Which concentration was not tried for Statin 4? [10 mg]
  5. Which statin looks the most effective overall? [Statin 1]
  6. Which two concentrations would you compare in order to get a fair view of the performance of all the drugs? [20 and 40 mg]
  7. Compare Statin 1 and Statin 4. What notable difference do you spot in the effectiveness of different concentrations? [Increasing the concentration from 40 mg to 80 mg had a much more marked effect for Statin 4 as opposed to Statin 1.]

- The following activity helps the students understand double-blind trials. The idea is the patients don't know what they are getting and the doctors don't know what they are giving. That way neither can show any bias.

  Split the class into groups of three. One student acts as the Researcher, one as the Doctor and one as the Patient. The Researchers have to come to the teacher to collect crackers. One set (labelled A) have got butter on them, one set (labelled B) have a cheaper substitute spread on them. Check in advance that no one has a gluten or dairy allergy. As an alternative, one could have disposable cups of regular and diet cola. The Researchers have to make a note of which one is which and give them to the Doctors. The Doctors, without knowing which is which, give them to the Patients to consume and analyse. Students may have to go outside the laboratory to carry this out safely. They must decide on the basis of their experience whether they had butter or substitute (or regular/diet cola). The Doctors record this and report to the Researchers, who record this and draw conclusions. Researchers can collate their results on the board in a blank table. You should get an accurate picture of whether the class can tell these apart.

  Conclude by relating this to drugs trials. Get students to put into words the importance of neither those giving nor those receiving the treatment knowing which drug is which.

Plenaries

The placebo effect – Get students to think of examples from their childhood of where they were convinced by their parents of something that would affect their feelings and give them relief from distress. *(5 minutes)*

Prescribed or not? – In groups, get the students to list some drugs you can buy over the counter and some you cannot. Students could be supported by supplying pre-prepared lists to choose from. Students could be extended by compiling their own lists. Compare each group's findings to compile a master list and create a summary definition. *(10 minutes)*

Further teaching suggestions

Prescribed drugs versus non-prescribed drugs
- Using the graph in the Student Book (Figure 2), discuss the findings and ask the students what they think are the advantages and disadvantages of using the non-prescribed drug.

Will it lower my blood cholesterol?
- Build up a list of food products that claim to lower cholesterol levels and get students to investigate the claims using secondary data and information from the internet. Working in groups, they could research one product each and then present a report to the rest of the class.

Alternative medicines
- Using suggestions from the class, build up a list of alternative, over-the-counter, medicines. Discuss their uses and their effectiveness compared to prescribed ones. Have ready – some suggestions – scan the shelves of the vitamins and supplements section of the local supermarket for ideas and examples.

Ethics
- Discuss the ethics of deliberately fooling people into believing they have taken an effective medicine if it is proved that this will be of assistance in helping them to feel better, even if the drug has no pharmaceutical efficacy itself.

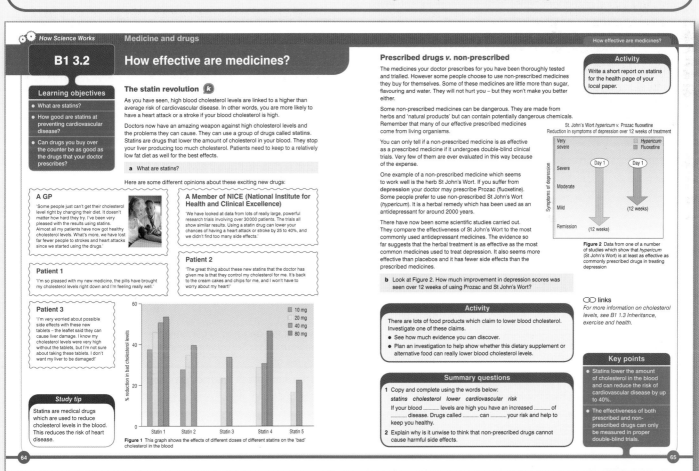

Answers to in-text questions

a Medical drugs that reduce the levels of cholesterol in the blood.

b St John's Wort was better than Prozac as it led to a remission whereas Prozac only reduced the symptoms of depression from 'severe' to 'mild'.

Summary answers

1 cholesterol, risk, cardiovascular, statins, lower

2 Because if natural remedies work, they contain chemicals that are drugs, and these can cause problems with side-effects like any other drug. Natural remedies that do not actually have any chemicals that can help you can still contain chemicals that can be harmful – natural does not mean harmless.

B1 3.3

Drugs

Learning objectives

Students should learn:

- that drugs are substances that affect the way in which the body works
- that drugs may cause harm by changing the chemical processes in the body
- that people using drugs may become dependent on them and unable to manage without them (addicted to drugs)
- that cannabis may cause psychological problems and the use of hard drugs such as cocaine and heroin can seriously damage health.

Learning outcomes

Most students should be able to:

- give a definition of the term 'drug'
- explain what is meant by addiction
- describe some of the problems caused by drug abuse.

Some students should also be able to:

- explain that the impact of drug use varies from individual to individual.

Support

- Give students a list of important social problems associated with the use of drugs and ask them to place these in order of importance. This could be used as an alternative to the first Plenary.

Extend

- Ask students to investigate further the nature of drugs, how they affect nerve transmission and whether they act in the brain or on the nervous system generally.

Specification link-up: Biology B1.3

- Candidates should be aware of the effects of misuse of the legal recreational drugs, alcohol and nicotine. Candidates should understand that the misuse of the illegal recreational drugs, ecstasy, cannabis and heroin may have adverse effects on the heart and circulatory system. *[B1.3.1 e)]*
- Drugs change the chemical processes in people's bodies so that they may become dependent or addicted to them and suffer withdrawal symptoms without them. Heroin and cocaine are very addictive. *[B1.3.1 h)]*
- Cannabis is an illegal drug. Cannabis smoke contains chemicals which may cause mental illness in some people. *[B1.3.1 f)]*

Lesson structure

Starters

Hooked? – Students are to describe what they understand addiction to mean. Students could be supported by being given a list of drugs and asked to tick those that they think are addictive. Students could be extended by being encouraged to come up with a list for themselves and to speculate about what would make some substances addictive and others not. *(5 minutes)*

Drugs in the house? – Write up a list of some of the places where there may be drugs in a house, such as alcohol, coffee and tea, tobacco products obviously, but also consider the First Aid kit or a typical family medicine cabinet (paracetamol, calamine, antihistamine cream, antiseptic or brands such as Calpol, Nurofen, Dettol) Use either examples or photographs. Ask the students to identify which they think are drugs, or contain drugs, and which are other substances. *(10 minutes)*

Main

- Get the students to either draw out or fill in a printed table with the following headings: 'Drugs', 'Other names', 'Legal?', 'Effects', 'Hazards'. They can gather the information for it from internet sites such as 'Talk to Frank.' (www.talktofrank.com).
- Discuss (or describe) the film *Trainspotting* with the students. Although it is an 18 certificate, quite a few could have seen it at home. Discuss what happens to the character Renton (played by Ewan McGregor) when he stops taking heroin (sweating, pain, craving and hallucinations that included a dead baby crawling over the ceiling). Explain about tolerance and the need for ever increasing dosages just to feel normal.
- Discuss the relative addictiveness of common drugs. Draw out that cannabis is not addictive although some users can become psychologically dependent on it and it can cause anxiety and paranoia and make latent psychological problems worse. Draw out that heroin and cocaine are very addictive and highly dangerous. Link to social problems.
- Show a suitable video covering the dangers of becoming addicted to drugs. Ask about drugs awareness videos at your Local Education Authority or Social Services – drugs teams will have these available on loan.
- Research and read or get the students to read some poetry about addiction, e.g. 'My name: Is Cocaine' by Desiree Kimbrue (use a search engine to locate).

Plenaries

Social problems linked with drug abuse – Ask students to compile a list of five important social problems associated with the use of drugs, including tobacco and alcohol. Compare lists and decide which ones top the list. *(5 minutes)*

Which one am I? – Bring a student to the front of the class. Get them to choose from a list (without telling anyone) a drug that they are to represent. The rest of the students can then ask questions of them to ascertain which drug they have chosen. Students could be supported by having a list of questions to choose from and a limited number of drugs to represent. Students could be extended by getting them to devise the activity themselves and possibly attach a list of taboo words to make it more demanding. *(10 minutes)*

Further teaching suggestions

Personal experience
- If students are willing, get them to share experiences of people they know who have been affected by drugs. This can be very powerful but must be carefully managed.

Local authority drugs specialist talk
- Ask the local authority to send in a drugs unit member to talk to the students. Ex-addicts can also have strong testimony but use great caution!

Answers to in-text questions

a People who have traditionally inhabited a region since ancient times.

b Any appropriate answers, such as alcohol and tobacco are legal, but cocaine and heroin are not.

c 'Addiction' means that you cannot function properly without a drug and suffer withdrawal symptoms if you are without it.

Medicine and drugs

Drugs

B1 3.3　Drugs

Learning objectives
- What is a drug?
- What is addiction?
- Why are drugs such as cannabis, cocaine and heroin such a problem?

Study tip

Drugs are chemicals which alter the body's chemistry.

Many drugs are used as medicines to treat disease.

A **drug** is a substance that alters the way in which your body works. It can affect your mind, your body or both. In every society there are certain drugs which people use for medicine, and other drugs which they use for pleasure.

Many of the drugs that are used both for medicine and for recreation come originally from natural substances, often plants. Many of them have been known to and used by indigenous (long-term inhabitants of an area) peoples for many years. Usually some of the drugs that are used for pleasure are socially acceptable and legal, while others are illegal.

Figure 1 Millions of pounds worth of illegal drugs are brought into the UK every year. It is a constant battle for the police to find and destroy drugs like these.

a What do we mean by 'indigenous peoples'?

Drugs are everywhere in our society. People drink coffee and tea, smoke cigarettes and have a beer, an alcopop or a glass of wine. They think nothing of it. Yet all of these things contain drugs – caffeine, nicotine and alcohol (the chemical ethanol). These drugs are all legal.

Other drugs, such as cocaine, ecstasy and heroin are illegal. Which drugs are legal and which are not varies from country to country. Alcohol is legal in the UK as long as you are over 18, but it is illegal in many Arab states. Heroin is illegal almost everywhere.

b Give an example of one drug which is legal and one which is illegal in the UK.

Because drugs affect the chemistry of your body, they can cause great harm. This is even true of drugs we use as medicines. However, because medical drugs make you better, it is usually worth taking the risk.

But legal recreational drugs, such as alcohol and tobacco, and illegal substances, such as solvents, cannabis and cocaine, can cause terrible damage to your body. Yet they offer no long-term benefits to you at all.

links

For more information on the mental health problems that can be caused by cannabis, see B1 3.5 Does cannabis lead to hard drugs?

What is addiction?

Some drugs change the chemical processes in your body so that you may become addicted to them. You can become dependent on them. If you are addicted to a drug, you cannot manage properly without it. Some drugs, for example heroin and cocaine, are very addictive.

Once addicted, you generally need more and more of the drug to keep you feeling normal. When addicts try to stop using drugs they usually feel very unwell. They often have aches and pains, sweating, shaking, headaches and cravings for their drug. We call these **withdrawal symptoms**.

c What do we mean by 'addiction'?

The problems of drug abuse

People take drugs for a reason. Drugs can make you feel very good about yourself. They can make you feel happy and they can make you feel as if your problems no longer matter. Unfortunately, because most recreational drugs are addictive, they can soon become a problem themselves.

No drugs are without a risk. Cannabis is often thought of as a relatively 'soft' – and therefore safe – drug. But evidence is growing which shows that cannabis smoke contains chemicals which can cause mental illness to develop in some people.

Hard drugs, such as cocaine and heroin, are extremely addictive. Using them often leads to very severe health problems. Some of these come from the drugs themselves. Others come from the lifestyle that often goes with drugs.

Because these drugs are illegal, they are expensive. Young people often end up turning to crime to pay for their drug habit. They don't eat properly or look after themselves. They can also contract serious illnesses, such as hepatitis, STDs (sexually transmitted diseases) and HIV/Aids especially if drugs are taken intravenously (via a needle).

Boys arrested for drug offences by age group 2006/07 and 2007/08

Girls arrested for drug offences by age group 2006/07 and 2007/08

Figure 2 Illegal drugs are often linked with crime. In the UK more and more young people are being arrested for drug offences – using or selling illegal drugs.

Summary questions

1 Copy and complete using the words below:

mind　cocaine　ecstasy　legal　alcohol　drug　body

A .... alters the way in which your body works. It can affect the ...., the .... or both. Some drugs are .... e.g. caffeine and .... Other drugs, such as ...., ... and heroin are illegal.

2 **a** Why do people often need more and more of a drug?
   b What happens if you stop taking a drug when you are addicted to it?

3 **a** Why do people take drugs?
   b Explain some of the problems linked with using cannabis, cocaine and heroin.
   c Look at Figure 2. What does this tell you about the difference in drug use between boys and girls?
   d What does Figure 2 tell you about the trend in drug use in young people?
   e Why do you think young people continue to take these drugs when they are well aware of the dangers?

Key points

- Drugs change the chemical processes in your body, so you may become addicted to them.
- Addiction is when you become physically or mentally dependent on a drug.
- Smoking cannabis may cause mental health problems.
- Hard drugs, such as cocaine and heroin, are very addictive and can cause serious health problems.

66

67

Summary answers

1 drug, mind/body, body/mind, legal, alcohol, cocaine/ecstasy, ecstasy/cocaine

2 **a** They need more and more to get the same effect.
   b You suffer withdrawal symptoms/feel ill.

3 **a** As medicines or for pleasure makes them feel good, feel they can cope with problems, fit in with the crowd.
   b Addiction, health problems from drug or lifestyle needed to fund drug, risk of hepatitis and HIV/Aids from lifestyle, etc.
   c Boys get arrested for drug offences much more than girls, which probably reflects that boys use drugs much more than girls, although it may also reflect more boys are arrested than girls.

d Both boys and girls would seem to be using drugs more from this limited evidence – although it could be that police are more effective at detecting and arresting people for drug crime.

e Any thoughtful points such as peer pressure, image, addiction.

B1 3.4

Legal and illegal drugs

Learning objectives

Students should learn:

- that many recreational drugs affect the nervous system, particularly the brain
- that drugs may be used recreationally and some are more harmful than others
- that some drugs are illegal and others legal; the overall impact of legal drugs on health is greater than that of illegal drugs.

Learning outcomes

Most students should be able to:

- list some common legal and illegal drugs
- explain why some people use illegal drugs for recreation and describe the effects of cannabis
- explain why the use of legal drugs has a greater impact on health than the use of illegal drugs.

Some students should also be able to:

- evaluate the impact of different types of drugs on society.

Answers to in-text questions

a Caffeine.
b Because many more people take (and abuse) legal drugs.

Support

- Give students the names of the different recreational drugs and ask them to place them in the correct categories under the headings 'Legal' and 'Illegal'.

Extend

- Ask students to design an experiment to investigate the effect of caffeine on memory.

Specification link-up: Biology B1.3

- The overall impact of legal drugs (prescribed and non-prescribed) on health is much greater than the impact of illegal drugs because far more people use them. *[B1.3.1 g)]*
- Evaluate different types of drugs and why some people use illegal drugs for recreation. *[B1.3]*

  Controlled Assessment: B4.1 Plan practical ways to develop and test candidates' own scientific ideas *[B4.1.1a) b)]*; B4.3 Collect primary and secondary data *[B4.3.2 a) b) c)]* and B4.5 Analyse and interpret primary and secondary data. *[B4.5.2 a)]*, *[B4.5.4 a) d)]*

Lesson structure

Starters

Which is which? – Put up charts of stick figures or dots onto the four walls: 90 000 on one, 9000 on another, 2000 on a third and 30 on the last. State that these are deaths in the UK due to drugs. Ask which chart might represent which drug? Following discussion, reveal that they refer to tobacco (nicotine) (90 000), alcohol (9000), all other illegal drugs (2000) and ecstasy (30). *(5 minutes)*

Quick quiz on different categories of drugs – Support students by handing out lists of different drugs as they enter the classroom and ask them to put two letters from M (medicinal), R (recreational) L (legal) or I (illegal) alongside each one. Check through the list. Students can be extended by suggesting the drugs themselves, filling in the categories and debating the nature of any overlaps. *(10 minutes)*

Main

- Give an exposition on which drugs are legal and which are not in the UK. Draw out an international perspective by overviewing differences, e.g. the approach of Muslim countries to alcohol.
- Review changes in UK drugs law over the years. Explain that commonly used legal drugs have physiological effects – lead on to practical on caffeine.
- You can ask students to investigate the effect of caffeine on reaction times. Caffeine has a mild stimulatory effect, increasing alertness. This experiment can be used to introduce 'How Science Works' concepts – predictions can be made, measurements repeated and controlled conditions are easy to ensure. However, generalising from data collected from one individual or a small group brings in the variety of factors that make humans different, and the need for large sample sizes in investigations where all variables cannot be controlled.
- 'How Science Works' concepts can be introduced. For example, they might focus on evaluating the reliability and validity of their investigation.

Plenaries

Drug symbols – Ask students to design an icon for each of a number of drugs to represent it on a website. Each icon should concisely sum up what the drug is about in a simple, visually effective way. This could be done individually or in groups and collectively producing a range. *(5 minutes)*

If I was in charge – Imagine you have been given the task of being in charge of drugs policy for the UK. What changes would you make? What would your desired outcomes be? What difficulties would you be likely to encounter when putting into effect your changes? Students can be supported by providing them with a list of suggestions and allowing them to discuss which they would implement. Extension level students should produce reasoned and cohesive strategies. *(10 minutes)*

Practical support

Investigation of the effect of caffeine on reaction times/heart rate

Equipment and materials required

Metre rulers, chocolate, cups of coffee (could have caffeinated and decaffeinated – but not to be consumed in the laboratory), data loggers and hand-held pulse meters (or a stop watch).

Details

Some students could look at the effect of caffeine on reaction times.

Using the stick-drop method of testing reaction times, the effect of caffeine can be measured. Students can volunteer to drink measured amounts of coffee, with a known/controlled caffeine content, and have their reaction times measured before and after drinking the coffee. A period of time (about 10 minutes) has to be allowed for the caffeine to be absorbed before the second test is

carried out. Remind the students that it is the difference between the two times that is significant.

This could also be an opportunity to teach about a double-blind test if technicians provide cups of coffee labelled as A and B (and only they know which is decaffeinated until after testing is complete).

Some students could look at the effect of caffeine on heart rate.

Changes in heart rate (measured by measuring the pulse rate) can be recorded before and after caffeine intake. This is best done using hand-held pulse meters attached to a data logger – the display can be projected to get a real time graph drawn of heart rate before and after consuming caffeine – a large lump of chocolate will do the trick!

● Is there any difference between before and after? Which variables need to be controlled?

Safety: Care needs to be taken with eating and drinking in a laboratory (should be done outside before the lesson or in a food technology room).

Medicine and drugs

Legal and illegal drugs

B1 3.4 — Legal and illegal drugs

Learning objectives

● How do drugs like caffeine and heroin affect your nervous system?

● Which has the bigger overall impact on health – legal or illegal drugs?

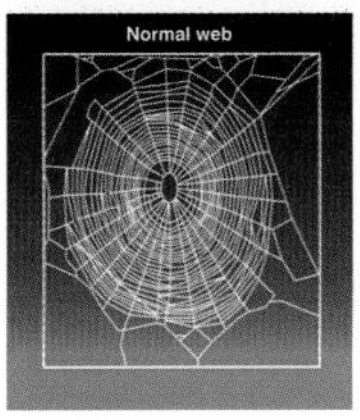

Normal web

What is the most widely used drug in the world? It is probably one that most of you will have used at least once today, yet no one really thinks about. The caffeine in your cup of tea, mug of coffee or can of cola is a drug.

Many people find it hard to get going in the morning without a mug of coffee. They are probably addicted to the drug caffeine. It stimulates your brain and increases your heart rate and blood pressure.

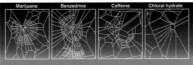

Marijuana | Benzedrine | Caffeine | Chloral hydrate

Figure 1 NASA scientists have shown that common house spiders spin their webs very differently when given some commonly used legal and illegal drugs. The effect of caffeine on the nervous system of a spider is particularly dramatic!

a What drug is in a can of cola?

How do drugs affect you?

Many of the drugs used for medical treatments have little or no effect on your nervous system. However, all of the recreational drugs that people use for pleasure affect the way your nervous system works, particularly your brain. It is these changes that people enjoy when they use the drugs. The same changes can cause addiction. Once addicted, your body doesn't work properly without the drug.

Some drugs like caffeine, nicotine and cocaine speed up the activity of your brain. They make you feel more alert and energetic.

Others, like alcohol and cannabis, slow down the responses of your brain. They make you feel calm and better able to cope. Heroin actually stops impulses travelling in your nervous system. Therefore you don't feel any pain or discomfort. Cannabis produces vivid waking dreams. It can make you see or hear things that are not really there.

Why do people use drugs?

People use drugs for a variety of reasons. They feel that caffeine, nicotine and alcohol help them cope with everyday life. Few people who use these legal drugs would think of themselves as addicts. Yet the chemicals they take can have a big physical and psychological impact (see Figure 1).

As for the illegal recreational drugs – people who try them may be looking for excitement or escape. They might want to be part of the crowd or just want to see what happens. Yet many drugs are addictive and your body needs increasingly more to feel the effects.

Study tip

Drugs may be:
● legal or illegal
● addictive or non-addictive.
Learn examples of all of these.

Impact of drugs on health

Some recreational drugs are more harmful than others. Most media reports on the dangers of drugs focus on illegal drugs. But in fact the impact of legal drugs on health is much greater than the impact of illegal drugs. That's because far more people take them. Millions of people in the UK take medicines such as statins, or smoke or drink alcohol. Only a few thousand take heroin.

A recent case history shows you how emotions and politics can be more important than scientific evidence in the way society reacts to drugs. In 2010, several young people died after apparently taking a relatively new legal drug known as 'meow-meow'. The drug was made illegal even though at least one of the 'victims' had not taken meow-meow.

In fact, in the UK, there are around 2000 deaths linked to using illegal drugs each year.

But every year in the UK around 9000 people die as a result of alcohol-abuse. About 90 000 people die from smoking-related diseases. Yet alcohol and nicotine remain completely legal drugs.

Everyone can see the dangers to health of non-prescribed, illegal drugs. However, choosing which drugs to make illegal does not appear to be based on the scientific evidence of health damage alone.

Figure 2 Drugs can seem appealing, exciting and fun. Many people use them briefly and then leave them behind. But the risks of addiction are high, and no one can predict whom drugs will affect most.

b Why do legal drugs cause many more health problems than illegal drugs?

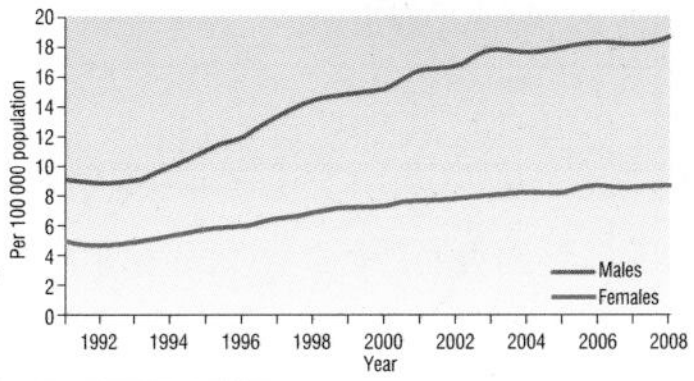

Figure 3 This graph shows how alcohol-related deaths almost doubled between 1990 and 2008 (Source: National Statistics Office)

Summary questions

1 Copy and complete using the words below:
   brain health illegal legal recreation
   Drugs which people use for .... all affect the nervous system, particularly the .... Some of these drugs are legal but some of them are .... More people suffer .... problems caused by .... drugs than illegal ones.

2 Use data from Figure 3 to help you answer these:
   a How many men and women died of alcohol-related diseases per 100 000 of the population in 1992?
   b How many men and women died of alcohol-related diseases per 100 000 of the population in 2008?
   c Suggest reasons for this increase in alcohol-related deaths.
   d Why do you think alcohol remains a legal drug when it causes so many deaths?

3 Compare the overall impact of legal and illegal drugs on the nation's health.

Key points

● Many recreational drugs affect the nervous system, particularly the brain. Some are more harmful than others.

● Some recreational drugs are legal and others are illegal.

● The overall impact of legal drugs on health is much greater than illegal drugs because more people use them.

Further teaching suggestions

Debate the issue

● Which are more dangerous – legal or illegal drugs? This question could be debated by the class. Each student could prepare a short case for and against and then the motion. Draw lots to decide which students speak.

The caffeine effect

● The experiment can compare the effect of caffeine on males and females. Is there a difference? If there is, can it be explained? Also, the effects of different quantities may differ between different sexes and age groups.

Summary answers

1 recreation, brain, illegal, health, legal

2 **a** 1992 men 9 per 100 000, women 5 per 100 000.
  b 2008 men 18–19 per 100 000, women 8–9 per 100 000.
  c More people drinking, younger people drinking, people drinking more at a time (binge drinking) and more people addicted to alcohol.
  d Very popular, part of culture, government revenue, enjoyed by many sensibly, hard to change legal status after so many years, many of the people who are in the government use alcohol themselves, prohibition already tried but unsuccessful and led to criminal activity. Any other thoughtful points on the reasons some drugs are legal and others not, social standpoints, historical usage, etc.

3 Give credit for each valid point made. Look for understanding of the differences between legal and illegal drugs – the contact with criminal culture with illegal drugs, high costs, etc., compared with the ease of causing damage with legal drugs, the impact of drug abuse on individuals. Increased rates of accidents as a result of drug use and increased crime under influence of both legal and illegal drugs. Also look for the positive aspects of legal drugs as medicines – cure diseases, save lives, relieve symptoms, etc.

B1 3.5

Does cannabis lead to hard drugs?

Learning objectives

Students should learn:

- that some recreational drugs are more harmful than others
- that some people may progress from non-addictive recreational drugs to addiction to hard drugs
- that the use of cannabis can be harmful.

Learning outcomes

Most students should be able to:

- describe ways in which some recreational drugs are more harmful than others
- evaluate the facts about the recreational use of cannabis.

Some students should also be able to:

- compare the damage caused by the use of cannabis with that caused by other recreational drugs, such as alcohol and tobacco.

Support

- Get students to design a poster on 'Keeping your children safe!' for the class display.

Extend

- Get students to consider the effects of the legalisation of cannabis. What effect could it have on the NHS, the Social Services and the police?

Specification link-up: Biology B1.3

- Consider the possible progression from recreational drugs to hard drugs. *[B1.3]*
- Evaluate different types of drugs and why some people use illegal drugs for recreation. *[B1.3]*

Lesson structure

Starters

Cannabis information video – Use the internet to search for a suitable information video for the students to watch on cannabis. *(5 minutes)*

'I know this bloke!' – Initiate a discussion of anecdotal evidence on the effects of cannabis. Find out if anyone in the class has suitable stories to tell, either of no harmful effects from cannabis or of problems people have had. If possible, draw out a range of responses. You could support students by supplying a suitable newspaper article or personal account for them to read out and discuss. Students could be extended by getting them to discuss articles they have read or problems they have heard about. Differentiation can also be by outcome – supported students will hold a less wide-ranging and less deeply questioning discussion than extended students. *(10 minutes)*

Main

- Get the students to read through the text about facts on whether cannabis use is related to hard drugs. Consult the websites mentioned and/or any other relevant ones. *The Guardian* ran a series of articles promoting the lowering of cannabis classification from B to C. Refer to the changes in government policy with the B to C move and then its subsequent reversal.

- Group display work. Brainstorm the coverage of the topic and split the class into groups, giving each responsibility for a topic. Collect and collate these for a class display.

- Carry out the debate suggested in the Student Book activity box. It is suggested that the students prepare two short speeches, one in favour and one against the proposal. These speeches could be set as homework and then the debate held at a convenient time.

- Designate volunteers as 'concerned parent', 'teenage user', 'drug dealer', 'police officer', 'psychiatric doctor' and other such roles. Have each one in turn take to the 'empathy hotseat' at the front of the class and have the rest of the students ask them questions which they have to consider and answer in role. A list of prompt questions for each character may be beneficial.

Plenaries

Cause and effect? – Find some statistics which are potentially misleading. For example, the average human being has slightly less than one testicle, children with bigger feet are better at spelling than their smaller-footed peers, countries with higher divorce rates have lower death rates, etc. Give these to the students and see if they can untangle the reasons behind them. Students can be supported by giving some clue sheets for these. Students can be extended by suggesting they use the internet to find their own examples and try them out on each other. *(5 minutes)*

Who should we listen to? – Make a list of sources of information regarding cannabis and rate each one from 1 to 4, with 1 being 'wouldn't pay much attention' to 4 being 'would pay most attention'. Discuss and evaluate results as a class. *(10 minutes)*

Further teaching suggestions

Drug facts

- The class display of drug facts could be used in an assembly or as a discussion focus during tutor times or PSHE lessons.

Cannabis on prescription?

- Students could find out more about the use of cannabis in treating the symptoms of multiple sclerosis, epilepsy and Alzheimer's disease. How does it work? What are the chemicals involved?

Guest speaker

- If it is felt appropriate, a guest speaker, such as a social worker or person trained in drug education, could be invited in to talk to students and answer questions. This could link with the plenary 'Who should we listen to?'

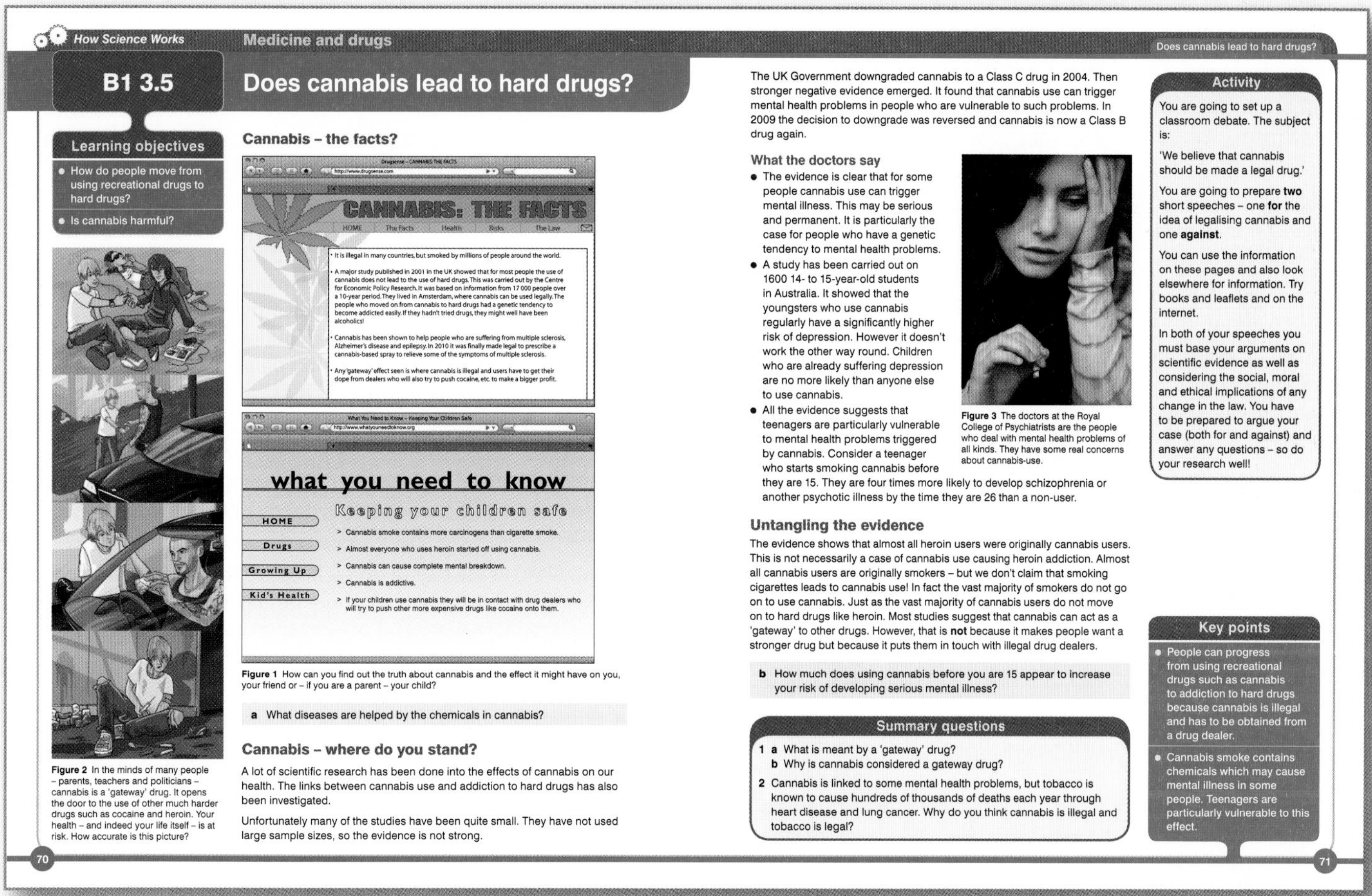

How Science Works — Medicine and drugs — Does cannabis lead to hard drugs?

B1 3.5 — Does cannabis lead to hard drugs?

Learning objectives
- How do people move from using recreational drugs to hard drugs?
- Is cannabis harmful?

Cannabis – the facts?

Figure 1 How can you find out the truth about cannabis and the effect it might have on you, your friend or – if you are a parent – your child?

a What diseases are helped by the chemicals in cannabis?

Cannabis – where do you stand?

A lot of scientific research has been done into the effects of cannabis on our health. The links between cannabis use and addiction to hard drugs has also been investigated.

Unfortunately many of the studies have been quite small. They have not used large sample sizes, so the evidence is not strong.

Figure 2 In the minds of many people – parents, teachers and politicians – cannabis is a 'gateway' drug. It opens the door to the use of other much harder drugs such as cocaine and heroin. Your health – and indeed your life itself – is at risk. How accurate is this picture?

The UK Government downgraded cannabis to a Class C drug in 2004. Then stronger negative evidence emerged. It found that cannabis use can trigger mental health problems in people who are vulnerable to such problems. In 2009 the decision to downgrade was reversed and cannabis is now a Class B drug again.

What the doctors say
- The evidence is clear that for some people cannabis use can trigger mental illness. This may be serious and permanent. It is particularly the case for people who have a genetic tendency to mental health problems.
- A study has been carried out on 1600 14- to 15-year-old students in Australia. It showed that the youngsters who use cannabis regularly have a significantly higher risk of depression. However it doesn't work the other way round. Children who are already suffering depression are no more likely than anyone else to use cannabis.
- All the evidence suggests that teenagers are particularly vulnerable to mental health problems triggered by cannabis. Consider a teenager who starts smoking cannabis before they are 15. They are four times more likely to develop schizophrenia or another psychotic illness by the time they are 26 than a non-user.

Figure 3 The doctors at the Royal College of Psychiatrists are the people who deal with mental health problems of all kinds. They have some real concerns about cannabis-use.

Untangling the evidence
The evidence shows that almost all heroin users were originally cannabis users. This is not necessarily a case of cannabis use causing heroin addiction. Almost all cannabis users are originally smokers – but we don't claim that smoking cigarettes leads to cannabis use! In fact the vast majority of smokers do not go on to use cannabis. Just as the vast majority of cannabis users do not move on to hard drugs like heroin. Most studies suggest that cannabis can act as a 'gateway' to other drugs. However, that is **not** because it makes people want a stronger drug but because it puts them in touch with illegal drug dealers.

b How much does using cannabis before you are 15 appear to increase your risk of developing serious mental illness?

Summary questions
1. a What is meant by a 'gateway' drug?
   b Why is cannabis considered a gateway drug?
2. Cannabis is linked to some mental health problems, but tobacco is known to cause hundreds of thousands of deaths each year through heart disease and lung cancer. Why do you think cannabis is illegal and tobacco is legal?

Activity
You are going to set up a classroom debate. The subject is:

'We believe that cannabis should be made a legal drug.'

You are going to prepare **two** short speeches – one **for** the idea of legalising cannabis and one **against**.

You can use the information on these pages and also look elsewhere for information. Try books and leaflets and on the internet.

In both of your speeches you must base your arguments on scientific evidence as well as considering the social, moral and ethical implications of any change in the law. You have to be prepared to argue your case (both for and against) and answer any questions – so do your research well!

Key points
- People can progress from using recreational drugs such as cannabis to addiction to hard drugs because cannabis is illegal and has to be obtained from a drug dealer.
- Cannabis smoke contains chemicals which may cause mental illness in some people. Teenagers are particularly vulnerable to this effect.

70 | 71

Answers to in-text questions

a Multiple sclerosis, Alzheimer's disease and epilepsy.

b Four times.

Summary answers

1. a A drug which makes it easier for an individual to begin taking 'harder' more damaging drugs through contact with people dealing with illegal drugs.

   b Because cannabis is seen as a soft drug (which is relatively harmless) and a lot of young people want to smoke it. Because it is illegal to buy cannabis, it puts them in contact with dealers who may well try to introduce them to more expensive, harder drugs which will make the dealer a bigger profit and that are more powerfully addictive.

2. Any thoughtful points on the reasons some drugs are legal and others not, social standpoints, historical usage, etc.

B1 3.6

Drugs in sport

Specification link-up: Biology B1.3

- There are several types of drug that an athlete can use to enhance performance. Some of these drugs are banned by law and some are legally available on prescription, but all are prohibited by sporting regulations … [B1.3.1 i)]
- Evaluate the use of drugs to enhance performance in sport and to consider the ethical implications of their use. [B1.3]

Lesson structure

Starters

What we know already – Break the class into groups of about three. Give each group a piece of blank A3 paper and get them to write down collectively all that they know about drugs in sport. Have them share their responses with others. *(5 minutes)*

Drugs race 3000 – Imagine that you are living in the year 3000 and that the use of drugs in sport has been legal for nearly a thousand years. What sort of events would there be? What sort of records would be set? Might they have pharmaceutical manufacturer's prizes in the same way that they have constructor's prizes in Formula 1 motorsport? Write a 'back-in-time' blog based on the year 3000 Olympic Games. Students could be supported with prompts and scaffolded response sheets. Students could be extended by being encouraged to use open-ended thinking on this activity. *(10 minutes)*

Main

- Tell the students that using performance-enhancing drugs is not a new problem. The Ancient Greeks in 300 BCE had to ban some competitors because of eating certain mushrooms and animal protein.
- Prepare a PowerPoint presentation on the use of drugs in sport, to include drugs which build up muscle, ways of making the body produce more red blood cells, speeding up reactions and making competitors more alert. The presentation could include some case histories, frequency and details of testing for a range of different sports.
- The presentation could be accompanied by articles from newspapers relating to the illegal use of performance-enhancing drugs. Students could discuss the issues and express their opinions. What about the use of caffeine as a stimulant? Should everyone be tested rather than random tests?
- Produce a blank grid (see example below). Students can, from the text, from their own knowledge and from internet research fill in the grid with suitable sports, drugs and the attributes of the drug which help in the performance of the sport, along with problems.

Sport	Drug type	Why use them?	Problems
Bodybuilding	Painkillers	Compete when injured	Exacerbates injury
Archery	Beta blockers	Steady hands	Insomnia, depression
Cycling	Erythropoietin	More oxygen to legs	Kidney disease complications
Sprinting	Anabolic steroids	Muscle growth	Sexual characteristic changes

Plenaries

Getting away with it! – Is cheating okay if you don't get caught? Investigate the morality of the use of performance-enhancing drugs and try to get inside the mindset of the user. Discuss as a group. *(5 minutes)*

My threshold – Most of us would not consider using drugs as performance enhancers when we play sport. Given a large enough incentive though, most people will do most things. Ask the students to imagine they are in a competition that they can only win if they take an illegal drug. The consequences of being caught are severe (end of your career, loss of the respect of your colleagues and your possessions, adverse press coverage, prison, etc.) but it is by no means certain that you would be caught – say a 1 in 10 chance. Would you go for it, if the prize was big enough? What would your personal threshold be if you have one? What if the odds of getting caught were different? Discuss. (Differentiation will be by outcome). *(10 minutes)*

Further teaching suggestions

Case studies
- Show case study videos or discuss examples of infamous drug scandals in sport, such as East Germany, Ben Johnson, Tour de France, Dwayne Chambers.

Random versus total testing
- Subtly take a few students to one side at the start of the lesson and tell them they have been taking performance enhancers. While explaining about random drug testing, get a volunteer who knows nothing of this to choose three people

at random from the class and ask them if they have taken performance enhancers. Then get the ones you informed at the start to own up.

Drug tests in sport
- Find out from the internet what tests are used for the different drugs and how reliable they are. What are the permitted limits? What are the rules about testing and why is more than one sample taken?

B1 3.6 — Drugs in sport

Learning objectives
- Can drugs make you better at sport?
- Is it ethical to use drugs to win?

The world of sport has a big problem with the illegal use of drugs. In theory, the only difference between competitors should be their natural ability and the amount they train. However, there are many performance-enhancing drugs that allow athletes to improve on their natural ability. The people who do this get labelled as cheats if they are caught.

Figure 1 Weightlifters need a lot of muscle so it can be tempting to cheat. Eleven Bulgarian weightlifters tested positive for anabolic steroids and were disqualified from the 2008 Olympics.

Performance-enhancing drugs

Different sports need different things from the competitors.

Anabolic steroids are drugs that help build up muscle mass. They are used by athletes who need to be very strong, such as weightlifters. Athletes who need lots of muscle to be very fast, such as sprinters, also sometimes use anabolic steroids. Taking anabolic steroids and careful training means you can make much more muscle and build it where you want it.

Strong painkilling drugs can allow an athlete to train and compete with an injury, causing further and perhaps permanent damage. These drugs are illegal for use by people involved in sport.

Different sports need great stamina – marathons and long distance cycling races are two examples. Some cyclists (and other athletes) use a drug to stimulate their body to make more red blood cells. This means they can carry more oxygen to their muscles. The drug is a compound found naturally in the body so drug-testers are looking for abnormally high levels of it.

Fast reactions are vital in many sports, and there are drugs that will make you very alert and on edge. On the other hand, in sports such as darts and shooting, you need very steady hands. Some athletes take drugs to slow down their heart and reduce any shaking in their hands to try and win medals.

> **a** What are anabolic steroids and why do athletes use them?

Catching the cheats

Athletes found using illegal drugs are banned from competing. The sports authorities keep producing new tests for drugs and run random drugs tests to try and identify the cheats. But some competitors are always looking for new ways to cheat without being found out. So the illegal use of drugs in sport continues. Some medicines contain banned drugs which can enhance performance, so athletes need to be very careful so they don't end up 'cheating' by accident.

Figure 2 The Tour de France has had many drug problems. Cyclists have died after using illegal drugs to help them go faster. Floyd Landis, the winner in 2006, was disqualified for using steroids.

The ethics of using drugs in sport

There are lots of ways an athlete can improve their performance. Where does wanting to win end and cheating begin? Is the use of performance-enhancing substances ever acceptable in sport? These are questions scientists cannot answer – society has to decide.

For example, if an athlete lives and trains at high altitude for several weeks, their body makes a hormone which increases their red blood cell count. This is legal. But it is illegal to buy the hormone and inject it to make more red blood cells.

Here are some of the arguments that athletes use to justify the use of substances that are banned and could do them harm:
- They want to win.
- They feel that other athletes are using these substances, and unless they take them they will be left behind.
- They think the health risks are just scare stories.
- Some athletes claim that they did not know they were taking drugs – their coaches supply them hidden in 'supplements'.

There are a number of ethical points that society needs to consider. Top athletes compete for the satisfaction of winning and millions of people enjoy watching them. Most performance-enhancing drugs risk the health of the athlete at the high doses used in training. They can even cause death. Even if the individual is prepared to take the risk, is this ethically acceptable? At the moment most people say 'no'.

Often the substances used by cheats are so expensive, or new, that most competitors can't afford them. This gives the richest competitors an unfair advantage. For example, most athletes could afford anabolic steroids if they wanted to use them, but not the most recent versions that are not detected by the drug-testing process.

There are some people who think that athletes should be able to do what they like with their bodies. At the moment most of society does not agree with this view – what do you think?

> **b** Why do athletes use drugs which could cause them harm?

Figure 3 Athletes can be asked to produce a urine sample for a drug test at any time, whether they are competing, training or resting

Study tip
Make sure you understand why athletes are banned from using some medical drugs.

Summary questions
1 Copy and complete using the words below:
compete performance-enhancing muscles steroids athletes
Some .... use .... drugs to help them .... more successfully. Many use anabolic .... which help them to develop bigger ....
2 Suggest the advantages and disadvantages to an athlete of using banned performance-enhancing drugs to help win a competition.
3 It has been suggested that athletes be allowed to use any drugs to improve their performance. Suggest arguments for and against this proposal.

Key points
- Anabolic steroids and other banned performance-enhancing drugs are used by some athletes.
- The use of performance-enhancing drugs is considered unethical by most people.

Answers to in-text questions

a Anabolic steroids are drugs which help athletes to build extra muscle mass – athletes use them to get extra strength and extra muscles for running, bodybuilding, etc.

b They are so keen to win at all costs that they feel the benefits outweigh the risks and they assume that the drugs will not affect them negatively etc.

Summary answers

1 athletes, performance-enhancing, compete, steroids, muscles

2 **Advantages**: the athlete will compete better (run faster and have more stamina), be able to lift heavier weights, etc., and build muscles more easily. They mean the athlete will have to do less work to perform well, which is likely to bring the financial benefits of success, e.g. sponsorship.

Disadvantages: the health risks, the risk of being found out and disqualified, the possible loss of personal satisfaction in achievement.

3 **For**: For example, it removes the need to spend large amounts of time and money trying to catch people cheating; it puts all athletes on a level playing field because they can all use performance-enhancing drugs if they want to.

Against: For example, the health risks to athletes, it means wealthy individual athletes or wealthy countries would be able to afford the latest developments and others wouldn't, questionable value of artificially-enhanced performance.

Summary answers

1 a To make sure that they are effective at treating the disease, that they are safe, that they are taken into the body effectively and can be removed from the body.

b Thousands of chemicals go through lab trials to result in a very small number which are put through animal testing and even fewer through human trials. All the stages are very expensive and the process can take up to 12 years.

c Any thoughtful point here – probably most likely response is yes, if a drug seems to be so good during trials that it would be unethical not to treat with it. This has happened on occasion – and there are also occasions when there is such a clear need for a drug in trial to be used on an individual patient as the only chance of avoiding death, that permission is granted there as well. However, equally valid to answer no because it is unethical to use drugs that have not been fully tested and to try and avoid problems such as thalidomide again.

2 a A drug which lowers cholesterol levels in the body.

b High cholesterol levels in the blood lead to an increased risk of cardiovascular disease. (Lowering the levels of cholesterol reduces risk of build up of fatty material in the arteries and so reduces the risk of CVD.)

c Statin 1.

d Some drugs might suit a patient better than others. The cost of the drug.

3 a The second group were asked to drink coffee without caffeine.

b Examples of control variables that could have been used include:
- drink the same amount of coffee
- wait for the same amount of time
- ensure that the students rest in the same conditions between drinking and pulse measurement.

c They could be expecting their pulse to rise and as a result it might have done.

d The students drinking decaffeinated coffee should not have an increase in pulse rate so there could be systematic error.

e The differences in the individual results are due to uncontrolled variables but the increase of 21 bpm in the 'with caffeine' group could be random error.

f The range for the increase in pulse rates without caffeine is 2 bpm to 7 bpm.

g i 14 beats per minute.
   ii 5 beats per minute.

4 a Both data sets suggest males use drugs more than females.

b Individuals
Illegal drugs can be very addictive, damaging to health because of effect of drugs and effect of lifestyle, often illegal activities to get money, injecting drugs, etc., open to HIV and hepatitis, relatively small numbers of people affected.

Smoking and drinking – can have short-term impact but both generally longer-term health damage but on a massive scale in terms of heart disease, cancers, cirrhosis etc. Far bigger populations involved.

Society
Illegal – cost in terms of crime on population, financial cost of policing, hospital treatment, prisons, drug rehab, etc.
Legal drugs cost in terms of hospital treatment for thousands, lost working days, etc.

Summary questions 🇰

1 a Why do new medicines need to be tested and trialled before doctors can use them to treat their patients?

b Why is the development of a new medicine so expensive?

c Do you think it would ever be acceptable to use a new medicine before all the trials had been completed?

2 a What is a statin?

b How do statins help reduce the number of people who suffer from cardiovascular disease?

c Which of the statins in Figure 1, B1 3.2 is most effective?

d The most effective drug is not always the one used. Why do you think other statins might be prescribed?

3 Some students decided to test whether drinking coffee could affect heart rate. They asked the class to help them with their investigation. They divided the class into two groups. Both groups had their pulses taken. They gave one group a drink of coffee. They waited for 10 minutes and then took their pulses again. They then followed the same procedure with the second group.

a What do you think the second group were asked to drink?

b State a control variable that should have been used.

c Explain why it would have been a good idea not to tell the two groups exactly what they were drinking.

d Study this table of results that they produced.

Group	Increase in pulse rate (beats per minute)
With caffeine	12, 15, 13, 10, 15, 16, 10, 15, 16, 21, 14, 13, 16
Without caffeine	4, 3, 4, 5, 7, 5, 7, 4, 2, 6, 5, 4, 7

Can you detect any evidence for systematic error in these results? If so, describe this evidence.

e Is there any evidence for a random error in these results? If so, describe this evidence.

f What is the range for the increase in pulse rates without caffeine?

g What is the mean (or average) increase in pulse rate:
   i with caffeine?
   ii without caffeine?

4 Look at Figure 3, B1 3.4. Compare the data in that graph to Figure 2, B1 3.3. Both show impact of drug taking on individuals in society.

a What are the similarities between the two data sets?

b Explain the relative impact of legal and illegal drugs on individuals and on society.

5 a Why do some athletes use illegal drugs, such as anabolic steroids, when they are training or competing?

b What are the arguments for and against the use of these performance-enhancing drugs?

c People sometimes use illegal performance-enhancing drugs on horses. They use pain killers, stimulants and substances which make the skin on their legs very sensitive. Sometimes they are given sedatives so they run slowly. Discuss the ethical aspects of giving performance-changing drugs to animals.

---

5 a To give them a competitive edge, to increase their physical development, to either reduce work needed or develop more than normal.

b For: build muscle, increased performance, make athletes capable of withstanding tougher training, etc.

Against: health risks, inequality of access, success/records meaningless as result of drugs, not just ability.

c Any thoughtful points: the biggest ethical issue is consent – athletes usually choose to take substances which may harm them or allow them to compete with injuries which may be permanently damaging – animals cannot agree to that. Also, animals do not choose to compete and do not care if they win, so being put at risk through drug use for human satisfaction is not acceptable. It is also unfair to the public who have placed bets. However, many competitive animals appear to enjoy what they do – students could argue that they 'want' to compete. A possible good thing to reduce pain and teach them to pick up feet so they jump more safely, etc.

Practice questions 🅚

1 People take drugs for many different reasons.

alcohol heroin penicillin statin steroid
thalidomide

Choose a word from above to match the following sentences.

a an illegal drug which is highly addictive (1)

b a drug used by athletes to make them perform better (1)

c a medical drug which is used to reduce cholesterol levels (1)

2 A drug company wants to test a new painkiller called PainGo2. The company hope that the new drug will cure headaches quicker than PainGo1.

PainGo2 has to be tested in clinical trials. PainGo2 is twice as strong as PainGo1.

Phase 1 trial – a few healthy people will be given one or two tablets of PainGo2.

Phase 2 trial – a small group (200–300) of patients with headaches will be given PainGo2.

Phase 3 trial – 3 large groups (2000 in each group) of patients with headaches will be given either PainGo2 or PainGo1 or a placebo.

a What is the purpose of the Phase 1 trial? (1)

b Suggest why in Phase 2 the patients were asked to record how they felt after taking the PainGo2.

Suggest why. (1)

c What is a placebo? (1)

d Phase 3 was done as a double-blind trial by doctors who had patients with headaches.

In a double-blind trial who will know who is given the new drug?

Choose your answer from the choices below.

A *the patient only*

B *the doctor only*

C *both the doctor and the patient*

D *neither the doctor nor the patient* (1)

e Why is it important to use the placebo in the Phase 3 trial? (1)

f Why are some patients given PainGo1 in Phase 3? (1)

3 a Give **one** example of:
  i a legal recreational drug. (1)
  ii an illegal recreational drug. (1)

b Some recreational drugs are addictive.
  i Give **one** example of a recreational drug that is very addictive. (1)
  ii Explain how the action of a drug makes a person become addicted to it. (1)

c Some doctors think that smoking cannabis causes depression. Doctors investigated the cannabis smoking habits of 1500 young adults.

The table shows the percentage of cannabis smokers in the investigation who became depressed.

How many times the men or women had smoked cannabis in the last 12 months	Percentage of men who became depressed	Percentage of women who became depressed
Less than 5 times	9	16
More than 5 times, but less than once per week	10	17
1–4 times per week	12	31
Every day	15	68

From the data, give **two** conclusions that can be drawn about the relationship between cannabis and depression. (2)
AQA, 2007

4 *In this question you will be assessed on using good English, organising information clearly and using specialist terms where appropriate.*

Read the description of an investigation into the link between smoking cannabis and heroin addiction.

Six 'teenage' rats were given a small dose of THC – the active chemical in cannabis – every three days between the ages of 28 and 49 days. This is the equivalent of human ages 12 to 18.

The amount of THC given was roughly equivalent to a human smoking one cannabis 'joint' every three days.

A control group of six 'teenage' rats did not receive THC.

After 56 days catheters (narrow tubes) were inserted in all twelve of the now adult rats and they were able to self-administer heroin by pushing a lever.

All the rats began to self-administer heroin frequently. After a while, they stabilised their daily intake at a certain level.

The ones that had been on THC as 'teenagers' stabilised their heroin intake at a much higher level than the others. They appeared to be less sensitive to the effects of heroin. This pattern continued throughout their lives.

Reduced sensitivity to the heroin means that the rats take larger doses. This has been shown to increase the risk of addiction.

Evaluate this investigation with respect to establishing a link between cannabis smoking and heroin addiction in humans. Remember to include a conclusion to your evaluation. (6)
AQA, 2007

Kerboodle resources 🅚

Resources available for this chapter on Kerboodle are:

- Chapter map: Medicine and drugs
- How Science Works: Can we believe the claims? (B1 3.2)
- Support: What's the harm in that? (B1 3.3)
- Interactive activity: Drugs
- Revision podcast: Medicine and drugs
- Test yourself: Medicines and drugs
- On your marks: Medicine and drugs
- Practice questions: Medicine and drugs
- Answers to practice questions: Medicine and drugs

Study tip

When candidates are asked to evaluate information, they should always give pros, cons and a conclusion. For example, they can use headings such as pros/advantages, cons/disadvantages and conclusion. In a six-mark answer, they should give at least two pros and two cons. The conclusion should be backed up by their previous selections.

This type of question could also be used to assess the Quality of Written Communication.

This is a High Demand example but evaluation and QWC can be tested at any level.

Practice answers

1 a heroin (*1 mark*)

b steroid(s) (*1 mark*)

c statin(s) (*1 mark*)

2 a To check for unexpected side effects with the higher dose/stronger pain killer. (*1 mark*)

b To see if the drug cured the headaches. (*1 mark*)

c A tablet which does not contain a drug/contains a harmless chemical/a 'blank'. (*1 mark*)

d D Neither the doctor nor the patient. (*1 mark*)

e To rule out psychological effects/description of this. (*1 mark*)

f To see if the PainGo2/the new drug is better (at curing headaches) than PainGo1. (*1 mark*)

3 a i tobacco/nicotine/alcohol (*accept:* solvent/glue/caffeine, *ignore:* cigarettes/coffee) (*1 mark*)
  ii cannabis/heroin/cocaine (*allow:* crack/weed/ecstasy/LSD/amphetamine/speed/steroids/GHB). (*1 mark*)

b i heroin/cocaine/tobacco/nicotine (*ignore:* alcohol/cigarettes/cannabis/caffeine/coffee) (*1 mark*)
  ii alters body chemistry which causes the body to become addicted to it (*ignore:* withdrawal symptoms/craving/non-chemical effects on nervous system) (*1 mark*)

c Any **two** from:
  - increase in cannabis smoking increases (%) depression
  - greater effect in women/allow women become more depressed
  - depression linked with/not directly caused by cannabis/ignore cannabis causes depression
  - not all cannabis smokers get depression (*2 marks*)

4 There is a clear, balanced and detailed argument referring to both pros and cons and a conclusion which matches the pos and cons. The answer shows almost faultless spelling, punctuation and grammar. It is coherent and in an organised, logical sequence. It contains a range of appropriate or relevant specialist terms used accurately. (*5–6 marks*)

The answer contains at least one pro and one con with a conclusion. There are some errors in spelling, punctuation and grammar. The answer has some structure and organisation. The use of specialist terms has been attempted, but not always accurately. (*3–4 marks*)

There is mention of either a pro or a con with an attempt at a conclusion or a list of pros and cons without a conclusion, has little clarity and detail. The spelling, punctuation and grammar are very weak. The answer is poorly organised with almost no specialist terms and/or their use demonstrating a general lack of understanding of their meaning. (*1–2 marks*)

No relevant content. (*0 marks*)

Examples of biology points made in the response:
Pros, e.g.
- used 'teenage rats' as equivalent to human teenagers
- THC dose typical of human cannabis smoking habits
- used control group
- rats allowed to choose amount of heroin

Cons, e.g.
- sample size small/only used 12 rat
- heroin administration very different from human situation

Conclusions
- rats given THC/cannabis took more heroin
- (this) is evidence for a link between THC/cannabis and heroin
- (but) rat behaviour/physiology not necessarily same as human behaviour/physiology
- does not prove link in human/results not reliable for humans.

B1 4.1

Adapt and survive

Learning objectives

Students should learn:

- that organisms need a supply of materials from their surroundings and from other living organisms in order to survive and reproduce
- that organisms are adapted to the conditions in which they live
- how microorganisms have a wide range of adaptations enabling them to live in a wide range of conditions.

Learning outcomes

Most students should be able to:

- describe the materials that living organisms need in order to survive and reproduce
- explain that plants and animals are adapted to survive in their particular habitat
- explain that the adaptations of microorganisms enable them to survive in a wide range of conditions.

Some students should also be able to:

- explain how some microorganisms are able to survive in extreme conditions.

Support

- Give the students a prepared table of adaptations and animals – they are to match one to another.
- Have a series of cards with the requirements for life, such as food, water, oxygen etc. and get the students to sort out what plants, animals and microorganisms need.

Extend

- Give students the term 'psychrophile' and ask them to find out what it means and give examples. The Natural History Museum website is a good starting point.
- Microbes on Mars? Students could investigate the possibility that some microbes could survive in the harsh weather conditions found on Mars. Try the Astrobiology magazine website.

Specification link-up: Biology B1.4

- To survive and reproduce, organisms require a supply of materials from their surroundings and from the other living organisms there. *[B1.4.1 a)]*
- Organisms, including microorganisms have features (adaptations) that enable them to survive in the conditions in which they normally live. *[B1.4.1 d)]*
- Some organisms live in environments that are very extreme. Extremophiles may be tolerant to high levels of salt, high temperatures or high pressures. *[B1.4.1 e)]*
- Animals and plants may be adapted to cope with specific features of their environment, e.g. thorns, poisons and warning colours to deter predators. *[B1.4.1 g)]*

Lesson structures

Starters

Spaceship supplies – Suppose you were to take yourself, some animals, some plants and some microorganisms to start a colony on another planet. In order to keep them alive during the journey, what would you need to provide for the plants, the animals, and the microorganisms? Write down your own ideas, then share them with others. *(5 minutes)*

Can you tell where I live from what I look like? – Bring in some live or stuffed animals or alternatively project some good pictures on to a smart board. Then discuss their adaptations, drawing some conclusions about the conditions in the habitats in which they might be found. The points to get across are that the adaptations are physical features that you can touch or see, but that there are also behavioural adaptations, such as lizards basking in the sun, that are important. Students can be supported by giving them a list of adaptations to choose from. Students can be extended by asking them to explain how these adaptations may have arisen. *(10 minutes)*

Main

- Ask the students the question: 'What makes an animal an animal and a plant a plant?' Draw out the differences in nutrition. You may well have to point out that some animals don't move much, e.g. sea anemones and that plants do move, although generally slowly. Speeded up camera footage of plants moving would be useful here and you could remind students of the growth movements involved in phototropism.

- Use a PowerPoint slide show or short explanation to review the needs of animals and plants. Get the students to summarise their responses in a table.

- Draw out what microorganisms are. Explain the very large number of different types and the vast variety of environments that they survive in. Remind students about pathogens as well as useful microorganisms. One way could be to have a circus of cards around the room each with a microorganism type, its picture and nutritional details.

- Show some animals and plants with extreme adaptations. Examples could include animals and plants that live in situations such as very low temperatures, very high salt concentrations, etc. Discuss the adaptations shown.

Plenaries

Life on another planet – Discuss with students how, once your spaceship had landed on another planet, the animals, plants and microorganisms might have to adapt to live there. Would it be possible? Might you decide to take some extremophiles with you? *(5 minutes)*

What's in a name? – Following a discussion or presentation on animals, plants and microorganisms living in extreme conditions, get students to give you their ideas on the meaning of the following terms: thermophile, xerophile, osmophile, halophile, acidophile. You can support students by providing a list from which they can choose and by showing pictures of examples that might give them clues. Students can be extended by adding extra terms: alkalophile, thermoacidophile, etc. These students can be asked to give the meaning of the term, suggest a habitat and an example for each one. It could be helpful to tell students that the suffix '-phile' comes from the Greek word for 'love'. *(10 minutes)*

Further teaching suggestions

Extreme resources
- An internet search for animals and plants which survive in extreme conditions can produce some good results. There are a number of very good educational videos available on the topic of adaptations. If the library has a good selection of books with animal photos, the students could look through these and select suitable ones to talk about to their peers.

Adaptation for survival

B1 4.1 Adapt and survive

Learning objectives
- What do organisms need to live?
- How do organisms survive in many different conditions?

The variety of conditions on the surface of the Earth is huge. It ranges from hot, dry deserts to permanent ice and snow. There are deep, saltwater oceans and tiny freshwater pools. Whatever the conditions, almost everywhere on Earth you will find living organisms able to survive and reproduce.

Survive and reproduce

Living organisms need a supply of materials from their surroundings and from other living organisms so they can survive and reproduce successfully. What they need depends on the type of organism.
- Plants need light, carbon dioxide, water, oxygen and nutrients to produce glucose energy in order to survive.
- Animals need food from other living organisms, water and oxygen.
- Microorganisms need a range of things. Some are like plants, some are like animals and some don't need oxygen or light to survive.

Living organisms have special features known as **adaptations**. These features make it possible for them to survive in their particular habitat, even when the conditions are very extreme.

links
For more information on plant adaptation, see B1 4.3 Adaptation in plants.

Plant adaptations

Plants need to photosynthesise to produce the glucose needed for energy and growth. They also need to have enough water to maintain their cells and tissues. They have adaptations that enable them to live in many different places. For example, most plants get water and nutrients from the soil through their roots. Epiphytes are found in rainforests. They have adaptations which allow them to live high above the ground attached to other plants. They collect water and nutrients from the air and in their specially adapted leaves.

Figure 1 Mangroves are trees that live in soil with very little oxygen, often with their roots covered by salty water. They have special adaptations to get rid of the salt through their leaves, and roots which grow in the air to get oxygen.

Study tip
Practise recognising plant and animal adaptations and try to work out where they might live from the adaptation. This will help in your examination where you may be asked to do the same.

Some plant adaptations are all about reproduction. *Rafflesia arnoldii* produces flowers which are 1 m across, weigh about 11 kg and smell of a rotting corpse. The plants are rare so the dramatic and very smelly flower increases the chances of flies visiting and carrying pollen from one plant to another.

a Why do plants need to photosynthesise?

Animal adaptations

Animals cannot make their own food. They have to eat plants or other animals. Many of the adaptations of animals help them to get the food they need. So you can tell what a mammal eats by looking at its teeth. **Herbivores** have teeth for grinding up plant cells. **Carnivores** have teeth adapted for tearing flesh or crushing bones. Animals also often have adaptations to help them find and attract a mate.

links
For more information on animal adaptation, see B1 4.2 Adaptation in animals.

Adapting to the environment

Some of the adaptations seen in animals and plants help them to survive in a particular environment. Some sea birds get rid of all the extra salt they take in from the sea water by 'crying' very salty tears from a special salt gland. Animals that need to survive extreme winter temperatures often produce a chemical in their cells which acts as antifreeze. It stops the water in the cells from freezing and destroying the cell. Plants such as water lilies have lots of big air spaces in their leaves. This adaptation enables them to float on top of their watery environment and make food by photosynthesis.

Organisms that survive and reproduce in the most difficult conditions are known as **extremophiles**.

Living in extreme environments

Microorganisms are found in more places in the world than any other living thing. These places range from ice packs to hot springs and geysers. Microorganisms have a range of adaptations which make this possible. Many extremophiles are microorganisms.

Some extremophiles live at very high temperatures. Bacteria known as thermophiles can survive at temperatures of over 45°C and often up to 80°C or higher. In most organisms the enzymes stop working at around 40°C. These extremophiles have specially adapted enzymes that do not **denature** and so work at these high temperatures. In fact, many of these organisms cannot survive and reproduce at lower temperatures.

Other bacteria have adaptations so they can grow and reproduce at very low temperatures, down to −15°C. They are found in ice packs and glaciers around the world.

Most living organisms struggle to survive in a very salty environment because of the problems it causes with water balance. However, there are species of extremophile bacteria that can only live in extremely salty environments such as the Dead Sea and salt flats. They have adaptations to their cytoplasm so that water does not move out of their cells into their salty environment. But in ordinary sea water, they would swell up and burst!

b What is a thermophile?

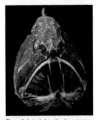
Figure 2 Animals from the deep oceans are adapted to cope with enormous pressure, no light and very cold, salty water. If these extremophiles are brought to the surface too quickly, they explode because of the rapid change in pressure.

Figure 3 Black smoker bacteria live in deep ocean vents, 2500 m down, at temperatures of well over 100°C, with enormous pressure, no light and an acid pH of about 2.6. They have adaptations to cope with some of the most extreme conditions on Earth.

Key points
- Organisms need a supply of materials from their surroundings and from other living organisms to survive and reproduce.
- Organisms have features (adaptations) that enable them to survive in the conditions in which they normally live.
- Extremophiles have adaptations enabling them to live in extreme conditions of salt, temperature or pressure.

Summary questions

1 Copy and complete using the words below:
adaptations organisms materials survive extreme
To .... and reproduce, organisms need a supply of .... from their surroundings and the living .... in their habitat. They have .... that enable them to survive in their particular habitat, even when the conditions are very ....

2 Make a list of what plants and animals need from their surroundings to survive and reproduce.

3 **a** What is an extremophile?
b Give two examples of adaptations found in different extremophiles.

76 / 77

Answers to in-text questions

a Plants need to photosynthesise to produce the glucose needed for energy and growth.

b A bacterium which can survive at temperatures of over 45 °C.

Summary answers

1 survive, materials, organisms, adaptations, extreme

2 **Plants:** carbon dioxide, water, light, minerals, oxygen
Animals: food from other living organisms, oxygen, water.

3 **a** An organism which can live in extremely difficult conditions where most other organisms cannot survive.
b Enzymes which function in very high temperatures, enzymes which function at very low temperatures, ability to get rid of excesses of salt, ability to respire without oxygen, any other valid point.

B1 4.2

Adaptation in animals

Learning objectives

Students should learn:

- that animals are adapted for survival in their particular habitat
- that there is a relationship between body size and surface area : volume ratio
- that hair and body fat can provide insulation.

Learning outcomes

Most students should be able to:

- define the term 'adaptation'
- describe how animals are adapted to survive in cold climates
- describe how animals are adapted to life in a dry climate.

Some students should also be able to:

- explain in detail how organisms are adapted to the conditions in which they live, when provided with appropriate information.

Answers to in-text questions

a It keeps the surface area : volume ratio as small as possible and so helps them to reduce heat loss.

b Arctic animals have small ears, thick fur, and a layer of fat/blubber.

c Because sweating results in loss of water from the body. There is not much water in the desert, so they cannot rely on finding more to drink.

Support

- Have a floor dominoes session where students match animals and their adaptations. Include animals of all types and from different habitats. Played with cards in the form of dominoes, but make the cards large so that the game can be played on the floor.

Extend

- Ask students to design an experiment to investigate whether people who regularly swim in the sea have a different surface area to volume ratio than those who only swim in heated pools.

Specification link-up: Biology B1.4

- Animals and plants may be adapted for survival in …. *[B1.4.1 f)]*

    Controlled Assessment: B4.1 Plan practical ways to develop and test candidates' own scientific ideas *[B4.1.1 a) b)]*; B4.3 Collect primary and secondary data *[B4.3.2 a) b)]*; B4.4 Select and process primary and secondary data *[B4.4.2 b)]* and B4.5 Analyse and interpret primary and secondary data. *[B4.5.3 a)]*, *[B4.5.4 a)]*

Lesson structure

Starters

Temperature regulation! – Get a student to dress up in a fur hat, scarf, thick coat and gloves (or dress up yourself). Contrast with pictures of Newcastle United football supporters taking their shirts off in the snow at matches. Discuss effects on temperature regulation. *(5 minutes)*

Life in the freezer – Search the internet for a video of Arctic animals (see the Discovery Channel at www.yourdiscovery.com) or project a series of images of arctic animals and get students to say what features the animals have which are adaptations to their environment. Students could be supported by being given a list of adaptations and matching the adaptation to the animal. Students could be extended by asking them to consider behavioural adaptations as well as physical ones. *(10 minutes)*

Main

- Surface area: volume ratio demonstrations with chocolate and building blocks. Show students a small chocolate bar. Ask if they think you could get it all in your mouth in one piece, without breaking it or biting it. Ask them to imagine if you did that, where would the saliva be able to touch? Draw out that is would be just the outside surface. Cut the bar into smaller and smaller bits, getting the students to see that the smaller the bits, the larger the surface area to volume ratio is. Make sure students do not eat in the laboratory.

- A further practical session could be used to introduce the concept of surface area : volume ratios having an effect on heat loss (see 'Practical support' for full details). 'How Science Works' concepts can also be introduced here.

- Set up a demonstration to show that the thickness of an insulating coat will affect the temperature loss (see 'Practical support'). This investigation is also useful for teaching and assessing investigative aspects of 'How Science Works', as it involves taking measurements, plotting graphs and drawing conclusions.

- Discuss the similarities between the adaptations in desert animals.

Plenaries

Mix and match adaptations and functions – Put a list of adaptations on the board alongside a list of functions. Ask students to come and link an adaptation to a function. *(5 minutes)*

Modify or die – Imagine that the climate has changed in the UK and is now very cold and icy for most of the year. Describe and/or draw how some of our familiar animals would eventually have to evolve or die. Do the same supposing that the UK became very hot and dry. Differentiation by outcome: some students will need to be supported by prompting and produce limited suggestions, whilst students can be extended by being encouraged to produce more detailed ones. *(10 minutes)*

??? Did you know …?

Polar bear hair is not white but colourless. It is hollow and transparent to allow the light to fall on to its skin, which is black to absorb the energy. It has been said that polar bears hide their noses with their paws when they are hunting to prevent their prey from spotting them.

Practical support

Surface area: volume ratios and energy loss

Equipment and materials required

Cups, saucers, digital thermometers, hot water (about 60 °C); a 1 litre beaker and ten 100 ml beakers; small conical flasks of different sizes.

Details

There are several ways of doing this. The simplest way is to give students cups and saucers and digital thermometers. Pour the same volume of hot (about 60 °C) water into each cup and measure the temperature drop. Alternatively, pour 1 litre of hot water into a litre beaker and divide another litre of water equally between ten 100 ml beakers. Monitor the temperature. Data loggers can be used here. It is also possible to use different sizes of flasks, allowing students to carry out their own temperature readings and plot their own graphs.

Predictions can be made, readings carried out and repeated, and conclusions drawn.

Safety: Care is needed with the handling of hot water.

The effect of insulation on energy loss

Equipment and materials required

For each group; two similar-sized flasks, thermometers, hot water, insulation.

Details

Two conical flasks of the same volume can be filled with hot water. One flask is left uncovered and the other surrounded by an insulating layer of cotton wool, or other material. The temperature drop can be recorded as before. This experiment could be done as a demonstration or by groups of students. It could be done at the same time as the previous experiment.

Safety: Care is needed with the handling of hot water.

Adaptation for survival

B1 4.2 Adaptation in animals

Adaptation in animals

Learning objectives

- How can hair help animals survive in very cold climates?
- What are the advantages – and disadvantages – of lots of body fat?
- How do animals adapt to hot, dry climates?

Animals have adaptations that help them to get the food and mates they need to survive and reproduce. They also have adaptations for survival in the conditions where they normally live.

Animals in cold climates

To survive in a cold environment you must be able to keep yourself warm. Animals which live in very cold places, such as the Arctic, are adapted to reduce the energy they lose from their bodies. You lose body heat through your body surface (mainly your skin). The amount of energy you lose is closely linked to your surface area : volume (SA : V) ratio.

Maths skills

Surface area : volume ratio

The surface area : volume ratio is very important when you look at the adaptations of animals that live in cold climates. It explains why so many Arctic mammals, such as seals, walruses and polar bears, are relatively large.

The ratio of surface area to volume falls as objects get bigger. You can see this clearly in the diagram. The larger the surface area : volume ratio, the larger the rate of energy loss. So mammals in a cold climate grow to a large size. This keeps their surface area : volume ratio as small as possible and so helps them hold on to their body heat.

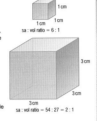

sa : vol ratio = 6 : 1

sa : vol ratio = 54 : 27 = 2 : 1

a Why are so many Arctic animals large?

Animals in very cold climates often have other adaptations too. The surface area of the thinly skinned areas of their bodies, like their ears, is usually very small. This reduces their energy loss.

Many Arctic mammals have plenty of insulation, both inside and out. Inside they have blubber (a thick layer of fat that builds up under the skin). On the outside a thick fur coat will insulate an animal very effectively. These adaptations really reduce the amount of energy lost through their skin.

The fat layer also provides a food supply. Animals often build up their fat in the summer. Then they can live off their body fat through the winter when there is almost no food.

b List three ways in which Arctic animals keep warm in winter.

Study tip

Remember, the *larger* the animal, the *smaller* the surface area : volume (SA : V).

Animals often have *increased* surface areas in *hot* climates, and *decreased* surface areas in *cold* climates.

links

For more information about other implications of surface area : volume ratios, see B3 1.4 Exchanging materials – the lungs.

Figure 1 The Arctic is a cold and bleak environment. However, the animals that live there are well adapted for survival. Notice the large size, small ears, thick coat and white camouflage of this polar bear.

Camouflage

Camouflage is important both to predators (so their prey doesn't see them coming) and to prey (so they can't be seen). The colours that would camouflage an Arctic animal in summer against plants would stand out against the snow in winter. Many Arctic animals, including the Arctic fox, the Arctic hare and the stoat, have grey or brown summer coats that change to pure white in the winter. Polar bears don't change colour. They have no natural predators on the land. They hunt seals all year round in the sea, where their white colour makes them less visible among the ice.

The colour of the coat of a lioness is another example of effective camouflage. The sandy brown colour matches perfectly with the dried grasses of the African savannah. Her colour hides the lioness from the grazing animals which are her prey.

Surviving in dry climates

Dry climates are often also hot climates – like deserts. Deserts are very difficult places for animals to live. There is scorching heat during the day, followed by bitter cold at night. Water is also in short supply.

The biggest challenges if you live in a desert are:

- coping with the lack of water
- stopping body temperature from getting too high.

Many desert animals are adapted to need little or nothing to drink. They get the water they need from the food they eat.

Mammals keep their body temperature the same all the time. So as the environment gets hotter, they have to find ways of keeping cool. Sweating means they lose water, which is not easy to replace in the desert.

c Why do mammals try to cool down without sweating in hot, dry conditions?

Animals that live in hot conditions adapt their behaviour to keep cool. They are often most active in the early morning and late evening, when it is not so hot. During the cold nights and the heat of the day they rest in burrows where the temperature doesn't change much.

Many desert animals are quite small, so their surface area is large compared to their volume. This helps them to lose heat through their skin. They often have large, thin ears to increase their surface area for losing energy.

Another adaptation of many desert animals is to have thin fur. Any fur they do have is fine and silky. They also have relatively little body fat stored under the skin. These features make it easier for them to lose energy through the surface of the skin.

Figure 2 Jerboas are very small and elephants are very big. They both show clear adaptations that help them survive in the hot, dry places where they live.

Key points

- All living things have adaptations that help them to survive in the conditions where they live.
- Animals that are adapted for cold environments are often large, with a small surface area : volume (SA : V) ratio. They have thick insulating layers of fat and fur.
- Changing coat colour in the different seasons gives animals year-round camouflage.
- Adaptations for hot, dry environments include a large SA : V ratio, little body fat and behaviour patterns that avoid the heat of the day.

Summary questions

1 **a** List the main problems that face animals living in cold conditions like the Arctic.
   b List the main problems that face animals living in the desert.
2 Animals that live in the Arctic are adapted to keep warm through the winter. Describe three of these adaptations and explain how they work.
3 **a** Using Figure 2, describe the visible adaptations of a jerboa and an elephant to keeping cool in hot conditions.
   b Suggest other ways in which animals might be adapted to survive in hot, dry conditions.

78   79

Further teaching suggestions

Sweating demonstration

- Demonstrate the cooling effect of sweating by wiping the backs of the hands of volunteer students with cotton wool soaked in ethanol and asking them how it feels. To show that it is the evaporation of alcohol that is doing the cooling, students could be given a test tube of ethanol in a rack with a digital thermometer in it. The temperature can be read and recorded. The thermometer should then be repeatedly dipped into the ethanol and waved in the air (gently and carefully) and the lowest temperature reached recorded. Ensure that there are no naked flames.

Comparing SA:V ratios

- Provide students with some data about the sizes of different animals and get them to work out the SA:V ratios. For example, comparing a mouse and an elephant. You can simplify the data by supplying them with the dimensions of a box into which the animal would fit.

Summary answers

1 **a** It is very cold, so there is a problem in keeping warm and finding enough food.
   b It is very hot, so the main problems are keeping the body cool and finding enough water.
2 Small ears (reduce SA (surface area) of thin skinned tissue to reduce heat loss), thick fur (insulating layer to help prevent heat loss), layer of fat/blubber (insulating layer), any other relevant adaptations, e.g. furry feet to insulate against contact with ice, large size reduces surface area:volume ratio so reduces heat loss, etc.
3 **a** E.g. **Jerboa** – big thin ears to increase SA (surface area) to lose heat, bare legs and tail to make it easier to lose heat, thin fine hair to increase heat loss. **Elephant** – big thin ears and large amount of wrinkled skin to increase SA and heat loss, little body hair to reduce insulation.
   b Animals living in hot dry conditions keep cool without sweating by avoiding the heat of the day and by having large ears, baggy skin, little fur, thin and silky fur and a large SA:V ratio to increase heat loss.

B1 4.3

Adaptation in plants

Learning objectives

Students should learn:

- how some plants are adapted to live in dry conditions
- that changes in the surface area of plants affect the rate at which water is lost
- how plants living in dry conditions may store water in their tissues.

Learning outcomes

Most students should be able to:

- describe the adaptations shown by plants that live in dry environments
- explain how these adaptations reduce the quantity of water lost by the plant.

Some students should also be able to:

- explain in detail the importance of water-storage tissues in desert plants.

Answers to in-text questions

a For photosynthesis and to keep the plant upright.
b By evaporation through the stomata.
c To prevent excessive water loss, e.g. in the desert. Water is lost through the surface of the leaf, so if the surface area is smaller, there will be less water lost.
d Leaves, stem and/or roots.

Support

- Ask students to measure the leaf areas of two contrasting plants by wax rubbing over large squared graph paper. Ask them to predict from this which plant will need more water.

Extend

- Ask students to try to work out a method for estimating the total leaf surface area on a tree.
- Ask students to consider how plants, such as cacti, are able to make enough food by photosynthesis if their leaves are reduced to spines?
- Look at flat-bladed cacti such as prickly pear (*Platyopuntia*). Shine a light on it and move the light around to model the apparent movement of the Sun during the day. Which orientation would be best for the cactus? Would the orientation change in different hemispheres?

Specification link-up: Biology B1.4

- Animals and plants may be adapted for survival in … . *[B1.4.1 f)]*

  Controlled Assessment: B4.1 Plan practical ways to develop and test candidates' own scientific ideas *[B4.1.1a) b)]*; B4.3 Collect primary and secondary data *[B4.3.2 a) b)]*; B4.4 Select and process primary and secondary data. *[B4.4.1 a) b)]*, *[B4.4.2 a) b)]*

Lesson structure

Starters

Saving water and storing water – Show the students a cactus plant and a potted geranium or similar plant. Ask the students which one could survive the longest in drought conditions and why? Draw out reduction in leaf surface area, possibility of storing water etc. Cut a slice of the cactus and show the water-storing tissue or project a slide of a section of the tissue. *(5 minutes)*

Losing water – Choose two identical soft-leaved plants (tomato plants or whatever is available) and two similar cactus plants. Leave one of each to dry out, so that the soft-leaved plant is wilted, but water the other two thoroughly. Present these to the students explaining how they have been treated. Students can be supported by asking what the differences are and getting them to describe what they see. Students can be extended by asking: 'Why are the differences not as great between the two cactus plants as they are between the two soft-leaved plants?' These students could be encouraged to speculate constructively as to the reasons and suggest further investigations to compare the two [e.g. weighing to calculate mass loss]. *(10 minutes)*

Main

- Search the internet to show pictures of adaptations of plants to arid conditions. Share with students the fact that the words 'stomach' and 'stoma' have the same origin from the Greek word for mouth. Show a picture of a stoma looking like a mouth. It would be useful to have a number of succulents and cactus plants available for students to be able to feel the texture and examine the structures in detail. Ask students to write a report on the adaptations.

- Set up a practical investigation into how variation in leaf size affects transpiration (see 'Practical support'). If preferred, this exercise can be set up as a demonstration where groups of students are given a 'leaf' of a different size, the measurements taken and then collected together and discussed. Many 'How Science Works' concepts, such as collecting and processing data and drawing conclusions, are introduced here.

- If you have a potometer (or a barometric pressure sensor) you can connect it to a leafy shoot. The rate of water uptake (equivalent to the rate of water loss) can be measured for the intact shoot. When several readings have been taken and a mean rate calculated, several leaves can be removed and the readings repeated. This can be done again removing more leaves. The effect will depend on the type of shoot chosen – one with soft leaves is better than laurel or rhododendron. Other conditions can be simulated using hair dryers and/or plastic bags.

- The surface area of the leaves can be measured as they are removed, by drawing around them on squared paper, cutting round the outlines and weighing them. If you know the mass of a known area of the squared paper, then it is possible to calculate the area of each leaf. (Dividing the mass of the leaf by the mass of 1 cm^2 will give the area of the leaf.)

Plenaries

Where do I come from? – Show a series of pictures of plants and ask students where they think the plants come from. Students can be supported by having a list of the different environments for them to select an appropriate one. Students can be extended by asking them to write down the name of an environment for each one. Compare answers and get them to suggest reasons for their choice of environment. *(5 minutes)*

Predictions

Ask students to make thumbnail sketches predicting what graphs would look like for the following:

- cuticle thickness v. habitat (rainforest/dry desert etc)
- surface area v. average humidity
- yearly rainfall v. water storage capacity.

These relate to 'How Science Works' – relationships between variables. This could be finished for homework. *(10 minutes)*

Practical support

 Investigation into how variation in leaf size affects transpiration

Equipment and materials required

Blotting paper, cotton string, drinking straws, boiling tube (or small measuring cylinder).

Details

Using pieces of blotting paper of known surface area, make up some 'leaves' of different sizes. Attach a piece of cotton string to one end of the blotting paper and pass the string down a drinking straw, so that the 'leaf' can be supported in a boiling tube (or small measuring cylinder). The blotting paper could have a thin card backing to give it strength. If a known volume of water is placed in each boiling tube (or the 'leaves' are placed in small measuring cylinders) the volume of water lost can be calculated in cm^3/hour against area in cm^2. The results can be shown graphically.

If preferred, this exercise can be set up as a demonstration where groups of students are given a 'leaf' of a different size, the measurements taken and then collected together and discussed.

Adaptation for survival

B1 4.3 Adaptation in plants

Learning objectives

- How do plants lose water?
- How are plants adapted to live in dry conditions?

Figure 1 Plants lose water vapour from the surface of their leaves. When the conditions are hot and dry, they may lose water very quickly.

links
For information on surface area : volume ratio, look back at B1 4.2 Adaptation in animals.

Figure 2 Marram grass grows on sand dunes. It has tightly curled leaves to reduce the surface area for water loss so it can survive the dry conditions.

Plants need light, water, space and nutrients to survive. There are some places where plants cannot grow. In deep oceans no light penetrates and so plants cannot photosynthesise. In the icy wastes of the Antarctic it is simply too cold for plants to grow.

Almost everywhere else, including the hot, dry areas of the world, you find plants growing. Without them there would be no food for the animals. But plants need water for photosynthesis and to keep their tissues supported. If a plant does not get the water it needs, it wilts and eventually dies.

a Why do plants need water?

Plants take in water from the soil through their roots. It moves up through the plant and into the leaves. There are small openings called stomata in the leaves of a plant. These open to allow gases in and out for photosynthesis and respiration. At the same time water vapour is lost through the stomata by evaporation.

The rate at which a plant loses water is linked to the conditions it is growing in. When it is hot and dry, photosynthesis and respiration take place quickly. As a result, plants also lose water vapour very quickly. Plants that live in very hot, dry conditions need special adaptations to survive. Most of them either reduce their surface area so they lose less water or store water in their tissues. Some do both!

b How do plants lose water from their leaves?

Changing surface area

When it comes to stopping water loss through the leaves, the surface area : volume ratio is very important to plants. A few desert plants have broad leaves with a large surface area. These leaves collect the dew that forms in the cold evenings. They then funnel the water towards their shallow roots.

Some plants in dry environments have curled leaves. This reduces the surface area of the leaf. It also traps a layer of moist air around the leaf. This reduces the amount of water the plant loses by evaporation.

Most plants that live in dry conditions have leaves with a very small surface area. This adaptation cuts down the area from which water can be lost. Some desert plants have small fleshy leaves with a thick cuticle to keep water loss down. The cuticle is a waxy covering on the leaf that stops water evaporating.

The best-known desert plants are the cacti. Their leaves have been reduced to spines with a very small surface area indeed. This means the cactus only loses a tiny amount of water. Not only that, its sharp spines also put animals off eating the cactus.

c Why do plants often reduce the surface area of their leaves?

Collecting water

Many plants that live in very dry conditions have specially adapted and very big root systems. They may have extensive root systems that spread over a very wide area, roots that go down a very long way, or both. These adaptations allow the plant to take up as much water as possible from the soil. The mesquite tree has roots that grow as far as 50 m down into the soil.

Storing water

Some plants cope with dry conditions by storing water in their tissues. When there is plenty of water after a period of rain, the plant stores it. Some plants use their fleshy leaves to store water. Others use their stems or roots.

For example, cacti don't just rely on their spiny leaves to help them survive in dry conditions. The fat green body of a cactus is its stem, which is full of water-storing tissue. These adaptations make cacti the most successful plants in a hot, dry climate.

Figure 3 A large saguaro cactus in the desert loses less than one glass of water a day. A UK apple tree can lose a whole bath of water in the same amount of time.

d In which parts can a plant store its water?

links
For more information about water loss in plants, see B3 1.9 Transpiration.

Summary questions

1 Copy and complete using the words below:

adaptations   desert   plants   spines   stems   water

Cacti are .... that live in the .... They have two main .... to help them survive. Their leaves have become .... and they store .... in their ....

2 **a** Explain why plants lose water through their leaves all the time.
  b Why does this make living in a dry place such a problem?

3 Plants living in dry conditions have adaptations to reduce water loss from their leaves. Give three of these and explain how they work.

Study tip

Remember that plants need their stomata open for photosynthesis and respiration. This is why they lose water by evaporation from their leaves.

Key points

- Plants lose water vapour from the surface of their leaves.
- Plant adaptations for surviving in dry conditions include reducing the surface area of the leaves, having water-storage tissues and having extensive root systems.

80   81

Further teaching suggestions

Demonstration of expanding stem

- Fold a piece of green card into corrugations and sticky tape the ends together. Self-shading can be demonstrated and also, by pulling it wide and closing it up, the ability of barrel cacti to expand when water is plentiful.

Plants and water loss

- Not all plants showing adaptations to prevent loss of water live in hot, dry conditions. Ask students to consider other environments in which water may be unavailable to plants. Show them pictures of conifers and salt-marsh plants (many of which are succulent).
- Investigate the effect of phosphate on oxygen levels in water using jars with algae, water and varying numbers of drops of phosphate, then monitor using meter.

Summary answers

1 plants, desert, adaptations, spines, water, stems

2 **a** Water is lost by evaporation through the stomata. The stomata are open for gaseous exchange in photosynthesis and respiration and water is lost by evaporation at the same time.

  b Dry places are often hot, so photosynthesis and respiration occur at a faster rate. The stomata are open more, so there is more evaporation. If the air is dry, evaporation occurs at a faster rate.

3 Small leaves; curled leaves – reduce surface area; thick cuticle – also reduces rate of evaporation.

B1 4.4 | Competition in animals

Specification link-up: Biology B1.4

- Animals often compete with each other for food, mates and territory. [B1.4.1 c)]
- Animals … may be adapted to cope with specific features …. [B1.4.1 g)]
- Suggest the factors for which organisms are competing in a given habitat. [B1.4]

Learning objectives

Students should learn:

- how competition is essential for survival
- that animals compete with each other for food, territory and mates
- that a successful competitor is one which is better adapted.

Learning outcomes

Most students should be able to:

- explain how competition is necessary for survival
- describe those characteristics which make an animal a successful competitor
- suggest the factors for which an animal is competing in a given habitat.

Some students should also be able to:

- explain in detail why certain characteristics make an animal a successful competitor.

Lesson structure

Starters

Competition for grass? – With the students working in pairs, ask them to list as many animals as they can that eat grass. Give them a time limit of 2 minutes. Students claiming to have the greatest number are asked to read out their list so that the rest of the class can agree or disagree. The winner gets a small prize. This leads to a discussion on competition. *(5 minutes)*

Survive! – Prepare small laminated cards with one of the following words written on it: 'food', 'shelter', 'water' or 'mate'. Place similar cards around the room, enough so that most, but not all, students can collect a complete set of all four cards. Students can be supported in this activity by telling them to move around the room collecting cards according to the rules: 'no swapping or taking from others by force and you can only hold one of each kind'.

Students who collect a full set can go to the front (or sit down) – they have survived. Those who do not manage to collect the set do not survive and at the end of the exercise have to share with their peers how they died (hunger, no mates, etc.). Students can be extended by allowing them to swap around the cards so that more can survive. Ask the students to speculate as to whether this sort of sharing-to-survive behaviour does take place in real life and what forms it may take. [To illustrate social effects or altruism, e.g. mothers feeding offspring but starving themselves.] *(10 minutes)*

Main

- Show the class courtship displays and mating behaviour. Find video or images of courtship displays (e.g. peacocks) or competition between males (e.g. sea lions) using the internet. References to the breeding plumage of different birds, behaviour of stags in the rutting season, etc. are other examples available. Search the Discovery Channel www.yourdiscovery.com.

- Introduce the ideas of 'interspecific' and 'intraspecific' competition: the words do not necessarily have to be used, only the idea that two types of animal eating the same food in the same habitat will be in competition with each other. There are some data available for the variation in numbers of two closely-related species of flour beetle (*Tribolium*) living in the same culture, and for two species of *Paramecium*: only one species will survive. You could also link this with the introduction of species, such as the grey squirrel, into this country and the rabbit (or more recently the camel) into Australia. For competition amongst members of the same species, there are data showing that when the density of limpets on a rocky shore increases, their length and biomass decrease.

- These examples can be presented to the students as OHPs or PowerPoint slides, and for each one discuss what they are competing for and why one wins and the other loses.

- Investigate a food web. Depending on the season, investigate a tree or a clump of plants in the school grounds to show the relationships between the different animals that feed on the plant. Using pooters and sweep nets, the small animals can be trapped and identified and a food web built up. There will be caterpillars and beetles eating the leaves; greenfly feeding directly on the plant sap; butterflies and moths feeding on the flowers; and other invertebrates feeding on the bark. Each group of animals can find plenty of food without being in competition with another species.

Plenaries

What makes a top competitor? – Discuss, for example, *Big Brother*, *The Weakest Link* or any other TV competition show. What parallels can be drawn between what goes on in such a show and competition in nature? *(5 minutes)*

Get off my patch! – Think of as many ways as you can by which animals mark out and defend territories. Write down a list of the animals and how each does this. Students can be supported by showing them pictures of some animals and asking them to suggest what territorial behaviour they may show. You can extend students by suggesting that they link territorial behaviour with survival and natural selection. Ask why changes in some DNA will result in survival and these changes are passed on to the next generation. *(10 minutes)*

Answers to in-text questions

a There is only a limited amount of food, water and living space in an area.

b Any sensible choices here. For example, for a herbivore: eating a wide range of plants, sensitive hearing to hear predators. For a carnivore: ability to run fast; good eyesight; sharp teeth, etc.

Support

- Show students some plastic animals or pictures of animals and ask them to pick out an adaptation for each animal which makes it a good competitor.

Extend

- Introduce the concept of the 'ecological niche'. The students could research interesting or unusual examples of ecological niches.

Further teaching suggestions

Camouflage!
- Another exercise would be to get students to hunt the cocktail stick, using red and green cocktail sticks on a green background.

Camouflage effectiveness
- Find some good pictures of camouflaged animals and ask the students to time how long it takes them to identify the animals. There are some good examples, e.g. flatfish,

amphibians, snakes, etc. Does camouflage play a role in competition between animals?

Competition in birds
- Birds compete all the time for food, mates and territory. Ask students to research the different ways in which birds compete using colour, food preferences and song. Good examples to get the students started are robins and blackbirds.

Adaptation for survival

B1 4.4   Competition in animals

Learning objectives
- What is competition?
- What makes an animal a good competitor?

Animals and plants grow alongside lots of other living things. Some will be from the same species and others will be completely different. In any area there is only a limited amount of food, water and space, and a limited number of mates. As a result, living organisms have to compete for the things they need.

The best adapted organisms are most likely to win the competition for resources. They will be most likely to survive and produce healthy offspring.

a Why do living organisms compete?

Figure 1 Some herbivores only feed on one particular plant. Pandas only eat bamboo, so they are open to competition from other animals or to diseases that damage bamboo.

What do animals compete for?
Animals compete for many things, including:
- food
- territory
- mates.

Competition for food

Competition for food is very common. Herbivores sometimes feed on many types of plant, and sometimes on only one or two different sorts. Many different species of herbivores will all eat the same plants. Just think how many types of animals eat grass!

The animals that eat a wide range of plants are most likely to be successful. If you are a picky eater, you risk dying out if anything happens to your only food source. An animal with wider tastes will just eat something else for a while!

Competition is common among carnivores. They compete for prey. Small mammals like mice are eaten by animals like foxes, owls, hawks and domestic cats. The different types of animals all hunt the same mice. So the animals which are best adapted to the area will be most successful.

Carnivores have to compete with their own species for their prey as well as with different species. Some successful predators are adapted to have long legs for running fast and sharp eyes to spot prey. These features will be passed on to their offspring.

Animals often avoid direct competition with members of other species when they can. It is the competition between members of the same species which is most intense.

Prey animals compete with each other too – to be the one that *isn't* caught! Their adaptations help prevent them becoming a meal for a predator. Some animals contain poisons which make anything that eats them sick or even kills them. Very often these animals also have bright warning colours so that predators quickly learn which animals to avoid. Poison arrow frogs are a good example.

Figure 2 The coral snake (top) is poisonous but the milk snake (bottom) is not. The milk snake is a mimic – it looks like the coral snake. As long as the two species live in the same area the milk snake is protected. Other animals and people leave it alone thinking it is a poisonous coral snake!

b Give one useful adaptation for a herbivore and one for a carnivore.

Competition for territory

For many animals, setting up and defending a territory is vital. A territory may simply be a place to build a nest. It could be all the space needed for an animal to find food and reproduce. Most animals cannot reproduce successfully if they have no territory. So they will compete for the best spaces. This helps to make sure they will be able to find enough food for themselves and for their young.

Competition for a mate

Competition for mates can be fierce. In many species the male animals put a lot of effort into impressing the females. The males compete in different ways to win the privilege of mating with a female.

In some species – like deer and lions – the males fight between themselves. Then the winner gets the females.

Many male animals display to the females to get their attention. Some birds have spectacular adaptations to help them stand out. Male peacocks have the most amazing tail feathers. They use them for displaying to other males (to warn them off) and to females (to attract them).

What makes a successful competitor?

A successful competitor is an animal that is adapted to be better at finding food or a mate than the other members of its own species. It also needs to be better at finding food than the members of other local species. It must be able to breed successfully.

Many animals are successful because they avoid competition with other species as much as possible. They feed in a way that no other local animals do, or they eat a type of food that other animals avoid. For example, one plant can feed many animals without direct competition. While caterpillars eat the leaves, greenfly drink the sap, butterflies suck nectar from the flowers and beetles feed on pollen.

Figure 3 The territory of a gannet pair may be small but without a space they cannot build a nest and reproduce

Figure 4 The spectacular display of a male peacock attracts females. Unlike deer and lions he doesn't need to fight and risk injury.

Study tip

Learn to look at an animal and spot the adaptations that make it a successful competitor.

Summary questions

1 **a** Give an example of animals competing with members of the same species for food.
   b Give an example of animals competing with members of other species for food.
   c Animals that rely on a single type of food can easily become extinct. Explain why.

2 **a** Give two ways in which animals compete for mates.
   b Suggest the advantages and disadvantages of the methods chosen in part **a**.

3 Explain the adaptations you would expect to find in:
   a an animal that hunts mice
   b an animal that eats grass
   c an animal that hunts and eats other animals
   d an animal that feeds on the tender leaves at the top of trees.

Key points
- Animals often compete with each other for food, territories and mates.
- Animals have adaptations that make them good competitors.

Summary answers

1 **a** Any suitable examples, such as lions, cheetahs and leopards etc.

   b Any suitable examples, such as rabbits, limpets on a sea shore.

   c If anything happens to their food supply, such as another animal eating it, fire or disease, then they will starve.

2 **a** Fighting: strength, antlers, teeth, etc.

   Displaying: spectacular appearance, colours, part of body to display (e.g. peacock's tail).

   b The answer to this will depend on the method selected for the first part of the answer.

   Fighting: advantages – possibility of winning lots of mates, becoming dominant, fathering lots of offspring, females don't usually have any choice, preventing others from mating. Disadvantages are that the animal could be hurt or killed, needs lots of body resources to grow antlers and to fight etc.

   Display: advantages – don't risk getting hurt, possibility of attracting several mates.

   Disadvantages – uses up lots of resources to grow feathers/ carry out displays, females usually choose and may not get noticed, vulnerable to disease or lack of food so don't produce good display, need to be seen. Any sensible points.

3 **a** Quite small, moves stealthily, so hard for mice to see and hear, sharp teeth to kill mice quickly, good eyesight to see small prey and judge distances when pouncing and hearing to pick up the sounds of mice in the undergrowth/grass; claws to help trap/hold mouse, hunts at time mice are active to increase chance of actually finding mice.

   b Special teeth to grind grass and break open cells, ability to run fast away from predators to avoid being caught, good all-round eyesight to detect predators creeping up, good hearing to detect predators, etc.

   c Fast to catch prey, good hearing and good eyesight to increase chances of seeing/hearing prey, eyes on front of head to give binocular vision to judge distance when pouncing on prey, sharp teeth and claws to catch, hold and kill prey, camouflage so prey doesn't notice predator creeping up.

   d Teeth and gut adapted to eating plants – crushing the cells to release the cell contents/breaking down cellulose cell walls, ability to reach the top of trees (long neck or good at climbing) to get to the tender leaves, ability to grip on to branches to get to the tender leaves/hold them to pull off the tree, possibly use tail for balance to get to the top of the tree.

B1 4.5

Competition in plants

Learning objectives

Students should learn:

- how plants compete with each other for water and nutrients from the soil
- how plants compete for light.

Learning outcomes

Most students should be able to:

- explain why plants need light
- explain why plants need nutrients (minerals)
- suggest the factors for which plants are competing in a given habitat.

Some students should also be able to:

- suggest why some plants are better competitors in a given habitat
- evaluate the strategies used by plants to make them successful competitors, e.g. seed dispersal mechanisms.

Support

- Supply students with a collection of seeds/fruits and ask them to match a dispersal/distribution method to each one. Sycamore, burdock, dandelion, strawberry, nuts and tomatoes are good examples.
- You could also give them some dandelion heads full of seeds and getting them to see how far the seeds will spread in different wind intensities. Use a small electric fan with a variable speed adjustment. Be aware of any hay fever or nut allergies.

Extend

- Students could be asked to find the best wing surface area to weight ratio for sycamore seeds by making small models from paper and paperclips. Provide them with a template for the wing, digital balances and litter pickers for dropping from a chosen height.
- Students could be provided with fruiting heads of dandelion and asked to design and carry out an experiment to investigate the rate of descent of the dandelion 'parachutes'.

Specification link-up: Biology B1.4

- Plants often compete with each other for light and space, and for water and nutrients from the soil. *[B1.4.1 b)]*
- Suggest the factors for which organisms are competing in a given habitat. *[B1.4]*

    Controlled Assessment: B4.1 Plan practical ways to develop and test candidates' own scientific ideas *[B4.1.1 a) b)]*; B4.3 Collect primary and secondary data *[B4.3.2 a)]*; B4.4 Select and process primary and secondary data *[B4.4.1 a)]*, *[B4.4.2 b)]*; B4.5 Analyse and interpret primary and secondary data. *[B4.5.3 a)]*, *[B4.5.4 a)]*

Lesson structure

Starters

How do coconut trees disperse their seeds? – Have a coconut complete with husk. Show the students the coconut, float it in a bucket of water and lead them into a discussion of seed distribution techniques. *(5 minutes)*

Seed dispersal – Have a range of seeds and fruits around the room, labelled with numbers. As the students enter the room, hand each one a list of numbers and get them to write the method of dispersal against each number using W (for wind), A (for animal) or E (for explosive). Students can be supported by providing them with a crib sheet for features of each type of seed distribution. Students can be extended by asking them to rate the relative efficiency of the various seed dispersal mechanisms. On completion of the exercise, ask the students to devise a plan for an experiment to investigate the relative efficiency of various seed dispersal mechanisms. *(10 minutes)*

Main

- There is an opportunity to investigate competition in plants. A spacing trial can be set up using radishes in late spring to early autumn. (See 'Practical support'.) 'How Science Works' concepts, such as experimental design, predicted outcomes, recording measurements and drawing conclusions can be reinforced here. Focus on one aspect you wish to develop.
- You might also wish to look at competition between weeds and crop plants (see 'Practical support'). Lead a discussion of the results prior to the students writing up a report. Experiments involving the growth of plants need time to yield results, so this should be planned ahead.
- Ask the question, 'Do plants shade out the competition?' Measure the surface area of nettle leaves growing in shady conditions and compare with the surface area of nettle leaves growing in brightly lit conditions. Squared paper can be used to measure leaf surface area or rubbings taken and light meters or data loggers used to record light intensity. This is a good opportunity to select 'How Science Works' concepts to teach. Predictions can be made and the results plotted as light intensity against surface area. Variable warning! There are some complex variables here: it is best to stick to the light intensity and pick leaves at the same height above the ground.

Plenaries

Competition! Competition! – Give the students a fixed time limit (the exact amount of time will vary with the ability level) and get them to fill in a missing words sentence '… competes with … for … .' Copy this line lots of times onto a sheet of paper. Give each student a copy. They have to fill in as many examples as they can in the given time. When time is up, the student with the most valid competition examples wins a small prize. *(5 minutes)*

What to do about weeds – What advice would you give gardeners who want to avoid weeds amongst their vegetables? Students can be supported by asking them to design a poster telling gardeners how to avoid problems with weeds. Give them a list of ideas, some desirable and some not so desirable, from which they choose the most sensible. Students can be extended by discussing their own ideas, giving reasons for their suggestions and designing a pamphlet to be displayed in garden centres. *(10 minutes)*

Practical support

Investigating competition in plants
Equipment and materials required

Balance for weighing seedlings; for each group or demonstration: radish seeds, potting compost, small trays.

Details

Plant seeds into small trays of moist potting compost at increasing distances apart on both *x*- and *y*-axes of the trays. The distances should be clearly marked along the sides of the trays, so that the experiment can be replicated. The trays should be watered regularly and kept in the same conditions of light and temperature. Using a 'watermoat' would help uneven watering. Weigh the seedlings, or plants, when grown to find the ideal spacing. This can be carried out on a larger scale with plants in a school garden or with rapid-cycling brassicas under a light bank at any time of year.

Investigating competition between weeds and crop plants
Equipment and materials required

Identical small pots, compost, radishes, a light box of the sort recommended by Science And Plants in Schools (SAPS) for their 'Rapid-cycling Brassicas'.

Details

Fill a number of identical small pots with compost and sow radishes and 'weed' (any other seeds such as marigolds etc.) seeds at different densities e.g. one radish to ten weeds, five radishes to five weeds, etc. Water the pots regularly and keep all other conditions (light, temperature) the same. A light box ensures even light distribution. Harvest the radishes at the appropriate time and compare the mass of radishes harvested at the different densities. The weeds could also be harvested and their wet mass determined, so that this can be compared with the mass of the radishes.

Adaptation for survival

B1 4.5 — Competition in plants

Learning objectives
- What do plants compete for?
- How do plants compete?

Practical

Investigating competition in plants

Carry out an investigation to look at the effect of competition on plants. Set up two trays of seeds – one crowded and one spread out. Then monitor the plants' height and wet mass (mass after watering). Keep all of the conditions – light level, the amount of water and nutrients available and the temperature – exactly the same for both sets of plants. The differences in their growth will be the result of overcrowding and competition for resources in one of the groups. The data show growth of tree seedlings. You can get results in days rather than months by using cress seeds.

Plants compete fiercely with each other. They compete for:
- light for photosynthesis, to make food using energy from sunlight
- water for photosynthesis and to keep their tissues rigid and supported
- nutrients (minerals) so they can make all the chemicals they need in their cells
- space to grow, allowing their roots to take in water and nutrients, and their leaves to capture light.

a What do plants compete with each other for?

Why do plants compete?

Just like animals, plants are in competition both with other species of plants and with their own species. Big, tall plants such as trees take up a lot of water and nutrients from the soil. They also prevent light from reaching the plants beneath them. So the plants around them need adaptations to help them to survive.

When a plant sheds its seeds they might land nearby. Then the parent plant will be in direct competition with its own seedlings. Because the parent plant is large and settled, it will take most of the water, nutrients and light. So the plant will deprive its own offspring of everything they need to grow successfully. The roots of some desert plants even produce a chemical that stops seeds from germinating, killing the competition even before it begins to grow!

Sometimes the seeds from a plant will all land close together, a long way from their parent. They will then compete with each other as they grow.

b Why is it important that seeds are spread as far as possible from the parent plant?

Coping with competition

Plants that grow close to other species often have adaptations which help them to avoid competition.

Small plants found in woodlands often grow and flower very early in the year. This is when plenty of light gets through the bare branches of the trees. The dormant trees take very little water out of the soil. The leaves shed the previous autumn have rotted down to provide nutrients in the soil. Plants like snowdrops, anemones and bluebells are all adapted to take advantage of these things. They flower, set seeds and die back again before the trees are in full leaf.

Another way plants compete successfully is by having different types of roots. Some plants have shallow roots taking water and nutrients from near the surface of the soil. Others have long, deep roots, which go far underground. Both compete successfully for what they need without affecting the other.

If one plant is growing in the shade of another, it may grow taller to reach the light. It may also grow leaves with a bigger surface area to take advantage of all the light it does get.

Some plants are adapted to prevent animals from eating them. They may have thorns, like the African acacia or the blackberry. They may make poisons that mean they taste very bitter or make the animals that eat them ill. Either way they compete successfully because they are less likely to be eaten than other plants.

c How can short roots help a plant to compete successfully?

Spreading the seeds

To reproduce successfully, a plant has to avoid competition with its own seedlings. Many plants use the wind to help them spread their seeds as far as possible. They produce fruits or seeds with special adaptations for flight to carry their seeds away. Examples of this are the parachutes of the dandelion 'clock' and the winged seeds of the sycamore tree.

d How do the fluffy parachutes of dandelion seeds help the seeds to spread out?

Some plants use mini-explosions to spread their seeds. The pods dry out, twist and pop, flinging the seeds out and away.

Juicy berries, fruits and nuts are adaptations to tempt animals to eat them. The fruit is digested and the tough seeds are deposited well away from the parent plant in their own little pile of fertiliser!

Fruits that are sticky or covered in hooks get caught up in the fur or feathers of a passing animal. They are carried around until they fall off hours or even days later.

Sometimes the seeds of several different plants land on the soil and start to grow together. The plants that grow fastest will compete successfully against the slower-growing plants. For example:
- The plants that get their roots into the soil first will get most of the available water and nutrients.
- The plants that open their leaves fastest will be able to photosynthesise and grow faster still, depriving the competition of light.

Figure 1 Plants have different types of roots to compete for water and nutrients in the soil

Figure 2 The winged seeds of the sycamore tree

Figure 3 Coconuts will float for weeks or even months on ocean currents, which can carry them hundreds of miles from their parents – and any other coconuts!

Summary questions

1 a How can plants overcome the problems of growing in the shade of another plant?
  b How do bluebell plants grow and flower successfully in spite of living under large trees in a wood?

2 a Why is it so important that plants spread their seeds successfully?
  b Give three examples of successful adaptations for spreading seeds.

3 The dandelion is a successful weed. Carry out some research and evaluate the adaptations that make it a better competitor than other plants on a school field.

Key points
- Plants often compete with each other for light, for water and for nutrients (minerals) from the soil.
- Plants have many adaptations that make them good competitors.

Further teaching suggestions

Light intensity
- Use data loggers to investigate light intensity in different sites in the school garden or on school grounds. Correlate light intensity with the type of vegetation present.

Answers to in-text questions

a Light, water, minerals/nutrients and space.

b So that there is no competition between the parent and the offspring.

c The plant roots can take in water and minerals near the surface of the soil, while other plants with deeper roots take water from lower down in the soil so competition is reduced.

d The fluffy parachutes help the seeds to float in the air, so that they can be blown as far as possible from the parent plant.

Summary answers

1 **a** May grow taller, may have deeper/shallower roots, flower at a different time of year. May grow leaves with a bigger surface area to absorb more light.

  b They produce flowers before the oak tree's leaves have grown to full size, so they are not shaded.

2 **a** To avoid competition between the seedlings and the parent plants and to avoid competition between the seedlings, as far as possible.

  b Any three suitable adaptations – look for different ones, for example, fluffy seeds, winged seeds, seeds in berries/fruits which are eaten, explosive seeds, sticky seeds, hooked seeds, seeds that float on water. Any other sensible suggestion.

3 For example, deep taproot (difficult to remove, can regenerate well if severed); low rosette of leaves (avoids blades of lawnmowers and grazing animals) long flowering period, produces large numbers of seeds, very effective wind dispersal of seed over a large area.

B1 4.6

How do you survive?

Learning objectives

Students should learn:

- that organisms can survive in very unusual conditions
- that wherever they live, organisms are competing for the things they need to survive.

Learning outcomes

Most students should be able to:

- describe some adaptations of organisms to unusual conditions
- explain that adaptations are essential for survival.

Some students should also be able to:

- apply their knowledge to interpret the survival strategies of organisms.

Support

- Get students to stick into their notebooks two coloured strips of paper cut to scale – one to show their reaction time and another to show that of the star nosed mole. Put them on a pair of axes and draw in the scale (some students may need a printed one).

Extend

- Give the students access to some neuroscience materials on myelination of neurons and the effect it has on speeding up the transmission of impulses.

Specification link-up: Biology B1.4

- Organisms, including microorganisms have features (adaptations) that enable them to survive in the conditions in which they normally live. *[B1.4.1 d)]*
- Suggest how organisms are adapted to the conditions in which they live. *[B1.4]*
- Suggest the factors for which organisms are competing in a given habitat. *[B1.4]*
- Some organisms live in environments that are very extreme. Extremophiles may be tolerant to high levels of salt, high temperatures or high pressures. *[B1.4.1 e)]*
- Observe the adaptations, e.g. body shape, of a range of organisms from different habitats. *[B1.4]*
- Develop an understanding of the ways in which adaptations enable organisms to survive. *[B1.4]*

Lesson structure

Starters

Pick an organism – Have the names and pictures of a number of organisms on playing card size pieces of card, one per card. Hand out sets of these to groups. Students to take turns in picking a card and stating the survival strategy for the organism shown. *(5 minutes)*

That's pretty harsh! – Put a circus of information points up around the room, each with an example of an organism living in harsh conditions (ice fish, thermophilic bacteria in hot pools, *Helicobacter pylori* living in stomach acid, etc.) Students can be supported by being given a prepared sheet and ticking off the name of the organisms. Students can be extended by writing their own notes and explanations of the difficulties the environments would present. *(10 minutes)*

Main

- If available, watch sections from the 2009 BBC wildlife series *Life* episode 2 'Reptiles and amphibians' where Komodo dragons bite the heel of a water buffalo and wait for three weeks while the infected saliva they introduced causes septicaemia and weakens the buffalo to a point where they can kill it.

- Show video footage of life around black smoker thermal vents. Look especially at the giant tube worms, getting the students to realise that they are 2 metres plus in length. Explain about hydrogen sulphide gas acting as a nutrient for bacteria which line their insides (they have no mouth, anus or intestines).

- Watch video Nature 'The Queen of trees' 2005 if available. This covers the remarkable story of the African sycamore fig and the ecosystem it provides, especially the extraordinary fig wasp, so small it can fly through the eye of a needle.

- Use the internet to find images and video clips of Venus flytraps in action. Using a real one, investigate whether they can count the trigger hairs by touching. Use a flexicam or similar digital video camera to project the test.

- Explain the idea of polymorphism and describe how it works as a survival strategy. Mention the European banded snails and show examples or pictures of examples. If possible, carry out a search for banded snails in your area and discuss the different types found. How do they survive?

Plenaries

Life on Europa? – Under a thick layer of ice, Europa, the sixth moon of Jupiter, has deep oceans of liquid water. It is speculated that life may exist around hydrothermal vents at the base of this ocean. Think about what the conditions there must be like. Students can be supported by giving them a list of the conditions and a list of adaptations to choose from. Students can be extended by getting them to write a list of the conditions and speculating as to what adaptations organisms might need to have to survive there. *(5 minutes)*

The fastest predator – From the internet, locate an interactive reflex timer programme. Time how fast the students can respond. Compare this with the reaction time of the Star nosed mole. If the timer used makes a sound, carry out the programme blindfolded as this more clearly imitates how the star-nosed mole catches its prey. *(10 minutes)*

Further teaching suggestions

Insectivorous plants
- There are a number of insectivorous plants with different mechanisms for trapping their prey. Some good sources of information are Kew Gardens, Darwin's book *Insectivorous Plants* and the internet.

The most amazing plants in the world?
- Find out more about amazing plants and the work of Dr Peter Scott on 'Resurrection plants' at the University of Sussex.

Crops for the future?
- Encourage students to think about the types of crops grown in areas prone to drought and the staple foods of the people who live in such regions. What adaptations might be needed?

Fact files
- Direct students to find out more about some of the plant species which have become problems because they are such good competitors' e.g. Japanese knotweed, water hyacinth and milfoil. An internet search of invasive plants could yield information on these examples.

Highly adapted animals
- More examples of highly adapted animals could be researched. Examples could include the vicuna (altitude), camels (arid conditions), springtails (low temperatures) and social insects.

B1 4.6 How do you survive?

Learning objectives
- How do organisms survive in very unusual conditions?
- What factors are organisms competing for in a habitat?

So far in this chapter we have looked at lots of different ways in which living organisms are adapted. This helps them to survive and reproduce wherever they live. We have looked at why they need to compete successfully against their own species and others. Now we are going to consider three case studies of adaption in living organisms.

Figs and fig wasps

There are about 700 different species of fig trees. Each one has its own species of pollinating wasps, without which the trees will die. The fig flowers of the trees are specially adapted so that they attract the right species of wasp.

Female fig wasps have specially shaped heads for getting into fig flowers. They also have **ovipositors** that allow them to place their eggs deep in the flowers of the fig tree.

Male fig wasps vary. Some species can fly but others are adapted to live in a fig fruit all their life. If they are lucky, a female wasp will arrive in the flower and the male will fertilise her. After this he digs an escape tunnel for the female through the fruit and dies himself! The male wasp has special adaptations (such as the loss of his wings and very small eyes) which help him move around inside the fig fruit to find a female.

Figure 1 A fig tree

Figure 2 A female (top) and male (bottom) fig wasp

If a fig tree cannot attract the right species of wasp, it will never be able to reproduce. In fact in some areas the trees are in danger of extinction because the wasp populations are being wiped out.

The fastest predator in the world?

It takes you about 650 milliseconds to react to a crisis. But the star-nosed mole takes only 230 milliseconds from the moment it first touches its prey to gulping it down. That's faster than the human eye can see!

What makes this even more amazing is that star-nosed moles live underground and are almost totally blind. Their main sense organ is a crown of fleshy tendrils around the nose – incredibly sensitive to touch and smell but very odd to look at. The ultra-sensitive tendrils can try out 13 possible targets every second.

It seems likely that they have adapted to react so quickly because they can't see what is going on. They need to grab their prey as soon as possible after they touch it. If they don't it might move away or try to avoid them, and they wouldn't know where it had gone.

Figure 3 The star-nosed mole

A carnivorous plant

Venus flytraps are plants that grow on bogs. Bogs are wet and their peaty soil has very few nutrients in it. This makes it a difficult place for plants to live.

The Venus flytrap has special 'traps' that contain sweet smelling nectar. They sit wide open showing their red insides. Insects are attracted to the colour and the smell. Inside the trap are many small, sensitive hairs. As the insect moves about to find the nectar, it will brush against these hairs. Once the hairs have been touched, the trap is triggered. It snaps shut and traps the insect inside.

Special enzymes then digest the insect inside the trap. The Venus flytrap uses the nutrients from the digested bodies of its victims. This is in place of the nutrients that it cannot get from the poor bog soil. After the insect has been digested, the trap reopens ready to try again.

Figure 4 The Venus flytrap – an insect-eating plant

Activity

Case studies
- For each of these three case studies, list how the organisms are adapted for their habitat and how these adaptations help them to compete successfully against both their own species and other species.
- Choose three organisms that you know something about – or find out about three organisms which interest you. Make your own fact file on their adaptations and how these adaptations help them to compete successfully. Include at least one plant.

Summary questions
1 Explain how both of the animals featured compete successfully for food.
2 Why could any species of fig tree or fig wasp easily die out? Give a reason for each.
3 Carry out research to explain the adaptations of a giraffe and why they help it to compete successfully with other animals living in the same area.

Key points
- Organisms have adaptations which enable them to survive in the conditions in which they normally live.
- Plants often compete with each other for light, water and nutrients from the soil.
- Animals often compete with each other for food, mates and territory.

Summary answers

1 Fig wasps have exclusive relationship with species of fig tree which means they are always close to their source of food. Star-nosed moles have finger-like sensory tendrils. They are very sensitive to touch and smell and have very rapid reflex reactions.

2 Trees are vulnerable because they often have only one pollinator. So if anything happens to that species of fig wasp e.g. new disease or predator – the tree will not be pollinated and so the species of fig could die out.

Wasps are vulnerable because one species of tree is their only food source. In some cases, the tree is the only place for meeting a mate – so any damage/disease/felling of trees could lead to extinction of wasps.

3 They are very tall and have a very long neck and tongue. This means they can reach leaves much higher from the ground than many other animals. They also have very long legs so they can cover the ground quickly and economically, moving from food source to food source. Their size means that they are unlikely to be attacked by predators. Any other sensible points – look to give extra credit to students who go beyond the long neck/tongue aspects of the animal.

B1 4.7 Measuring environmental change

Learning objectives

Students should learn:
- some factors that affect the distribution of living organisms
- that living and non-living factors can cause environmental changes
- that non-living indicators can be used to measure environmental changes
- how living organisms can be used as indicators of pollution.

Learning outcomes

Most students should be able to:
- list some factors that affect the distribution of living organisms
- describe some living and non-living factors that cause environmental changes
- measure some environmental changes using non-living indicators
- describe an example of a living organism that can be used as a pollution indicator.

Some students should also be able to:
- analyse data on changes in environmental conditions.

Study tip

Students often get confused when considering invertebrate indicators. They assume large numbers means more oxygen. They need to understand that some invertebrates, e.g. blood worms, survive well in low-oxygen concentrations.

Answers to in-text questions

a Temperature.
b Any suitable examples of each, for example: Living – new predator, new pathogen, food or competition; Non-living: temperature, amount of sunlight or rainfall.

Support

- Make a set of cards depicting non-living environmental factors and another set showing measuring equipment. Ask students to match the correct equipment to the factor.

Extend

- Get students to research the life cycles of lichens and their importance as colonisers of bare rock.

Specification link-up: Biology B1.4

- … plants may be adapted to cope with specific features of their environment, e.g. thorns, poisons…. [B1.4.1 g)]
- Animals and plants are subjected to environmental changes. Such changes may be caused by living or non-living factors such as a change in a competitor, or in the average temperature or rainfall. [B1.4.2 b)]
- Living organisms can be used as indicators of pollution:
  - lichens can be used as air pollution indicators, particularly of the concentration of sulfur dioxide in the atmosphere
  - invertebrate animals can be used as water pollution indicators and are used as indicators of the concentration of dissolved oxygen in water. [B1.4.2 c)]
- Environmental changes can be measured using non-living indicators such as oxygen levels, temperature and rainfall. [B1.4.2 d)]

Lesson structure

Starters

What's it like outside? – Get the students to make a list of all the environmental parameters they can think of to describe their surroundings. Support students by having a display of measuring devices, such as measuring cylinders, rulers, maximum–minimum thermometers and perhaps an anemometer and a sundial. Extend students by asking them to suggest a measuring device for each parameter they come up with and give an estimate of the range of values they may find for each parameter. Read out and compare the lists. *(5 minutes)*

Link up – Ask the students to compete with each other to name pairs of organisms. Each pair of organisms should be linked through one affecting the other in some way, e.g. hawks and sparrows – the link is the hawks eat the sparrows. See if they can come up with a number of different types of interaction, not just feeding relationships. *(10 minutes)*

Main

- The use of equipment to measure non-living indicators of change can be demonstrated. Show the students maximum–minimum thermometers, rainfall gauges and oxygen meters and discuss with them how these can be used.
- There are two suggested activities here: one measuring oxygen levels and another measuring temperature and rainfall. Both activities involve fieldwork.
- Produce a PowerPoint presentation or exposition on lichens. Include some photographs of different forms and different places where lichens are found. Explain that lichens are sensitive to the levels of sulfur dioxide in the atmosphere and can therefore be used to indicate levels of pollution in an area. Provide the students with a worksheet which can be completed as the lesson proceeds.
- Consider the idea of lichens as pollution indicators by investigating the distribution of lichens on the trees in your neighbourhood. Provide the students with pictures of a couple of lichens, one that is fairly common and tolerant (the yellow *Xanthoria*) and a foliose or leafy type. Get the students to carry out a survey of lichens on the trees in the school grounds or a local park. You could do a preliminary survey and find out which species are likely to occur, so that the pictures and identification features are relevant to what they might find.
- Alternatively, a survey could be made of lichens on buildings and walls if it is more convenient. Discuss the results and consider the level of sulfur dioxide pollution in the area.
- As well as lichens, invertebrate species are indicators of pollution. Carry out a survey of the number of different species of invertebrates in the local pond or stream. The cleaner the water, the greater the number of species. Some species are only found in the cleanest, least polluted water and some are only found in the dirtiest, most polluted water.

Plenaries

Environmental charades – Write a list of the key words from the topic on the board. Select a student to stand up and using mime indicate which key word they have chosen. Wipe that parameter off the board when complete. Repeat for the rest of the key words until two are left then get two students to do these together; peers have to guess which one is which. *(5 minutes)*

Crossword – Use an internet-based crossword compiler (there are many free examples of these) to create a crossword based on the key words used in the lesson. Students can be supported by using easier clues and filling in the vowels. Students can be extended by using cryptic clues or asking the students to compile the clues themselves. *(10 minutes)*

Practical support

Indicators of pollution levels

Equipment and materials required
Pond nets (one per three students if possible, buckets, plastic containers, Petri dishes with lids, identification charts (laminated) and books, hand lenses, clipboards, pens and paper.

Details
Choose a suitable day regarding weather. It's a good idea to do a dipping exercise yourself in advance to find out what is there. If working with large groups it may be advisable to split the class in two.

Then, working with a colleague, do the practical pond dipping half a class at a time. Equipment needed should be gathered in advance. Run through behavioural expectations in advance, emphasising safety aspects of and due consideration for the creatures. Space the students around the pond. Collect organisms, observe them and identify, recording your findings. Ensure that you return the specimens to the pond before leaving and that they do not get too stressed.

Safety: Please check LA (Local Authorities) policy on school visits, with reference to safety and procedure. Students should be warned to wear suitable footwear and clothing. Wash hands after contact with pond water.

B1 4.7 — Measuring environmental change

Learning objectives
- What affects the distribution of living things?
- What causes environmental changes?
- How can we measure environmental changes?

Have you noticed different types of animals and plants when you travel to different places? The distribution of living organisms depends on the environmental conditions and varies around the world.

Factors affecting the distribution of organisms

Non-living factors have a big effect on where organisms live. The average temperature or average rainfall will have a big impact on what can survive. You don't find polar bears in countries where the average temperature is over 20 °C, for example! The amount of rainfall affects the distribution of both plants and animals. Light, pH and the local climate all influence where living organisms are found.

The distribution of different species of animals in water is closely linked to the oxygen levels. Salmon can only live in water with lots of dissolved oxygen, but bloodworms can survive in very low oxygen levels.

Living organisms also affect the distribution of other living organisms. So, for example, koala bears are only found where eucalyptus trees grow. Parasites only live where they can find a host.

One species of ant eats nectar produced by the flowers of the swollen-thorn acacia tree. The ants hollow out the vicious thorns and live in them. So any animal biting the tree not only gets the sharp thorns, they get a mouth full of angry ants as well. The distribution of the ants depends on the trees.

Figure 1 The distribution of bullhorn acacia ants depends on where the swollen-thorn acacia trees grow

a Which non-living environmental factor affects the distribution of polar bears?

CD links
For more information about how environmental changes affect organisms, see B3 chapter 4 How humans can affect the environment.

Environmental changes

When the environment changes, it can cause a change in the distribution of living organisms in the area. Non-living factors often cause these changes in an environment.

The average temperature may rise or fall. The oxygen concentration in water may change. A change in the amount of sunlight, the strength of the wind or the average rainfall may affect an environment. Any of these factors can affect the distribution of living organisms.

Living factors can also cause a change in the environment where an organism lives, affecting distribution. A new type of predator may move into an area. A new disease-causing pathogen may appear and wipe out a species of animal or plant. Different plants may appear and provide food or a home for a whole range of different species.

b Give an example of a living and a non-living factor that can change an environment.

Measuring environmental change k

When an environment changes, the living organisms in it are affected. If the change is big enough, the distribution of animals or plants in an area may change.

You can measure environmental change using non-living indicators. You can measure factors such as average rainfall, temperature, oxygen levels, pH and pollutant levels in water or the air, and much more. All sorts of different instruments are available to do these measurements. These range from simple rain gauges and thermometers to oxygen meters and dataloggers used in schools.

You can also use the changing distribution of living organisms as an indicator of environmental change. Living organisms are particularly good as indicators of pollution.

Lichens grow on places like rocks, roofs and the bark of trees. They are very sensitive to air pollution, particularly levels of sulfur dioxide in the atmosphere. When the air is clean, many different types of lichen grow. The more polluted the air, the fewer lichen species there will be. So a field survey on the numbers and types of lichen can be used to give an indication of air pollution. The data can be used to study local sites or to compare different areas of the country.

In the same way you can use invertebrate animals as water pollution indicators. The cleaner the water, the more species you will find. Some species of invertebrates are only found in the cleanest waters. Others can be found even in very polluted waters. Counting the different types of species gives a good indication of pollution levels, and can be used to monitor any changes.

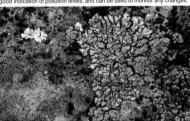

Practical

Indicators of pollution levels

Investigate both the variety of lichens in your local area and the number of invertebrate species in your local pond or stream. This will give you an idea of pollution levels in your area if you compare them to national figures.

Figure 2 Lichens grow well where the air is clean. In an area polluted with sulfur dioxide there would be fewer species. Lichens are good indicators of pollution.

Summary questions

1 Copy and complete these sentences using the words below:
indicators   distribution   pollution   organisms
Changes in the environment affect the .... of living .... This means living organisms can be used as .... of ....

2 Give three different methods you could use to collect environmental data. For each method, comment on its reliability and usefulness as a source of evidence of environmental change.

Key points
- Animals and plants may be adapted to cope with specific features of their environment, e.g. thorns, poisons and warning colours.
- Environmental changes may be caused by living or non-living factors.
- Environmental changes can be measured using non-living indicators.
- Living organisms can be used as indicators of pollution.

Further teaching suggestions

Further lichen surveys
- The lichen surveys could be extended by comparing a woodland with a suburban street, or a cemetery (look at the gravestones). A comparison of trees in woodland with trees in a suburban area could yield interesting results.

Discussion on how plants and animals cope with their environment
- Students should discuss how animals and plants cope with features of their environment, such as thorns, poisons and warning colours. Consider the examples in the student text and research other examples.

Internet investigation into symbiosis
- Get the students to carry out an internet investigation into organisms that have deeply involved relationships with other ones. Try using 'symbiosis' as a search term.

Investigation into the behaviour of woodlice
- Investigation of the behaviour of woodlice in choice chambers can show how organisms will move to the conditions to which they are best suited.

Summary answers

1 distribution, organisms, indicators, pollution

2 Methods along with evaluation of usefulness – should include at least one physical factor and one example of a bio indicator.

Methods could include: measuring a non-living factor, e.g. rainfall, temperature, oxygen levels, levels of pollutants. For each method student must choose a suitable method of measuring changes in the factor they choose, e.g. rain gauge for rainfall, oxygen meter and datalogging for oxygen levels. They need to show that they realise that these measurements need to be taken over time, and using the same equipment to build up a record of data over time.

Measuring the changing distribution of living organisms is another way. This can be done using quadrats, field surveys – again data collected over time in the same place in the same way examples could be lichens on trees, invertebrates in water. In that case students need to mention capture techniques, identification keys – again over time – measuring number of different species found and the types of different species is also indicative of the cleanliness of the water. Any other valid suggestions.

B1 4.8

The impact of change

Learning objectives

Students should learn:

- how changes in the environment can affect the distribution of living organisms.

Learning outcomes

Most students should be able to:

- explain that environmental changes can effect the distribution of living organisms

- describe some changes in both living and non-living factors that can affect distribution

- evaluate data concerned with environmental change on the distribution of living organisms.

Some students should also be able to:

- evaluate data concerned with the effect of environmental change on the behaviour of living organisms.

Specification link-up: Biology B1.4

- Changes in the environment affect the distribution of living organisms. [B1.4.2 a)]
- Animals and plants are subjected to environmental changes. Such changes may be caused by living or non-living factors such as a change in a competitor, or in the average temperature or rainfall. [B1.4.2 b)]
- Evaluate data concerned with the effect of environmental changes on the distribution and behaviour of living organisms. [B1.4]

Lesson structure

Starters

To bee or not to bee – Discuss with students the importance of bees both in making honey and as pollinators. Show some animation or video footage of bees pollinating flowers. Ensure that the students realise the importance of pollination. Ask them what would happen if there were no more bees? Get them to draw out a chain of consequences. Students can be supported by providing a list of consequences which they can put in the correct order. Students can be extended by considering which crops would disappear and what the alternatives might be. *(5 minutes)*

"When I were a lad..." – Ask the students to recount any stories their parents or grandparents may have told them about how things are different these days compared to the environment when they were young. Compile a collective list for the class. *(10 minutes)*

Main

- Provide exposition as to the changing environment and how it is affecting the distribution of species (the birds and the bees).

- Break the students into small groups. Give each an A3 sheet of paper with a large blank 5×5 squares frame in it. Ask them to devise a snakes and ladders style board game with snakes representing hazards for bees, such as diseases, chemicals and changing patterns of flowering. The ladders can be things that benefit the bees, such as disease-resistant strains, crop plants and successful swarming.

- Give the students data on the declining bee population in a table. They are to turn this into a graph, and extrapolate this to check the possible date for bee decline to be complete in the UK, i.e. no more bees by 2018.

- Changes in the concentrations of chemicals in the environment can cause changes in the populations of living organisms. The effect of changes in phosphate levels can alter the oxygen concentration in water. Set up containers of algae in water containing different levels of phosphate. Observe the effect on the growth of the algae. Monitor the oxygen levels using oxygen probes.

- Produce a poem to encourage young people to value our bee population.

Plenaries

Here today gone tomorrow – Show a photo of a mammoth tusk being brought up in fishing nets from the bottom of the North Sea. This can be linked with clips from the film *Ice Age*. Discuss how climate change is a normal part of the way the Earth works. *(5 minutes)*

What's the fuss? – Imagine you have a neighbour who doesn't care much about the environment. They are reading a newspaper headline about the decline of the bee population. They state that they 'don't see what all the fuss is about, bees are just a pest anyway'. How would you go about convincing them that they are wrong on this? Students can be supported by finding and reading out sections from the main text to get across the idea of bee preservation. Students can be extended by getting them to produce convincing and credible arguments in a friendly and persuasive manner. *(10 minutes)*

Support

- Show students pictures of dinosaurs and the type of vegetation which existed when they roamed the Earth. Ask them to suggest why there are no dinosaurs now. What has changed? Was it the climate or was it something else? Get them to express their ideas as to what does cause major changes.

Extend

- Ask 'What happened to the quagga?' An internet search will provide information about this animal, why it died out and attempts made to breed them again.

Further teaching suggestions

Linking data
● Look at some data regarding the increase in number of buzzards in the UK and link this to their making use of road kill as a change in feeding habits.

Changing patterns of migration
● Research the internet for evidence that climate change can affect the migration of birds and other animals.

ICT link-up
● Carry out computer simulations to model the effect on organisms from changes to the environment.

Compiling case histories
● Do changes in non-living and living factors in the environment affect the behaviour of living organisms? Students to research and compile case histories of such changes.

B1 4.8   The impact of change

Learning objectives
● How do changes in the environment affect the distribution of living organisms?
● How reproducible are the data about the effect of environmental change on living organisms?

Changing birds of Britain

Temperatures in the UK seem to be rising. Many people like the idea – summer barbeques and low heating bills. But rising temperatures will have a big impact on many living organisms. We could see changes in the distribution of many species. Food plants and animals might become more common, or die out, in different conditions.

The Dartford warbler is small brown bird that breeds mainly in southern Europe. A small population lived in Dorset and Hampshire. By 1963, two very cold winters left just 11 breeding pairs in the UK. But temperatures have increased steadily since. Dartford warblers are now found in Wales, the Midlands and East Anglia. If climate change continues, Dartford warblers could spread through most of England and Ireland. However, in Spain the numbers are dropping rapidly – 25% in the last 10 years – as it becomes too warm. Scientists can simulate the distribution of birds as the climate changes. They predict that by the end of the century Spain could lose most of its millions of Dartford warblers.

Scientists predict that by the end of this century, if climate change continues at its present rate, the range of the average bird species will move nearly 550 km north-east. About 75% of all the birds that nest in Europe are likely to have smaller ranges as a result and many species will be lost for good.

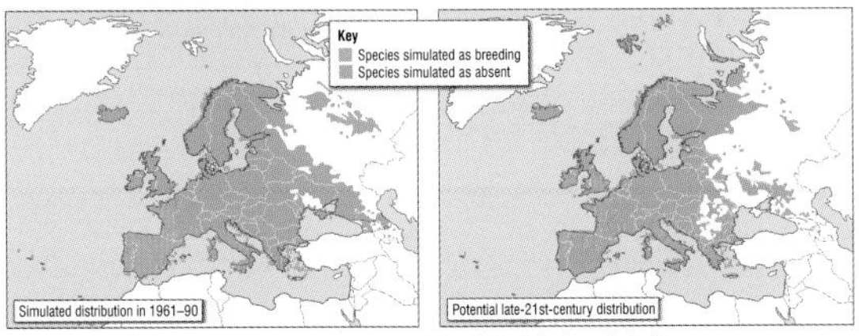

Figure 1 The Dartford warbler

Key
■ Species simulated as breeding
■ Species simulated as absent

Simulated distribution in 1961–90

Potential late-21st-century distribution

Figure 2 The maps show how scientists think the distribution of these birds might change in the future

Table 1 Numbers of breeding pairs of Dartford warblers in the UK

Year	Number of breeding pairs
1961	450
1963	11
1974	560
1984	420
1994	1890
2010	3208

Activity
● Plot a bar graph to show the change in population of the Dartford warbler from 1961 to the present day. Draw an extra bar to show what you would expect the population to be in 2030 if climate change continues in the same way.
● Investigate the effect of climate change on the way birds migrate from one country to another and write a report for a wildlife programme or magazine.

Where are all the bees? ⓚ

All around the world honey bees are disappearing. In the UK alone, around one in five bee hives has been lost in the last few years. In the United States, around 2 million colonies of bees were lost in 3 years. The bees had been struck down by a new, mystery disease called Colony Collapse Disorder or CCD. The bees either die, or simply fail to return to the hive. Without the mass of worker bees, those bees left in the hive quickly die.

Members of the British Beekeepers Association are alarmed. They say that if hives continue to be lost at the same rate there will be no honey bees left in Britain by 2018. You might think that having fewer bees doesn't really matter. It also means honey is more expensive to buy.

In fact, bees are vitally important in plant ecology. Honey bees pollinate flowers as they collect the nectar. Without them, flowers are not pollinated and fruit does not form. Without bees as pollinators we would have no apples, raspberries, cucumbers, strawberries, peaches … the list goes on and on. There would be cereal crops, because they are pollinated by the wind, but not much else.

No one fully understands what is happening to the bees and what is changing their distribution. Scientists think that viral diseases, possibly spread by a parasitic mite, are a major cause. So living factors – the agents of disease – are causing a major change in the environment of the honey bee. This in turn is affecting their distribution.

Other living and non-living factors affecting the environment have also been suggested. Flowering patterns are changing as temperatures vary with climate change. This may affect the food supply of the bees. Farmers spray chemicals that may build up in the bees. Some people have even suggested that mobile phones affect the navigation system of the bees.

Research is continuing all over the world. Disease-resistant strains of bees are being bred. Collecting the evidence to show exactly what environmental change is affecting the honey bee population is proving to be difficult. But until we can find out, the decline of the honey bee looks as if it will continue. There is a little good news – UK numbers have recovered slightly as more people have started keeping bees, probably as a result of all the publicity.

Figure 3 Honey bees are vital pollinators. Bee-pollinated fruits are worth about £50 billion of trade every year.

Activity
● List the main suggested causes for the decline of the honey bee. Use secondary sources to investigate the current state of the research findings for each cause.
● Produce a slide show to justify the investment of research funds into the loss of honey bees. Show what is happening to the bees, the main theories about what is causing the problem and how the problem is being tackled.

Summary questions
1 Using the information on this spread, what aspect of climate change seems to be linked to a change in the distribution of British birds?
2 a Why is the loss of honey bees so important?
  b Why is it important to find out whether the environmental cause of the problem is a living or non-living factor?

Key points
● Both living and non-living factors can cause changes in the distribution of living organisms.
● Reproducible data on the effect of environmental change are not always easy to collect or interpret.

Summary answers

1 Temperature changes.

2 a Because they act as pollinators to many different plants including many food crops, especially fruit. Also loss of honey and beeswax.

  b Because the way the problem is tackled will be very different – if it is a disease caused or carried by parasitic mites, then it becomes important to eradicate or control the mites or treat the disease. If it is a physical factor then we need to look at the environment and what, if anything, can be done to improve the situation for the bees.

Summary answers

1 a D   b C   c A   d B

2 a The temperatures are too cold for reactions in the body to work and so for the organisms to survive.

   b Problems: overheating in day, too cold at night and early morning to move much, water loss.
   How they cope with problems: bask in the Sun in the morning to warm up, hide in burrows or shade of rocks to avoid heat of day and cold of night, reduce water loss by behaviour and don't sweat.

   c Large surface area: volume ratio allows them to lose heat effectively.

3 a Lots of water loss through the leaves, not much water taken up by roots.

   b Most water is lost through the leaves – less leaf surface area, less water loss.

   c Spines, rolled leaves.

   d Water storage in stems, roots or leaves, thick waxy cuticle, ability to withstand dehydration.

   e They have several different adaptations to enable them to withstand water loss/little water available (spines, water storage in stem, etc).

4 a Makes sure there is plenty of food for the animals and their young, advertise their territory to reduce conflict with predators.

   b Pandas feed almost exclusively on bamboo, so if it dies out they have no food and will die out as well. Other animals – bamboo only part of the diet so they simply eat other plants.

5 Because they are competing for exactly the same things.

6 Students use the bar charts in the practical activity on page 84 to answer these questions.

   a First month: crowded seedlings taller than spread out seedlings. Crowded seedlings shade each other so each seedling grows taller to avoid the shade. Spread seedlings don't have that pressure. But over six months, the crowded seedlings do not get light as they shade each other. They photosynthesise less so they cannot grow as tall as the spread out seedlings which can make as much food as possible.

   b i They relied mainly on the food stored in the seed – the crowded ones were taller but the spread ones had thicker stems and bigger leaves.

     ii As before the spread out seedlings get the full effect of the light and grow as well as possible making lots of new plants (and so wet mass). The crowded plants each get less light therefore less photosynthesis and less wet mass.

   c To eliminate as far as possible the effects of genetic variety in the seedlings – the bigger the sample, the more reproducible the results.

   d i Any of: light level, amount of water and nutrients available, and temperature.

     ii So that any differences would be the result of the crowding of the seedlings.

7 a New predator, new pathogen, introduction of different plants and more competition, the death of a competitor species from disease – any other sensible point.

   b Change in temperature, change in oxygen level, change in pollution levels, addition of nitrates – any other sensible point.

Summary questions 🄚

1 Match the following words to their definitions:

a	competition	A	an animal that eats plants
b	carnivore	B	an area where an animal lives and feeds
c	herbivore	C	an animal that eats meat
d	territory	D	the way animals compete with each other for food, water, space and mates

2 Cold-blooded animals like reptiles and snakes absorb heat from their surroundings and cannot move until they are warm.

   a Why do you think that there are no reptiles and snakes in the Arctic?

   b What problems do you think reptiles face in desert conditions and what adaptations could they have to cope with them?

   c Most desert animals are quite small. How does this help them survive in the heat?

3 a What are the main problems for plants living in a hot, dry climate?

   b Why does reducing the surface area of their leaves help plants to reduce water loss?

   c Describe two ways in which the surface area of the leaves of some desert plants is reduced.

   d How else are some plants adapted to cope with hot, dry conditions?

   e Why are cacti such perfect desert plants?

4 a How does marking out and defending a territory help an animal to compete successfully?

   b Bamboo plants all tend to flower and die at the same time. Why is this such bad news for pandas, but doesn't affect most other animals?

5 Why is competition between animals of the same species so much more intense than the competition between different species?

6 Use the bar charts from the practical activity on B1 4.5 to answer these questions.

   a Describe what happens to the height of both sets of seedlings over the first six months and explain why the changes take place.

   b The total wet mass of the seedlings after one month was the same whether or not they were crowded. After six months there was a big difference.

   i Why do you think both types of seedling had the same mass after one month?

   ii Explain why the seedlings that were more spread out each had more wet mass after six months.

   c When scientists carry out experiments such as the one described, they try to use large sample sizes. Why?

   d i Name a control variable mentioned in the practical

     ii Why were the other variables kept constant?

7 a Give three living factors that can change the environment and affect the distribution of living organisms.

   b Give three non-living factors that can change the environment and affect the distribution of living organisms.

8 Maize is a very important crop plant. It has many uses – it is made into cornflakes and it is also grown for animal feed. The most important part of the plant is the cob, which fetches the most money. In an experiment to find the best growing conditions, three plots of land were used. The young maize plants were grown in different densities in the three plots.
The results were as follows:

	Planting density (plants/m²)		
	10	15	20
Dry mass of shoots (kg/m²)	9.7	11.6	13.5
Dry mass of cobs (kg/m²)	6.1	4.4	2.8

   a What was the independent variable in this investigation?

   b Draw a graph to show the effect of the planting density on the mass of the cobs grown.

   c What is the pattern shown in your graph?

   d This was a fieldwork investigation. What would the experimenter have taken into account when choosing the location of the three plots?

   e Did the experimenter choose enough plots? Explain your answer.

   f What is the relationship between the mass of cobs and the mass of shoots at different planting densities?

   g The experimenter concluded that the best density for planting the maize is 10 plants per m². Do you agree with this as a conclusion? Explain your answer.

---

8 a The independent variable was planting density.

   b Graph with correctly labelled axes and points plotted accurately. Density on the x-axis and dry mass on the y-axis.

   c The pattern should show increasing density of planting reducing the dry mass of cobs.

   d The three plots should have the same type of soil, the same amount of water and similar weather patterns.

   e Three plots was too few to be certain of the pattern, five would have been better ideally with repeats.

   f As the dry mass of cobs gets less per m², the dry mass of the shoots increases.

   g It seems from this investigation to be correct, but does the pattern continue? If so, then planting fewer plants could give an even higher yield. The experimenter should investigate lower densities of planting.

Practical suggestions

Practicals	AQA	🄚	📖	⚙
Investigations of environmental conditions and organisms in a habitat such as a pond.	✓		✓	
'Hunt the cocktail stick' using red and green cocktail sticks on a green background.	✓		✓	

Practice questions k

1 The picture shows a solenodon.

Solenodons have lived on earth since the Age of the Dinosaurs. They are only found in forests in Haiti and are the only mammals which have a poisonous bite. They are rarely seen because they feed at night. They mainly eat insects and spiders.

a The solenodon has adaptations which help it to survive.
Match the adaptation to the correct letter (A,B, C, D or E) for the following:
  i   This helps the solenodon to dig its burrow.   (1)
  ii This helps the solenodon to detect its food.   (1)

b The solenodon is at risk of dying out since new animals have been taken to the islands.
Use the information and the picture to help answer the following questions.
  i   The solenodon is not adapted to flee from predators. Suggest why.   (1)
  ii If the solenodon is caught by a predator it can defend itself. Suggest how.   (1)

2 Trees that live in the rainforests are very tall and often have broad leaves. This is a problem for young trees, which do not get much light.

a Choose the correct answer to complete the sentence.
  light   nutrients   space
  Rainforest trees have broad leaves so they can compete for ....   (1)

b Choose the correct answer to complete the sentence.
  larger trees   large seeds with stored food
  Trees in the rainforest have adapted to lack of light near the ground by having ....   (1)

3 The gemsbok is a large herbivore living in dry desert regions of South Africa. It feeds on grasses that are adapted to the dry conditions by obtaining moisture from the air as it cools at night. The table below shows the water content of these grasses and the feeding activity of the gemsbok over a 24-hour period.

Time of day	% water content of grasses	% of gemsboks feeding
03.00	18	40
06.00	23	60
09.00	25	20
12.00	08	17
15.00	06	16
18.00	05	19
21.00	07	30
24.00	14	50

a i   Name the independent variable investigated.   (1)
   ii Is this a categoric, ordered, discrete or continuous variable?   (1)

b How does the water content of the grasses change throughout the 24-hour period?   (1)

c Between which recorded times are more than 30% of the gemsboks feeding?   (1)

d Suggest **three** reasons why the gemsboks benefit from feeding at this time.   (3)
AQA, 2008

93

Practice answers

1 a i D   *(1 mark)*
     ii E   *(1 mark)*

  b i any one of: poor eyesight, legs look awkward for running, no natural predators, other sensible suggestions.   *(1 mark)*
     ii Poisonous bite, has poison, strong claws/description   *(1 mark)*

2 a light   *(1 mark)*

  b large seeds with stored food   *(1 mark)*

3 a i Time of day   *(1 mark)*
     ii Continuous   *(1 mark)*

  b It rises during the night (some time after (1800) hours to a maximum of 25% at 0900 hours and then falls (more rapidly at first) to a minimum of 5% at 1800 hours *(1 mark)*
     Some accurate reference to actual figures in the table is necessary to obtain the mark.

  c Between 2400 hours and 0600 hours.   *(1 mark)*
     The important words here are 'more than'. Candidates who ignore these words will include the figure of 30% and therefore give a response of 2100 hours to 0900 hours.

  d The water content of the grasses that it eats are high over this period.
     It is night and the gemsboks are therefore less easily seen by predators.
     It is cooler and therefore they are less likely to have to sweat and so this helps them conserve precious water.
     (1 mark for each point; 3 marks in total)

Practicals	AQA	k	📖	⚙
Investigate the distribution of European banded snails.	✓		✓	
Investigate the behaviour of woodlice using choice chambers.	✓		✓	
Investigate the effect on plant growth of varying their environmental conditions, e.g. degrees of shade, density of sowing, supply of nutrients.	✓	✓		
Investigating particulate levels, e.g. with the use of sensors to measure environmental conditions.	✓		✓	
The use of maximum–minimum thermometers, rainfall gauges and oxygen meters.	✓		✓	
Investigating the effect of phosphate on oxygen levels in water using jars with algae, water and varying numbers of drops of phosphate, then monitor oxygen using a meter.	✓		✓	
Computer simulations to model the effect on organisms of changes to the environment.	✓		✓	

Kerboodle resources k

Resources available for this chapter on Kerboodle are:
- Chapter map: Adaptation for survival
- Support: Making a living organism (B1 4.1)
- Data handling skills: Insulation (B1 4.2)
- How Science Works: Does changing the surface area to volume ratio affect water loss by evaporation? (B1 4.2)
- Bump up your grade: Survival rivals (B1 4.4)
- Extension: Tied up in 'Knots' (B1 4.5)
- Practical: Density of sowing (B1 4.5)
- Practical: Measuring non-living factors in the environment (B1 4.7)
- Extension WebQuest: Beeless Britain (B1 4.8)
- Interactive activity: Adaptation
- Revision podcast: Adaptation
- Test yourself: Adaptation for survival
- On your marks: Adaptation for survival
- Practice questions: Adaptation for survival
- Answers to Practice questions: Adaptation for survival

B1 5.1

Pyramids of biomass

Learning objectives

Students should learn:

- that solar radiation is the source of energy for all communities of living organisms
- that green plants and algae capture solar energy to build up energy stores in their cells
- that the biomass at each stage in a food chain is less than it was at the previous stage
- how to draw and interpret a pyramid of numbers.

Learning outcomes

Most students should be able to:

- explain where biomass comes from
- describe what a pyramid of biomass is and how it can be constructed
- interpret pyramids of biomass and construct them from appropriate information
- state that biomass is lost at each stage.

Some students should also be able to:

- explain in detail why all the biomass at one stage does not get passed on to the next stage.

Support

- Provide students with the components of a food chain written on cards, which they can put in the correct order.
- Similarly, students can build up pyramids of biomass if provided with the components.

Extend

- Ask students to consider whether or not pyramids of biomass tell the whole story. They could write a short paragraph on what the pyramid of biomass does tell us about the relationships between the organisms.

Specification link-up: Biology B1.5

- Radiation from the Sun is the source of energy for most communities of living organisms. Green plants and algae absorb a small amount of the light that reaches them. The transfer from light energy to chemical energy occurs during photosynthesis. This energy is stored in the substances that make up the cells of the plants. [B1.5.1 a)]
- The mass of living material (biomass) at each stage in a food chain is less than it was at the previous stage. The biomass at each stage can be drawn to scale and shown as a pyramid of biomass. [B1.5.1 b)]
- Interpret pyramids of biomass and construct them from appropriate information. [B1.5]

Lesson structure

Starters

Food chains in the school canteen – Check out the menu for lunch and get students to discuss the food chains related to items on the menu. *(5 minutes)*

What am I? – Prepare a list of key words and phrases related to the topic, such as 'producer', 'primary consumer', 'secondary consumer, 'herbivore', 'carnivore', etc. and a list of their definitions. Students can be supported by writing up or projecting both lists on to the board and asking them to match the definitions to the key words and phrases. Students can be extended by giving them either the list of key words and asking them to write their own definitions or the definitions and getting them to supply the key word. *(10 minutes)*

Main

- Carry out the practical 'Investigation of leaf litter' (see 'Practical support'). Using a known mass or volume of leaf litter, allows students to sort through it by hand and separate out the soil organisms into containers. It is unwise to mix organisms in case they eat each other! This sorting should remove the larger organisms, but it might be necessary to use a Tullgren funnel to find the smaller invertebrates.
- The organisms should be identified as far as possible, counted and all those of one species weighed. It should be possible to classify most families of invertebrates into different feeding types (herbivore, carnivore or detritivore). It is then easy to add up the total numbers and the total masses for the different feeding types.
- A pyramid of biomass can be constructed. Students can construct these pyramids on squared paper, choosing suitable scales.
- Look at pyramids of biomass for different communities. Data can be obtained from different communities, such as a rocky shore, in woodland or open grassland.
- Investigate biomass in a pond or freshwater habitat. The method described in 'Practical support' can be modified to obtain a rough estimate of the biomass in a pond or stream. Sampling in water requires the use of a net and the technique needs to be standardised.
- In flowing water, kick sampling is carried out over a certain area (0.5 m^2) and the disturbed organisms are allowed to flow into a net. The net can be emptied into sampling trays and the organisms identified, grouped and their wet mass determined.
- In still water, a sweeping technique is used. The net is swept through the water for a fixed period of time or over a fixed distance. The organisms caught are then tipped into a sampling tray and identified as before.
- Follow local guidelines on 'outside activities'.

Plenaries

Anagrams with a difference – Prepare anagrams of the key words. To support students leave in the vowels: students can be extended by leaving out the vowels. Write up or project the anagrams onto the board and ask the students to work out what they are. *(5 minutes)*

Numbers or biomass? – Students could compare a pyramid of numbers with a pyramid of biomass. They could discuss one that they have produced from their own investigations. Ask: 'Which shows the information more accurately? Are there advantages in using numbers?' *(10 minutes)*

Practical support

Investigation of leaf litter

Equipment and materials required
Quadrats, sweep nets, pooters, sorting trays and small beakers, identification keys, Tullgren funnel, balance for weighing organisms.

Details
The method is essentially the same for the different habitats and the results can be expressed as biomass per m².

Select an area and place a 1 m² or 0.5 m² square quadrat carefully onto the ground.

Collect the leaf litter within the quadrat or cut the plants at the base and place in a white tray.

Search carefully and remove all the animals present. Smaller animals can be removed using a pooter, larger ones with forceps.

Animals should be placed in suitable containers, such as plastic beakers.

Weigh the plant material.

Identify and sort the animals into groups.

Weigh the groups of animals separately.

Return the animals to their habitat.

Construct a pyramid of biomass.

Safety: Cover any open wounds on hands and wash hands after the investigation. Follow LA (Local Authorities) advice on outdoor activities.

B1 5.1 Pyramids of biomass

Learning objectives
- Where does biomass come from?
- What is a pyramid of biomass?

Did you know ...?
Only about 1% of all the light energy falling on the Earth is used by plants and algae for photosynthesis.

Radiation from the Sun (solar or light energy) is the source of energy for all groups of living organisms on Earth.

Light (solar) energy pours out continually on to the surface of the Earth. Green plants and algae absorb some of this light energy using chlorophyll for photosynthesis. During photosynthesis some of the light energy is transferred to chemical energy. This energy is stored in the substances that make up the cells of the plants and algae. This new material adds to the biomass.

Biomass is the mass of material in living organisms. Ultimately all biomass is built up using energy from the Sun. Biomass is often measured as the dry mass of biological material in grams.

a What is the source of all the energy in the living things on Earth?

The biomass made by plants is passed on through food chains or food webs. It goes into the animals that eat the plants. It then passes into the animals that eat other animals. No matter how long the food chain or complex the food web, the original source of all the biomass involved is the Sun.

In a food chain, there are usually more producers (plants) than primary consumers (herbivores). There are also more primary consumers than secondary consumers (carnivores). If you count the number of organisms at each level you can compare them. However, the number of organisms often does not accurately reflect what is happening to the biomass.

Pyramids of biomass
The amount of biomass at each stage of a food chain is less than it was at the previous stage. We can draw the total amount of biomass in the living organisms at each stage of the food chain. When this biomass is drawn to scale, we can show it as a pyramid of biomass.

b What is a pyramid of biomass?

Figure 1 Plants can produce a huge mass of biological material in just one growing season

Oak tree → Aphid → Ladybird

Organism	Number	Biomass – dry mass in g
Oak tree	1	500000
Aphids	10000	1000
Ladybirds	200	50

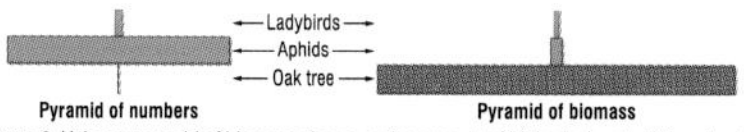

Ladybirds
Aphids
Oak tree

Pyramid of numbers   Pyramid of biomass

Figure 2 Using a pyramid of biomass shows us the amount of biological material involved at each level of this food chain much more effectively than a pyramid of numbers

Interpreting pyramids of biomass
The amount of material and energy contained in the biomass of organisms at each stage of a food chain is less than it was at the previous stage.

This is because:
- not all organisms at one stage are eaten by the stage above
- some material and energy taken in is passed out as waste by the organism
- when a herbivore eats a plant, lots of the plant biomass is used in respiration by the animal cells to release energy. Only a relatively small proportion of the plant material is used to build new herbivore biomass by making new cells, building muscle tissue etc. This means that very little of the plant biomass eaten by the herbivore in its lifetime is available to be passed on to any carnivore that eats it.

So, at each stage of a food chain the amount of energy in the biomass that is passed on gets less. A large amount of plant biomass supports a smaller amount of herbivore biomass. This in turn supports an even smaller amount of carnivore biomass.

Biomass of tertiary consumer (carnivore)
Biomass of secondary consumer (carnivore)
Biomass of primary consumer (herbivore)
Biomass of plants (producers)

Figure 3 Any food chain can be turned into a pyramid of biomass like this

Study tip
Make sure you can draw pyramids of biomass when you are given the data.

Summary questions
1 **a** What is biomass?
   b Why is a pyramid of biomass more useful for showing what is happening in a food chain than a pyramid of numbers?

2

Organism	Biomass, dry mass (g)
grass	100000
sheep	5000
sheep ticks	30

Draw a pyramid of biomass for this grassland ecosystem.

3 Using the data in Figure 2, calculate the percentage biomass passed on from:
   a the producers to the primary consumers
   b the primary consumers to the secondary consumers.

Key points
- Radiation from the Sun (solar or light energy) is the main source of energy for all living things. The Sun's light energy is captured and used by green plants and algae during photosynthesis, to make new biomass.
- Biomass is the dry mass of living material in an animal or plant.
- The mass of living material at each stage of a food chain is less than at the previous stage. The biomass at each stage can be drawn to scale and shown as a pyramid of biomass.

Further teaching suggestions

Comparing leaf litter
- Leaf litter from two different areas could be compared.

Comparing pyramids
- Pyramids of biomass from the same area at different times of the year could be considered. For example, in the English Channel in January the biomass of animal plankton is greater than the biomass of the plant plankton (the producers). Discuss why pyramids could vary at different times of the year.

Answers to in-text questions

a The Sun.

b The biomass of organisms at each level of a food chain drawn as a pyramid.

Summary answers

1 **a** The mass of material in an animal or plant.
  b Because it shows the amount of biological material at each level more accurately.

2 Check students' answers for accuracy of pyramids.

3 **a** 5000/100 000 × 100 = 5%
  b 30/5000 × 100 = 0.6%

B1 5.2

Energy transfers

Learning objectives

Students should learn:

- that materials and energy are lost in an organism's waste materials
- that energy is used in movement
- that energy is transferred heating the surroundings.

Learning outcomes

Most students should be able to:

- state why biomass and energy are reduced at each successive stage of a food chain
- explain why energy is transferred in movement and heating the surroundings.

Some students should also be able to:

- explain in detail why energy transfers by heating are particularly large in warm-blooded organisms (mammals and birds).

Specification link-up: Biology B1.5

- The amounts of material and energy contained in the biomass of organisms is reduced at each successive stage in a food chain because:
  - some materials and energy are always lost in the organisms' waste materials
  - respiration supplies all the energy needs for living processes, including movement. Much of this energy is eventually transferred to the surroundings. *[B1.5.1 c)]*

  Controlled Assessment: B4.3 Collect primary and secondary data. *[B4.3.2 a) b) d)]*

Lesson structure

Starters

Burning cowpats! – Show the students a picture of a pile of dried cowpats (try searching the internet for dung as fuel). Ask them what they think the picture shows. Draw out from them that there is energy in dung – energy that is lost and is not passed on to the next consumer – and that this is used in many countries as fuel. If time, discuss other uses for dung: elephant dung has been made into paper, dung used to generate ethanol and biogas. You could also mention that many insects and fungi can live on dung, making use of the food wastes of the consumer. *(5 minutes)*

Pass the energy – In groups, start off with a large sheet of paper labelled 'Energy'. Give the paper to a student who is designated to play the role of the Sun. The paper is passed to another student representing the Earth, some being torn off for reflection. The paper is then passed along a 'food chain' with a bit torn off at each level. Students can be supported by being given cues as to which order the stages in the food chain should come. Students can be extended by explaining the reasons in detail for energy being eventually lost to the surroundings at each level. *(10 minutes)*

Main

- Organise a 'great burger race'. This is a large scale outside practical activity for a sunny day. The idea is to show energy loss through trophic levels. Arrange a course with five posts in a line about 10 m apart: 1 At the first post have a picture of the Sun, two buckets with holes in and two large barrels (fruit barrels or similar) full of water; 2 At the second post have a large picture of the Earth and two similar buckets with holes in them; 3 At the third post have a picture of a wheat plant and two more buckets with holes in; 4 At the fourth post, have on one side a large picture of a burger, on the other side a picture of a cow. On the side with the burger, have a collecting vessel large enough to contain several buckets of water. On the side with the cow have another bucket with holes in; 5 At the fifth post have a picture of a burger and a collecting vessel on the cow side (nothing on the other side).

- Water represents the energy and it is lost through the holes in the buckets at each stage. Stress the conservation of energy – just because the water is lost through the holes it has not disappeared. Pairs of students start the race, collecting water from the 'sun barrels' and passing it to the buckets of the next pair of students at the first post and so on up the course. The cow side has one more trophic level, so the student on that side should have less water in their bucket as measured with a dipstick when the time is up.

  Because this is hard to set up, it may be a good idea to video it for future reference!

- Investigate the energy released by respiration (see 'Practical support'). Set up the demonstration of energy production by germinating peas. Record the temperatures and plot a graph of temperature against time.

- Alternatively, the students, in groups, could set up their own experiments. They could plan the investigation, as suggested in the Student Book, making sure they understand the need for controls and explaining the reasons for the treatment of the peas. The 'How Science Works' skill of selecting measuring equipment appropriate for the task, and the concept of the resolution of a measuring instrument, can be reinforced here.

- Discuss the results of this experiment in terms of cellular respiration. Ask: 'Why include the dead peas? Why is so much respiration taking place in the peas?'

Answers to in-text questions

a Because animals cannot digest everything they eat.

b The muscles use energy to contract, and the more an animal moves about the more energy (and biomass) it uses from its food. As the muscles contract they produce heat.

Support

- Supply the students with cards on which the components of a simple food chain and the processes which result in energy losses are written. Get the students to arrange these cards in the correct order so the energy losses at each level are clear.

Extend

- Ask students to look up specific heat capacity. Ask: 'How much more energy would a 10 kg animal have at 37 °C as opposed to 20 °C?' Assume flesh to have approximately the same specific heat capacity as water.

Plenaries

Fish v. fowl – Give the students a simple food chain involving a fish and another one involving a chicken [both just containing the producer, one primary consumer and one secondary consumer (humans)]. Ask them to compare the energy losses between the levels and suggest reasons for the differences. Differentiation by outcome. Support students by prompting, extend students by asking them to give appropriate details in their answers. *(5 minutes)*

Jumbled answers – Give the students Question 1 of the 'Summary questions' with the answers in the wrong places. Have a competition to see who can get the answers in the correct order the fastest. *(10 minutes)*

Practical support

Investigating the energy released by respiration

Equipment and materials required
Two vacuum flasks, thermometers or probes for data loggers, one batch of live germinating peas and one batch of boiled, dead peas that have been cooled, cotton wool. Both batches of peas should be rinsed in disinfectant to kill microorganisms.

Details
Into one flask, place some live germinating seeds and a thermometer. Close the mouth of the flask with cotton wool.

Into the second flask, place the same quantity of germinating peas that have been boiled to kill them and cooled.

Insert a thermometer and close the mouth of the flask with cotton wool.

Keep both flasks in similar conditions and monitor the temperature in both flasks at regular intervals.

Instead of thermometers, data loggers could be used to monitor the temperatures.

Energy in biomass

B1 5.2   Energy transfers

Learning objectives
- What happens to the material and energy in the biomass of organisms at each stage of a food chain?
- How is some energy transferred to the environment?

Study tip
Make sure you can explain the different ways in which energy is lost between the stages of a food chain.

The amounts of biomass and energy contained in living things get less as you progress up a food chain. Only a small amount of the biomass taken in gets turned into new animal material. What happens to the rest?

Figure 1 The amount of biomass in a lion is a lot less than the amount of biomass in the grass that feeds the zebra it preys on. But where does all the biomass go?

Energy loss in waste
The biomass that an animal eats is a source of energy, but not all of the energy can be used. Firstly, herbivores cannot digest all of the plant material they eat. The material they can't digest is passed out of the body in faeces.

The meat that carnivores eat is easier to digest than plants. This means that carnivores need to eat less often and produce less waste. But like herbivores, most carnivores cannot digest all of their prey, such as hooves, claws, bones and teeth. Therefore some of the biomass that they eat is lost in their faeces.

When an animal eats more protein than it needs, the excess is broken down. It gets passed out as urea in the urine. This is another way biomass – and energy – are transferred from the body to the surroundings.

a Why is biomass lost in faeces?

Figure 2 Animals such as horses produce very large quantities of dung made up of all the biomass they can't digest

Energy loss due to movement
Part of the biomass eaten by an animal is used for respiration in its cells. This supplies all the energy needs for the living processes taking place within the body, including movement.

Movement uses a great deal of energy. The muscles use energy to contract and also get hot. So the more an animal moves about the more energy (and biomass) it uses from its food.

b Why do animals that move around a lot use up more of the biomass they eat than animals that don't move much?

Figure 3 These sea anemones don't move much so they don't need to eat much

Keeping a constant body temperature
Much of the energy animals release from their food in cellular respiration is eventually transferred heating their surroundings. Some of this heat is produced by the muscles as the animals move.

Energy transfers to the surroundings are particularly large in mammals and birds. That is because they use energy to keep their bodies at a constant temperature. They use energy all the time, to keep warm when it's cold or to cool down when it's hot. So mammals and birds need to eat far more food than animals such as fish and amphibians to get the same increase in biomass.

Practical

Investigating the energy released by respiration
Even plants transfer energy by heating their surroundings in cellular respiration. You can investigate this using germinating peas in a vacuum flask.
- What would be the best way to monitor the temperature continuously?
- Plan the investigation.

Figure 4 Only between 2% and 10% of the biomass eaten by an animal such as this horse will get turned into new horse. The rest of the stored energy will be used for movement or transferred, heating the surroundings, or lost in waste materials.

Summary questions

1 Copy and complete using the words below:
*biomass   temperature   energy   growth   movement
producers   respiration   waste*
The amounts of .... and .... contained in living things always get less at each stage of a food .... from .... onwards. Biomass is lost as .... products and used to release energy in .... This is used for .... and to control body .... Only a small amount is used for ....

2 Explain why so much of the energy from the Sun that lands on the surface of the Earth is not turned into biomass in animals.

Key points
- The amounts of biomass and energy get less at each successive stage in a food chain.
- This is because some material and energy are always lost in waste materials, and some are used for respiration to supply energy for living processes, including movement. Much of the energy is eventually transferred by heating to the surroundings.

Summary answers

1 biomass/energy, energy/biomass, chain, producers, waste, respiration, movement, temperature, growth

2 Most of the Sun's energy is not captured by plants. Plant biomass eaten by animals cannot all be digested. Some is broken down and used in respiration to release energy. Most energy is used for movement and control of body temperature. A small amount is used for growth to produce new biomass in animals.

B1 5.3

Decay processes

Learning objectives

Students should learn:

- that materials decay because they are broken down by microorganisms
- that the decay process releases substances which plants need to grow
- that the materials are constantly cycled.

Learning outcomes

Most students should be able to:

- explain the role of microorganisms in the process of decay
- explain why decay is important in the cycling of materials.

Some students should also be able to:

- explain the factors which affect the rate of decay.

Specification link-up: Biology B1.6

- Living things remove materials from the environment for growth and other processes. These materials are returned to the environment either in waste materials or when living things die and decay. [B1.6.1 a)]
- Materials decay because they are broken down (digested) by microorganisms. Microorganisms digest materials faster in warm, moist, aerobic conditions. [B1.6.1 b)]
- The decay process releases substances that plants need to grow. [B1.6.1 c)]
- In a stable community, the processes that remove materials are balanced by processes that return materials. The materials are constantly cycled. [B1.6.1 d)]

  Controlled Assessment: B4.1 Plan practical ways to develop and test candidates' own scientific ideas. [B4.1.1a) b)]

Lesson structure

Starters

The magic pin mould – Show the students a piece of ordinary bread and a piece which you have left exposed to the air, and then cover with a clear plastic lunch box or Petri dish for a couple of days (it should either have a fluffy white growth on it or a mucky brown one depending on what spores are around.) The mould can then be seen via a stereomicroscope or digital microscope through the plastic. Do not open the box or dish. Show a picture of pin mould or *Rhizopus* – preferably much larger than life – with sporangia full of spores (use a search engine to find images on the internet). Ask the students to make the link and explain how the bread became mouldy. *(5 minutes)*

Rotless world – Get the students to imagine what would happen if decay didn't occur. What would the short term and long term consequences be? Differentiation is by outcome: students can be supported by verbal prompting, you can extend students by suggesting they explore a range of scenarios. Ask students to write down their ideas and then discuss. *(10 minutes)*

Main

- **Investigate decay.** Students could design and plan an investigation into the effect of temperature on the rate of decay. This can be done with cubes of bread exposed to the air and then placed in Petri dishes at different temperatures, such as in the refrigerator, classroom, etc. All other conditions, such as moisture levels, need to be kept the same. Observations will need to be made over a period of time, or allow a set time for the investigation, e.g. a week.

- This investigation introduces concepts of 'How Science Works' planning skills, involving the manipulation of variables. Predictions can also be made, measurements taken and conclusions drawn. The results can be assessed in a variety of ways: use digital cameras to record the appearance, assess the area of decay, etc. A time-lapse camera could be used.

- As an extension, the effect of different moisture levels could be investigated, but the temperature should be kept constant. Organise a potato decay competition using fresh potatoes. Students to decide on the conditions and set up an experiment to investigate the rate of decay of potatoes. The rate of decay over two weeks is judged.

Plenaries

Quickest rotter game – Provide the students with a piece of paper with six empty boxes connected in a line. Arrange pairs of boxes with 'warmth', 'air' and 'moisture' written above them. In pairs, students roll the dice: 1 and 2 lets them write in the letters 'R' and 'O' in the first two boxes; 3 and 4 lets them write in 'T' and 'T' into the middle two boxes and 5 and 6 lets them write 'E' and 'N' into the last boxes. Students race to see who gets rotten first. *(5 minutes)*

Stop the rot! – How do we stop things from decaying? Students can be supported by showing them vacuum-wrapped food, plastic wrapping from a pack of fruit, pasteurised milk, frozen food wrapper, tin of tomatoes, a jar of pickled onions, smoked fish, jam, etc. and asking them to say how decay has been prevented. Students can be extended by writing down five ways in which perishable foods can be treated to prevent decay. In each case, they need to explain why the treatment prevents the decay. Choose some to read out and compile a list on the board. *(10 minutes)*

Support

- Ask students to make a poster explaining how to make compost. They could be provided with pictures of vegetables, grass clippings and suitable words, etc., which can be pasted on to a sheet of A3.

Extend

- Students could find out about the human remains that have been found preserved in peat bogs. They could research: 'What are the conditions needed for peat formation? How can peat be used to provide us with information about what plants there were around thousands of years ago?'

Practical support

Investigating decay

Equipment and materials required

Cubes of bread or other suitable material, Petri dishes with lids or small glass containers with lids, thermometers to register temperatures in the different locations, access to refrigerator, incubator (do not exceed 25 °C), etc. to provide different temperatures. Fix lids with tape but do not seal.

Details

The cubes of bread should be all the same size, exposed to the air but not allowed to dry out, placed in Petri dishes and the lids secured with tape. The temperatures at which the dishes are kept should be recorded. Leave the dishes for a week and then observe. The results could be recorded photographically.

Safety: The lids should not be opened and the contents disposed of safely.

Energy in biomass

B1 5.3 Decay processes

Learning objectives

- Why do things decay?
- Why are decay processes so important?
- How are materials cycled in a stable community?

Study tip

You need to know the type of organisms that cause decay, the conditions needed for decay and the importance of decay in recycling nutrients.

Figure 1 This tomato is slowly being broken down by the action of decomposers. You can see the fungi clearly but the bacteria are too small to be seen.

Did you know ...?

The 'Body Farm' is a US research site where scientists have buried human bodies in many different conditions. They are studying every stage of human decay to help police forces all over the world work out when someone died and if they were murdered.

Plants take nutrients from the soil all the time. These nutrients are passed on into animals through food chains and food webs. If this was a one-way process the resources of the Earth would have been exhausted long ago.

Fortunately all these materials are recycled. Many trees shed their leaves each year, and most animals produce droppings at least once a day. Animals and plants eventually die as well. A group of organisms known as the **decomposers** then break down the waste and the dead animals and plants. In this process decomposers return the nutrients and other materials to the environment. The same material is recycled over and over again. This often leads to very stable communities of organisms.

a Which group of organisms take materials out of the soil?

The decay process

Decomposers are a group of microorganisms that include bacteria and fungi. They feed on waste droppings and dead organisms.

Detritus feeders, such as maggots and some types of worms, often start the process of decay. They eat dead animals and produce waste material. The bacteria and fungi then digest everything – dead animals, plants and detritus feeders plus their waste. They use some of the nutrients to grow and reproduce. They also release waste products.

The waste products of decomposers are carbon dioxide, water, and nutrients that plants can use. When we say that things decay, they are actually being broken down and digested by microorganisms.

The recycling of materials through the process of decay makes sure that the soil contains the mineral ions that plants need. The decomposers also 'clean up' the environment, removing the bodies of all the dead organisms.

b What type of organisms are decomposers?

Conditions for decay

The speed at which things decay depends partly on the temperature. Chemical reactions in microorganisms, like those in most living things, work faster in **warm conditions**. They slow down and might even stop if conditions are too cold. Decay also stops if it gets too hot. The enzymes in the decomposers change shape and stop working.

Most microorganisms also grow better in **moist conditions**. The moisture makes it easier for them to dissolve their food and also prevents them from drying out. So the decay of dead plants and animals – as well as leaves and dung – takes place far more rapidly in warm, moist conditions than it does in cold, dry ones.

Although some microbes survive without oxygen, most decomposers respire like any other organism. This means they need oxygen to release energy, grow and reproduce. This is why decay takes place more rapidly when there is **plenty of oxygen** available.

c Why are water, warmth and oxygen needed for the process of decay?

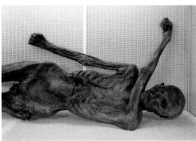

Figure 2 The decomposers cannot function at low temperatures so if an organism – such as this 4000-year-old man – is frozen as it dies, it will be preserved with very little decay.

The importance of decay in recycling

Decomposers are vital for recycling resources in the natural world. What's more, we can take advantage of the process of decay to help us recycle our waste.

In **sewage treatment plants** we use microorganisms to break down the bodily waste we produce. This makes it safe to release into rivers or the sea. These sewage works have been designed to provide the bacteria and other microorganisms with the conditions they need. That includes a good supply of oxygen.

Another place where the decomposers are useful is in the garden. Many gardeners have a **compost heap**. Grass cuttings, vegetable peelings and weeds are put onto the compost heap. It is then left to allow decomposing microorganisms break all the plant material down. It forms a brown, crumbly substance known as compost which can be used as a fertiliser.

Practical

Investigating decay

Plan an investigation into the effect of temperature on how quickly things decay.
- Write a question that can be used as the title of this investigation.
- Identify the independent variable in the investigation.

Key points

- Living things remove materials from the environment as they grow. They return them when they die through the action of decomposers.
- Materials decay because they are broken down (digested) by microorganisms. Microorganisms digest materials faster in warm, moist conditions. Many of them also need oxygen.
- The decay process releases substances that plants need to grow.
- In a stable community the processes that remove materials (particularly plant growth) are balanced by the processes that return materials.

Summary questions

1 Copy and complete using the words below:

bacteria carbon dead decomposers digest microorganisms nutrients waste water

.... are a group of .... that includes fungi and .... They feed on .... droppings and .... organisms. They .... them and use some of the .... They also release waste products which include .... dioxide and ...., which plants can use.

2 Explain why the processes of decay are so important in keeping the soil fertile.

Further teaching suggestions

Treatment of sewage

- Show a (simplified) diagram of a sewage treatment or photograph of the treatment of sewage (search for images using an internet search engine). The emphasis here is to be on the microorganisms involved in the breakdown of the waste. Students need to make notes or complete worksheets outlining the main points.

Visit a sewage treatment works

- If possible, arrange a visit to a treatment works.

A longer-term leaf experiment

- If leaf discs or leaf litter are put into nylon bags with different mesh sizes and then buried in soil, the contribution made by detritivores and decomposers can be assessed. If the mesh is small, then the detritivores will be unable to gain entry and the breakdown will be brought about by the decomposers. Mesh diameter of 6 mm allows the entry of earthworms, other detritivores and decomposers. Mesh sizes of about 0.5 mm will allow entry of other detritivores, but not earthworms. A mesh diameter of 0.003 mm will only allow decomposers through. The bags should contain a known mass of leaf material and be weighed every month. (This relates to 'How Science Works' – making measurements.)

Answers to in-text questions

a Plants.

b Bacteria, fungi, (maggots, worms).

c Water is needed to prevent the microorganisms from drying out/to help them absorb their soluble food; warmth is needed for the enzymes to work efficiently; oxygen is needed for (aerobic) respiration.

Summary answers

1 decomposers, microorganisms, bacteria, waste, dead, digest, nutrients, carbon, water

2 Plants constantly take materials from the soil. These then pass into the animals which eat the plants. Animals produce droppings and animals and plants all die. The materials from the soil are held within those bodies. The decay process releases the minerals and nutrients back into the soil so they can be taken up again by plants.

B1 5.4

The carbon cycle

Learning objectives

Students should learn:

- that carbon dioxide is removed from the atmosphere by photosynthesis in green plants and used to make carbohydrates, fats and proteins
- that carbon dioxide is returned to the atmosphere when green plants, animals and decomposers respire
- that detritus feeders and microorganisms break down the waste products and dead bodies of organisms, returning materials to the ecosystem.

Learning outcomes

Most students should be able to:

- describe the processes in the carbon cycle
- explain the importance of the activities of the detritus feeders and microorganisms in the cycling of nutrients.

Some students should also be able to:

- explain in detail the changes that occur in the carbon cycle.

Support

- Ask students to write the word 'carbon' using a pencil. Then they can write it using a burned stick, a piece of burnt animal (a bone or a piece of burned beef jerky), a piece of coal and a charcoal briquette. These can be made into a poster for display along with a balloon of exhaled air.

Extend

- Students could speculate on whether there may be life on other planets that is not carbon-based. Ask: 'Do other elements have properties similar to carbon? What might non-carbon based life be like?'

Specification link-up: Biology B1.6

- The constant cycling of carbon is called the carbon cycle. In the carbon cycle:
  - carbon dioxide is removed from the environment by green plants and algae for photosynthesis
  - the carbon from the carbon dioxide is used to make carbohydrates, fats and proteins, which make up the body of plants and algae
  - when green plants and algae respire, some of this carbon becomes carbon dioxide and is released into the atmosphere
  - when green plants and algae are eaten by animals and these animals are eaten by other animals, some of the carbon becomes part of the fats and proteins that make up their bodies
  - when animals respire some of this carbon becomes carbon dioxide and is released into the atmosphere
  - when plants, algae and animals die, some animals and microorganisms feed on their bodies
  - carbon is released into the atmosphere as carbon dioxide when these organisms respire
  - by the time the microorganisms and detritus feeders have broken down the waste products and dead bodies of organisms in ecosystems and cycled the materials as plant nutrients, all the energy originally absorbed by green plants and algae has been transferred
  - combustion of wood and fossil fuels releases carbon dioxide into the atmosphere.

  [B1.6.2 a)]

Lesson structure

Starters

Fossils in coal – Have some plant fossils in coal (real ones if possible but pictures if not). Ask students to write down how the carbon got there and what would happen to it if we burned the coal. *(5 minutes)*

Eggy tale – Show the students an egg. Ask them whether as it develops it gets heavier or lighter? Draw out both responses and encourage debate as to reasons for these beliefs. Clarify by showing diagrams of oxygen going into the egg and carbon dioxide coming out. Students could be supported by getting them to follow this up by measuring the weight of eggs as they develop in an incubator. Students can be extended by asking them to draw up a balanced equation, giving them the formula for glucose ($C_6H_{12}O_6$). *(10 minutes)*

Main

- If available, show students an animation of the carbon cycle. It is a good idea to provide the students with a worksheet and allow time for the explanation of points.
- Play a role-play game 'Pass the carbon'. In small groups, students to be labelled as parts of the carbon cycle, such as 'The atmosphere', 'Plants', 'Animals', 'Fossil fuels', etc. Have a soft ball labelled 'Carbon', which students are to pass around going from locations to other locations via the correct processes.
- Create a cartoon carbon cycle. Students to draw, or use, pictures to make a cartoon strip illustrating how a carbon atom goes from a lion's breath, into plants, into an impala, into a lion and out again through the lion's breath. This could be done in groups and the best displayed.

Plenaries

The carbon cycle – Label a diagram of the carbon cycle. *(5 minutes)*

Best of order, please! – Prepare sets of cards with stages of the carbon cycle on them. Also give the students sheets of paper with which to make connecting arrows. In pairs, students have to put them into a sensible arrangement, take a digital photograph of them as a record and then compare with another pair of students and feedback. Students can be supported by being given one-to-one assistance and labelled arrows. Students can be extended by asking them to annotate their arrows with details of the processes. *(10 minutes)*

Further teaching suggestions

Compost heap
- If the school has a compost heap, set up a data logger to take the temperature over a period of time. If there is no compost heap, students could investigate the possibility of setting one up in a suitable position. Investigate what types of material can be composted. Why is it best to use vegetable matter only? What kinds of organisms would you expect to find in a well-established compost heap? Why does the temperature change within the compost heap?

Measuring carbon dioxide
- Use a sensor to measure carbon dioxide levels.

Energy in decomposers
- Set fire to some dried mushrooms to show that there is energy in decomposers (risk assessment).

Carbon emissions
- There has been much discussion within the European Union and globally about the levels of carbon released into the atmosphere. Make a collection of newspaper and magazine articles about this topic. Find out how carbon emissions are controlled and what the targets are amongst the industrialised nations.

Energy in biomass

The carbon cycle

B1 5.4 The carbon cycle

Learning objectives
- What is the carbon cycle in nature?
- Which processes remove carbon dioxide from the atmosphere – and which processes return it?

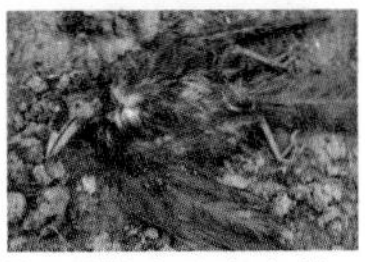

Imagine a stable community of plants and animals. The processes that remove materials from the environment are balanced by processes that return materials. Materials are constantly cycled through the environment. One of the most important of these is carbon.

All of the main molecules that make up our bodies (carbohydrates, proteins, fats and DNA) are based on carbon atoms combined with other **elements**.

The amount of carbon on the Earth is fixed. Some of the carbon is 'locked up' in **fossil fuels** like coal, oil and gas. It is only released when we burn them.

Huge amounts of carbon are combined with other elements in carbonate rocks like limestone and chalk. There is a pool of carbon in the form of carbon dioxide in the air. It is also found dissolved in the water of rivers, lakes and oceans. All the time a relatively small amount of available carbon is cycled between living things and the environment. We call this the **carbon cycle**.

a What are the main sources of carbon on Earth?

Figure 1 Within the natural cycle of life and death in the living world, mineral nutrients are cycled between living organisms and the physical environment

??? Did you know ...?
Every year about 166 gigatonnes of carbon are cycled through the living world. That's 166 000 000 000 tonnes – an awful lot of carbon!

Photosynthesis

Green plants and algae remove carbon dioxide from the atmosphere for photosynthesis. They use the carbon from carbon dioxide to make carbohydrates, proteins and fats. These make up biomass of the plants and algae. The carbon is passed on to animals that eat the plants. The carbon goes on to become part of the carbohydrates, proteins and fats in these animal bodies.

This is how carbon is taken out of the environment. But how is it returned?

b What effect does photosynthesis have on the distribution of carbon levels in the environment?

Respiration

Living organisms respire all the time. They use oxygen to break down glucose, providing energy for their cells. Carbon dioxide is produced as a waste product. This is how carbon is returned to the atmosphere.

When plants, algae and animals die their bodies are broken down by decomposers. These are animals and microorganisms such as blowflies, moulds and bacteria that feed on the dead bodies. The animals which feed on dead bodies and waste are called *detritus feeders*. They include animals such as worms, centipedes and many insects.

Carbon is released into the atmosphere as carbon dioxide when these organisms respire. All of the carbon (in the form of carbon dioxide) released by the various living organisms is then available again. It is ready to be taken up by plants and algae in photosynthesis.

Combustion

Fossil fuels contain carbon, which was locked away by photosynthesising organisms millions of years ago. When we burn fossil fuels, carbon dioxide is produced, so we release some of that carbon back into the atmosphere:

Photosynthesis: carbon dioxide + water (+ light energy) → glucose+ oxygen

Respiration: glucose + oxygen → carbon dioxide + water (+ energy)

Combustion: fossil fuel or wood + oxygen → carbon dioxide + water
(+ energy)

The constant cycling of carbon is summarised in Figure 2.

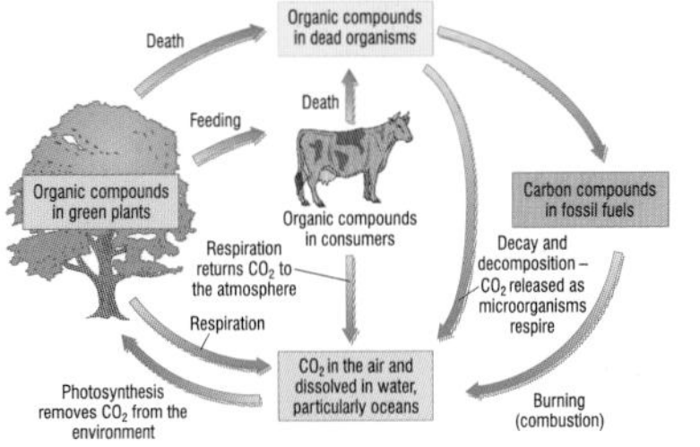

Figure 2 The carbon cycle in nature

Study tip
Make sure you can label the processes in a diagram of the carbon cycle.

Energy transfers

When plants and algae photosynthesise, they transfer light energy into chemical energy can be the food that they make. This chemical energy is transferred from one organism to another through the carbon cycle. Some of the energy can be used for movement or transferred as energy to the organisms and its surroundings at each stage. The decomposers break down all the waste and dead organisms and cycle the materials as plant nutrients. By this time all of the energy originally absorbed by green plants and algae during photosynthesis has been transferred elsewhere.

For millions of years the carbon cycle has regulated itself. However, as we burn more fossil fuels we are pouring increasing amounts of carbon dioxide into the atmosphere. Scientists fear that the carbon cycle may not cope. If the levels of carbon dioxide in our atmosphere increase it may lead to global warming.

Figure 3 Fossil fuels such as coal contain large amounts of carbon

Summary questions

1 a What is the carbon cycle?
   b What are the main processes involved in the carbon cycle?
   c Why is the carbon cycle so important for life on Earth?

2 a Where does the carbon come from that is used in photosynthesis?
   b Explain carefully how carbon is transferred through an ecosystem.

Key points
- The constant cycling of carbon in nature is known as the carbon cycle.
- Carbon dioxide is removed from the atmosphere by photosynthesis. It is returned to the atmosphere through respiration and combustion.

Answers to in-text questions

a Fossil fuels, carbonate rocks, the atmosphere, oceans and living things.

b It removes it from the atmosphere.

Summary answers

1 a The cycling of carbon between living organisms and the environment.

   b Photosynthesis, respiration and combustion.

   c Because it prevents all the carbon from getting used up; returns carbon dioxide to the atmosphere to be available for photosynthesis again.

2 a Carbon dioxide in the air.

   b Students can produce a written description of the carbon cycle or a diagram (See Figure 2, The carbon cycle in nature) to summarise the stages (must cover all points in the carbon cycle).

B1 5.5

Recycling organic waste

Learning objectives

Students should learn:

- why we should recycle organic waste
- the most effective ways to recycle organic waste.

Learning outcomes

Most students should be able to:

- give reasons for the recycling of organic kitchen or garden waste
- describe ways in which organic waste is recycled
- evaluate the effectiveness of recycling schemes.

Some students should also be able to:

- explain the benefits of reducing the amount of waste that is put into landfill sites.

Answers to in-text questions

a Potato peelings, vegetable peelings, apple core, grass cuttings – any sensible suggestions that demonstrate an understanding of what goes into compost.

b Methane.

Support

- Ensure students understand that the household waste we produce consists of organic and non-organic materials. Help them make this distinction by providing them with a variety of materials that they can sort into containers labelled 'biodegradable' and 'non-biodegradable'.

Extend

- Ask students to research the nutrient contents of various types of waste and match this to the nutritional requirements of different types of plants.

Specification link-up: Biology B1.6

- Evaluate the necessity and effectiveness of schemes for recycling organic kitchen or garden waste. [B1.6]

Controlled Assessment: B4.3 Collect primary and secondary data [B4.3.2 a)]; B4.5 Analyse and interpret primary and secondary data. [B4.5.4 a)]

Lesson structure

Starters

The core of the problem – Show the students a lunch box containing an apple core, an empty crisp packet, a half-eaten sandwich in its wrapper and an empty drinks can. Ask the students what would happen if the contents of the lunchbox were thrown out of the window. Ask what will happen to the apple core and the packaging? What would happen to the half-eaten sandwich and the can? Draw out the concept of biodegradability; get the students to use this word, to write it down and to give examples of biodegradable and non-biodegradable substances. *(5 minutes)*

Bin sort – Get litter-pickers, a plastic sheet, some large containers and some gloves. With the class, go out and find litter bins around school or bring in the contents of a bin. Empty the contents on to the sheet and using the litter-pickers and gloves sort the waste into recyclable, non-recyclable and compostable. Record results. Students can be supported by providing a writing frame. Students can be extended by getting them to weigh each portion, calculate the total, calculate percentages and draw up a pie chart. *(10 minutes)*

Main

- Investigate the factors that affect how quickly organic materials decay. This investigation could take two to three weeks. Each student, or group of students, will need a plant pot containing damp soil, a sealable plastic bag and a selection of objects, such as a leaf, a piece of fruit, an eggshell, some cardboard and a small piece of twig. (This links to 'How Science Works' – planning investigations.)

- When setting up the experiment, the students could discuss the nature of the objects and make predictions about what will happen and why. Ask, 'Why is it important not to let the soil dry out? Why use soil?' Students should also consider how the results are to be assessed. Is it possible to make measurements? How science works concepts can be introduced here. Ensure a range of factors are investigated across the whole class and draw together each set of results to draw a class conclusion about the ideal conditions for composting. Discuss the limitations of the conclusions you can draw.

- Alternatively, students can set up a practical activity on composting and investigate the rate at which grass clippings decompose under different conditions, including the use of a composting agent.

- Split the class into pairs. Each member of each pair is to prepare a short cloze passage for the other to complete. Put on the board a set of possible words which could be used in these. When they have both completed writing theirs, swap over and fill them in. Small prizes for the best sets of cloze questions.

Plenaries

Recycling building blocks – One team is to make a fish or other simple animal shape from construction toy bricks. Get a team of volunteers to dismantle it and use the parts to make it into another organism. Explain the link between this and recycling materials in nature. *(5 minutes)*

Compost corner – Design a label to go on a compost bin to be placed in the school food technology rooms. Students could be supported by providing a writing frame for the label. Or getting them to draw pictures of the items that should be placed in the bin. Students could be extended by getting them to include advice on composting materials and reasons why it is important. *(10 minutes)*

Practical support

Investigating the decay of organic matter
Equipment and materials required
Plant pots containing damp soil, plastic bags large enough to contain the plant pots, rubber bands, leaves, eggshells, twigs, small pieces of fruit, cardboard, labels and marker pens.

Details
Students should place selected objects on the surface of the damp soil, enclose the plant pot with the plastic bag and secure the top with a rubber band. The pots can be left in different conditions of light and temperature, labelled with the date and conditions and observations made at intervals.

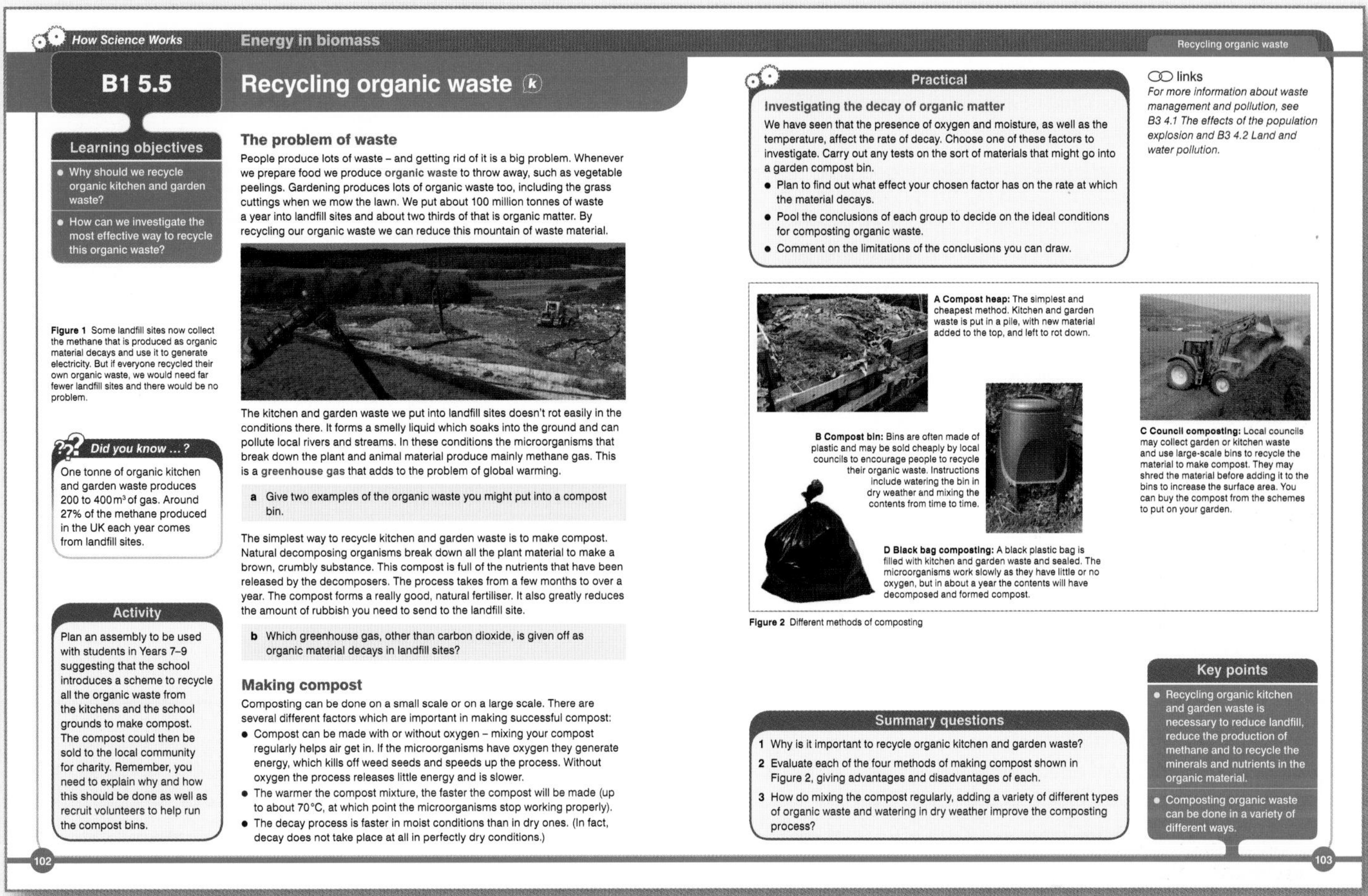

How Science Works — Energy in biomass — Recycling organic waste

B1 5.5 Recycling organic waste (k)

Learning objectives
- Why should we recycle organic kitchen and garden waste?
- How can we investigate the most effective way to recycle this organic waste?

The problem of waste
People produce lots of waste – and getting rid of it is a big problem. Whenever we prepare food we produce organic waste to throw away, such as vegetable peelings. Gardening produces lots of organic waste too, including the grass cuttings when we mow the lawn. We put about 100 million tonnes of waste a year into landfill sites and about two thirds of that is organic matter. By recycling our organic waste we can reduce this mountain of waste material.

Figure 1 Some landfill sites now collect the methane that is produced as organic material decays and use it to generate electricity. But if everyone recycled their own organic waste, we would need far fewer landfill sites and there would be no problem.

Did you know …?
One tonne of organic kitchen and garden waste produces 200 to 400 m³ of gas. Around 27% of the methane produced in the UK each year comes from landfill sites.

The kitchen and garden waste we put into landfill sites doesn't rot easily in the conditions there. It forms a smelly liquid which soaks into the ground and can pollute local rivers and streams. In these conditions the microorganisms that break down the plant and animal material produce mainly methane gas. This is a greenhouse gas that adds to the problem of global warming.

a Give two examples of the organic waste you might put into a compost bin.

The simplest way to recycle kitchen and garden waste is to make compost. Natural decomposing organisms break down all the plant material to make a brown, crumbly substance. This compost is full of the nutrients that have been released by the decomposers. The process takes from a few months to over a year. The compost forms a really good, natural fertiliser. It also greatly reduces the amount of rubbish you need to send to the landfill site.

b Which greenhouse gas, other than carbon dioxide, is given off as organic material decays in landfill sites?

Making compost
Composting can be done on a small scale or on a large scale. There are several different factors which are important in making successful compost:
- Compost can be made with or without oxygen – mixing your compost regularly helps air get in. If the microorganisms have oxygen they generate energy, which kills off weed seeds and speeds up the process. Without oxygen the process releases little energy and is slower.
- The warmer the compost mixture, the faster the compost will be made (up to about 70°C, at which point the microorganisms stop working properly).
- The decay process is faster in moist conditions than in dry ones. (In fact, decay does not take place at all in perfectly dry conditions.)

Activity
Plan an assembly to be used with students in Years 7–9 suggesting that the school introduces a scheme to recycle all the organic waste from the kitchens and the school grounds to make compost. The compost could then be sold to the local community for charity. Remember, you need to explain why and how this should be done as well as recruit volunteers to help run the compost bins.

Practical

Investigating the decay of organic matter
We have seen that the presence of oxygen and moisture, as well as the temperature, affect the rate of decay. Choose one of these factors to investigate. Carry out any tests on the sort of materials that might go into a garden compost bin.
- Plan to find out what effect your chosen factor has on the rate at which the material decays.
- Pool the conclusions of each group to decide on the ideal conditions for composting organic waste.
- Comment on the limitations of the conclusions you can draw.

A Compost heap: The simplest and cheapest method. Kitchen and garden waste is put in a pile, with new material added to the top, and left to rot down.

B Compost bin: Bins are often made of plastic and may be sold cheaply by local councils to encourage people to recycle their organic waste. Instructions include watering the bin in dry weather and mixing the contents from time to time.

C Council composting: Local councils may collect garden or kitchen waste and use large-scale bins to recycle the material to make compost. They may shred the material before adding it to the bins to increase the surface area. You can buy the compost from the schemes to put on your garden.

D Black bag composting: A black plastic bag is filled with kitchen and garden waste and sealed. The microorganisms work slowly as they have little or no oxygen, but in about a year the contents will have decomposed and formed compost.

Figure 2 Different methods of composting

links
For more information about waste management and pollution, see B3 4.1 The effects of the population explosion and B3 4.2 Land and water pollution.

Summary questions
1 Why is it important to recycle organic kitchen and garden waste?
2 Evaluate each of the four methods of making compost shown in Figure 2, giving advantages and disadvantages of each.
3 How do mixing the compost regularly, adding a variety of different types of organic waste and watering in dry weather improve the composting process?

Key points
- Recycling organic kitchen and garden waste is necessary to reduce landfill, reduce the production of methane and to recycle the minerals and nutrients in the organic material.
- Composting organic waste can be done in a variety of different ways.

Further teaching suggestions

Compost heap
- If the school has a compost heap, set up a data logger to take the temperature over a period of time. If there is no compost heap, students could investigate the possibility of setting one up in a suitable position. Investigate what types of material can be composted. Why is it best to use vegetable matter only? What kinds of organisms would you expect to find in a well-established compost heap? Why does the temperature change within the compost?

Set up a wormery
- A wormery is a fun, easy and efficient way of converting organic kitchen or garden waste into compost.

Summary answers

1 It is important to recycle organic material to prevent it going into landfill sites, to reduce levels of methane.

2 **Compost heap:** Advantages are it is simple, cheap, and anyone can do it.
Disadvantages are it can be smelly, it can be slow and inefficient at decomposing, it can get big, and can attract vermin.

Compost bin: Advantages are it is neat, tidy, efficient, not expensive, and reduces risk of vermin.
Disadvantages are that it needs water in hot dry weather and may need forking over. Probably need two compost bins working together.

Council composting: Advantages are economy of scale, any smell and inconvenience out of your garden, can be used to make money for local council.

Disadvantages are it may be limited to how much will be collected, and you don't have your own compost to use.

Black bag composting: Advantages are it is neat, there is no smell, and it is easy to use.
Disadvantages are it is slow, limited quantity.

3 Mixing compost adds oxygen – aerobic digestion is faster, so compost is made quicker and hotter (so kills more weed seeds). Variety of material makes compost better – more varied nutrients. Adding water in dry weather – microbes that bring about decay work better in a damp environment, so adding water allows them to work as fast as possible.

Summary answers

1 a
  i 10%   **ii** 8%   **iii** 12.5%

b The mass of the producers has to support the whole pyramid, relatively little energy is transferred from producers to primary consumers (difficult to digest).

c Relatively little energy is passed up the chain, so not enough to support many carnivores.

d Less energy passed on as warm blooded animals use energy to generate warmth. This is transferred to the environment and so that energy is no longer available to pass on up the chain.

2 The amount of biomass transferred along food chain gets less. Biomass is needed for energy. So by eating plants, the maximum amount of biomass is passed on to people. Eating meat – plant biomass transferred to animals, animal biomass to people – biomass lost at both stages. Draw pyramid of biomass to show plant/person and plant/cow or sheep/person.

3 a Graph plotting, correct scale, labelled axes, axes correct way round, accurate points.

b Chickens use little energy maintaining their body temperature, so have more energy for growth.

c To reduce movement. So reduce energy used in movement, so more energy for growth.

d So they grow fast to a weight when they can be eaten and another set of chickens started up – economic reasons.

4 a Low temperatures prevent growth of decay – causing microorganisms.

b Cooking destroys the microorganisms, denatures enzymes so no decay.

c Most decomposers need oxygen to respire – no air, no oxygen, so microbes cannot grow.

d Heat kills microorganisms, no oxygen so no decay.

5 a Photosynthesis.

b Respiration, burning (decay and decomposition).

c Oceans, air (carbonate rocks).

d CO_2 is important for photosynthesis and keeping surface of Earth warm. Excess CO_2 surface gets warmer; affects sea levels, living organisms. Less CO_2 means surface cools, affects life.

6 a Higher-temperature means faster reactions. Warm compost means microorganisms digest, grow and reproduce faster. More decomposers = faster decomposition.

b Makes sure all the decomposing microorganisms have enough oxygen to respire as fast as possible.

Kerboodle resources

Resources available for this chapter on Kerboodle are:
- Chapter map: Energy in biomass
- Practical: Composting (B1 5.2)
- Simulation: Microorganisms and decay (B1 5.3)
- How Science Works: What can speed up the decay of bread? (B1 5.3)
- Bump up your grade: What a load of rubbish! (B1 5.5)
- Interactive activity: Exploring energy in biomass
- Revision podcast: Energy in biomass
- Test yourself: Energy in biomass
- On your marks: Energy in biomass
- Practice questions: Energy in biomass
- Answers to practice questions: Energy in biomass

Summary questions

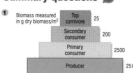

1 Biomass measured in g dry biomass/m²

Top carnivore	25
Secondary consumer	200
Primary consumer	2500
Producer	25 000

a From this diagram, calculate the percentage biomass passed on:
  i from producers to primary consumers
  ii from primary to secondary consumers
  iii from secondary consumers to top carnivores.

b In any food chain or food web the biomass of the producers is much larger than that of any other level of the pyramid. Why is this?

c In any food chain or food web there are only small numbers of top carnivores. Use your calculations to help you explain why.

d All of the animals in the pyramid of biomass shown here are cold blooded. What difference would it have made to the average percentage of biomass passed on between the levels if mammals and birds had been involved? Explain the difference.

2 The world population is increasing and there are food shortages in many parts of the world. Explain, using pyramids of biomass to help you, why it would make a better use of resources if people everywhere ate much less meat and more plant material.

3 Chickens for us to eat are often farmed intensively to provide meat as cheaply as possible. The birds arrive in the broiler house as 1-day-old chicks. They are slaughtered at 42 days of age when they weigh about 2 kg. The temperature, amount of food and water and light levels are carefully controlled. About 20 000 chickens are reared together in one house. The table below shows their weight gain.

Age (days)	1	7	14	21	28	35	42
Mass (g)	36	141	404	795	1180	1657	1998

a Plot a graph to show the growth rate of one of these chickens.

b Explain why the temperature is so carefully controlled in the broiler house.

c Explain why so many birds are reared together in a relatively small area.

d Why are birds for eating reared like this?

4 Microorganisms decompose organic waste and dead bodies. We preserve food to stop this decomposition taking place. Use your knowledge of decomposition to explain how each method stops the food going bad:

a Food may be frozen.

b Food may be cooked – cooked food keeps longer than fresh food.

c Food may be stored in a vacuum pack – with all the air sucked out.

d Food may be tinned – it is heated and sealed in an airtight container.

5

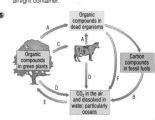

a How is carbon dioxide removed from the atmosphere in the carbon cycle?

b How does carbon dioxide get into the atmosphere?

c Where is most of the carbon stored?

d Why is the carbon cycle so important and what could happen if the balance of the reactions was disturbed?

6 a The temperature in the middle of a compost heap will be quite warm. Heat is produced as microbes respire. How does this help the compost to be broken down more quickly?

b In sewage works oxygen is bubbled through the tank containing sewage and microorganisms. How does this help make sure the human waste is broken down completely?

Practical suggestions

Practicals	AQA	k	📖	⚙️
Design and carry out an investigation to measure the rate of decay of bread, e.g. by exposing cubes of bread to air before placing them in sealed Petri dishes at different temperatures and/or different moisture levels.	✓			✓
Investigate the rates of decay using containers (e.g. thermos flasks) full of grass clippings, one with disinfectant, one with dry grass, one with wet grass and one with a composting agent. Seal the container. Place a thermometer or temperature probe through a cotton wool plug to monitor the temperature.	✓	✓		
Potato decay competition, using fresh potatoes. Candidates decide on the environmental conditions and the rate of decay is measured over a 2-week period.	✓		✓	
Role play exercise – A4 sheets labelled with different stages of the carbon cycle. Candidates arrange themselves in the correct order to pass a ball along labelled as carbon.	✓		✓	
Using a sensor and data logger to investigate carbon dioxide levels during the decay process.	✓		✓	

Practice questions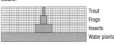

1 Rabbits eat very large amounts of grass. A single hawk eats a few rabbits.

a Draw a pyramid of biomass for the rabbits, grass and the hawk. (2)

b Much of the energy from the grass is not transferred to the hawk.
Suggest **two** reasons why. (2)

2 Choose words from below to complete each sentence.

carbon dioxide cool dry insects microorganisms moist nitrogen oxygen rats warm

a Plant waste in a compost heap is decayed by .... (1)

b The plant waste decays faster in conditions which are .... and .... (2)

c The plant waste will also decay faster when the air contains plenty of .... (1)

3 The diagram shows what happens to the energy in the food a calf eats.

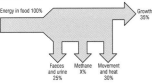

In the calculations show clearly how you work out your answer.

a Calculate the percentage of energy lost in methane (X). (2)

b The energy in the food the calf eats in one day is 10 megajoules.
Calculate the amount of this energy that would be lost in faeces and urine. (2)

c Name the process which transfers the energy from the food into movement. (1)

d The farmer decides to move his calf indoors so that it will grow quicker.
Suggest **two** reasons why. (2)

4 *In this question you will be assessed on using good English, organising information clearly and using specialist terms where appropriate.*

The constant cycling of carbon in nature is called 'The carbon cycle'.

Each autumn, trees lose their leaves.

Describe how the carbon in the leaves is recycled so that the trees can use it again. (6)

5 The diagram shows a pyramid of biomass drawn to scale.

Trout
Frogs
Insects
Water plants

a What is the source of energy for the water plants? (1)

b The ratio of the biomass of water plants to the biomass of insects is 5 : 1.
Calculate the ratio of the biomass of insects to the biomass of frogs.
Show clearly how you work out your answer. (2)

c Give **two** reasons why the biomass of the frog population is smaller than the biomass of the insect population. (2)

d Some insects die.
Describe how the carbon in the dead insect bodies may be recycled. (4)

AQA, 2006

105

Practice answers

1 a Pyramid drawn with three layers
widest to narrowest either way up but correctly labelled
(2 marks)

b Any **two** from:
- not all the grass eaten is used to make rabbit grow/ waste in urea faeces/roots not eaten
- energy is lost due to movement by rabbits/rabbits run around
- energy used to keep rabbits warm
- hawks do not eat the whole rabbit *(2 marks)*

2 a microorganisms *(1 mark)*

b moist and warm (either order) *(2 marks)*

c oxygen *(1 mark)*

3 a 10 (%) = 2 marks. If wrong answer allow 25+35+30 for 1 mark. *(2 marks)*

b 2.5 = 2 marks, if incorrect answer allow 1 mark for correct working. *(2 marks)*

c respiration *(1 mark)*

d It reduces the calf's movement because it won't walk about, therefore it will use that energy for growth. It also reduces the energy the calf will need to use to keep warm and that energy can be used for growth.
reduces movement/walking about
reduces energy/transferred by heating/keeps (calf)warm
(2 marks)

4 There is a clear and detailed description of the sequence of events in the carbon cycle. The answer is coherent and in a logical sequence. It contains a range of appropriate or relevant specialist terms used accurately. The answer shows very few errors in spelling, punctuation and grammar. *(5–6 marks)*

There is some description of the sequence of events in the carbon cycle but there is a lack of clarity and detail. The answer has some structure and the use of specialist terms has been attempted, but not always accurately. There may be some errors in spelling, punctuation and grammar.
(3–4 marks)

There is a brief description of the carbon cycle, which has little clarity and detail. The answer is poorly constructed with an absence of specialist terms or their use demonstrates a lack of understanding of their meaning. The spelling, punctuation and grammar are weak. *(1–2 marks)*

No relevant content. *(0 marks)*

Examples of biology points made in the response:
- microorganisms – only allow once if no mention of bacteria or fungi
- bacteria
- fungi
- digest/break down organic matter/leaves/decompose/ reference decomposers/decay/rot
- respiration
- combustion
- release of carbon dioxide
- into the air
- CO_2 can be used (by trees) in photosynthesis
- Reference to faster in warmer weather/slower during the winter/cold weather.

5 a the sun/light/sunshine/solar
allow radiation from the sun
ignore photosynthesis/respiration
apply list principle
*do **not** allow water/minerals/heat* *(1 mark)*

b 2.5 (:1)
correct answer with or without working
ignore rounding with correct working
*do **not** allow other equivalent ratios for both marks*
*evidence of selection of 10(insects) **and** 4(frogs) **or** 50 **and** 20 **or** 1 **and** 0.4 for **1** mark*

*if no other working allow **1** mark for (1):0.4 on answer line*
(2 marks)

c Any **two** from:
*allow for insects **or** frogs*
allow energy for biomass
- some parts indigestible/faeces
- waste/examples of waste eg urea/nitrogenous compounds/urine/excretion
- movement/eg of movement
allow keeping warm
- heat
- not all eaten/eg of not all eaten
- respiration
do not accept energy for respiration *(2 marks)*

d Any **four** from:
- (bodies) consumed by animals/named/scavengers/ detritus feeders
- microorganisms/bacteria/fungi/decomposers
- reference to enzymes
- decay/breakdown/decompose/rot
ignore digest(ion)
- respiration
- carbon dioxide produced
- photosynthesis
- sugar/glucose produced
accept other organic molecules
- fossilisation/fossil fuels/named
- combustion/burning
must be linked with fossilisation/fossil fuels
- (burning) produces carbon dioxide
allow carbon dioxide produced once only *(4 marks)*

B1 6.1

Inheritance

Learning objectives

Students should learn:

- that genetic information is passed from parent to offspring in the gametes from which the offspring develop
- that the genetic information is located on the chromosomes in the nucleus of a cell.

Learning outcomes

Most students should be able to:

- state that genetic information is present in the gametes from each parent
- describe the relationship between chromosomes and genes
- identify where the chromosomes are located in the cells
- state that each gene affects a different characteristic.

Some students should also be able to:

- recognise that genes are found in pairs on paired chromosomes.

Answers to in-text questions

a   Because you have inherited genetic information from them, which determines what you will look like.

b   In the nucleus of your cells.

c   On your chromosomes in the nucleus of your cell.

Support

- Provide students with pictures of stages in mitosis which they can be asked to place in order.

Extend

- Ask students to find out how many pairs of chromosomes there are in a list of common plants and animals (cat, dog, mouse, chicken, fruit fly, garden pea, bean, etc.).

Specification link-up: Biology B1.7

- The information that results in plants and animals having similar characteristics to their parents is carried by genes, which are passed on in the sex cells (gametes) from which the offspring develop. *[B1.7.1 a)]*
- The nucleus of a cell contains chromosomes. Chromosomes carry genes that control the characteristics of the body. *[B1.7.1 b)]*
- Different genes control the development of different characteristics of an organism. *[B1.7.1 c)]*

Lesson structure

Starters

Where are my genes? – Remind students of the structure of cells by projecting, or drawing, a generalised cell and getting them to name the parts: cytoplasm, cell membrane, and nucleus. Project an image of a sperm and an egg cell and ask students where they think the genetic material is. Search the internet for and show a picture of a '*Drosophila*' chromosome. *(5 minutes)*

Offspring naming race – Show the students a list or a series of pictures of ten types of animal and ask them to name their offspring. Students can be supported by providing them with a list of the names of the offspring from which to choose. Students can be extended by including some difficult ones in the list. In a discussion at the end, show photographs and talk over why they resemble each other to establish current knowledge. *(10 minutes)*

Main

- Following on from the 'Where are my genes?' starter, show the students a series of pictures or a video clip of cells undergoing mitotic cell division. Ask: 'What are the rods that can be seen? What would we see if we could look closer?'

- This leads into a discussion of how the genetic material is organised and how it is being shared out equally between the daughter cells. Show a picture of a 'giant' plastic chromosome from a *Drosophila* salivary gland and then build up a picture of a chromosome, so that the relationship between chromosomes and genes is clear.

- Show the students a photograph of a human karyotype (the human chromosome complement), emphasising that there are 23 pairs of chromosomes. One of each pair comes from the father and the other from the mother. If the karyotypes are large enough, photocopy examples and get the students to work in groups and do a cut and stick pairing exercise. In order to help students, some of the more difficult ones could be done for them and they finish it off with a small number of obviously different chromosomes.

- It would be interesting to give the students a mixture of male and female karyotypes and see if they can discover which they have been given, by identifying the 'odd' male chromosome. In a karyotype of a Down's syndrome person, it should be possible to identify *trisomy 22* when compared with the karyotype of a normal person. There are other examples of differences in number and structure of the chromosomes causing abnormalities (search the internet for examples) and it could be pointed out to the students that these conditions can be detected in a karyotype. Search the internet for pictures of different karyotypes.

- Show pictures of horse chestnut trees with red and white flowers. Hand round some conkers and ask the students what will decide whether the conkers will produce plants with red flowers or white flowers. Discuss the concept of a gene for flower colour. For a long-term investigation, students could plant the conkers and label them for future groups to find the answer. A time capsule description of the experiment (the best selected by the class) should be placed in a plastic bag, put inside a cigar tube and glued shut. Instructions could be written on a laminated tag and attached to the trees. (Before considering whether or not to do this exercise, think about whether you want the students to carry out one of the cloning exercises, which also involves growing plants – you may run out of pots or growing space!)

Plenaries

Clues for key words – Give the students the key words: 'cell, nucleus, chromosome, gene'. Ask students to identify and then place them in order of size. Students can be supported by giving them the key words on cards and asked to place them in order of size. Students can be extended by writing cryptic clues for the words. These can be used later to compile a crossword. *(5 minutes)*

Karyotypes – If the human karyotype exercise was used above, discuss the value of such karyotypes. Ask: 'Who would use them? What conditions could they show?' This could lead into a discussion about the value of amniocentesis and other diagnostic tests for the inheritance of chromosome abnormalities. *(10 minutes)*

Variation, reproduction and new technology

Inheritance

B1 6.1 Inheritance

Learning objectives

● How do parents pass on genetic information to their offspring?

● In which part of a cell is the genetic information found?

Young animals and plants resemble their parents. Horses have foals and people have babies. Chestnut trees produce conkers that grow into little chestnut trees. Many of the smallest organisms that live in the world around us are actually identical to their parents. So what makes us the way we are?

Figure 1 This mother cat and her kittens are not identical, but they are obviously related

Study tip

Make sure you know the difference between chromosomes, genes and DNA.

Why do we resemble our parents?

Most families have characteristics that we can see clearly from generation to generation. People like to comment when one member of a family looks very much like another. Characteristics like nose shape, eye colour and dimples are inherited. They are passed on to you from your parents.

Your resemblance to your parents is the result of information carried by **genes**. These are passed on to you in the sex cells (**gametes**) from which you developed. This genetic information determines what you will be like.

a Why do you look like your parents?

Chromosomes and genes

The genetic information is carried in the nucleus of your cells. It is passed from generation to generation during reproduction. The nucleus contains all the plans for making and organising a new cell. What's more, the nucleus contains the plans for a whole new you!

b In which part of a cell is the genetic information found?

Figure 2 The nucleus of each of your cells contains your chromosomes. The chromosomes carry the genes, which control the characteristics of your whole body.

Inside the nucleus of all your cells there are thread-like structures called **chromosomes**. The chromosomes are made up of a special chemical called **DNA** (deoxyribonucleic acid). This is where the genetic information is actually stored.

DNA is a long molecule made up of two strands that are twisted together to make a spiral. This is known as a double helix – imagine a ladder that has been twisted round.

Each different type of organism has a different number of chromosomes in their body cells. Humans have 46 chromosomes while turkeys have 82. You inherit half your chromosomes from your mother and half from your father, so chromosomes come in pairs. You have 23 pairs of chromosomes in all your normal body cells.

Each of your chromosomes contains thousands of genes joined together. These are the units of inheritance.

Each gene is a small section of the long DNA molecule. Genes control what an organism is like. They determine its size, its shape and its colour. Genes work at the level of the molecules in your body to control the development of all the different characteristics you can see. They do this by controlling all the different enzymes and other proteins made in your body.

Your chromosomes are organised so that both of the chromosomes in a pair carry genes controlling the same things. This means your genes also come in pairs – one from your father and one from your mother.

c Where would you find your genes?

Some of your characteristics are decided by a single pair of genes. For example, there is one pair of genes which decides whether or not you will have dimples when you smile. However, most of your characteristics are the result of several different genes working together. For example, your hair and eye colour are both the result of several different genes.

Did you know that scientists are still not sure exactly how many genes we have? At the moment they think it is between 20 000 to 25 000.

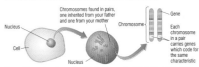

Figure 3 The nucleus of your cell contains the chromosomes that carry the genes which control the characteristics of your whole body

Summary questions

1 Copy and complete using the words below:

chromosomes genes genetic gametes nucleus

Offspring look like their parents because of .... information passed on to them in the .... (sex cells) from which they developed. The information is contained in the ...., which are found in the .... of the cell. The information is carried by the ....

2 **a** What is the basic unit of inheritance?

b Offspring inherit information from their parents, but do not look exactly like them. Why not?

3 **a** Why do chromosomes come in pairs?

b Why do genes come in pairs?

c How many genes do scientists think humans have?

Key points

● Parents pass on genetic information to their offspring in the sex cells (gametes).

● The genetic information is found in the nucleus of your cells. The nucleus contains chromosomes, and chromosomes carry the genes that control the characteristics of your body.

● Different genes control the development of different characteristics.

106 / 107

Further teaching suggestions

Your own inherited characteristics

● An interesting homework exercise would be to ask students to research their own families for inherited characteristics. There are some obvious ones, such as tongue rolling, straight thumbs *v.* bendy thumbs, dimples *v.* no dimples, ear lobes *v.* no ear lobes. They might be able to produce a family tree or pedigree. This exercise could produce material for discussion in preparation for the next spread.

'Window on Life'

● Show the visual summary *Window on Life (Sunday Times* CD).

Mendel

● Either tell the story of Mendel and his peas or get students to research the topic for themselves.

??? *Did you know …?*

We do know that we share more than 95% of our DNA with chimpanzees, so we obviously have some genes in common with them!

Summary answers

1 genetic, gametes, chromosomes, nucleus, genes

2 **a** The gene.

b Offspring inherit information from both parents and so end up with a combination of characteristics, some from father and some from mother.

3 **a** You inherit one set from each parent.

b Genes are carried on the chromosomes, so because chromosomes come in pairs, so do the genes – one from each parent.

c 20 000–25 000.

B1 6.2 Types of reproduction

Learning objectives

Students should learn:

- the differences between sexual and asexual reproduction
- that the offspring produced by asexual reproduction are genetically identical to their parents and show no variation
- why the offspring produced by sexual reproduction differ slightly from each other and from their parents.

Learning outcomes

Most students should be able to:

- state the meaning of the term 'clone'
- describe why asexual reproduction produces identical offspring
- describe how variety is achieved in individuals produced by sexual reproduction.

Some students should also be able to:

- explain the genetic differences between sexually and asexually produced offspring.

Answers to in-text questions

a Offspring only have one parent; there is no joining or fusion of sex cells from two parents; so identical genetic information is passed on.

b There is genetic information from both parents, so there is a mixture of characteristics from both.

c There is a great advantage in making sure that the species survives. The more variety there is in a group of individuals, the more likely it is that at least a few of them will have the ability to survive difficult conditions.

Support

- Supply students with pictures to represent the different possibilities in the inheritance of dimples presentation.

Extend

- Ask students to research and explain the types of nuclear division involved in both types of reproduction.

Specification link-up: Biology B1.7

- There are two forms of reproduction:
  - Sexual reproduction – the joining (fusion) of male and female gametes. The mixture of the genetic information from two parents leads to variety in the offspring
  - Asexual reproduction – no fusion of gametes and only one individual is needed as the parent. There is no mixing of genetic information and so no variation in the offspring. These genetically identical individuals are known as clones. [B1.7.2 a)]

Lesson structure

Starters

Recognising variation – Write up on the board the list of human characteristics controlled by a single pair of genes. Ask students to look at each other and decide which version of each characteristic they have. Add up the numbers for each one. Ask the students if there appears to be a pattern. Is one of the pair of characteristics more common than the other? *(5 minutes)*

Fruit or vegetable? – Have a range of fruit and vegetables available, to include onions, potatoes, yams, root ginger, peas in a pod, runner beans, and tomatoes. Students can be supported by asking them which are fruits and which are vegetables and then discussing with them the differences between a fruit and a vegetable. Students can be extended by getting them to say whether they are produced as the result of sexual or asexual reproduction. For the examples that are produced by asexual reproduction, students should name the organs involved. *(10 minutes)*

Main

- Create an OHP presentation of variety in sexual reproduction. Use the example in the Student Book for the inheritance of dimples. Explain again that this characteristic is controlled by a single pair of genes and that one gene for the characteristic is inherited from each parent. One form of the gene enables the formation of dimples and the other form of the gene does not. If a person has dimples, then they have inherited the 'dimples' form of the gene, but if they do not have dimples then they have not inherited this form of the gene. In order for a person to have dimples, they only have to inherit the 'dimples' form of the gene from one parent. Ask the students: Is it possible for two parents without dimples to produce a child with dimples? Can two parents with dimples have a child without dimples? What happens if one parent has dimples and the other does not?

- Provide worksheets for the students and explain about the relationship between chromosomes and genes. Remind them that dimples dominate over no dimples. After showing the different possibilities and asking the questions, get them to decide whether or not the offspring will have dimples. They have to justify their answers. After they have had time to decide and write their answers, discuss in class, or proceed to the next activity to back up the theoretical predictions.

- Set up a practical to demonstrate how sexual reproduction produces variety (see 'Practical support').

Plenaries

Why do some plants do both? – This is a brainstorming session on why a number of plants have both strategies. Ask: 'Has it got something to do with the differences between plants and animals?' *(5 minutes)*

What are the advantages and disadvantages of asexual v. sexual reproduction? – This question produces a quick balance sheet of ideas with suggestions from the students. Students can be supported by providing them with statements about each type of reproduction and getting them to decide which are advantages and which are disadvantages. Students can be extended by making their own lists and building up a balance sheet of ideas. *(10 minutes)*

Practical support

Investigation into how sexual reproduction produces variety

Equipment and materials required

For this experiment, you will need two sets (about 50 in each set) of different-coloured beads for each group of students. If beads are difficult, it is possible to use haricot beans dyed different colours. Each group of students will need two beakers into which 50 beads can be mixed.

Details

It is suggested that one set of coloured beads represents the 'dimples' form of the gene and the other set represents the 'non-dimples' form of the gene. The idea is to get the students to appreciate how the variations arise, so set them the task of investigating the different possibilities.

Tell the students to set up the possibilities using sets of beads to represent the parental genes: all one colour for the 'dimples' form, all the second colour for the 'non-dimples' form and a mixture of half of each colour for a parent with both forms of the gene. They can set up the situations described above and work out what happens if beans are chosen randomly from the beakers. With closed eyes, the students should take one bead from each beaker and record what colours they have selected. Beads should continue to be chosen and recorded until all the beads in the beakers have been used up. Simple arithmetic will show what the ratios/numbers of the offspring having a particular characteristic are.

Variation, reproduction and new technology

B1 6.2 Types of reproduction

Learning objectives

- What is a clone?
- Why does asexual reproduction result in offspring that are identical to their parents?
- How does sexual reproduction produce variety?

Reproduction is very important to living things. It is during reproduction that genetic information is passed on from parents to their offspring. There are two very different ways of reproducing – **asexual reproduction** and **sexual reproduction**.

Asexual reproduction

Asexual reproduction only involves one parent. There is no joining of special sex cells and there is no variety in the offspring.

Asexual reproduction gives rise to identical offspring known as **clones**. Their genetic material is identical both to the parent and to each other.

a Why is there no variety in offspring from asexual reproduction?

Asexual reproduction is very common in the smallest animals and plants and in bacteria. However, many bigger plants like daffodils, strawberries and brambles do it too. The cells of your body reproduce asexually all the time. They divide into two identical cells for growth and to replace worn-out tissues.

Figure 1 A mass of daffodils like this can contain hundreds of identical flowers. This is because they come from bulbs that reproduce asexually. They also reproduce sexually using their flowers.

Study tip

- asexual reproduction – one parent → clones
- sexual reproduction – two parents → variety

Sexual reproduction

Sexual reproduction involves a male sex cell and a female sex cell from two parents. These two special sex cells (gametes) join together to form a new individual.

The offspring that result from sexual reproduction inherit genetic information from both parents. This means you will have some characteristics from both of your parents, but won't be exactly like either of them. This introduces variety. The offspring of sexual reproduction show much more variation than the offspring from asexual reproduction. In plants the gametes involved in sexual reproduction are found within ovules and pollen. In animals they are called ova (eggs) and sperm.

Sexual reproduction is risky because it relies on the sex cells from two individuals meeting but it also introduces variety. That's why we find sexual reproduction in organisms ranging from bacteria to people.

b How does sexual reproduction cause variety in the offspring?

Variation

Why is sexual reproduction so important? The variety it produces is a great advantage in making sure a species survives. Variety makes it more likely that at least a few of the offspring will have the ability to survive difficult conditions.

If you take a closer look at how sexual reproduction works, you can see how variation appears in the offspring.

Different genes control the development of different characteristics about you. Most things about you, such as your hair and eye colour, are controlled by several different pairs of genes. A few of your characteristics are controlled by one single pair of genes. For example, there are genes that decide whether:

- your earlobes are attached closely to the side of your head or hang freely
- your thumb is straight or curved
- you have dimples when you smile
- you have hair on the second segment of your ring finger.

We can use these genes to help us understand how inheritance works.

c Why is variety important?

Figure 2 Although these young people have some family likenesses, the variety caused by the mixing of their parents' genetic information is clear

Curved thumb

Attached ear lobe

Dimples

Straight thumb

Unattached ear lobe

No dimples

Figure 3 These are all human characteristics that are controlled by a single pair of genes. They can help us to understand how sexual reproduction introduces variety and how inheritance works.

You will get a random mixture of genetic information from your parents, which is why you don't look exactly like either of them!

Summary questions

1 Define the following words:
  a asexual reproduction   c gamete
  b sexual reproduction   d variation.

2 Compare the advantages and disadvantages of sexual reproduction with asexual reproduction.

3 A daffodil reproduces asexually using bulbs and sexually using flowers.
  a How does this help to make them very successful plants?
  b Explain the genetic differences between a daffodil's sexually and asexually produced offspring.

Key points

- In asexual reproduction there is no joining of gametes and only one parent. There is no genetic variety in the offspring.
- The genetically identical offspring of asexual reproduction are known as clones.
- In sexual reproduction male and female gametes join. The mixture of genetic information from two parents leads to genetic variety in the offspring.

108   109

Further teaching suggestions

Interactive programs on inherited genes

- There are some interactive programmes on the inheritance of different genes and how variation is achieved.

Family similarities and differences

- Suggest to students that they investigate family photographs and family members for similarities and differences. Sometimes it is possible that a characteristic 'skips' a generation, e.g. 'he has his grandfather's nose'. Students could write a short paragraph about any inherited tendencies in their family. If this is a sensitive issue, then supply pictures of the Hapsburgs or other dynasties where there are obvious family characteristics.

Characteristics of your pets!

- Those students who keep pets, such as budgerigars or mice, could investigate some of their characteristics. Coat colour in mice is a good example.

More than one gene involved?

- The human characteristics described in the student book are examples of variation due to a single gene, but these are the exceptions rather than the rule. Ask: 'What other characteristics are inherited? How are hair colour and height affected by inheritance?'

Summary answers

1 a No fusion of gametes, only one parent, no variety.
  b Two parents, fusion of gametes, variety.
  c Sex cell.
  d The differences between individuals as a result of their genetic material.

2 **Advantages:** mixes genes, leads to variation, allows process of evolution, increases chances of a species surviving if environment changes.
  Disadvantages: need to find a partner which uses resources, more waste in producing gametes, generally slower.

3 a They have the best of both worlds – safe reproduction through bulbs and variety from seeds.
  b There will be genetic variety in the sexually produced offspring as they inherit characteristics from both parents whereas there is no genetic variety resulting from asexual reproduction as this only involves one parent plant.

B1 6.3

Genetic and environmental differences

Learning objectives

Students should learn:

- that differences between individuals of the same species may be due to the genes they have inherited
- how differences may be due to environmental causes
- how differences may be due to a combination of both genetic and environmental causes.

Learning outcomes

Most students should be able to:

- explain what makes them different to the rest of their family
- explain why identical twins are not exactly the same in every way.

Some students should also be able to:

- evaluate evidence for the different characteristics caused by genetic and environmental effects.

Answers to in-text questions

a Your parents.

b Because any differences in the adult plants are the result of environmental differences as they are genetically identical.

Support

- Provide students with a list of environmental factors that could affect the growth of the beans and get them to decide the most favourable factors. Tell them that this would reduce variation due to the environment, so that they could then deduce any variation that would be genetic.

Extend

- Get students to investigate the link between IQ and environment and consider whether nutrition affects IQ?

Specification link-up: Biology B1.7

- Differences in the characteristics of different individuals of the same kind may be due to differences in:
  - the genes they have inherited (genetic causes)
  - the conditions in which they have developed (environmental causes)
  Or a combination of both. [B1.7.1 d)]

  Controlled Assessment: B4.1 Plan practical ways to develop and test candidates' own scientific ideas [B4.1.1 a) b)]; B4.3 Collect primary and secondary data. [B4.3.2 a) f)]

Lesson structure

Starters

Scars and birth marks – Project two torso outlines onto a whiteboard. Ask students to draw onto one any scars they have and onto the other any moles or birthmarks they have (be sensitive about using this activity where students have obvious distinctive birthmarks). Point at individual ones and ask who drew them and how they got them. Draw out that some differences are caused by the environment, such as scars, but some are not, such as birthmarks. *(5 minutes)*

Hairy moments – show the students pictures of a range of heads of hair. Encourage them to look at each other's hair and see how it varies. Some in the class may have coloured hair or extensions. Some may have been to sunny places on holiday. Discuss how hair colour changes during the year and over time. Relate this to genetic and environmental causes. Students can be supported by flagging up on the board in advance the common differences and causes, so students can refer to them when answering questions. Students can be extended by getting them to speculate as to the causes of the colour changes in terms of biochemical events, interaction with light, how DNA can bring about colour change etc. *(10 minutes)*

Main

- Split the class into small groups. Give each group a beaker containing some dry runner bean seeds without fungicide coating (cheaply bought by the half pint from garden centres) and an electronic balance. Get them to weigh the individual beans and record their mass as marks in a tally chart of categories. A range from 0.8 g through to 1.5 g should do. Get the students to make a bar chart of the results. Line the beans up, lightest to heaviest. Ask the students to write down reasons why the smaller beans were smallest and why the largest one grew largest. Ask them to speculate as to whether if you planted the smallest bean it would produce small seeds – what might complicate things? Ask how you could investigate this practically.

- Compare the bar chart of bean size with bell-shaped curves of normal distribution and draw out that there is a range of values of physical parameters within organisms and that this variation may have genetic or environmental causes. Lead into a discussion of causes of variation and draw out examples of inherited, environmental and combined variation.

- Try to find two beans which are as alike as possible. Ask how you could try to produce different sized beans or bean plants from each. Use this to link to a discussion of identical twins and twin studies to investigate the percentage hereditability of characteristics.

- There is some interesting information on twin studies in an article entitled 'Seeing doubles' (The Human Genome at the Wellcome Trust website). Summarise the project and some of the findings. Discuss with the students the work being done on the genetic basis of diseases of ageing.

Plenaries

G, E or B? – Give the students mini-whiteboards and dry-wipe markers. Project a series of photographs from the internet showing features which may show genetic variability, environmental variability or both. Get them on the command 'show me' to raise their boards. Have discussions where there is disagreement. *(5 minutes)*

Cloze passage – Draw out a cloze passage summarising the learning objectives suitable for your class's abilities. Students could be supported by making the passage simple and giving the missing words in a list at the end. Students can be extended by asking them to devise the cloze passage themselves and to use some more challenging omissions. Get the students to complete the passage and peer mark it. *(10 minutes)*

B1 6.3

Genetic and environmental differences

Learning objectives

- What makes you different from the rest of your family?
- Why aren't identical twins exactly the same in every way?

Figure 1 However much this Falabella eats, it will never be as tall as the Shire. It just isn't in the genes.

Have a look at the ends of your fingers and notice the pattern of your fingerprints. No one else in the world will have exactly the same fingerprints as you. Even identical twins have different fingerprints. What factors make you so different from other people?

Nature – genetic variety

The genes you inherit determine a lot about you. An apple tree seed will never grow into an oak tree. Environmental factors, such as the weather or soil conditions do not matter. The basic characteristics of every species are determined by the genes they inherit.

Certain human characteristics are clearly inherited. Features such as eye colour, the shape of your nose and earlobes, your sex and dimples are the result of genetic information inherited from your parents. But your genes are only part of the story.

a Where do the genes you inherit come from?

Nurture – environmental variety k

Some differences between you and other people are completely due to the environment you live in. For example, if a woman drinks heavily when she is pregnant, her baby may be very small when it is born and have learning difficulties. These characteristics are a direct result of the alcohol the fetus has to deal with as it develops. You may have a scar as a result of an accident or an operation. These characteristics are all environmental, not genetic.

Genes certainly play a major part in deciding how an organism will look. However, the conditions in which it develops are important too. Genetically identical plants can be grown under different conditions of light or soil nutrients. The resulting plants do not look identical. Plants deprived of light, carbon dioxide or nutrients do not make as much food as plants with plenty of everything. The deprived plants will be smaller and weaker. They have not been able to fulfil their 'genetic potential'.

b Why are genetically identical plants so useful for showing the effect of the environment on appearance?

Combined causes of variety

Many of the differences between individuals of the same species are the result of both their genes and the environment. For example, you inherit your hair colour and skin colour from your parents. However, whatever your inherited skin colour, it will be darker if you live in a sunny environment. If your hair is brown or blonde, it will be lighter if you live in a sunny country.

Your height and weight are also affected by both your genes and the conditions in which you grow up. You may have a genetic tendency to be overweight. However, if you never have enough to eat you will be underweight.

Figure 2 The differences in these cows are partly genetic and partly down to their environment, from the milk they drank as calves to the quality of the grass they eat each day

Investigating variety

It is quite easy to produce genetically identical plants to investigate variety. You can then put them in different situations to see how the environment affects their appearance. Scientists also use groups of animals that are genetically very similar to investigate variety. You cannot easily do this in a school laboratory.

The only genetically identical humans are identical twins who come from the same fertilised egg. Scientists are very interested in identical twins, to find out how similar they are as adults.

It would be unethical to take identical twins away from their parents and have them brought up differently just to investigate environmental effect. But there are cases of identical twins who have been adopted by different families. Some scientists have researched these separated identical twins.

Often identical twins look and act in a remarkably similar way. Scientists measure features such as height, weight and IQ (a measure of intelligence). The evidence shows that human beings are just like other organisms. Some of the differences between us are mainly due to genetics and some are largely due to our environment.

In one study, scientists compared four groups of adults:
- separated identical twins
- identical twins brought up together
- non-identical, same sex twins brought up together
- same sex, non-twin siblings brought up together.

The differences between the pairs were measured. A small difference means the individuals in a pair are very alike. If there was a big difference between the identical twins the scientists could see that their environment had more effect than their genes.

links
For more information on producing genetically identical plants, see B1 6.4 Cloning.

Figure 3 Whether identical twins are brought up together or apart, they are often very similar as adults

Table 1 Differences in pairs of adults

Measured difference in:	Identical twins brought up together	Identical twins brought up apart	Non-identical twins	Non-twin siblings
height (cm)	1.7	1.8	4.4	4.5
mass (kg)	1.9	4.5	4.6	4.7
IQ	5.9	8.2	9.9	9.8

Summary questions

1 Copy and complete using the words below.

combination *identical* *developed* *genes*

Everybody is different, even .... twins. Some of the differences are caused by our .... Some differences are caused by the conditions in which we have .... Many differences are caused by a .... of both.

2 **a** Using the data from Table 1, explain which human characteristic appears to be mostly controlled by genes and which appears to be most affected by the environment.

b Why do you think non-twin siblings reared together were included in the study as well as twins reared together and apart?

3 You are given 20 pots containing identical cloned seedlings, all the same height and colour. Explain how you would investigate the effect of temperature on the growth of these seedlings compared to the impact of their genes.

Study tip

- Genes control the development of characteristics.
- Characteristics may be changed by the environment.

Key points

- The different characteristics between individuals of a family or species may be due to genetic causes, environmental causes or a combination of both.

Further teaching suggestions

Dr Josef Mengele
- Research the crimes committed in the name of studies on twins by the Nazi Dr Josef Mengele.

Is variation due to nature or nurture?
- Discuss the table of differences in height, mass and IQ given in the text. Is it possible to say whether the variation is due more to nature rather than nurture?

Investigations
- Provide the students with a tray of identical small geranium plants (available from garden centres). Ask them to design and carry out an investigation into the effect of light on their growth and colour.
- A similar investigation could be done to find out what effect differences in nutrition have on the growth of the seedlings. Use a proprietary plant food.

Summary answers

1 identical, genes, developed, combination

2 **a** Height seems to be most closely controlled by genetics as there is least difference between the identical twins regardless of whether they are brought up together or apart. Mass seems to be most affected by the environment as identical twins brought up apart are no more identical than ordinary siblings.

b For comparison with the normal population: Identical twins reared together and twins reared apart mean you can compare the impact of different environments on genetically identical humans. Even twins brought up in the same household will not have identical environments – and there are small differences between them for all features. But when twins are reared apart, if they remain very similar, then that is largely controlled by genetics whilst if there are big differences then environment is having a big effect. Non-twin siblings show the level of similarity you would expect from two siblings (not genetically identical) reared in the same environment.

3 Credit for any sensible suggestions along with recognition of the need to control variables, how to get the most reliable and valid data from the investigation etc.

B1 6.4

Cloning

Learning objectives

Students should learn:

- that a clone is genetically identical to its parent
- taking cuttings is a rapid and cheap method of obtaining new plants
- modern cloning techniques, such as tissue culture and embryo transplants, use small groups of cells to produce many identical offspring.

Learning outcomes

Most students should be able to:

- define a clone
- explain the importance to gardeners and plant growers of cloning plants
- describe cloning by tissue culture in plants
- describe the process of embryo transplanting in animals
- discuss issues involving embryo cloning.

Some students should also be able to:

- interpret information about the advantages and disadvantages of different cloning techniques
- make informed judgements on the economic and ethical issues concerning embryo cloning.

Answers to in-text questions

a A cutting looks the same as its parent plant because it is genetically identical. It has been grown from a small piece of the parent plant.

b Tissue culture allows you to make thousands of new plants from a tiny piece of plant tissue.

Support

- Give students definitions from Question 1 of the Summary questions and ask them to fill in the correct terms.

Extend

- Ask students to research tissue culture as practised in horticultural research and development establishments. They could investigate the different mixtures of hormones and conditions needed to form new plants.

Specification link-up: Biology B1.7

- New plants can be produced quickly and cheaply by taking cuttings from older plants. These new plants are genetically identical to the parent plant. *[B1.7.2 b)]*
- Modern cloning techniques include:
  - tissue culture – using small groups of cells from part of a plant
  - embryo transplants – splitting apart cells from a developing animal embryo before they become specialised, then transplanting the identical embryos into host mothers
  - adult cell cloning … *[B1.7.2 c)]*
- Interpret information about cloning techniques and genetic engineering techniques. *[B1.7]*
- Make informed judgements about economic, social and ethical issues concerning cloning and genetic engineering, including genetically modified (GM) crops. *[B1.7]*

  Controlled Assessment: B4.1 Plan practical ways to develop and test candidates' own scientific ideas *[B4.1.1a) b)]*; B4.3 Collect primary and secondary data *[B4.3.2 a)]*; B4.4 Select and process primary and secondary data. *[B4.4.2 b)]*

Lesson structure

Starters

Photographs of 'Mini-Me' and Dolly – Show the photograph from the Austin Powers films. Ask: 'How was he made?' Show a photograph of Dolly the sheep for a real-life version and ask: 'How was she made?' *(5 minutes)*

Identical twins – Search the internet for a photograph of identical twins (or from within the school, if possible, with permission). Ask: 'How did they get to be identical?' Students can be supported by giving them a series of statements which they are asked to put in the correct order. Students can be extended by writing down the stages as bullet points. *(10 minutes)*

Main

This topic lends itself to practical work on cloning plants. The ideal time to do this is spring or early summer, but provided cuttings are kept in suitable conditions, it can be done at any time of year. With both practical experiments, students could be given a sheet of instructions to help them.

- Set up a practical on growing potatoes – this is best carried out during April–May, when pots can be left outside or in glasshouses (see 'Practical support'). Students should note the developments (digital photos can help here), until harvesting when the flowers have died off. A small prize can be awarded to the student whose pot yields the greatest mass at harvest. All students can take their potatoes home at the end of the experiment.
- If this is run as a competition, then the pots need to be kept in the same place, given the same quantities of water and nutrients and harvested at the same time. These conditions introduce the students to the idea of controlling variables, so that the test can be made as fair as possible. Be prepared to allow some time for checking progress and measuring during the course of the investigation. This activity can be used to teach aspects of 'How Science Works'.
- This practical exercise is similar, but can be done at any time of year using geraniums or zonal pelargoniums, growing them in a propagator (see 'Practical support'). Students can take a series of digital photographs for a PowerPoint presentation of their plant's development.

Plenaries

Thanks for the memories – Imagine it was possible to produce a clone of yourself. This could take place when you were old and had lived a full and happy life. Suppose you could transfer these memories to a young clone of yourself. Would it still be you? Discuss. *(5 minutes)*

Cloning cattle – Give students an empty flow diagram for cloning cattle and the associated labels, but in the wrong order. Students can be supported by asking them to sort them out and complete the diagram. Students could be extended by getting them to put in additional links or information boxes. *(10 minutes)*

Practical support

⚙ Growing potatoes
Equipment and materials required
Large potatoes with obvious 'eyes', and preferably the beginnings of shoots (chits), knives, 10 cm pots, compost, plant food.

Details
You will need large potatoes that have obvious 'eyes', and preferably the beginnings of shoots (chits). Give each group of student's one potato; tell them to cut it into sections, each with at least one 'eye'. The sections should be allowed to dry off and then placed in pots of compost. The pots should be stored in a frost-free area, kept watered and supplied with nutrients. They can be repotted as necessary, noting developments (digital photos can help here), until harvesting when the flowers have died off.

Safety: Care taken when using cutting instruments.

⚙ Cloning plants: Growing geraniums
Equipment and materials required
Propagator, geraniums or zonal pelargoniums, 10 cm pots, cutting compost, dibber, hormone rooting compound (if applicable).

Details
Take cuttings from geraniums, or zonal pelargoniums, by using 10 cm growing tips cut straight across just beneath a node. Remove most of the leaves, leaving only the top two or three, which can be reduced in size to cut down on water loss. Fill 10 cm pots to the brim with cutting compost and use a dibber to make a hole. Place the cutting in the hole so that the base of the stem is about halfway down the depth of the compost. Firm in, water and label. Pots can be placed in a propagator or covered with a polythene bag over the top, secured round the pot with an elastic band and left on a windowsill.

Safety: Care taken when using cutting instruments.

Variation, reproduction and new technology

Cloning

B1 6.4 — Cloning

Learning objectives
- How do we clone plants?
- How do we clone animals?
- Why do we want to create clones?

A clone is an individual that has been produced asexually and is genetically identical to the parent. Many plants reproduce naturally by cloning and this has been used by farmers and gardeners for many years.

Cloning plants
Gardeners can produce new plants by taking cuttings from older plants. How do you take a cutting? First you remove a small piece of a plant. This is often part of the stem or sometimes just part of the leaf. If you keep it in the right conditions, new roots and shoots will form. It will grow to give you a small, complete new plant.

Using this method you can produce new plants quickly and cheaply from old plants. The cuttings will be genetically identical to the parent plants.

Many growers now use hormone rooting powders to encourage cuttings to grow. Cuttings are most likely to develop successfully if you keep them in a moist atmosphere until their roots develop. We produce plants such as orchids and many conifer trees commercially by cloning in this way.

a Why does a cutting look the same as its parent plant?

Cloning tissue
Taking cuttings is a form of artificial asexual reproduction. It has been carried out for hundreds of years. In recent years scientists have come up with a more modern way of cloning plants called **tissue culture**. It is more expensive but it allows you to make thousands of new plants from one tiny piece of plant tissue.

The first step is to use a mixture of plant hormones to make a small group of cells from the plant you want to clone produce a big mass of identical plant cells.

Then, using a different mixture of hormones and conditions, you can stimulate each of these cells to form a tiny new plant. This type of cloning guarantees that you can produce thousands of offspring with the characteristics you want from one individual plant.

b What is the advantage of tissue culture over taking cuttings?

Cloning animals
In recent years cloning animals has become quite common in farming, particularly transplanting cloned cattle embryos. Cows normally produce only one or two calves at a time. If you use embryo cloning, your best cows can produce many more top-quality calves each year.

How does embryo cloning work? You give a top-quality cow fertility hormones so that it produces a lot of eggs. You fertilise these eggs using sperm from a really good bull. Often this is done inside the cow and the embryos that are produced are then gently washed out of her womb. Sometimes the eggs are collected and you add sperm in a laboratory to produce the embryos.

⊙⊙ links
For information on taking plant cuttings, look back at B1 2.6 Hormones and the control of plant growth.

Figure 1 Simple cloning by taking cuttings is a technique used by gardeners and nurserymen all around the world.

Figure 2 Tissue culture makes it possible to produce thousands of identical plants quickly and easily

At this very early stage of development every cell of the embryo can still form all of the cells needed for a new cow. They have not become specialised.

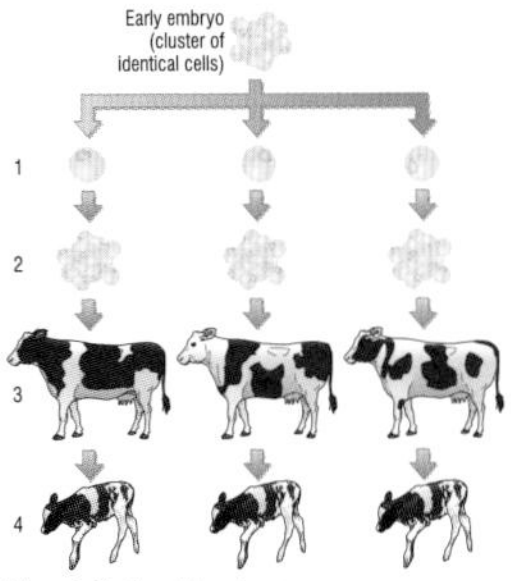

Early embryo (cluster of identical cells)

1. Divide each embryo into several individual cells.
2. Each cell grows into an identical embryo in the lab.
3. Transfer embryos into their host mothers, which have been given hormones to get them ready for pregnancy.
4. Identical cloned calves are born. They are not biologically related to their mothers.

Figure 3 Cloning cattle embryos

Cloning cattle embryos and transferring them to host cattle is skilled and expensive work. It is worth it because using normal reproduction, a top cow might produce 8–10 calves during her working life. Using embryo cloning she can produce more calves than that in a single year.

Cloning embryos means we can transport high-quality embryos all around the world. They can be carried to places where cattle with a high milk yield or lots of meat are badly needed for breeding with poor local stock. Embryo cloning is also used to make lots of identical copies of embryos that have been genetically modified to produce medically useful compounds.

Study tip
- Remember clones have identical genetic information.
- Make sure you are clear about the difference between a tissue and an embryo.

⊙⊙ links
For more information on cloning embryos, see B1 6.5 Adult cell cloning.

Key points
- New plant clones can be produced quickly and cheaply by taking cuttings from mature plants. The new plants are genetically identical to the older ones.
- A modern technique for cloning plants is tissue culture using cells from a small part of the original plant.
- Transplanting cloned embryos is one way in which animals are cloned.

Summary questions
1 Define the following words:
   a cuttings
   b tissue cloning
   c asexual reproduction
   d embryo cloning.
2 Make a table to compare the similarities and differences between tissue cloning and taking cuttings.
3 a Cloning cattle embryos is very useful. Why?
   b Draw a flow chart to show the stages in the embryo cloning of cattle.
   c Suggest some of the economic and ethical issues raised by embryo cloning in cattle.

112 / 113

Summary answers

1 a **Cuttings**: Taking a small piece of a stem or leaf and growing it on in the right conditions to produce a new plant.
  b **Tissue cloning**: Getting a few cells from a desirable plant to make a big mass of identical cells each of which can produce a tiny identical plant.
  c **Asexual reproduction**: Reproduction which involves only one parent, there is no joining of gametes and the offspring are genetically identical to the parent.
  d **Embryo cloning**: Splitting cells apart from a developing embryo before they become specialised to produce several identical embryos.

2 **Cuttings**: Put a small piece of plant into the right conditions and it grows into a new plant genetically identical to the parent plant.
  Tissue cloning: Take a few cells from the plant; provide the right conditions to produce a mass of cells; separate individual cells and provide the right conditions; can form thousands of tiny plants identical to the parent.

3 a It allows the production of far more calves from the best cows; can carry good breeding stock to poor areas of the world; as frozen embryos; can replicate genetically engineered animals quickly.
  b **Either** cow given hormones to produce large numbers of eggs → then cow inseminated with sperm → embryos collected and taken to the lab → embryos split to make more identical embryos → cells grown on again to make more identical embryos → embryos transferred to host mothers. **Or** cow given hormones to produce large numbers of eggs → eggs collected and taken to lab → eggs and sperm mixed → embryos grown → embryos split up to make more identical embryos → cells grown on to make bigger embryos → embryos transferred to host mothers.
  c Student shows understanding of issues involved in embryo cloning. For example, economic issues – only wealthy farmers/wealthy countries can afford the technology, is it acceptable to produce large numbers of identical cattle, etc.

B1 6.5 | Adult cell cloning

Learning objectives

Students should learn:

- that the steps in the techniques of adult cell cloning
- how scientists were able to clone a sheep
- that the potential benefits and risks of cloning animals.

Learning outcomes

Most students should be able to:

- explain the processes of adult cell cloning
- describe how Dolly the sheep was cloned
- list some of the benefits and disadvantages of cloning animals.

Some students should also be able to:

- evaluate the advantages and disadvantages of cloning
- discuss the ethical issues raised by adult cell cloning techniques.

Specification link-up: Biology B1.7

- Modern cloning techniques include:
  - tissue culture – using small groups of cells from part of a plant
  - embryo transplants – splitting apart cells from a developing animal embryo before they become specialised, then transplanting the identical embryos into host mothers.
  - Adult cell cloning – the nucleus is removed from an unfertilised egg cell. The nucleus from an adult body cell, e.g. a skin cell, is then inserted into the egg cell. An electric shock then causes the egg cell to begin to divide to form embryo cells. These embryo cells contain the same genetic information as the adult skin cell. When the embryo has developed into a ball of cells, it is inserted into the womb of an adult female to continue its development. *[B1.7.2 c)]*
- Interpret information about cloning techniques and genetic engineering techniques. *[B1.7]*
- Make informed judgements about the economic, social and ethical issues concerning cloning and genetic engineering, including genetically modified (GM) crops. *[B1.7]*

Lesson structure

Starters

Fill in the vowels – Write a list of key words and phrases used in this chapter on the board, but leave out the vowels (e.g. CLNNG, NCLS). Students can be supported by indicating where the vowels should go by writing the words with dashes for the missing letters. Ask students to fill in the missing vowels. Students can be extended by completing the words and writing a definition for each word or phrase. *(5 minutes)*

Would you like to be a twin? – If there are twins in the class, get them to describe what it is like to be a twin. Open up the discussion and then ask the students to write down a list of advantages and disadvantages of being an identical twin. Build up a general list on the board. *(10 minutes)*

Main

The main purpose of this lesson is to ensure that the students have a sound understanding of the basic technique of adult cell cloning and how it can be used to clone animals.

- Prepare a PowerPoint presentation illustrating the steps of adult cell cloning. Give students worksheets so that they can follow the sequence and write about the stages in their own words. Allow time for questions and further explanations.
- The story of Dolly is well-documented and it would be possible to show some of the material from websites such as the Science Museum Antenna (http://antenna.sciencemuseum.org.uk), the BBC (www.bbc.co.uk) or the Roslin Institute, Edinburgh (www.roslin.co.uk) (where the cloning was carried out). Alternatively, if there is good access to computers, the students could be given a list of suitable sites and then carry out their own search in groups. Each group of students could then be asked to produce a poster about Dolly and her life, for display in the laboratory.
- The Science Museum Antenna link is a particularly good one and covers the story of Dolly well in a sequence of topics. It combines details of the techniques involved, with details of Dolly's life and demise.
- Give students, working in groups, large A3 sheets of paper on which they can write their ideas about the advantages and disadvantages of this type of cloning. Ask one group to present their ideas and then discuss generally adding ideas from the other groups. At the end of the discussion, ask students to list the advantages and disadvantages in order of importance and compile a class list.

Support

- Give students pictures of Dolly the sheep and ask them to make a scrapbook or poster as suggested in the 'Main' section.

Extend

- Ask students to research ways in which animals, such as cows and sheep, can be genetically engineered and then cloned to produce useful substances in their milk. Has it been done? What substances have been produced? What substances would it be beneficial to produce?

Plenaries

Why is it ...? – Why is it easier to clone plants than it is to clone animals? Students can be supported by providing them with a list of reasons from which they can choose. Students can be extended by asking them to make a list of the differences between plants and animals that might affect the outcome of cloning. *(5 minutes)*

The quagga ... is cloning the answer? – Tell the story of the quagga, a type of zebra that became extinct in the 1880s and the attempts by the Quagga Project Committee to revive it. Is this a case for the use of a cloning technique or selective breeding? Discuss cloning as an alternative to selective breeding. *(10 minutes)*

Further teaching suggestions

Designer babies or cloned babies

- Research Bionet website (www.bionetonline.org) for the topic 'Design-a-baby'? Print out or project the information. Ask students to discuss whether it would be more desirable to design a baby or clone one. What are the pros and cons of each technique if it were possible to do it?

How much does it all cost?

- One factor which has so far not been considered is the cost of developing these new methods for cloning animals. The initial research has to be funded and then the cost of producing cloned animals could be quite high. Humans have been producing new varieties of animals through the techniques of selective breeding for centuries, so why should money be spent on cloning? Will it make food more expensive?

Answers to in-text questions

a   Adult cell cloning.

b   It could be used to help infertile couples have their own genetic child.

Variation, reproduction and new technology

B1 6.5 Adult cell cloning

Learning objectives

- How did scientists clone a sheep?
- What are the steps in the techniques of adult cell cloning?

True cloning of animals, without sexual reproduction involved at all, has been a major scientific breakthrough. It is the most complicated form of asexual reproduction you can find.

Adult cell cloning

To clone a cell from an adult animal is easy. The cells of your body reproduce asexually all the time to produce millions of identical cells. However, to take a cell from an adult animal and make an embryo or even a complete identical animal is a very different thing.

When a new whole animal is produced from the cell of another adult animal, it is known as adult cell cloning. This is still relatively rare. You place the nucleus of one cell into the empty egg cell of another animal of the same species. Then you place the resulting embryo into the uterus of another adult female where it develops until it is born.

Here are the steps involved:

- The nucleus is removed from an unfertilised egg cell.
- At the same time the nucleus is taken from an adult body cell, e.g. a skin cell of another animal of the same species.
- The nucleus from the adult cell is inserted (placed) in the empty egg cell.
- The new cell is given a tiny electric shock that makes it start dividing to form embryo cells. These contain the same genetic information as the original adult cell and the original adult animal.
- When the embryo has developed into a ball of cells it is inserted into the womb of an adult female to continue its development.

Adult cell cloning has been used to produce a number of whole animal clones. The first large mammal ever to be cloned from the cell of another adult animal was Dolly the sheep, born in 1997.

Figure 1 Dolly the sheep was the first large mammal to be cloned from another adult mammal. She went on to have lambs of her own in the normal way.

a   What is the name of the technique that produced Dolly the sheep?

Study tip

Animals can be cloned by using embryo transplants or by adult cell cloning.

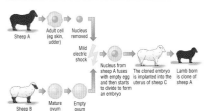

Figure 2 Adult cell cloning is still a very difficult technique – but scientists hope it may bring benefits in the future

When Dolly was produced she was the only success from hundreds of attempts. The technique is still difficult and unreliable, but scientists hope that it will become easier in future.

How Science Works

The benefits and disadvantages of adult cell cloning

One big hope for adult cell cloning is that animals that have been genetically engineered to produce useful proteins in their milk can be cloned. This would give us a good way of producing large numbers of cloned, medically useful animals.

This technique could also be used to help save animals from extinction, or even bring back species of animals that died out years ago. The technique could be used to clone pets or prized animals so that they continue even after the original has died. However, some people are not happy about this idea.

There are some disadvantages to this exciting science as well. Many people fear that the technique could lead to the cloning of human babies. This could be used to help infertile couples, but it could also be abused. At the moment this is not possible, but who knows what might be possible in the future?

Another problem is that modern cloning techniques produce lots of plants or animals with identical genes. In other words, cloning reduces variety in a population. This means the population is less able to survive any changes in the environment that might happen in the future. That's because if one of them does not contain a useful characteristic, none of them will.

In a more natural population, at least one or two individuals can usually survive change. They go on to reproduce and restock. This could be a problem in the future for cloned crop plants or for cloned farm animals.

b   How might adult cell cloning be used to help people?

Summary questions

1   Copy and complete using the words below:
    mammal adult technique genetic Dolly
    In .... cell cloning an animal is produced that is an exact .... copy of another adult animal. .... the sheep was the first large .... to be produced using this modern cloning ....

2   Produce a flow chart to show how adult cell cloning works.

3   What are the main advantages and disadvantages of the development of adult cell cloning techniques?

links

For more information on adult cell cloning, see B1 6.7 Making choices about technology.

Did you know ...?

The only human clones alive at the moment are natural ones known as identical twins! But the ability to clone mammals such as Dolly the sheep has led to fears that some people may want to have a clone of themselves produced – whatever the cost.

Key points

- Scientists cloned Dolly the sheep using adult cell cloning.
- In adult cell cloning the nucleus of a cell from an adult animal is transferred to an empty egg cell from another animal. A small electric shock causes the egg cell to begin to divide and starts embryo development. The embryo is placed in the womb of a third animal to develop. The animal that is born is genetically identical to the animal that donated the original adult cell.

114   115

Summary answers

1   adult, genetic, Dolly, mammal, technique

2   The nucleus is removed from an unfertilised egg cell → the nucleus is taken from an adult body cell → the nucleus from the adult cell is inserted (placed) in the empty egg cell → new cell is given a tiny electric shock → new cell fuses together → begins to divide to form embryo cells → ball of cells inserted into womb to continue its development.

3   **Advantages:** enabled us to clone adult animals so we can clone genetically engineered organisms, making it possible to clone new tissues and organs for people with diseases or needing transplants, could help infertile couples, could help conserve very endangered species. Any valid points.

Disadvantages: people are concerned about human cloning, reduces variety in a population, objections to the formation of embryos which are then used to harvest tissues, people object to the cloning of endangered or extinct animals. Any other valid points.

B1 6.6 Genetic engineering

Learning objectives

Students should learn:

- that genetic engineering involves artificially changing the genetic material of an organism
- that genes can be transferred from one organism to another
- that genes can be transferred into plants and animals so that they develop desired characteristics.

Learning outcomes

Most students should be able to:

- explain the term 'genetic engineering'
- describe how genes from one organism can be transferred into another organism
- list some advantages and disadvantages of genetic engineering
- interpret information about cloning techniques and genetic engineering techniques.

Some students should also be able to:

- explain the process of genetic engineering, and the difference between genetically modified organisms which produce useful proteins and organisms which are improved themselves
- evaluate the advantages and disadvantages of genetic engineering.

Support

- Provide students with cards for the stages in genetic engineering and getting them to put them in the correct order.

Extend

- Students could be introduced to some of the terms used in genetic engineering such as the correct names of the enzymes, plasmids, vectors, marker genes, recombinant DNA.

Specification link-up: Biology B1.7

- In genetic engineering, genes from the chromosomes of humans and other organisms can be 'cut out' using enzymes and transferred to cells of other organisms. *[B1.7.2 d)]*
- Genes can also be transferred to the cells of animals, plants or microorganisms at an early stage in their development so that they develop with desired characteristics.
  - new genes can be transferred to crop plants
  - crops that have had their genes modified in this way are called genetically modified crops (GM crops)
  - examples of genetically modified crops include ones that are resistant to insect attack or to herbicides
  - genetically modified crops generally show increased yields. *[B1.7.2 e)]*
- Concerns about GM crops include the effect on populations of wild flowers and insects, and uncertainty about the effects of eating GM crops on human health. *[B1.7.2 f)]*
- Make informed judgements about the economic, social and ethical issues concerning cloning and genetic engineering, including genetically modified (GM) crops. *[B1.7]*

Lesson structure

Starters

'Glow in the dark mouse' – Search online news stories about genetic engineering such as 'glow in the dark' mice. For example, try www.bbc.co.uk. Discuss how this might come about. *(5 minutes)*

Genetic engineering – good or bad? – Ask students to think about the advantages and disadvantages of genetically modified (GM) crops. Students can be supported by writing up six statements on the board, three positive points about GM crops and three negative points. Ask the students to sort out the positive points from the negative ones. Students can be extended by asking them to suggest points of their own. Give them two minutes to do this and then build up a list on the board. Students can also be extended by asking them to think of an ethical framework for their decision-making, so that it will work independent of content. *(10 minutes)*

Main

- What is genetic engineering? Take students through the sequence of selecting a gene, cutting it out, putting it into a bacterium; mention the different enzymes (not necessarily by name but according to what they are doing). A good example to choose as an illustration is the human growth hormone. The production of the hormone is under the control of one gene, so the sequence is clear. As this is a difficult concept, a worksheet for the students to fill in during the presentation will help them.
- Make your own genetically modified bacterium. Use a digital camera and a stop motion animation program, provide the students with the materials to make a plasticine model of a genetically modified bacterium. They will need to remove the required gene from a chromosome model and insert it into a plasmid in a bacterium. Use a knife labelled 'enzymes'.
- To explain genetic engineering, type a random DNA sequence into a word processor and copy/paste a part of this into a drawing of a bacterium. Now copy the two and paste as many copies of the new bacterium as quickly as you can.
- Provide material from pro-GM organisations, such as Monsanto, and anti-GM organisations, such as Greenpeace and the Soil Association, together with articles from the general media coverage. Ask students to gather information from the sources during class time, and then for homework design a case for or against.

Plenaries

Designer kids quandary – Imagine how you would feel if your parents had chosen all sorts of features about you – your hair, eyes, gender etc. How would that affect the way you feel about your own identity? Discuss as a class. *(5 minutes)*

Review genetic engineering – good or bad? – Review the list of pros and cons made at the beginning. Have any ideas changed? Students can be supported by asking them which they think are the most important and giving each a rank. Students could be extended by getting them to add extra points about the pros and cons of human engineering. *(10 minutes)*

Further teaching suggestions

Genetic diseases

- There are references on the internet to specific genetic diseases. There is a good account of the story of Sammi Sparke, who suffered from cystic fibrosis and had a successful lung transplant, at www.organdonation.nhs.uk.

GM videos

- There are videos on GM crops giving a negative slant. These can be obtained free of charge from the organisation 'Compassion in World Farming' (Charles House, 5a Charles Street, Petersfield, Hants GU32 3EH, Tel. (01730 264 208). However, students will be expected to present a balanced view of this topic.

Answers to in-text questions

a It is cut out using enzymes.

b There is a limit to the types of protein bacteria can make.

c A genetic disease is a disease or problem caused by a mistake in the genetic material in your cells.

B1 6.6 — Genetic engineering

Learning objectives

- What is genetic engineering?
- How are genes transferred from one organism to another?
- What are the issues involved in genetic engineering?

What is genetic engineering?

Genetic engineering involves changing the genetic material of an organism. You take a gene from one organism and transfer it to the genetic material of a completely different organism. So, for example, genes from the chromosomes of a human cell can be 'cut out' using enzymes and transferred to the cell of a bacterium. The gene carries on making a human protein, even though it is now in a bacterium.

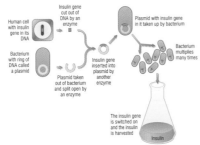

Figure 1 The principles of genetic engineering. A bacterial cell receives a gene from a human being so it makes the human hormone insulin.

Labels in Figure 1:
- Human cell with insulin gene in its DNA
- Insulin gene cut out of DNA by an enzyme
- Plasmid with insulin gene in it taken up by bacterium
- Bacterium with ring of DNA called a plasmid
- Plasmid taken out of bacterium and split open by an enzyme
- Insulin gene inserted into plasmid by another enzyme
- Bacterium multiplies many times
- The insulin gene is switched on and the insulin is harvested
- Insulin

a How is a gene taken out of one organism to be put into another?

If genetically engineered bacteria are cultured on a large scale they will make huge quantities of protein from other organisms. We now use them to make a number of drugs and hormones used as medicines.

Transferring genes to animal and plant cells

There is a limit to the types of proteins that bacteria are capable of making. As a result, genetic engineering has moved on. Scientists have found that genes from one organism can be transferred to the cells of another type of animal or plant at an early stage of their development. As the animal or plant grows it develops with the new desired characteristics from the other organism. For example, glowing genes from jellyfish have been used to produce crop plants which give off a blue light when they are attacked by insects. Then the farmer knows when they need spraying.

b Why are genes inserted into animals and plants as well as into bacteria?

The benefits of genetic engineering

Genetically engineered bacteria can make exactly the proteins we need, in exactly the amounts needed and in a very pure form. For example, people with diabetes need supplies of the hormone insulin. In the past people used animal insulin extracted from the pancreases of pigs and cattle. Now they can use pure human insulin produced by genetically engineered bacteria (see Figure 1).

We can use engineered genes to improve the growth rates of plants and animals. They can be used to improve the food value of crops as genetically modified (GM) crops usually have much bigger yields than ordinary crops. They can also be designed to grow well in dry, hot or cold parts of the world so could help to solve the problems of world hunger. Crops can be engineered to produce plants which make their own **pesticide** or are resistant to **herbicides** used to control weeds.

Human engineering

If there is a mistake in your genetic material, you may have a genetic disease. These can be very serious. Many people hope that genetic engineering can solve the problem.

It might become possible to put 'healthy' genes into the affected cells by genetic engineering, so they work properly. Perhaps the cells of an early embryo can be engineered so that the individual develops into a healthy person. If these treatments become possible, many people would have new hope of a normal life for themselves or their children.

c What do we mean by a 'genetic disease'?

The disadvantages of genetic engineering

Genetic engineering is still a very new science. No one knows what all of the long-term effects might be. For example, insects may become pesticide-resistant if they eat a constant diet of pesticide-forming plants.

Some people are concerned about the effect of eating GM food on human health. Genes from genetically modified plants and animals might spread into the wildlife of the countryside. GM crops are often made infertile, which means farmers in poor countries have to buy new seed each year.

People might want to manipulate the genes of their future children. This may be to make sure they are born healthy, but there are concerns that people might want to use it to have 'designer' children with particular characteristics such as high intelligence. Genetic engineering raises issues for us all to think about.

Figure 2 You can't tell that food is genetically modified just by looking at it! In the UK, few GM foods are sold and they have to be clearly labelled. Many other countries, including the USA, are less worried and use GM food widely.

Summary questions

1 Copy and complete using the words below:

cell engineering enzymes gene genetic transfer

Genetic .... involves changing the .... material of an organism. You cut a .... from one organism using .... and .... it to the .... of a completely different organism.

2 **a** Make a flow chart that explains the stages of genetic engineering.

   b Make two lists, one to show the possible advantages of genetic engineering and the other to show the possible disadvantages.

Key points

- Genes can be transferred to the cells of animals and plants at an early stage of their development so they develop desired characteristics. This is genetic engineering.
- In genetic engineering, genes from the chromosomes of humans and other organisms can be 'cut out' using enzymes and transferred to the cells of bacteria and other organisms.
- There are advantages and disadvantages associated with genetic engineering.

Summary answers

1 engineering, genetic, gene, enzymes, transfer, cell

2 **a** Suitable flow diagram based on B1 6.6 Figure 1 in the Student Book.

  b **Advantages** – any suitable points such as:
  - Bacteria can make human medicines and hormones.
  - Improve the growth rates of plants and animals.
  - Improve the food value of crops.
  - Reduce the fat levels in meat.
  - Produce plants that make their own pesticide chemicals.
  - Crop plants can give off a blue light when attacked by insects, so that the farmer knows when they need to be sprayed.
  - Possible cures for genetic diseases.
  - Fruit does not go bad so quickly.

Disadvantages – any suitable points such as:
- Insects may become pesticide-resistant if they eat a constant diet of pesticide-forming plants.
- Effect on human health of eating genetically modified food.
- Genes from genetically modified plants and animals might spread into the wildlife.
- Genetically modified crops are often infertile, so farmers in poor countries have to buy new seed each year.
- People may want to manipulate the genes of their future children.

B1 6.7

Making choices about technology

Learning objectives

Students should learn:

- that there are economic, social and ethical issues concerning new techniques such as cloning and genetic engineering.

Learning outcomes

Most students should be able to:

- interpret information about cloning and genetic engineering techniques
- describe some of the ethical problems associated with these techniques
- make informed judgements about the issues.

Some students should also be able to:

- make balanced judgements, explaining their reasoning clearly, about the issues involved.

Specification link-up: Biology B1.7

- Interpret information about cloning techniques and genetic engineering techniques. [B1.7]
- Make informed judgments about the economic, social and ethical issues concerning cloning and genetic engineering, including genetically modified (GM) crops. [B1.7]
- Concerns about GM crops include the effect on populations of wild flowers and insects, and uncertainty about the effects of eating GM crops on human health. [B1.7.2 f)]

Lesson structure

Starters

Who's bothered? – Show a photograph of a GM protester (Greenpeace or similar). Ask the students to write down any ideas they have as to why the protester might be angry? What might they be trying to change? (5 minutes)

Opinions on the line – Draw a series of long, parallel horizontal lines on the board. Get students to draw them either on rough paper or on mini-whiteboards. Put the word 'agree' on one side and the word 'disagree' on the other. Read out a series of statements based on the content of the student text (adjust the language level to suit the class). Get each student to put crosses on their lines according to where their opinion lies. Get some volunteers to come to the front of the class and show where they have placed their crosses and explain their reasoning. Students can be supported by making the statements very simple and unambiguous. They will also need some guidance. Students can be extended by giving them more challenging and/or ambiguous statements and the activity should generate discussion. (10 minutes)

Main

- Hold a discussion of the issues raised during the 'opinions on the line' starter. If not used, discuss the Student Book directly after having given the students an opportunity of reading it.

- Explain that it took 188 attempts to bring Copycat, the cloned cat, into existence. Debate as to whether it is worth doing this kind of research when it is so expensive in embryos.

- The Canadian Museum of Nature (http://nature.ca) has an excellent online game involving cloning cats. Search for 'geee in genome – copycat'.

- Discuss the film *The Boys from Brazil* about clones of Hitler. Get the students to come up with a list of situations in which it would be OK to carry out cloning and a list where it would not be approved. Discuss who should be in charge of this. Carry out internet research to find out who the controlling bodies are in the UK and internationally.

- There is an opportunity here for introducing the concept of the formal debate with a motion, proposer and seconder, opposer and their second, questions from the floor and a vote to see if it is carried. This can tie in with the coverage of debates in PSHE or citizenship.

- Show some rice and show some children with vitamin A deficiency symptoms. Discuss the issue of biofortification and draw out opinions with reasons.

Plenaries

£100 000 pet – Imagine you are going to write a short email addressed to the people in the USA who spent £100 000 cloning their Labrador. What would you say? Read out some when the exercise is completed. (5 minutes)

Speech bubble summaries – Give the students cut out speech bubbles. Get them to put their opinions on the topics covered during the discussions within the lesson onto their speech bubble and then tack them to the walls around the room. Allow the students to circulate and read each other's opinions. Students can be supported by giving them speech bubble summaries to choose from. Students can be extended by getting them to pick one speech bubble summary (not their own) and to critically evaluate it. The class must be trustworthy in order to carry out this without silliness. (10 minutes)

Support

- Get students to design a poster to summarise how Copycat was cloned

Extend

- Get students to research the current situation on the growing of GM crops in the UK.

Further teaching suggestions

Local farmers opinions on GM
- If possible, ask local farmers for their opinions on GM either via email or see if you can get some visiting speakers who have personal involvement.

GM trials
- Research information on the trialling of GM crops.

Designing an advertisement
- Design an advertisement for a company who will clone your pet for you.

Researching cheese
- More than 30% of cheese is made using fungal enzymes from genetically modified yeast. This topic could be researched and students could find out whether or not this information is included on the wrappers of cheese.

How Science Works — **Variation, reproduction and new technology**

Making choices about technology

B1 6.7 — Making choices about technology

Learning objectives
- What sort of economic, social and ethical issues are there about new techniques such as cloning and genetic engineering?

Cloning pets

Cc, or Copycat, was the first cloned cat to be produced. Most of the research into cloning had been focused on farm and research animals – but cats are thought of first and foremost as pets.

Much of the funding for cat cloning in the US comes from companies who are hoping to be able to clone people's dying or dead pets for them. It has already been shown that a successful clone can be produced from a dead animal. Cells from beef from a slaughter house were used to create a live cloned calf.

It took one hundred and eighty-eight attempts to make Cc, producing 87 cloned embryos, only one of which resulted in a kitten. Cloning your pet won't be easy or cheap. The issue is, should people be cloning their dead cats, or would it be better to give a home to one of the thousands of unwanted cats already in existence? Even if a favourite pet cat is cloned, it may look nothing like the original because the coat colour of many cats is the result of genes switching on and off at random in the skin cells. The clone will develop and grow in a different environment to the original cat as well. This means other characteristics that are affected by the environment will probably be different too.

?? Did you know …?
Dogs have also been cloned. In 2009, an American couple paid more than £100 000 to have a clone of their much-loved pet Labrador. The new dog is called Lancelot encore (encore means 'again').

Figure 2 Lancelot encore, a clone of a much-loved pet, and a portrait of the original dog

Figure 1 The cat on the left is Rainbow. The cat on the right is Cc, Rainbow's clone. Rainbow and Cc share the same DNA – but they don't look the same.

To some people these are exciting events. To others they are a waste of time, money and the lives of all the embryos that don't make it. What do you think?

Activity
In B1 6.4 and B1 6.5 there is information about cloning animals and plants for farming. Here you have two different stories about cloning animals for money (Cc and Lancelot encore).

There is talk of a local company setting up a laboratory to clone cats, dogs and horses for anyone in the country who wants to do this.

Write a letter or post a blog either *for* the application or *against* it. Make sure you use clear, sensible arguments and put the science of the situation across clearly.

The debate about GM foods

Ever since genetically modified foods were first introduced there has been controversy and discussion about them. For example, varieties of GM rice known as 'golden rice' and 'golden rice 2' have been developed. These varieties of rice produce large amounts of vitamin A. Up to 500 000 children go blind each year as a result of lack of vitamin A in their diets. In theory golden rice offers a solution to this problem. In fact, many people objected to the way trials of the rice were run and the cost of the product. No golden rice is yet being grown in countries affected by vitamin A blindness.

There is a lot of discussion about genetically modified crops. Here are some commonly expressed opinions.

Figure 3 The amount of beta carotene in golden rice and golden rice 2 is reflected in the depth of colour of the rice

John, 49, plumber, UK
'I'm very concerned about GM foods. Who knows what we're all eating nowadays. I don't want strange genes inside me, thank you very much. We've got plenty of fruit and vegetables as it is – why do we need more?'

Ali, 26, shop assistant, UK
'I think GM food is such a good idea. If the scientists can modify crops so they don't go off so quickly, food should get cheaper, and there will be more to go around. And what about these plants that produce pesticides? That'll stop a lot of crop spraying, so that should make our food cleaner and cheaper. It's typical of us in the UK that we moan and panic about it all.'

Tilahun, 35, farmer, Ethiopia
'I have some real worries about the GM crops that don't form fertile seeds. In the past, farmers in poorer countries just kept seeds from the previous year's crops, so it was cheap and easy. With the GM crops we have to buy new seeds every year – although I hear that won't be the case with golden rice. On the other hand, these GM crops don't need spraying very much. They grow well in our dry conditions, they give a much bigger crop yield and keep well too – so there are some advantages.'

Activity
You are going to produce a 5-minute slot for a daytime television show on '**Genetic engineering – a good thing or not?**' Using the information here and on B1 6.6 Genetic engineering (and extra research if you have time), plan out a script for your time on air, remembering that you have to inform the public about genetic engineering, entertain them and make them think about the issues involved.

Summary questions
1 People get very concerned about cloning. Do you think these fears are justified? Explain your answer.
2 Summarise the main advantages and disadvantages of genetic engineering expressed here.

Key points
- There are a number of economic, social and ethical issues concerning cloning and genetic engineering which need to be considered when making judgements about the use of this science.

118 / 119

Summary answers

1 Credit for relevant comments backed by science

No: e.g. cloning has many potential benefits such as reproducing genetically engineered organisms, saving organisms from extinction, producing cheap plants. Some forms of cloning have been going on for centuries (cuttings) and these have been/may be used to produce medical treatments, etc.

Yes: e.g. most animals produced by adult cell cloning have problems, wasteful process, risk of human cloning for the wrong reasons, etc.

2 **Advantages:** Food won't go off so fast: less pesticide use; food cheaper and cleaner; plants can be developed to grow well in particular environments, e.g. dry conditions of some areas of developing World.

Disadvantages: People are concerned about eating engineered DNA; infertile crops which is a problem for farmers in the developing world; cost.

Summary answers

1 a From a runner – a special stem from the parent plant with small new identical plant on the end.

  b Asexual.

  c By sexual reproduction (flowers, pollination, etc.).

  d The new plants from the packet will be similar to, but not identical to their parents – each one will be genetically different. The plants produced by asexual reproduction will be identical to their parents.

2 a A unit of inheritance – a small piece of DNA.

  b On the chromosomes in the nucleus of a cell.

  c A sex cell.

3 a Traditional cuttings used parts of whole stems and roots, but tissue culture uses minute collections of cells as the starting point. Cuttings result in up to hundreds of identical plants, tissue culture can give thousands.

  b Embryo cloning – flushing out early embryos and dividing them before replacing in surrogate mother cows.

  c Both allow large numbers of genetically identical individuals to be produced from good parent stock much faster and more reliably than would be possible using traditional techniques.

  d Cloning plants uses bits of the adult plant as the raw material for the cloning. Animal embryo cloning, as it is used at the moment, involves using embryos as the raw material for the cloning, although this may change in the future.

  e There are more and more people in the world needing to be fed, so techniques for reproducing high yielding plants and animals are always helpful and are financially beneficial for farmers. Also in developed countries people demand high quality but cheap food – so techniques which reproduce valuable animals and plants more quickly are valued.

4 a Clear description of adult cell cloning, e.g. The nucleus is removed from an unfertilised egg cell. At the same time the nucleus is taken from an adult body cell, e.g. a skin cell of another animal of the same species. The nucleus from the adult cell is inserted (placed) in the empty egg cell. The new cell is given a tiny electric shock which fuses the new cells together, and causes it to begin to divide to form embryo cells. These contain the same genetic information as the original adult cell and the original adult animal. When the embryo has developed into a ball of cells, it is inserted into the womb of an adult female to continue its development.

  b Plant cloning has been accepted for a long time and doesn't threaten people – only advantages seen in general. Cloning animals is seen as worrying in itself but also raises concerns of human cloning. Cloning pets etc., is seen as frivolous.

5 a See Figure 1, 6.6 Genetic engineering – it should look similar but with growth hormone instead of insulin.

  b It is pure – free from any contamination. It is the human version of a hormone. It can be produced in large amounts relatively easily and cheaply as and when it is needed.

6 a They have been raised and trained on different establishments so it is environmental factors which are influencing their racing ability.

  b As a control – to see how the animal turns out if not trained up as a racing mule.

  c Data on effect of diet, handling, intensity of training etc. on the temperament, running speed, stamina, etc., of the mules.

7 Plant a GM crop. After pollination, collect samples of plants at increasing distances, in all directions. Inspect the pollen collected; analyse for GM cells; plot distribution.

Summary questions

1 a How has the small plant shown in diagram A been produced?

  b What sort of reproduction is this?

  c How were the seeds in B produced?

  d How are the new plants that you would grow from the packet of seeds shown in B different from the new plants shown in A?

2 a What is a gene?

  b Where do you find genes?

  c What is a gamete?

3 Tissue culture techniques mean that 50 000 new raspberry plants can be grown from one old one instead of two or three by taking cuttings. Cloning embryos from the best bred cows means that they can be genetically responsible for 30 or more calves each year instead of two or three.

  a How does tissue culture differ from taking cuttings?

  b How can one cow produce 30 or more calves in a year?

  c What are the similarities between cloning plants and cloning animals in this way?

  d What are the differences in the techniques for cloning animals and plants?

  e Why do you think there is so much interest in finding different ways to make the breeding of farm animals and plants increasingly efficient?

4 a Describe the process of adult cell cloning.

  b There has been a great deal of media interest and concern about cloning animals but very little about cloning plants. Why do you think there is such a difference in the way people react to these two different technologies?

5 Human growth is usually controlled by growth hormo produced by the pituitary gland in your brain. If you don't make enough hormones, you don't grow prope and remain very small. This condition affects 1 in eve 5000 children. Until recently the only way to get grow hormone was from the pituitary glands of dead bodie Genetically engineered bacteria can now make plent pure growth hormone.

  a Draw and label a diagram to explain how a healthy human gene for making growth hormone can be ta from a human chromosome and put into a working bacterial cell.

  b What are the advantages of producing substances growth hormone using genetic engineering?

6 In 2003 two mules called Idaho Gem and Idaho Star were born in America. They were clones of a famous racing mule. They both seem very healthy. They were separated and sent to different stables to be reared a trained for racing. So far Idaho Gem has been more successful than his cloned brother, winning several ra against ordinary racing mules. There is a third clone, Utah Pioneer, which has not been raced.

  a The mules are genetically identical. How do you explain the fact that Idaho Gem has beaten Idaho S in several races?

  b Why do you think one of the clones is not being raced?

  c Their progress is being carefully monitored by scientists. What type of data do you think will be available from these animals?

7 One concern people have about GM crops is that they might cross pollinate with wild plants. Scientists need find out how far pollen from a GM crop can travel to b able to answer these concerns. Describe how a trial to investigate this might be set up

120

Kerboodle resources

Resources available for this chapter on Kerboodle are:

- Chapter map: Variation, reproduction and new technology
- Practical: Stem and leaf cuttings (B1 6.2)
- Practical: New plants from tissue culture (B1 6.2)
- How Science Works: Twin studies (B1 6.3)
- Animation: Genetic modification (B1 6.6)
- Viewpoints: Designer babies (B1 6.5)
- Viewpoints: Genetically modified crops (B1 6.6)
- Support: You're never alone with a clone (B1 6.4)
- Extension: Genetic history (B1 6.6)
- Interactive activity: Reproduction and inheritance
- Revision podcast: Variation, reproduction and new technology
- Test yourself: Variation, reproduction and new technology
- On your marks: Variation, reproduction and new technology
- Practice questions: Variation, reproduction and new technology
- Answers to practice questions: Variation, reproduction and new technology

End of chapter questions

ractice questions 🄚

trawberries are able to reproduce many plants from one
arent plant.

Choose the correct answer to complete each sentence.
Producing new plants with one parent is called ....
(1)

*asexual reproduction   genetic engineering
sexual reproduction*

The advantage of this is that all the strawberry fruits
will ....
(1)

be bigger   all taste better   all taste the same

A disadvantage of this to the strawberry plants
is that ....
(1)

*there is more variation   they are genetically identical
they cannot mate*

Read the passage. Use the information and your own
knowledge to answer the questions.

At one time, the boll weevil destroyed cotton crops. Farmers
sprayed the crops with a pesticide.

The weevil died out but another insect, the bollworm moth,
became resistant to this pesticide.

In the 1990s large crops of the cotton plant were destroyed by
the bollworm moth. The pesticides then used to kill the moth
were expensive and very poisonous, resulting in deaths to
humans.

Scientists investigated alternative ways to control the bollworm
moth. They found out that a type of bacterium produced a
poison which killed bollworm larvae (grubs).

A GM cotton crop plant was developed which produced the
poison to kill bollworms. This proved to be very effective and
farmers were able to stop using pesticide sprays.

Now farmers have another problem. Large numbers of other
insects have multiplied because they were not killed when the
farmers stopped using pesticides. Some of these insects have
started to destroy the GM cotton and farmers are beginning to
use pesticides again!

  i Give **one** advantage of spraying crops with
pesticides.
(1)

  ii Give **two** disadvantages of spraying crops with
pesticides.
(2)

  iii Give **one** economic advantage of using GM cotton.
(1)

  iv Some people object to using GM crops. Suggest
one reason why.
(1)

b *In this question you will be assessed on using good
English, organising information clearly and using
specialist terms where appropriate.*

The GM cotton was genetically engineered to produce
the same poison as the bacterium.
Describe fully how this is done.
(6)

3 The use of cloned animals in food production is
controversial.

> It is now possible to clone 'champion' cows.
>
> Champion cows produce large quantities of milk.

a Describe how adult cell cloning could be used to
produce a clone of a 'champion' cow.
(4)

b Read the passage about cloning cattle.

> The Government has been accused of 'inexcusable behaviour'
> because a calf of a cloned American 'champion' cow has been
> born on a British farm. Campaigners say it will undermine trust
> in British food because the cloned cow's milk could enter the
> human food chain.
>
> But supporters of cloning say that milk from clones and their
> offspring is as safe as the milk we drink every day.
>
> Those in favour of cloning say that an animal clone is a genetic
> copy. It is not the same as a genetically engineered animal.
> Opponents of cloning say that consumers will be uneasy about
> drinking milk from cloned animals.

Use the information in the passage and your own
knowledge and understanding to evaluate whether the
government should allow the production of milk from
cloned 'champion' cows.

Remember to give a conclusion to your evaluation. (5)

AQA, 2006

121

Practical suggestions

Practicals	AQA	🄚	📖	⚙
Investigate the optimum conditions for the growth of cuttings of, e.g. Mexican hat plants, spider plants, African violets.	✓	✓	✓	
Investigate the best technique for growing new plants from tissue cultures (e.g. cauliflower).	✓	✓		

Practice answers

**Note to teachers – DNA is strictly introduced in Unit BLY2. If
candidates give an answer where DNA would be appropriate
they will gain credit in BLY1 but it is not essential knowledge.**

1 a asexual reproduction
(1 mark)

  b all taste the same
(1 mark)

  c they are genetically identical
(1 mark)

2 a **i** Kills insects (which eat crop) **or** increases yield
(1 mark)

    ii Any **two** from:
- kills insects which may not be pests
- poisonous to humans
- expensive
- pollutes the environment
- other relevant suggestions e.g. is not organic
(2 marks)

    iii Increases crop yield **or** reduces cost of pesticide use
(1 mark)

    iv Any **one** from:
- May lead to increased use of pesticides in the long run/description /ref to last paragraph
- ethical considerations e.g. alters genes of crop
- Do not allow 'not natural' 'against genes may get into wildlife idea, religion' or similar, not organic.
(1 mark)

  b There is a clear and detailed scientific description of the
sequence of events in genetic engineering. The answer is
coherent and in a logical sequence. It contains a range of
appropriate or relevant specialist terms used accurately.
The answer shows very few errors in spelling, punctuation
and grammar.
(5–6 marks)

There is some description of the sequence of events in
genetic engineering but there is a lack of clarity and detail.
The answer has some structure and the use of specialist
terms has been attempted, but not always accurately.
There may be some errors in spelling, punctuation and
grammar.
(3–4 marks)

There is a brief description of the genetic engineering,
which has little clarity and detail. The answer is poorly
constructed with an absence of specialist terms or
their use demonstrates a lack of understanding of their
meaning. The spelling, punctuation and grammar are
weak.
(1–2 marks)

No relevant content.
(0 marks)

Examples of biology points made in the response:
- gene from the bacterium
- is cut from the chromosome
- using enzymes
- gene transferred to the cotton
- (cotton) chromosome – allow cell
- (the gene) controls characteristics
- causes the cotton (cells) to produce the poison.

3 a Any **four** from:
- nucleus/DNA/chromosomes/genetic material removed (from egg)
- from (unfertilised) egg/ovum

linked to second point
*allow 'empty egg cell' for first **two** marks*
*do **not** allow fertilised egg*
allow egg from champion cow

- nucleus from body cell of champion (cow)
- inserted into egg/ovum
- electric shock
- to make cell divide **or** develop into embryo
- (embryo) inserted into womb/host/another cow

allow this point if wrong method eg embryo splitting
(4 marks)

  b Any **four** from:
Pros: Max 2 marks
- economic benefit eg increased yield/more profit
- clone calf not genetically engineered
- genetic material not altered
- milk safe to drink/same as ordinary milk

Cons: Max 2 marks
- consumer resistance
- caused by misunderstanding process
- not proved that milk is safe

*ignore 'God would not like it' **or** 'it's not natural'*

- ethical/religious argument
- reduce gene pool/eg

Conclusion: Max 1 mark
    sensible conclusion for or against, substantiated by
    information from the passage and/or own knowledge
conclusion at end
(5 marks)

B1 7.1

Theories of evolution

Learning objectives

Students should learn:

- the theory of evolution
- that there is evidence that evolution has taken place.

Learning outcomes

Most students should be able to:

- state Darwin's theory of evolution
- describe some of the evidence that evolution has taken place
- identify the differences between Darwin's theory of evolution and conflicting theories, e.g. Lamarck's.

Some students should also be able to:

- suggest reasons for the different theories explaining life on Earth.

Specification link-up: Biology B1.8

- Darwin's theory of evolution by natural selection states … . *[B1.8.1 a)]*
- The theory of evolution by natural selection was only … . *[B1.8.1 b)]*
- Other theories, including that of Lamarck, are based … . *[B1.8.1 c)]*
- Interpret evidence relating to evolutionary theory. *[B1.8]*
- Identify the differences between Darwin's theory of evolution and conflicting theories, such as that of Lamarck. *[B1.8]*

Lesson structure

Starters

Sorted! – Give a number of students a card or sheet with the picture of a different organism on it. These organisms should represent a spread over the timescale from life first emerging to human development. Students are to arrange themselves in order according to when they think the organism they are holding evolved. Match this with the real order and see who came in approximately the correct place. Students can be supported by giving them simple animal examples. Students can be extended by giving them a range of plants and animals. *(5 minutes)*

How much do we already know? – This is formative assessment task on the words 'Darwin', 'Natural selection', 'Origin of Species' and 'Evolution'. Write these words on a large sheet of quartered A2 paper. Allow the sheet to be circulated around the room with students adding comments. *(10 minutes)*

Main

- Gather together some details of as many different theories of evolution as you can: Darwin, Lamarck, the Creation, spontaneous generation, etc. and give a brief summary of each. This would be a good introduction to some of the following suggestions. Discuss the merits of each one.

- The life and times of Charles Darwin – Show a video (one is produced by Hawkhill Associates, Madison, WI) of Darwin's journey and discoveries, together with some details of his life (when he published his work etc.). Alternatively, search the internet for 'Charles Darwin video'. Discuss how his trip led to his point of view. As an alternative, show some excerpts from the film *Creation* about the life of Charles Darwin. The showing of the video could be followed by building up a cartoon summary of Darwin's voyage. Decide on the frames and get the students to complete it.

- Find out more about the life and times of Lamarck. There are some interesting videos (particularly from Cornell University) comparing and explaining the theories of Darwin and Lamarck. Try researching 'Jean-Baptiste Lamarck video' online.

Support

- Ask students to complete simple sentences summarising natural selection in a simple way.

- Present students with pictures of three or four animals with fairly obvious different characteristics (e.g. horn length in antelope, speed of response in rabbits they can run at about 30 mph, etc.). Ask them to choose which one would survive to have offspring.

Extend

- Suggest that the students do some more research on the attitude of all religions to evolutionary theory, in Darwin's time and also at the present time. Try The Richard Dawkins Foundation for information.

Plenaries

Which ones shall we have? L, D or LD? – Give students individual cards or whiteboards on which they can respond to various statements and key words from both theories. For example: parents pass on acquired characteristics (L), survival of the fittest (D), law of use and disuse (L), natural selection (D), species do not stay the same (LD). L for Lamarck only, D for Darwin only and LD if applicable to both. *(5 minutes)*

Faking the evidence – How easy would it be to fake a fossil and so provide some evidence in support of evolution? Show some pictures or models of real fossils and discuss how fakes could be made and how you could prove that they were fakes. Students could be supported by prompting and suggestions. Students could be extended by getting them to research fakes (go to the BBC Nature and Science website, www.bbc.co.uk/sn). You could include a couple of 'fakes' in the examples you show to the students. *(10 minutes)*

Further teaching suggestions

Summarising the issues
- There are some good summaries of the issues in *A Short History of Nearly Everything* by Bill Bryson.

What makes the Galapagos so special?
- Students could find out why the Galapagos Islands are so special and research: 'Are there any other locations where similar conditions might have existed?' If available, show some footage from the film *Master and Commander: The Far Side of the World* (2003), where one of the characters has the chance to explore the Galapagos Islands.

Find out more about Darwin
- Although Darwin is probably best known for his work on the theory of evolution, he did work in other areas of biology. Use some of the information from the film and from other sources, such as libraries and the internet, to build up an account of all his scientific work.

Answers to in-text questions
a Useful changes or characteristics that organisms developed during their lives to help them survive are passed on to their offspring.

b *HMS Beagle*.

c Galapagos Islands.

Evolution

B1 7.1 Theories of evolution

Learning objectives
- What is the theory of evolution?
- What is the evidence that evolution has taken place?

We are surrounded by an amazing variety of life on planet Earth. Questions such as 'Where has it all come from?' and 'When did life on Earth begin?' have puzzled people for many generations.

The theory of evolution tells us that all the species of living things alive today have evolved from the first simple life forms. Scientists think these early forms of life developed on Earth more than 3 billion years ago. Most of us take these ideas for granted – but they are really quite new.

Up to the 18th century most people in Europe believed that the world had been created by God. They thought it was made, as described in the Christian Bible, a few thousand years ago. However, by the beginning of the 19th century scientists were beginning to come up with new ideas.

Lamarck's theory of evolution
Jean-Baptiste Lamarck was a French biologist. He thought that all organisms were linked by what he called a 'fountain of life'. He made the great step forward of suggesting that individual animals adapted and evolved to suit their environment. His idea was that every type of animal evolved from primitive worms. The change from worms to other organisms was caused by the **inheritance of acquired characteristics**.

Lamarck's theory was that the way organisms behaved affected the features of their body – a case of 'use it or lose it'. If animals used something a lot over a lifetime he thought it would grow and develop. Any useful changes that took place in an organism during its lifetime would be passed from a parent to its offspring. The neck of the giraffe is a good example. If a feature wasn't used, Lamarck thought it would shrink and be lost.

Lamarck's theory influenced the way **Charles Darwin** thought. However, there were several problems with Lamarck's ideas. There was no evidence for his 'fountain of life' and people didn't like the idea of being descended from worms. People could also see quite clearly that changes in their bodies – such as big muscles, for example – were not passed on to their children.

We now know that in the great majority of cases Lamarck's idea of inheritance cannot happen. However, scientists have discovered that in a few cases the way an animal behaves actually changes its genes. This results in the next generation behaving in the same way.

a What do you think is meant by the phrase 'inheritance of acquired characteristics'?

Charles Darwin and the origin of species
Our modern ideas about evolution began with the work of one of the most famous scientists of all time – Charles Darwin. Darwin set out in 1831 as the ship's naturalist on *HMS Beagle*. He was only 22 years old at the start of the voyage to South America and the South Sea Islands.

Darwin planned to study geology on the trip. But as the voyage went on he became excited by his collection of animals and plants as by his rock samples.

b What was the name of the ship that Darwin sailed on?

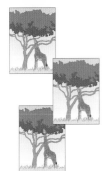

Figure 1 In Lamarck's model of evolution, giraffes have long necks because each generation stretched up to reach the highest leaves. So each new generation had a slightly longer neck.

Study tip

Remember the basic key stages in natural selection:
survive → breed → pass on genes

In South America, Darwin discovered a new form of the common rhea, an ostrich-like bird. Two different types of the same bird living in slightly different areas set Darwin thinking.

On the Galapagos Islands he was amazed by the variety of species. He noticed that they differed from island to island. Darwin found strong similarities between types of finches, iguanas and tortoises on the different islands. Yet each was different and adapted to make the most of local conditions.

Darwin collected huge numbers of specimens of animals and plants during the voyage. He also made detailed drawings and kept written observations. The long journey home gave him plenty of time to think about what he had seen. Charles Darwin returned home after five years with some new and different ideas forming in his mind.

c What is the name of the famous islands where Darwin found so many interesting species?

After returning to England, Darwin spent the next 20 years working on his ideas. Darwin's theory of evolution by natural selection is that all living organisms have evolved from simpler life forms. This evolution has come about by a process of natural selection.

Reproduction always gives more offspring than the environment can support. Only those that have inherited features most suited to their environment – the 'fittest' – will survive. When they breed, they pass on the genes for those useful inherited characteristics to their offspring. This is natural selection.

When Darwin suggested how evolution took place, no one knew about genes. He simply observed that useful inherited characteristics were passed on. Today, we know it is useful genes which are passed from parents to their offspring in natural selection.

Figure 2 Darwin was very impressed by the giant tortoises he found on the Galapagos Islands. The tortoises on each island had different-shaped shells and a slightly different way of life. Darwin made detailed drawings of them all.

Figure 3 Darwin worked here in his study for around 20 years, carrying out experiments and organising his ideas on evolution by natural selection

Study tip

Avoid confusion between:
- the *theory of evolution* and
- the *process of natural selection*.

Summary questions
1 Explain what is meant by the following terms:
   a evolution
   b natural selection
2 What was the importance of the following in the development of Darwin's ideas?
   a South American rheas
   b Galapagos tortoises, iguanas and finches
   c the long voyage of *HMS Beagle*
   d the 20 years from his return to the publication of his book *The Origin of Species*.

Key points
- The theory of evolution states that all the species which are alive today – and many more which are now extinct – evolved from simple life forms that first developed more than 3 billion years ago.
- Darwin's theory is that evolution takes place through natural selection.

122   123

Summary answers

1 a All the species of living organisms which are alive today (and many more which are now extinct) have evolved from simple life forms, which first developed more than 3 billion years ago.

   b Only the animals and plants most suited to their environment – the 'fittest' – will survive to breed and so pass on their characteristics.

2 a South American rheas – Darwin found a new species – two types of the bird living in slightly different areas made Darwin start to think about how they came about.

   b Galapagos tortoises, iguanas and finches – these were some of the animals in the Galapagos Islands that varied from island to island, and made Darwin wonder what had brought about the differences.

   c The long voyage of *HMS Beagle* – this gave Darwin lots of opportunities to collect specimens and time to think about his theories and ideas.

   d The twenty years from his return to the publication of the book *The Origin of Species* in the development of Darwin's ideas gave Darwin time to work out his ideas very carefully and to collect a lot of evidence to support them.

B1 7.2

Accepting Darwin's ideas

Learning objectives

Students should learn:

- how Darwin's ideas were only gradually accepted
- how his ideas conflicted with religious beliefs
- that he could not explain how variety and inheritance happened.

Learning outcomes

Most students should be able to:

- explain why Darwin's ideas were only gradually accepted
- explain why there was conflict with religious beliefs
- describe some of the evidence that was lacking.

Some students should also be able to:

- explain why knowledge of genetics is necessary to understand how inheritance works.

Specification link-up: Biology B1.8

- Suggest reasons for the different theories. [B1.8]
- Suggest reasons why Darwin's theory of natural selection was only gradually accepted. [B1.8]
- Interpret evidence relating to evolutionary theory. [B1.8]

Lesson structure

Starters

Seeing is believing – Introduce this activity as a 'true or false' game to see who will believe unusual suggestions. Tell the students that everything they see is upside down. The ceiling is really on the floor and the floor is really on the ceiling. Get a 'hands-up' show of who believes that this is the case. Use a diagram of the eye, an overhead projector and a lens to project an upside-down image of a student onto an A3 sheet of paper. Refer to an experiment in 1896 where scientist George Stratton wore inverting glasses for a week. At first he couldn't walk or function at all but by the end of the week, everything appeared normal. He then took off the inverting glasses and everything looked upside down! Discuss and link to Darwin's views seeming unbelievable at the time but now widely accepted to be true. *(5 minutes)*

Darwin's life and times – a potted biography – Get the students to put the events of Darwin's life in chronological order. Students could be supported by providing a list of the major events (voyage on HMS Beagle, publication of books, etc.). Students could be extended by getting them to do a timeline emphasising the length of time it took him to publish his findings. *(10 minutes)*

Main

- Use the images in the text or search the internet for 'Darwin's finches', which will clearly show the beaks, and try to match them with their function. Show a map of the Galapagos Islands with the location of the different finches and also a picture of the original type of finch which colonised the Galapagos Islands. Why were these islands interesting?

- Find other examples of Darwin's collection from the Galapagos Islands and the voyage of *HMS Beagle* (the turtles are quite a good starting point). Discuss how he collected his evidence. What was he looking for?

- Produce a students PowerPoint presentation or exposition on the objections. During the exposition, give an opportunity to express their views and to discuss the objections.

- Get the students to imagine that they were one of Darwin's fellow scientists and had just heard about his ideas on evolution. Ask them to suggest what further evidence they would have needed to be convinced that he was right. Would they be convinced by fossils? (It might be worth pointing out that although fossils were collected as curiosities, people just thought they were preserved skeletons of creatures they had not seen yet.) Would they think of other ways in which his theories could be tested? Ask students what they consider is the most compelling piece of evidence to support the theories. What convinces them today that Darwin was right?

Plenaries

Let's make sure! – Darwin did not publish his theory for many years after he first thought of it. Imagine you are Darwin and write a diary entry giving reasons why he delayed the publication – what might he have been afraid of? What negative consequences could there be for him, for his family, for society? Discuss and then summarise. *(5 minutes)*

Assume the position – Darwin's work was so controversial because it went against the assumptions and collective world view of the time. What assumptions and collective world view do we have today on his theories? List things we take as given in current Western society. Support students by giving some examples, e.g. scientists will always find the correct answers to problems, many people assume that there is no reality beyond the physical etc. How do we react to people who challenge these assumptions? What lessons from the past can we draw from the ridicule Darwin experienced and the eventual acceptance of his views and his veneration? More able students will succeed in empathising with Darwin and gaining an awareness of the blinding effect of scepticism. They will probably be able to provide some more examples of theories that have been ridiculed. *(10 minutes)*

Support

- Provide students with a synopsis of the events of Genesis.

Extend

- Introduce students to Darwin's *The Descent of Man* and get them to find out about more recent work on the origins of humans. Guide them to the work of Professor Chris Stringer at the Natural History Museum.

Further teaching suggestions

Challenging society
- List ideas which would appear provocative to the assumptions of our current society. Try to evaluate which may have merit and how you might go about finding if they have merit in a non-presumptive fashion.

If only Darwin had known about...
- Get students to think about how much easier it would have been for Darwin if he had known about genetics and inheritance.

Darwin and Mendel
- Imagine a meeting between Darwin and Mendel. Darwin could have talked about his observations on pigeons and domestic birds and Mendel could have talked about his peas.

B1 7.2   Accepting Darwin's ideas

Learning Objectives
- Why was Darwin's theory of evolution only gradually accepted?

Charles Darwin came back from his trip on *HMS Beagle* with new ideas about the variety of life on Earth. He read many books and thought about the ideas of many other people such as Lamarck, Lovell and Malthus. He gradually built up his theory of evolution by natural selection.

He knew his ideas would be controversial. He expected a lot of opposition both from fellow scientists and from religious leaders.

Building up the evidence

Darwin realised he would need lots of evidence to support his theories. This is one of the reasons why it took him so long to publish his ideas. He spent years trying to put his evidence together in order to convince other scientists.

He used the amazing animals and plants he had seen on his journeys as part of that evidence. They showed that organisms on different islands had adapted to their environments by natural selection. So they had evolved to be different from each other.

Darwin carried out breeding experiments with pigeons at his home. He wanted to show how features could be artificially selected. Darwin also studied different types of barnacles (small invertebrates found on seashore rocks) and where they lived. This gave him more evidence of organisms adapting and forming different species.

Darwin built up a network of friends, fellow scientists and pigeon breeders. He didn't travel far from home (he was often unwell) but he spent a lot of time discussing his ideas with this group of friends. They helped him get together the evidence he needed and he trusted them as he talked about his ideas.

Figure 1 The finches found on the different Galapagos islands look very different but all evolved from the same original type of finch by natural selection

Why did people object?

In 1859, Darwin published his famous book *On the Origin of Species by means of Natural Selection* (often known as *The Origin of Species*). The book caused a sensation. Many people were very excited by his ideas and defended them enthusiastically. Others were deeply offended, or simply did not accept them.

There were many different reasons why it took some scientists a long time to accept Darwin's theory of natural selection. They include:

- The theory of evolution by natural selection challenged the belief that God made all of the animals and plants that live on Earth. This religious view was the generally accepted belief among most people in early Victorian England.
- In spite of all Darwin's efforts, many scientists felt there was not enough evidence to convince them of his theory.
- There was no way to explain how variety and inheritance happened. The mechanism of how inheritance happens – by genes and genetics – was not known until 50 years *after* Darwin published his ideas. Because there was no mechanism to explain how characteristics could be inherited, it was much harder for people to accept and understand.

The arguments raged and it took some time before the majority of scientists accepted Darwin's ideas. However, by the time of his death in 1882 he was widely regarded as one of the world's great scientists. He is buried in Westminster Abbey along with other great people like Sir Isaac Newton.

Figure 2 Darwin's famous book – it sold out on the first day of publication!

Figure 3 It wasn't just scientists who were interested in Darwin's ideas. Cartoonists loved the idea of evolution too.

?? Did you know ...?

Darwin let his children use the back of his original manuscript of *The Origin of Species* as drawing paper. Not many of these original pages exist. Darwin kept the ones that remain because of his children's drawings rather than his own writing!

Key points
- Darwin's theory of evolution by natural selection was only gradually accepted for a number of reasons. These include:
  - a conflict with the widely held belief that God made all the animals and plants on the Earth
  - insufficient evidence
  - no mechanism for explaining variety and inheritance – genetics were not understood for another 50 years.

Summary questions

1. **a** Darwin set out in *HMS Beagle* in 1831. How many years later did he publish *The Origin of Species*?
   b What was Darwin's big idea?
2. What type of evidence did Darwin put together to convince other scientists his ideas were right?
3. Why did it take some time before most people accepted Darwin's ideas?

Summary answers

1. **a** *On the Origin of Species* published in 1859, so 28 years.

   b All the species which are alive today, and many more that are now extinct, evolved from simple life forms which first developed more than three billion years ago through a process of natural selection. The organism most suited to its environment is most likely to survive and breed and so pass on the useful characteristic.

2. He used evidence from the voyage of *HMS Beagle* to show different organisms on different islands which were very similar but had adapted to fill different niches etc., breeding experiments with pigeons, and evidence of different species of barnacles, discussion with and use of observations from fellow scientists.

3. There was a clash between the establishment which was based on the Church and the idea that everything had its place and was created by God. A lot of inertia and strong belief to overcome. Also, it was just the status quo.

   Although Darwin had put together a lot of evidence, it wasn't enough for some scientists, particularly the links higher up the evolutionary tree thinking about human evolution. He was missing the fossil records that would fill in some of the gaps.

   No obvious mechanism until genes and genetics were discovered, so it was a process without an obvious model of how it came about.

B1 7.3 Natural selection

Specification link-up: Biology B1.8

- Evolution occurs via natural selection:
  - individual organisms within a particular species may show a wide range of variation because of differences in their genes
  - individuals with characteristics most suited to the environment are more likely to survive to breed successfully
  - the genes which have enabled these individuals to survive are then passed on to the next generation. [B1.8.1 e)]
- Where new forms of a gene result from mutation, there may be relatively rapid change in a species if the environment changes. [B1.8.1 f)]

Learning objectives

Students should learn:

- how individuals best suited to their environment survive to breed successfully
- that these individuals pass their genes on to the next generation
- that a mutation is a change in an existing gene.

Learning outcomes

Most students should be able to:

- explain what is meant by natural selection
- describe how mutation results in changes to genes.

Some students should also be able to:

- explain how mutation can affect the evolution of an organism.

Answers to in-text questions

a Charles Darwin.

b Because it would be more likely to hear the approach of a predator and also to hear warning signs from other animals.

c A change in the genes/DNA.

d A disease of oysters where they do not grow properly; they are small, flabby and they develop pus-filled blisters and die.

Lesson structure

Starters

Six fingers better than five? – Show a picture of a person with six fingers on each hand. Ask what are the advantages and disadvantages. Students can be supported by providing a list of suggestions and getting them to select which they think are the most important and why. Students can be extended by getting them to make their own lists, followed by a discussion. They could also be asked to think of mutations in other animals which could affect survival, e.g. albinism. *(5 minutes)*

Blinky, the three-eyed mutant fish – Search the internet for images of 'Blinky the fish' from *The Simpsons* or show sections from season 2, episode 4, 'Two Cars in Every Garage and Three Eyes on Every Fish'. Discuss how this mutant could have arisen and whether three eyes would be an advantage. *(10 minutes)*

Main

- There are a number of interactive natural selection games available on the internet. These can be recommended to students or used in class if there is appropriate computer access. Try PBS Teacher Source at www.pbs.org or www.echalk.co.uk.
- Consider the peppered moth. This moth (*Biston betularia*) with its black mutant is well-documented. Prepare a PowerPoint presentation about the distribution of the two forms of the moth, together with some statistics on how populations have changed since the decline of industry in some areas. Students can be asked to compile a single A4 sheet summary of the evidence. This case provides support for the mechanism of survival of the fittest, natural selection and evolution.
- The activity above can be linked to another example of natural selection at work: the banded snail. Students may find evidence of this in their own gardens or in the school grounds. There are pictures of the different forms of the snail available; look for references to polymorphism. Essentially, there are more variations in the banded snail which provide camouflage in different situations. The snails best camouflaged survive, the rest do not.
- The fruit fly (*Drosophila*) is used in genetics experiments to investigate the inheritance of characteristics. Show some fruit flies and photographs of some of the mutations that have been studied. Discuss how these mutations might have arisen or been induced. In order to gain an understanding of how rapidly a mutation could spread, calculate how long it would take a pair of fruit flies to produce a billion offspring if each female produces 200 offspring every two weeks.

Support

- Provide students with pictures of backgrounds and different banded snails and get them to match the snails with the most favourable background.

Extend

- Students could be asked to draw analogies between the evolution of animals and plants and the development of communications equipment over the last century.

Plenaries

The 'mutant schoolchild' – Imagine that Dr Who has returned to Earth in the Tardis many thousands of years in the future to find that schoolchildren have mutated to suit their environment. Build up a picture of a 'mutant schoolchild', who has adapted to an extreme extent. Suggestions from the students can be used to build up a picture on the board. Alternatively, each student could be given a sheet of paper and asked to draw or describe their mutant. Results to be displayed. *(5 minutes)*

Favourable adaptations? – Project or display photographs of a number of adaptations shown by plants and animals and discuss and explain how each could have arisen by natural selection. Some fairly obvious ones are thorns on stems, brightly coloured flowers, prehensile tails, eyes that swivel in chameleons, etc. Students could be supported by using very obvious examples and if necessary linking these with clue or prompt sheets. Students could be extended by getting them to imagine a very useful adaptation for an animal or a plant. Get the students to draw out a sequence chart of what must happen and over what timescale in order for this to take place. *(10 minutes)*

Further teaching suggestions

Linking animal evolution to plant evolution
- How far is the evolution of animals linked to the evolution of plants or vice versa? A possible example of parallel evolution is that of insects and insect-pollinated plants, i.e. the evolution of flowers. This could be the basis of a discussion on links between plants and animals.

Evolution in action
- Studies of the occurrence of heavy metal tolerant plants on spoil heaps can provide some evidence for evolution in

action. Students need to be provided with some background information and then asked to summarise the process. Link to the peppered moth story.

The mutant schoolchild
- The plenary can be extended by encouraging students to describe and explain the selective advantages of the features of their mutant. Would it survive?

Evolution

B1 7.3   Natural selection ⓚ

Learning objectives
- How does natural selection work?
- What is mutation?

Scientists explain the variety of life today as the result of a process called natural selection. The idea was first suggested about 150 years ago by Charles Darwin.

Animals and plants are always in competition with each other. Sometimes an animal or plant gains an advantage in the competition. This might be against other species or against other members of its own species. That individual is more likely to survive and breed. This is known as natural selection.

a Who first suggested the idea of natural selection?

links
For more information on the competition between plants and animals in the natural world, look back at B1 4.4 Competition in animals and B1 4.5 Competition in plants.

Figure 1 The natural world is often brutal. Only the best adapted predators capture prey – and only the best adapted prey animals escape.

?? Did you know ...?
Fruit flies can produce 200 offspring every two weeks. The yellow star thistle, an American weed, produces around 150000 seeds per plant per year. If all those offspring survived we'd be overrun with fruit flies and yellow star thistles!

links
For information on genes, see B1 6.1 Inheritance.

Survival of the fittest ⓚ

Charles Darwin was the first person to describe natural selection as the 'survival of the fittest'. Reproduction is a very wasteful process. Animals and plants always produce more offspring than the environment can support.

The individual organisms in any species show lots of variation. This is because of differences in the genes they inherit. Only the offspring with the genes best suited to their habitat manage to stay alive and breed successfully. This is natural selection at work.

Think about rabbits. The rabbits with the best all-round eyesight, the sharpest hearing and the longest legs will be the ones that are most likely to escape being eaten by a fox. They will be the ones most likely to live long enough to breed. What's more, they will pass those useful genes on to their babies. The slower, less alert rabbits will get eaten and their genes are less likely to be passed on.

b Why would a rabbit with good hearing be more likely to survive than one with less keen hearing?

The part played by mutation

New forms of genes result from changes in existing genes. These changes are known as mutations. They are tiny changes in the long strands of DNA.

Mutations occur quite naturally through mistakes made in copying DNA when the cells divide. Mutations introduce more variety into the genes of a species. In terms of survival, this is very important.

c What is a mutation?

Many mutations have no effect on the characteristics of an organism, and some mutations are harmful. However, just occasionally a mutation has a good effect. It produces an adaptation that makes an organism better suited to its environment. This makes it more likely to survive and breed.

Whatever the adaptation, if it helps an organism survive and reproduce it will get passed on to the next generation. The mutant gene will gradually become more common in the population. It will cause the species to evolve.

When new forms of a gene arise from mutation, there may be a relatively more rapid change in a species. This is particularly true if the environment changes. If the mutation gives the organism an advantage in the changed environment, it will soon become common.

Natural selection in action

Malpeque Bay in Canada has some very large oyster beds. In 1915, the oyster fishermen noticed a few small, flabby oysters with pus-filled blisters among their healthy catch.

By 1922 the oyster beds were almost empty. The oysters had been wiped out by a destructive new disease (soon known as Malpeque disease).

Fortunately a few of the oysters had a mutation which made them resistant to the disease. These were the only ones to survive and breed. The oyster beds filled up again and by 1940 they were producing more oysters than ever.

A new population of oysters had evolved. As a result of natural selection, almost every oyster in Malpeque Bay now carries a gene that makes them resistant to Malpeque disease. So the disease is no longer a problem.

Figure 2 The tiny number of dandelion seeds that survive and grow into plants have a combination of genes that gives them an edge over all the others

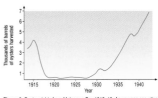

Figure 3 Oyster yields from Malpeque Bay 1915–40. As you can see, disease devastated the oyster beds. However, thanks to the process of natural selection, a healthy population of oysters managed to survive and reproduce again.

d What is Malpeque disease?

Summary questions

1 Copy and complete using the words below:

*adaptation breed environment generation
mutation selection organism survive*

When a .... has a good effect it produces an .... that makes an .... better suited to it's .... This makes it more likely to .... and .... The mutation then gets passed on to the next .... This is natural ....

2 Many features that help animals and plants survive are the result of natural selection. Give three examples, e.g. all-round eyesight in rabbits.

3 Explain how the following characteristics of animals and plants have come about in terms of natural selection.
 a Male red deer have large sets of antlers.
 b Cacti have spines instead of leaves.
 c Camels can tolerate their body temperature rising far higher than most other mammals.

Key points
- Natural selection works by selecting the organisms best adapted to a particular habitat.
- Different organisms in a species show a wide range of variation because of differences in their genes.
- The individuals with the characteristics most suited to their environment are most likely to survive and breed successfully.
- The genes that have produced these successful characteristics are then passed on to the next generation.
- Mutation is a change in the genetic material (DNA) which results in a new form of a gene.

Summary answers

1 mutation, adaptation, organism, environment, survive, breed, generation, selection

2 [Any suitable examples from the spread]

3 **a** Mutation gave some deer antlers to make them more successful in battles with other stags and more attractive to females. This means that they are more likely to mate and pass on their genes. This process continues until antlers become normal in the population. The stags with the biggest or most effective antlers are the ones which mate most successfully.

b Mutation produced spines instead of leaves. Cactus loses very little water and so survives well and reproduces, passing on advantageous genes until normal in population.

c Mutation gives increased temperature tolerance. These camels have an advantage, so more likely to survive and breed, passing on the mutation until it is normal in the population.

B1 7.4

Classification and evolution

Specification link-up: Biology B1.8

Learning objectives

Students should learn:

- that studying the similarities and differences between organisms allows us to classify living organisms
- that living organisms are classified into animals, plants and microorganisms
- that systems of classification help us to understand evolutionary and ecological relationships.

Learning outcomes

Most students should be able to:

- define classification
- describe some of the criteria used in the classification of organisms
- explain how evolutionary trees are used to show relationships between organisms.

Some students should also be able to:

- describe how DNA evidence can be used to work out evolutionary relationships.

Specification link-up: Biology B1.8

- Studying the similarities and differences between organisms allows us to classify living organisms into animals, plants and microorganisms, and helps us to understand evolutionary and ecological relationships. Models allow us to suggest relationships between organisms. *[B1.8.1 d]*

Lesson structure

Starters

Tree of life – Find a 'Tree of life with genome size' illustration on the internet and explain what is being displayed. Discuss and record student observations on who we are and where we fit in to the larger picture of life on Earth. *(5 minutes)*

Types of living things – Get the students to think of as many different kinds of living things as they can within one minute. Have a small prize for the person with the largest list. Explain that there are at least 1.75 million known species alive at the moment and there may be many more as yet undiscovered (so there may be 3–10 million species). A board with a million dots on can bring this into perspective. Link this to a need for a classification system.

Support students by showing them a range of toy animals and getting them to place them into groups with reasons for their decisions. Extend students by showing them pictures of organisms which although similar in form have a very different evolutionary ancestry (e.g. marsupial and eutherian placental relatives such as rats and dogs). Get them to speculate as to reasons why this situation should arise. *(10 minutes)*

Main

- Break into groups and give the students a list of organisms for them to classify in whatever way they decide. Emphasise that there is no right or wrong way for this exercise. Photographs or models will help but a list will suffice. To get them started, you could suggest a group called 'water organisms' or 'organisms of the air'. To conclude, get the students to state how they went about the exercise, comparing the ways in which different groups approached the problem. Draw out that it would be a good idea if everyone used the same agreed system and that many of the names we use for groups describe some of an organism's features (e.g. mammal).

- Define species using lions and tigers as examples – they can mate but their offspring are infertile so they are separate species. Photographs of ligers and tigrons would help here. The students do not need to memorise the system, just to know about what a species is and that an international system of classification exists.

- Show examples of printed evolutionary tree diagrams, from early ones to the most recent. Get students to comment of these.

- Review any recent case from the news where DNA fingerprinting has been instrumental in securing a conviction. Explain the basic principles behind DNA profiling. Link this to phylogenic tracing of ancestry and get the students to copy down some phylogenic ancestry diagrams projected from the internet.

Plenaries

Thumbs up – Review the flow chart in Figure 3 of the Student Book and trace the evolution of the thumb in both red pandas and giant pandas. *(5 minutes)*

Classified data – Use a phylogenic key from the internet to follow the ancestry of humans back through time. Get the students to make a list of human forefathers until they get back to the single ancestor from which all beings have evolved. Bear in mind that some of the genetic information from many millions of years ago is still present in us. Reflect on this. Students could be supported by giving them a phylogenic key with certain stages in the evolution of humans highlighted. Students could be extended by allowing them to speculate on where this phylogenic tree could extend to in the future. Get the students to appreciate that in evolutionary terms the human race has only just begun! *(10 minutes)*

Support

- Provide students with cards on which the names of the taxonomic groups (Kingdom, Phylum etc.) are printed and sets of the names of the groups to which selected animals belong (Animalia, Mammalia etc.). Give them some examples such as frog, snake etc. and adapt the number of groups to the student ability. The students have to match the name with the correct taxonomic group.

Extend

- Get students to examine data from embryonic studies showing evidence of our evolutionary ancestry.
- Ask students to find out about Linnaeus and his binomial system of classification on which the system we use today is based.

Further teaching suggestions

Variation in a species
- Get the students to suggest as many different types of dog as they can and tell them that all these are different varieties of the same species. Therefore, they can potentially interbreed. Get the students to think of differences between some of these breeds and discuss how different a breed has to be before it can be considered a new species. How different are some of these breeds from their ancestors? Reinforce the criteria that determine a species and the variation within it. There are other examples of large numbers of breeds amongst domesticated animals. It might be useful to speculate why the different breeds of domesticated animals have been developed.

Trying to classify objects
- Giving the students groups or collections of objects which they have to sort out and classify. Examples could be: coins, buttons and beads, pins, needles and safety pins.

Evolution

B1 7.4   Classification and evolution

Learning objectives
- What is classification?
- How does classification help us understand evolution?

?? Did you know ... ?
The most widely accepted kingdoms of microorganisms are Monera, Protista and Fungi. However, there is still a lot of argument between scientists as to exactly which organisms fit into each kingdom.

Figure 1 Animals, plants and microorganisms are identified by the differences between them rather than the similarities

How are organisms classified?
Classification is the organisation of living things into groups according to their similarities.

There are millions of different types of living organisms. Biologists classify living things to make it easier to study them. Classification allows us to make sense of the living world. It also helps us to understand how life began and how the different groups of living things are related to each other.

Living things are classified by studying their similarities and differences. By looking at similarities and differences between organisms we can decide which should be grouped together.

The system we use for classifying living things is known as the natural classification system. The biggest groups are the kingdoms, and the best known are the animal kingdom and the plant kingdom. The microorganisms are then split between three different kingdoms.

Kingdoms contain lots of organisms with many differences but a few important similarities. For example, all animals move their whole bodies about during at least part of their life cycle, and their cells do not have cell walls. Plants on the other hand do not move their whole bodies about, and their cells have cell walls. Also some plant cells contain chloroplasts full of chlorophyll for photosynthesis.

The smallest group is a species. Members of the same species are very similar. Any differences are small variations of the same feature. A species is a group of organisms that can breed together and produce fertile offspring. Orang-utans, dandelions and brown trout are all examples of species of living organisms.

a What is classification?

Classification and evolutionary relationships
In the past, we relied on careful observation of organisms to decide which group they belonged to. Out in the field, this is still the main way we identify an organism. However, scientists develop models to suggest relationships between living organisms.

Since Darwin's time, scientists have used classification to show the evolutionary links between different organisms. These models are called evolutionary trees. They are built up by looking at the similarities and differences between different groups of organisms. One of the most famous evolutionary trees was produced by Darwin himself. It was found in one of the notebooks that he used to plan his book *The Origin of Species*. It starts off with the words 'I think'. Then it shows how Darwin was beginning to see relationships between different groups of living organisms (see Figure 2).

However, observation may not tell you the whole story. Some organisms look very different but are closely related. Others look very similar but come from very different groups. Now scientists are increasingly using DNA evidence to decide what species an animal belongs to. They look for differences as well as similarities in the DNA. This allows them to work out the evolutionary relationships between organisms. It also means they can see how long ago different organisms had a common ancestor.

b What is an evolutionary tree?

Evolutionary and ecological relationships
Classifying organisms helps us to understand how they evolved. It can also help us understand how species have evolved together in an environment. We call this their ecological relationships and it is another way of modelling relationships between organisms.

For example, pandas have a thumb which they use to grip bamboo. However it is not like a human thumb – it has evolved from specialised wrist bones. The only other animals to have a similar 'wrist thumb' are the red pandas. Both red pandas and giant pandas eat bamboo. Based on their modern ecological feeding relationships, it looks as if they are closely related in evolution. However, based on their anatomy and DNA, giant pandas are closely related to other species of bears. Red pandas are much more closely related to racoons.

Recently scientists found a fossil ancestor of red pandas which also had a 'wrist thumb'. There is also evidence from the ecological relationships of this fossil animal. This suggests the thumb evolved as an adaptation for a quick escape into trees carrying prey stolen from sabre-toothed tigers. This is rather different from the giant panda evolving to feed on bamboo.

Now the ecological models and the evolutionary models match – the two species had a common ancestor a very long time ago, but the special 'wrist thumb' evolved separately as adaptations to solve two different ecological problems.

Figure 2 This evolutionary tree was found in one of the notebooks that Darwin used to plan his book *The Origin of Species*

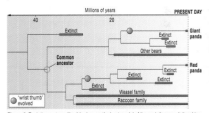
Figure 3 Evolutionary trees like this show us the best model of the evolutionary relationships between organisms

Figure 4 Both the giant panda and the red panda use the 'wrist thumb' to eat bamboo

Summary questions
1 Copy and complete using the words below:
kingdoms animals organisms species classify microorganisms similarities
Scientists .... living .... by studying .... and differences between them. The big groups are called .... and the smallest are called .... All living organisms are either .... , plants or ....
2 What observations can be made to compare living organisms?
3 How are evolutionary trees useful to us?

Key points
- Studying the similarities and differences between organisms allows us to classify them into animals, plants and microorganisms.
- Classification also helps us to understand evolutionary and ecological relationships.

128   129

Answers to in-text questions
a Putting organisms into groups based on similarities and differences between them.

b A model suggesting the evolutionary relationships between different groups of organisms.

Summary answers
1 classify, organisms, similarities, kingdoms, species, animals/microorganisms, microorganisms/animals

2 External appearance, internal structures, DNA evidence. Any other valid points (there are other observations which are not covered within the scope of this specification but if students know them they should get credit).

3 Evolutionary trees look at the relationships between different groups of animals and how long ago they divided away from a common ancestor. They are very useful for helping to understand evolutionary pathways and relationships between species. DNA evidence has become very important in the development of evolutionary trees and changed some of the ideas based on observation alone.

Summary answers

1 Lamarck thought that animals adapted and evolved to suit their environment and that they had all evolved from primitive worms by the inheritance of acquired characteristics. Lamarck's theory was that an organism's behaviour affected their structures, so if an animal used something a lot over several generations it would grow and develop and this improved feature would be passed from parents to offspring. If a structure wasn't used, Lamarck thought it would shrink and be lost.

2 a He started with his work on barnacles but it was the observations he made on the voyage on the *Beagle* that really made him recognise the great variety of life and start to consider how it had come about.

b Darwin's theory is that all organisms produce more offspring than can survive. Some of these are better fitted to the environment than others, and these are the ones that are most likely to survive, breed and pass on those beneficial characteristics. This process of natural selection is most noticeable if there is a change in the environment.

3 a **Similarities:** They both suggest evolution of living things from simpler organisms, both suggest it took a long time; both suggest changes passed from parents to offspring. **Differences:** Lamarck suggests primitive worms as a starting point, suggests it is acquired characteristics which are passed on; Darwin suggests it is inherited features which are passed on, and the process of natural selection ('survival of the fittest') to decide which organisms survive and breed.

b Any thoughtful point, e.g. It helped to pave the way for Darwin's ideas, people had already come to terms with a theory other than the Bible, debate was opened up, the idea of organisms evolving and changing was already there, Darwin's ideas of natural selection then made more sense – (people could see it happening with their own livestock) – than the idea of acquired characteristics which people could see didn't happen in their own experience.

4 Credit careful explanations which include an understanding of the basic concepts. E.g. a pair of founder finches on one island with a high insect population has mutation which results in birds with a slightly different shape beak. This makes it easier (for example) to poke its beak into cracks to find insects. These birds can get food that others can't reach which gives them an advantage. They get more food therefore more likely to survive, breed and pass on the genes for the thinner beak shape. Eventually a whole group of birds evolve with thinner beaks which feed on insects. As they are separate from the other birds – a new species has been formed. A similar process occurs on another island where there are a lot of fruit bushes – these birds evolve beaks suited to eating fruit and buds etc. The birds evolve to take advantage of the available food on the islands.

5 a That species exist in different forms and the species which are not well adapted to conditions are most likely to die out.

b Both relatively isolated islands with lots of organisms which are found only there and are well adapted to the conditions. These different organisms would have helped Wallace as the differences were clear and obviously related to the conditions in Borneo just as Darwin observed the very specialised organisms on the Galapagos islands.

Summary questions

1 What was Jean-Baptiste Lamarck's theory of evolution?

2 a What started Charles Darwin thinking about the variety of life and how it has come about?

b Explain Darwin's theory of evolution.

3 a Summarise the similarities and differences between Darwin's and Lamarck's theories of evolution.

b Why do you think Lamarck's theory was so important to the way Darwin's theory was subsequently received?

4

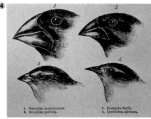

Figure 1 Darwin's finches – more evidence for evolution

Look at the birds in Figure 1. They are known as Darwin's finches. They live on the Galapagos Islands. Each one has a slightly different beak and eats a different type of food.

Explain carefully how natural selection can result in so many different beak shapes from one original type of founder finch.

5 Alfred Russel Wallace came from a poor family but he was a gifted naturalist. He went on a collecting expedition to Borneo, an island in South East Asia that has a rich variety of unique animal and plant life. While he was there, Wallace became ill with a fever and while he was unwell he developed his theory. He had the idea that if species exist in various forms, the organisms that are not well adapted to change are likely to die out. This would leave only the better-adapted forms to survive and breed. Wallace put his ideas down in a paper and sent it to Charles Darwin for advice. Darwin and Wallace both published papers together on their ideas in London at the same time. It was Wallace's work that shocked Darwin into finally writing *The Origin of Species*.

Wallace's ideas were not as well thought out as Darwin and he did not have the evidence to back them up, wh is why it is largely Darwin who is remembered for the theory of evolution by natural selection.

a What was Wallace's theory?

b What are the similarities between Borneo and the Galapagos and how would this have helped Wallace develop his theory?

c Why do you think the arrival of Wallace's letter and paper was such a shock to Darwin?

d Wallace's theories were not strongly supported by evidence. What sort of evidence did Darwin bring forward to support his ideas in *The Origin of Species*

6 a What is classification?

b Explain two alternative ways of deciding how to classify an organism.

c What are the differences and similarities between an evolutionary relationship and an ecological relationship between organisms?

7 It is difficult to gather data that illustrate evolution. It is possible to gather data to show natural selection, but this usually takes a long time. Simulations are useful because, while they are not factually correct, they do show how natural selection might work.

A class decided to simulate natural selection, using different tools to pick up seeds.

Four students each chose a particular tool to pick up seeds. The teacher then scattered hundreds of seeds onto a patch of grass outside the lab. The four student were given 5 minutes to pick up as many seeds as the could.

James, who was using a spoon, picked up 23 seeds, whilst Farzana, using a fork, could only pick up two. Claire managed seven seeds with the spatula, but Jenny struggled to pick up her two seeds with a pair o scissors.

a Put the essential data into a table.

b How would the data be best presented? Explain you choice.

c Was this a fair test? Explain your answer.

d What conclusion can you draw from this simulation?

e How does this simulation model the situation with th finches on the Galapagos Islands, which evolved int many different species?

---

c Darwin was still working on his ideas and building up evidence – he was not expecting someone else to come up with basically the same idea on the strength of a short period of work.

d Darwin had many different species which were closely related showing adaptations from Galapagos. He had years of breeding experiments with pigeons; both his own and from others, huge collections of drawings and classification of barnacles with adaptations to different environments etc.

6 a The organisation of living organisms into groups based on the similarities and differences between them.

b Simple observation of external physical characteristics, habitat, etc.

Analysis of the DNA to show the genetic links between the organisms.

c Both show the ways in which organisms are related and may have evolved from a common ancestor.

An evolutionary relationship shows how closely linked different organisms are genetically and so shows when the different species evolved away from each other.

An ecological relationship shows how different organisms have developed together within their environment, and how this has affected their evolution.

Practice questions

a This diagram shows a timeline for the evolution of some dinosaurs. The mass of each dinosaur is shown in the brackets by its name.
Choose the correct answer to complete each sentence.

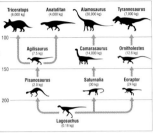

Triceratops (6,000 kg)	Anatotitan (4,000 kg)	Alamosaurus (30,000 kg)	Tyrannosaurus (7,000 kg)
Agilisaurus (7.5 kg)	Camarasaurus (14,000 kg)	Ornitholestes (12.6 kg)
Pisanosaurus (2.0 kg)	Saturnalia (30 kg)	Eoraptor (24 kg)
Lagosuchus (0.18 kg)

dinosaur evolution timeline

i A dinosaur which lived between 100 and 150 million years ago is .... (1)
Agilisaurus   Saturnalia   Tyrannosaurus

ii Camarasaurus evolved from .... (1)
Agilisaurus   Alamosaurus   Saturnalia

iii The difference in mass between Agilisaurus and the smallest dinosaur is .... kg. (1)
1.82   5.5   7.32

b i The earliest life forms developed on Earth more than 3 .... years ago. (1)
billion   million   thousand

ii The earliest life forms can be described as .... (1)
bony   complex   simple

c Darwin suggested a theory of evolution. His theory is described as evolution by .... (1)
acquired characteristics   a god   natural selection

2 Giraffes have developed their long necks over millions of years.

Two scientists tried to explain why the giraffes have long necks. They are called Darwin and Lamarck.

Match the name in List A to the correct statement in List B.

List A	List B
Name	**Statement**
Darwin only	Noticed that the neck of the giraffe changed over time
Lamark only	Had enough evidence to prove why the giraffe's neck got longer
Both Lamark and Darwin	Thought that natural selection worked on variations in neck length present at birth
	Thought the giraffe stretched its neck while eating leaves in trees. Then its young inherited the longer neck

(3)

3 The photograph shows a snake eating a toad.

Cane toads were first introduced into Australia in 1935. The toads contain toxins and most species of Australian snake die after eating the toad. The cane toad toxin does not affect all snakes the same way. Longer snakes are less affected by toad toxin. Scientists investigated how red-bellied black snakes had changed in the 70 years since cane toads were introduced into their area. They found that red-bellied black snakes had become longer by around 3–5%.

Suggest an explanation for the change in the body length of the red-bellied black snakes since the introduction of the cane toads. (4)

AQA, 2005

Practice answers

1 a i Agilisaurus (1 mark)
   ii Saturnalia (1 mark)
   iii 7.32 (1 mark)

  b i billion (1 mark)
   ii simple (1 mark)

  c Natural selection (1 mark)

2 Darwin only – Thought that natural selection worked on variations in neck length present at birth.
Lamark only – Thought the giraffe stretched its neck while eating leaves in trees. Then its young inherited the longer neck.
Both Lamark and Darwin – Noticed that the neck of the giraffe changed over time. (3 marks)

3 Accept any **four** from:
- mutation (do **not** accept 'had to mutate/decided to mutate')
- produces longer snake **or** there is variation in snake length (do **not** accept 'had to adapt and became longer')
- longer snake less susceptible to toxin **or** longer snake survives
- survivors reproduce
- gene passed to next generation (allow characteristic passed to next generation) (4 marks)

7 a

Tool used	spoon	fork	spatula	scissors
Number of seeds	23	2	7	2

b Data would best be presented in a bar chart, because the independent variable is categoric.

c No, this was not a fair test. The different people could have performed differently, so it was not a test of the tools used. The results are not valid.

d That different people using different tools can pick up different numbers of seeds. Possibly the spoon was the best tool.

e The spoon is like the finch's beak, which is most successful at picking up seeds. The other beaks (fork, spatula and scissors) were less successful and so less likely to be carried into the next generation.

Kerboodle resources k

Resources available for this chapter on Kerboodle are:
- Chapter map: Evolution
- Extension: Evolutionary trees (B1 7.3)
- How Science Works: How the peppered moth changed colour (B1 7.3)
- Bump up your grade: Natural selection (B1 7.3)
- Interactive activity: Evolution
- Revision podcast: Evolution
- Test yourself: Evolution
- On your marks: Evolution
- Practice questions: Evolution
- Answers to practice questions: Evolution

Practice answers

1 a i C *(1 mark)*
  ii A *(1 mark)*
  iii D *(1 mark)*

b (Sun) light – not sun alone *(1 mark)*

c Any **two** from:
- the snails/bluetits use some of the energy
- some of the food energy is not eaten or digested/idea e.g. bones cannot be digested
- (energy used) for movement (by snails or bluetits)
- (energy used) to keep (bluetits) warm *(2 marks)*

2 a Extremophiles *(1 mark)*

b Enzymes *(1 mark)*

c 3 billion years *(1 mark)*

d Genes *(1 mark)*

3 a Any **two** from:
- live inside/infect body cells
- difficult for drugs to enter (body) cells/drug would kill (body) cell
- antibiotics ineffective against viruses
- viruses mutate **frequently** *(2 marks)*

b i 420
  *correct answer with **or** without working*
  if answer incorrect evidence of 'number of deaths' × 7
  or *60 seen gains **1** mark*
  ignore 6 000 000 *(2 marks)*

  ii Any **three** from:
- virus/flu mutates
- people no longer/not immune
  ignore resistance
- white blood cells/memory cells/immune system do not recognise virus
- relevant reference to antibodies/antigens
- current vaccine ineffective **or** no vaccine available then
  or takes time to develop new vaccine
  allow no tamiflu/anti-viral drugs
- conditions less hygienic/lack of hygiene
- people in poor health (following world wars)
  allow people had 'weak' immune system *(3 marks)*

4 There is a clear, balanced and detailed argument referring to both pros and cons and a conclusion which matches the pros and cons. The answer shows almost faultless spelling, punctuation and grammar. It is coherent and in an organised, logical sequence. It contains a range of appropriate or relevant specialist terms used accurately. *(5–6 marks)*

There is an answer contains at least one pro and one con with a conclusion. There are some errors in spelling, punctuation and grammar. The answer has some structure and organisation. The use of specialist terms has been attempted, but not always accurately. *(3–4 marks)*

There is mention of either a pro or a con with an attempt at a conclusion or a list of pros and cons without a conclusion, has little clarity and detail. The spelling, punctuation and grammar are very weak. The answer is poorly organised with almost no specialist terms and/or their use demonstrating a general lack of understanding of their meaning. *(1–2 marks)*

No relevant content. *(0 marks)*

1 The diagrams show some biological processes.

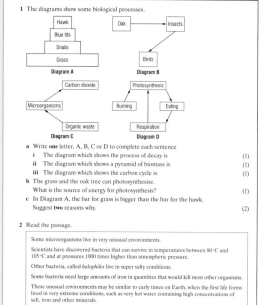

a Write **one** letter, A, B, C or D to complete each sentence
  i The diagram which shows the process of decay is (1)
  ii The diagram which shows a pyramid of biomass is (1)
  iii The diagram which shows the carbon cycle is (1)
b The grass and the oak tree can photosynthesise.
  What is the source of energy for photosynthesis? (1)
c In Diagram A, the bar for grass is bigger than the bar for the hawk.
  Suggest **two** reasons why. (2)

2 Read the passage.

> Some microorganisms live in very unusual environments.
>
> Scientists have discovered bacteria that can survive in temperatures between 80 °C and 105 °C and at pressures 1000 times higher than atmospheric pressure.
>
> Other bacteria, called *halophiles* live in super salty conditions.
>
> Some bacteria need large amounts of iron in quantities that would kill most other organisms.
>
> These unusual environments may be similar to early times on Earth, when the first life forms lived in very extreme conditions, such as very hot water containing high concentrations of salt, iron and other minerals.

a What is the name given to all the bacteria which live in these unusual environments? (1)
b Which chemical in human cells would not work at temperatures between 80 °C and 105 °C? (1)
c How long ago did early life forms appear on Earth? (1)
d Halophiles breed in very salty conditions. The offspring of halophiles can also live in very salty conditions.
  Choose the correct answer to complete the sentence.
  The offspring can live in salty conditions because the parents pass on their ....
  genes   iron   salt (1)

Examples of biology points made in the response:
Pros
- large scale trial gave better results
- chose uneducated women so that if these women could use it correctly, women elsewhere would be able to.

Cons
- used pill with high dose of hormone – *either* so results not valid for general use of hormone *or* dangerous
- side effects ignored
- women not told pill was experimental/pill might have side effects
- no placebo
- should have tried a range of doses
- should have done pre-trial to check for side effects

Conclusion 1 mark, e.g.
- trials flawed therefore cons outweigh pros
- *accept reverse* e.g. trials flawed but pros outweigh cons.

3 Influenza is a disease caused by a virus.

a Suggest **two** reasons why it is difficult to treat diseases caused by viruses. (2)

b In some years there are influenza epidemics.
The graph shows the death rate in Liverpool during three influenza epidemics.

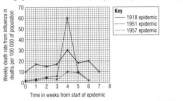

Time in weeks from start of epidemic

Key
— 1918 epidemic
------ 1951 epidemic
······ 1957 epidemic

i The population of Liverpool in 1951 was approximately 700 000.
Calculate the approximate number of deaths from influenza in week 4 of the 1951 epidemic.
Show clearly how you work out your answer. (2)

ii In most years, the number of deaths from influenza in Liverpool is very low.
Suggest, in terms of the influenza virus and the body's immune system, **three** reasons why there were large numbers of deaths in years such as 1918 and 1951. (3)

4 *In this question you will be assessed on using good English, organising information clearly and using specialist terms where appropriate.*
Hormones are used in contraceptive pills.
Read the information about the trialling of the first contraceptive pill.

> The Pill was developed by a team of scientists led by Gregory Pincus. The team needed to carry out large-scale trials on humans.
>
> In the summer of 1955, Pincus visited the island of Puerto Rico. Puerto Rico is one of the most densely populated areas in the world. Officials supported birth control as a form of population control. Pincus knew that if he could demonstrate that the poor, uneducated women of Puerto Rico could use the Pill correctly then so could women anywhere in the world.
>
> The scientists selected a pill with a high dose of hormones to ensure that no pregnancies would occur while test subjects were taking the drug. The Pill was found to be 100% effective when taken properly. But 17% of the women in the study complained of side effects. Pincus ignored these side effects.
>
> The women in the trial had been told only that they were taking a drug that prevented pregnancy. They had not been told that the Pill was experimental or that there was a chance of dangerous side effects.

Evaluate the methods used by Pincus in trialling the contraceptive pill. (6)

Commentary

Proportion seems to baffle many Foundation candidates. They do not appear to relate what they learn in Maths to Biology questions. Make sure that your students are aware of this.

Commentary

It may be worth having a 'Maths for biology' lesson so that the average and Foundation Tier students are supported to improve their maths skills. Several marks can be lost by carelessness and they should be encouraged to think whether the answer looks unrealistic, e.g. it is over 100% or is in millions instead of tens – these mistakes are often made when using a calculator.

Commentary

Look for novel ways to present data to avoid predictability – make a collection of some of these from past papers, e.g. pie charts, overlapping circles, scattergrams – small posters/flash cards of these can make them look familiar and less daunting.

B2 1.1 Animal and plant cells

Learning objectives

Students should learn:

- the functions of the different parts of animal and plant cells
- the differences between plant and animal and plant cells.

Learning outcomes

Most students should be able to:

- describe the structure of animal and plant cells
- describe the functions of the parts of animal and plant cells
- list the differences between animal and plant cells.

Some students should also be able to:

- describe the functions of the special structures in plant cells and algal cells.

Answers to in-text questions

a Nucleus, cytoplasm, cell membrane, mitochondria, ribosomes.

b Plant cells have a cell wall, chloroplasts and a permanent vacuole.

Support

- Give students an outline of a plant cell and an animal cell with labels to cut out and stick on.
- They could try making model cells using cardboard boxes and polythene bags. This could be a test of their ingenuity in finding different materials to represent the organelles. Run a competition, display the entries and award a small prize for the best one.

Extend

- Get students to find out more about how an electron microscope works and how it is used to look at cells. You can find some references in more advanced Biology texts such as *Tools, Techniques and Assessment in Biology*, Adds, Larkcom, Miller and Sutton (Nelson Advanced Science series).

Specification link-up: Biology B2.1

- Most human and animal cells have the following parts:
  - a *nucleus*, which controls the activities of the cell
  - cytoplasm, in which most of the chemical reactions take place
  - a cell membrane, which controls the passage of substances into and out of the cell
  - mitochondria, which is where most energy is released in respiration
  - ribosomes, which is where protein synthesis occurs. *[B2.1.1 a)]*
- Plant and algal cells also have a cell wall made of cellulose, which strengthens the cell. Plant cells often have:
  - chloroplasts, which absorb light energy to make food
  - a permanent vacuole filled with cell sap. *[B2.1.1 b)]*

Lesson structure

Starters

What does it do? – Write up a list of functions of parts of an animal cell on the board, splitting them up so that there is more than one function per part, e.g. 'controls activities' and 'contains chromosomes' for nucleus. Support students by providing a list of parts and asking them to match a part with a function. Extend students by giving them the functions and getting them to name the parts. Let them work through the list by themselves and then check each other's responses. *(5 minutes)*

Plant or animal? – Show a drawing or electron microscope image of a typical plant cell. (Search the internet for 'plant cell' images.) Students to say whether it is a plant or an animal cell, giving reasons. Get them to suggest labels for the parts and decide whether these are common features of cells or special to plant cells. *(10 minutes)*

Main

- This exercise is designed to show students that what they can see using a light microscope is limited, and that structures such as mitochondria and ribosomes are only visible using electron microscopy. The students could work in groups, each having light microscopes with slides of stained cheek cells, onion bulb inner epidermal cells and algal cells (a filamentous alga such as *Spirogyra* would be suitable) and a set of electron micrographs of plant and animal cells (there are plenty in A level text books). They could identify structures in both, and make a comparison of what they can observe from the slides and from the electron micrographs.

- If the magnification of the light microscope is given and the magnification of the electron micrographs known, they can work out how much bigger the latter are. Gather together and discuss the information, particularly with respect to the structures revealed by electron microscopy. Ask: 'Why do they all appear to have membranes around them?'

- Plant cells, such as rhubarb petiole epidermis or the inner epidermal cells from onion bulbs, are relatively easy to mount, stain and observe using light microscopes. In order for students to see cell structures, some staining is advisable. Filamentous algae are easy to find and easy to mount. They will not need staining. The procedure, (see 'Practical support') could be demonstrated to the students and they can then have a go at making their own slides and drawing and labelling some cells.

- Using safe, sterile procedures, students could make slides of their own cheek cells. (See 'Practical support'). Some cells could be drawn and labelled.

Plenaries

Our wonderful world – There are some excellent scanning electron micrographs (SEM) and transmission electron micrographs (TEM) of cells. Show a selection (from www.cellsalive.com) with a 'Guess what this is' attached to each one. This would help students appreciate the complexity of some structures. *(5 minutes)*

A question of size – A typical cell is 20 μm wide (0.002 mm). You will need to talk about scales and the relationship between millimetres and micrometres. Support students by giving them a sheet of the units of measurement involved and their relationship to one another. They can then calculate how many cells will fit across the page of their Student Book. Extend students by giving them extra examples to work out. *(10 minutes)*

Practical support

Looking at cells

Equipment and materials required

Light microscopes (at least one per group of two or three students), clean microscope slides and cover slips, onion bulbs or rhubarb petiole, scalpels, scissors and mounted needles, dilute iodine solution in dropping bottles (CLEAPSS Hazcard 54), tissues, eye protection.

Details

Cut an onion in half and remove the thin inner epidermis of the leaves with forceps. This can be cut up into small squares about 5 mm square. Place a square of epidermis on a slide, trying to get it as flat as possible, and then place a drop of dilute iodine solution on top to stain the cells. Place a cover slip over the top, lowering it carefully down so that air bubbles are not trapped. Place the slide under the low power of the microscope, focusing carefully. Then switch to high power and focus using the fine adjustment.

Safety: Follow CLEAPSS Hazcard 54B Iodine.

Cheek cells

Equipment and materials required

Light microscopes (at least one per group of two or three students), new cotton buds, clean microscope slides and cover slips, dilute methylene blue solution, disinfectant, or another approved way, for disposal of used cotton buds and slides.

Details

The inside of the cheek is gently scraped using a sterile cotton bud and the scrapings smeared on to the middle of a clean microscope slide. A drop of dilute methylene blue is added on top of the cells and covered with a cover slip. The slide can then be observed under the microscope. Some gentle pressure might be needed to spread the cells out, so that they are easier to see. When finished, place prepared slides and cotton buds in a container of freshly prepared sodium hypochlorite solution.

Safety: (See CLEAPSS Student Safety Sheet 3 and follow Society of Biology guidelines.) CLEAPSS Hazcard 89 Sodium chlorate(I) – corrosive.

Cells, tissues and organs

B2 1.1 — Animal and plant cells (k)

Learning objectives

- What do the different parts of your cells do?
- Are human cells the same as other animal cells?
- How do plant and algal cells differ from animal cells?

Figure 1 Diagrams of cells are much easier to understand than the real thing seen under a microscope. This picture shows a magnified animal cell.

The Earth is covered with a great variety of living things. However, they all have one thing in common – they are all made up of cells. Most cells are very small. You can only see them using a microscope.

The light microscopes in schools may magnify things several hundred times. Scientists have found out even more about cells using electron microscopes. These can magnify things more than a hundred thousand times!

Animal cells – structure and function

All cells have some features in common. We can see these clearly in animal cells. The cells of your body have these features, just like the cells of every other living thing.

- The **nucleus** – controls all the activities of the cell. It contains the genes on the chromosomes. They carry the instructions for making new cells or new organisms.
- The **cytoplasm** – a liquid gel in which most of the chemical reactions needed for life take place.
- The **cell membrane** – controls the passage of substances into and out of the cell.
- The **mitochondria** – structures in the cytoplasm where oxygen is used and most of the energy is released during respiration.
- **Ribosomes** – where protein synthesis takes place. All the proteins needed in the cell are made here.

Plant cells – structure and function

Plants are very different organisms from animals. They make their own food by photosynthesis. They stay in one place, and do not move their whole bodies about from one place to another.

Plant cells have all the features of a typical animal cell, but they also contain features that are needed for their very different way of life. Algae are simple aquatic organisms. They also make their own food and have many similar features to plant cells.

All plant and algal cells have:

- a cell wall made of cellulose that strengthens the cell and gives it support.

Many (but not all) plant cells also have these other features:

- **Chloroplasts** are found in all the green parts of the plant. They are green because they contain the green substance chlorophyll. Chlorophyll absorbs light energy to make food by photosynthesis. Root cells do not have chloroplast because they are underground and do not photosynthesise.
- A **permanent vacuole** is a space in the cytoplasm filled with cell sap. This is important for keeping the cells rigid to support the plant.

a What are the main features found in all living cells?
b How do plant cells differ from animal cells?

Study tip

Remember that not all plant cells have chloroplasts. Don't confuse chloroplasts and chlorophyll.

links

For more information on photosynthesis, look at B2 2.1 Photosynthesis.

Figure 2 A simple **animal cell** like this shows the features which are common to all living cells – including human cells

Figure 3 A **plant cell** has many features in common with an animal cell, but others that are unique to plants

Cell membrane
Ribosomes
Cellulose cell wall
Mitochondria
Cytoplasm
Permanent vacuole
Chloroplasts
Nucleus

?? Did you know ...?

Animal cells vary in size but we can only see most of them using a microscope. Eggs are the biggest animal cells. Unfertilised ostrich eggs are the biggest of all – they have a mass of around 1.35 kg!

Practical

Looking at cells (k)

Set up a microscope to look at plant cells, e.g. from onions and *Elodea*. You should see the cell wall, the cytoplasm and sometimes a vacuole but you won't see chloroplasts in the onion cells.

- Why won't you see any chloroplasts in the onion cells?

Figure 4 Microscopes can be used to look at the features of a plant cell

Study tip

Practise labelling an animal cell and a plant cell. You need to know the functions of each part of a cell. For example, chloroplasts contain chlorophyll, which absorbs light energy for photosynthesis. Write the functions of the parts on the diagram.

Summary questions

1 a List the main structures you would expect to find in an animal cell.
   b You would find all the things we have in animal cells also in a plant or algal cell. There are three extra features that are found in plant cells but not animal cells. What are they?
   c What are the main functions of these three extra structures?

2 Why are the nucleus and the mitochondria so important in all cells?

3 Chloroplasts are found in many plant cells but not all of them. Give an example of plant cells without chloroplasts and explain why they have none.

Key points

- Most human cells are like most other animal cells and contain a nucleus, cytoplasm, cell membrane, mitochondria and ribosomes.
- Plant and algal cells contain all the structures seen in animal cells as well as a cell wall. Many plant cells also contain chloroplasts and a permanent vacuole filled with sap.

Further teaching suggestions

Observing cytoplasm

- Using rhubarb petiole or onion bulb epidermis will not show chloroplasts, so a demonstration of some moss leaf cells or leaves of a water plant such as *Elodea* which could be mounted in water and projected. The cells will be living and so it is possible that the streaming of the cytoplasm can be observed.

Computer simulations

- If you have access to computers, you could use them to model the relative size of different cells, organelles and molecules for students.

Summary answers

1 a nucleus, cytoplasm, cell membrane, mitochondria, ribosomes
   b Cell wall, chloroplasts, permanent vacuole.
   c Cell wall provides support and strengthening for the cell and the plant; chloroplasts for photosynthesis; permanent vacuole keeps the cells rigid to support the plant.

2 The nucleus controls all the activities of the cell and contains the instructions for making new cells or new organisms. Mitochondria are the site of aerobic respiration, so they produce energy for the cell.

3 Root cells in a plant do not have chloroplasts because they don't carry out photosynthesis – they are underground so have no light.

B2 1.2

Bacteria and yeast

Learning objectives

Students should learn:

- the structure of a bacterial cell
- that the genes in a bacterial cell are not in a distinct nucleus
- the structure of a yeast cell.

Learning outcomes

Most students should be able to:

- describe the structure of a bacterial cell
- describe the structure of a yeast cell
- list the differences between bacterial and yeast cells.

Some students should also be able to:

- compare animal, plant and algal cells with bacteria and yeasts.

Specification link-up: Biology B2.1

- A bacterial cell consists of cytoplasm and a membrane surrounded by a cell wall; the genes are not in a distinct nucleus. [B2.1.1 c)]
- Yeast is a single-celled organism. Yeast cells have a nucleus, cytoplasm and a membrane surrounded by a cell wall. [B2.1.1 d)]

Lesson structure

Starters

What are bacteria really like? – Show a clip from the internet of an advert for bleach or a sterilising agent that has animations or cartoons of germs. How does this picture fit with reality? Are there any similarities between the pretend bacteria and real ones? *(5 minutes)*

Marmite – love it or hate it? – Bring out a jar of Marmite. Pass it around for students to smell. Ask if anyone knows what it is made from. Make the students write down a brief description of what yeast is, and what it does. Support students by prompting them to produce a limited description. Extend students by asking them about wild yeasts, they should provide detailed descriptions with a variety of examples. *(10 minutes)*

Main

- Produce a PowerPoint presentation or exposition to show the structure of a typical bacterium. Bring out the features which all bacterial cells have and then add in some features that may be found, relating these to their function (flagella, slime capsules). Create a list of questions for the students to fill in as you proceed through the exposition. Compare a bacterial cell with a plant and an animal cell and bring out the differences.

- Look at prepared slides of bacteria under the microscope. Students will not be able to see very much, so project some TEM and SEM images. Discuss how difficult it is to see structures and thus difficult to identify different bacteria. Simple classification is based on shape, but more detailed identification depends on their growth and biochemistry.

- Remind the students of previous work on pathogens. In addition, bring in the useful bacteria (for yoghurt, cheese making and antibiotic production). Link some pathogens with the diseases they cause.

- Set up a culture of yeast at the beginning of the lesson. Show some pictures of yeast cells and remind students that yeast is a fungus. Then let them make slides of the culture. Examine the culture at the end of the lesson when there should be some budding visible. Get students to make sketches of the budding process.

- If the yeast culture is active, there should be frothing. Bubble some of the gas given off through limewater and get the students to say what is going on. Link this in with the uses of yeast and the fact that it can respire aerobically and anaerobically.

Answers to in-text questions

a Smaller, have genetic material but no nucleus, may have plasmids.

b Bigger, have a nucleus.

Plenaries

Am I a yeast or a bacterium? – Prepare a series of statements about yeast and bacterial cells, such as 'I have a flagellum', 'I have a cell wall', 'I have a true nucleus' (some common features and some specific ones as well as sizes). Write these up as a numbered list on the board and get students to write 'Y', 'B' or 'Both' in their notebooks. Check the answers and get students to agree on the list of similarities and differences. *(5 minutes)*

Job lists – Show the students an imaginary 'To do' list for a teacher (you can put some humorous bits in). Write down two 'To do' list headings on the board: one for bacteria and one for yeasts. Ask for suggestions from the students – these should include both positive and negative aspects of the roles of these organisms. Support students by providing prompt cards which can be sorted into the respective job lists. Extend students by providing them with some background reading about the roles of bacteria and yeasts and get them to select more detail. *(10 minutes)*

Support

- Provide students with blank bacterial cells which they can add features to, as the activity proceeds.

Extend

- Get students to find out about ginger beer plants and how ginger beer can be made from simple ingredients.

Further teaching suggestions

Bread making demonstration
- Set up a demonstration of the use of yeast in bread making. Have dough with and without yeast added and take measurements of the rise in the dough. There are many variations of this investigation: varying the temperature, addition of vitamin C. Get students to think about the type of respiration that is going on.

Bacteria in the body
- Get students to think about the presence of bacteria in and on the body. Discuss the importance of bacteria in the gut – both good and bad ones.

Table of differences
- Build up a comprehensive table of differences between bacterial, yeast, animal, plant and algal cells.

Cells, tissues and organs

B2 1.2   Bacteria and yeast Ⓚ

Learning objectives
- What are bacterial cells like?
- How are yeast cells different from bacterial, plant and animal cells?

Bacteria are single-celled living organisms that are much smaller than animal and plant cells. Most bacteria are less than 1 μm in length. You could fit hundreds of thousands of bacteria on to the full stop at the end of this sentence. You can't see individual bacteria without a powerful microscope.

When you culture bacteria on an agar plate you grow many millions of bacteria. This enables you to see the bacterial colony with your naked eye.

Cell membrane   Slime capsule   Cell wall   Plasmids

Cytoplasm

Genetic material

Flagella

1μm

Figure 1 Bacteria come in a variety of shapes, but they all have the same basic structure

Bacterial cells

Each bacterium is a single cell. It is made up of cytoplasm surrounded by a membrane and a cell wall. Inside the bacterial cell is the genetic material. Unlike animal, plant and algal cells, the genes are not contained in a nucleus. The long strand of DNA (the bacterial chromosome) is usually circular and found free in the cytoplasm.

Many bacterial cells also contain plasmids, which are small circular bits of DNA. These carry extra genetic information. Bacteria may have a slime capsule around the outside of the cell wall. Some types of bacterium have at least one flagellum (plural: flagella), a long protein strand that lashes about. These bacteria use their flagella to move themselves around.

Although some bacteria cause disease, many are harmless. Some are actually really useful to us. We use them to make food like yoghurt and cheese. Others are used in sewage treatment and to make medicines.

a How are bacteria different from animal and plant cells?

Yeast

Another type of microorganism that is very useful to people is yeast. Yeasts are single-celled organisms. Each yeast cell has a nucleus containing the genetic material, cytoplasm, and a membrane surrounded by a cell wall.

The cells vary in size but most are about 3–4 μm. This makes them bigger than bacteria but still very small.

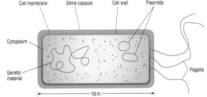

Figure 2 Bacteria come in several different shapes and sizes. This helps us to identify them under the microscope. *Streptococcus* causes sore throats and *E. coli* live in your gut.

The main way in which yeasts reproduce is by asexual budding. This involves a new yeast cell growing out from the original cell to form a new separate yeast organism.

b How do yeast cells differ from bacterial cells?

Yeast cells are specialised to be able to survive for a long time even when there is very little oxygen available. When yeast cells have plenty of oxygen they use aerobic respiration. They use oxygen to break down sugar to provide energy for the cell. During this process they produce water and carbon dioxide as waste products.

However, when there isn't much oxygen, yeast can use **anaerobic respiration**. When yeast cells break down sugar in the absence of oxygen, they produce ethanol and carbon dioxide.

Ethanol is commonly referred to as alcohol. The anaerobic respiration of yeast is sometimes called fermentation.

We have used yeast for making bread and alcoholic drinks almost as far back as human records go. We know yeast was used to make bread in Egypt 6000 years ago. Not only that, some ancient wine found in Iran is over 7000 years old.

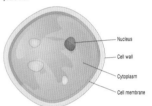

Nucleus

Cell wall

Cytoplasm

Cell membrane

Figure 3 Yeast cells – these microscopic organisms have been useful to us for centuries

?? Did you know …?

In Ethiopia, natural yeast from the air is enough to make injera, the traditional bread. The dough is left for a couple of days before it is cooked for the yeast to produce carbon dioxide bubbles, which give injera its texture.

Study tip

Be clear about the similarities and differences between animal, plant, algal, bacterial and yeast cells.

Figure 4 Brewers use the ethanol produced by yeast in their alcoholic drinks

Summary questions

1 Copy and complete using the words below:
nucleus bacteria cell wall microorganism yeast plasmids
.... and .... are both types of .... Bacterial cells do not contain a .... but often have .... Bacteria and yeast cells both have a ....

2 **a** What is unusual about the genetic material in bacterial cells?
  b Which are bigger, bacterial cells or yeast cells?
  c What are flagella and what are they used for?

3 Make a table to compare the structures in animal, plant and algal, bacterial and yeast cells.

Key points
- A bacterial cell consists of cytoplasm and a membrane surrounded by a cell wall. The genes are not in a distinct nucleus.
- Yeast is a single-celled organism. Each cell has a nucleus, cytoplasm and a membrane surrounded by a cell wall.

136   137

Summary answers

1   bacteria/yeast, yeast/bacteria, microorganism, nucleus, plasmids, cell wall

2 **a**   It isn't contained in a nucleus and there are extra genes known as plasmids separate from the main genetic material.
  b   Yeast cells.
  c   Flagella are long protein strands found in some bacteria which are used for moving the bacteria about.

3

Feature	Animal cell	Plant or algal cell	Bacterial cell	Yeast cell
Cell membrane	yes	yes	yes	yes
Nucleus	yes	yes	no	yes
Plasmids	no	no	yes	no
Chloroplasts	no	yes	no	no
Cell wall	no	yes	yes	yes
Cytoplasm	yes	yes	yes	yes

Specialised cells

Learning objectives

Students should learn:

- that cells may be specialised to carry out particular functions.

Learning outcomes

Most students should be able to:

- recognise different types of cells
- relate the structure of given types of cells to their functions in a tissue or an organ.

Some students should also be able to:

- relate the structure of unfamiliar cells to other functions in a tissue or organ.

Answers to in-text questions

a The middle section.

b To break down the outer layers of the egg.

Specification link-up: Biology B2.1

- Cells may be specialised to carry out a particular function. *[B2.1.1 e)]*
- Relate the structure of different types of cells to their function. *[B2.1]*

  Controlled Assessment: B4.3 Collect primary and secondary data. *[B4.3.1 a)]*, *[B4.3.2 c) d)]*

Lesson structure

Starters

How big can cells be? – Show a goose egg, explaining that it is a single cell, and break it on to a plate. The students may be able to see the place where the embryo will develop (the germinal disc). Discuss with the students why it is so big and how it is specialised. If possible show an empty ostrich egg. *(5 minutes)*

Do you know what this is? – Project some images of specialised cells – do not label them but give each one a number. Support students by giving them a list of the names. Extend students by asking them to name the ones they know and have a guess at the ones they do not. Check the answers at the end. *(10 minutes)*

Main

- 'Observing specialised cells: Root hair cells'. This practical activity can be prepared a few days before the lesson (see 'Practical support' for full details). It can be set up as a demonstration or for groups of students. This exercise introduces some of the concepts of 'How Science Works', such as making single measurements, if the micrometer idea is used.

- Video footage of sperm cell activity is readily available. There are clips available which show fertilisation, emphasising the difference in sizes of egg cells and sperm and also the relative numbers.

- Prepared slides of rat testes could be available for students to look at, observing the different stages in sperm development. Prepare a worksheet with some drawings of different stages so that students can look for specific features and make labelled drawings of their own. This activity can link with the showing of the video.

- **How structure is related to function in animal cells** – Show students pictures of a range of different animal cells, to include blood cells, neurons, muscle cells, cells from glands (secretory cells), fat cells and gametes. Get the students to make a list of the cells, their special features and how each specialised cell differs from a generalised animal cell. Allow the students to make their notes individually and then go through the cells again, discussing the important points.

- **How structure is related to function in plant cells** – This could be presented in a similar manner to the above, using a range of plant cells, such as palisade cells, guard cells, root hair cells, lignified cells (fibres) and epidermal cells. Cells from the cortex of the stem or the root could be used as generalised plant cells.

- Students are required to be able to relate the structure of different types of cell to their functions in a tissue or an organ, so these exercises will give them a record for future reference and revision.

Plenaries

20 Questions – One student goes out of the room and the others decide which type of specialised cell they are. The student comes back in and asks the rest of the class questions about their specialisation to guess what they are. Repeat several times. *(5 minutes)*

What can I do and how can I do it? – Project images of the specialised cells mentioned/described in the text (fat cell, cone cell, root hair cell, sperm cell) but do not label them. Ask students to write down the function of each cell and to state a particular feature of each which is related to its function (for example, for the fat cell, storage of fat and little normal cytoplasm). Support students by giving them the names of the cells, then asking them to state a feature. Extend students by adding extra examples from the activities suggested in the main lesson. *(10 minutes)*

Support

- Use domino-style cards with specialised cells on one side and their special features on the other. Ask the students to play with these as dominoes. Alter the number of cards and the labelling according to ability.

Extend

- Suggest to students that they design a special cell found in an alien or undiscovered species. Ask them to give it an interesting, unusual or gruesome feature and make it scientifically feasible.

Practical support

Observing specialised cells – Root hair cells

Equipment and materials required

Cress seedlings with root hairs, forceps, cling film, blotting paper or filter paper, digital camera, binocular microscopes, Petri dishes, micrometer eyepiece, if available.

Details

A few days before the lesson, sow some cress seeds on damp blotting paper or filter paper in Petri dishes. Handle the seedlings by the cotyledons using forceps. When ready to use them, remove the lids and cover with cling film to keep the moisture levels high. Place the dishes under a binocular microscope and take digital photographs down the microscope. The photographs can then be stuck in the students' records. This can either be set up as a demonstration or groups of students could work together on the activity.

If a micrometer eyepiece is inserted in the microscope, the length of some of the root hairs can be measured. The measurements can either be left as eyepiece units (eu) or converted to millimetres if the eyepiece is calibrated. This exercise will reinforce the extent to which the root hairs are specialised for the increase of the SA (surface area) available for the uptake of water. Students should consider the following questions:

- How is this cell different in structure from a generalised plant cell?
- How does the difference in structure help it to carry out its function?

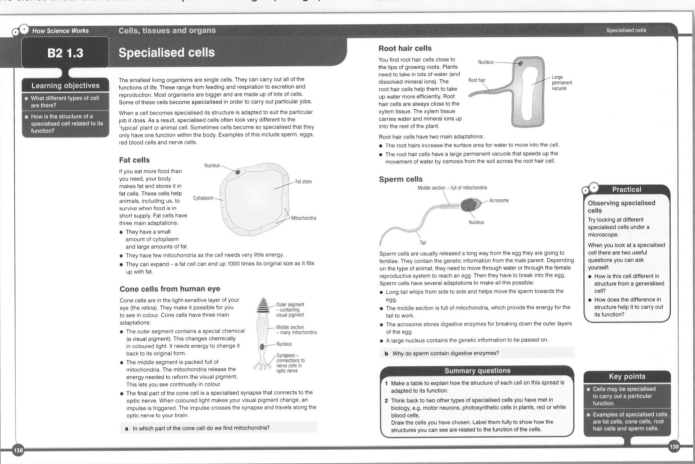

Further teaching suggestions

Fun with colour vision

- Students could have fun with their colour vision by staring at brightly coloured cardboard and then at white paper to perceive residual false colour images. Search the internet for 'flags' to illustrate such after-images. In the retina, there are three types of cone: sensitive to red, green or blue. When you stare at a particular colour for too long, these receptors get 'tired' or 'fatigued'. After looking at the flag with the strange colours, your receptors that are tired do not work as well. Therefore the information from all the different colour receptors is not in balance.

Single-celled organisms

- Show images of single-celled organisms as a contrast to specialised cells. Good examples to find on the internet are chlamydomonas, paramecium and amoeba, and then discuss how these organisms can carry out all the functions of life.

Am I colour-blind?

- Search the internet for 'colour-blind' to find tests you can use to investigate colour-blindness further.

Summary answers

1 **Fat cells:** not much cytoplasm so room for fat storage; ability to expand to store fat; few mitochondria as they do not need much energy, so do not waste space.

   Cone cells from human eye: outer segment containing visual pigment; middle segment packed full of mitochondria; specialised nerve ending.

   Root hair cells: no chloroplasts so no photosynthesis; root hair increases SA (surface area) for water uptake; vacuole to facilitate water movement; close to xylem tissue.

   Sperm cells: tail for movement to egg; mitochondria to provide energy for movement; acrosome full of digestive enzymes to break down the outside layers of the egg cell; large nucleus full of genetic material.

2 [Any two cells chosen, appropriately labelled and annotated.]

B2 1.4

Diffusion

Learning objectives

Students should learn:

- that substances, such as oxygen, move in and out of cells by a process called diffusion
- the factors that affect the rate of diffusion.

Learning outcomes

Most students should be able to:

- define diffusion in cells
- list factors that affect the rate of diffusion
- describe how cells may be adapted to facilitate diffusion.

Some students should also be able to:

- explain the factors that affect the rate of diffusion
- explain in detail how cells may be adapted to facilitate diffusion.

Specification link-up: Biology B2.1

- Dissolved substances can move into and out of cells by diffusion. *[B2.1.2 a)]*
- Diffusion is the spreading of the particles of a gas, or of any substance in solution, resulting in a net movement from a region where they are of a higher concentration to a region with a lower concentration. The greater the difference in concentration, the faster the rate of diffusion. *[B2.1.2 b)]*
- Oxygen required for respiration passes through cell membranes by diffusion. *[B2.1.2 c)]*

  Controlled Assessment: B4.3 Collect primary and secondary data. *[B4.3.1 a)]*, *[B4.3.2 c) d)]*

Lesson structure

Starters

Watching diffusion – In advance of the lesson set up a boiling tube of water with a few crystals of potassium permanganate in the bottom of the tube. Using a digital camera take shots of the tube every 20 minutes for several hours. Use these to create a PowerPoint slideshow, projecting the shots in sequence. Get the students to comment on what they think is happening and why. *(5 minutes)*

Human diffusion – Ask the students if they have ever been in a crowd coming out from a major football match or other event. Show a slide of a big crowd. Ask what happens to the concentration of people as they move away from the stadium. Draw an analogy to diffusion in particles in that they go from an area of high concentration to an area of low concentration. Support students by giving them this definition of diffusion and a broken sentence to reassemble. Extend students by asking them to sort the strengths and weaknesses of the analogy – where is it valid and where does it break down? *(10 minutes)*

Main

- It is possible to demonstrate and measure the rate of diffusion of ammonia along a glass tube using litmus paper (see 'Demonstration support' for full details). This shows that the ammonia diffuses along the tube from an area where it is in high concentration to a lower concentration. It is possible to work out the rate of diffusion. The overall time to diffuse 28 cm can be found and the individual times for the diffusion from one 2 cm mark to the next can be recorded. This gives several possibilities for discussion and calculation. It also introduces 'How Science Works' concepts.

Additional suggestions include:

- Comparing the rate of diffusion of the strong solution with that of a weaker solution by setting up an identical tube and timing the change in colour of the litmus squares.
- Measuring the diffusion of liquids. Cut wells into the agar gel dyed with universal indicator or hydrogencarbonate indicator. Add acid at various concentrations into the wells, allow a set time and then measure the extent of the colour change around each well. Alkali could be used as well as acid for different colour changes.
- There are some good internet-based animations illustrating diffusion. Make the point that the length of the diffusion pathway is also important hence thin layers on absorbent tissues.
- If you have access to computers, you could use them to model the process of diffusion for students.

Support

- Provide students with figures and prepared grids on which to plot the results of the experiments.

Extend

- Ask students to consider how well single-celled organisms are adapted to facilitate diffusion. How big could they grow? Is there a limit?

Plenaries

Surface area to volume – Get students to fold up a sheet of A4 paper as small as they can get it, without tearing. Measure the dimensions and try to fit it into a matchbox. Relate this to diffusion rate. *(5 minutes)*

Defining diffusion – Give the students the key words of the topic and get them to write a definition of diffusion and the factors which affect the rate. Support students by providing a sentence or sentences into which they fit the key words. Extend students by asking them to include in their definition an explanation of how cells in living organisms are adapted to make diffusion more rapid. *(10 minutes)*

Practical support

Demonstrating and measuring the rate of diffusion

Equipment and materials required

Glass tubes, 30 cm long and of diameter 20 mm should be marked using a felt tip pen at 2 cm intervals starting at 10 cm from one end, each tube requires two corks, one ordinary one and one which has had a core of cork taken out the cavity plugged with cotton wool, felt-tip pen, litmus paper, wire or glass rod, strong ammonia solution and a stopwatch.

Details

It is possible to demonstrate and measure the rate of diffusion of ammonia along a glass tube. Litmus paper is used to show the progress of the gas along the tube. Small squares of pink litmus paper are dipped into distilled water, shaken and placed inside each tube with a piece of wire or a glass rod. The pieces of litmus paper should be pushed into position and lined up with the markings on the outside of the tube. Saturate the cotton wool in the cork at one end with a strong ammonia solution, then place it in the end of the tube, start the clock or stopwatch and time how long it takes each piece of litmus paper to turn from pink to completely blue.

Safety: Care is needed when using the strong ammonia solution – eye protection should be worn. CLEAPSS Hazcard 5/6. Ventilating the laboratory.

Diffusion of glucose

Equipment and materials required

Visking tubing, beaker of water, glucose solution (Benedict's).

Details

The diffusion of glucose through a cell membrane can be demonstrated by placing a solution of glucose in Visking tubing and immersing the tubing in a beaker of water. The water is tested for glucose at the start of the experiment and then again after 20 minutes.

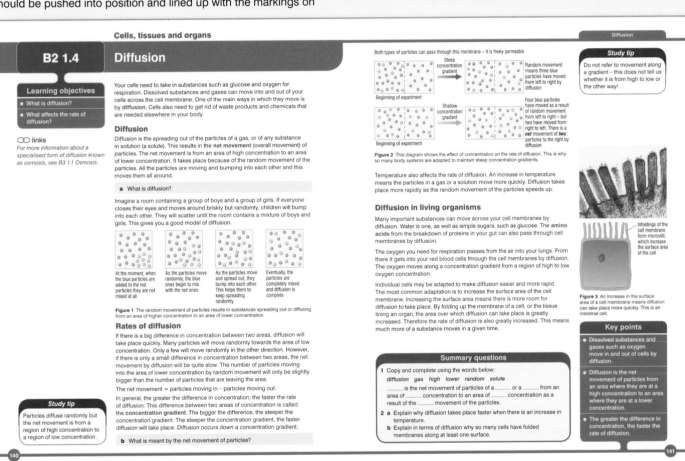

Further teaching suggestions

More diffusion in liquids

- Give students boiling tubes containing clear gelatine up to a marked level. They can then pour a thin layer of gelatine coloured with methylene blue on to the top, allow it to set and then pour on a quantity of clear gelatine equal to the volume in the bottom of the tube. (Levels could be marked for them.) The tubes should be left for a week and then the distribution of the blue colour recorded.

Two-way diffusion

- Pour some gelatine into a boiling tube and colour it with 10 drops of cresol red (it will go yellow). Mix thoroughly and allow to set. Pour a further layer of clear gelatine on top of the coloured layer. Allow this layer to set. Finally add about 5 cm³ of ammonia solution to the top of the tube and insert a bung. Leave the tube for about 4 days. The cresol red will diffuse into the clear gelatine and the ammonia will diffuse into the gelatine. This can be shown by the cresol red turning from yellow to red.

Answers to in-text questions

a The spreading out of the particles of a gas, or of any substance in solution.

b The difference between the numbers of particles moving in and those moving out of cells.

Summary answers

1 diffusion, gas/solute, solute/gas, high, lower, random

2 a The oxygen moves along a concentration gradient from a region of high to low oxygen concentration.

  b Folded membranes provide an increased surface area so diffusion can take place more quickly.

B2 1.5 Tissues and organs

Learning objectives

Students should learn:

- that a tissue is a group of cells with similar structure and function
- that organs are made of tissues.

Learning outcomes

Most students should be able to:

- define a tissue
- describe some plant and animal tissues
- understand that organs are made up of tissues working together to carry out a function.

Some students should also be able to:

- explain how organs are adapted for the exchange of materials.

Specification link-up: Biology B2.2

- Large multicellular organisms develop systems for exchanging materials. During the development of a multicellular organism, cells differentiate so that they can perform different functions. [B2.2.1 a)]
- A tissue is a group of cells with similar structure and function. Examples of tissues include:
  - muscular tissue, which can contract to bring about movement
  - glandular tissue, which can produce substances such as enzymes and hormones
  - epithelial tissue, which covers some parts of the body. [B2.2.1 b)]
- Organs are made of tissues. One organ may contain several tissues. The stomach is an organ that contains:
  - muscular tissue, to churn the contents
  - glandular tissue, to produce digestive juices
  - epithelial tissue, to cover the outside and the inside of the stomach. [B2.2.1 c)]

Lesson structure

Starters

Sentences – Give the students the words 'cell', 'tissue', 'organ' and 'function'. They have to write down four simple sentences, one with each of these words in. The idea is to find out what they understand so far about the words. On completion, get some of the students to read out their sentences and discuss as a class. Support students by providing them with simple sentences which they have to complete, choosing the correct word. Extend students by asking them to compose an additional sentence containing all four words. *(5 minutes)*

Schools and cells – What jobs do the various members of the school team do? Make a list of who does what. Draw out that the various staff members can be seen as being parts of teams, each team with an overall function, e.g. the individual teaching staff are part of a department responsible for a subject, or in pastoral terms are part of looking after a year group or a house. Draw an analogy with cells. *(10 minutes)*

Main

- Levels of organisation – Label some toy building bricks of one colour 'Cell' and fit them together. On the back of the block formed stick a label 'Tissue'. Make some more 'Tissue' blocks from 'Cells' of other colours. Stick these together and label it 'Organ'. Have several of these and place them in a circle on the floor or the bench labelled 'Organ system'. Get the students to identify some organ systems and work back suggesting the organs, tissues and cells involved.

- Microscope work – look at slides of various individual cells and of tissues such as fat and muscle. Identify the similarities between the cells of a tissue.

- Use a torso model to gather the students around and identify various organs and then the systems to which they belong. Discuss the functions of the organs and the systems, particularly with respect to the exchange of materials. Create a worksheet for students to summarise the various systems and their relationship to one another.

- Show slides of a range of plant tissues e.g. palisade, mesophyll, spongy mesophyll, epidermis, parenchyma, xylem and phloem. Discuss their functions and how exchange of materials is achieved.

Plenaries

CTOS – Give the students a piece of scrap A4 with a blank side. Draw lines on to break it into four sections. Get them to write in big letters 'C', 'T', 'O' and 'S' on the paper and fold along the lines to make a little leaflet which can display each of the letters. Display or write on the board items which are a cell, a tissue, an organ or a system. The students have to fold their leaflet to the appropriate letter and hold it up. *(5 minutes)*

Matching game – Using a Java interactive exercise generation programme, such as the excellent one found at www.quia.com, draw out a list of various cells, tissues, organs and systems and write out definitions for them. Use Quia or similar to create digital flashcards with the name on one side and the definition on the other or alternatively a pairs-type matching game. Play this either as a class or if computers are available as a class IT exercise. Support students by restricting the number of cards and simplifying the definitions. Extend students by having a larger number of cards and making the definitions and links more challenging. *(10 minutes)*

Support

- Provide students with blank outlines of different cells and ask them to add structures and labels from their observations.

Extend

- Let students carry out a more detailed study of the exchange of materials in an organ system (e.g. excretory system, digestive system).

Further teaching suggestions

The circulatory system
- How necessary is the circulatory system? Review a range of animals from different phyla and consider how materials are circulated and exchanged. This links cells, tissues and organs as well as considering that increase in complexity depends on a good circulatory system.

Drawing analogies
- Show pictures of the pipes and console of a church organ, especially details of the writing on the voicing stops. Ask

students to draw analogies between this type of organ and the biological meaning of the word 'organ'– similarities and differences?

Function and appearance
- Show the students some more plant tissues, e.g. water storage tissue, aerenchyma, modified epidermis, collenchymas. Ask the students if they could determine the function of the tissue from its appearance.

Cells, tissues and organs

B2 1.5 Tissues and organs

Learning objectives
- What is a tissue?
- What is an organ?

links
For more information on specialised cells, look back at B2 1.3 Specialised cells.

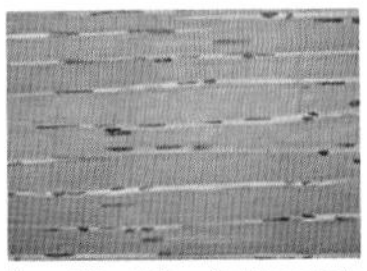

Figure 1 Muscle tissue like this contracts to move your skeleton around

Large multicellular organisms have to overcome the problems linked to their size. They develop different ways of exchanging materials. During the development of a multicellular organism, cells differentiate. They become specialised to carry out particular jobs. For example, in animals, muscle cells have a different structure to blood and nerve cells. In plants the cells where photosynthesis takes place are very different to root hair cells.

However, the adaptations of multicellular organisms go beyond specialised cells. Similar specialised cells are often found grouped together to form a tissue.

Tissues

A tissue is a group of cells with similar structure and function working together. Muscular tissue can contract to bring about movement. Glandular tissue contains secretory cells that can produce substances such as enzymes and hormones. Epithelial tissue covers the outside of your body as well as your internal organs.

Plants have tissues too. Epidermal tissues cover the surfaces and protect them. Mesophyll tissues contain lots of chloroplasts and can carry out photosynthesis. Xylem and phloem are the transport tissues in plants. They carry water and dissolved mineral ions from the roots up to the leaves and dissolved food from the leaves around the plant.

a What is a tissue?

Organs

Organs are made up of tissues. One organ can contain several tissues, all working together. For example, the stomach is an organ involved in the digestion of your food. It contains:
- muscular tissue to churn the food and digestive juices of the stomach together
- glandular tissue, to produce the digestive juices that break down food
- epithelial tissue, which covers the inside and the outside of the organ.

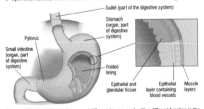

Figure 2 The stomach contains several different tissues, each with a different function in the organ

The pancreas is an organ that has two important functions. It makes hormones to control our blood sugar. It also makes some of the enzymes that digest our food. It contains two very different types of tissue to produce these different secretions.

To summarise, an organ is a collection of different tissues working together to carry out important functions in your body.

b What is an organ?

Different organs are combined in organ systems to carry out major functions in the body. These functions include transporting the blood or digesting food. The organ systems together make up your body.

Adaptations for exchange

Many of the organs of the body have developed to enable exchange to take place. For example:
- there is an exchange of gases in the lungs
- digested food moves from the small intestine into the blood
- many different dissolved substances are filtered out of the blood into the kidney tubules. Some of them then move back from the tubules into the blood.

These organs have adaptations that make the exchange of materials easier and more efficient.

Many of these adaptations increase the surface area over which materials are exchanged. The bigger the surface area, the more quickly diffusion can take place.

Other adaptations increase the concentration gradient across the membranes. The steeper the concentration gradient, the faster diffusion takes place. Many organs have a good blood supply, bringing substances in and taking them out. This helps to maintain the steep concentration gradient needed for diffusion to take place more rapidly.

?? Did you know ...?
A human liver cell is about 10μm (1 × 10⁻⁵ m) in diameter. A human liver is about 22.5cm (2.5 × 10⁻¹ m) across. It contains a lot of liver cells!

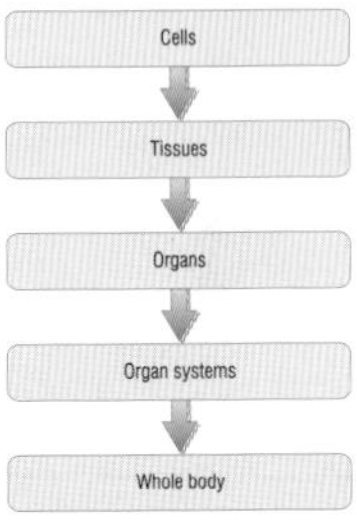

Cells → Tissues → Organs → Organ systems → Whole body

Figure 3 Larger living organisms have many levels of organisation

Summary questions

1 Copy and complete using the words below:
specialised tissue differentiated function multicellular
A .... organism is made up of many different cells. Some of these cells have .... and become .... to carry out a particular .... in the body. A group of these specialised cells working together forms a ....

2 For each of the following, state whether they are a specialised cell, a tissue or an organ. Explain your answer.
a sperm
b kidney
c stomach

3 Find out and explain how the small intestine and the lungs are adapted to provide the biggest possible surface area for the exchange of materials within the organs.

Key points
- A tissue is a group of cells with similar structure and function.
- Organs are made of tissues. One organ may contain several types of tissue.

142 | 143

Answers to in-text questions

a A tissue is a collection of cells of similar structure and function all working together.

b An organ is a collection of different tissues working together to carry out a specific function in the body.

Summary answers

1 multicellular, differentiated, specialised, function, tissue

2 **a** sperm – specialised cell – found individually.
  b kidney – organ – several tissues working together.
  c stomach – organ – several tissues working together.

3 **Small intestine** – villi and microvilli to increase SA (surface area) for the diffusion of dissolved food molecules from small intestine into the blood. Any other valid points.

  Lungs – many alveoli to give large surface area for exchange of oxygen and carbon dioxide.

B2 1.6

Organ systems

Learning objectives

Students should learn:

- that organ systems are groups of organs that perform a particular function
- that the digestive system of a mammal is an example of a system in which substances are exchanged with the environment
- that plant organs include stems, roots and leaves.

Learning outcomes

Most students should be able to:

- define an organ system
- describe the digestive system as an example of an organ system
- describe the main organs of a plant, with the leaf in more detail.

Some students should also be able to:

- explain in detail how organs in an organ system work together.

Support

- Provide students with pre-prepared labels for the plant organs and functions.

Extend

- Let students discover how the digestive systems of carnivores and herbivores are different from the human digestive system.

Specification link-up: Biology B2.2

- Organ systems are groups of organs that perform a particular function. The digestive system is one example of a system in which humans and other mammals exchange substances with the environment. The digestive system includes:
  - glands, such as the pancreas and salivary glands, which produce digestive juices
  - the stomach and small intestine, where digestion occurs
  - the liver, which produces bile
  - the small intestine, where the absorption of soluble food occurs
  - the large intestine, where water is absorbed from the undigested food, producing faeces. *[B2.2.1 d)]*
- Plant organs include stems, roots and leaves. *[B2.2.2 a)]*
- Examples of plant tissues include:
  - epidermal tissues, which cover the plant
  - mesophyll, which carries out photosynthesis
  - xylem and phloem, which transport substances around the plant. *[B2.2.2 b)]*

Lesson structure

Starters

Down the hatch! – Ask a student what they last ate. Ask the class to describe as far as they know what will happen to the food as it goes through the student's body – which organs will it pass through and what will each one do to it? Read out some examples. *(5 minutes)*

Differentiation of cells – Ask students to visualise themselves getting younger and younger until they were back inside their mother's womb, as a single cell. Think of all the different jobs that all the cells in an adult body have to do. Write a command list to the cell telling it what functions we will need in the future from its offspring. Share the list with the rest of the class. Support students by using a writing frame to assist with the presentation of the command list. Extend students by expecting them to produce a more comprehensive list and by putting more detail into the job descriptions. *(10 minutes)*

Main

- Break the class into small groups. Give each one a dissecting board and a small weed in flower such as groundsel. Ask them to separate out the different parts of the plant (e.g. root system, shoot system, flower) and place them on a sheet of paper. Then stick them on with sticky tape and write next to each part what its name is and what its function is.
- They could also label the individual parts of each system, such as the leaves, leaf stalks, stem, etc. of the shoot system. Add to these labels the functions of the component parts.
- A video or DVD of science programmes giving a tour of the digestive system would be useful here.
- Provide the class with a set of large information sheets spaced out around the room, one per system, giving relevant facts regarding the component organs and how the system is put together, what its overall function is, how it interacts with other systems, etc. Provide the students with question sheets on each system which they can fill in as they go around. Have a marking session at the end, either peer, self, or collective as required.
- Comparison of plant and animal organs and organ systems – get students to list the characteristics of living organisms. Alongside each characteristic, get them to decide which organs and/or organ systems are involved in a plant and a mammal. Are there similar organs? Are there similar functions? Are there basic differences?

Plenaries

System hangman – Play a version of the traditional game by either using a whiteboard or an electronic projected version (many are freely available as downloads from the internet). To enhance competition, have small prizes available for winners. *(5 minutes)*

System card sort – Give the students several large cards of one colour with the names of systems on them. Give them also a pack of smaller cards of a different colour with the names of organs on. Their job is to sort the organs into the systems and place them on the correct pile. You can have the names of the relevant organs on the back of the system cards if the students won't cheat! Support students by limiting the number of cards and the complexity of the descriptions. Extend students by encouraging them to devise their own game to reinforce the ideas. You could also run the exercise again this time against the clock – see if they can beat their record! *(10 minutes)*

Cells, tissues and organs

B2 1.6   Organ systems

Organ systems

Learning objectives

- What are organ systems?
- What organs form the digestive system?
- What are plant organs?

Organ systems are groups of organs that all work together to perform a particular function. The way one organ functions often depends on others in the system. The human digestive system is a good example of an organ system.

The digestive system

The digestive system of humans and other mammals exchanges substances with the environment. The food you take in and eat is made up of large insoluble molecules. Your body cannot absorb and use these molecules. They need to be broken down or digested to form smaller, soluble molecules. These can then be absorbed and used by your cells. This process of digestion takes place in your digestive system.

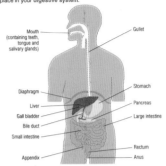

Mouth (containing teeth, tongue and salivary glands)
Gullet
Diaphragm
Stomach
Liver
Pancreas
Gall bladder
Large intestine
Bile duct
Small intestine
Rectum
Appendix
Anus

Figure 1 The main organs of the human digestive system

The digestive system is a **muscular tube** that squeezes your food through it. It starts at one end with your mouth, and finishes at the other with your anus. The digestive system contains many different organs. There are glands such as the pancreas and salivary glands. These glands make and release digestive juices containing enzymes to break down your food.

The stomach and the small intestine are the main organs where food is digested. Enzymes break down the large insoluble food molecules into smaller, soluble ones.

Your small intestine is also where the soluble food molecules are absorbed into your blood. Once there they get transported in the bloodstream around your body. The small intestine is adapted to have a very large surface area. This increases diffusion from the gut to the blood.

The muscular walls of the gut squeeze the undigested food onwards into your large intestine. This is where water is absorbed from the undigested food into your blood. The material left forms the faeces. Faeces are stored and then pass out of your body through the rectum and anus back into the environment.

a What is the digestive system and what does it do?

Plant organs

Animals are not the only organisms to have organs and organ systems – plants do too.

Plants have differentiated cells that form specialised tissues. These include mesophyll, xylem and phloem. Within the body of a plant, tissues such as these are arranged to form organs. Each organ carries out its own particular functions.

Plant organs include the leaves, stems and roots, each of which has a very specific job to do.

b What are the main organs in a plant?

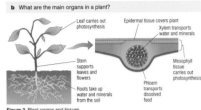

Leaf carries out photosynthesis
Epidermal tissue covers plant
Xylem transports water and minerals
Stem supports leaves and flowers
Mesophyll tissue carries out photosynthesis
Roots take up water and minerals from the soil
Phloem transports dissolved food

Figure 2 Plant organs and tissues

Study tip

Learn the sequence for multicellular organisms:

organism
↓
organ systems
↓
organs
↓
tissues
↓
cells

Summary questions

1 Match each of the following organs to its correct function.

A stem   i   breaking down large insoluble molecules into smaller soluble molecules

B root   ii   photosynthesising in plants

C small intestine for absorption   iii   providing support in plants

D leaf   iv   anchoring plants and obtaining water and minerals from soil

2 Explain the difference between organs and organ systems, giving two examples.

3 Using the human digestive system as an example, explain how the organs in an organ system rely on each other to function properly.

Key points

- Organ systems are groups of organs that perform a particular function.
- The digestive system in a mammal is an example of a system where substances are exchanged with the environment.
- Plant organs include stems, roots and leaves.

Further teaching suggestions

More organ systems
- Find videos or presentations of other organ systems, such as the respiratory system and the circulatory system in mammals.

Support systems
- Compare support systems in plants with support systems in animals.

Leaf systems
- Get the students to work out how many different functions are carried out by a leaf and how these link with the other systems in a plant.

Answers to in-text questions

a The digestive system is a system of organs all working together to bring about the digestion of your food.

b The main organs in a plant are the stems, roots and leaves.

Summary answers

1 A iii, B iv, C i, D ii.

2 An organ is a collection of several different tissues that work together to carry out a particular function in the body, e.g. heart pumps blood around the body, the stomach collects the food you eat and continues the digestive process (any two examples).

An organ system is a number of organs which work together to carry out a major function in the body, e.g. the digestive system which gradually breaks down insoluble food molecules into soluble molecules which can be taken into the blood stream, and then gets rid of the waste material (any two examples).

3 Each part of the digestive system relies on the parts before it, e.g. the stomach relies on the mouth, teeth and salivary glands to deliver chunks of chewed food, the small intestine depends on the stomach to continue the process of digestion and then on the enzymes made by the pancreas to help with the digestive process. The large intestine can only deal with the remains of the food which has already been digested in the small intestine and the soluble molecules absorbed into the blood. This leaves the waste material and lots of water, so the large intestine can absorb the water and remove faeces from the body.

Summary answers

1 a Nucleus, chloroplast, starch, cytoplasm, membrane, cell wall.

  b Flagellum for moving around, eye spot for sensing light.

  c Chlamydomonas is classified as a plant. It is a green alga – has chloroplasts and a cellulose cell wall.

2 a Correctly labelled diagrams.

  b **i** **Palisade cell:** it carries out photosynthesis;

    ii **White blood cell:** defending the body against pathogens/immune system/destroying/engulfing pathogens;

    iii **Sensory nerve cell:** carrying nerve impulses.

  c **i** **Palisade cell:** it has lots of chloroplasts to capture the light energy and enzymes needed for photosynthesis;

    ii **White blood cell:** can flow and engulfs organisms, it doesn't produce antibodies;

    iii **Sensory nerve cell:** sensory receptor to respond to changes, long axon to carry impulse long distances around body, synapse to pass impulse to other nerve cells, transmitter substance in the synapse to transfer impulse across gap.

3 a See B1.2 for correctly drawn bacterial cell and yeast cell.

  b • Nucleus containing genetic material – the instructions for making a new cell and controlling the reactions in the cell.

    • Cell membrane – controls the movement of substances into and out of the cell.

    • Ribosomes – make proteins.

    • Mitochondria – produce energy by cellular respiration.

    • Cytoplasm – liquid gel in which the reactions of life take place.

4 a Diffusion is the net movement of particles of a gas or dissolved substance from an area of high concentration to an area of lower concentration.

  b The blood spreads into the water by diffusion so the water turns red and it looks as if there is a lot more blood.

  c Diffusion takes place more rapidly at higher temperatures because the particles have more energy and move more quickly. So on a warm, still day the scent molecules will travel faster from the area in the flower where they are at their highest concentration into the garden air, so you will smell them. On a cold still day, although the concentration gradient will be the same, the particles will be moving much more slowly so you are less likely to smell the flowers.

5 a The bigger the surface area (SA), the faster diffusion can take place across a boundary.

  b **i** Individual cells have a folded cell membrane – microvilli – to increase the SA (surface area) available for diffusion.

    ii Any sensible suggestions, e.g. body organs have folded epithelial linings, etc. to give a bigger SA (surface area) for diffusion.

6 a Epidermis, mesophyll, xylem, etc. – any three plant tissues.

  b Stem – supports other areas of the plant, transports materials around the plant; roots – anchor plant in soil, uptake of water and mineral ions from the soil; leaves – photosynthesis.

  c Xylem and phloem – because xylem brings water and minerals to all the cells from the roots, and phloem

---

Summary questions 🄺

1 *Chlamydomonas* is a single-celled organism that lives under water. It can move itself to the light to photosynthesise, and stores excess food as starch.

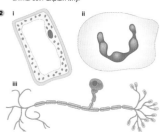

Labels: Flagellum; Chloroplast; Red eye spot; Site of starch formation; Starch grains

  a What features does it have in common with most plant cells?

  b What features are not like plant cells and what are they used for?

  c Would you class *Chlamydomonas* as a plant cell or an animal cell? Explain why.

2 i ii iii

Each of these cells is specialised for a particular function in your body.

  a Copy each of these diagrams and label the cells carefully. Carry out some research if necessary.

  b Describe what you think is the function of each of these cells.

  c Explain how the structure of the cell is related to its function.

3 a Draw and label a bacterial cell and a yeast cell.

  b What are the common structures in all plant, algal and animal cells? Describe their functions.

4 a What is diffusion?

  b If you cut your hand and then put it in a bowl of water, it looks as if there is a lot of blood. Explain why this happens.

  c The scent of flowers in a garden is much more noticeable on a warm, still day than it is on a cold, day. Explain this in terms of diffusion.

5 a What effect does surface area have on diffusion?

  b Describe one way in which the following can be adapted to increase the surface area available for diffusion:
    i individual cells
    ii body organs.

6 Plants have specialised cells, tissues and organs just animals do.

  a Give three examples of plant tissues.

  b What are the main plant organs and what do they d

  c Which plant tissues are found in all of the main pla organs and why?

7 It is possible to separate the different parts of a cell u a centrifuge which spins around rather like a very fast spin dryer. They are used to separate structures that might be mixed together in a liquid. One of their uses to separate the different parts of a cell.

The cells are first broken open so that the contents spill out into the liquid. The mixture is then put into the centrifuge. The centrifuge starts to spin slowly and a pellet forms at the bottom of the tube. This is removed The rest is put back into the centrifuge at a higher spe and the next pellet removed and so on.

Here are some results:

Centrifuge speed (rpm*)	Part of cell in pellet
3000	nuclei
10000	mitochondria
12000	ribosomes

*rpm = revolutions per minute

  a From these observations can you suggest a link between the speed of the centrifuge and the size o the part of the cell found in the pellet?

  b What apparatus would you need to test your suggestion?

  c If your suggestion is correct, what results would yo expect?

  d What would be the easiest measurement to make t show the size of the mitochondria?

  e Suggest how many mitochondria you might measu

  f How would you calculate the mean for the measurements you have taken?

---

transports dissolved food (glucose, sugars) which all the cells need for energy from respiration.

7 a The slower the centrifuge spins, the larger the cell part found in the pellet. Or reverse argument.

  b A microscope with attachment to measure, e.g. length.

  c For the results you would expect the mean size of part of the cell in the pellet to be larger with slower centrifuge speed.

  d Measure the length – because they are 'cigar-shaped'.

  e As many as possible! But a minimum of 10.

  f Add up all the measurements and divide by how many there are.

Kerboodle resources 🄺

Resources available for this chapter on Kerboodle are:

- Chapter map: Cells, tissues and organs
- Support: Cell structures and functions (B2 1.1)
- Extension: Artificial life, but is it intelligent? (B2 1.1)
- Practical: Observation of cells under a microscope (B2 1.1)
- Bump up your grade: Hunt the answer – cells (B2 1.3)
- Interactive activity: Cells
- Revision podcast: Cells, tissues and organs
- Test yourself: Cells, tissues and organs
- On your marks: Cells, tissues and organs
- Practice questions: Cells, tissues and organs
- Answers to practice questions: Cells, tissues and organs

End of chapter questions

Practice questions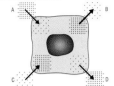

The diagram shows a plant cell.

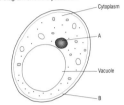

a Identify the structures listed. Choose the correct letter A, B, C, D or E for each structure.
  i nucleus (1)
  ii chloroplast (1)
  iii cell wall (1)
b Animal cells are different from plant cells. Give the letters of the two parts that are also found in animal cells. (2)
c What is a tissue? (2)

The parts of plant cells have important functions. **List A** contains names of cell parts. **List B** lists some functions of cell parts.

Match each cell part to its correct function.

List A	List B
nucleus	controls entry of materials into cell
mitochondria	produce protein
chloroplasts	release energy
ribosomes	controls cell activities
	absorb light for photosynthesis

(4)

Plant and animal organs contain tissues.

a Name one example of a plant tissue and describe its function. (2)
b **i** Name one example of an animal tissue. (1)
  ii Give an example of an organ where this tissue would be found. (1)
  iii What is the function of the tissue you have named? (1)

4 The diagram shows four ways in which molecules may move into and out of a cell. The dots show the concentration of molecules.

a Name the cell structure that controls the movement of materials into or out of cells. (1)
b **i** Name the process illustrated by A and B. (1)
  ii Explain the direction of the arrows in A and B. (2)

5 The diagram shows a yeast cell.

a Identify the parts labelled A and B. (2)
b The cytoplasm also contains mitochondria and ribosomes.
  What is the function of these structures? (2)
c Suggest what is found in the vacuole. (1)

6 *In this question you will be assessed on using good English, organising information clearly and using specialist terms where appropriate.*

The digestive system is a group of organs which changes food from insoluble into soluble molecules. Soluble molecules can be absorbed into the blood stream. Some food cannot be digested.

Describe the functions (jobs) of the organs in the digestive system. (6)

147

Practical suggestions

Practicals	AQA		📖	⚙
Observation of cells under a microscope, e.g. sprouting mung beans to show root hair cells.	✓	✓	✓	
Computer simulations to model the relative size of different cells, organelles and molecules.	✓		✓	
Computer simulations to model the process of diffusion.	✓		✓	
Making model cells.	✓			
Diffusion of ammonium hydroxide in a glass tube using litmus as the indicator.	✓		✓	
Investigate how temperature affects the rate of diffusion of glucose through Visking tubing.	✓		✓	

Practice answers

1 a i D   **ii** C   **iii** A   *(3 marks)*
  b B and D   *(2 marks)*
  c Group of cells – with similar function.   *(2 marks)*

2 Nucleus – controls cell activities.
Mitochondria – release energy.
Chloroplasts – absorb light for photosynthesis.
Ribosomes – produce protein.   *(4 marks)*

3 a Named plant tissue, e.g. epidermal/mesophyll/xylem/phloem.
  Function correctly linked to chosen tissue, covers surface/photosynthesis/transport.   *(2 marks)*
  b **i** Correctly named animal tissue, e.g. muscular/glandular/epithelial.   *(1 mark)*
    (Allow other relevant answer).
    ii Correct organ named, which contains named tissue, e.g. stomach.   *(1 mark)*
    iii Correct function for named tissue, e.g. contracts to cause movement/produces enzymes/lines organ.   *(1 mark)*

4 a (Cell) membrane.   *(1 mark)*
  b **i** diffusion   *(1 mark)*
    ii Molecules move from a region of higher concentration to a region of lower concentration.   *(2 marks)*

5 a A = nucleus, B = cell wall.   *(2 marks)*
  b Mitochondria – release energy/respiration.
  Ribosomes – produce protein.   *(2 marks)*
  c Solution/liquid/(cell) sap or description e.g. water and sugar.   *(1 mark)*

6 Marks awarded for this answer will be determined by the Quality of Written Communication (QWC) as well as the standard of the scientific response.

There is a clear, balanced and detailed description referring to most of the key organs in the digestive system and their functions. The answer shows almost faultless spelling, punctuation and grammar. It is coherent and in an organised, logical sequence. It contains a range of appropriate or relevant specialist terms used accurately.   *(5–6 marks)*

There is some description of at least three organs and their functions. There are some errors in spelling, punctuation and grammar. The answer has some structure and organisation. The use of specialist terms has been attempted, but not always accurately.   *(3–4 marks)*

There is a brief description of the functions of at least two organs, which has little clarity and detail. The spelling, punctuation and grammar are very weak. The answer is poorly organised with almost no specialist terms and/or their use demonstrating a general lack of understanding of their meaning.   *(1–2 marks)*

No relevant content.   *(0 marks)*

Examples of biology points made in the response:

* Glands produce digestive juices
* Salivary glands
* Pancreas
* Digestion occurs in the stomach and small intestine
* The liver produces bile
* The soluble food is absorbed in the small intestine
* Water is absorbed from the undigested food
* In the large intestine.

B2 2.1 | Photosynthesis

Learning objectives

Students should learn:

- that light energy is absorbed by the chlorophyll in the chloroplasts of green plants and some algae
- that light energy is used by converting carbon dioxide and water into sugar
- that oxygen is released as a by-product.

Learning outcomes

Most students should be able to:

- summarise the process of photosynthesis in a word equation
- describe where the energy comes from and how it is absorbed
- describe experiments that show the raw materials needed and the resulting products.

Some students should also be able to:

- explain the build up of sugars into starch during photosynthesis.

Answers to in-text questions

a carbon dioxide + water $\xrightarrow{\text{(+ light energy)}}$ glucose + oxygen

b The green substance that absorbs light energy in plants.

c Provides a large surface area for the light to fall on.

Support

- Provide students with the components of a word equation for photosynthesis. Ask them to assemble it in the correct order.

Extend

- Ask students to find out the actual structure of glucose and then use chemical symbols for the photosynthesis equation and balance it.

Specification link-up: Biology B2.3

- Photosynthesis is summarised by the equation:
  carbon dioxide + water $\xrightarrow{\text{(+ light energy)}}$ glucose + oxygen. *[B2.3.1 a)]*
- During photosynthesis:
  - light energy is absorbed by a green substance called chlorophyll, which is found in chloroplasts in some plant cells
  - this energy is used by converting carbon dioxide and water into sugar (glucose)
  - oxygen is released as a by-product. *[B2.3.1 b)]*

  Controlled Assessment: B4.3 Collect primary and secondary data *[B4.3.1 a)]*, *[B4.3.2 a)]*; B4.5 Analyse and interpret primary and secondary data. *[B4.5.4 a)]*

Lesson structure

Starters

Why are leaves green? – Lead a discussion based on a concept cartoon-style talking head. Revise light reflection and absorbance. *(5 minutes)*

What will happen to my leaf? – During the growing season (or if you have plants in a greenhouse), give each student a spot label on which they can write their initials. Allow them to choose and label a young leaf. They should then measure the length of the leaf and record it. Back in the laboratory, ask them to predict what will happen to the leaf and explain why. Support students by prompting them to consider what the leaf needs in order to grow. Extend students by asking them to explain in detail all the processes involved. The leaves will need to be checked at intervals. *(10 minutes)*

Main

- Prepared microscope slides of transverse sections through leaves could be projected or viewed under the microscope, so that students can distinguish the different tissues within the leaf. Point out the palisade tissue, the vascular tissue and the stomata. Students could draw plans of the tissues to show where photosynthesis takes place (see 'Practical support').

- When carrying out experiments on photosynthesis, we can test for the products i.e. the presence of sugars or the evolution of oxygen. In most plants, the sugars are converted to starch (shown by the presence of starch grains in chloroplasts). The starch test can then be used on leaves to show that photosynthesis has occurred (see 'Practical support').

- The experiment to show that oxygen has been produced (see 'Practical support') can be done using water plants such as *Elodea canadensis* (Canadian pondweed). If students carry out and extend the experiment into an investigation, individually or in groups, several of the concepts of 'How Science Works' could be introduced. They can formulate a hypothesis, make predictions, draw conclusions and evaluate the validity of experimental design. Focus on one or two skills.

- The experiment on testing for starch to show that chlorophyll is necessary for photosynthesis can use variegated plants, such as a spider plant or geranium (see 'Practical support').

- In the 'Observing leaves' practical (see 'Practical support'), the adaptations of leaves for the process of photosynthesis are investigated.

Plenaries

Summary – Use a summary of photosynthesis with missing words. Support students by providing a list of the missing words from which they choose the appropriate one. Extend students by asking them to write their own summaries. They could be provided with a list of words that should be included. *(5 minutes)*

Prove it! – Write on the board, or project, a number of statements about photosynthesis. Then the students have to write out or discuss how we know each of the statements is true. *(10 minutes)*

Practical support

Producing oxygen

Equipment and materials required

Elodea canadensis (Canadian pondweed), glass funnel, beaker of water, test tube full of water, light conditions.

Details

This practical will show that oxygen has been produced using water plants such as *Elodea canadensis* (Canadian pondweed) which is readily available from garden centres. The water plant is placed under the wide part of an inverted glass funnel in a beaker of water. A test tube full of water is inverted and placed over the end of the funnel. The apparatus can be set up as described and kept illuminated for several hours, so that enough gas can be collected to be able to test it satisfactorily. If groups of students set up their own, it is unlikely to yield enough gas to test within a lesson.

Safety: Wash hands after contact with pond water.

Testing for starch

Equipment and materials required

Variegated plants, such as geranium, dilute iodine solution in dropping bottles, water baths to kill the leaves/make them more permeable/softer, ethanol for decolourising leaves/removing chlorophyll, white tiles or dishes to put the leaves in, forceps.

Details

The plants need to be kept in bright light for several hours. Keep one plant in the dark for two days to destarch it as a control. Each student can be given a leaf from an illuminated plant. A record should be made of the distribution of the green and white areas of the leaf, before testing for starch. Test for starch by dipping the leaf to be tested into boiling water for 15 seconds using forceps. Remove the leaf and place in a test tube of ethanol until the green colour is removed. Wash leaf in water and add dilute iodine solution. After carrying out the test, another drawing can be made showing the areas that remain brown and those that have been stained blue/black. Comparison of the two drawings will enable a conclusion to be drawn. Testing a leaf from the control plant will show that if there is no light, then no starch will be produced.

Safety: CLEAPSS Hazcard 54B Iodine. CLEAPSS Hazcard 40A Ethanol – highly flammable/harmful. Keep away from naked flames. Take care when handling hot water. Wear eye protection.

Observing leaves

Equipment and materials required

Prepared slides of sections through leaves and microscopes. Use whole leaves of different types.

Details

Slides should be projected or viewed under a microscope and students draw plans of the sections showing where the tissues are situated. Students should make drawings of whole leaves and label the parts, annotating each to indicate the adaptations for photosynthesis.

Safety: No special precautions needed.

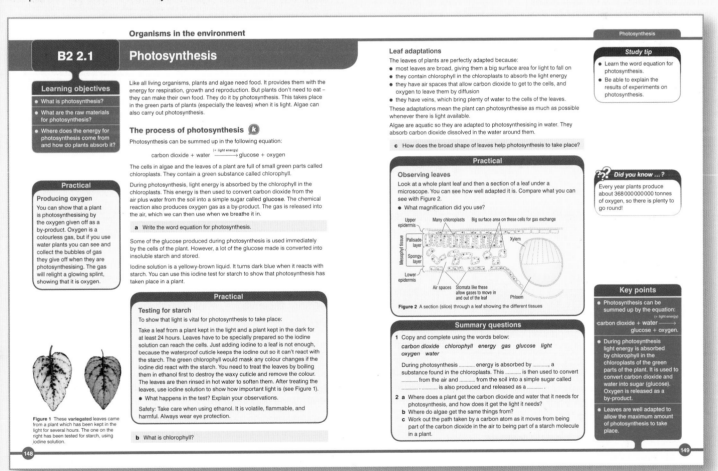

B2 2.2

Limiting factors

Learning objectives

Students should learn:

- that the rate of photosynthesis may be limited by low temperature and the shortage of carbon dioxide or light
- that these factors interact
- that if any of these factors are in short supply, the rate of photosynthesis is limited.

Learning outcomes

Most students should be able to:

- list the factors that limit the rate of photosynthesis
- describe how the factors interact
- describe how the environment in which plants grow can be artificially manipulated to grow more food.

Some students should also be able to:

- interpret data showing how the factors affect the rate of photosynthesis
- explain why the rate of photosynthesis is limited by low temperature, shortage of carbon dioxide or shortage of light.

Support

- Use pondweed in hydrogencarbonate indicator solution to show the effect of varying the light intensity on the rate of photosynthesis. Explain to the students that the deeper the purple colour, the more photosynthesis has occurred.

Extend

- Give students some cross sections of tree branches and, using hand lenses or binocular microscopes, ask: 'Why are there rings present? What do they represent? Why would they vary from year to year?' Expect the students to make links between growth rate, temperature and light intensity as limiting factors.

Specification link-up: Biology B2.3

- The rate of photosynthesis may be limited by:
  - shortage of light
  - low temperature
  - shortage of carbon dioxide. *[B2.3.1 c)]*
- Light, temperature and the availability of carbon dioxide interact and in practice any one of them may be the factor that limits photosynthesis. *[B2.3.1 d)]*
- Interpret data showing how factors affect the rate of photosynthesis. *[B2.3]*

Controlled Assessment: B4.1 Plan practical ways to develop and test candidates' own scientific ideas. *[B4.1.1 a) b) c)]*

Lesson structure

Starters

Oxygen production and light intensity – Show students the 'Producing oxygen' practical from the previous lesson. Support students by telling them that the rate of oxygen production varies with light intensity. Show them different graphs and ask them to choose which they think is the most likely and why. Extend students by asking them to draw a sketch graph of how the rate of oxygen production would vary with light intensity. Draw onto mini whiteboards. *(5 minutes)*

The limiting factors game – Have three sorts of counters (or small cards): one set labelled 'L' for suitable light level, another 'T' for suitable temperature and the third 'CO_2'. For each group of students, place some of each set of counters (or cards) into a bag so that they get a mixture of 'L', 'T' and 'CO_2'. The students are to take out a counter one at a time, placing them on a base line on paper or on the desk. The aim is to make sets of three counters side by side, at which point they can start on the next layer as they have grown. If they draw out a counter which they have already got in that layer, they put it back. The objective is to grow the 'plant' to as many levels as possible during a set time. Adjust each bag's contents so that some groups run out of 'L' counters first, some of 'T' counters and some of 'CO_2' ones. Discuss the results. *(10 minutes)*

Main

- The experiment 'How does the intensity of light affect the rate of photosynthesis' is easy to set up (see 'Practical support'). Students can work in groups and vary the light intensity by altering the distance of the lamp from the plant.
- This is a good experiment for developing 'How Science Works' concepts. A hypothesis can be formulated, predictions made, variables such as temperature controlled, measurements taken, results expressed as graphs, conclusions drawn and evaluation carried out. Choose which skills to actively teach. These might be the same for the whole group or use the opportunity to respond to areas of specific weakness identified in different groups.
- Results can be plotted as number of bubbles evolved, in a set time, against distance of the lamp from the plant. A more accurate way of plotting the results is to use light intensity, given by $\frac{1}{d^2}$ where d is the distance of the lamp from the plant.
- How does temperature affect the rate of photosynthesis? Show the students a graph of the effect of temperature on the rate of photosynthesis. Discuss the graph and get the students to think about the temperature fluctuations in a day. Discuss how the apparatus used to investigate the effect of different light intensity could be modified to investigate the effect of varying the temperature.
- How does carbon dioxide concentration affect the rate of photosynthesis? Project the graph of the effect of different concentrations of carbon dioxide on the rate of photosynthesis. Ask the students whether they think this is the most important limiting factor and why? Go on to discuss how carbon dioxide concentrations can be increased and what effect this could have on productivity.

Plenaries

Question loop – Students play a loop game on the factors limiting photosynthesis. *(5 minutes)*

Finish off the graph – Give the students some semi-completed graphs showing photosynthesis rates featuring various limiting factors to finish off and label. Support students by giving them completed graphs and asking them which factor is limiting under certain sets of circumstances, e.g. in a dense jungle, high up a mountain, etc. Extend students by asking them to say how the graphs could vary at different times of the year. *(10 minutes)*

Practical support

How does the intensity of light affect the rate of photosynthesis?

Equipment and materials required
Sprigs of *Elodea,* boiling tubes and test-tube racks, bench lamps, rulers, beakers, funnels, stopwatches or stop clocks, graph paper.

Details
Place some sprigs of *Elodea* in the mouth of a glass funnel and place the funnel in a beaker of water as shown in the diagram in the Student Book. The level of the water should be above the funnel so that a test tube of water can be inverted over the opening of the funnel to collect the gas given off. Start with the light source close to the beaker (high light intensity) and either count the number of bubbles of gas given off in a set time (1 minute) or allow a set time and measure the volume of the gas in the test tube. Vary the distance of the lamp from the beaker, allow time for the plant to adjust and then take more readings.

Safety: Wash hands after contact with pond water. Dry hands before using mains electricity (lamps).

Organisms in the environment

B2 2.2 Limiting factors (k)

Learning objectives
- What factors limit the rate of photosynthesis in plants?
- How can we use what we know about limiting factors to grow more food?

You may have noticed that plants grow quickly in the summer, yet they hardly grow at all in the winter. Plants need certain things to grow quickly. They need light, warmth and carbon dioxide if they are going to photosynthesise as fast as they can.

Sometimes any one or more of these things can be in short supply. Then they may limit the amount of photosynthesis a plant can manage. This is why they are known as limiting factors.

a Why do you think plants grow faster in the summer than in the winter?

Study tip
Make sure you can explain limiting factors.
Learn to interpret graphs that show the effect of limiting factors on photosynthesis.

Light (k)
The most obvious factor affecting the rate of photosynthesis is light. If there is plenty of light, lots of photosynthesis can take place. If there is very little or no light, photosynthesis will stop. It doesn't matter what other conditions are like around the plant. For most plants, the brighter the light, the faster the rate of photosynthesis.

Practical

How does the intensity of light affect the rate of photosynthesis?

We can look at this experimentally (see Figure 1). At the start, the rate of photosynthesis goes up as the light intensity increases. This tells us that light intensity is a limiting factor.

When the light is moved away from this water plant, the rate of photosynthesis falls – shown by a slowing in the stream of oxygen bubbles being produced. If the light is moved closer (keeping the water temperature constant) the stream of bubbles becomes faster, showing an increased rate of photosynthesis.

However, we reach a point when no matter how bright the light, the rate of photosynthesis stays the same. At this point, light is no longer limiting the rate of photosynthesis. Something else has become the limiting factor.

The results can be plotted on a graph, which shows the effect of light intensity on the rate of photosynthesis.

- Why is light a limiting factor for photosynthesis?
- Name the independent and the dependent variables in this investigation.

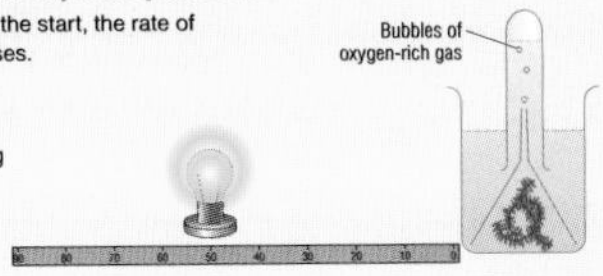

Bubbles of oxygen-rich gas

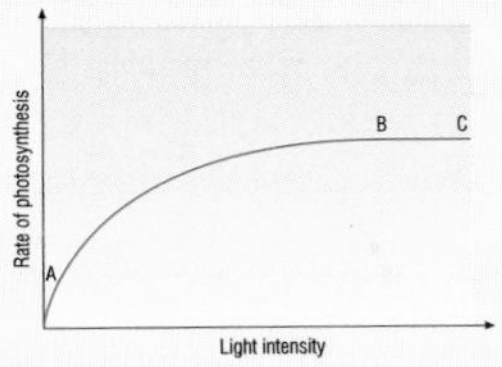

Figure 1 Investigating the effect of light intensity on the rate of photosynthesis

Temperature (k)
Temperature affects all chemical reactions, including photosynthesis. As the temperature rises, the rate of photosynthesis increases as the reaction speeds up. However, photosynthesis is controlled by enzymes. Most enzymes are destroyed (denatured) once the temperature rises to around 40–50 °C. So if the temperature gets too high, the enzymes controlling photosynthesis are denatured. Therefore the rate of photosynthesis will fall (see Figure 2).

b Why does temperature affect photosynthesis?

Carbon dioxide levels
Plants need carbon dioxide to make glucose. The atmosphere only contains about 0.04% carbon dioxide. This means that carbon dioxide levels often limit the rate of photosynthesis. Increasing the carbon dioxide levels will increase the rate of photosynthesis.

On a sunny day, carbon dioxide levels are the most common limiting factor for plants. The carbon dioxide levels around a plant tend to rise at night. That's because in the dark a plant respires but doesn't photosynthesise. Then, as the light and temperature levels increase in the morning, the carbon dioxide all gets used up.

However, in a science lab or greenhouse the levels of carbon dioxide can be increased artificially. This means they are no longer limiting. Then the rate of photosynthesis increases with the rise in carbon dioxide.

In a garden, woodland or field rather than a lab, light, temperature and carbon dioxide levels interact and any one of them might be the factor that limits photosynthesis.

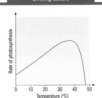

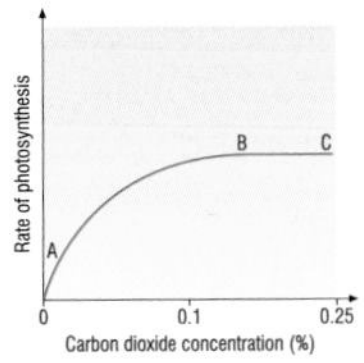

Figure 2 The effect of increasing temperature on the rate of photosynthesis

Figure 3 This graph shows the effect of increasing carbon dioxide levels on the rate of photosynthesis at a given light level and temperature

Summary questions

1 **a** What is photosynthesis?
  b What are the three main limiting factors that affect the rate of photosynthesis in a plant?

2 **a** In each of these situations *one* factor in particular is most likely to be limiting photosynthesis. In *each* case listed below, suggest which factor this is and explain why the rate of photosynthesis is limited.
  i a wheat field first thing in the morning
  ii the same field later on in the day
  iii plants growing on a woodland floor in winter
  iv plants growing on a woodland floor in summer.
  b Why is it impossible to be certain which factor is involved in each of these cases?

3 Look at the graph in Figure 1.
  a Explain what is happening between points A and B on the graph.
  b Explain what is happening between points B and C on the graph.
  c Look at Figure 2. Explain why it is a different shape to the other two graphs shown in Figures 1 and 3.

Key points
- The rate of photosynthesis may be limited by shortage of light, low temperature and shortage of carbon dioxide.
- We can manipulate the levels of light, temperature and carbon dioxide artificially to increase the rate of photosynthesis in food crops.

150
151

Further teaching suggestions

Under glass (choose one)
- Arrange a visit to a commercial glasshouse or encourage students to find out how conditions are controlled.
- Students could discuss the interactions of the factors and how they can be altered. Relate this to the production of glasshouse crops.

ICT link (choose one)
- Use a computer simulation where conditions for plant growth are varied, such as the one suggested above.
- Carry out a data-logging exercise, recording the temperature and light levels as they fluctuate throughout the day.

Answers to in-text questions

a It is warmer in summer and there is more light, so photosynthesis takes place more quickly making more food, so plants grow faster.

b Photosynthesis is a chemical reaction; temperature affects all chemical reactions. An increase in temperature speeds up the reactions as reacting particles collide more frequently and with more energy.

Summary answers

1 **a** The process by which plants use light energy trapped by chlorophyll to convert carbon dioxide and water into glucose (sugar).

 b Carbon dioxide, light and temperature.

2 **a** **i** Light levels are low until sunrise, temperature falls overnight.
  ii Carbon dioxide will limit photosynthesis.
  iii Low light levels in winter, days are shorter, temperature colder.
  iv Trees will limit the light, temperature will be warm so carbon dioxide will be limiting.

 b Above 40–50 °C the enzymes controlling photosynthesis are denatured so the rate of photosynthesis decreases.

3 **a** As light intensity increases, so does the rate of photosynthesis. This tells us that light intensity is a limiting factor.

 b An increase in light intensity has no effect on the rate of photosynthesis, so it is no longer a limiting factor; something else probably is.

 c Temperature acts as a normal limiting factor to begin with; increase in temperature increases the rate of photosynthesis. But above a certain temperature, the enzymes in the cells are destroyed so no photosynthesis can take place.

B2 2.3

How plants use glucose

Learning objectives

Students should learn:

- that glucose is converted into starch for storage
- that some of the glucose produced in plants and algae is used for respiration and some is used to produce fat or oil for storage
- that cellulose and proteins are also produced.

Learning outcomes

Most students should be able to:

- describe how and where starch is stored in plants
- state that some of the glucose produced is used in respiration and some is used to produce fat and oil for storage
- state that some sugars can combine with nitrate ions and other mineral ions to form amino acids which can be built into proteins
- state that cellulose is also produced.

Some students should also be able to:

- explain that the energy released by plants in respiration is used to build smaller molecules into larger molecules
- describe how proteins and cellulose are produced.

Answers to in-text questions

a To provide energy for their cells.

b Starch.

Support

- Give students samples of glucose and corn starch. Tell them to stir the powders into two beakers of water. They should observe what happens and make comments on the solubility. Then ask them to filter the contents of both beakers and isolate and dry the corn starch.

Extend

- Ask students to find out about the differences in structure between starch and cellulose. Relate these differences to their functions within the plant.

Specification link-up: Biology B2.3

- The glucose produced in photosynthesis may be converted into insoluble starch for storage. Plant cells use some of the glucose produced during photosynthesis for respiration. [B2.3.1 e)]
- Some glucose in plants and algae is used:
  - to produce fat or oil for storage
  - to produce cellulose, which strengthens the cell wall
  - to produce proteins. [B2.3.1 f)]
- To produce proteins, plants also use nitrate ions that are absorbed from the soil. [B2.3.1 g)]

Controlled Assessment: B4.3 Collect primary and secondary data [B4.3.1 a)]; B4.5 Analyse and interpret primary and secondary data. [B4.5.4 a)]

Lesson structure

Starters

Showing that respiration has occurred – Issue all the students with drinking straws, and then give half of them boiling tubes containing a little fresh limewater in the bottom and the other half boiling tubes with a little hydrogencarbonate indicator solution in the bottom. Wearing eye protection, ask them to blow *gently* through the drinking straws into the solutions. They should note and compare colour changes, suggesting explanations. *(5 minutes)*

Make a starch molecule – Get the students to draw a chain of about 10 to 12 blank joined hexagons on a narrow strip of paper. Ask them to write 'glucose' inside each hexagon and then to turn the paper over and write 'starch' across the whole of the back. Get them to coil up the strip of paper into as tight a coil as they can and tell them that this represents a starch molecule in a cell. Ask them why they think glucose is converted to starch. What benefit does it have? Lead into how good a storage molecule it is. Support students by prompting them with simple questions about the nature of starch and how much more can be stored. Extend students by asking about the effects of starch and glucose on the water balance of the cells. *(10 minutes)*

Main

- There are many ways to show that a plant produces starch. The most straightforward is to use potted plants: some should be kept in the dark for 48 hours (so that they are destarched) and others kept in daylight conditions.
- Students could be provided with a list of instructions for the procedure, and then asked to test a leaf that has been kept in the light and one that has been kept in the dark.
- The destarched leaves are half-covered with foil or initials cut out of thin card or foil, kept in bright light for several hours and then tested for starch.
- Use the practical experiment 'Where is the starch stored?' (see 'Practical support').
- Roughly compare the starch content of fruits, such as apples, with potato tubers and some seeds. Choose some oily seeds and show by staining that they contain oils using a staining technique or by grinding them up and pressing out the oil.
- Give a PowerPoint presentation or exposition on algae. Introduce them as a group, showing a range of different types from freshwater examples and plankton to large seaweeds. Explain that they do not always look green but they all contain chlorophyll and can carry out photosynthesis. Get the students to say how the algae get the raw materials for the process, bringing in the need for minerals, and discuss the products.

Plenaries

Matching exercise – Write up a list of definitions and key words about photosynthesis, limiting factors and the use of glucose and ask students to match them up. *(5 minutes)*

From the air to a chip – In small groups, the students could produce a series of bullet points of the stages from carbon dioxide in the air to the starch in the chips on their plates. Support students by giving them the stages which they should put into the correct order. Extend students by getting them to add the stages from the starch in the chip back to the carbon dioxide in the air. Gather together the suggestions from all groups and build up the chain of events. *(10 minutes)*

Practical and demonstration support

Making starch

Equipment and materials required
Destarched and illuminated plants, water baths for killing leaves/making them permeable, ethanol to decolourise the leaves/remove chlorophyll, dilute iodine solution in dropping bottles, white tiles, forceps for handling leaves, eye protection.

Details
Remove the leaf to be tested and dip into boiling water for 15 seconds using the forceps. Remove the leaf from the water bath and place in a test tube of ethanol until the green colour is removed. Wash the leaf in water and spread it out on a white tile. Add dilute iodine solution and note the areas of the leaf which have stained blue-black and those that have remained brown.

Safety: Wear eye protection. CLEAPSS Hazcard 54B Iodine solution. CLEAPSS Hazcard 40A Ethanol – highly flammable/harmful. No naked flames.

Where is the starch stored?

Equipment and materials required
Microscopes, slides, cover slips, filter paper, a variety of plant parts (potato tubers, fruits, seeds, nuts, etc.), dilute iodine solution in dropping bottles, eye protection.

Details
The presence of large numbers of starch grains in potato tuber cells can be demonstrated by cutting thin slices of the tissue. Place the thin slices of tissues on microscope slides, cover with a drop of water and then with a cover slip. A drop of dilute iodine solution can be drawn through using filter paper. The starch grains will stain blue-black. In order to see the grains more clearly, it is advisable to draw some water through the slide to remove the surplus iodine solution.

The technique described above can be used on a variety of plant parts. Very thin sections of tissue from fruits, seeds, nuts and other plant organs can then be tested for the presence of starch grains.

Safety: Wear eye protection. CLEAPSS Hazcard 54B Iodine solution.

Organisms in the environment

How plants use glucose

B2 2.3 How plants use glucose

Learning objectives
- What do plants do with the glucose they make?
- How do plants store food?
- What other materials do plant and algal cells need to produce proteins?

Study tip
Two important points to remember:
- Plants respire 24 hours a day to release energy.
- Glucose is soluble in water, but starch is insoluble.

Figure 2 Algal cells contain a nucleus and chloroplasts so they can photosynthesise

links
For more information about the transport of sugars in plants, see B3 2.5 Transport systems in plants.

Plants and algae make glucose when they photosynthesise. This glucose is vital for their survival. Some of the glucose produced during photosynthesis is used immediately by the cells. They use it for respiration to provide energy for cell functions such as growth and reproduction.

Using glucose

Plants cells and algal cells, like any other living cells, respire all the time. They use some of the glucose produced during photosynthesis as they respire. The glucose is broken down using oxygen to provide energy for the cells. Carbon dioxide and water are the waste products of the reaction.

The energy released in respiration is used to build up smaller molecules into bigger molecules. Some of the glucose is changed into starch for storage. Plants and algae also build up glucose into more complex carbohydrates like cellulose. They use this to strengthen the cell walls.

Plants use some of the glucose from photosynthesis to make amino acids. They do this by combining sugars with nitrate ions and other mineral ions from the soil. These amino acids are then built up into proteins to be used in the cells. This uses energy from respiration.

Algae also make amino acids. They do this by taking the nitrate ions and other materials they need from the water they live in.

Plants and algae also use glucose from photosynthesis and energy from respiration to build up fats and oils. These may be used in the cells as an energy store. They are sometimes used in the cell walls to make them stronger. In addition, plants often use fats or oils as an energy store in their seeds. They provide lots of energy for the new plant as it germinates.

Some algal cells are very rich in oils. They are even being considered as a possible source of biofuels for the future.

a Why do plants respire?

Starch for storage

Plants make food by photosynthesis in their leaves and other green parts. However, the food is needed all over the plant. It is moved around the plant in the phloem.

Plants convert some of the glucose produced in photosynthesis into starch to be stored. Glucose is soluble in water. If it were stored in plant cells it could affect the way water moves into and out of the cells. Lots of glucose stored in plant cells could affect the water balance of the whole plant.

Figure 1 Worldwide, algae produce more oxygen and biomass by photosynthesis than plants do – but we often forget all about them

Figure 3 Oilseed rape plants use energy from respiration and glucose from photosynthesis to produce oil to store in their seeds. We use this to make oil for cooking and as a source of biofuels.

Starch is insoluble in water. It will have no effect on the water balance of the plant. This means that plants can store large amounts of starch in their cells.

So, the main energy store in plants is starch and it is found all over a plant. It is stored in the cells of the leaves. The starch provides an energy store for when it is dark or when light levels are low.

Insoluble starch is also kept in special storage areas of a plant. Many plants produce tubers and bulbs. These help them to survive through the winter. They are full of stored starch. We often take advantage of these starch stores and eat them ourselves. Potatoes and onions are all full of starch to keep a plant going until spring comes again.

b What is the main storage substance in plants?

Practical

Making starch
The presence of starch in a leaf is evidence that photosynthesis has taken place. You can test for starch using the iodine test. See B2 2.1 Photosynthesis for details of how to treat the leaves so they will absorb the iodine. After this treatment, adding iodine will show you clearly if the leaf has been photosynthesising or not.

Figure 4 The leaf on the right has been kept in the dark. Its starch stores have been used for respiration or moved to other parts of the plant. The leaf on the left has been in the light and been able to photosynthesise. The glucose has been converted to starch, which is clearly visible when it reacts with iodine and turns blue-black.

Summary questions

1 Copy and complete using the words below:
energy glucose growth photosynthese respiration reproduction starch storage 24
Plants make _____ when they _____ . Some of the glucose produced is used by the cells of the plant for _____, which goes on _____ hours a day. It provides _____ for cell functions, _____ and _____ . Some glucose is converted to _____ for _____ .

2 List as many ways as possible in which a plant uses the glucose produced by photosynthesis.

3 a Why is some of the glucose made by photosynthesis converted to starch to be stored in the plant?
b Where might you find starch in a plant?
c How could you show that a potato is a store of starch?

Key points

- Plant and algal cells use the soluble glucose they produce during photosynthesis in several different ways:
  – for respiration
  – to convert into insoluble starch for storage
  – to produce fats or oils for storage
  – to produce fats, proteins or cellulose for use in the cells and cell walls.
- Plants and algal cells need other materials including nitrate ions to make the amino acids which make up proteins.

152

153

Further teaching suggestions

Formation, use and storage of glucose
- Students can produce a poster showing how glucose is produced, used and stored in the plant. This can either be done individually or in groups.

Respiring plants
- To demonstrate that plants respire, keep some *Elodea* in a boiling tube of hydrogencarbonate indicator. The boiling tube will need to have foil around it or be kept in the dark, so that photosynthesis does not occur. The cherry-red colour should turn yellow as it becomes more acidic due to the evolution of carbon dioxide. Compare with the starter activity that shows respiration in mammals has occurred.

Summary answers

1 glucose, photosynthesise, respiration, 24, energy, growth/reproduction, reproduction/growth, starch, storage

2 Respiration; energy for cell functions; growth; reproduction; building up smaller molecules into bigger molecules; converted into starch for storage; making cellulose; making amino acids; building up fats and oils for a food store in seeds.

3 a Glucose is soluble and would affect the movement of water into and out of the plant cells. Starch is insoluble and so does not disturb the water balance of the plant.
b Leaves, stems, roots and storage organs.
c [Any sensible suggestions involving a slice of potato and dilute iodine solution.]

B2 2.4

Making the most of photosynthesis

Learning objectives

Students should learn:

- that different factors affect the rate of photosynthesis
- that the environment in which plants are grown can be artificially manipulated.

Learning outcomes

Most students should be able to:

- describe the factors that affect the rate of photosynthesis
- describe some ways in which the environment in which plants are grown can be manipulated.

Some students should also be able to:

- evaluate the benefits of artificially manipulating the environment in which plants are grown.

Support

- Give each student some sunflower seeds to plant: one set in the school garden and another set indoors or in a glasshouse. They could compare the growth of the two sets. Each week (or more frequently) hold a strip of coloured paper 2–3 cm wide next to the plant and cut the paper off at the same height as the plant. Stick the strips on to a bar chart frame, using a different colour each time. Get them to state why there is a difference in the growth rate.

Extend

- Get students to research ways of manipulating the growth of plants, other than by manipulating the environment. Hint: using breeding techniques or genetic engineering to produce varieties of plants that grow well at lower temperatures.
- Get students to find out more about Tiberius and making their 'prophecies' cryptic.

Specification link-up: Biology B2.3

- Evaluate the benefits of artificially manipulating the environment in which plants are grown. [B2.3]

  Controlled Assessment: B4.1 Plan practical ways to develop and test candidates' own scientific ideas *[B4.1.1 a) b) c)]*; B4.3 Collect primary and secondary data *[B4.3.1 a)]*; B4.4 Select and process primary and secondary data *[B4.4.2 a) b) c)]*; B4.5 Analyse and interpret primary and secondary data. *[B4.5.4 a)]*

Lesson structure

Starters

Mini-greenhouse – If available, set up a miniature greenhouse. Alternatively, use a transparent plastic container, such as a lemonade bottle cut in half. Rig up a data logger with a couple of temperature sensors, one placed inside and one outside. Shine a heat lamp at the 'greenhouse' and observe the temperature changes. Relate this to the Student Book and ask whether people would have managed to keep plants alive during the winter before greenhouses were invented. *(5 minutes)*

Farming indoors – Tell the students you are going to show them a photograph of a farm. Show the students a photograph of the outside of an ordinary looking terraced house. Assure them that it is a farm and ask them how this can be? Show them a newspaper article featuring a raid on a hydroponic cannabis cultivation factory within an ordinary house (these are frequent occurrences). Emphasise that this activity is illegal and can result in severe punishment. Ask the students to list the features of the environment that would have to be controlled. Support students by encouraging them to come up with simple suggestions, e.g. light, temperature, and plant 'food'. Extend students by getting them to give indications of ranges of these factors and specific nutrients for inclusion. *(10 minutes)*

Main

- Investigating the need for minerals. Provide each group of students with three specimens of tomato plants that have been given different nutrient treatments. Alternatively, provide large coloured photographs (laminated for future use). Ask the students to compare the three plants by describing their appearance, measuring the leaves and estimating root growth.
- Tell the students that the plants have been in the same conditions of light, temperature and carbon dioxide concentration. Ask students to examine and tabulate the differences. Apart from the obvious deficiency symptoms, they could measure leaves, height, etc. Lead a discussion and ask the students to draw conclusions.
- Produce a PowerPoint presentation or exposition on hydroponics to include basic principles and some information on the Nutrient Film Technique. If possible, show pictures of the set-up, including the ways in which all the conditions are monitored and controlled. Apart from optimum growing conditions for the growth of crops, get students to think about some of the other benefits of using this method of cultivation (e.g. cleaner crops, easier harvesting, pest control, etc.). Provide students with a set of questions (with the level adjusted to the ability of the class) and allow some time for discussion – put the process into the context of making the most of photosynthesis.
- Students could then set up their own experiment (see 'Practical support') with sets of plants using water culture (hydroponics). This is a good experiment for introducing the concepts of 'How Science Works'. Hypotheses can be formulated, predictions made, variables considered and controlled, and measurements taken.
- Ask students 'Where does the nitrate come from?' – Draw out the sequence of events from nitrogen in the air (remind the students of the percentage to the protein in plants). You can start with the nitrates in the soil as the centre of a spider diagram or flow chart. This can be accompanied by a modelling activity of 'Pass the N'.

Plenaries

Is it worth it? – Students to consider whether the cost of installing hydroponics systems to grow crops is worth it. Do the crops cost more? Do we need to produce crops out of season – strawberries in January? What are the cost and environmental implications of importing strawberries? *(5 minutes)*

Calling Tiberius – Refer to the Did you know …? feature on the first recorded greenhouse. Imagine that scientists have found a way of getting messages back to people in the past. To the recipient, this would of course be a message from the future. Write down a message to Tiberius Caesar, giving him a prophecy as to how his simple mica greenhouse will be improved in the future. Support students by giving them a writing frame or cloze passage to assist with the message to Tiberius. Extend students by getting them to add other information about scientific inventions which could help him. *(10 minutes)*

Practical support

Hydroponics
Equipment and materials required
Small flasks or bottles, culture solutions lacking magnesium and nitrate, an aquarium aerator, kitchen foil to cover flasks or bottles.

Details
Students could set up their own sets of plants using water culture (hydroponics). Broad bean or cereal seedlings could be used and grown in small flasks or bottles (root development can also be observed in this way). The seedlings should all be at the same stage of growth, as the plants need to grow.

The cultures need to be aerated at intervals and the containers covered to prevent the growth of photosynthetic algae. It is possible to use duckweed in a water culture experiment. It has the advantage of growing more quickly and the growth can be assessed by the number of leaves produced. It will also show the deficiency symptoms.

Safety: No special precautions needed.

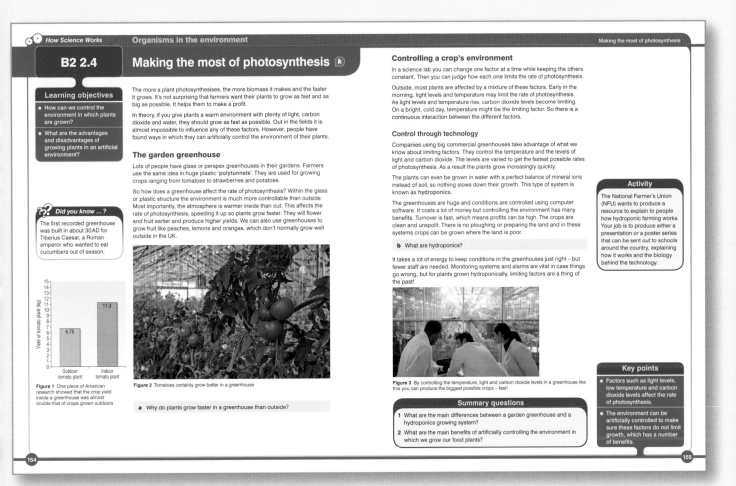

B2 2.4 — Making the most of photosynthesis

Learning objectives
- How can we control the environment in which plants are grown?
- What are the advantages and disadvantages of growing plants in an artificial environment?

Did you know ...?
The first recorded greenhouse was built in about 30 AD for Tiberius Caesar, a Roman emperor who wanted to eat cucumbers out of season.

The more a plant photosynthesises, the more biomass it makes and the faster it grows. It's not surprising that farmers want their plants to grow as fast and as big as possible. It helps them to make a profit.

In theory, if you give plants a warm environment with plenty of light, carbon dioxide and water, they should grow as fast as possible. Out in the fields it is almost impossible to influence any of these factors. However, people have found ways in which they can artificially control the environment of their plants.

The garden greenhouse
Lots of people have glass or perspex greenhouses in their gardens. Farmers use the same idea in huge plastic 'polytunnels'. They are used for growing crops ranging from tomatoes to strawberries and potatoes.

So how does a greenhouse affect the rate of photosynthesis? Within the glass or plastic structure the environment is much more controllable than outside. Most importantly, the atmosphere is warmer inside than out. This affects the rate of photosynthesis, speeding it up so plants grow faster. They will flower and fruit earlier and produce higher yields. We can also use greenhouses to grow fruit like peaches, lemons and oranges, which don't normally grow well outside in the UK.

Figure 1 One piece of American research showed that the crop yield inside a greenhouse was almost double that of crops grown outdoors

(Graph: Yield of tomato plant (kg) — Outdoor tomato plant: 6.75; Indoor tomato plant: 11.3)

Figure 2 Tomatoes certainly grow better in a greenhouse

a Why do plants grow faster in a greenhouse than outside?

Controlling a crop's environment
In a science lab you can change one factor at a time while keeping the others constant. Then you can judge how each one limits the rate of photosynthesis.

Outside, most plants are affected by a mixture of these factors. Early in the morning, light levels and temperature may limit the rate of photosynthesis. As light levels and temperature rise, carbon dioxide levels become limiting. On a bright, cold day, temperature might be the limiting factor. So there is a continuous interaction between the different factors.

Control through technology
Companies using big commercial greenhouses take advantage of what we know about limiting factors. They control the temperature and the levels of light and carbon dioxide. The levels are varied to get the fastest possible rates of photosynthesis. As a result the plants grow increasingly quickly.

The plants can even be grown in water with a perfect balance of mineral ions instead of soil, so nothing slows down their growth. This type of system is known as **hydroponics**.

The greenhouses are huge and conditions are controlled using computer software. It costs a lot of money but controlling the environment has many benefits. Turnover is fast, which means profits can be high. The crops are clean and unspoilt. There is no ploughing or preparing the land and in these systems crops can be grown where the land is poor.

b What are hydroponics?

It takes a lot of energy to keep conditions in the greenhouses just right – but fewer staff are needed. Monitoring systems and alarms are vital in case things go wrong, but for plants grown hydroponically, limiting factors are a thing of the past!

Figure 3 By controlling the temperature, light and carbon dioxide levels in a greenhouse like this you can produce the biggest possible crops – fast!

Activity
The National Farmer's Union (NFU) wants to produce a resource to explain to people how hydroponic farming works. Your job is to produce *either* a presentation *or* a poster series that can be sent out to schools around the country, explaining how it works and the biology behind the technology.

Key points
- Factors such as light levels, low temperature and carbon dioxide levels affect the rate of photosynthesis.
- The environment can be artificially controlled to make sure these factors do not limit growth, which has a number of benefits.

Summary questions
1 What are the main differences between a garden greenhouse and a hydroponics growing system?
2 What are the main benefits of artificially controlling the environment in which we grow our food plants?

Further teaching suggestions

Other mineral ions
- Water culture experiments could include plants grown in solutions deficient in other mineral ions such as iron, phosphate etc. There are water culture tablets available to make up the appropriate solutions.

What is in the fertilisers?
- Students to investigate the components of lawn fertiliser and Baby Bio and any other fertilisers, by looking at the boxes or containers. This will introduce the idea of commercial fertilisers not just containing one mineral ion, especially if the need for other mineral ions is demonstrated in the water culture experiments.

Answers to in-text questions
a The atmosphere is warmer which increases the rate of photosynthesis, so plants make more food and grow faster.
b Hydroponics is growing plants in water full of mineral ions providing an ideal environment for them to grow in.

Summary answers
1 **Garden greenhouse:** higher temperatures, plants not affected by wind, gardener can water with added food, etc.

Hydroponics growing system: plants grown in mineral enriched water rather than soil, everything controlled including temperature, carbon dioxide levels and light levels.

2 By artificially manipulating the environment we can eliminate limiting factors and allow photosynthesis to take place at its maximum rate. This means plants grow as fast and as large as possible, maximising the profit we can make and allowing us to grow more crops in season and out of season.

B2 2.5

Organisms in their environment

Learning objectives

Students should learn:

- that the distribution of living organisms is affected by physical factors in the environment
- that the distribution of both plants and animals is affected by the interaction of the physical factors.

Learning outcomes

Most students should be able to:

- list the physical factors which affect the distribution of living organisms
- describe the effects of some of these factors on the distribution of plants and animals.

Some students should also be able to:

- explain in detail why some of the factors that influence the distribution of plants affect the distribution of animals.

Answers to in-text questions

a Low levels of nutrients mean plants like the Venus flytrap (which can capture prey and get nutrients from them) is at an advantage and can grow well. In a soil with plenty of nutrients such plants cannot compete with normal plants.

b Raised carbon dioxide levels affect distribution because plants are more vulnerable to insect attacks.

Support

- Provide students with a list of the features of woodlice and some information about their habitat, which they could link in to their write-up following the investigation of the distribution of the woodlice.

Extend

- Get students to consider abiotic factors such as altitude and aspect and find out how other abiotic factors are linked with these two.

Specification link-up: Biology B2.4

- Physical factors that may affect organisms are:
  - temperature
  - availability of nutrients
  - amount of light
  - availability of water
  - availability of oxygen and carbon dioxide. [B2.4.1 a)]

  Controlled Assessment: B4.3 Collect primary and secondary data [B4.3.1 a)], [B4.3.2 a) b) c) d)]; B4.4 Select and process primary and secondary data. [B4.4.2 a) b) c)]

Lesson structure

Starters

Match up – Show the students a number of plants and animals which are adapted to survive in particular environmental conditions, such as those mentioned in the text. Give them a list of the environmental conditions which the animals and plants are suited to and ask them to match the organism with the environment. Get them to either verbalise or write down the relationship between the environmental factor and the distribution of organisms. *(5 minutes)*

Factor list – Ask the students to write down as many measurable environmental factors as they can. Give them a time limit suitable for the ability of the class. To conclude, count up and read out the longest few lists. Support students by prompting. Extend students by encouraging them to include on their list, ranges of values and the name of the apparatus used to measure the factor. *(10 minutes)*

Main

- There is a wide range of wildlife films and DVDs available, many of which feature the interactions between organisms and their environments, often hostile ones. Seek out suitable video support material available in your school, view it in advance and prepare a set of questions to be answered while the students are watching the film. The video can either be periodically stopped, or the answers filled in at the end. Writing key words and phrases down on a board as they are covered in the film is helpful.

- Demonstrate the effect of light limitation by placing a bin or similar lightproof container upside down with some weight on it on grass during the growing season (informing the grounds staff is a good idea). Come back after a week, remove the bin and examine the changes. Get the students to explain why this response to low light levels will be useful to the plants (no chlorophyll needed as no light is present; is metabolically expensive to make so it is not made; plant goes yellow and uses the metabolites for extra growth instead, hence the straggly fast growth). Explain that removing the light makes the plant put everything it has at its disposal to get some leaf surface back into the light or it will die. Extend students by using the word 'etiolation' and link it to trees growing very straight when packed densely together.

- Measurement of specific abiotic factors (see practical on the use of maximum-minimum thermometers, rainfall gauges and oxygen meters described in B1.4). Introduce the students to the use of light meters and hygrometers to measure humidity. Other abiotic factors that can be measured are pH, wind speed and soil moisture. Demonstrate the apparatus and methods of measurement and provide the students with a list of instructions, telling them that they will need to use some of the methods in fieldwork investigations.

- Take the students into the school grounds and get them to try to find woodlice. Having a nature area is useful, as is a pile of rotting logs. If available, use light meters and hygrometers to assess the light and moisture conditions in which the woodlice live. Back in class, carry out a write-up linking their features to their distribution.

Plenaries

Flash cards – Make (or get the students to make) a set of flash cards with the name of an organism on one side and the environmental factor likely to limit its distribution on the other. Play in pairs, looking at the organism and trying to guess what is on the reverse side of each card in turn. Extend students by inverting the pack and getting them to guess the organism based on the environmental conditions. *(5 minutes)*

Just don't go there! – Get the students to consider organism distribution linked with environmental conditions by writing short, witty notes addressed to various creatures and plants advising them on places they should **not** go to, with reasons. Support students by reading them several examples to get them going. Extend students by encouraging them to apply their imagination and creativity to come up with more detailed and appropriate advice. *(10 minutes)*

Further teaching suggestions

Why do animals migrate?
- Ask the students this question and compile a list of their answers. What are the influencing factors? Discuss examples.

Plotting and interpreting data
- Students could be provided with data, such as temperature changes in a rock pool, oxygen levels in a stream near a sewage outfall or mean January temperatures over a 50-year span. They can be asked to plot the data and produce

reasoned explanations of the changes and how they could affect the distribution of organisms.

Hay infusions
- Set up hay infusions (place cut grass into pond water in a jar and cover loosely) and observe the effect of changes on the population of organisms over a period of time (wash hands after contact with pond water).

Organisms in the environment

Organisms in their environment

B2 2.5 Organisms in their environment ⓚ

Learning objectives
- What factors affect the distribution of organisms in their natural environment?
- Are animals as well as plants affected by physical factors?

In any habitat you will find different distributions of living organisms. These organisms form communities, with the different animals and plants often dependent on each other.

Factors affecting living organisms

A number of factors affect how living organisms are distributed in the environment. They include the following.

Temperature

You have seen that temperature is a limiting factor on photosynthesis and therefore growth in plants. In cold climates temperature is always a limiting factor. For example, Arctic plants are all small. This in turn affects the numbers of herbivores that can survive in the area.

Did you know …?
Reindeer live in cold environments where most of the plants are small because temperature limits growth. They eat grass, moss and lichen. Reindeer travel thousands of miles as they feed. They cannot get enough food to survive in just one area.

Figure 1 Reindeer distribution depends on temperature, which affects the rate of photosynthesis and growth of their food

Nutrients

The level of mineral ions (e.g. nitrate ions) available has a big impact on the distribution of plants. Carnivorous plants such as Venus flytraps thrive where nitrate levels are very low because they can trap and digest animal prey. The nitrates they need are provided when they break down the animal protein. Most other plants struggle to grow in these areas with low levels of mineral ions.

Figure 2 The distribution of plants like these Venus flytraps depends heavily on nutrient levels

a How do nutrient levels affect the distribution of plants like the Venus fly trap?

Amount of light

Light limits photosynthesis, so it also affects the distribution of plants and animals. Some plants are adapted to living in low light levels. They may have more chlorophyll or bigger leaves. However, most plants need plenty of light to grow well.

The breeding cycles of many animal and plant species are linked to the day length. They only live and breed in regions where day length and light intensity are right for them.

Availability of water

The availability of water is important in the distribution of plants and animals in a desert. As a rule plants and animals are relatively rare in a desert. However, the distribution changes after it rains. A large number of plants grow, flower and set seeds very quickly while the water is available. These plants are eaten by many animals that move into the area to take advantage of them. If there is no water, there will be little or no life.

Availability of oxygen and carbon dioxide

The availability of oxygen has a big impact on water-living organisms. Some invertebrates can survive in water with very low oxygen levels. However, most fish need a high level of dissolved oxygen. The distribution of land organisms is not affected by oxygen levels as there is plenty of oxygen in the air and levels vary very little.

Carbon dioxide levels act as a limiting factor on photosynthesis and plant growth. They can also affect the distribution of organisms. For example, mosquitoes are attracted to the animals on whose blood they feed by high carbon dioxide levels. Plants are also more vulnerable to insect attacks in an area with high carbon dioxide levels.

b How do carbon dioxide levels affect the distribution of plants?

The physical factors that affect the distribution of living organisms do not work in isolation. They interact to create unique environments where different animals and plants can live.

Did you know …?
Scientists thought that all organisms, apart from specialised microorganisms, needed oxygen to live. Then in 2010, multicellular organisms that do not need oxygen were discovered living deep under the Mediterranean seas. If more of these amazing organisms are found, our ideas of how oxygen affects the distribution of organisms will have to change.

Figure 3 One of the first known multicellular organisms that do not need oxygen to respire

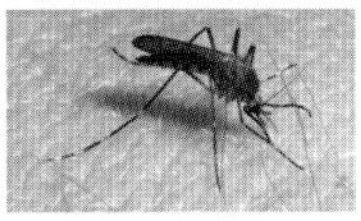

Figure 4 Mosquitoes are attracted to us by the carbon dioxide we breathe out

Summary questions

1 What are the physical factors most likely to affect living organisms?

2 How do carnivorous plants survive in areas with very low levels of nitrate ions whilst other plants cannot grow there?

3 Explain how the limiting factors for photosynthesis – light, temperature and carbon dioxide levels – also affect the distribution of animals directly and indirectly.

Key points
- Physical factors that may affect the distribution of living organisms include:
  – temperature
  – nutrients
  – the amount of light
  – the availability of water
  – the availability oxygen and carbon dioxide.

Summary answers

1 Temperature, amount of light, level of nutrients, availability of water, oxygen and carbon dioxide.

2 Carnivorous plants capture and digest animals and use the nitrate ions produced as the animal proteins are broken down. Other plants rely on taking nitrate ions from the soil and there are not enough of them available for the plants to grow well.

3 Temperature affects animals directly because some animals are adapted to life in cold climates and others to hot climates. Animals are only found in appropriate temperatures and if the temperature of an area changes it can have a significant impact on the distribution of animals, e.g. bird distribution.

Carbon dioxide levels affect animals directly because some animals are attracted to the carbon dioxide produced by other animals, e.g. mosquitoes.

Light affects the distribution of animals because it often affects the breeding cycles of animals, and also how well they can see to hunt.

All three influence indirectly because of their affect on plant growth as limiting factors – and the distribution of plants has a major impact on the distribution of animals as a major food source.

B2 2.6

Measuring the distribution of organisms

Learning objectives

Students should learn:

- how to measure the distribution of living organisms in their natural environment by means of random sampling using quadrats
- the meaning of the terms mean, median and mode
- how to count organisms along a transect.

Learning outcomes

Most students should be able to:

- describe the method of random sampling using quadrats
- calculate the mean and identify the mode and median from a set of data
- describe the use of a transect.

Some students should also be able to:

- explain the importance of collecting data by quantitative sampling.

Answers to in-text questions

a A quadrat is a frame used as a sample area when measuring distribution and population numbers of organisms (plants and animals).

Support

- Provide students with a very simple way of remembering the differences between mean, median and mode. For example: the mean is the sum of all the values divided by the number of values, the median is the middle of the range and the mode is the most frequently occurring value or number.

Extend

- Ask students to investigate quadrat size. Is the same size of quadrat ideal for counting all organisms? What size quadrat would you use to count the density of barnacles on a rock? What factors determine the size of quadrat used?

Specification link-up: Biology B2.4

- Quantitative data on the distribution of organisms can be obtained by:
  - random sampling with quadrats
  - sampling along a transect. *[B2.4.1 b)]*
- Suggest reasons for the distribution of living organisms in a particular habitat. *[B2.4]*

Lesson structure

Starter

Find a link – Ask students to look for situations in the school grounds where the distribution of organisms shows a change. Provide guidance, it may be useful to find an obvious place in advance, such as the density of vegetation changing under trees with less in the dark area and more in the bright, lichen distribution on tree trunks, etc. Get the students to come up with a hypothesis to test. Support students by giving them clear direct guidance to help them to find a change in distribution. Extend students by encouraging them to find a link by themselves and possibly a number of different links for group investigations. *(5 minutes)*

Main

- Use quadrats to survey the distribution of daisy and dandelion plants in a field. Select a suitable section of the school field (see 'Practical support').
- A much more scientific technique is to select the area to be studied and mark out a grid. Using random numbers, either from an internet-based random number generator or from a table of random numbers, select two numbers to provide the *x* and *y* co-ordinates of squares in which to take the samples. An alternative is to sample in a regular pattern, but to be unbiased, the pattern should be chosen before looking at the site. Students may need to be guided through the maths of scaling up the average to provide an estimate for the total.
- Sampling with quadrats in this way can be used to compare two areas. For example, the daisy population of one field could be compared with that of another field. The dandelion plants in a section of mown grass could be compared with those in a section of unmown grass or in well-worn areas of the playing field.
- A line transect can be used to find patterns of grass growth under trees. Use a reel of tape of the type used on sports fields, weighted down to avoid shifting. Decide which type of transect the students are going to use – recording all plants present in terms of distance covered on the line, point sampling at regular intervals, a belt transect of continuous quadrats along the line or an interrupted belt transect with regular gaps between the quadrats. Record the distance from the tree where the tree canopy stops. Measure the light levels, humidity and temperature associated with each quadrat. Soil samples can be taken from each quadrat area or as required. Get the students to label them as they collect them. Back in the laboratory, the soil could be tested for pH, moisture content and humus content. Take care over hygiene when handling soil as it can carry pathogens and parasites (e.g. *Toxocara canis*).
- Now students can process their data to calculate the distribution. A kite diagram can be used to provide a visual impression of the distribution along a transect line. The results of random sampling can be tabulated and density of plants per m² calculated. If a comparison is carried out, a bar chart could be used to show differences.
- Introduce the mean, median and mode. Check who knows the definitions already. Make sure the students have an understanding of these terms by providing them with more sets of practice data. They need to become familiar with the terms and their calculation before actually carrying out an investigation.

Plenary

Why bother? – Get the students to think of situations where scientists may want to record the distribution of a species. Discuss in small groups, write out a summary of ideas and report back to the whole class. Students could be supported by providing them with stimulus material to help them think of situations in which it would be valuable to have some distribution data. Students could be extended by asking them to recommend appropriate methods and sampling strategies as well as identifying where scientists may want to record distribution. *(10 minutes)*

Practical support

Surveying the distribution of daisies

Equipment and materials required

Half-metre square quadrats, measuring tapes, tape to lay out a transect line, data logger/light meter, hygrometer, thermometers, trowel and plastic bags for soil samples, universal indicator papers, oven for drying soil samples, balance.

Details

Use quadrats to survey the distribution of daisy and dandelion plants in a field. Select a suitable section of the school field. Show the students what daisy plants look like (large photographs and real specimens). Emphasise that they will be looking at the number of plants, not the number of flowers. Ensure that they can spot the leaves and track them back to the body of the plant. Get them to decide how they will count if a plant is in the quadrat (e.g. more than 50% or just presence?). The method suggested in the student book will provide a rough idea on the distribution. Rather than 1m² quadrats, a ball of paper can be dropped and four metre rulers placed around it. If using smaller quadrats remind the students to do the appropriate calculation to convert their findings to plants per m².

Safety: Do not allow the students to throw quadrats, especially not with eyes closed and/or after spinning! (Use of a small Frisbee can be a fun, safe alternative). Wash hands after contact with soil. Follow school guidelines for outside activities.

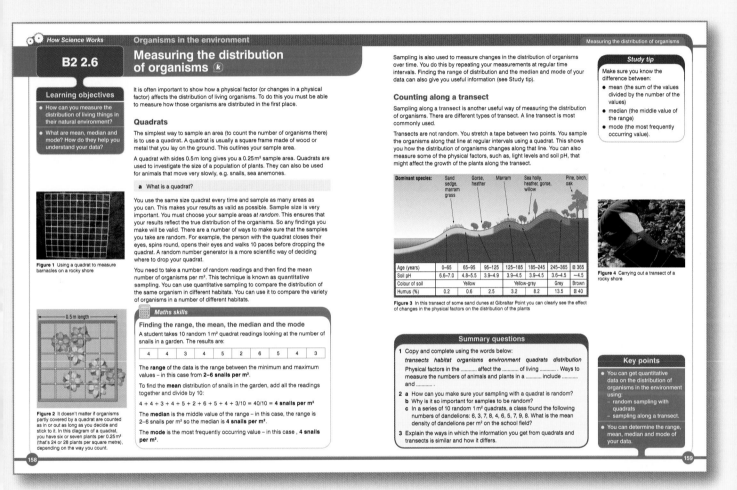

Summary answers

1 environment, distribution, organisms, habitat, quadrats/ transects, transects/quadrats

2 a Spin round with eyes closed, keep eyes closed, walk a given number of paces and drop the quadrat, or any other sensible method.

 b To give a representative and unbiased sample.

 c $\dfrac{6 + 3 + 7 + 8 + 4 + 6 + 5 + 7 + 9 + 8}{10} = \dfrac{63}{10} = 6.3$

 so the mean density of dandelions is 6/m² if you count only whole plants or 6.3/m² if not.

3 Information similar – often use quadrats along the transect so using the same technique in different ways.

 Quadrats used for random measurements to get an overall picture of population or distribution of an organism or variety of organisms. Transect is a very specific study of a particular section of a habitat and measures zonal changes.

B2 2.7

How valid is the data?

Learning objectives

Students should learn:

- that appropriate sampling methods need to be used
- that sample size is related to reproducibility and validity
- that as many variables as possible should be controlled.

Learning outcomes

Most students should be able to:

- choose an appropriate sampling method
- explain that the sample size is important if the results are to be considered valid
- describe how some variables can be controlled.

Some students should also be able to:

- explain why it is difficult to control all the variables in fieldwork.

Specification link-up: Biology B2.4

- Evaluate methods used to collect environmental data, and consider the validity of the method and the reproducibility of the data as evidence for environmental change. *[B2.4]*

  Controlled Assessment: B4.1 Plan practical ways to develop and test candidates' own scientific ideas. *[B4.1.1 a) b) c)]*

Lesson structure

Starters

Valid and reproducible – Get the students to create and write down two sentences, one with the word 'valid' in it and one with the word 'reproducible'. Emphasise that we are after current understanding, drawing out what these words mean in general English usage, so the sentences can be about anything, not just scientific topics. Get volunteers to read theirs out and collect examples on the board. Come to a collective understanding. *(5 minutes)*

Right tool for the job – Give the students a number of scenarios where data is to be gathered. The complexity of these will depend on the ability of the class, but could include whether the population of a species of flat fish in the North Sea is declining or whether carbon dioxide levels are rising in the atmosphere. Get the students to suggest suitable data collection techniques and as a class discuss and critically evaluate them. Support students by giving clear prompts and clues pointing towards a straightforward example. Extend students by asking them to give more details and reasons for their choice of data collection methods and to say why they have dismissed alternatives. *(10 minutes)*

Main

- Go over the specific meanings of the terms 'valid' and 'reproducible' as outlined in the Student Book. 'Reproducible' as in if someone else did the same experiment they would get similar results, and 'valid' meaning it answers the question you are asking. Get the students to memorise the definitions. Get students to give examples of the opposites, where an investigation would not be able to be reproduced and where the data would not be valid.

- Discuss what is meant by variables. Identify some dependant, independent and controlled variables in experiments the students have already undertaken. Discuss the difficulty of controlling all the variables in biological situations and particularly fieldwork.

- Discuss the strength of evidence. Ask how the students could tell if a coin was biased and fell on heads more often than tails. Throw a coin a few times and analyse the results. You can find digital coin tossing on the internet, which can be projected if required. Get the class to throw a coin many more times and plot the ratio of heads to tails on a graph – the fluctuations will settle out eventually and it should become evident to the students that the more times you repeat an experiment, the stronger your evidence will be.

- Give the students a data set to analyse the trends. It could be the penguin data set from the Student Book or a more limited range for support level students. Whatever it is, a clear trend should be discernible. Get the students to plot graphs of the data, either manually or by using a spreadsheet tool. Excellent simple tools for data analysis, especially useful for less able students, exist such as 'Simple Data Handling' and 'FlexiData'. Project and share students' analyses.

Support

- Provide students with printed definitions of the words 'reproducible' and 'valid' that they can stick in their notebooks.

Extend

- Get students to review the pertussis (whooping cough) controversy in the light of what they have learnt about scientific method, the collection of data and controlling variables.

Plenaries

Spot the blot – Give the students a version of a summary of the content covered in this spread. It should have a number of errors in it. The students are to identify these and to make a list of corrections. *(5 minutes)*

Simples? – It is easy to make mistakes in handling data. Read the penguins passage in the Student Book. Produce icons/symbols to represent each possible reason for reductions in the penguin population and write an advisory note to scientists studying the penguins encouraging them to be aware of all the possibilities. Support students by providing a range of symbols/icons from which the students can choose suitable ones; state what they represent and give a cloze passage for the advisory note. Extend students by getting them to produce their own icons without assistance and to envisage other potential problems, such as bioaccumulation of toxins, disease, and parasites, etc. *(10 minutes)*

Further teaching suggestions

More fieldwork
- Some of the fieldwork suggestions mentioned in the previous spread could be carried out if time permits.

Planning
- If time is short, these investigations could be planned, the number of variables to be controlled and how this is to be managed described, the number and type of measurements needed could be stated and the best way of displaying the results indicated.

How Science Works Organisms in the environment

B2 2.7 How valid is the data?

Learning objectives
- Will the method used answer the question that has been asked?
- Have all the variables been controlled?
- Does the size of your sample matter?

Environments are changing naturally all the time. But people also have an effect on the environment. This can be locally, e.g. dropping litter or building a new road, or on a worldwide scale with possible global warming and climate change. A change in the distribution of living organisms can be evidence of a change in the environment. However, if you want to use this type of data as evidence for environmental change it is important to use reproducible and valid methods to collect your results.

Reproducible, valid data

When you measure the distribution of living organisms you want your investigation to be reproducible and valid. In a reproducible investigation, other people can do the same investigation and get results that are very similar or the same as yours. And for the investigation to be valid it must answer the question you are asking. For example: What is the population density of snails in this garden?

One important factor is the size of your sample. If you do 10 quadrats, your data will not be as reproducible or as valid as if you carry out 100 quadrats.

Your method of sampling must be appropriate. If you want to measure the distribution of plants in an area, random quadrats work well. If you want to measure change in distribution over a range of habitats, a transect is a better technique to use.

If you are trying to measure change over time, you must be able to replicate your method every time you repeat your readings.

Changes in the distribution of a species are often used as evidence of environmental change. You must use a method of measuring that works regardless of who is collecting the data.

Controlling variables

When you are working in a lab you can control as many of the variables as possible. Then other scientists can carry out the investigation under the same conditions. This increases the likelihood that your results will be reproducible.

In fieldwork, it is not possible to control all the variables of the natural environment, but you can control some. For example, you can always measure at the same time of day. However, you cannot control the weather or the arrival of different organisms.

You must be clear about the problems of collecting data if you want to use them as evidence of environmental change.

A penguin case study

In the early 1980s Dee Boersma noticed that the numbers of penguins in a breeding colony in Argentina were falling. In 1987 she set up a research project making a transect of the colony with 47 permanent stakes, 100 metres apart.

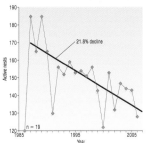

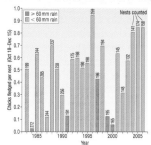

Figure 2 Patagonian penguins reflect environmental change in a very sensitive way. This graph shows clearly the effect of heavy rain on chick survival.

Every year Dee counted the active nests within a 100 m² circle around 19 of the stakes. She surveyed the remaining sites less regularly. However, Dee found the same pattern everywhere – numbers were falling.

What is causing these changes? Climate change seems to be significant:
- There have been several breeding seasons where unusually heavy rainfall has occurred. This has destroyed many nests and killed many chicks (see Figure 2).
- There have been changes in the numbers of small fish that the penguins eat. This is in response to changes in the water temperature. So there has been less food available in some years.

However, in biology things are rarely simple. The penguins are also affected by oil and waste from nearby shipping lanes. Around 20000 penguins were killed by one major oil spill in 1991 alone. People catch the same small fish that the penguins feed on. Thousands of tourists visit the colony every year. They trample the area and cause stress to the birds.

Many factors, probably including climate change, are involved in the distribution changes of the penguins.

Figure 3 The penguin population at Punta Tombo fell by almost 22% between 1987 and 2006

Figure 1 If you are trying to find evidence of environmental change in an area as big as this, it is important to use a method that is as valid as possible

Summary questions

1 What is meant by the terms: a reproducible and b valid, when you are talking about scientific data?

2 Look at Figure 2 and Figure 3 and the text above to help you answer this question.
   a When was the penguin population at Punta Tombo at its peak?
   b When was the population at its lowest? Suggest a reason for this.
   c How could Professor Boersma's data be used as evidence for environmental change?

3 Professor Boersma is widely respected in the scientific community. In what ways can you see that her data are both reproducible and valid?

Key points
- Different methods can be used to collect environmental data.
- Validity and reproducibility must be considered carefully as it is difficult to control variables in fieldwork.
- Sample size is an important factor in both reproducibility and validity of data.

Summary answers

1 a **Reproducible** – other people can do the same investigation and get results that are very similar or the same as yours.
  b **Valid** – it must answer the question you are asking.

2 a 1987 and 1989.
  b 2000 – heavy rain 2 years running which killed a lot of chicks.
  c Evidence shows increase in numbers of years with heavy rainfall – often linked to climate change and also change in sea temperatures with change in numbers of fish species – again often linked to climate change and changes in the ocean currents.

3 Data is reproducible because it has been carried out over many years on the same transect, on the same nests by different people every time. When a wider variety of nests are examined, the same pattern of results emerges. In a year of heavy rain there is a much lower level of chick survival.

Different groups of students were involved in different years and the results still follow the same pattern. So, in these ways, the results can be seen to be reproducible.

Results are valid because they answer the question, 'what is happening to the penguin population at Punta Tomobo', 'is the penguin population at Punta Tombo falling?' Or any of a number of other pertinent questions.

Summary answers

1 a carbon dioxide + water $\xrightarrow{\text{(+ light energy)}}$ glucose + oxygen

b Starch.

2 a Credit accurately drawn graphs, correctly labelled axes, etc.

b Plants in higher light intensity photosynthesise faster and therefore produce more food and grow well. Light will not limit them – CO_2 or temperature might. For plants in lower light, the light is a limiting factor on their growth.

3 a In the oceans, rivers, lakes and ponds of the world.

b Some glucose is used in respiration in much the same way as plants – the energy released in respiration is used to build up smaller molecules into bigger ones. Some of the glucose is converted into starch for storage. Plants also build up sugars into more complex carbohydrates like cellulose. They use this to make new plant cell walls. Some of the energy from respiration is used to combine sugars with other nutrients from the soil to make amino acids. These amino acids are then built up into proteins to be used in the cells. Energy from respiration is also used to build up fats and oils to make a food store. Any other sensible suggestions.

4 a Ideal growing conditions – warm, plenty of light, lots of water as it rains most days – the same conditions which enable tropical rain forests to grow so well; support rapid growth of oil palms.

b Made from the products of photosynthesis.

c To provide energy for the growing seedling when it germinates.

d Energy for respiration making cellulose, starch stores, making protein, etc.

5 a Hydroponic growing eliminates limiting factors, so more photosynthesis takes place.

b Rice, potatoes, tomatoes, peas and cucumbers because these are the crops where you get the biggest percentage increase in yield by growing hydroponically.

c Wheat and cabbage – relatively very small increase in yield from hydroponic growing.

d i Benefits: relatively easy and cheap, no specialist equipment needed, can use natural growing cycle. Any other valid points.

Problems: open to pests and weeds, weather can affect growth, limiting factors such as temperature and light levels mean plants don't get the maximum growth. Any other valid points.

ii Benefits: maximum growth, no limiting factors, relatively easy to control pests and weeds, can grow out of season, crops clean when harvested, not affected by changes in the weather, good working conditions inside. Any other valid points.

Problems: big set up costs, expensive to run, vulnerable to failings in technology.

Summary questions

1 a Write the word equation for photosynthesis.

b Much of the glucose made in photosynthesis is turned into an insoluble storage compound. What is this compound?

2 The figures in the table show the mean growth of two sets of oak seedlings. One set was grown in 85% full sunlight, the other set in only 35% full sunlight.

Year	Mean height of seedlings grown in 85% full sunlight (cm)	Mean height of seedlings grown in 35% full sunlight (cm)
2005	12	10
2006	16	12.5
2007	18	14
2008	21	17
2009	28	20
2010	35	21
2011	36	23

The figures in the table show the mean growth of two sets of oak seedlings. One set was grown in 85% full sunlight, the other set in only 35% full sunlight.

a Plot a graph to show the growth of both sets of oak seedlings.

b Using what you know about photosynthesis and limiting factors, explain the difference in the growth of the two sets of seedlings.

3 More of the biomass and oxygen produced by photosynthesis comes from algae than from plants.

a Where do you find most algae?

b How do algal cells use the products of photosynthesis?

4 Palm oil is made from the fruit of oil palms. Large areas of tropical rainforests have been destroyed to make space to plant these oil palms, which grow rapidly.

a Why do you think that oil palms grow rapidly in the conditions that support a tropical rainforest?

b Where does the oil in the oil palm fruit come from?

c What is it used for in the plant?

d How else is glucose used in the plant?

5 Here are the yields of some different plants grown in Bengal, India. The yields per acre when grown normally in the field and when grown hydroponically are compared.

Name of crop	Hydroponic crop per acre (kg)	Ordinary soil crop per acre (kg)
wheat	3629	2540
rice	5443	408
potatoes	70760	8164
cabbage	8164	5896
peas	63503	11340
tomatoes	181437	9072
lettuce	9525	4080
cucumber	12700	3175

a Why are yields always higher when the crops are grown hydroponically?

b Which crops would it be most economically sensible to grow hydroponically? Explain your choice.

c Which crops would it be least sensible to grow hydroponically? Explain your choice.

d What are the benefits and problems of growing crops

i in their natural environment

ii in an artificially manipulated environment?

Kerboodle resources

Resources available for this chapter on Kerboodle are:

- Chapter map: Organisms in the environment
- Support: Photosynthesis (B2 2.1)
- Data handling skills: Investigating the rate of photosynthesis (B2 2.2)
- Simulation: Limiting factors of photosynthesis (B2 2.2)
- How Science Works: Does the amount of light affect the rate of photosynthesis? (B2 2.2)
- Bump up your grade: Limiting factors (B2 2.2)
- Extension: Limiting factors (B2 2.2)
- Practical: Photosynthesis (B2 2.2)
- Maths skills: Calculating the mean (B2 2.2)
- How Science Works: Evaluating fieldwork methods (B2 2.6)
- Practical: Fieldwork (B2 2.6)
- Interactive activity: Photosynthesis
- Revision podcast: Photosynthesis
- Test yourself: Organisms in the environment
- On your marks: Organisms in the environment
- Practice questions: Organisms in the environment
- Answers to practice questions: Organisms in the environment

---

Practical suggestions

Practicals	AQA	k	📖	⚙
Investigating the need for chlorophyll for photosynthesis with variegated leaves.	✓		✓	
Taking thin slices of potato and apple and adding iodine to observe under the microscope.	✓		✓	

End of chapter questions

Practice questions

The picture shows a snail. Snails feed on plants.

Some students wanted to investigate the distribution of snails in the hedges on two sides of their school field. All the hedges were trimmed to a height of 1.5 metres. One side of the field was very open but the opposite side was shaded by trees. The students thought there would be more snails in the hedges on the open side because birds living in the trees would eat the snails. In the investigation they:

* measured a transect of 50 metres along the hedge on the open side of the field
* leaned a 1 m² quadrat against the hedge every 5 metres
* counted all the snails they could see in the quadrat
* recorded the data in a table
* repeated the investigation with the hedge that was shaded by trees.

a Choose the correct answer to complete each sentence.

  i The idea that birds in the trees eat the snails is a
  .... (1)
    conclusion   hypothesis   test

  ii A transect is a .... (1)
    line   square   triangle

  iii One thing that was controlled in this investigation was the .... (1)
    light intensity   number of trees   size of quadrat

b The data recorded by the students can be seen in the table.

Quadrat number	1	2	3	4	5	6	7	8	9	10
Open hedge	3	3	5	3	2	3	6	3	6	2
Hedge shaded by trees	2	3	4	3	5	2	1	4	1	5

Use the data to answer the questions. Choose the correct answer.

  i The mean for the number of snails in the open hedge is [3 / 3.6 / 5]. (1)

  ii The median for the number of snails in the shaded hedge is [2 / 3 / 4]. (1)

c One student said he didn't think the results would be valid. Suggest **one** reason why. (1)

2 A farmer has decided to grow strawberry plants in polytunnels, similar to the one shown in the diagram.

The tunnels are enclosed spaces with walls made of plastic sheeting. The farmer decides to set up several small polytunnels, as models, so he can work out the best conditions for the strawberry plants to grow. He needs help from a plant biologist who provides some data.

The data is shown in the graph.

Rate of photosynthesis vs Light intensity
- - - - 4% CO₂ at 25°C
- - - - 4% CO₂ at 15°C
- - - - 0.03% CO₂ at 25°C
- - - - 0.03% CO₂ at 15°C

a *In this question you will be assessed on using good English, organising information clearly and using specialist terms where appropriate.*

You are advising the farmer.

Using all the information given, describe the factors the farmer should consider when building his model tunnels so he can calculate the optimal conditions for growing strawberry plants. (6)

b Biologists often use models in their research. Suggest **one** reason why. (1)

AQA, 2007

163

Practicals

Practicals	AQA	k	📖	⚙
Investigate the effects of light, temperature and carbon dioxide levels, (using Cabomba, algal balls or leaf discs from brassicas) on the rate of photosynthesis.	✓	✓	✓	✓
Computer simulations to model the rate of photosynthesis in different conditions.	✓		✓	
The use of sensors to investigate the effect of carbon dioxide and light levels on the rate of photosynthesis and the release of oxygen.	✓		✓	
Investigative fieldwork involving sampling techniques and the use of quadrats and transects…	✓	✓	✓	✓
Analysing the measurement of specific abiotic factors in relation to the distribution of organisms.	✓		✓	
The study of hay infusions.	✓		✓	
The use of sensors to measure environmental conditions in a fieldwork context.	✓		✓	

Practice answers

1 a i hypothesis (1 mark)
  ii line (1 mark)
  iii size of quadrat (1 mark)

b i 3.6 (1 mark)
  ii 3 (1 mark)

c Any sensible suggestion relating to method of counting or uncontrolled variables. e.g. difficulty of counting inside the hedge/quadrat would miss all snails in top 0.5 metres/hard to see snails under leaves/not all parts of the hedge are shaded on the shaded side of the field/birds might live in the hedges not just the trees/allow – snails might move about and be counted twice. (1 mark)

2 a There is a clear, balanced and detailed description referring to the data in the graph about light, temperature and carbon dioxide and how to set up a controlled experiment. The answer shows almost faultless spelling, punctuation and grammar. It is coherent and in an organised, logical sequence. It contains a range of appropriate or relevant specialist terms used accurately. (5–6 marks)

There is some description of setting up a controlled experiment, including at least two variables. There are some errors in spelling, punctuation and grammar. The answer has some structure and organisation. The use of specialist terms has been attempted, but not always accurately. (3–4 marks)

There is a brief description with reference to setting up several tunnels and mention of at least one variable, but little clarity and detail. The spelling, punctuation and grammar are very weak. The answer is poorly organised with almost no specialist terms and/or their use demonstrating a general lack of understanding of their meaning. (1–2 marks)

No relevant content. (0 marks)

Examples of biology points made in the response:
* Use of term limiting factors
* The more photosynthesis the more growth
* Carbon dioxide optimum around 4%
* Plants need water
* Control of light intensity
* Types of light
* Temperature control/25°C
* Idea that light changes with type of plastic/colour of plastic/thickness of plastic
* Idea that might need heating/ventilation to control/ monitor temperature
* Idea that need to contain the carbon dioxide/have a source of carbon dioxide gas.
* Reference to having different sets of conditions in each model tunnel to be able to determine optimum/idea that might try slightly lower/higher temperature/carbon dioxide level to check cost effectiveness.

b Any **one** from the following:
* Possible to mimic large scale events/idea of/on a small scale.
* Can be used to predict changes/changes in variables.
* Allow a description e.g. predict the spread of disease/can predict the effect of a chemical on all bacteria using a safe organism/can use fast breeding organisms to mimic processes which occur slowly in others/can predict the effect of global warming on organisms in a locality. (1 mark)

B2 3.1 Proteins, catalysts and enzymes

Learning objectives

Students should learn:

- that protein molecules are made up of long chains of amino acids
- that proteins act as structural components, hormones, antibodies and catalysts
- that an enzyme is a biological catalyst
- how enzymes work.

Learning outcomes

Most students should be able to:

- describe how long chains of amino acids form protein molecules
- state the roles of proteins in the formation of muscles, hormones, antibodies and enzymes
- describe the structure and mode of action of an enzyme.

Some students should also be able to:

- explain in detail the concept of the active site of the enzyme.

Answers to in-text questions

a A building block of protein.

b A substance that speeds up a chemical reaction without being changed itself.

Support

- Use toy building blocks to represent large molecules, such as starch, proteins and fats. Label each one on one side with the name of the substrate ('starch', 'protein') then label the individual bricks with the name of the products ('sugars', 'amino acids'). Use plastic knives with the word 'Enzyme' on to cut up the blocks.

Extend

- Ask students to research the structure of proteins and use a length of Bunsen tubing to demonstrate the differences between the primary, secondary and tertiary structure. Different sequences of amino acids can be marked with a pen and the tubing can be coiled and twisted into a C shape to illustrate the active site.

Specification link-up: Biology B2.5

- Protein molecules are made up of long chains of amino acids … *[B2.5.1 a)]*
- Catalysts increase the rate of chemical reactions … *[B2.5.1 b)]*
- The shape of an enzyme is vital for the enzyme's function … *[B2.5.2 a)]*
- Different enzymes work best at different pH values. *[B2.5.2 b)]*

Controlled Assessment: B4.3 Collect primary and secondary data *[B4.3.2 a) b) c) d) e) f)]*; B4.4 Select and process primary and secondary data *[B4.4.1 a) b)]*, *[B4.4.2 b)]*; B4.5 Analyse and interpret primary and secondary data. *[B4.5.4 a)]*

Lesson structure

Starter

Biological stains – Bring in a cheap, clean white T-shirt and allow students to smear it with selected food and drink (tomato ketchup, mustard, egg). Discuss with the students how they could remove the stains and get the T-shirt clean. Show the students a box of biological washing powder and a box of non-biological washing powder and get them to say which one would be best to use with reasons. (Care needed if washing powders are handed around – some people can have sensitive skin). Support students by prompting as to the nature of the stains and how they could be broken down. Extend students by asking them to compare the contents of the two washing powders and to say what the enzymes are, breaking down, e.g. starches, proteins, fats. *(10 minutes)*

Main

Enzymes in action

- The experiment 'Breaking down hydrogen peroxide' shows the action of manganese(IV) oxide, an inorganic catalyst, and a piece of liver, which contains the enzyme catalase, on hydrogen peroxide.

- Use a PowerPoint presentation to build up a picture of how enzymes are composed of long chains of amino acids folded and coiled into special shapes. Introduce the concept of the active site, enzyme specificity, how they work and what they can do. Introduce them to the convention of naming enzymes – the '-ase' suffix for many – and give some examples. Provide students with a worksheet that they can fill in as the presentation proceeds.

- Catalase is present in living tissue. The more active the tissue, the greater the catalase activity (see Practical support 'Catalase in living tissues' for full details). The reactions can be described or they can be measured. (This links to 'How Science Works' – making observations and measurements.) If the experiment is to be a qualitative one, i.e. just a simple comparison of the activity by observation, then written descriptions or comparative statements can be made.

- It is possible to make this experiment more quantitative by using the same quantities of each tissue, and then measuring the activity when placed in the same volume of hydrogen peroxide. Simple heights of froth up the tube in a given time can be measured. A more accurate measurement is given by collecting the gas evolved in a given time. (This demonstrates many 'How Science Works' concepts.)

- There are many variations of the catalase experiments:
  - Investigate the volume of gas released when different quantities of fresh liver are used in the same volume of hydrogen peroxide, i.e. varying the amount of enzyme with a fixed quantity of substrate.
  - The converse of this is to use the same quantity of liver and vary the concentration of hydrogen peroxide used, i.e. varying the quantity of the substrate with a fixed quantity of enzyme.

Plenary

Find the substrate for the enzyme – Using thin card, make sets of 'enzymes' of different shapes and with differently shaped 'active sites', and a corresponding set of 'substrates' that fit into the enzymes' 'active sites'. (You could adapt very simple jigsaw pieces.) Support students by making the pieces very simple. Extend students by using more complex shapes and making the 'substrates' consist of two parts which fit together into the active site. Students need to find the 'enzyme' and 'substrate' that fit together. *(10 minutes)*

Practical support

Breaking down hydrogen peroxide

Equipment and materials required

Manganese(IV) oxide, fresh liver, tiles and knives for cutting, test tubes, hydrogen peroxide solution, eye protection, some method of collecting the gas given off (syringes/inverted test tubes, rulers if height of froth to be measured), water bath if liver is to be boiled and denatured.

Details

By adding hydrogen peroxide, students can compare the activity of the inorganic catalyst with cubes of fresh liver and liver in which the enzymes have been denatured by heating. The denatured liver shows that the enzyme is present in living tissue and is destroyed by heating. Include a test tube containing hydrogen peroxide as a control. An additional control using a piece of boiled and cooled liver would show that the enzyme from the living tissue can be denatured.

Safety: CLEAPSS Hazcard 33 – disposal of organic waste. CLEAPSS Hazcard 50 Hydrogen peroxide.

Catalase in living tissue

Equipment and materials required

Fresh liver, potato tuber tissue, apple, etc., tiles and knives for cutting, test tubes, hydrogen peroxide solution, eye protection, some method of measuring the gas given off (syringes/inverted test tubes or manometers; rulers if height of froth to be measured), stopwatches or stop clocks, water bath if tissues are to be boiled and denatured.

Details

Drop small cubes of different tissues, such as liver, muscle, apple and potato, into test tubes containing hydrogen peroxide ($10 \, cm^3$ to $15 \, cm^3$ depending on the size of the tubes). If the experiment is to be qualitative, students should record their observations, make comparisons and write statements about the activity of the enzyme in the different tissues. If it is to be quantitative, then the same quantities of tissue and hydrogen peroxide should be used and measurements taken of the activity.

Safety: Wear eye protection, CLEAPSS Hazcard 50 Hydrogen peroxide. Take care with tubes, which can become hot.

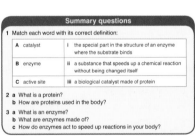

Reproduced pages 164–165 of the student book.

Further teaching suggestions

Catalase activity in plant tissues

- The different parts of a plant can be tested for catalase activity. Take equal quantities of leaf, stem and root tissue and test with hydrogen peroxide. Alternatively, use equal quantities of germinating and non-germinating seeds to show that the more active the tissue, the greater the catalase activity.

Computer simulations – modelling enzymes

- Use computer simulations of enzymes to model their action in varying conditions of pH, temperature and concentration.

Summary answers

1   A ii   B iii   C i

2   a   A molecule made up of long chains of amino acids.

      b   As structural components, as hormones, as antibodies and as catalysts (enzymes).

3   a   A biological catalyst.

      b   Protein/amino acid chains.

      c   Substrate molecule/s arrive at the active site. They fit perfectly together, like a lock and key. The substrate molecules react and change shape. The products leave the active site. The enzyme is left unchanged and ready to catalyse the next reaction.

B2 3.2

Factors affecting enzyme action

Learning objectives

Students should learn:

- that enzymes are vital to all living cells
- that changes in temperature affect the rate at which enzymes work
- that different enzymes work best at different pH values.

Learning outcomes

Most students should be able to:

- describe experiments that show the effect of changes in temperature and pH on the rate of enzyme-controlled reactions
- describe how changes in temperature and pH affect enzyme action.

Some students should also be able to:

- explain in detail how changes in temperature and pH affect the active site of an enzyme.

Answers to in-text questions

a Enzymes in bacteria in the milk break down proteins that makes the milk go sour/bad. This happens faster in the sun as it is warmer.

b When an enzyme is denatured the shape of the active site is lost, so it does not work properly anymore.

Support

- Tell students that bits of milk need to be joined together by enzymes to make yoghurt. Make some yoghurt in a vacuum flask, a water bath or preferably a commercial yoghurt maker. Set up controls in the refrigerator and at room temperature. Prepare a work sheet with a results table for time taken for it to run through a funnel. Adjust the bore so that some yoghurt will very slowly flow through. Try it with boiled yoghurt (risk assessment).

Extend

- Get students to research some of the organisms that live in hot springs, very cold conditions and conditions of extreme pH.

Specification link-up: Biology B2.5

- The shape of an enzyme is vital for the enzyme's function. High temperatures change the shape. *[B2.5.2 a)]*
- Different enzymes work best at different pH values. *[B2.5.2 b)]*

  Controlled Assessment: B4.4 Select and process primary and secondary data *[B4.4.2 a) b) c)]*; B4.5 Analyse and interpret primary and secondary data. *[B4.5.2 a) b) c)]*, *[B4.5.3 a)]*

Lesson structure

Starters

What happens to milk when it goes off? – Show the students fresh and sour milk. If possible, have one that is really solid but careful risk assessment is necessary. Discuss what has happened to the milk and why putting milk in the refrigerator stops it going off. *(5 minutes)*

Denaturing eggs – Crack raw eggs (or get students to do this) into three beakers: one beaker at room temperature, one at a temperature where visible changes to the egg white just occur, and one at boiling point. Support students by asking them to describe the visible and textural changes to the egg white. Extend students by asking them to explain the changes that are happening to the shape of the protein. Are the changes irreversible? Introduce the concept of denaturation. *(10 minutes)*

Main

Investigating the effect of temperature on enzymes

- Students can use their own saliva to carry out this experiment on the action of amylase on starch (see Practical support 'Investigating the effect of temperature on enzymes').
- A graph can be plotted of the rate of disappearance of starch (1/time taken in seconds) against the temperature. Many concepts of 'How Science Works' can be developed in the investigative work, e.g. hypotheses are formulated, predictions are made, variables are controlled and conclusions drawn. Concentrate on one or two of these, e.g. drawing conclusions from the graph plotted.
- Other enzymes could be used for investigations into the effect of temperature. If the use of the students' saliva is not possible, commercial amylase could be used, but it is usually derived from fungi and can give odd results.
- If pepsin or trypsin (protein digesting enzymes) are used, the substrate to use is the white of hard-boiled eggs or an egg-white suspension made by adding 5 g of egg white to 500 cm³ of very hot water and whisking briskly. The rate at which the egg-white suspension clears can be timed at the different temperatures. More 'How Science Works' concepts are introduced here too.

Investigating the effect of pH

- The effects of varying pH can also be investigated by modifying the experiments described above. Keep the temperature constant and vary the pH by using a range of buffer solutions.
- The effect of varying pH on catalase. Potato discs can be added to hydrogen peroxide and buffer solutions and the quantity of oxygen evolved in a set time can be measured at each pH. A graph can be plotted of volume of oxygen evolved against pH and the optimum pH for catalase determined.

Plenaries

What temperature do I work best at? – Discuss what might be the optimum temperature for the enzymes in the human body. What happens if we get a fever? Why do parents worry when you get too hot? Contrast our body temperature with that of other organisms – include some fish, reptiles and invertebrates. Do all enzymes have the same optimum temperature? *(5 minutes)*

Definitions – Write up a list of the key words and phrases used in this topic so far. Support students by providing a list of definitions which they need to match with the words. Extend students by asking them to write their own definitions and using them to compose a short passage which they could use as a revision card. *(10 minutes)*

Practical support

Investigating the effect of temperature on enzymes

Equipment and materials required

Test tubes and racks, water baths for different temperatures, 2% starch solution, fresh saliva, boiled saliva, iodine solution, white tiles, glass rods, eye protection.

Details

Each student will need at least 2 cm depth of saliva in a test tube. Test tubes should be set up containing equal volumes of saliva and starch solution, shaken and then placed into water baths at different temperatures. Drops of the mixtures are then tested at 30 second intervals for the presence or absence of starch by dipping a glass rod into the mixture and then into a drop of iodine solution on a white tile. Note the colour each time and record how long it takes for the starch to disappear at each temperature. A control could be set up using boiled saliva.

Safety: CLEAPSS Hazcard 54B Iodine solution. Dispose of saliva in disinfectant. CLEAPSS Hazcard 33 Enzymes.

Enzymes

B2 3.2 — Factors affecting enzyme action

Learning objectives

- How does increasing the temperature affect your enzymes?
- Why does a change in pH affect your enzymes?

A container of milk left at the back of your fridge for a week or two will be disgusting. The milk will go off as enzymes in bacteria break down the protein structure.

Leave your milk in the sun for a day and the same thing happens – but much faster. Temperature affects the rate at which chemical reactions take place even when they are controlled by biological catalysts.

Biological reactions are affected by the same factors as any other chemical reactions. Factors such as concentration, temperature and surface area all affect them. However, in living organisms an increase in temperature only works up to a certain point.

a Why does milk left in the sun go off quickly?

links

For more information about how body temperature is maintained at a constant level for optimum enzyme activity, see B3 3.5 Controlling body temperature.

Practical

Investigating the effect of temperature on enzymes

You can show the effect of temperature on the rate of enzyme action using simple practical procedures.

The enzyme amylase (found in your saliva) breaks down starch into simple sugars. You can mix starch solution and amylase together and keep them at different temperatures. Then you test samples from each temperature with iodine solution at regular intervals.

- How does iodine solution show you if starch is present?
- Why do we test starch solution without any amylase added?
- What conclusion can you draw from the results?

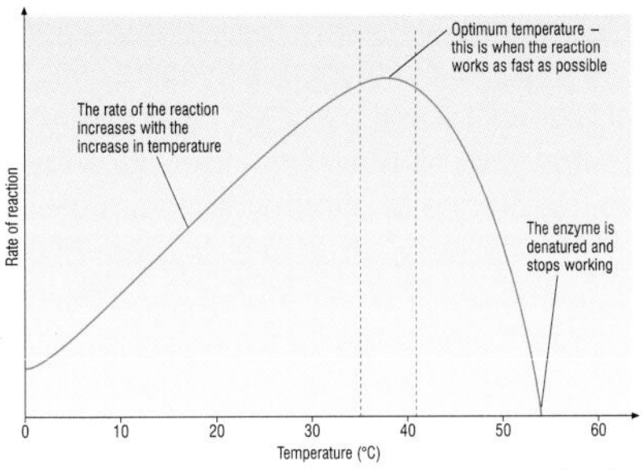

The effect of temperature on enzyme action

The reactions that take place in cells happen at relatively low temperatures. Like other reactions, the rate of enzyme-controlled reactions increases as the temperature increases.

However, this is only true up to temperatures of about 40°C. After this the protein structure of the enzyme is affected by the high temperature. The long amino acid chains begin to unravel. As a result, the shape of the active site changes. We say the enzyme has been denatured. It can no longer act as a catalyst, so the rate of the reaction drops dramatically. Most human enzymes work best at 37°C.

b What does it mean if an enzyme is denatured?

Figure 1 The rate of an enzyme-controlled reaction increases as the temperature rises – but only until the protein structure of the enzyme breaks down

Effect of pH on enzyme action

The shape of the active site of an enzyme comes from forces between the different parts of the protein molecule. These forces hold the folded chains in place. A change in the pH affects these forces. That's why it changes the shape of the molecule. As a result, the active site is lost, so the enzyme no longer acts as a catalyst.

Different enzymes have different pH levels at which they work best. A change in the pH can stop them working completely.

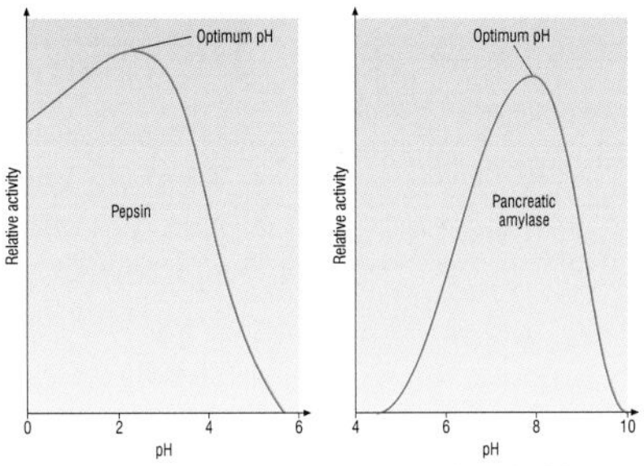

Figure 2 These two digestive enzymes need very different pH levels to work at their maximum rate. Pepsin is found in the stomach, along with hydrochloric acid, while pancreatic amylase is in the small intestine along with alkaline bile.

Without enzymes, none of the reactions in your body would happen fast enough to keep you alive. This is why it is so dangerous if your temperature goes too high when you are ill. Once your body temperature reaches about 41°C, your enzymes start to be denatured and you will soon die.

Summary questions

1 Copy and complete using the words below:

active site   cells   denatured   enzyme   increase   protein reactions   shape   temperatures   40°C

The chemical .... that take place in living .... happen at relatively low .... The rate of these ....-controlled reactions .... with an increase in temperature. However, this is only true up to temperatures of about .... After this the .... structure of the enzyme is affected and the .... of the .... is changed. The enzyme has been ....

2 Look at Figure 2.
 a At which pH does pepsin work best?
 b At which pH does amylase work best?
 c What happens to the activity of the enzymes as the pH increases?
 d Explain why this change in activity happens.

Did you know …?

Not all enzymes work best at around 40°C. Bacteria living in hot springs survive at temperatures up to 80°C and higher. On the other hand, some bacteria that live in the very cold, deep seas have enzymes that work effectively at 0°C and below.

Figure 3 The magical light display of a firefly is caused by the action of an enzyme called luciferase

Study tip

Enzymes aren't killed (they are molecules, not living things themselves) – use the term 'denatured'.

Key points

- Enzyme activity is affected by temperature and pH.
- High temperatures and the wrong pH can affect the shape of the active site of an enzyme and stop it working.

Further teaching suggestions

Luciferase

- Search the internet and show pictures of flashlight fish, luminous jellyfish, fungi and glow worms that all have this enzyme, which catalyses a reaction and releases energy as light. Some plants have the enzyme and glow green. Tell the true story of a pilot lost at sea from an aircraft carrier at night who navigated his way back and landed successfully after following the faint trail of light from phosphorescent algae, which glowed in the wake of the ship following its passage. Break a lightstick of the kind used by the armed forces, campers and at discos. Demonstrate the reaction of luciferase by mixing the appropriate chemicals *in vitro*. Students could do internet research on luciferase to see what else they can find out about this unique enzyme.

Extended experiments

- With the pH experiments, the introduction of a wider range of pH values could make the experiment more reliable. The quantities of alkali and acid could be varied and the pH ascertained by testing with pH papers or a pH sensor. Alternatively, make up solutions of known pH for use.

How to make sour cream

- Milk protein can be curdled by adding lemon juice to it. Demonstrate and discuss with the students what is happening. Link with the starter and link with the effects of temperature and pH together. Reinforce the idea of what causes the milk to go off or go sour.

Summary answers

1 reactions, cells, temperatures, enzyme, increase, 40°C, protein, shape, active site, denatured

2 a About pH 2.
  b About pH 8.
  c The activity levels fall fast.
  d The increase in pH affects the shape of the active site of the enzyme, so it no longer bonds to the substrate. It is denatured and no longer catalyses the reaction.

B2 3.3

Enzymes in digestion

Learning objectives

Students should learn:

- that during digestion, the breakdown of large molecules into smaller molecules is catalysed by enzymes
- that these enzymes, which are produced by specialised cells in glands, pass out into the gut
- that the enzymes include amylases that catalyse the breakdown of starch, proteases that catalyse the breakdown of proteins and lipases that catalyse the breakdown of lipids.

Learning outcomes

Most students should be able to:

- explain how enzymes are involved in the digestion of our food
- describe the location and action of the enzymes which catalyse the breakdown of carbohydrates (starch), proteins and lipids.

Some students should also be able to:

- explain digestion in terms of the molecules involved.

Answers to in-text questions

a They work outside the cells of your body.
b Amylase.
c Proteases.
d Lipases.

Support

- Use flip cards with foods on one side and their components on the other. Some students might need a clue, such as starting letters or vowels. Alternatively, use an internet version for whiteboards, or individual computers such as those created through 'Quia' (use this as a search term).
- Play **floor dominoes.** Make up large 'domino' cards of food types, their components and the enzymes and allow the students to play in groups.

Extend

- Get students to research how cystic fibrosis affects the digestive system and the use of enzymes in its treatment.

Specification link-up: Biology B2.5 and B2.6

- The chemical reactions inside cells are controlled by enzymes. *[B2.6.1 a)]*
- Some enzymes work outside the body cells … . *[B2.5.2 c)]*
- The enzyme amylase is produced in the salivary glands … . *[B2.5.2 d)]*
- Protease enzymes are produced by the stomach … . *[B2.5.2 e)]*
- Lipase enzymes are produced by the pancreas and small intestine … . *[B2.5.2 f)]*
- The stomach also produces hydrochloric acid. The enzymes … . *[B2.5.2 g)]*
- The liver produces bile, which is stored in the gall bladder … . *[B2.5.2 h)]*

  Controlled Assessment: B4.5 Analyse and interpret primary and secondary data. *[B4.5.2 a) b) c) d)]*, *[B4.5.3 a)]*, *[B4.5.4 d)]*

Lesson structure

Starters

What we know about enzymes so far, a quick quiz – Ask 10 questions on enzyme structure and factors affecting their action. Support students by making the questions simple and straightforward. Extend students by asking more difficult questions and expecting more detailed answers. *(5 minutes)*

The fly – Show photographs of a fly's mouthparts and talk through how they function, or how a spider sucks the juice out of its victims. (For a taster, search the internet for 'The Fly watch trailer'). *(10 minutes)*

Main

- Introduce the different types of digestive enzymes by reviewing the different components of the diet. Get the students to realise that complex carbohydrates, proteins and lipids have to be digested before they can be absorbed. Introduce the groups of digestive enzymes and what they do. Reference to carbohydrases, proteases and lipases, their substrates and their products is required. Project a diagram of the human digestive system and its associated glands and indicate where the different enzymes work in the gut. Also indicate on this diagram where the enzymes are produced as well as where they act. It could be helpful to provide the students with an outline of the digestive system, so that they can fill in the information for themselves.

- Making a model gut – each group of students will need two 15 cm lengths of dialysis (Visking) tubing to model the gut (see 'Practical support'). If desired, the experiments can be left for 24 hours at room temperature before testing.

- If there is not time for the students to carry out their own experiments, then a length of dialysis tubing can be filled with a mixture of 30% glucose solution and 3% starch solution and placed in a test tube of distilled water. If this is left for about 15 minutes, the water can be tested for starch and glucose.

- Some glucose should have diffused through the tubing into the water, but the starch should not. Tests for starch and glucose will confirm this. Note: This only demonstrates that glucose will pass through the tubing but starch will not; it does not show that the enzyme catalyses the breakdown of the starch.

- The model gut can be used to show the effect of changes in temperature and pH on the activity of saliva or amylase on starch. The tubing should be placed in boiling tubes, and samples of the water surrounding the tubing can be tested for starch and sugars at intervals to determine whether or not digestion has taken place.

- To investigate changes in temperature, the boiling tubes containing the enzyme-substrate mixtures in the tubing should be incubated in a range of temperatures from about 5 °C to 60 °C using water baths.

- To investigate the range of pH values, buffer solutions should be used, providing another opportunity to develop the investigative aspects of 'How Science Works', such as evaluation.

Plenary

Cryptic word search – Support students by giving them a wordsearch of the enzymes, substrates and products from the lesson. Extend students by getting them to write cryptic definitions of the words and using them to test each other. *(10 minutes)*

Practical support

Investigating digestion
Equipment and materials required
Visking or dialysis tubing, dropping pipettes, elastic bands, starch and enzyme solutions (the concentration of these solutions may need to be increased to give results in a single lesson), water baths, beakers, test tubes and racks, iodine solution, Benedict's solution.

Details
Each group of students will need two 15 cm lengths of dialysis (Visking) tubing, which has been soaked in water. Each piece should be knotted securely at one end. Using a dropping pipette, fill one length of the tubing with 3% starch solution and place it in a test tube. Fold the top of the tubing over the rim of the test tube and

secure with an elastic band. Remove all traces of the starch solution from the outside of the tubing by filling the test tube with water and emptying it several times. Finally, fill the test tube with water and place it in a rack.

Repeat the procedure with the second length of tubing but add 5 cm³ saliva or amylase solutions to the starch solution, and shake before filling the dialysis tubing. The test tubes should be labelled A and B and placed in a water bath at 35 °C for 30 minutes. The water in the test tubes should then be tested for: starch, using iodine solution; sugars, using Benedict's solution.

Safety: CLEAPSS Hazcard 54B Iodine solution. CLEAPSS Hazcards 27C and 95A Benedict's solution – harmful. CLEAPSS Hazcard 33 Enzymes. Wear eye protection.

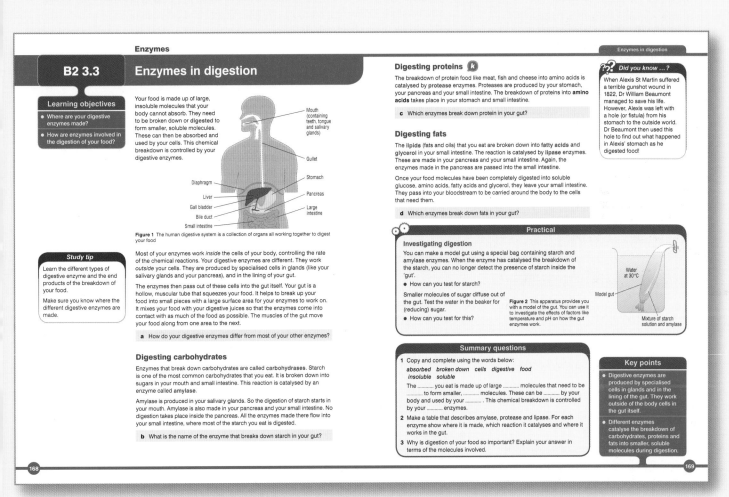

Summary answers

1 food, insoluble, broken down, soluble, absorbed, cells, digestive

2 Suitable table.

Enzyme	Where it is made	Reaction catalysed	Where it works
Amylase	Salivary glands, pancreas, small intestine	Starch → sugars/glucose	Mouth, small intestine
Protease	Stomach, pancreas, small intestine	Proteins → amino acids	Stomach, small intestine
Lipase	Pancreas, small intestine	Lipids → fatty acids and glycerol	Small intestine

3 Large insoluble molecules in food cannot be absorbed into the blood so have to be digested to form small insoluble molecules that can be absorbed.

B2 3.4

Speeding up digestion

Learning objectives

Students should learn:

- that the enzymes in the stomach work most effectively in the acid conditions resulting from the production of hydrochloric acid by the stomach
- that bile produced by the liver provides the alkaline conditions needed for the enzymes in the small intestine to work most effectively
- that bile also emulsifies the fats increasing the surface area for the enzymes to act upon.

Learning outcomes

Most students should be able to:

- describe how pH affects the enzymes in the different parts of the gut
- describe how bile emulsifies fats.

Some students should also be able to:

- explain in detail how the emulsification of fats increases the rate of their digestion.

Specification link-up: Biology B2.5

- Some enzymes work outside the body cells … . *[B2.5.2 c)]*
- The enzyme amylase is produced in the salivary glands … . *[B2.5.2 d)]*
- Protease enzymes are produced by the stomach … . *[B2.5.2 e)]*
- Lipase enzymes are produced by the pancreas and small intestine … . *[B2.5.2 f)]*
- The stomach also produces hydrochloric acid. The … . *[B2.5.2 g)]*
- The liver produces bile, which is stored in the gall bladder … . *[B2.5.2 h)]*

  Controlled Assessment: B4.1 Plan practical ways to develop and test candidates' own scientific ideas *[B4.1.1 a) b) c)]*; B4.4 Select and process primary and secondary data. *[B4.4.2 a) b) c)]*

Lesson structure

Starters

Effect of body temperature on digestion – Show a picture or footage of a reptile, such as a snake or a crocodile, eating a large lump of meat and show a picture of lions feeding. Ask: 'What consequences will their different body temperatures have on the rate at which they digest their meals? How often do they feed the reptiles in the zoo?' Students to make a list and compare. *(5 minutes)*

More about surface area – Get students to tell you what they know about SA (surface area) to volume ratio. Ask them to think about how this might be relevant to the process of digestion. Discuss the effect of the teeth and mastication on the break up of large masses of food in the mouth. Ask: 'What is the effect on digestion in the mouth? Does chewing affect digestion in the stomach?' Support students by reminding them of how SA (surface area) increases when the volume is decreased. Extend students by asking them to think about other examples of the importance of SA (surface area) in the process of digestion (e.g. chewing, absorption). *(10 minutes)*

Main

- The practical on 'Breaking down protein' described in the Student Book is easy to set up (see 'Practical support'). The experiment can be made more quantitative (introducing 'How Science Works'), by getting the students to formulate an hypothesis, make predictions, use stated volumes of enzyme and acid and weigh the pieces of meat used at the beginning and end of the experiment. A bar chart can be drawn showing the percentage change in mass.

- Compare the action of pepsin with the action of trypsin. Pepsin and trypsin work in different parts of the gut in different pH conditions. The experiment ('Effect of pH on enzyme action') described in 'B2 3.2 Factors affecting enzyme action' could be used here to show that pepsin works best in acid conditions and trypsin in alkaline conditions. If specific pH values are required, then the use of buffer solutions is recommended.

- Ask the students what the word 'emulsion' means (paint it on to a large sheet of paper – using emulsion paint). Bring in a salad, some vinegar and some olive oil. Get a student to pour some oil on top of the vinegar in a gas jar or similar vessel, shake vigorously and produce an emulsion. Students can do this themselves on a small scale in a boiling tube. Observe the globules formed and link to SA (surface area), then to speeding up digestion. Link the formation of an emulsion with the effect of bile salts.

- An experiment could be set up to demonstrate the effect of bile salts on the activity of lipase (see 'Practical support').

Plenaries

Gallstones – Show some gallstones or photographs of gallstones. Discuss why gallstones occur and what might be the consequences. Get the students to write a letter to their doctor stating what problems they fear and asking advice. *(5 minutes)*

Colouring exercise: The pH in the gut – Give the students unlabelled diagrams of the digestive system and ask them to label them and colour in the different regions according to the different pH conditions that exist in the gut. Support students by giving them the list of different pH conditions. Extend students by getting them to work out the different regions and to add the names of the major enzymes present in each region. *(10 minutes)*

Answers to in-text questions

a The body temperature is usually maintained around 37 °C.

b The stomach glands produce a thick layer of mucus.

c The food entering the small intestine from the stomach is acidic. The enzymes of the small intestine work best in alkaline conditions.

Support

- Get students to illustrate the formation of an emulsion.

Extend

- Get students to find out more about bile. What does it contain? How and where is it made?

Practical support

Breaking down protein
Equipment and materials required
For each group:
At least three test tubes and a rack, small cubes of meat, 2% pepsin solution, 0.1 M solution of hydrochloric acid, water bath at 35 °C, balance, labels, filter papers, eye protection.

Details
Each group of students will require three test tubes and can set up their own experiment. Into one test tube, place about 20 cm³ of pepsin solution. Into a second tube place the same volume of hydrochloric acid and into a third tube place the same volume of a mixture of pepsin solution and hydrochloric acid. Cut three similar sized chunks of meat, weigh each one and place one piece into each of the three tubes, noting which piece of meat was placed into which tube. Leave for a few hours. An additional control tube could be added using boiled and cooled pepsin. If this done, it would be advisable to leave the experiment running for 24 hours. The pieces of meat should then be removed from the tubes, rinsed and dried on filter paper before reweighing.

Safety: Wear eye protection.

Demonstrating the effect of bile salts on the activity of lipase
Equipment and materials required
Two test tubes, 5 cm³ of milk, 7 cm³ sodium carbonate solution and 5 drops of phenolphthalein, washing up liquid, 2 cm³ of lipase.

Details
Set up two test tubes, each containing 5 cm³ of milk, 7 cm³ sodium carbonate solution and 5 drops of phenolphthalein. To one tube, add a drop of washing up liquid. Add 1 cm³ of lipase to each tube and stir each tube, timing how long it takes for the indicator to go from pink (alkaline) to colourless (acid) showing that the lipids in the milk have been broken down to fatty acids. The washing up liquid emulsifies the lipids and the reaction should therefore be quicker.

Safety: CLEAPSS Hazcard 33 Enzymes. Wear eye protection. Wash hands if reagents come into contact with the skin.

Enzymes

B2 3.4

Speeding up digestion

Learning objectives
- Why does your stomach contain hydrochloric acid?
- What is bile and why is it so important in digestion?

links
For information on the sensitivity of enzymes to temperature and pH, look back at B2 3.2 Factors affecting enzyme action.

Your digestive system produces many enzymes that speed up the breakdown of the food you eat. As your body is kept at a fairly steady 37 °C, your enzymes have an ideal temperature that allows them to work as fast as possible.

Keeping the pH in your gut at ideal levels isn't that easy because different enzymes work best at different pH levels. For example, the protease enzyme found in your stomach works best in acidic conditions.

On the other hand, the proteases made in your pancreas need alkaline conditions to work at their best

So, your body makes a variety of different chemicals that help to keep conditions ideal for your enzymes all the way through your gut.

a Why do your enzymes almost always have the right temperature to work at their best?

Changing pH in the gut
You have around 35 million glands in the lining of your stomach. These secrete protease enzymes to digest the protein you eat. The enzymes work best in an acid pH. So your stomach also produces a concentrated solution of hydrochloric acid from the same glands. In fact, your stomach produces around 3 litres of acid a day! This acid allows your stomach protease enzymes to work very effectively. It also kills most of the bacteria that you take in with your food.

Finally, your stomach also produces a thick layer of mucus. This coats your stomach walls and protects them from being digested by the acid and the enzymes.

b How does your stomach avoid digesting itself?

Practical
Breaking down protein
You can see the effect of acid on pepsin, the protease found in the stomach, quite simply.
Set up three test tubes: one containing pepsin, one containing hydrochloric acid and one containing a mixture of the two. Keep them at body temperature in a water bath. Add a similar-sized chunk of meat to all three of them. Set up a webcam and watch for a few hours to see what happens.
● What conclusions can you make?

Figure 1 These test tubes show clearly the importance of protein-digesting enzymes and hydrochloric acid in your stomach. Meat was added to each tube at the same time.

After a few hours – depending on the size and type of the meal you have eaten – your food leaves your stomach. It moves on into your small intestine. Some of the enzymes that catalyse digestion in your small intestine are made in your pancreas. Some are also made in the small intestine itself. They all work best in an alkaline environment.

The acidic liquid coming from your stomach needs to become an alkaline mix in your small intestine. So how does it happen?

Your liver makes a greenish-yellow alkaline liquid called bile. Bile is stored in your gall bladder until it is needed.

As food comes into the small intestine from the stomach, bile is squirted onto it. The bile neutralises the acid from the stomach and then makes the semi-digested food alkaline. This provides the ideal conditions needed for the enzymes in the small intestine.

c Why does the food coming into your small intestine need neutralising?

Altering the surface area
It is very important for the enzymes of the gut to have the largest possible surface area of food to work on. This is not a problem with carbohydrates and proteins. However, the fats that you eat do not mix with all the watery liquids in your gut. They stay as large globules (like oil in water) that make it difficult for the lipase enzymes to act.

This is the second important function of the bile. It **emulsifies** the fats in your food. This means bile physically breaks up large drops of fat into smaller droplets. This provides a much bigger surface area for the lipase enzymes to act on. The larger surface area helps the lipase chemically break down the fats more quickly into fatty acids and glycerol.

Did you know …?
Sometimes gall stones block the gall bladder and bile duct. The stones can range from a few millimetres to several centimetres long and can cause terrible pain.

Figure 2 Gall stones

Study tip
Remember, food is not digested in the liver or the pancreas.
Bile is *not* an enzyme and it does *not* break down fat molecules.
Bile emulsifies fat droplets to increase the surface area, which in turn increases the rate of fat digestion by lipase.

Summary questions
1 Copy and complete using the words below:
alkaline emulsifies gall bladder liver neutralises small intestine
Bile is an .... liquid produced by your .... It is stored in the .... and released onto food as it enters the .... It .... the acidic food from the stomach and makes it alkaline. It also .... fats.

2 Look at Figure 1.
a In what conditions does the protease from the stomach work best?
b How does your body create the right pH in the stomach for this enzyme?
c In what conditions does the proteases in the small intestine work best?
d How does your body create the right pH in the small intestine for this enzyme?

3 Draw a diagram to explain how bile produces a big surface area for lipase to work on and explain why this is important.

Key points
- The enzymes of the stomach work best in acid conditions.
- The enzymes made in the pancreas and the small intestine work best in alkaline conditions.
- Bile produced by the liver neutralises acid and emulsifies fats.

Further teaching suggestions

Estimating the rate of digestion
● Use small pieces of cooked sausage, 2% pepsin and 0.01M HCl in water baths at different temperatures to estimate the rate of digestion. Compare this with the cooked sausage in 2% trypsin and 0.1M NaOH. The concentration of both enzymes can be varied and the effect of specific pH values can be estimated with the use of buffer solutions.

Summary answers

1 alkaline, liver, gall bladder, small intestine, neutralises, emulsifies

2 **a** Acid
b Hydrochloric acid is made in glands in the stomach.
c Alkaline/alkali
d The liver produces bile that is stored in the gall bladder and released when food comes into the small intestine.

3 [Marks for a good diagram showing a large fat droplet coated in bile splitting into many small fat droplets.] This produces a larger SA (surface area) so enzymes can get to many more fat molecules and so break them down more quickly.

B2 3.5

Making use of enzymes

Specification link-up: Biology B2.5

- Some microorganisms produce enzymes that pass out of the cells … . *[B2.5.2 i)]*
- In industry, enzymes are used to bring about reactions … . *[B2.5.2 j)]*

  Controlled Assessment: B4.1 Plan practical ways to develop and test candidates' own scientific ideas. *[B4.1.1 a) b) c)]*

Learning objectives

Students should learn:

- that enzymes from microorganisms have many uses in the home and in industry
- that proteases and lipases are used in the manufacture of biological detergents
- that proteases, carbohydrases and isomerase are used in food manufacture.

Learning outcomes

Most students should be able to:

- explain how biological detergents work
- describe some of the ways in which enzymes are used in the food industry.

Some students should also be able to:

- evaluate the advantages and disadvantages of using enzymes in home and in industry.

Answers to in-text questions

a It's a washing powder that contains enzymes, usually proteases and lipases.

b Enzymes in yeast turn sugar (glucose) into ethanol. They wouldn't work on starch.

Support

- Use name boards with a fold-over end. Write 'carbohydrate' on one and use the hinged fold-over to convert it into 'carbohydrase'. Have examples of all the enzymes required in the specification.

Extend

- Ask students to find out the differences in the structural formulae of glucose and fructose. They can try to work out why these sugars have different effects on the taste buds.

Lesson structure

Starters

Taste tests – Fructose is now available in many supermarkets. You could make up separate solutions of fructose, sucrose and glucose of the same strength (e.g. 2 teaspoons in a beaker of water) and get the students to do a blind tasting scoring them for sweetness on a 5-point scale. Note: this must be done in hygienic conditions following risk assessment and not in a laboratory. *(5 minutes)*

Baby food for lunch? – Show the students some samples of baby food. Have disposable plastic spoons and be prepared for joking. Some pelican bibs will help to create the atmosphere. Ask: 'How does baby food differ from adult food? What did parents do before the commercially prepared baby foods were available?' Compile lists on the board and compare. Support students by prompting them to suggest how enzymes might be involved. Extend students by asking them to list the processes involved in the commercial production of baby food. *(10 minutes)*

Main

- Use agar plates containing starch, milk and mayonnaise (or salad cream or egg yolk) to demonstrate the activity of enzymes in biological detergents (see 'Practical support'). This activity can be used to compare different biological washing powders or liquids (the advantage of liquids is that volumes can be measured and dilutions made more easily). It can also be used to compare dishwasher detergents with clothes washing detergents and to discover whether the age of the detergent has any effect on its efficiency.

- All of these can be used to introduce many 'How Science Works' concepts. Predictions can be made, measurements made and recorded, variables controlled and conclusions drawn. It also gives students some scope for designing their own investigations.

- The experiment above can be modified to demonstrate that the proteases in a biological detergent can work at higher temperatures than trypsin from an animal source. Samples of both can be heated to temperatures of 30 °C, 40 °C, etc. and then placed in holes in milk agar plates. Use a separate plate for each enzyme or detergent tested and the number of holes should correspond to the number of different temperatures tested. The plates should then be treated as above and the clear areas measured and recorded. A graph can then be plotted of temperature against area of clear zone.

- The effect of biological detergent on egg albumin can be demonstrated by immersing cubes of egg white in a solution of a biological detergent. A solution of a biological washing powder is made by dissolving 3 g of powder in 30 cm^3 of water. A cube of egg white is weighed and placed in this solution for 20 minutes, after which time it is removed, rinsed and dried. The effect of the washing powder can be assessed by reweighing.

- This investigation can be expanded to consider different variables. Comparisons can be made using different biological detergents. The strength of the detergent needed can be investigated and the optimum temperature found.

Plenary

Enzymes table – Give the students two minutes to write down as many advantages and disadvantages of using enzymes in commercial processes as they can. Gather together the suggestions and build up a table of advantages and disadvantages. Discuss how the disadvantages can be overcome. *(5 minutes)*

Practical support

Investigating biological washing powder

Equipment and materials required

Some biological detergent (either in powder or liquid form in order to make up different concentrations if needed – avoid contact with skin), egg white in chunks/cubes (or agar plates containing starch, milk, mayonnaise, salad cream or egg yolk), test tubes and racks, tissues for drying, iodine solution (CLEAPSS Hazcard 54B) balance for weighing, eye protection, protective gloves.

Details

A cork borer is used to remove cylinders of agar from the prepared plates. The number of cylinders removed depends on the number of detergents being tested. Into the holes, solutions of the detergents can be placed and the plates incubated at 25 °C for about 24 hours.

Iodine solution is poured over the starch-agar plate and left for 5 minutes before being poured away. The diameter of clear areas around the holes can be measured and recorded. It should be possible to measure clear areas around the holes on the milk-agar plates and the mayonnaise-agar plates.

Safety: Care when handling detergents. CLEAPSS Hazcard 54B Iodine solution. Eye protection and protective gloves needed.

Enzymes

Making use of enzymes

B2 3.5 Making use of enzymes

Learning objectives

- How do biological detergents work?
- How are enzymes used in the food industry?

Enzymes were first isolated from living cells in the 19th century. Ever since then, we have found more and more ways of using them in industry. Some microorganisms produce enzymes that pass out of the cells and are easy for us to use. In other cases we use the whole microorganism.

Enzymes in the home

In the past, people boiled and scrubbed their clothes to get them clean – by hand! Now we have washing machines and enzymes ready and waiting to digest the stains.

Many people use **biological detergents** to remove stains such as grass, sweat and food from their clothes. Biological washing powders contain proteases and lipases. These enzymes break down the proteins and fats in the stains. They help to give you a cleaner wash. Biological detergents work better than non-biological detergents at lower temperatures. This is because the enzymes work best at lower temperatures – they are denatured if the water is too hot. This means you use less electricity too.

a What is a biological washing powder?

Practical

Investigating biological washing powder

Weigh a chunk of cooked egg white and leave it in a strong solution of biological washing powder.

- What do you think will happen to the egg white?
- How can you measure just how effective the protease enzymes are?
- How could you investigate the effect of surface area on enzyme action?

Enzymes in industry

Pure enzymes have many uses in industry.

Proteases are used to make baby foods. They 'predigest' some of the protein in the food. When babies first begin to eat solid foods they are not very good at digesting it. Treating the food with protease enzymes makes it easier for a baby's digestive system to cope with it. It is easier for them to get the amino acids they need from their food.

Carbohydrases are used to convert starch into sugar (glucose) syrup. We use huge quantities of sugar syrup in food production. You will see it on the ingredients labels on all sorts of foods.

Starch is made by plants like corn and it is very cheap. Using enzymes to convert this plant starch into sweet sugar provides a cheap source of sweetness for food manufacturers.

It is also important for the process of making fuel (ethanol) from plants.

b Why does starch need to be converted to sugar before it is used to make ethanol?

Figure 1 Many people now have a dishwasher. Dishwasher detergents contain enzymes that digest cooked-on proteins like eggs, which are often hard to remove.

Figure 2 Learning to eat solid food isn't easy. Having some of it predigested by protease enzymes can make it easier to get the amino acids you need to grow.

Sometimes the glucose syrup made from starch is passed through another process that uses a different set of enzymes. The enzyme **isomerase** is used to change glucose syrup into **fructose syrup**.

Glucose and fructose contain exactly the same amount of energy (1700 kJ or 400 kcal per 100 g). However, fructose is much sweeter than glucose. Much smaller amounts are needed to make food taste sweet. Fructose is widely used in 'slimming' foods – the food tastes sweet but contains fewer calories.

The advantages and disadvantages of using enzymes

In industrial processes, many of the reactions need high temperatures and pressures to make them go fast enough to produce the products needed. This needs expensive equipment and requires a lot of energy.

Enzymes can solve industrial problems like these. They catalyse reactions at relatively low temperatures and normal pressures. Enzyme-based processes are therefore often fairly cheap to run.

One problem with enzymes is that they are denatured at high temperatures, so the temperature must be kept down (usually below 45 °C). The pH also needs to be kept within carefully controlled limits that suit the enzyme. It costs money to control these conditions.

Many enzymes are also expensive to produce. Whole microbes are relatively cheap, but need to be supplied with food and oxygen and their waste products removed. They use some of the substrate to grow more microbes. Pure enzymes use the substrate more efficiently, but they are also more expensive to produce.

Figure 3 Some people are always trying to lose weight. Enzyme technology is used to convert more and more glucose syrup to fructose syrup to make so-called 'slimming' foods.

Study tip

Remember that most enzyme names end in '-ase'.

Some enzymes used in industry work at quite high temperatures – so don't be put off if a graph shows an optimum temperature well above 45 °C!

Summary questions

1 List three enzymes and the ways in which we use them in the food industry.

2 Biological washing powders contain enzymes in tiny capsules. Explain why:
  a they are more effective than non-biological powders at lower temperatures
  b they are not more effective at high temperatures.

3 Make a table to show the advantages and disadvantages of using enzymes in industry.

Key points

- Some microorganisms produce enzymes that pass out of the cells and can be used in different ways.
- Biological detergents may contain proteases and lipases.
- Proteases, carbohydrases and isomerase are all used in the food industry.

172

173

Further teaching suggestions

How good are biological detergents?

Students could find out how many people use biological detergents in dishwashers and washing machines, and whether or not there are differences between them. Some preparatory work for the next lesson could be set as homework tasks here.

More about temperatures

There have been efforts made to persuade people to reduce the temperature at which they run their washing machine programmes. Discuss this with students and get them to suggest ways of finding out if the detergents work as well at lower temperatures as they do at higher temperatures.

Summary answers

1 Proteases: predigested baby food. Carbohydrases: convert starch to glucose syrup. Isomerase: converts glucose syrup to fructose syrup.

2 a The protease and lipase enzymes digest proteins and fats on the clothes, so the clothes get cleaner than detergent alone. The enzymes work best at lower temperatures. Detergent alone needs higher temperatures to work at its best, so biological detergents are much more effective at low temperatures.

  b At temperatures above about 45 °C, the enzymes may be denatured and so have no effect on cleaning.

3

Advantages	Disadvantages
Work at relatively low temperatures.	Denatured by high temperatures.
Work at relatively low pressures.	Sensitive to pH changes.
Efficient catalysts.	If whole organisms, need food, oxygen and waste products removed.
Processes often cheap to run.	Enzymes can be expensive to produce.

B2 3.6

High-tech enzymes

Learning objectives

Students should learn:

- that there are advantages and disadvantages to using enzymes at home and in industry
- that enzymes can be used as diagnostic tools in medicine and in the treatment of some diseases.

Learning outcomes

Most students should be able to:

- describe some of the advantages and disadvantages of using biological detergents
- describe some of the ways in which enzymes are used in medicine.

Some students should also be able to:

- evaluate the advantages and disadvantages of using enzymes in the home and in industry.

Support

- Provide students with the text and pictures with which to build up a poster on 'Enzymes in medicine'.

Extend

- Get students to find out more about unusual enzymes, such as bromelain and papain, and their uses in the food industry.

Specification link-up: Biology B2.5

- Evaluate the advantages and disadvantages of using enzymes in the home and in industry. [B2.5]

  Controlled Assessment: B4.1 Plan practical ways to develop and test candidates' own scientific ideas. [B4.1.1 a) b) c)]

Lesson structure

Starters

A question of temperature – Some washing machine cycles can operate at temperatures as low as 30 °C. Ask: 'Is this always a good thing?' Draw up a balance sheet of advantages and disadvantages of the lowering of the temperature. Ask: 'Do the advantages outweigh the disadvantages? Would you wash your baby's dirty clothes in a low temperature wash?' *(5 minutes)*

Will it come out in the wash? – Get students to suggest stains they might get on their clothes and build up a list. Add a few of your own suggestions (such as tar, ballpoint pen, etc.). Then ask which ones will come out if the clothes are washed with a biological detergent. Support students by making the list fairly simple and reminding them about the enzymes in the detergent. Extend students by including some more unusual examples (chilli sauce!) and get them to identify the class of enzyme that would get rid of the stain. *(10 minutes)*

Main

- Clinistix and albustix can be used to test for the presence of glucose and protein in urine. Carry out a 'Tinkle test' experiment with fake urine doctored with glucose, protein, both and neither. Discuss the benefits of such tests compared with the standard methods of testing for glucose and protein in the lab (using Benedict's solution and the Biuret test). Discuss the value of the tests in making quick diagnoses and helping people with diabetes to control their condition.

- Discuss the problems of cystic fibrosis and the use of enzymes in its treatment. Tell students about the consequences of the blocking of the pancreatic duct. Ask the students what they think the consequences could be and how the problem could be overcome. Show the video *Sammi's story* (Channel 4 Television, 1995) if available or go to the cystic fibrosis website for more information about the treatment.

- Use the internet to research other uses of enzymes in medicine, such as streptokinase for heart attacks and a treatment for childhood leukaemia. Allow the students to carry out their own research or prepare a PowerPoint presentation with a worksheet for the students to complete.

- Carry out the poster activity 'Enzymes in medicine' recommended in the Student Book. It would be quite difficult to include masses of information on one poster so students could decide to make a series of posters about different uses of enzymes, along the lines of 'Did you know that … streptokinase is used to treat heart attacks?' etc. Use could be made of ICT in the design and production of the posters.

- Students could carry out the activity suggested in the Student Book and design an experiment to compare the effectiveness of a biological detergent with an ordinary detergent at 40 °C. Encourage students to think about the variables that need to be controlled and the way in which they are going to assess the results. They should be able to use the knowledge they have gained from setting up the enzyme experiments described in other spreads.

Plenaries

Enzyme anagrams round-up – Prepare anagrams of the enzymes mentioned in this chapter. Students could be supported by using the simpler, straightforward ones. Students could be extended by including more enzymes and/or leaving out the vowels. *(5 minutes)*

The perfect detergent – Students, in groups, could decide on the most favourable properties that a clothes-washing detergent should have and then give it a name and design a simple poster advertising its advantages. There should be good scientific reasons behind the claims made for its efficacy! Posters could be displayed around the classroom. *(10 minutes)*

B2 3.6

High-tech enzymes

Learning objectives

- What are the advantages and disadvantages of using enzymes in detergents?
- Can doctors use enzymes to help keep you healthy?

The pros and cons of biological detergents

For many people, biological washing powders have lots of benefits. Children can be messy eaters and their clothes get lots of mud and grass stains as well. Many of the stains that adults get on their clothes – sweat, food and drink – are biological too. So these enzyme-based washing powders are effective and therefore widely used.

Biological powders have another advantage. They are very effective at cleaning at low temperatures. Therefore they use a lot less electricity than non-biological detergents. That's good for the environment and cheaper for the consumer.

Figure 1 Biological detergents come in many different forms

Figure 2 The enzymes in biological detergents are held in tiny capsules – these are seen under an electron microscope

However, when biological detergent was first manufactured many factory staff developed allergies. They were reacting to enzyme dust in the air – proteins often trigger allergies. Some people using the powders were affected in the same way. But there was a solution – the enzymes were put in tiny capsules and then most of the allergy problems stopped.

Unfortunately, it got bad publicity, which some people still remember. However, research (based on 44 different studies) was published by the British Journal of Dermatology in 2008. This showed that biological detergents do not seem to be a major cause of skin problems.

Some people worry about all the enzymes going into our rivers and seas from biological detergents. The waste water from washing machines goes into the sewage system. Also, the low temperatures used to wash with biological detergents may not be as good at killing pathogens on the clothes.

Practical

Plan and carry out an investigation to compare the effectiveness of a biological detergent with a non-biological detergent at 40°C.

Enzymes and medicine
Some of the ways in which enzymes are used in medicine

TO DIAGNOSE DISEASE

If your liver is damaged or diseased, some of your liver enzymes may leak out into your bloodstream. If your symptoms suggest your liver isn't working properly, doctors can test your blood for these enzymes. This will tell them if your liver really is damaged.

TO DIAGNOSE AND CONTROL DISEASE

People who have diabetes have too much glucose in their blood. As a result, they also get glucose in their urine. One commonly used test for sugar in the urine relies on a colour change on a test strip. The test strip contains a chemical indicator and an enzyme. It is placed in a urine sample. The enzyme catalyses the breakdown of any glucose found in the urine. The strip changes colour if the products of this reaction are present. This shows that glucose was present in the original sample.

TO CURE DISEASE

- If your pancreas is damaged or diseased it cannot make enzymes. So, you have to take extra enzymes – particularly lipase – to allow you to digest your food. The enzymes are in special capsules to stop them being digested in your stomach.
- If you have a heart attack, an enzyme called streptokinase will be injected into your blood as soon as possible. It dissolves clots in the arteries of the heart wall and reduces the amount of damage done to your heart muscle.
- An enzyme is being used to treat a type of blood cancer in children. The cancer cells cannot make one particular amino acid. They need to take it from your body fluids. The enzyme speeds up the breakdown of this amino acid. The cancer cells cannot get any and they die. Your normal cells can make the amino acid so they are not affected.

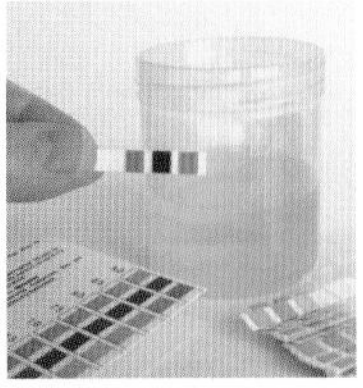

Figure 3 Enzymes are vital in the human body, so it is not surprising that they are widely used in the world of medicine as well

Activity

Make a poster with the title 'Enzymes in medicine' which could be displayed on the walls of the science department to inform and interest students in KS3 and/or KS4. Use this material as a starting point and do some more research about the way enzymes are used, to help you make your poster as interesting as possible.

Key points

- Enzymes in detergents break down biological stains such as sweat. They work at low temperatures so use less electricity, which is cheaper and environmentally friendly. They originally caused problems with allergies, but this has been solved now. The lower-temperature washes are less good at killing pathogens; but higher temperatures can denature the enzymes.
- Enzymes can be produced industrially, both to diagnose and to treat disease.

Summary questions

1 Some people think that biological detergents are better for the environment than non-biological detergents. Why is this?

2 Write a short report on the use of one enzyme in industry or medicine. Explain things such as where the enzyme comes from, what it does, why it is an advantage to use it and what disadvantages there might be.

174

Further teaching suggestions

The differences between detergents
- Students could research the constituents of the biological detergents used in washing machines and those used in dishwashers. Are they different? Are the enzymes the same? Relate the different constituents to the functions of each detergent.

The ethics of using biological detergents
- Get students to consider the ethics of using biological detergents. Do they have effects on the environment? It could be interesting to compare the constituents and claims made for one brand range of cleaning products compared to other brands.

Summary answers

1 Enzymes work best at around 40°C therefore biological detergents are most effective in a cooler wash cycle. This uses less electricity and can therefore be argued to be ecologically more sound.

2 Students should provide information on where the enzyme comes from, what it does, why it is an advantage to use it, what disadvantages there are. Credit given for accuracy, interest and detail in the report.

Summary answers

1 a A vi   B iv   C ii   D i   E iii   F v

b Enzymes work by bringing reacting particles together and lowering the energy needed for them to react. Enzymes are large protein molecules with a hole or indentation known as the 'active site'. The substrate of the reaction fits into the active site of the enzyme like a lock and key. Once it is in place, the enzyme and substrate bind together. This is called the 'enzyme-substrate complex'. Then the reaction takes place rapidly and the products are released from the surface of the enzyme. [The use of diagrams would make this explanation very clear.]

2 a Smooth curve drawn through points and a good graph plot with suitable scale chosen, axes right way round, axes labelled correctly and accurately plotted points.

b Alkaline.

c This enzyme could be found in the small intestine, because it works in alkaline conditions. Other protein-digesting enzymes work in the stomach, but the conditions there are acidic.

3 a Well drawn graph.

b The reaction speeds up with the increase in temperature. Particles moving faster with more energy, so more likely to collide and react.

c A well drawn graph.

d Catalase.

e That it increases the rate up to about 40 °C and after that, the rate of the reaction decreases and eventually stops.

f Manganese(IV) oxide is a chemical and not adversely affected by temperature. Catalyse is an enzyme made of protein – as temperature goes up, the enzyme is denatured, the shape of the active site is lost and it can no longer catalyse the reaction.

g Carry out the test on temperatures around 40 °C to see which temperature took the shortest time.

Kerboodle resources

Resources available for this chapter on Kerboodle are:
- Chapter map: Enzymes
- Animation: Enzyme action (B2 3.1)
- Bump up your grade: Nearly everything about enzymes (B2 3.1)
- How Science Works: Does temperature affect the speed of an enzyme reaction? (B2 3.2)
- How Science Works: Lines of best fit and error bars (B2 3.2)
- Maths skills: Enzymes and rates (B2 3.5)
- Support: Enzyme memory (B2 3.5)
- Extension WebQuest: Enzymes in industry (B2 3.6)
- Practical: Making use of enzymes (B2 3.6)
- Interactive activity: Enzymes
- Revison podcast: Enzymes
- Test yourself: Enzymes
- On your marks: Enzymes
- Practice questions: Enzymes
- Answers to practice questions: Enzymes

Enzymes: B2 3.1–B2 3.6

Summary questions

1 a Copy and complete the following sentences, matching each beginning with its correct ending.

A	A catalyst will speed up a reaction	i	.... could not occur without enzymes.
B	Living organisms make very efficient catalysts	ii	.... made of protein.
C	All enzymes are	iii	.... binds to the active site.
D	The reactions that keep you alive	iv	.... known as enzymes.
E	The substrate of an enzyme	v	.... a specific type of molecule.
F	Each type of enzyme affects	vi	.... but is not changed itself.

b Explain how an enzyme catalyses a reaction. Use diagrams if they make your explanation clearer.

2 The table gives some data about the relative activity levels of an enzyme at different pH levels.

pH	Relative activity
4	0
6	3
8	10
10	1

a Plot a graph of this data.

b Does this enzyme work best in an acid or an alkaline environment?

c This is a protein-digesting enzyme. Where in the gut do you think it might be found? Explain your answer.

3 The results in these tables come from a student who investigating the breakdown of hydrogen peroxide us manganese(IV) oxide and mashed raw potato.

Table 1 Manganese(IV) oxide

Temperature (°C)	Time taken (s)
20	106
30	51
40	26
50	12

Table 2 Raw mashed potato

Temperature (°C)	Time taken (s)
20	114
30	96
40	80
50	120
60	no reaction

a Draw a graph of the results using manganese(IV) oxide.

b What do these results tell you about the effect of temperature on a catalysed reaction? Explain your observation.

c Draw a graph of the results when raw mashed pota was added to the hydrogen peroxide.

d What is the name of the enzyme found in living cell that catalyses the breakdown of hydrogen peroxide

e What does this graph tell you about the effect of temperature on an enzyme-catalysed reaction?

f Why does temperature have this effect on the enzy catalysed reaction but not on the reaction catalyse by manganese(IV) oxide?

g How could you change the second investigation to find the temperature at which the enzyme works be

Practical suggestions

Practicals	AQA	k	📖	⚙️
Design an investigation to find the optimum temperature for biological and non-biological washing powders to remove stains from cotton and other materials.	✓	✓	✓	
Investigate the action of enzymes using catalase at different concentrations and measuring the rate at which oxygen is given off from different foods, e.g. liver, potato, celery and apple.	✓		✓	
Plan and carry out an investigation into enzyme action using the reaction between starch and amylase at different temperatures, pH and concentrations.	✓		✓	
Using small pieces of cooked sausage, use 2% pepsin and 0.01 M HCl in water baths at different temperatures to estimate the rate of digestion. This can also be carried out with 2% trypsin and 0.1 M NaOH. The concentration of both enzymes can be varied.	✓		✓	

Practice questions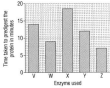

Enzymes are chemicals produced in living cells.

a Copy and complete the following sentences, using some of the words below.

amylase bile catalysts fats lipase protease protein sugars

i Enzymes are described as biological .... (1)
ii Enzyme molecules are made of .... (1)
iii The enzyme that digests starch is called .... (1)
iv The substance that neutralises stomach acid is called .... (1)
v Glycerol is one of the products of the digestion of .... (1)

b An enzyme works well in pH 7.
i What happens to this enzyme when it is placed in an acid solution? (1)
ii Give **one** other factor that will affect the activity of the enzyme. (1)

c Explain what happens to starch when it is digested. (2)

AQA, 2002

Enzymes have many uses in the home and in industry.

a Which type of organisms are used to produce these enzymes?

Choose the correct answer from the following options:

mammals microorganisms plants (1)

b Babies may have difficulty digesting proteins in their food. Baby-food manufacturers use enzymes to 'pre-digest' the protein in baby food to overcome this difficulty.

Copy and complete the following sentences, using some of the words below.

amino acids amylases proteases sugars

i Proteins are 'pre-digested' using enzymes called .... (1)
ii This pre-digestion produces .... (1)

c A baby-food manufacturer uses enzyme **V** to predigest protein.
He tries four new enzymes, **W**, **X**, **Y** and **Z**, to see if he can reduce the time taken to predigest the protein. The graph shows the time taken for the enzymes to completely predigest the protein.
The manufacturer uses the same concentration of enzyme and the same mass of protein in each experiment.

i How long did it take enzyme **V** to predigest the protein? (1)
ii Which enzyme would you advise the baby food manufacturer to use?
Choose the correct answer from the following options:

enzyme V enzyme W enzyme X enzyme Y enzyme Z

Give a reason for your answer. (2)
iii Give **two** factors which should be controlled in the baby-food manufacturer's investigations.
Choose the correct answer from the following options:

oxygen concentration temperature light intensity pH (2)

3 *In this question you will be assessed on using good English, organising information clearly and using specialist terms where appropriate.*

Describe the roles of the liver and pancreas in the digestion of fats. (6)

177

Practicals	**AQA**	k	📖	⚙
Using computer simulations of enzymes to model their action in varying conditions of pH, temperature and concentration.	✓		✓	

Practice answers

1 a i catalysts *(1 mark)*
ii protein *(1 mark)*
iii amylase *(1 mark)*
iv bile *(1 mark)*
v fats *(1 mark)*

b i It is denatured/changes shape does not work as well. *(1 mark)*

ii Temperature *(allow concentration)*. *(1 mark)*

c Large molecules are broken down into small molecules. Starch is changed into sugar. *(2 marks)*

2 a Microorganisms. *(1 mark)*

b i proteases. *(1 mark)*
ii amino acids (both words). *(1 mark)*

c i 14 minutes *(1 mark)*
ii *mark independently*
enzyme Z
It takes the least time (to pre-digest protein)/works fastest.
Allow only 7 minutes/less time/faster
*(do **not** allow works best)*. *(2 marks)*
iii temperature
pH *(2 marks)*

3 There is a clear, balanced and detailed description of the roles of both the liver and pancreas. The answer shows almost faultless spelling, punctuation and grammar. It is coherent and in an organised, logical sequence. It contains a range of appropriate or relevant specialist terms used accurately. *(5–6 marks)*

There is some description of the roles of both the liver and pancreas which lacks some details. There are some errors in spelling, punctuation and grammar. The answer has some structure and organisation. The use of specialist terms has been attempted, but not always accurately. *(3–4 marks)*

There is a brief description reference to the role of either the liver or pancreas. The spelling, punctuation and grammar are very weak. The answer is poorly organised with almost no specialist terms and/or their use demonstrating a general lack of understanding of their meaning. *(1–2 marks)*

No relevant content. *(0 marks)*

Examples of biology points made in the response:
- liver produces bile
- bile neutralises acid
- acid produced by stomach
- pancreas produces lipase
- lipase is an enzyme
- lipase works best in neutral/alkaline conditions
- lipase catalyses the breakdown of fat
- to fatty acids and glycerol
- allow reference to, or a description of emulsification.

B2 4.1

Aerobic respiration

Learning objectives

Students should learn:

- that during aerobic respiration, glucose and oxygen are used to release energy
- how carbon dioxide and water are released as waste products
- that most of the reactions in aerobic respiration occur inside mitochondria.

Learning outcomes

Most students should be able to:

- describe the raw materials and products of the process of respiration
- describe where the reactions take place in cells
- explain why more active cells, such as muscle cells, have greater numbers of mitochondria than less active cells.

Some students should also be able to:

- design experiments independently to show that oxygen is taken up and carbon dioxide is released during aerobic respiration.

Answers to in-text questions

a It provides energy for all the functions of the cells.

b The folded inner membranes provide a large surface for all the enzymes needed to control the reactions of respiration.

Support

- Get students to make model mitochondria from date boxes or washing liquid capsule boxes. They should line them with corrugated cardboard to represent the inner membrane. Fill with used batteries to indicate their role as energy carriers and display on a large poster.
- Give them cards with the components of the word equation for aerobic respiration and get them to assemble the equation.

Extend

- Give students a sheet on the theories of Alan Templeton and Rebecca Cann with regard to 'Mitochondrial Eve' and the origins of the human species. Ask them to summarise points for and against each theory.

Specification link-up: Biology B2.6

- The chemical reactions inside cells are controlled by enzymes. *[B2.6.1 a)]*
- During aerobic respiration (respiration that uses oxygen) chemical reactions occur that:
  - use glucose (a sugar) and oxygen
  - release energy. *[B2.6.1 b)]*
- Aerobic respiration takes place continuously in both plants and animals. *[B2.6.1 c)]*
- Most of the reactions in aerobic respiration take place inside mitochondria. *[B2.6.1 d)]*
- Aerobic respiration is summarised by the equation:
  glucose + oxygen → carbon dioxide + water (+ energy) *[B2.6.1 e)]*
- Energy that is released during respiration is used by the organism. The energy may be used:
  - to build larger molecules from smaller ones
  - in animals, to enable muscles to contract
  - in mammals and birds, to maintain a steady body temperature in colder surroundings
  - in plants, to build up sugars, nitrates and other nutrients into amino acids which are then built up into proteins. *[B2.6.1 f)]*

Controlled Assessment: B4.3 Collect primary and secondary data *[B4.3.2 a)]*; B4.5 Analyse and interpret primary and secondary data. *[B4.5.2 a)]*, *[B4.5.4 a)]*

Lesson structure

Starters

Turning limewater cloudy – Draw crosses on the bottoms of test tubes with a chinagraph pencil. Half-fill each tube with limewater. Give each student a drinking straw (use bendy straws) and a tube of limewater and tell them to blow gently through the straw into the limewater until they can no longer see the cross on the bottom from the top. Eye protection must be worn. Ask: 'How long does it take? What is happening?' Go over the reaction and introduce respiration. *(5 minutes)*

Instant energy – Show glucose drink bottles, energy drinks and energy bars. Read or show their labels and read as a class (search an image bank for 'energy drink label'). Support students by giving them preprinted lists of sugar content and energy and ask to put the products in order of their highest sugar and energy content to the lowest. Extend students by asking them to study the contents and decide which would supply the most energy and which would supply energy the fastest, giving reasons. *(10 minutes)*

Main

- Provide a short, introductory PowerPoint presentation or exposition on the need for energy and the process of aerobic respiration. Build up the word equation, getting students to work out what the raw materials and the products are. Introduce mitochondria and show a diagram and electron micrograph images of mitochondria in cells. Provide the students with a worksheet containing an outline of a mitochondrion which they can complete.
- As a follow-up to the starter 'Turning limewater cloudy', a more refined piece of apparatus can be used to show that the air that is breathed in contains less carbon dioxide than air breathed out (see 'Practical support').
- Investigating respiration using a small mammal or plant (see 'Practical support'). All these experiments need controls, which should be discussed with the students (this relates to 'How Science Works'– validity of experimental design). In most cases, with the bell jar experiments, the removal of the living organism should be considered as a control.

Plenaries

How small can you get it? – Have a competition to see who can fold an A4 sheet of paper into the smallest volume. Ask: 'What is the best method?' Relate to surface area (SA) and cristae in mitochondria. *(5 minutes)*

What do I need energy for? – Ask students to write down as many uses for the energy released by respiration that they can think of. Build up a list on the board. Support students by providing prompts once they have completed their initial list. Extend students by ensuring their lists include references to cell activities and animals other than humans. *(10 minutes)*

Practical support

Composition of inhaled and exhaled air

Equipment and materials required
Test tubes half-full of limewater in racks, test tubes with 2-hole bungs, delivery tubes (one long, one short), rubber tubing, sterile mouth pieces, chinagraph pencil, drinking straws (bendy ones if possible or tubing and clips, eye protection.

Details
Arrange two tubes of limewater, tubing and clips, so that air can be drawn in through one tube containing limewater and breathed out through another tube containing limewater. After a few breaths, it can clearly be seen that the limewater in the two tubes differs in cloudiness.

Investigating respiration using a small mammal or plant

Equipment and materials required
Limewater, soda lime in U-tube, small mammals in a bell jar, potted plant, earthworms, maggots or woodlice, black paper, tubing, air pump, 2 boiling tubes, bungs, delivery tubes, boiling tube rack, eye protection.

Details
A small mammal, or other small living animals, can be placed under a bell jar on a glass plate sealed with Vaseline. Emphasise to the students that the animal has fresh air drawn across it all the time, just with the carbon dioxide removed. Air is drawn through the apparatus, first passing through a U-tube of soda lime (to remove carbon dioxide and then through a tube of limewater (to show that carbon dioxide has been removed before entering the bell jar). After leaving the bell jar, the air is drawn through another tube of limewater to show that carbon dioxide is given off. Any small mammal is usually quite active and a result is achieved fairly quickly. Alternatively, other small animals, such as earthworms, woodlice or maggots can be used in such a demonstration/investigation.

It is possible to substitute a potted plant for the small mammal and to show that carbon dioxide is given off during respiration in plants. The pot and soil of the plant need to be enclosed in a polythene bag and the bell jar needs to be covered in black paper to exclude light. The apparatus should be left running for a couple of days.

● Ask: 'Why is the plant pot covered up? Why is light excluded?'

Safety: CLEAPSS Hazcard 18 Limewater – irritant. CLEAPSS Hazcard 91 Soda lime – corrosive.

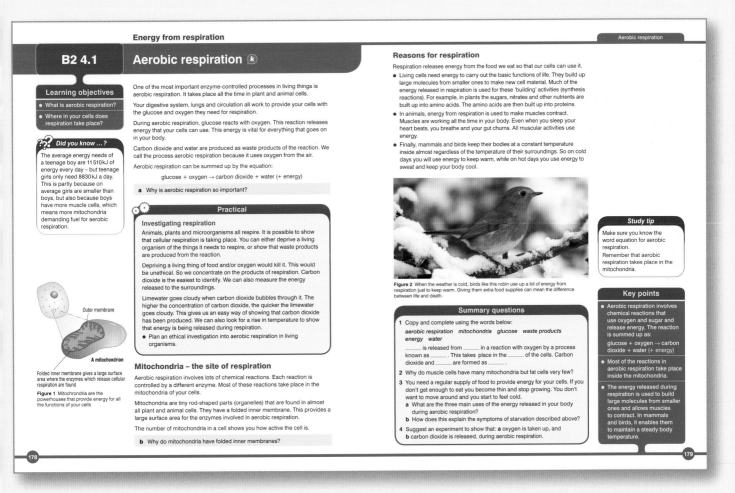

Summary answers

1 energy, glucose, aerobic respiration, mitochondria, water, waste products

2 Muscle cells are very active and need a lot of energy so they need large numbers of mitochondria to supply the energy. Fat cells use very little energy so need very few mitochondria.

3 a The main uses of energy in the body are for movement, building new molecules and heat generation.

b The symptoms of starvation are: people become very thin, stored energy is used up and growth stops, new proteins are not made and there is not enough energy or raw materials, people lack energy, as there is a lack of fuel for the mitochondria, people feel cold, as there is not enough fuel for the mitochondria to produce heat energy.

4 See practical box 'Investigating respiration' in the Student Book. Any sensible suggestions for practical investigations.

B2 4.2

The effect of exercise on the body

Learning objectives

Students should learn:

- that muscles need energy from respiration in order to contract
- that, during exercise, there is an increase in the blood flow to the muscles so more glucose and oxygen is supplied and carbon dioxide removed
- that glycogen provides a store of energy in the muscles.

Learning outcomes

Most students should be able to:

- describe how the body responds to the demands of exercise
- describe how glycogen is used in the body.

Some students should also be able to:

- interpret data on the use of oxygen/ heart rate increase during exercise.
- relate the responses of the body to exercise and the ability of the muscles to contract efficiently.

Specification link-up: Biology B2.6

- Energy that is released during respiration is used by the organism. The energy may be used:
  - to build larger molecules from smaller ones
  - in animals, to enable muscles to contract
  - in mammals and birds, to maintain a steady body temperature in colder surroundings
  - in plants, to build up sugars, nitrates and other nutrients into amino acids which are then built up into proteins. *[B2.6.1 f)]*
- During exercise a number of changes take place:
  - the heart rate increases
  - the rate and depth of breathing increases
  - the arteries supplying the muscles dilate. *[B2.6.1 g)]*
- These changes increase the blood flow to the muscles and so increase the supply of sugar and oxygen and increase the rate of removal of carbon dioxide. *[B2.6.1 h)]*
- Muscles store glucose as glycogen, which can then be converted back to glucose for use during exercise. *[B2.6.1 i)]*
- Interpret the data relating to the effects of exercise on the human body. *[B2.6]*

  Controlled Assessment: B4.1 Plan practical ways to develop and test candidates' own scientific ideas *[B4.1.1 a) b, c)]*; B4.3 Collect primary and secondary data *[B4.3.2 a) b)]*; B4.4 Select and process primary and secondary data *[B4.4.1 a) b)]*, *[B4.4.2 a) b) c)]*; B4.5 Analyse and interpret primary and secondary data. *[B4.5.4 a) c) d)]*

Lesson structure

Starters

Cardiac muscle contraction – Show an MPEG file or a video clip of contracting heart muscle. Discuss what the energy source for this movement will be and the reaction involved. Support students by prompting and extend students by asking how the energy source gets to the muscle and what happens to the waste products. *(5 minutes)*

Exercise … how much do you get? – Show a clip from an old exercise video such as Mr Motivator, with some good 1980s clothes to have a laugh at. Also, show some footage of modern gym clubs. Carry out a quick survey to find out the health and exercise activities of the class members and their families. *(10 minutes)*

Support

- Create and use jigsaw sheets of the human body and the changes which happen due to exercise. Blank jigsaw sheets can be bought or you can make your own. Support students by offering clues if necessary.

Extend

- Tell students that a young woman has been found dead in a field. No one knows her identity. Students could write a letter of advice from a pathologist telling the police what they can find out about her exercise habits and lifestyle from her corpse, to aid with her identification.
- Get them to calculate the percentage changes in the parameters measured in the table in the Student Book and to comment on the significance of these changes.

Main

- Investigate the effect of exercise on heart rate (see 'Practical support'). There are many variations on this investigation that can be carried out:
  - The intensity of the exercise can be varied.
  - The increase in breathing rate (number of breaths per minutes) can be investigated either separately from the pulse rate or in conjunction with it.
  - In addition to the performance of individuals, comparisons could be made between members of the class who exercise regularly and those who do not.
- This investigation can be used for teaching/assessing 'How Science Works': hypotheses can be formulated and predictions made, measurements taken and results tabulated, graphs produced and conclusions drawn, finishing with an evaluation. This can deliver the complete range of investigative requirements from which to choose a skill or skills to develop.
- Digital pulse monitors can be used and it is possible to use data loggers and get live read-out graphs that can be displayed through a projector.

Plenaries

Animal starch – Glycogen has been referred to as 'animal starch'. Ask students to compile two lists: one headed 'similarities to starch' and the other headed 'differences from starch'. Stress that it is not starch and that animals do not store starch. Support students by giving them a number of straightforward statements about the two molecules which they have to sort into the correct list. Extend students by encouraging them to include differences in structure, location and use. They could continue the task for homework. *(5 minutes)*

'Unfit' club – Imagine an 'Unfit' club, where the membership rules included the banning of exercise. Write down instructions for the club's Unfitness Enforcers, giving a list of telltale signs that would indicate the person being investigated has been exercising. Use imagination and illustration, being careful regarding the size sensitivity of some students. *(10 minutes)*

Practical support

Testing fitness
Equipment and materials required
The practical activities suggested in this spread do not require complex apparatus. The pulse and breathing rate investigations simply require stopwatches or stop-clocks. If a spirometer is used, then follow the instructions supplied with it.

Details
This is best carried out in pairs, so that students can record each other's pulse rates. Before starting, the students should decide on the level and period of exercise. The simplest investigation could concentrate on one level of exercise, such as walking on the spot for a set time. The resting pulse rate in beats per minute should be determined (count beats in 15 seconds and then multiply by 4). Show the students how to do this either using the radial artery on their wrists, using the carotid artery in the neck or a pulse rate monitor. Ideally, this should be done three times and a mean taken. The student then undertakes the exercise and the pulse rate recorded immediately and at set intervals, such as every minute afterwards, until the rate returns to normal. A graph can be plotted of heart/pulse rate against time. The students exchange roles.

Safety: Students should exercise sensibly.

Energy from respiration

B2 4.2
The effect of exercise on the body

Learning objectives
- How does your body respond to the increased demands for oxygen during exercise?
- What is glycogen and how is it used in the body?

Your muscles use a lot of energy. They move you around and help support your body against gravity. Your heart is made of muscle and pumps blood around your body. The movement of food along your gut depends on muscles too.

Muscle tissue is made up of protein fibres. These contract when they are supplied with energy from respiration. Muscle fibres need a lot of energy to contract. They contain many mitochondria to carry out aerobic respiration and supply the energy needed.

Muscle fibres usually occur in big blocks or groups known as muscles, which contract to cause movement. They then relax, which allows other muscles to work.

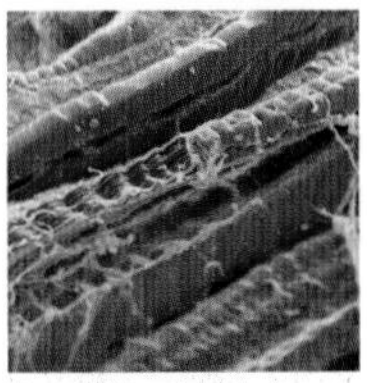

Your muscles also store glucose as the carbohydrate **glycogen**. Glycogen can be converted rapidly back to glucose to use during exercise. The glucose is used in aerobic respiration to provide the energy to make your muscles contract:

glucose + oxygen → carbon dioxide + water (+ energy)

a What is aerobic respiration?

The response to exercise
Even when you are not moving about your muscles use up a certain amount of oxygen and glucose. However, when you begin to exercise, many muscles start contracting harder and faster. As a result they need more glucose and oxygen to supply their energy needs. During exercise the muscles also produce increased amounts of carbon dioxide. This needs to be removed for muscles to keep working effectively.

b Why do you need more energy when you exercise?

So during exercise, when muscular activity increases, several changes take place in your body:

- Your heart rate increases and the arteries supplying blood to your muscles dilate (widen). These changes increase the blood flow to your exercising muscles. This in turn increases the supply of oxygen and glucose to the muscles. It also increases the rate that carbon dioxide is removed from the muscles.
- Your breathing rate increases and you breathe more deeply. So you breathe more often and also bring more air into your lungs each time you breathe in. More oxygen is brought into your body and picked up by your red blood cells. This oxygen is carried to your exercising muscles. It also means that more carbon dioxide can be removed from the blood in the lungs and breathed out.

c Why do you produce more carbon dioxide when you are exercising hard?

Figure 1 All the work done by the muscles is based on these special protein fibres, which contract when they work and relax afterwards

The benefits of exercise
Your heart and lungs benefit from regular exercise. Both the heart and the lungs become larger. They both develop a bigger and more efficient blood supply. This means they function as effectively as possible, whether you are exercising or not. Look at the table below.

Table 1 A comparison of heart and lung functions before and after getting fit

	Before getting fit	After getting fit
Amount of blood pumped out of the heart during each beat at rest (cm³)	64	80
Volume of the heart at rest (cm³)	120	140
Resting breathing rate at rest (breaths/min)	14	12
Resting pulse rate (beats/min)	72	63
Maximum lung volume (cm³)	1000	1200

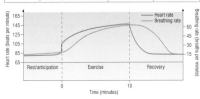

Figure 2 During exercise the heart rate and breathing rate increase to supply the muscles with what they need and remove the extra waste produced. The maximum rate to which you should push your heart is usually calculated as approximately 220 beats per minute minus your age. When you exercise, you should ideally get your heart rate into the range between 60 per cent and 90 per cent of your maximum.

Practical

Testing fitness
A good way of telling how fit you are is to measure your resting heart rate and breathing rate. The fitter you are, the lower they will be. Then see what happens when you exercise. The increase in your heart rate and breathing rate and how fast they return to normal is another way of finding out how fit you are – or aren't!

Summary questions
1 Using Figure 2, describe the effect of exercise on the heart rate and the breathing rate of a fit person and explain why these changes happen.
2 Plan an investigation into the fitness levels of your classmates. Describe how you might carry out this investigation and explain what you would expect the results to be.

Study tip
- Be clear about the difference between the rate and the depth of breathing.
- Be clear about the difference between the breathing rate and the rate of respiration.

Key points
- The energy that is released during respiration is used to enable muscles to contract.
- When you use your muscles you need more glucose and oxygen and produce more carbon dioxide.
- Body responses to exercise include:
  - an increase in heart rate, in breathing rate and in depth of breathing
  - glycogen stores in the muscle are converted to glucose for cellular respiration
  - the blood flow to your muscles increases.
- These act to increase the supply of glucose and oxygen to the muscle and remove more carbon dioxide.

Further teaching suggestions

Glycogen and its importance
- Introduce the structure of glycogen and its importance as a storage carbohydrate in the liver and the muscles. Link with its role in the maintenance of a steady level of glucose in the blood. Students can be reminded of the conversion of glucose to glycogen, stimulated by the release of insulin and the conversion of glycogen to glucose when the glucose levels in the blood decrease.

Answers to in-text questions
a Aerobic respiration is the complete breakdown of glucose using oxygen to release energy with carbon dioxide and water as waste products:

Glucose + oxygen → energy + carbon dioxide + water

b Your muscles are contracting harder for longer, so you need more energy.

c The muscles are contracting more, therefore using more energy. There is more aerobic respiration and more carbon dioxide produced. This is a waste product of the process.

Summary answers

1 **Heart rate:** increases before exercise starts as a result of anticipation. It rises rapidly, followed by a steady rise and then falls quite sharply as the exercise finishes. Increased heart rate supplies muscles with the extra blood they need to bring glucose/sugar and oxygen to the muscle fibres, and to remove the carbon dioxide which rapidly builds up.

Breathing rate: increases more slowly and evenly than the heart rate, but remains high for some time after exercise. To begin with, increased heart rate supplies enough oxygen, then the breathing rate needs to increase to meet demand. When exercise stops, breathing rate remains high until the oxygen debt is paid off.

2 [Mark depending on ideas presented when predicting results. Look for clear, sensible ideas, safe investigation, realistic expectations, appropriate methods of recording and analysing, awareness of weakness in investigation. Look also for clear understanding of independent, dependent and control variables].

B2 4.3

Anaerobic respiration

Learning objectives

Students should learn:

- that during long periods of vigorous activity, muscles respire anaerobically in order to obtain energy
- that less energy is released by anaerobic respiration than aerobic respiration [HT only]
- that during anaerobic respiration, incomplete breakdown of glucose results in the formation of lactic acid and the building up of an oxygen debt. [HT only]

Learning outcomes

Most students should be able to:

- explain why muscles respire anaerobically during vigorous exercise
- explain why less energy is released by anaerobic respiration [HT only]
- describe the oxygen debt and how it is repaid. [HT only]

Some students should also be able to:

- interpret data relating to the effects of exercise on the human body [HT only]
- explain the principle of oxygen debt and why speed of recovery from exercise is a measure of physical fitness. [HT only]

Answers to in-text questions

a Anaerobic respiration does not use oxygen; incomplete breakdown of glucose/sugars; lactic acid is the end product instead of carbon dioxide and water.

b The amount of oxygen needed to break down the lactic acid built up during a period of anaerobic respiration.

Support

- Make cards with the relevant words and symbols for students to compose equations for aerobic and anaerobic respiration.

Extend

- Ask students to research the differences between the different energy systems used by muscles. Get them to find out the differences in the training programmes of sprinters and marathon runners.

Specification link-up: Biology B2.6

- During exercise, if insufficient oxygen is reaching the muscles, they use anaerobic respiration to obtain energy. [B2.6.2 a)]
- Anaerobic respiration is the incomplete breakdown of glucose and produces lactic acid. [B2.6.2 b)]
- As the breakdown of glucose is incomplete, much less energy is released than during aerobic respiration. Anaerobic respiration results in an oxygen debt that has to be repaid in order to oxidise lactic acid to carbon dioxide and water. [B2.6.2 c)] [HT only]
- If muscles are subjected to long periods of vigorous activity, they become fatigued, i.e. they stop contracting efficiently. One cause of muscle fatigue is the build up of lactic acid in the muscles. Blood flowing through the muscles removes the lactic acid. [B2.6.2 d)]

Controlled Assessment: B4.1 Plan practical ways to develop and test candidates' own scientific ideas [B4.1.1 a) b) c)]; B4.3 Collect primary and secondary data [B4.3.2 a) b)]; B4.4 Select and process primary and secondary data. [B4.4.1 a) b)], [B4.4.2 a) b) c)]

Lesson structure

Starters

Wile E. Coyote and Road Runner – Show the students a video clip of Wile E. Coyote and Road Runner at the start of the episode 'Lickety Splat' – the first minute or so where Wile E. runs very hard and gets out of breath. This can be found on the internet. Draw out a thumbnail sketch of the graph you would expect of his breathing rate against time, labelling what is happening in each section. (5 minutes)

Sprinting! – Show a video of a 100 m sprint (from the Olympics or the World Championships), where the athletes are shown immediately before and afterwards. Get students to observe the behaviour of the athletes. Comment on breathing, whether they collapse, etc. Support students by asking questions such as: 'Are they breathing deeply? Can they talk?' Extend students by getting them to make their observations without prompting and expecting more detailed comments and reasons. (10 minutes)

Main

- Take the opportunity of clearing up the mistaken idea that it is lactic acid building up in muscles which makes them sore – this is not so! Lactate is actually used as a fuel by the mitochondria and makes no contribution to soreness/stiffness afterwards. Explain to extension level students that the actual reason for the acidification during exercise is the build up of H^+ ions which are released during the break down of ATP to ADP + P_i. They are produced so fast, they overcome the body's buffering mechanism and cause painful burning sensations.
- Practical on making lactic acid (see 'Practical support' for full details).
- There are variations on this investigation that can be discussed and students could be asked to design a standard test that everyone could do, and this could be used to determine whether muscle fatigue varied from person to person. For example, the same action could be carried out for a set time and a set recovery time allowed. Students could find out if they could continue longer doing that, rather than carrying out the investigation as first suggested.
- If the variation in breathing rate with activity was not used in the previous spread, it could be investigated here. (This relates to 'How Science Works'.) Again, it would be sensible for students to work in pairs, so that the record keeping is done by the partner, and then the roles can be reversed. In this case, it could be appropriate to vary the intensity of the exercise, starting with walking on the spot, then running on the spot and so on. Carry out the exercise for a set time and record breathing rates until they return to normal, before starting on a more vigorous exercise.

Plenaries

The long distance runner – Show video footage of a long-distance race, at the beginning, during and at the end. Students to observe the behaviour of the athletes and compare with the sprint shown as a starter. Ask: 'Do the athletes seem so out of breath? Or are they breathing as deeply?' Discuss why there are differences in behaviour. (5 minutes)

Energy yields – Anaerobic respiration in yeast cells produces alcohol. Show students that there is energy locked up in alcohol by igniting some in controlled conditions (could use it in a spirit lamp or similar). Link to the energy still in lactic acid. Get students to compare the energy yields of aerobic and anaerobic respiration. Support students by giving them the figures which they could represent in a simple way. Extend students by comparing the structures of glucose, lactic acid, alcohol and carbon dioxide, in terms of the numbers of C, H and O atoms in the molecules. (10 minutes)

Practical support

Making lactic acid

Equipment and materials required
Stopwatches, stop-clocks or a spirometer.

Details
Students should work in pairs and devise a simple repetitive action, such as stepping up and down on to a low bench, lifting a book from the bench to shoulder height or raising one arm and clenching and unclenching the fist twice a second. One student should perform

the action as many times as they can before tiring, while the other student keeps a record of the number of actions and the time.

A period of recovery time is allowed – the student to decide when they are ready to resume the activity, but record the time. Ask: 'Can they do the same number of actions before tiring again? Are they performing the action at the same speed as before? Why does the student slow down?'

Safety: No student should feel under pressure to take part in any of the activities, particularly if they have any medical condition. If a spirometer is used, follow the instructions given in CLEAPSS Handbook CD-ROM section 14.5.

Energy from respiration

Anaerobic respiration

B2 4.3 Anaerobic respiration

Learning objectives
- Why do muscles use anaerobic respiration to obtain energy?
- Why is less energy released by anaerobic respiration than aerobic respiration? [H]
- What is an oxygen debt? [H]

Your everyday muscle movements use energy released by aerobic respiration. However, when you exercise hard your muscle cells may become short of oxygen. Although you increase your heart and breathing rates, sometimes the blood cannot supply oxygen to the muscles fast enough. When this happens the muscle cells can still get energy from glucose. They use anaerobic respiration, which takes place without oxygen.

In anaerobic respiration the glucose is not broken down completely. It produces lactic acid instead of carbon dioxide and water.

If you are fit, your heart and lungs will be able to keep a good supply of oxygen going to your muscles while you exercise. If you are unfit, your muscles will run short of oxygen much sooner.

a How does anaerobic respiration differ from aerobic respiration?

Muscle fatigue K
Using your muscle fibres vigorously for a long time can make them become fatigued. This means they stop contracting efficiently. One cause of muscle fatigue is the build up of lactic acid. It is made by anaerobic respiration in the muscle cells. Blood flowing through the muscles removes the lactic acid.

Figure 1 Training hard is the simplest way to avoid anaerobic respiration. When you are fit you can get oxygen to your muscles and remove carbon dioxide more efficiently.

Figure 2 Repeated movements can soon lead to anaerobic respiration in your muscles – particularly if you're not used to it

Anaerobic respiration is not as efficient as aerobic respiration. This is because the glucose molecules are not broken down completely. So far less energy is released than during aerobic respiration.

The end product of anaerobic respiration is lactic acid and this leads to the release of a small amount of energy, instead of the carbon dioxide and water plus lots of energy released by aerobic respiration.

Anaerobic respiration:

glucose → lactic acid (+ energy)

Oxygen debt
If you have been exercising hard, you often carry on puffing and panting for some time after you stop. The length of time you remain out of breath depends on how fit you are. But why do you keeping breathing faster and more deeply when you have stopped using your muscles?

The waste lactic acid you produce during anaerobic respiration is a problem. You cannot simply get rid of lactic acid by breathing it out as you can with carbon dioxide. As a result, when the exercise is over lactic acid has to be broken down to produce carbon dioxide and water. This needs oxygen.

The amount of oxygen needed to break down the lactic acid to carbon dioxide and water is known as the oxygen debt.

After a race, your heart rate and breathing rate stay high to supply the extra oxygen needed to pay off the oxygen debt. The bigger the debt (the larger the amount of lactic acid), the longer you will puff and pant!

Oxygen debt repayment:

lactic acid + oxygen → carbon dioxide + water

Figure 3 Everyone gets an oxygen debt if they exercise hard, but if you are fit you can pay it off faster

b What is an oxygen debt?

?? Did you know ...?
In a 100m sprint some athletes do not breathe at all. This means that the muscles use the oxygen taken in before the start of the race and then don't get any more oxygen until the race is over. Although the race only takes a few seconds, a tremendous amount of energy is used up so a big oxygen debt can develop, even though the athletes are very fit.

Practical

Making lactic acid
Carry out a single repetitive action such as stepping up and down or lifting a weight or a book from the bench to your shoulder time after time or even just clenching and unclenching your fist. You will soon feel the effect of a build up of lactic acid in your muscles.
- How can you tell when your muscles have started to respire anaerobically?

Summary questions

1 Define the following terms:
   aerobic respiration   anaerobic respiration   lactic acid

2 If you exercise very hard or for a long time, your muscles begin to ache and do not work so effectively. Explain why.

3 If you exercise very hard, you often puff and pant for some time after you stop. Explain what is happening. [H]

Key points
- If muscles work hard for a long time they become fatigued and don't contract efficiently. If they don't get enough oxygen they will respire anaerobically.
- Anaerobic respiration is respiration without oxygen. Glucose is incompletely broken down to form lactic acid.
- The anaerobic breakdown of glucose releases less energy than aerobic respiration. [H]
- After exercise, oxygen is still needed to break down the lactic acid which has built up. The amount of oxygen needed is known as the oxygen debt. [H]

182

183

Further teaching suggestions

Review of aerobic and anaerobic respiration
- It could be useful to students to review both types of respiration by building up a table of the differences between aerobic and anaerobic respiration.

Measuring respiration in yeast
- Use carbon dioxide sensors to measure respiration in yeast.

Respiration in plants and microorganisms
- It could be instructive to students to consider respiration in other organisms. In microorganisms, for example, there are types that are strictly aerobic, strictly anaerobic and those that can respire aerobically if oxygen is present and anaerobically if oxygen is absent. Discuss the importance of these organisms and their possible locations.

Summary answers

1 **Aerobic respiration:** respiration using oxygen.

   Anaerobic respiration: respiration that does not use oxygen and releases less energy than aerobic respiration.

   Lactic acid: The chemical produced in animal cells during anaerobic respiration of glucose.

2 The muscles become fatigued. After a long period of exercise, your muscles become short of oxygen and switch from aerobic to anaerobic respiration, which is less efficient. The glucose molecules are not broken down completely, so less energy is released than during aerobic respiration. The

end products of anaerobic respiration are lactic acid and a small amount of energy.

3 The waste lactic acid you produce during exercise as a result of anaerobic respiration has to be broken down to produce carbon dioxide and water. This needs oxygen, and the amount of oxygen needed to break down the lactic acid is known as the oxygen debt. Even though your leg muscles have stopped, your heart rate and breathing rate stay high to supply extra oxygen, until you have broken down all the lactic acid and paid off the oxygen debt.

Summary answers

1 **a** Award marks for standard of graphs, axes, etc.

b As the peas start to grow, they began to respire aerobically. As a result, a small amount of heat energy is produced so the temperature increased.

c Because the seeds were dry and not growing, so no respiration occurred or heat produced.

d As a control level.

e Any reasonable explanation, e.g. The important thing about flask C is that peas are dead so temperature for first five days remains at 20°C as they are not respiring. peas had gone mouldy and mould respiring so temperature goes up, anomaly: Sun on thermometer, poor reading, etc.

2 **a** [Credit will be given in the subsequent answers for extracting and using the information on the bar charts.]

b **i** Increased fitness means that the heart has a greater volume and pumps more blood at each beat. The heart therefore beats more slowly at rest.

ii Increased fitness affects the lungs by lowering the breathing rate.

3 **a** Both people are exercising hard. The fit person's breathing rate goes up more slowly, it doesn't go as high and it comes down faster than the unfit person.

b The breathing of the fit person doesn't need to increase immediately as their fit heart will simply pump more blood to the muscles. Their lungs will be larger than those of an unfit person so they will not need to breathe as quickly, and because they can keep their muscles better supplied with blood and oxygen, they will not fatigue as quickly. They won't build up such a large oxygen debt, so their breathing will return to normal faster.

c They could exercise more regularly and build up their own levels of fitness. Then their heart and lung capacity would increase and they would not get as breathless when they exercised.

4 **a** The complete breakdown of glucose using oxygen to produce carbon dioxide, water and energy.

b Aerobic respiration produces more energy to allow the muscles to contract more efficiently, so athletes want it to continue as long as possible before changing to less efficient anaerobic respiration.

c Red blood cells carry oxygen to the tissues, so if you have more red blood cells, you have more oxygen so aerobic respiration continues longer and muscles work more effectively.

d It increases the red blood cells in the body just before a performance and so allows more oxygen to be carried to the working muscles.

e They start anaerobic respiration where glucose is incompletely broken down to form lactic acid. Less energy is produced and the lactic acid can cause muscle fatigue.

f Any thoughtful opinion about the situation.

Summary questions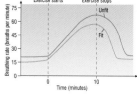

1 Edward and Jess wanted to investigate the process of cellular respiration. They set up three vacuum flasks. One contained live, soaked peas. One contained dry peas. One contained peas which had been soaked and then boiled. They took daily observations of the temperature in each flask for a week. The results are shown in the table.

Day	Room temperature (°C)	Temperature in flask A containing live, soaked peas (°C)	Temperature in flask B containing dry peas (°C)	Temperature in flask C containing soaked, boiled peas (°C)
1	20.0	20.0	20.0	20.0
2	20.0	20.5	20.0	20.0
3	20.0	21.0	20.0	20.0
4	20.0	21.5	20.0	20.0
5	20.0	22.0	20.0	20.0
6	20.0	22.2	20.0	20.5
7	20.0	22.5	20.0	21.0

a Plot a graph to show these results.

b Explain the results in flask A containing the live, soaked peas.

c Why were the results in flask B the same as the room temperature readings?

d Why did Edward and Jess record room temperature in the lab every day?

e How would you explain the results seen in flask C? Why is the temperature at 20°C for the first five days? Give two possible explanations why the temperature then increases.

2 It is often said that taking regular exercise and getting fit is good for your heart and your lungs.

	Before getting fit	After getting fit
Amount of blood pumped out of the heart during each beat (cm³)	64	80
Heart volume (cm³)	120	140
Breathing rate (breaths/ min)	14	12
Pulse rate (beats/min)	72	63

a The table shows the effect of getting fit on the heart and lungs of one person. Display this data in four bar charts.

b Use the information on your bar charts to explain exactly what effect increased fitness has on:
i your heart
ii your lungs.

3 Look at the graph that shows the difference between fit and unfit person and the time taken to repay oxygen debt.

a Explain what is happening to both people.

b Why is the graph for the unfit person different from graph for the fit person?

c What could the unfit person do to change their bo responses to be more like those of the fit person?

4 Athletes want to be able to use their muscles aerobic for as long as possible when they compete. They tra to develop their heart and lungs. Many athletes also train at altitude. There is less oxygen in the air so you body makes more red blood cells, which helps to ave oxygen debt. Sometimes athletes remove some of th own blood, store it and then just before a competition transfuse it back into their system. This is called bloo doping and it is illegal. Other athletes use hormones stimulate the growth of extra red blood cells. This is a illegal.

a What is aerobic respiration?

b Why do athletes want to be able to use their musc aerobically for as long as possible?

c How does developing more red blood cells by trai at altitude help athletic performance?

d How does blood doping help performance?

e Explain in detail what happens to the muscles in you body cannot supply enough glucose and oxygen when they are working hard.

f It is legal to train at altitude but illegal to carry out blood doping or to take hormones that stimulate th development of red blood cells. What do you think about this situation?

Kerboodle resources

Resources available for this chapter on Kerboodle are:

- Chapter map: Energy from respiration
- Support: Respiration (B2 4.1)
- Video: Exercise (B2 4.2)
- How Science Works: Displaying and interpreting data (B2 4.2)
- Bump up your grade: Glucose-enriched drinks – sweets? (B2 4.2)
- Practical: Measuring pulse rate before and after exercise (B2 4.2)
- How Science Works: How quickly do muscles fatigue? (B2 4.3)
- Extension: The cyanide deadline (B2 4.3)
- Interactive activity: Energy from respiration
- Revision podcast: Energy from respiration
- Test yourself: Energy from respiration
- On your marks: Energy from respiration
- Practice questions: Energy from respiration
- Answers to practice questions: Energy from respiration

End of chapter questions

actice questions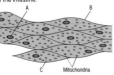

he diagram shows a group of muscle cells from the wall f the intestine.

Choose the correct words to name the structures labelled **A**, **B** and **C**.

cell membrane cell wall chloroplast cytoplasm nucleus (3)

Suggest **two** ways that these muscle cells are adapted to release a lot of energy? (2)

espiration is a chemical process.

Where does respiration take place? Choose the correct answer.

chloroplasts mitochondria nuclei ribosomes (1)

Which food material is used in respiration? (1)

Name the **two** waste materials that are produced in respiration. (2)

Respiration is important in muscle contraction. Explain why. (2)

Copy and complete the word equation for aerobic respiration.

oxygen + ... → water + ... (+ energy) (2)

i Which substance is missing in anaerobic respiration? (1)

ii What is made during anaerobic respiration? (1)

iii Muscles get tired during anaerobic respiration. Explain why. (1)

④ An athlete started a fitness programme. He was advised to eat a diet containing 18 000 kJ per day.

a The athlete was told that 80% of this energy was needed to keep his body temperature at normal levels. Calculate the remaining number of kilojoules available to the athlete. Show your working. (2)

b The athlete decided to double his amount of exercise and assumed he should increase the number of kilojoules in his diet.
Using only the information available to the athlete, calculate the extra energy he is likely to need. (1)

c The energy supplied in the diet must be transferred to the muscles.
Explain in detail this process of energy transfer to the muscles. (4)

⑤ In this question you will be assessed on using good English, organising information clearly and using specialist terms where appropriate.

The bar charts show what happens in an athlete's muscles when running in two races of different distances.

The equations show two processes that occur in muscle cells.

aerobic respiration	glucose + oxygen → carbon dioxide + water
anaerobic respiration	glucose → lactic acid

Use all the information to explain what happens in the athlete's muscles when running in the two races. (6)

185

Practice answers

1 a A nucleus
B (cell) membrane
C cytoplasm *(3 marks)*

b any **two** from
- (contain) mitochondria
- many (mitochondria)
- respiration (occurs in mitochondria) *(2 marks)*

2 a mitochondria *(1 mark)*

b glucose *(1 mark)*

c carbon dioxide and water *(either order)* *(2 marks)*

d energy is released which is then used for movement *(2 marks)*

3 a glucose, carbon dioxide *(2 marks)*

b i oxygen *(1 mark)*
ii lactic acid *(1 mark)*
iii less energy is released. This energy is needed for muscle contraction/movement *(1 mark)*

4 a 3600 *(2 marks)*
(If answer incorrect allocate 1 mark for working
$18\,000 - \dfrac{18\,000}{100} \times 80$ *)*

b 21 600 *(1 mark)*

c respiration uses oxygen/is aerobic glucose/sugar is broken down in the mitochondria to release energy for muscle contraction. *(4 marks)*

5 There is a clear, balanced and detailed explanation about the differences between the two races in terms of aerobic and anaerobic respiration. The answer shows almost faultless spelling, punctuation and grammar. It is coherent and in an organised, logical sequence. It contains a range of appropriate or relevant specialist terms used accurately.
(5–6 marks)

There is some attempt to explain the differences between the two races in terms of respiration. There are some errors in spelling, punctuation and grammar. The answer has some structure and organisation. The use of specialist terms has been attempted, but not always accurately. *(3–4 marks)*

There is a brief description of the differences between the two races. The spelling, punctuation and grammar are very weak. The answer is poorly organised with almost no specialist terms and/or their use demonstrating a general lack of understanding of their meaning. *(1–2 marks)*

No relevant content. *(0 marks)*

Examples of biology points made in the response:
- energy transferred faster in 100 m race
- carbon dioxide produced faster during 1500 m race/more
- carbon dioxide produced
- correct reference to twice/half as fast in either/both cases
- respiration during 100 m race (mainly) anaerobic
- respiration during 1500 m race (mainly) aerobic
- aerobic respiration produced carbon dioxide
- anaerobic respiration produced lactic acid.

Practical suggestions

Practicals	AQA	k	📖	⚙
Investigating the rate of respiration in yeast using carbon dioxide sensors and dataloggers.	✓		✓	
Investigating the effect of exercise on pulse rate, either physically or using pulse sensors and data loggers.	✓	✓	✓	
Investigating the link between exercise and breathing rate with a breathing sensor.	✓		✓	
Investigating holding masses at arm's length and timing how long it takes the muscles to fatigue.	✓		✓	
Designing an investigation using force meters and dataloggers to find the relationship between the amount of force exerted by a muscle and muscle fatigue.	✓	✓	✓	

B2 5.1 Cell division and growth

Learning objectives

Students should learn:

- that mitosis results in the production of additional cells for growth, repair and replacement
- that before each cell division, the genetic information on the chromosomes is copied so that the new cells have the same genes as the parent cells
- that most animal cells differentiate at an early stage but most plant cells have the ability to differentiate throughout life.

Learning outcomes

Most students should be able to:

- understand that mitosis results in the production of new cells
- describe the process of mitosis
- describe how the cells produced by mitosis differentiate in plants and animals.

Some students should also be able to:

- explain why plants retain the ability to grow throughout their lives whereas cell division in mature animals is involved in repair and replacement of tissues.

Support

- Give a student two short pieces of modelling clay of one colour and two long ones of another colour. These are placed inside a ring of string representing the cell. Give the students balls of modelling clay and tell them to make copies of each and pass a set to two other students who do the same. Do this until the whole class has been involved and there are many copies inside string rings on the floor. This works well in a gym.

Extend

- Introduce students to the names of the stages of mitosis as an introduction to AS-level work.

Specification link-up: Biology B2.7

- In body cells, the chromosomes are normally found in pairs. Body cells divide by mitosis. *[B2.7.1 a)]*
- The chromosomes contain the genetic information. *[B2.7.1 b)]*
- When a body cell divides by mitosis:
  - copies of the genetic material are made
  - then the cell divides once to form two genetically identical body cells. *[B2.7.1 c)]*
- Mitosis occurs during growth or to produce replacement cells. *[B2.7.1 d)]*
- Body cells have two sets of chromosomes: sex cells (gametes) have only one set. *[B2.7.1 e)]*
- Most types of animal cells differentiate at an early stage, whereas many plant cells retain the ability to differentiate throughout life. In mature animals, cell division is mainly restricted to repair and replacement. *[B2.7.1 j)]*
- The cells of the offspring produced by asexual reproduction are produced by mitosis from the parental cells. They contain the same alleles as the parents. *[B2.7.1 n)]*
  Controlled Assessment: B4.4 Select and process primary and secondary data. *[B4.4.2 c)]*

Lesson structure

Starters

Matching exercise – Give each student pieces of paper with 'cell', 'nucleus', 'chromosome', 'gene' and 'DNA' on them, plus definitions all muddled up. They have to join them correctly. *(5 minutes)*

Growth, repair or replacement? – Get students to write three headings in their notebooks: Growth, Repair and Replacement. Get them to think about where in their bodies cells are produced for growth, repair and replacement. They should write down the name of the organ or the region of the body where each might occur. Support students by prompting them with clues or by giving them a list of organs and sites to sort into the correct columns. Extend students by asking them to add the circumstances under which new cells are produced. Expect these students to recognise that some new growth takes place all the time (hair, fingernails) whereas growth in height does not. Discuss and lead students to the idea that the same genetic information needs to be passed on to the new cells and that the type of division producing these identical cells is mitosis. *(10 minutes)*

Main

- Observing mitosis – This can be done using prepared longitudinal sections of root tips, or the students can make their own root tip squashes. A number of different sources will give suitable root tips, although it is a good idea to choose something that does not have a large diploid number of chromosomes. Germinating broad bean or pea seeds work well, or the tips of roots produced from hyacinth or garlic bulbs suspended in water. (See 'Practical support').
- Students may require help mounting their root tips and in using microscopes. It may be useful to create a list for students with the details of the preparation on it. This could be accompanied by a series of diagrams or photographs showing stages so that they can have a go at identifying stages on their own slides. If a space is left beside each stage, then the students could make a sketch of what they can see on their slides. They do not need to know the names of the stages.
- Cloning a cauliflower – Students could try cloning for themselves (see 'Practical support').

Plenaries

Mitosis dominoes – In groups of four, play a dominoes-style game showing the stages of mitosis and a general description. No details, i.e. named stages, are required. *(5 minutes)*

Growing points – Using a small potted plant, remove all the leaves, so that the growing point (main bud and the buds in the axils of the leaves are left. Give the students a diagram of the plant with all the leaves pulled off. Support students by telling them where the growing points are, get them to mark them and then to draw in what they think the plant will look like in a couple of weeks. Extend students by asking them to indicate the positions of the growing points and then to draw in what they think will happen. Ask them to make a list of the different tissues that will be produced (reinforcing the idea that undifferentiated cells, similar to stem cells in animals, are produced and are capable of differentiating into the different tissues). Keep the plant in the lab and look at it when the time is up. *(10 minutes)*

Practical support

Observing mitosis

Equipment and materials required
Root tips of beans, peas, onions, garlic or other suitable material, dilute acetic orsein stain and dilute hydrochloric acid, watch glasses, heater/spirit lamp/hotplate, mounted needles, microscope slides and cover slips, blotting paper, microscopes.

Details
5 mm lengths of the root tips should be cut off and placed in a watch glass containing acetic orcein stain and hydrochloric acid. This should be warmed gently for 5 minutes. The tip is then placed on a microscope slide with a few drops of the stain, teased out with a pair of mounted needles and then covered with a cover slip. Cover with blotting paper and press gently to spread out the cells.

Safety: Care with the handling of stains and acids. Wear eye protection and wash hands if in contact with chemicals.

Cloning a cauliflower

Equipment and materials required
One of: a 3 mm tip of an 'eye' of a potato, a mini-floret from the floret of a cauliflower or a segment of carrot tap root treated with the plant growth regulator 2,4-D. Also bleach, sterilised water, agar, sterilised petri dishes

Details
Using sterile techniques, it is possible to grow clones of carrot, cauliflower or potato tissue on nutrient agar. Use a treated plant tissue (as above). The plant tissue should be sterilised in bleach, rinsed in four washes of sterilised water and then gently pressed into the agar in sterilised Petri dishes. The cultures should be loosely covered in cling film and kept incubated in a growth cabinet at about 25 °C in the light.

- Calluses should develop over the next few weeks and tiny plantlets should develop from buds. The cultures should be examined regularly and a photographic record kept.

Safety: Care with the handling of bleach and the plant growth regulator. Wear eye protection.

Cell division and growth

Simple inheritance in animals and plants

B2 5.1 Cell division and growth

Learning objectives
- How are chromosomes arranged in body cells?
- What is mitosis?
- What is cell differentiation and how does it differ in animals and plants?

New cells are needed for an organism, or part of an organism, to grow. They are also needed to replace cells which become worn out and to repair damaged tissue. However, the new cells must have the same genetic information as the originals. Then they can do the same job.

Each of your cells has a nucleus containing the instructions for making both new cells and all the tissues and organs needed to make an entire new you. These instructions are carried in the form of genes.

A gene is a small packet of information that controls a characteristic or part of a characteristic, of your body. It is a section of DNA. Different forms of the same gene are known as **alleles**. The genes are grouped together on chromosomes. A chromosome may carry several hundred or even thousands of genes.

You have 46 chromosomes in the nucleus of your body cells. They are arranged in 23 pairs. One of each pair is inherited from your father and one from your mother. Your sex cells (gametes) have only one of each pair of chromosomes.

a Why are new cells needed?

links
For more information on alleles, look at B2 5.5 Inheritance in action.

Mitosis
The cell division in normal body cells produces two identical cells and is called **mitosis**. As a result of mitosis all your body cells have the same chromosomes. This means they have the same genetic information.

In asexual reproduction, the cells of the offspring are produced by mitosis from the cells of their parent. This is why they contain exactly the same alleles as their parent with no genetic variation.

How does mitosis work? Before a cell divides it produces new copies of the chromosomes in the nucleus. Then the cell divides once to form two genetically identical cells.

In some parts of an animal or plant, cell division like this carries on rapidly all the time. Your skin is a good example. You constantly lose cells from the skin's surface, and make new cells to replace them. In fact about 300 million body cells die every minute so mitosis is very important.

This normal body cell has four chromosomes in two pairs

As cell division starts, a copy of each chromosome is made

The cell divides in two to form two daughter cells. Each daughter cell has a nucleus containing four chromosomes identical to the ones in the original parent cell.

Figure 1 Two identical cells are formed by the simple division that takes place during mitosis. For simplicity this cell is shown with only two pairs (not 23).

Practical
Observing mitosis
View a special preparation of a growing root tip under a microscope. You should be able to see the different stages of mitosis as they are taking place. Use Figure 2 for reference.
- Describe your observations of mitosis.

b What is mitosis?

Differentiation
In the early development of animal and plant embryos the cells are unspecialised. Each one of them (known as a **stem cell**) can become any type of cell that is needed.

In many animals, the cells become specialised very early in life. By the time a human baby is born most of its cells are specialised. They will all do a particular job, such as liver cells, skin cells or muscle cells. They have differentiated. Some of their genes have been switched on and others have been switched off.

This means that when, for example, a muscle cell divides by mitosis it can only form more muscle cells. So in a mature (adult) animal, cell division is mainly restricted. It is needed for the repair of damaged tissue and to replace worn out cells. This is because in most adult cells differentiation has already occurred. Specialised cells can divide by mitosis, but they only form the same sort of cell. Therefore growth stops once the animal is mature.

In contrast, most plant cells are able to differentiate all through their life. Undifferentiated cells are formed at active regions of the stems and roots. In these areas mitosis takes place almost continuously.

Plants keep growing all through their lives at these 'growing points'. The plant cells produced don't differentiate until they are in their final position in the plant. Even then the differentiation isn't permanent. You can move a plant cell from one part of a plant to another. There it can redifferentiate and become a completely different type of cell. You can't do that with animal cells – once a muscle cell, always a muscle cell.

We can produce huge numbers of identical plant clones from a tiny piece of leaf tissue. This is because in the right conditions, a plant cell will become unspecialised and undergo mitosis many times. Each of these undifferentiated cells will produce more cells by mitosis. Given different conditions, these will then differentiate to form a tiny new plant. The new plant will be identical to the original parent.

It is difficult to clone animals because animal cells differentiate permanently, early in embryo development. The cells can't change back. Animal clones can only be made by cloning embryos in one way or another, although adult cells can be used to make an embryo.

links
For information on cell differentiation, look back to B2 1.5 Tissues and organs.

Figure 2 The undifferentiated cells in this onion root tip are dividing rapidly. You can see mitosis taking place, with the chromosomes in different positions as the cells divide.

Study tip
Cells produced by mitosis are genetically identical.

Summary questions
1 Copy and complete using the words below:
chromosomes genetic information genes growth mitosis nucleus replace

New cells are needed for .... and to .... worn out cells. The new cells must have the same .... in them as the originals. Each cell has a .... containing the .... grouped together on .... The type of cell division that produces identical cells is known as ....

2 a Explain why the chromosome number must stay the same when the cells divide to make other normal body cells.
   b Why is mitosis so important?

3 a What is differentiation?
   b How does differentiation differ in animal and plant cells?
   c How does this difference affect the cloning of plants and animals?

Key points
- In body cells, chromosomes are found in pairs.
- Body cells divide by mitosis to produce more identical cells for growth, repair and replacement, or in some cases asexual reproduction.
- Most types of animal cell differentiate at an early stage of development. Many plant cells can differentiate throughout their life.

186 / 187

Further teaching suggestions

Make a mitosis flick book
- Find or make some clear diagrams of the stages of mitosis. Copy on to a sheet for each student so that they can make their own 'flick book' by cutting up the pictures and assembling them in the correct order.

Make your own mitosis movie
- Using modelling clay to model the chromosomes and stop motion photography with a webcam, students can make their own animation of the process of mitosis.

Answers to in-text questions
a New cells are needed for growth, replacement and repair.

b Mitosis is cell division that takes place in the normal body cells and produces two identical cells containing exactly the same genes as their parents.

Summary answers

1 growth, replace, genetic information, nucleus, genes, chromosomes, mitosis

2 a Cells need to be replaced with identical cells to do the same job.
   b Mitosis is important because cells die at the rate of 300 million per minute; cells are damaged; cells need to grow; in some organisms cells are needed for asexual reproduction.

3 a Differentiation is the process by which cells become specialised.
   b In animals, it occurs during embryo development and is permanent. In plants, it occurs throughout life and can be reversed or changed.
   c Plants can be cloned relatively easily. Differentiation can be reversed, mitosis is induced, conditions can be changed and more mitosis induced. The cells redifferentiate into new plant tissues. In animals, differentiation cannot be reversed, so clones cannot be made easily. In order to make clones, embryos have to be made.

B2 5.2

Cell division in sexual reproduction

Learning objectives

Students should learn:

- that cells which divide to form gametes undergo meiosis
- that gametes have a single set of genetic information, whereas body cells have two sets
- fertilisation results in the formation of a cell with new pairs of chromosomes, so sexual reproduction gives rise to variation
- how meiosis occurs. [HT only]

Learning outcomes

Most students should be able to:

- understand what happens during meiosis
- describe what happens to the number of chromosomes during fertilisation
- explain how sexual reproduction gives rise to variation.

Some students should also be able to:

- describe what happens to the chromosomes during the process of gamete formation. [HT only]

Support

- Write the word 'chromosomes' twice on the board, inside a ring to represent a cell. To model meiosis, get four students to copy the word 'chromosomes' once onto a piece of A4 and put each on the board inside a ring. To model fertilisation, cut two of these 'chromosomes' words out and stick them inside a single ring. To model mitosis, take both words, stick them onto a sheet and photocopy it repeatedly. (Bear in mind that how meiosis takes place is a concept required at Higher Tier level only).

Extend

- Get students to research the structure of chromosomes. They should find out what happens to them during the stages leading up to their becoming visible and the division.

Specification link-up: Biology B2.7

- Cells in reproductive organs – testes and ovaries in humans – divide to form gametes. *[B2.7.1 f)]*
- The type of cell division in which a cell divides to form gametes is called meiosis. *[B2.7.1 g)]*
- When a cell divides to form gametes:
  - copies of the genetic information are made
  - then the cell divides twice to form four gametes, each with a single set of chromosomes. *[B2.7.1 h)]* **[HT only]**
- When gametes join at fertilisation, a single body cell with new pairs of chromosomes is formed. A new individual then develops by this cell repeatedly dividing by mitosis. *[B2.7.1 i)]*
- Sexual reproduction gives rise to variation because, when gametes fuse, one of each pair of alleles comes from each parent. *[B2.7.2 a)]*

Lesson structure

Starters

Introducing meiosis: a mnemonic for mitosis – Contrast meiosis with mitosis. Find a picture of some ghastly toes. (Search the internet for 'toes'.) Get the students to copy down and remember that 'Mitosis goes on in my toes' and toes are not sexy. Also introduce meiosis as the 'reduction' division, as it reduces the number of chromosomes. *(5 minutes)*

Naming the sex cells – Give the students an empty grid to stick in their books. They are to complete this with the names of the sex cells from animals and plants. Students could be supported by prompting or by providing a list which they can sort out into animals and plants. Students could be extended by getting them to find out and use the correct spellings i.e. 'spermatozoa' etc. and discussing where in animals and plants the sex cells are produced. *(10 minutes)*

Main

- A flow diagram of the events of meiosis can be built up, showing that there are similarities in that the chromosomes are copied, but that there are two divisions rather than one. The flow diagram can be adjusted to the ability of the group: simplify it for students that need support. It is probably best to concentrate on the formation of sperm to begin with (because four observable cells result from the division) and follow up with slides of testis showing stages in sperm development.

- Microscopic examination of testis slides – the best prepared slides are of rat or grasshopper testis squashes. Provide the students with a sheet of paper showing stages in the development of sperm that they are likely to be able to see on their slides. Extend students by producing a flow diagram to show the different stages of division. They may need help with their microscopes, as they will need to use high power if they are to see any chromosomes.

- Alternatively, sections of testis could be projected on to the board and students could identify the different cells with reasons for their choices. They should be able to see chromosomes at different stages and you could extend students by asking them to identify the stages.

- Microscopic examination of ovary slides – the slides could be projected and viewed by the class, or slides could be viewed using a microscope. There will be obvious differences in size of the sperm and egg. Extend students by explaining what happens during the meiotic divisions that produce ova, e.g. the formation of the polar bodies (and possible advantages of their formation).

- Model meiosis and the need for reduction by using model chromosomes. First without a reduction in number of the chromosomes, show how the number of chromosomes would go on increasing. Follow this with the reduction part of the division, so that gametes have half the number and the correct number is restored at fertilisation.

- Using modelling clay of different colours, it is possible to show how variation can occur during the process of meiosis. Students, in groups, could make models showing how the chromosomes separate, perhaps showing some exchange of genes (alleles), and then matching one set of gametes with another set, to represent the sperm and the ovum at fertilisation.

Plenaries

True or false? – Present students with statements about mitosis and meiosis. They are to write 'True' or 'False' on mini whiteboards. You could use the following statements:

'Mitosis is necessary for growth, repair and replacement of tissues.' [True]. 'In meiosis, the number of chromosomes stays the same.' [False]. 'Meiosis takes place in the testes.' [True]. 'Mitosis involves two divisions of the chromosomes.' [False]. 'Mitosis results in two genetically identical cells.' [True]. *(5 minutes)*

Mitosis or meiosis? – Ask students to draw up a table of differences between mitosis and meiosis. Support students by giving them a list of simple statements about the two processes which they place in the correct column. Extend students by encouraging them to put as much detail as they can into their tables. *(10 minutes)*

Simple inheritance in animals and plants

B2 5.2 Cell division in sexual reproduction

Learning objectives

- What is meiosis?
- What happens to your chromosomes when your gametes are formed? [H]
- How does sexual reproduction give rise to variation?

Mitosis is taking place all the time, in tissues all over your body. But there is another type of cell division that takes place only in the reproductive organs of animals and plants. In humans this is the ovaries and the testes. **Meiosis** results in sex cells, called gametes, with only half the original number of chromosomes.

Meiosis

The female gametes or ova are made in the ovaries. The male gametes or sperm are made in the testes.

The gametes are formed by meiosis – cell division where the chromosome number is reduced by half. When a cell divides to form gametes, the chromosomes (the genetic information) are copied so there are four sets of chromosomes. The cell then divides twice in quick succession to form four gametes, each with a single set of chromosomes.

Each gamete that is produced is slightly different from all the others. They contain random mixtures of the original chromosomes pairs. This introduces variety.

a What are the names of the male and female gametes in animals? How do they differ from normal body cells?

Did you know ...?

The testes can produce around 400 million sperm by meiosis every 24 hours between them. Only one sperm is needed to fertilise an egg but each sperm needs to travel 100 000 times its own length to reach the ovum and less than one in a million make it!

A cell in the reproductive organs looks just like a normal body cell before it starts to divide and form gametes

As in normal cell division, the first step is that the chromosomes are copied

The cell divides in two, and these new cells immediately divide again

This gives four sex cells, each with a single set of chromosomes – in this case two instead of the original four

Figure 1 The formation of sex cells in the ovaries and testes involves meiosis to halve the chromosome number. The original cell is shown with only two pairs of chromosomes to make it easier to follow what is happening.

b What type of cell division is needed to produce the gametes?

Fertilisation

More variety is added when fertilisation takes place. Each sex cell has a single set of chromosomes. When two sex cells join during fertilisation the single new cell formed has a full set of chromosomes. In humans, the egg cell (ovum) has 23 chromosomes and so does the sperm. When they join together they produce a single new body cell with the body human number of 46 chromosomes in 23 pairs.

The combination of genes on the chromosomes of every newly fertilised ovum is unique. Once fertilisation is complete, the unique new cell begins to divide by mitosis to form a new individual. This will continue long after the foetus is fully developed and the baby is born.

In fact about 80% of fertilised eggs never make it to become a live baby – about 50% never even implant into the lining of the womb.

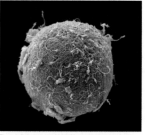

Figure 2 At the moment of fertilisation the chromosomes in the two gametes are combined. The new cell has a complete set of chromosomes, like any other body cell. This new cell will then grow and reproduce by mitosis to form a new individual.

Variation

The differences between asexual and sexual reproduction are reflected in the different types of cell division involved.

In asexual reproduction the offspring are produced as a result of mitosis from the parent cells. So they contain exactly the same chromosomes and the same genes as their parents. There is no variation in the genetic material.

In sexual reproduction the gametes are produced by meiosis in the sex organs of the parents. This introduces variety as each gamete is different. Then when the gametes fuse, one of each pair of chromosomes, and so one of each pair of genes, comes from each parent.

The combination of genes in the new pair of chromosomes will contain alleles from each parent. This also helps to produce variation in the characteristics of the offspring.

Study tip

Learn to spell mitosis and meiosis.

Remember their meanings:
Mitosis – making identical two.
Meiosis – making eggs (and sperm).

Key points

- Cells in the reproductive organs divide by meiosis to form the gametes (sex cells).
- Body cells have two sets of chromosomes; gametes have only one set.
- In meiosis the genetic material is copied and then the cell divides twice to form four gametes, each with a single set of chromosomes [H]
- Sexual reproduction gives rise to variety because genetic information from two parents is combined.

Summary questions

1 a How many pairs of chromosomes are there in a normal human body cell?
  b How many chromosomes are there in a human sperm cell?
  c How many chromosomes are there in a fertilised human egg cell?

2 Sexual reproduction results in variety. Explain how.

3 a What is the name of the special type of cell division that produces gametes from ordinary body cells? Describe what happens to the chromosomes in this process.
  b Where in your body would this type of cell division take place?
  c Why is this type of cell division so important in sexual reproduction? [H]

Further teaching suggestions

Differences between mitosis and meiosis

- Get students to make a leaflet or poster summarising the differences between mitosis and meiosis. They should make it memorable, perhaps using the 'non-sexy toes' statement.

Meiosis in plants

- Preparations of squashes of immature anthers from developing buds of lily show the stages of meiosis and chromosomes very clearly.

Answers to in-text questions

a Sperm, ova, half the number of chromosomes.

b Meiosis.

Summary answers

1 a 23 (pairs)   **b** 23   **c** 46

2 As the gametes are formed, each gamete has a different combination of chromosomes and there is some exchange of genes. This introduces variation, as each gamete is different. In sexual reproduction, two unique gametes from two different people join together, so the combination of chromosomes and the mix of alleles on the chromosomes will be unique.

3 a Meiosis. After the chromosomes are copied, the cell divides twice quickly resulting in sex cells each with half the number of chromosomes.
  b In the reproductive organs/in the ovary or the testes.
  c Sexual reproduction involves the joining of gametes from mother and father. The chromosome number of the body cells needs to be halved to make the gametes, otherwise the number of chromosomes in the cell would just get bigger and bigger when gametes joined at fertilisation. Meiosis halves the chromosome number.

B2 5.3

Stem cells

Learning objectives

Students should learn:

- that stem cells are unspecialised cells found in human embryos and in some adult tissues such as the bone marrow
- how stem cells have the potential to differentiate into different types of specialised cells.

Learning outcomes

Most students should be able to:

- understand the special nature of stem cells
- describe the structure and location of stem cells in humans
- describe how stem cells have the potential to treat sick people.

Some students should also be able to:

- explain in detail the arguments for and against using stem cells from embryos.

Support

- Provide students with a pre-drawn diagram of a ball of cells and some labels of cells and organs. They can stick the labels around the stem cells to gain an understanding of these cells giving rise to all other types of cell.

Extend

- Begin by asking students to define for themselves when life starts. They can be given a list of criteria from contrasting organisations such as the Human Fertilisation and Embryology Authority and Pro-Life.

Specification link-up: Biology B2.7

- Most types of animal cells differentiate at an early stage whereas many plant cells retain the ability to differentiate throughout life. In mature animals, cell division is mainly restricted to repair and replacement. *[B2.7.1 j)]*
- Cells from human embryos and adult bone marrow, called stem cells, can be made to differentiate into many different types of cells, e.g. nerve cells. *[B2.7.1 k)]*
- Human stem cells have the ability to develop into any kind of human cell. *[B2.7.1 l)]*
- Treatment with stem cells may be able to help conditions such as paralysis. *[B2.7.1 m)]*
- Make informed judgements about the social and ethical issues concerning the use of stem cells from embryos in medical research and treatments. *[B2.7]*

Lesson structure

Starters

Stem cells salamander style – Search the internet for a clip called 'Building Body Parts: Saving lives, salamander style'. Make notes on the points covered in the clip and discuss with the class their opinions on the potential new technology. *(5 minutes)*

Gone! – Discuss what it would be like to have lost a limb. Be aware of any potential issues regarding family circumstances within the class. Get the students to spend a single minute silently concentrating on a specific limb of theirs. Start by concentrating on the feeling coming from the limb. If it is a leg, can they feel their socks? If an arm, can they feel the hairs on their forearm? Are they aware of the sensations coming from the front of their leg? The sole of the foot? Imagine life without it – what would they not be able to do? What would they miss? Link with ways of getting science to address the problem of lost limbs through stem cell research. Support students by helping them to empathise. Extend students by encouraging them to suggest how the problems encountered may be overcome. *(10 minutes)*

Main

- Some animals are able to regrow parts of their bodies. Show photographs from search engines of lizards regrowing their tails and starfish regrowing limbs. Lead into a discussion of injuries and how they heal. Allow students to discuss injuries that they have had and what happens to them (time limit will be needed!).
- Find photographs about therapeutic cloning. There are a number of good internet sites with lots of information on the use of stem cells. The important thing is to be aware of what is actually being done and what is hoped can be done in the future.
- Show photographs of different sources of stem cells. Search the internet for 'cell division blastocyst video' to show what happens after fertilisation. Otherwise, find a photograph of a ball of stem cells. After four divisions, the cells become increasingly specialised. Discuss what would happen to the cells if they were allowed to continue development. Other sources include umbilical cord blood (rich in blood stem cells), fetal germ cells (extracted from terminated pregnancies of 5–9 weeks), frozen embryos and adult stem cells from bone marrow.
- Initiate a debate on the pros and cons of the use of stem cells. Both arguments need to be put forward. The cons of stem cell research could be put to the students by a visiting speaker who will argue the case. Some internet sites provide a concise version of the sanctity of life (see www.justthefacts.org for some pre-birth information). The pros can also be summarised from internet sites. Some useful ones are given in the 'ICT link-up' in the 'Further teaching suggestions'.
- Use a summary sheet to state the main information and hold a snowball discussion where pairs of students brainstorm the concepts, then double up as fours and continue the process. The fours then gather into groups of eight in order to compare ideas and agree on a course of action (to endorse stem cell research or not). A spokesperson from each group of eight feeds back to the whole group.

Plenaries

Banking your baby's cord blood – It is now possible for the blood from the umbilical cord of a newborn baby to be collected and stored. Get the students to write a short paragraph explaining the benefits of this procedure to prospective parents. Select students to read out their efforts and discuss. *(5 minutes)*

Anagrams – Write up or project anagrams of the key words and terms from the lesson. Support students by giving them simpler words and terms. Extend students by omitting the vowels and asking them for definitions. *(10 minutes)*

Further teaching suggestions

Debate the use of prosthetic limbs at the Olympics

- Ask how the students would feel about competitors in the Olympic using prosthetic limbs which allow them to perform better than unaided humans. Encourage discussion.

ICT link-up

- There are a number of good internet sites that have useful information: New Scientist; Nature; Stem Cell Information; Christopher Reeve Foundation; Stem Cell Research Foundation. (See www.nature.com; www.stemcells.nih.gov; www.christopherreeve.org; www.newscientist.com; www.stemcellresearchfoundation. org.) If computers are available, set up a scavenger hunt style trail of internet sites to pull out the main bits of the pro and con arguments and details of the research carried

out. Ask students to find out about the original research and write a report of what was discovered. (See www. stemcellresearchfoundation.org.)

The meaning of 'totipotent', 'pluripotent' and 'multipotent'

- Get students to investigate the meaning of 'totipotent', 'pluripotent' and 'multipotent' when applied to stem cells. ['Totipotent' cells are found in very early embryos (for the first three or four divisions) and can differentiate into all types of cell. 'Pluripotent' stem cells are present in later embryos and can differentiate into any cell type. 'Multipotent' stem cells are found in adults as well as embryos and will only differentiate into certain cell types.] The Stem Cell Research Foundation has illustrations on its internet site.

Simple inheritance in animals and plants

B2 5.3 Stem cells

Learning objectives

- What is special about stem cells?
- How can we use stem cells to cure people?

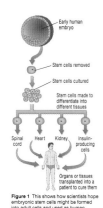

- Early human embryo
- Stem cells removed
- Stem cells cultured
- Stem cells made to differentiate into different tissues
- Spinal cord, Heart, Kidney, Insulin-producing cells
- Organs or tissues transplanted into a patient to cure them

Figure 1 This shows how scientists hope embryonic stem cells might be formed into adult cells and used as human treatments in the future

The function of stem cells

An egg and sperm cell fuse to form a zygote, a single new cell. That cell divides and becomes a hollow ball of cells – the embryo. The inner cells of this ball are the stem cells. Stem cells differentiate to form the specialised cells of your body that make up your various tissues and organs. They will eventually produce every type of cell in your body.

Even when you are an adult, some of your stem cells remain. Your bone marrow is a good source of stem cells. Scientists now think there may be a tiny number of stem cells in most of the different tissues in your body. This includes your blood, brain, muscle and liver.

The stem cells can stay in the different tissues for many years. They are only needed if your tissues are injured or affected by disease. Then they start dividing to replace the different types of damaged cell.

a What are stem cells?

Using stem cells

Many people suffer and even die because parts of their body stop working properly. For example, spinal injuries can cause paralysis. That's because the spinal nerves do not repair themselves. Millions of people would benefit if we could replace damaged body parts.

In 1998, there was a breakthrough. Two American scientists managed to culture human embryonic stem cells. These were capable of forming other types of cell.

Scientists hope that the embryonic stem cells can be encouraged to grow into almost any different type of cell needed in the body. For example, scientists in the US have grown nerve cells from embryonic stem cells. In rats, these have been used to reconnect damaged spinal nerves. The rats regained some movement of their legs. In 2010 the first trials using nerve cells grown from embryonic stem cells in humans were carried out. The nerve cells were injected into the spinal cords of patients with new, severe spinal cord injuries. These first trials were to make sure that the technique is safe. The scientists and doctors hope it will not be long before they can use stem cells to help people who have been paralysed walk again.

We might also be able to grow whole new organs from embryonic stem cells. These organs could be used in transplant surgery. Conditions from infertility to dementia could eventually be treated using stem cells. Doctors in the UK hope to begin using embryonic stem cells to treat a common cause of blindness in 2011.

b What was the big scientific breakthrough by American scientists in 1998?

Problems with stem cells

Many embryonic stem cells come from aborted embryos. Others come from spare embryos in fertility treatment. This raises ethical issues. There are people, including many religious groups, who feel this is wrong. They question the use of a potential human being as a source of cells, even to cure others.

Some people feel that as the embryo cannot give permission, using it is a violation of its human rights. As well as this, progress with stem cells is slow. There is some concern that embryonic stem cells might cause cancer if they are used to treat sick people. This has certainly been seen in mice. Making stem cells is slow, difficult, expensive and hard to control.

c What is the biggest ethical concern with the use of embryonic stem cells?

The future of stem cell research

Scientists have found embryonic stem cells in the umbilical cord blood of newborn babies. These may help to overcome some of the ethical concerns.

Scientists are also finding ways of growing the adult stem cells found in bone marrow and some other tissues. So far they can only develop into a limited range of cell types. However, this is another possible way of avoiding the controversial use of embryonic tissue. Adult stem cells have been used successfully to treat some forms of heart disease and to grow some new organs such as tracheas (windpipes).

The area of stem cell research known as therapeutic cloning could be very useful. However, it is proving very difficult. It involves using cells from an adult to produce a cloned early embryo of themselves. This would provide a source of perfectly matched embryonic stem cells. In theory these could then be used to grow new organs for the original donor. The new organs would not be rejected by the body because they have been made from the body's own cells.

Most people remain excited by the possibilities of embryonic stem cell use in treating many diseases. At the moment, after years of relatively slow progress, hopes are high again that stem cells will change the future of medicine. We don't know how many of these hopes will be fulfilled; only time will tell.

Figure 2 For years, funding for stem cell research in the US was blocked by the government. In 2009 President Obama changed that ruling so US research could move forward. However, the battle continues in the courts.

Figure 3 In 2010 Ciaran Finn-Lynch was the first child to be given a life-saving new windpipe grown using his own stem cells

Summary questions

1 Copy and complete using the words below:

bone marrow differentiate embryos hollow inner stem cells

Unspecialised cells known as .... can .... (divide and change) into many different types of cell when they are needed. Human stem cells are found in .... and in adult .... The embryo forms a .... ball of cells and the .... cells of this ball are the stem cells.

2 **a** What are the advantages of using stem cells to treat diseases?
 b What are the difficulties with stem cell research?
 c How are scientists hoping to overcome the ethical objections to using embryonic stem cells in their research?

Key points

- Embryonic stem cells (from human embryos) and adult stem cells (from adult bone marrow) can be made to differentiate into many different types of cell.

- Stem cells have the potential to treat previously incurable conditions. We may be able to grow nerve cells or whole new organs for people who need them.

190 191

Answers to in-text questions

a Unspecialised cells that can differentiate to form many different types of specialised body cell.

b Culturing human embryonic stem cells.

c Some people think it is wrong to use a potential human being as a source of cells to help other people.

Summary answers

1 stem cells, differentiate, embryos, bone marrow, hollow, inner

2 **a** They can be used to make any type of adult cell to repair or replace damaged tissues, with no rejection issues.

 b There are ethical objections and concerns over possible side effects.

 c By using stem cells from umbilical blood, adult stem cells and therapeutic cloning.

B2 5.4

From Mendel to DNA

Learning objectives

Students should learn:

- about the work of Mendel and why its importance was not recognised until after his death
- why DNA fingerprinting is possible
- how specific proteins are made.

Learning outcomes

Most students should be able to:

- describe Mendel's discoveries
- recognise why Mendel's ideas were not accepted in his time
- describe how DNA fingerprinting is used to identify individuals.

Some students should also be able to:

- explain simply the structure of DNA
- explain how a gene codes for a specific protein. [HT only]

Specification link-up: Biology B2.7

- Sexual reproduction gives rise to variation because when gametes fuse, one of each pair of alleles comes from each parent. [B2.7.2 a)]
- Some characteristics are controlled by a single gene. Each gene may have different forms called alleles. [B2.7.2 c)]
- An allele that controls the development of a characteristic when it is present on only one of the chromosomes is a dominant allele. [B2.7.2 d)]
- An allele that controls the development of characteristics only if the dominant allele is not present is a recessive allele. [B2.7.2 e)]
- Chromosomes are made up of large molecules of DNA (deoxyribo nucleic acid) which has a double helix structure. [B2.7.2 f)]
- A gene is a small section of DNA. [B2.7.2 g)]
- Each gene codes for a particular combination of amino acids which make a specific protein. [B2.7.2 h)] **[HT only]**
- Each person (apart from identical twins) has unique DNA. This can be used to identify individuals in a process known as DNA fingerprinting. [B2.7.2 i)]
- Explain why Mendel proposed the idea of separately inherited factors and why the importance of this discovery was not recognised until after his death. [B2.7]

Answers to in-text questions

a Mendel became a monk because he was clever but poor and the only way to get an education if you were poor was to join the Church.

b He kept records and analysed his results.

Lesson structure

Starters

How did Mendel start? – Give the students a collection of dried peas to sort out into groups. Include smooth and wrinkled skins, yellow and green if possible. Ask them to predict what would happen if the peas were planted. Would you get peas identical to the ones you planted? Discuss. If students are interested, they could plant the peas and await the results. *(5 minutes)*

A model of DNA – If possible, have a model of DNA showing its structure with the different bases, the deoxyribose and the phosphate groups. Get the students to identify the component parts. Support students by providing labels of the component parts which they can stick on to the model. It could be useful to indicate here that a gene is a bit of DNA. Extend students by discussing the coding on a simple level. It could be helpful to provide students with a print-out of a DNA molecule which they can label and keep in their notebooks. *(10 minutes)*

Main

- Create/show a video or PowerPoint presentation on Mendel's life and work. There is plenty of information available and scope for introducing students to the demands of research (think about all those plants he grew and seeds he counted). Consider the characteristics that he investigated; introduce some of the easier terms, such as 'pure-breeding' and some of the simple ratios. Discuss his technique. (See www.mendelweb.org).

- 'Grow your own genetics experiment' (see 'Practical support').

- Prepare a PowerPoint presentation on genetic fingerprinting. The technique can be fairly simply explained (see NCBE publications or website for details) and then the implications discussed. Some examples of different uses can be given, e.g. forensic evidence, paternity issues. There are some good images available on the internet.

Plenaries

Press conference – Select a student who is prepared to be Mendel. Other students are to interview him about his work and why he did not get recognition at the time. The student can choose other members of the class to represent workers who followed up his discoveries. Differentiation by outcome: support level students will ask simpler questions and may need prompting. Students can be extended by asking 'Mendel' questions about what he thought the benefits of his work might be. *(5 minutes)*

Be a detective! – Present the students with some genetic evidence (some DNA from a murder weapon and three sets of genetic fingerprints). You could make it more complex by adding in some other forensic details, such as mud from the scene of the crime, bloodstains, etc. Let them work out who did the crime. Pick one group to present the solution with their reasons. Discuss the importance of genetic fingerprinting in solving crimes. Link with cases where someone has been wrongfully imprisoned for years until the DNA evidence showed them to be innocent. *(10 minutes)*

Support

- Get students to use different coloured (yellow and green) dried peas, glue and a large sheet of paper to make a large poster showing Mendel's experiment as depicted in the Student Book.

Extend

- Ask students to draw up a plan for one of Mendel's experiments and calculate how long it took him to get his results. What precautions would he have to take? Did he use controls? Ask the students to apply some of the criteria needed when they design their own experiments. Would you do it the same way as he did it? What different techniques might you use?

Practical support

Grow your own genetics experiment

Equipment and materials required
Sets of seeds from monohybrid genetic crosses can be obtained from suppliers, seed trays, compost.

Details
Plant seeds from monohybrid genetic crosses. When the seeds grow, it is possible to observe differences between the seedlings and make predictions about the genetic constitution of the parent plants. Tobacco (colour of cotyledons, hairiness of stem, colour of stem and leaf shape), tomato (leaf shape, hairiness of stem, colour of stem) and cucumber (bitterness of leaves) are all suitable for class use. The seeds are sown in seed trays, kept in light, airy conditions and watered every two or three days. They will be ready for scoring the characteristics after about 15 to 20 days. These seeds usually come provided with instructions and an explanation of the parental cross which produced them.

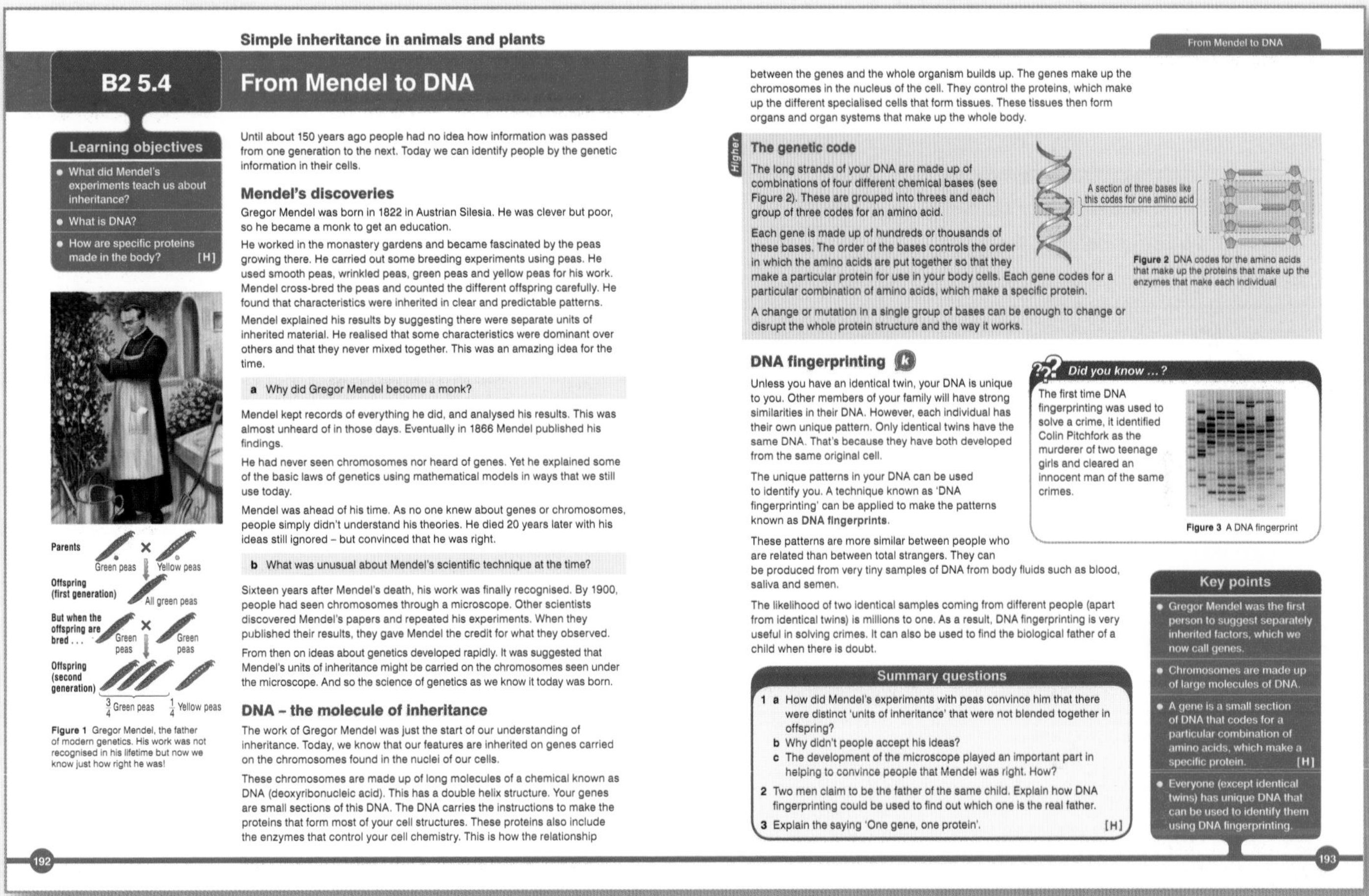

B2 5.4 From Mendel to DNA

Learning objectives
- What did Mendel's experiments teach us about inheritance?
- What is DNA?
- How are specific proteins made in the body? [H]

Until about 150 years ago people had no idea how information was passed from one generation to the next. Today we can identify people by the genetic information in their cells.

Mendel's discoveries
Gregor Mendel was born in 1822 in Austrian Silesia. He was clever but poor, so he became a monk to get an education.

He worked in the monastery gardens and became fascinated by the peas growing there. He carried out some breeding experiments using peas. He used smooth peas, wrinkled peas, green peas and yellow peas for his work. Mendel cross-bred the peas and counted the different offspring carefully. He found that characteristics were inherited in clear and predictable patterns.

Mendel explained his results by suggesting there were separate units of inherited material. He realised that some characteristics were dominant over others and that they never mixed together. This was an amazing idea for the time.

a Why did Gregor Mendel become a monk?

Mendel kept records of everything he did, and analysed his results. This was almost unheard of in those days. Eventually in 1866 Mendel published his findings.

He had never seen chromosomes nor heard of genes. Yet he explained some of the basic laws of genetics using mathematical models in ways that we still use today.

Mendel was ahead of his time. As no one knew about genes or chromosomes, people simply didn't understand his theories. He died 20 years later with his ideas still ignored – but convinced that he was right.

b What was unusual about Mendel's scientific technique at the time?

Sixteen years after Mendel's death, his work was finally recognised. By 1900, people had seen chromosomes through a microscope. Other scientists discovered Mendel's papers and repeated his experiments. When they published their results, they gave Mendel the credit for what they observed.

From then on ideas about genetics developed rapidly. It was suggested that Mendel's units of inheritance might be carried on the chromosomes seen under the microscope. And so the science of genetics as we know it today was born.

Parents — Green peas × Yellow peas
Offspring (first generation) — All green peas
But when the offspring are bred ... — Green peas × Green peas
Offspring (second generation) — ¾ Green peas ¼ Yellow peas

Figure 1 Gregor Mendel, the father of modern genetics. His work was not recognised in his lifetime but now we know just how right he was!

DNA – the molecule of inheritance
The work of Gregor Mendel was just the start of our understanding of inheritance. Today, we know that our features are inherited on genes carried on the chromosomes found in the nuclei of our cells.

These chromosomes are made up of long molecules of a chemical known as DNA (deoxyribonucleic acid). This has a double helix structure. Your genes are small sections of this DNA. The DNA carries the instructions to make the proteins that form most of your cell structures. These proteins also include the enzymes that control your cell chemistry. This is how the relationship between the genes and the whole organism builds up. The genes make up the chromosomes in the nucleus of the cell. They control the proteins, which make up the different specialised cells that form tissues. These tissues then form organs and organ systems that make up the whole body.

The genetic code
The long strands of your DNA are made up of combinations of four different chemical bases (see Figure 2). These are grouped into threes and each group of three codes for an amino acid.

Each gene is made up of hundreds or thousands of these bases. The order of the bases controls the order in which the amino acids are put together so that they make a particular protein for use in your body cells. Each gene codes for a particular combination of amino acids, which make a specific protein.

A change or mutation in a single group of bases can be enough to change or disrupt the whole protein structure and the way it works.

A section of three bases like this codes for one amino acid

Figure 2 DNA codes for the amino acids that make up the proteins that make up the enzymes that make each individual

DNA fingerprinting
Unless you have an identical twin, your DNA is unique to you. Other members of your family will have strong similarities in their DNA. However, each individual has their own unique pattern. Only identical twins have the same DNA. That's because they have both developed from the same original cell.

The unique patterns in your DNA can be used to identify you. A technique known as 'DNA fingerprinting' can be applied to make the patterns known as DNA fingerprints.

These patterns are more similar between people who are related than between total strangers. They can be produced from very tiny samples of DNA from body fluids such as blood, saliva and semen.

The likelihood of two identical samples coming from different people (apart from identical twins) is millions to one. As a result, DNA fingerprinting is very useful in solving crimes. It can also be used to find the biological father of a child when there is doubt.

?? Did you know ... ?
The first time DNA fingerprinting was used to solve a crime, it identified Colin Pitchfork as the murderer of two teenage girls and cleared an innocent man of the same crimes.

Figure 3 A DNA fingerprint

Summary questions
1 **a** How did Mendel's experiments with peas convince him that there were distinct 'units of inheritance' that were not blended together in offspring?
  b Why didn't people accept his ideas?
  c The development of the microscope played an important part in helping to convince people that Mendel was right. How?
2 Two men claim to be the father of the same child. Explain how DNA fingerprinting could be used to find out which one is the real father.
3 Explain the saying 'One gene, one protein'. [H]

Key points
- Gregor Mendel was the first person to suggest separately inherited factors, which we now call genes.
- Chromosomes are made up of large molecules of DNA.
- A gene is a small section of DNA that codes for a particular combination of amino acids, which make a specific protein. [H]
- Everyone (except identical twins) has unique DNA that can be used to identify them using DNA fingerprinting.

Further teaching suggestions

Make your own model DNA
- Students could try to make their own model of a part of a DNA molecule, either from a kit or from materials to hand. (See internet site www.csiro.au and search for a 'DNA model template'.)

Did Mendel fiddle his results?
- There are several ways in which you could consider Mendel to be lucky. His choice of plants to work on, the characteristics he chose, the numbers he obtained – all these worked out well for him. Give students some of his results and let them work out the ratios. If there are any budding mathematicians in the group, ask if they can work out the probability of getting such good results. There are suggestions that he knew what he wanted to prove before he set up his experiments. Ask: 'What do you think?'

How to get enough DNA for a fingerprint
- Sometimes the quantity of DNA left at a crime scene is very small, but using PCR (the polymerase chain reaction), this can be increased. Find out how this works. Use a search engine and key in the words or go to the NCBE website for more information.

Summary answers

1 **a** He found that characteristics were inherited in clear and predictable patterns. He realised some characteristics were dominant over others and that they never mixed together.
  b No one could see the units of inheritance, so there was no proof of their existence. People were not used to studying careful records of results.
  c Once people could see chromosomes, a mechanism for Mendel's ideas of inheritance became possible.

2 The DNA fingerprint of the real father would have similarities to the DNA fingerprint of the child, whereas that of the other man would not.

3 A gene is made up of groups of three base pairs. Each group of three base pairs codes for a single amino acid. The order of the base pairs in the gene determines the sequence of the amino acids which are joined together to make a protein – so each gene codes for a unique protein.

B2 5.5

Inheritance in action

Learning objectives

Students should learn:

- that characteristics are controlled by genes which have different forms called alleles
- the difference between dominant alleles and recessive alleles
- how, in humans, the sex chromosomes determines whether you are female (XX) or male (XY).

Learning outcomes

Most students should be able to:

- explain how the inheritance of characteristics is controlled by dominant and recessive alleles
- explain how sex is determined in humans.

Some students should also be able to:

- use the terms homozygous, heterozygous, phenotype and genotype correctly [HT only]
- construct genetic diagrams. [HT only]

Support

- Play a card game using dominant and recessive cards for lobed ears, dimples and tongue rolling. Some students might be able to cope with the sex determination game in its simplest form.

Extend

- If the school has the facilities, students could try scoring the *Drosophila* crosses, particularly if the flies have been used for sixth-form classes.

Specification link-up: Biology B2.7

- Interpret genetic diagrams, including family trees. *[B2.7]*
- Construct genetic diagrams of monohybrid crosses and predict the outcomes of monohybrid crosses and be able to use the terms homozygous, heterozygous, phenotype and genotype. *[B2.7]* **[HT only]**
- In human body cells, one of the 23 pairs of chromosomes carries the genes that determine sex. In females, the sex chromosomes are the same (XX); in males the sex chromosomes are different (XY). *[B2.7.2 b)]*
- Some characteristics are controlled by a single gene. Each gene may have different forms called alleles. *[B2.7.2 c)]*
- An allele that controls the development of a characteristic when it is present on only one of the chromosomes is a dominant allele. *[B2.7.2 d)]*
- An allele which controls the development of characteristics only if the dominant allele is not present is a recessive allele. *[B2.7.2 e)]*

Lesson structure

Starters

Can you? – Ask some of these: 'Can you roll your tongue? Can you taste quinine (the bitter tasting anti-malaria chemical present in Indian tonic water)? Do you have dimples? Do you have dangly ear lobes? Do you have straight thumbs or bendy thumbs?' Discuss some of these characteristics. Build up a list of positive and negatives on the board. Are there any discernible trends? *(5 minutes)*

Get the words right – Put up at the front of the room some word cards with the important terms from the spread on inheritance (e.g. allele, chromosome, dominant, recessive, Mendel, inheritance, etc.). Support students by giving them a numbered list of sentences to match with the terms. Extend students by asking them to compose sentences containing combinations of these words. Select from responses, noting key ideas. *(10 minutes)*

Main

- If students did not carry out the 'Grow your own genetics experiment' when studying the previous spread, it could be done here as an illustration of inheritance in action.
- Inherited conditions in humans are due to mutations of the DNA. The Human Genome Project has mapped all the human chromosomes. Prepare a PowerPoint presentation on this project, including references to why it was done, how it was done and how long it took. Discuss the implications. Information is available on The Wellcome Trust website and the Human Genome Project Information website.
- Sex determination game – prepare sets of sperm cards with either an X or a Y on the back and egg cards, all with X on the back. Working in pairs, the students are to turn one sperm card and one egg card over at a time. In a table, they note the sperm chromosome, the egg chromosome, the combination, the gender and give the baby a name. Run for about 5–7 minutes and then see who has the biggest family. Ask: 'Are there more boys than girls? What does this tell us about the ratio of the sexes?' How strong is your evidence? What would happen to the ratio if we did it thousands of times? Get the students to write an advice note on gender likelihood for prospective parents.
- Draw a Punnett square on the board with a number of different dominant and recessive alleles. Use some of the examples mentioned in the 'Can you?' starter. Get the students to fill in pre-printed frames to 'model' the crosses. Also give the students some examples of the crosses Mendel made with his peas to work out. It is recommended that the students get as much practice as possible in predicting the outcome of monohybrid crosses.
- Different coloured beads (or dyed haricot beans) can be used to model how different characteristics are inherited. Students could be given a characteristic, either a human one or one of Mendel's crosses, and carry out the exercise scoring the different combinations of alleles. They can relate the figures they obtain to the outcome predicted by a Punnett square.

Plenaries

Human karyotypes – Show students some pictures of sets of human chromosomes (karyotypes) where the chromosomes have not been matched into pairs. Can they identify the sex chromosomes and decide where the karotype is from a male or a female? Compare with karyotypes where the chromosomes are in pairs. When is this type of information helpful? *(5 minutes)*

Family trees – Draw on the board or project a family tree (or pedigree diagram) for tongue rolling, or another human single gene characteristic that is not sex-linked and that has not been used in the Student Book. Ask students to explain how the characteristic has been inherited. Support students by prompting them to trace the inheritance in a simple way. Extend students by getting them to describe the possible genotypes of the different members. *(10 minutes)*

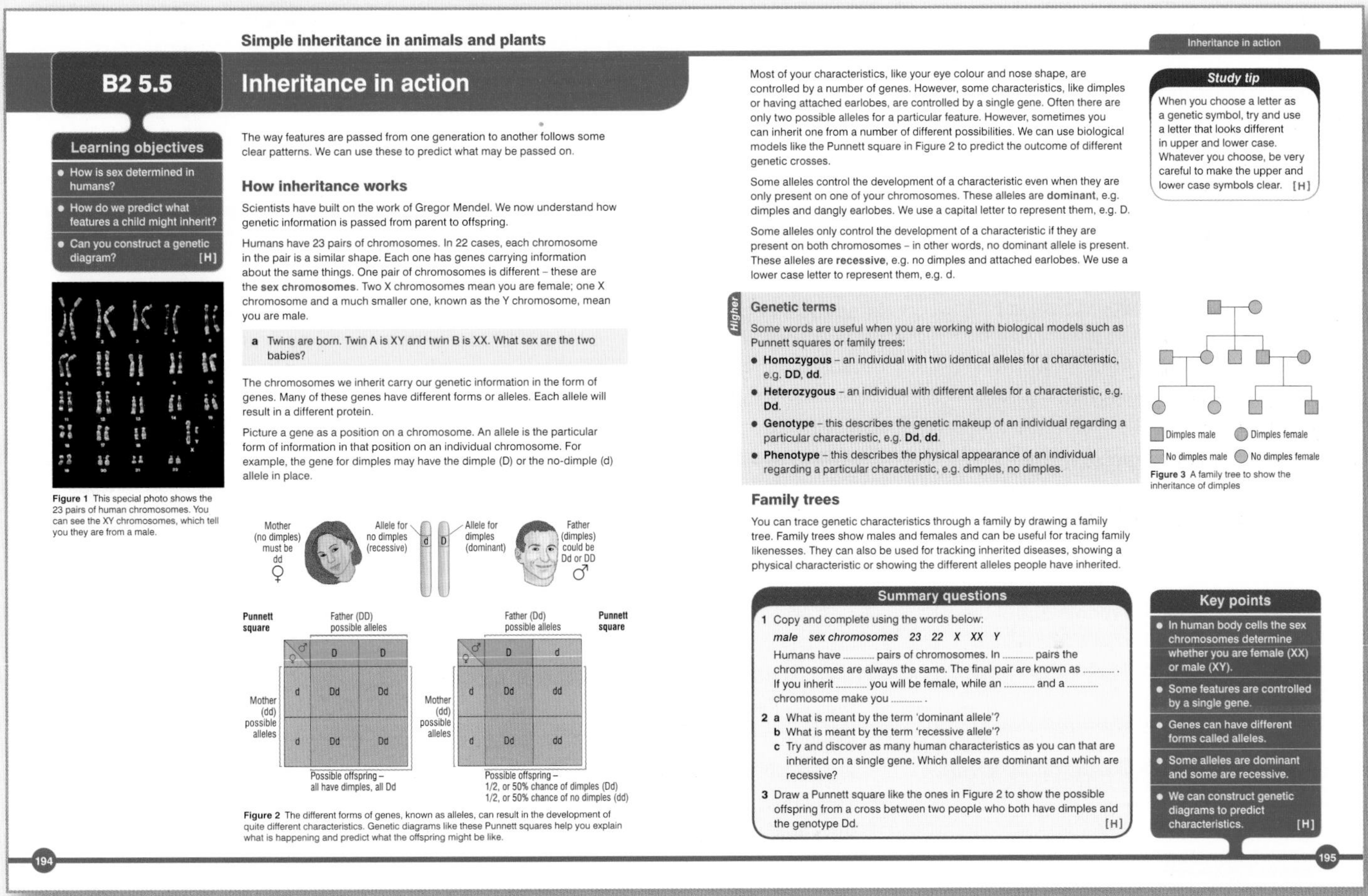

Simple inheritance in animals and plants

B2 5.5 Inheritance in action

The way features are passed from one generation to another follows some clear patterns. We can use these to predict what may be passed on.

Learning objectives

- How is sex determined in humans?
- How do we predict what features a child might inherit?
- Can you construct a genetic diagram? [H]

How inheritance works

Scientists have built on the work of Gregor Mendel. We now understand how genetic information is passed from parent to offspring.

Humans have 23 pairs of chromosomes. In 22 cases, each chromosome in the pair is a similar shape. Each one has genes carrying information about the same things. One pair of chromosomes is different – these are the sex chromosomes. Two X chromosomes mean you are female; one X chromosome and a much smaller one, known as the Y chromosome, mean you are male.

> **a** Twins are born. Twin A is XY and twin B is XX. What sex are the two babies?

The chromosomes we inherit carry our genetic information in the form of genes. Many of these genes have different forms or alleles. Each allele will result in a different protein.

Picture a gene as a position on a chromosome. An allele is the particular form of information in that position on an individual chromosome. For example, the gene for dimples may have the dimple (D) or the no-dimple (d) allele in place.

Figure 1 This special photo shows the 23 pairs of human chromosomes. You can see the XY chromosomes, which tell you they are from a male.

Mother (no dimples) must be dd — Allele for no dimples (recessive) d — Allele for dimples (dominant) D — Father (dimples) could be Dd or DD

Punnett square / Father (DD) possible alleles

Mother (dd) possible alleles	D	D
d	Dd	Dd
d	Dd	Dd

Possible offspring – all have dimples, all Dd

Punnett square / Father (Dd) possible alleles

Mother (dd) possible alleles	D	d
d	Dd	dd
d	Dd	dd

Possible offspring – 1/2, or 50% chance of dimples (Dd) 1/2, or 50% chance of no dimples (dd)

Figure 2 The different forms of genes, known as alleles, can result in the development of quite different characteristics. Genetic diagrams like these Punnett squares help you explain what is happening and predict what the offspring might be like.

Most of your characteristics, like your eye colour and nose shape, are controlled by a number of genes. However, some characteristics, like dimples or having attached earlobes, are controlled by a single gene. Often there are only two possible alleles for a particular feature. However, sometimes you can inherit one from a number of different possibilities. We can use biological models like the Punnett square in Figure 2 to predict the outcome of different genetic crosses.

Some alleles control the development of a characteristic even when they are only present on one of your chromosomes. These alleles are **dominant**, e.g. dimples and dangly earlobes, are controlled by a single gene. We use a capital letter to represent them, e.g. D.

Some alleles only control the development of a characteristic if they are present on both chromosomes – in other words, no dominant allele is present. These alleles are **recessive**, e.g. no dimples and attached earlobes. We use a lower case letter to represent them, e.g. d.

Genetic terms

Some words are useful when you are working with biological models such as Punnett squares or family trees:

- **Homozygous** – an individual with two identical alleles for a characteristic, e.g. **DD, dd**.
- **Heterozygous** – an individual with different alleles for a characteristic, e.g. **Dd**.
- **Genotype** – this describes the genetic makeup of an individual regarding a particular characteristic, e.g. **Dd, dd**.
- **Phenotype** – this describes the physical appearance of an individual regarding a particular characteristic, e.g. dimples, no dimples.

Family trees

You can trace genetic characteristics through a family by drawing a family tree. Family trees show males and females and can be useful for tracing family likenesses. They can also be used for tracking inherited diseases, showing a physical characteristic or showing the different alleles people have inherited.

■ Dimples male ● Dimples female
□ No dimples male ○ No dimples female

Figure 3 A family tree to show the inheritance of dimples

Study tip

When you choose a letter as a genetic symbol, try and use a letter that looks different in upper and lower case. Whatever you choose, be very careful to make the upper and lower case symbols clear. [H]

Summary questions

1 Copy and complete using the words below:
  male sex chromosomes 23 22 X XX Y
  Humans have .... pairs of chromosomes. In .... pairs the chromosomes are always the same. The final pair are known as .... If you inherit .... you will be female, while an .... and a .... chromosome make you ....

2 **a** What is meant by the term 'dominant allele'?
  b What is meant by the term 'recessive allele'?
  c Try and discover as many human characteristics as you can that are inherited on a single gene. Which alleles are dominant and which are recessive?

3 Draw a Punnett square like the ones in Figure 2 to show the possible offspring from a cross between two people who both have dimples and the genotype Dd. [H]

Key points

- In human body cells the sex chromosomes determine whether you are female (XX) or male (XY).
- Some features are controlled by a single gene.
- Genes can have different forms called alleles.
- Some alleles are dominant and some are recessive.
- We can construct genetic diagrams to predict characteristics. [H]

194 / 195

Further teaching suggestions

ICT link-up

- There are some excellent internet sites with genetics games that can be played online, e.g. the Canadian Museum of Nature website (www.nature.ca). Search for 'genome'.

Modify the sex determination game

- Using a symbol to represent a characteristic, such as tongue rolling, which can be stuck on the cards, the inheritance of a human characteristic (not a sex-linked one can be investigated at the same time. Just add another column to the table. It would be possible to model sex-linkage using this game, but it is beyond the specification.

Answers to in-text questions

a A is male and B is female.

Summary answers

1 23, 22, sex chromosomes, XX, X/Y, Y/X, male

2 **a** Dominant allele – an allele which controls the development of a characteristic even when it is present on only one of the chromosomes.

  b Recessive allele – an allele which only controls the development of a characteristic if it is present on both chromosomes.

  c Marks for each case where students identify correctly the single gene characteristic and the dominant and recessive alleles.

3 [Marks awarded for drawing a Punnett square correctly with the appropriate gametes.] DD, Dd, dD, dd is the one that doesn't have dimples; with dimples: 1 with no dimples.

B2 5.6

Inherited conditions in humans

Learning objectives

Students should learn:

- that some human disorders are inherited
- that some disorders are the result of the inheritance of a dominant allele (polydactyly), but others are the result of the inheritance of two recessive alleles (cystic fibrosis)
- that embryos can be screened for genetic disorders.

Learning outcomes

Most students should be able to:

- state that some human disorders may be inherited
- describe how genetic disorders caused by a dominant allele are inherited
- describe how a genetic disorder caused by a recessive allele must be inherited from both parents
- list some issues concerning embryo screening.

Some students should also be able to:

- draw genetic diagrams to show how genetic disorders are passed on [HT only]
- make informed judgements about the economic, social and ethical issues concerning embryo screening that they have studied or from information that is presented to them.

Support

- Provide students with large printed grids and cards with alleles on so that they could work out genetic crosses. They could work out the ratios and show them underneath.

Extend

- Suggest that students do some research on the frequency of particular alleles in populations. We are told that 1 person in 25 carries the allele for cystic fibrosis. Ask: 'How has this been calculated?' They could find out about the Hardy–Weinberg law and how it works. The law itself is fairly straightforward – students could work out how they can use it to inform people that the incidence of the alleles for certain conditions is quite high.

Specification link-up: Biology B2.7

- Some disorders are inherited. *[B2.7.3 a)]*
- Polydactyly – having extra fingers or toes – is caused by a dominant allele of a gene and can therefore be passed on by only one parent who has the disorder. *[B2.7.3 b)]*
- Cystic fibrosis (a disorder of cell membranes) must be inherited from both parents. The parents may be carriers of the disorder without actually having the disorder themselves. It is caused by a recessive allele of a gene and can therefore be passed on by parents, neither of whom has the disorder. *[B2.7.3 c)]*
- Embryos can be screened for the alleles that cause these and other genetic disorders. *[B2.7.3 d)]*
- Construct genetic diagrams of monohybrid crosses and predict the outcomes of monohybrid crosses and be able to use the terms homozygous, heterozygous, phenotype and genotype. *[B2.7]* **[HT only]**

Lesson structure

Starters

Infectious or genetic or ...? – Read students a list of illnesses, including some infectious diseases and some genetic disorders. Students to respond by writing on 'Show me' boards whether a disease is infectious (writing I) or genetic (writing G). If they do not know then they should write a question mark. Draw up a list on the board in two columns. *(5 minutes)*

Interpreting pedigree diagrams – If the Family tree plenary was not done on the previous lesson, introduce a family tree or pedigree diagram for an invented 'condition' and get students to work out some of the offspring. Support students by prompting them and identifying the affected members and how they inherited the condition. They should be able to identify the carriers. Extend students by asking them to work out the way in which the alleles have been inherited. If time permits, use one condition caused by a dominant allele and one by a recessive allele. *(10 minutes)*

Main

- Polydactyly – Find and show images of polydactyly. The basic facts, symptoms and inheritability can be presented, together with some examples of polydactyly in other animals (cats, chickens, etc.).

- This could lead to a discussion on the condition and whether treatment is needed or desirable. If some images are shown where there is an extra thumb, then students could express their own feelings about how it should be treated. It is not a life-threatening condition, but students could think about whether or not genetic testing is a good idea.

- Cystic fibrosis – Useful internet sites can be found, including 'The Cystic Fibrosis Trust', the 'Cystic Fibrosis Foundation' (see www.cftrust.org.uk and www.cff.org), and the students could be asked to research different aspects of the disorder in groups and put together a lesson on the condition.

- One group could describe the disease and its symptoms, another the genetics of how it is inherited and a further group could review the different treatments. Ask: 'According to the statistics, 1 in 25 people carries the allele, so is it worth being screened for it?'

- Inherited or not? – It is difficult to know whether a particular disorder or condition is inherited or not. The only way to find out is to carry out pedigree analysis and go back through the generations if possible. Suggest to students that they think of a particular family trait and see if they can draw up a pedigree within their own family. It is probably better to choose a characteristic, such as dangly ear lobes or dimples, rather than a disorder unless a student has a particular interest.

Plenaries

Play the inheritance game – The sex determination game, from the previous spread, could be modified by adding a dominant or recessive genetic disorder sticker to some of the cards and to see what happens to the offspring. Allow 5 minutes for the game and then add up how many are affected offspring, how many are carriers and how many are unaffected by the disorder. *(5 minutes)*

Statistics or chance? – Much emphasis is put on the ratios of incidence of the condition, but it does not necessarily follow that it works like that. Ask: 'Why are there some families where there are no boys or no girls?' Every child of a person with polydactyly could inherit the disease. Students can try tossing a coin to see if they get equal numbers of heads and tails or if they get a run of heads. Ask students: What are the implications if it was your family? Get them to write down their thoughts. Support students by giving them a list of simple statements about the implications which they could put in order of importance. Extend students by getting them to express their thoughts coherently, backed up by scientific reasoning. *(10 minutes)*

Answers to in-text questions

a A genetic disorder is inherited from parents. An infectious disorder is caught from other people.

b Cystic fibrosis is caused by a recessive allele.

Simple inheritance in animals and plants

B2 5.6 — Inherited conditions in humans

Learning objectives
- How are human genetic disorders inherited?
- How can we use a genetic diagram to predict whether a child will inherit a genetic disorder?
- Can you construct a genetic diagram to make predictions about the likelihood of inheriting a genetic disorder? [H]

Not all diseases are infectious. Sometimes diseases are the result of a problem in our genes and can be passed on from parent to child. They are known as **genetic or inherited disorders**.

We can use our knowledge of dominant and recessive alleles to work out the risk of inheriting a **genetic disorder**.

a How is an inherited disorder different from an infectious disease?

Polydactyly
Sometimes babies are born with extra fingers or toes. This is called **polydactyly**. The most common form of polydactyly is caused by a dominant allele. It can be inherited from one parent who has the condition. People often have their extra digit removed, but some live quite happily with them.

Higher: If one of your parents has polydactyly and is heterozygous, you have a 50% chance of inheriting the disorder. That's because half of their gametes will contain the faulty allele. If they are homozygous, you will definitely have the condition.

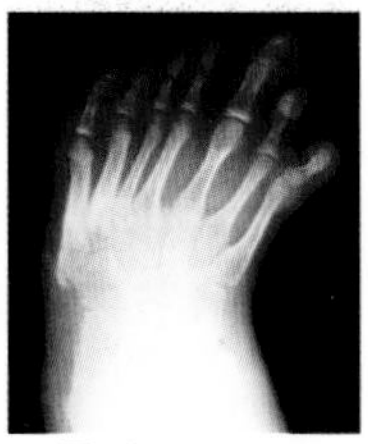

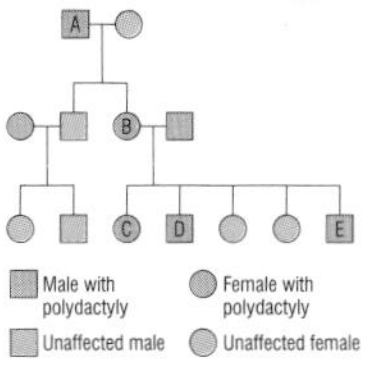

Cystic fibrosis [k]
Cystic fibrosis is a genetic disorder that affects many organs of the body, particularly the lungs and the pancreas. Over 8500 people in the UK have cystic fibrosis.

Organs become clogged up by thick, sticky mucus, which stops them working properly. The reproductive system is also affected, so many people with cystic fibrosis are infertile.

Treatment for cystic fibrosis includes physiotherapy and antibiotics. These help keep the lungs clear of mucus and infections. Enzymes are used to replace the ones the pancreas cannot produce and to thin the mucus.

However, although treatments are getting better all the time, there is still no cure.

Cystic fibrosis is caused by a recessive allele so it must be inherited from both parents. Children affected by cystic fibrosis are usually born to parents who do not suffer from the disorder. They have a dominant healthy allele, which means their bodies work normally. However, they also carry the recessive cystic fibrosis allele. Because it gives them no symptoms, they have no idea it is there. They are known as **carriers**.

In the UK, one person in 25 carries the cystic fibrosis allele. Most of them will never be aware of it. They only realise when they have children with a partner who also carries the allele. Then there is a 25% (one in four) chance that any child they have will be affected.

b You will only inherit cystic fibrosis if you get the cystic fibrosis allele from both parents. Why?

Figure 1 Polydactyly is passed through a family tree by a dominant allele

Male with polydactyly / Female with polydactyly / Unaffected male / Unaffected female

The genetic lottery
When the genes from parents are combined, it is called a genetic cross. We can show this using a genetic diagram (see Figures 2 and 3). A genetic diagram shows us:
- the alleles for a characteristic carried by the parents (the genotype of the parents)
- the possible gametes which can be formed from these
- how these could combine to form the characteristic in their offspring. The genotype of the offspring allows you to work out the possible phenotypes too.

When looking at the possibility of inheriting genetic disorders, it is important to remember that every time an egg and a sperm fuse it is down to chance which alleles combine. So if two parents who are heterozygous for the cystic fibrosis allele have four children, there is a 25% chance (one in four) that each child might have the disorder.

But in fact all four children could have cystic fibrosis, or none of them might be affected. They might all be carriers, or none of them might inherit the faulty alleles at all. It's all down to chance!

	P	p
p	Pp	pp
p	Pp	pp

50% chance polydactyly, PP or Pp, 50% chance normal pp

Pp = Parent with polydactyly
pp = Normal parent

Figure 2 A genetic diagram for polydactyly

Both parents are carriers, so Cc.

	C	c
C	CC	Cc
c	Cc	cc

Genotype: 25% normal (CC) 50% carriers (Cc) 25% affected by cystic fibrosis (cc)

Phenotype: 3/4, or 75% chance normal 1/4, or 25% chance cystic fibrosis

Figure 3 A genetic diagram for cystic fibrosis

Curing genetic diseases
So far we have no way of curing genetic disorders. Scientists hope that genetic engineering could be the answer. It should be possible to cut out faulty alleles and replace them with healthy ones. They have tried this in people affected by cystic fibrosis. Unfortunately, so far they have not managed to cure anyone.

Genetic tests are available that can show people if they carry the faulty allele. This allows them to make choices such as whether or not to have a family. It is possible to screen fetuses or embryos during pregnancy for the alleles which cause inherited disorders. You can also screen embryos before they are implanted in the mother during IVF treatment. These tests are very useful but raise many ethical issues.

Summary questions
1 a What is polydactyly?
  b Why can one parent with the allele for polydactyly pass the condition on to their children even though the other parent is not affected?
  c Look at the family tree in Figure 1. For each of the five people labelled A to E affected by polydactyly; give their possible alleles and explain your answers.

2 a Why are carriers of cystic fibrosis not affected by the disorder themselves?
  b Why must both of your parents be carriers of the allele for cystic fibrosis before you can inherit the disease?

3 A couple have a baby who has cystic fibrosis. Neither the couple, nor their parents, have any signs of the disorder.
  Draw genetic diagrams showing the possible genotypes of the grandparents and the parents to show how this could happen. [H]

Key points
- Some disorders are inherited.
- Polydactyly is caused by a dominant allele of a gene and can be inherited from only one parent.
- Cystic fibrosis is caused by a recessive allele of a gene and so must be inherited from both parents.
- You can use genetic diagrams to predict how genetic disorders might be inherited.
- You can construct genetic diagrams to predict the inheritance of genetic disease. [H]

Further teaching suggestions

Sex-linked genetic disorders
- The best-known sex-linked genetic disorders are haemophilia and colour blindness. Discuss the inheritance of conditions with genes located on the X chromosome. Draw up Punnett squares to show how the alleles are inherited and the probability of the disease occurring. It was suggested on the last spread that gifted and talented students did some research on haemophilia. This could be a good opportunity for them to present their findings.

Study tip
It is sensible for students to be able to use Punnett diagrams: it makes the interpretation of any genetic cross much easier. It could be a good idea to stress to students that they are dealing with ratios and probabilities. What happens in real life is not always the same!

Summary answers
1 a A genetic disorder which causes extra fingers or toes.
  b The faulty allele is dominant, so only one parent needs to have the allele and pass it on for the offspring to be affected.
  c A Pp only – as produced a child that was unaffected.
    B Pp – because mother must pass on a recessive allele to produce two unaffected children.
    C–E – could be PP or Pp as each parent has the genotype Pp.

2 a Carriers have a normal dominant allele, so their body works normally.
  b CF (cystic fibrosis) recessive – must inherit one from each parent to get the disease – but if parents had the disease themselves, they would almost certainly be infertile so parents must be carriers.

3 Genetic diagram based on Figure 3 in Student Book, showing how the cc (cystic fibrosis) arises.

B2 5.7

Stem cells and embryos – science and ethics

Learning objectives

Students should learn:

- that there are social and ethical issues concerning the use of stem cells from embryos
- that there are economic, social and ethical issues concerning embryo screening
- to make informed judgements about these issues.

Learning outcomes

Most students should be able to:

- list some of the opinions for and against the use of stem cells in medical research and treatments
- describe the problems associated with the screening of embryos for genetic disorders.

Some students should also be able to:

- make informed judgements about the issues they have studied and from information presented to them.

Support

- Ask simple questions, such as 'If you or someone you loved was ill, would you donate bone marrow, even if it hurt?'

Extend

- Get students to find out about different aspects of stem cell research which do not involve the use of embryos or foetal tissue.

Specification link-up: Biology B2.7

- Cells from human embryos and adult bone marrow called stem cells, can be made to differentiate into many different types of cells e.g. nerve cells. *[B2.7.1 k)]*
- Make informed judgements about the sort of social and ethical issues concerning the use of stem cells from embryos in medical research and treatments. *[B2.7]*
- Make informed judgements about the economic, social and ethical issues concerning embryo screening. *[B2.7]*

Lesson structure

Starters

In the beginning… – Get the students to think back through their lives and to their earliest memory. Share a few of these with the class. Ask did they actually exist before this memory? Engender a debate as to when they started – when they became themselves, possibly best phrased as getting them to think of a time when they were not themselves. Link this to the debate on whether a fertilised egg is a human being or not. *(5 minutes)*

Wished out of existence – Get the students to think of someone they know, either personally or know of through the media who has a disability of some description. Empathise with them. Ask the students to consider whether, if the parents had known that the child would be disabled, they would have allowed the child to be born (if they had been given the choice). Would they have tried for another baby instead? What factors would have influenced their decision? Support students by providing some examples of popular media figures who have some disability. Extend students by providing them with access to suitable sections from ethics text books on the subject. *(10 minutes)*

Main

- Carry out the stem cell dilemma activity ('Activity 1') from the Student Book. Several internet sites have been suggested as good sources of information about stem cell research. One of the ways in which the views of the target group can be discovered is by means of a questionnaire. The questions need to be phrased correctly to elicit the information. Students should ask whether or not the group they are questioning are aware of some of the pros and cons before asking for their opinions. Carefully designed questions should yield information and the results of such a questionnaire could form part of the display.

- Working in groups, get the students to produce display material as suggested, using the information for and against as starting points.

- The students can display the results of the original survey in a variety of different ways. They should be bold and innovative, making use of ICT. The subsequent survey and any changes of opinion can reveal how good their material was. Again, bold display of the data is needed. They might like to find out if their target group needed more information or whether it was pitched at the right level.

- Students could discuss the pros and cons of genetic screening using the material in the Student Book and from other sources. They may need to research more topics using the internet sites given previously.

- The activity suggested ('Activity 2') is a difficult one for some students to do without carrying out more research. It also requires a degree of confidence. Give students time to discuss their approach and suggest they work in small groups. Perhaps they could plan it like a film script or scenes from a TV documentary. The questions suggested could be expanded with some about the lives of the couple included. Ask: 'How demanding are their jobs? How have they coped with the child they already have?' If each group approached the activity from a slightly different perspective, then these role-play exercises could prove interesting to the class and provide them with a balanced view.

Plenaries

Continuum – Ask students to place themselves, or a card with their name on it, along a line from two opposing viewpoints: for and against using embryonic stem cells. They could be asked to justify their position when challenged by their peers. *(5 minutes)*

Thank you for your bone marrow – Get students to write a postcard from hospital to the person who has just donated bone marrow to them. Support students by prompting or giving them some words and phrases to arrange. Extend students by getting them to explain how the donation will improve their life. Select some students to read out their messages. *(10 minutes)*

Further teaching suggestions

Counselling speaker
- If anyone knows a genetic counsellor, it might be a good opportunity to invite them in to the school to give a short talk and answer questions about the topic.

Bone marrow transplants
- Students could find information about bone marrow transplants. Information can be obtained from the Anthony Nolan Trust.

Identity transplants
- Explore how the students view the concept of identity transplants – will this ever be possible? Discuss the 2009 film *Avatar* and link with superstitious ideas about possession by demons. Discuss brain transplants and the possible future potential of memory transplants.

How Science Works — Simple inheritance in animals and plants

Stem cells and embryos – science and ethics

B2 5.7
Stem cells and embryos – science and ethics

Learning objectives
- Does everyone agree with the use of embryonic stem cells?
- Are there any problems related to embryo screening?

The stem cell dilemma
Doctors have treated people with adult stem cells for many years by giving bone marrow transplants. Now scientists are moving ever closer to treating very ill people using embryonic stem cells. This area of medicine raises many issues. People have strong opinions about using embryonic stem cells – here are some of them:

In favour of using embryonic stem cells in medical research and possible treatments	Against using embryonic stem cells in medical research and possible treatments
• Embryonic stem cells offer one of the best chances of finding treatments for many different and often very serious conditions, including paralysis from spinal injury, Alzheimer's and diabetes. • The embryos used are generally spare embryos from infertility treatment which would be destroyed anyway. • Embryos are being created from adult cells for use in research and therapy – they would never become babies. • It may be possible to use embryonic stem cells from the umbilical cord of newborn babies, so that no embryos need to be destroyed for the research and treatments to go ahead. • Embryonic stem cells could be used to grow new tissues and organs for transplants.	• Embryonic stem cell treatments are very experimental and there is a risk that they may cause further problems such as the development of cancers. • All embryos have the potential to become babies. It is therefore wrong to experiment on them or destroy them. • Embryos cannot give permission to be used in experiments or treatments, so it is unethical. • It is taking a long time to develop any therapy that works – the money and research time would be better spent on other possible treatments such as new drugs or using adult stem cells.

Activity 1

Your class is going to produce a large wall display covered with articles both for and against stem cell research. Your display is aimed at students in Years 10–11. Make sure the level of content is right for your target group.

Try and carry out a survey or a vote with your target group before the display is put up to assess attitudes to the use of embryonic stem cells. Record your findings.

Work on your own or in a small group to produce one piece of display material either in favour of stem cell research or against it. Use a variety of resources to help you – the material in this chapter is a good starting point. Make sure that your ideas are backed up with as much scientific evidence as possible.

Once the material has been displayed for a week or two, repeat your initial survey or vote. Analyse the data to see if easy access to information has changed people's views.

The ethics of screening
Today we not only understand the causes of many genetic disorders, we can also test for them. However, being able to test for a genetic disorder doesn't necessarily mean we should always do it.

- Huntington's disease is inherited through a dominant allele. It causes death in middle age. People in affected families can take a genetic test for the faulty allele. Some people in affected families take the test and use it to help them decide whether to marry or have a family. Others prefer not to know.
- Some couples with an inherited disorder in their family have any developing embryos tested during pregnancy. Cells from the embryo are checked. If it is affected, the parents have a choice. They may decide to keep the baby, knowing that it will have a genetic disorder when it is born. On the other hand, they may decide to have an abortion. This prevents the birth of a child with serious problems. Then they can try again to have a healthy baby.
- Some couples with an inherited disorder in the family have their embryos screened before they are implanted in the mother. Embryos are produced by IVF (*in vitro* fertilisation). Doctors remove a single cell from each embryo and screen it for inherited disorders. Only healthy embryos free from genetic disorders are implanted back into their mother, so only babies without that disorder are born.

Activity 2

Genetic counsellors help families affected by particular genetic disorders to understand the problems and the choices available. Plan a role play of an interview between a genetic counsellor and a couple who already have one child with cystic fibrosis, and would like to have another child.

Either: Plan the role of the counsellor. Make sure you have all the information you need to be able to explain the chances of another child being affected and the choices that are open to the parents.

Or: Plan the role of a parent or work in pairs to give the views of a couple. Think carefully about the factors that will affect your decision, e.g. can you cope with another sick child? Are you prepared to have an abortion? Do you have religious views on the matter? What is fairest to the unborn child, and the child you already have? Is it ethical to choose embryos to implant?

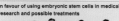

	H	h
h	Hh	hh
h	Hh	hh

H = dominant, Huntington's disease
h = recessive, no Huntington's disease

Offspring genotype: 50% Hh, 50% hh

Phenotype: 50% Huntington's disease
50% healthy

Figure 1 A genetic diagram for Huntington's disease

Summary questions
1 What are the main ethical issues associated with the use of embryonic stem cells?
2 It would cost a lot of money to screen all embryos for genetic conditions. Put forward two arguments for, and two against, this process.

Key points
- It is important that people make informed judgements about the use of embryonic stem cells in medical research and treatment.
- There are a number of economic, social and ethical issues surrounding the screening of embryos.

Summary answers

1 The main ethical issue is the source of the stem cells – some people are completely against the use of embryos in this way, seeing them as potential human beings.

2 Any two arguments for and two against universal embryo screening.

Summary answers

1 a Mitosis is cell division that takes place in the normal body cells and produces genetically identical daughter cells.

b [Marks awarded for correct sequence of diagrams with suitable annotations.]

c All the divisions from the fertilised egg to the baby are mitosis. After birth, all the divisions for growth are mitosis, together with all the divisions involved in repair and replacement of damaged tissues.

2 Meiosis is a special form of cell division to produce gametes where the chromosome number is reduced by half. It takes place in the reproductive organs (the ovaries and testes).

3 a Meiosis is important because it halves the chromosome number of the cells, so that when two gametes fuse at fertilisation, the normal chromosome number is restored. It also allows variety to be introduced.

b [Marks awarded for correct sequence of diagrams with appropriate annotations.]

4 a Stem cells are unspecialised cells which can differentiate (divide and change into many different types of cell) when they are needed.

b They may be used to repair damaged body parts, e.g. grow new spinal nerves to cure paralysis; grow new organs for transplants; repair brains in demented patients. [Accept any other sensible suggestions.]

c **For:** They offer tremendous hope of new treatments; they remove the need for donors in transplants; they could cure paralysis, heart disease, dementia etc; can grow tissues to order.

Against: They use tissue from human embryos; it's wrong to use embryos, as these could become people; embryos cannot give permission; stem cells could develop into cancers. [Accept any other valid points on either side of the debate.]

5 [Give credit for valid points made and the way in which the letter is written.]

6 a Sami's alleles are **ss**. We know this because she has curved thumbs and the recessive allele is curved thumbs. She must have inherited two recessive alleles to have inherited the characteristic.

b If the baby has curved thumbs, then Josh is **Ss**. The baby has inherited a recessive allele from each parent, so Josh must have a recessive allele. We know he also has a dominant allele as he has straight thumbs.

Sami

		s	s
Josh	S	Ss	Ss
	s	ss	ss

c If the baby has straight thumbs, then Josh could be either Ss or SS. We know that the baby has inherited one recessive allele from mother, and we know that Josh has one dominant allele but we do not know if he has two dominant alleles.

Sami

		s	s
Josh	S	Ss	Ss
	S	Ss	Ss

Summary questions 🅺

1 a What is mitosis?

b Explain, using diagrams, what takes place when a cell divides by mitosis.

c Mitosis is very important during the development of a baby from a fertilised egg. It is also important all through life. Why?

2 What is meiosis and where does it take place?

3 a Why is meiosis so important?

b Explain, using labelled diagrams, what takes place when a cell divides by meiosis. [H]

4 a What are stem cells?

b It is hoped that many different medical problems may be cured using stem cells. Explain how this might work.

c There are some ethical issues associated with the use of embryonic stem cells. Explain the arguments both for and against their use.

5 Hugo de Vries is one of the scientists who made the same discoveries as Mendel several years after Mendel's death. Write a letter from Hugo to one of his friends after he has found Mendel's writings. Explain what Mendel did, why no one took any notice of him and how the situation has changed so that you (Hugo) can come up with a clear explanation for the results of your own experiments. Explain your attitude to Mendel.

6 Whether you have a straight thumb or a curved one is decided by a single gene with two alleles. The allele for a straight thumb, S, is dominant to the curved allele, s. Use this information to help you answer these questions.

Josh has straight thumbs but Sami has curved thumbs. They are expecting a baby.

a We know exactly what Sami's thumb alleles are. What are they and how do you know?

b If the baby has curved thumbs, what does this tell you about Josh's thumb alleles? Draw and complete a Punnett square to show the genetics of your explanation.

c If the baby has straight thumbs, what does this tell us about Josh's thumb alleles? Draw and complete a Punnett square to show the genetics of your explanation. [H]

7 Amjid grew some purple flowering pea plants from seeds he had bought at the garden centre. He planted them in his garden.

Here are his results.

Seeds planted	247
Purple-flowered plants	242
White-flowered plants	1
Seeds not growing	4

a Is the white-flowered plant an anomaly? Why?

b Are the seeds that did not grow anomalies? Why?

c Suggest other investigations Amjid could carry out into the cause of the colour of the white-flowered plant.

Amjid was interested in these plants, so he collected the seed from some of the purple-flowered plants and used them in the garden the following year. He made careful note of what happened.

Here are his results:

Seeds planted	406
Purple-flowered plants	295
White-flowered plants	102
Seeds not growing	6

Amjid was slightly surprised. He did not expect to find that a third of his flowers would be white.

d i The purple allele (P) is dominant and the allele for white flowers (p) is recessive. Draw a genetic diagram that explains Amjid's numbers of purple and white flowers.

ii How accurate were Amjid's results compared with the expected ratio?

e How could Amjid have improved his method of growing the peas to make his results more valid?

---

7 a Yes, the white flowered plant is an anomaly because it is not as expected.

b Yes, the seeds that did not grow are also anomalies probably due to the way they were grown or some genetic problem.

c As an anomaly, the white flowered plant should be investigated, e.g. to see if the colour was a result of a mutation or because of the particular conditions in which it was grown. He could breed from it, plant it in a different soil, etc.

d i To have white flowers both of the parent plants must have contained a recessive white allele so

	P	p
P	PP	Pp
p	Pp	pp

ii Expect a 3 : 1 ratio actual results 295 : 102 – very close.

e To improve his method of growing the peas to make his results more valid Amjid could have grown them under controlled conditions.

Kerboodle resources 🅺

Resources available for this chapter on Kerboodle are:

- Chapter map: Simple inheritance in animals and plants
- Animation: Chromosomes (B2 5.1)
- Extension: Mitosis and cancer (B2 5.1)
- Bump up your grade: Mitosis or meiosis? (B2 5.2)

ractice questions

Copy and complete the following sentences using the words or symbols below:

characteristics cytoplasm fitness genes nucleus proteins tissue

2 23 46 X XX XY Y

In the body cells of a boy there are .... chromosomes that are found in the .... The boy's cells can be identified as male by the .... chromosome. On all the chromosomes there are sections called .... that determine the .... of the boy. (5)

The drawing shows some of the stages of reproduction in horses.

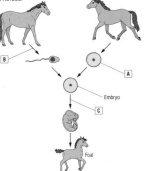

a i Name this type of reproduction (1)
   ii Name the type of cell labelled **A**. (1)
b Name the type of cell division taking place at the stages labelled:
   i **B** (1)
   ii **C**. (1)
c How does the number of chromosomes in each cell of the embryo compare with the number of chromosomes in cell **A**? (1)
d When the foal grows up it will look similar to its parents but it will **not** be identical to either parent.
   i Explain why it will look similar to its parents. (1)
   ii Suggest **two** reasons why it will **not** be identical to either of its parents. (2)
       AQA, 2001

3 When an embryo is formed, the cells divide and start to differentiate. Some adult cells are still able to differentiate.
   a What is meant by the term *differentiation*? (1)
   b What name do we give to cells which have not differentiated? (1)
   c Give an example of adult cells that can differentiate. (1)
   d Some of the embryo cells may be used in the future to treat conditions such as paralysis.
      There are people who do not think we should use embryos in this way. What is an ethical reason for objecting to the use of embryos? (1)

4 *In this question you will be assessed on using good English, organising information clearly and using specialist terms where appropriate.*

Doctors all over the world are investigating the use of stem cells to treat a wide variety of disorders.

Many doctors use adult stem cells but some use embryonic stem cells. There is evidence that adult stem cells do not cause cancer tumours if they are transferred soon after being removed from the body. Embryonic stem cells multiply very quickly and there is a risk of cancer developing after treatment with them.

Bone marrow cells are stem cells which continually replace your blood cells every day of your life.

Adult stem cells from bone marrow have been used successfully to treat leukaemia for over 40 years. Many patients with damage to the nervous system have reported improvements in movement following treatment with adult stem cells, but more research is needed before widespread use of the treatment.

One doctor said, 'It is safer to use adult stem cells. Using embryonic stem cells is not ethical.'

Using the information and your own knowledge explain the statement made by the doctor. (6)

201

Practice answers

1 46   nucleus   Y   genes   characteristics *(5 marks)*

2 a i sexual/sex *(1 mark)*
      ii egg/gamete/sex cell/ovum *(reject* ovule*)* *(1 mark)*
   b i meiosis/reduction *(1 mark)*
      ii mitosis/somatic *(1 mark)*
   c twice as many *(reject answers based on 23/46 chromosomes)* *(1 mark)*
   d i information/genes/DNA passed from parents (chromosomes neutral) *(1 mark)*
      ii genes/genetic information/chromosomes from two parents
             <u>alleles</u> may be different
             environmental effect/named
             may have been mutation
             any two for 1 mark each *(2 marks)*

3 a The cells change into other types of cell. *(1 mark)*
   b stem cells *(1 mark)*
   c bone marrow cells *(1 mark)*
         allow other types of adult stem cells – not umbilical cord cells
   d It may lead to death of an embryo/An embryo cannot give consent. *(1 mark)*
         – allow other ethical reason – not religious reasons

4 There is a clear, balanced and detailed explanation about the differences between adult and embryonic stem cells and the uses and advantages of the adult stem cells. The answer shows almost faultless spelling, punctuation and grammar. It is coherent and in an organised, logical sequence. It contains a range of appropriate or relevant specialist terms used accurately. *(5–6 marks)*

There is some attempt to explain the differences between adult and embryonic stem cells and the benefits of adult stem cells. There are some errors in spelling, punctuation and grammar. The answer has some structure and organisation. The use of specialist terms has been attempted, but not always accurately. *(3–4 marks)*

There is a brief description of what stem cells do and some evidence of the uses of stem cells. The spelling, punctuation and grammar are very weak. The answer is poorly organised with almost no specialist terms and/or their use demonstrating a general lack of understanding of their meaning. *(1–2 marks)*

No relevant content. *(0 marks)*

Examples of biology points made in the response:
- Stem cells are able to change into other types of cell
- Stem cells can be removed from adults, e.g. bone marrow
- Embryonic stem cells are taken from early embryos before the cells have started to change into other cells
- This is unethical because the embryo is destroyed
- There is a risk of cancer with embryonic stem cells
- Adult stem cells have been used safely for 40 years
- To treat leukaemia/other named example
- Patients with nervous system disorders have shown improvements after treatment with adult stem cells
- Accept another relevant point which answers the doctor's statement.

- Support: The gametes (B2 5.2)
- WebQuest: Stem cell research (B2 5.3)
- Viewpoints: Stem cell research (B2 5.3)
- Viewpoints: DNA fingerprinting (B2 5.4)
- Practical: Extracting DNA from kiwi fruits
- Animation: The inheritance of cystic fibrosis (B2 5.6)
- Interactive activity: Inheritance
- Revision podcast: Simple inheritance in animals and plants
- Test yourself: Simple inheritance
- On your marks: Simple inheritance in animals and plants
- Practice questions: Simple inheritance in animals and plants
- Answers to practice questions: Simple inheritance in animals and plants

Practical suggestions

Practicals	AQA		📖	⚙️
Observation or preparation of root tip squashes to illustrate chromosomes and mitosis.	✓		✓	
Using genetic beads to model mitosis and meiosis and genetic crosses.	✓	✓	✓	
Making models of DNA.	✓		✓	
Extracting DNA from kiwi fruit.	✓	✓		

B2 6.1 The origins of life on Earth

Learning objectives

Students should learn:

- the nature of fossils
- how fossils provide evidence for the existence of prehistoric plants and animals.

Learning outcomes

Most students should be able to:

- explain what a fossil is
- describe some of the ways in which fossils are formed
- suggest reasons why scientists cannot be certain about how life began on Earth.

Some students should also be able to:

- evaluate what can be learnt from the fossil record.

Support

- Get students to make a fossil using modelling clay or plaster of Paris for a mould and molten stearic acid to pour in and set (take care with hot liquids). Alternatively, students could use a modelling clay mould and pour plaster of Paris into the impression of a shell.

Extend

- Set students the problem of finding out how long a representation of a timeline would need to be if the Earth is 4 600 000 000 years old and 100 years was represented by a millimetre. Ask: 'How many A4 sheets of paper would be needed, allowing 1 cm overlap for gluing?' [Do not try to make one – it is over 40 km!]

Specification link-up: Biology B2.8

- Evidence for early forms of life comes from fossils. *[B2.8.1 a)]*
- Fossils are the 'remains' of organisms from many years ago, which are found in rocks. Fossils may be formed in various ways:
  - from the hard parts of animals that do not decay easily
  - from parts of organisms that have not decayed because one or more of the conditions needed for decay are absent
  - when parts of the organism are replaced by other materials as they decay
  - as preserved traces of organisms, e.g. footprints, burrows and rootlet traces. *[B2.8.1 b)]*
- Many early forms of life were soft-bodied, which means that they have left few traces behind. What traces there were have been mainly destroyed by geological activity. *[B2.8.1 c)]*
- Suggest reasons why scientists cannot be certain about how life began on Earth. *[B2.8]*

Lesson structure

Starters

Fossil five words – Get the students to explain their current understanding of what fossils are in five words. Read some examples out. Support students by placing some words to choose from on the board. Extend students by allowing them to create more five-word sentences – what they feel about fossils, what their importance is, etc. *(5 minutes)*

Fossil circus – Arrange a circus of numbered fossils or fossil pictures around the laboratory. Get students to look and make notes on what they might be. *(10 minutes)*

Main

- Create a PowerPoint presentation or exposition on the ways that fossils form, such as cast formation, impressions and ice fossils. Victims of Pompeii illustrate cast formation; mammoths are found in ice; dinosaurs left footprints and animal droppings fossilise over time. For pictures, search the internet using key words and especially look for Ardley Quarry in Oxfordshire for its dinosaur footprints. Provide the students with a worksheet that they can complete as the presentation proceeds.

- Give students a timeline exercise linking with the above. Using a long strip of paper (e.g. till roll), students should mark off the major evolutionary events for which there is evidence. An alternative to this is to use a clock face and discover that *Homo sapiens* evolved in the last few seconds before 12 midnight.

- Give students an outline account of some of the methods of dating fossils: layers in rocks and sediments, potassium-argon dating, radiocarbon dating and looking at fossils of other species that overlap. With some more recent human fossils, the presence of artefacts (tools or shaped stones) can give clues as to the age of a fossil.

- Try to get hold of some peat, look for plant remains and discuss their age (can be many thousands of years old).

- Show students pictures of reconstructions of large fossil dinosaurs (such as are on show in the Natural History Museum) and ask: Were these fossils found as complete skeletons? Show some pictures of how reconstruction of fossils takes place using bits of the original skeleton. Discuss how accurate these reconstructions are. How are scientists sure that what they build up is a true representation? Refer students to reconstruction that has been done with prehistoric human skulls.

Plenaries

What makes a good fossil? – Lead a quick discussion on why some creatures became fossilised and others did not. Ask: 'Why are there few fossils of worms and other soft-bodied creatures?' *(5 minutes)*

Only half the story … – Display a sentence with many of the letters missing, but enough left to see what it is saying. Ask the students to write their own completed version. Support students by leaving out fewer letters or giving them a list of the missing letters that they can insert in appropriate places. Extend students by leaving out more letters and some words. Read out and discuss. *(10 minutes)*

Maths skills

Introduce students to the idea of a scale. Remind them that 10^3 is a thousand, 10^6 is a million and 10^9 is a billion. Link this to evolutionary timescales, so that students have a clear idea of how sizeable they are.

Old and new species

B2 6.1 The origins of life on Earth ⓚ

Learning objectives

- What is the evidence for the origins of life on Earth?
- What are fossils?
- What can we learn from fossils?

There is no record of the origins of life on Earth. It is a puzzle that can never be completely solved. There is not much valid evidence for what happened – no one was there to see it! We don't even know exactly when life on Earth began. However, most scientists think it was somewhere between 3 to 4 billion years ago.

There are some interesting ideas and well-respected theories that explain most of what you can see around you. The biggest problem we have is finding the evidence to support the ideas.

a When do scientists think life on Earth began?

What can we learn from fossils?

Some of the best evidence we have about the history of life on Earth comes from **fossils**. Fossils are the remains of organisms from many thousands or millions of years ago that are found preserved in rocks, ice and other places. For example, fossils have revealed the world of the dinosaurs. These lizards dominated the Earth at one stage and died out millions of years before humans came to dominate the Earth.

Maths skills

Time scales for the evolution of life are big:
- A thousand years is 10^3 years.
- A million years is 10^6 years.
- A billion years is 10^9 years.

You have probably seen a fossil in a museum or on TV, or maybe even found one yourself. Fossils can be formed in a number of ways:
- They may be formed from the hard parts of an animal. These are the bits that do not decay easily, such as the bones, teeth, claws or shells.
- Another type of fossil is formed when an animal or plant does not decay after it has died. This happens when one or more of the conditions needed for decay are not there. This may be because there is little or no oxygen present. It could be because poisonous gases kill off the bacteria that cause decay. Sometimes the temperature is too low for decay to take place. Then the animals and plants are preserved in ice. These ice fossils are rare, but they give a clear insight into what an animal looked like. They can also tell us what an animal had been eating or the colour of a long-extinct flower. We can even extract the DNA and compare it to modern organisms.
- Many fossils are formed when harder parts of the animal or plant are replaced by other minerals. This takes place over long periods of time. These are the most common fossils (see Figure 3).
- Some of the fossils we find are not of actual animals or plants, but of traces they have left behind. Fossil footprints, burrows, rootlet traces and droppings are all formed. These help us to build up a picture of life on Earth long ago.

b Which is the most common type of fossil?

Did you know ...?

The biggest herbivore found so far is *Argentinosaurus huinculensis*. It was nearly 40 metres long and probably weighed about 80–100 tonnes! The biggest carnivore found, *Giganotosaurus*, was about 14 metres long. It had a brain the size of a banana and 20cm long serrated teeth. By comparison, the biggest modern lizard, the Komodo dragon, is about 3 metres long and weighs around 140kg.

Figure 1 A fossil of *Tyrannosaurus rex*

An incomplete record

The fossil record is not complete for several reasons. Many of the very earliest forms of life were soft-bodied organisms. This means they have left little fossil trace. It is partly why there is so little valid evidence of how life began. There is no fossil record of the earliest life forms on Earth.

Most organisms that died did not become fossilised – the right conditions for fossil formation were rare. Also, many of the fossils that were formed in the rocks have been destroyed by geological activity. Huge amounts of rock have been broken down, worn away, buried or melted over the years. As this happens the fossil record is lost too. Finally, there are many fossils that are still to be found.

In spite of all these limitations, the fossils we have found can still give us a 'snapshot' of life millions of years ago.

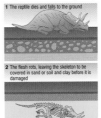

1 The reptile dies and falls to the ground

2 The flesh rots, leaving the skeleton to be covered in sand or soil and clay before it is damaged

3 Protected, over millions of years, the skeleton becomes mineralised and turns to rock. The rocks shift in the earth with the fossil trapped inside.

4 Eventually, the fossil emerges as the rocks move and erosion takes place

Figure 3 It takes a very long time for fossils to form, but they provide us with invaluable evidence of how life on Earth has developed

Figure 2 This baby mammoth was preserved in ice for at least 10000 years. Examining this kind of evidence helps scientists check the accuracy of ideas based on fossil skeletons alone.

Summary questions

1 Copy and complete using the words below:
animal   decay   evidence   fossils   ice fossils   minerals   plant

One important piece of .... for how life has developed on Earth are .... The most common type are formed when parts of the .... or .... are replaced by .... as it decays. Some fossils are formed when an organism does not .... after it dies. An example is ...., which are very rare.

2 There are several theories about how life on Earth began.
   a Why is it impossible to know for sure?
   b Why are fossils such important evidence for the way life has developed?

3 How do ice fossils help scientists check the evidence provided by the main fossil record?

Key points

- Fossils are the remains of organisms from many years ago that are found in rocks.
- Fossils may be formed in different ways.
- Fossils give us information about organisms that lived millions of years ago.
- It is very difficult for scientists to know exactly how life on Earth began because there is little evidence that is valid.

Further teaching suggestions

Fossil formation conditions
- Many fossil plants were found in the coal seams. Try finding pictures of a few, and then link their presence in coal with why conditions were good for fossil formation. This ties in with the term 'fossil fuels'.

Go on a fossil hunt
- Fossils can be found in many unlikely places, such as on public buildings. These are usually as the fossil remains of invertebrates found in Portland stone and other natural building materials. A trip around some municipal buildings could reveal some evidence.

Find out more about the fossil hunters
- Charles Lyell and Arthur Holmes are mentioned in the answer to the timeline question. Who were they? How did they become interested in fossils and dating rocks? They could also look up Mary Anning and read of her pioneering fossil discoveries. There are good links with geology here for interested students. Why are there more fossils in some rocks than in others?

Construct a fossil?
- Provide the students with printed outlines of fossil bones or parts of a dinosaur skeleton that they can assemble. The activity can be made more realistic by only giving them some of the parts and allowing them to try and work out what animal the skeleton belonged to. The Natural History Museum Picture Library is a good source of material.

Answers to in-text questions

a Between 3 and 4 billion years ago.

b Fossils where the harder parts of living organisms are replaced by minerals over a long period of time.

Summary answers

1 evidence, fossils, animal/plant, plant/animal, minerals, decay, ice fossils

2 **a** No one was there to see it and there is no direct evidence for what happened.
   b They show us how plants and animals have changed over time, how many animals have appeared and that some no longer exist.

3 Scientists build up models of earlier animals from fossils (often from fragments) so they don't know exactly what they looked like. Ice fossils allow scientists to see exactly what the original animal looked like and its internal structures. Scientists can compare these with models built up from rock fossils and see how accurate they are; and so learn from this for future rock-based models.

B2 6.2 Exploring the fossil evidence

Learning objectives

Students should learn:

- how fossil evidence indicates the extent to which some organisms changed over time
- that mass extinction of organisms occurred in the past.

Learning outcomes

Most students should be able to:

- describe some examples of how much organisms have changed over time
- suggest why some organisms may have become extinct, including massive natural disasters.

Some students should also be able to:

- explain how living organisms can cause the extinction of species.

Support

- Give students a matching exercise where bits of evidence are placed in one column and the theories that they back up are in another – they have to join the evidence to the theory it supports.

Extend

- Ask students to find out the different methods of dating fossils. They could summarise their findings in a poster which can be displayed in the laboratory.

Specification link-up: Biology B2.8

- We can learn from fossils how much or how little different organisms have changed as life developed on Earth. [B2.8.1 d)]
- Extinction may be caused by:
  - changes to the environment over geological time
  - new predators
  - new diseases
  - new, more successful, competitors
  - a single catastrophic event, e.g. massive volcanic eruptions or collisions with asteroids
  - the cyclical nature of speciation. [B2.8.1 e)]

Lesson structure

Starters

Can you run on your toenails? – Sensitively find out who has got the longest fingernails in the class. Ask: 'Are they the strongest? Could you do press-ups resting on your middle finger?' Relate this to how a horse walks, and introduce equine foot development using photographs of ancient hooves. This leads to a discussion of fossil evidence. (5 minutes)

Guinness advert evolution – Search the internet for a clip of the Guinness 'Evolution' advert from 2006 where three men are traced back in time through reverse evolution until they are mud skippers not enjoying drinking mud. Ask the students to make a list of the things that have some validity in the advert and to spot any flaws with it. Support students by giving them a list of the organisms and getting them to place them in order. Extend students by asking for their ideas on how the advert would look if they extended the time travel sequence further back into the past. (10 minutes)

Main

- Following on from the 'Can you run on your toenails?' Starter activity, take the students through the evolution of the modern horse. Point out that this is not necessarily a direct line of evolution, that there could have been many other variations that died out and the evidence we have is probably incomplete.
- Another good example of a sequence of changes can be illustrated by the fossil evidence for human evolution from *Australopithecus* to *Homo sapiens*. Research the Natural History Museum website and the work of Professor Chris Stringer for more information. Discuss the position of the Neanderthals – one of our relatives that died out. Why?
- Two good examples of organisms that were thought to have been extinct and only known in the fossil record are the Wollemi pine *(Wollemia nobilis)* and the Coelacanth *(Latimeria chalumnae)*, both of which have been found alive unexpectedly. Students can compare pictures of real Wollemia pine and Coelacanth specimens with pictures of fossils, commenting on any similarities and differences.

Plenaries

An overactive pituitary gland? – It has been suggested that the demise of the dinosaurs was caused by them developing overactive pituitary glands resulting in the excessive growth of bones and cartilage. Get the students to think of reasons why bigger bones could be a disadvantage. Support students by providing them with a list of suggestions from which they could discuss and choose appropriate reasons. Extend students by asking them to explain their reasoning. (5 minutes)

The extinction game – Five players have cards saying 'Climate change', 'Meteorite', 'Predators', 'Disease' and 'Competition' with appropriate pictures. Another player represents a species trying to survive. The 'species' throws a dice and one of the 'extinction' players also throws a dice. If the numbers match, the species is extinct and the players swap places and continue. If the numbers are different, the species has survived, the player collects the combined score on the dice and plays against the next 'extinction' player, until they eventually become extinct. Play to a time limit. (10 minutes)

Old and new species

B2 6.2

Exploring the fossil evidence

Learning objectives

- How much have organisms changed over time?
- What is extinction?
- How do living organisms cause extinction?

⌾ links

For information on fossil records, look back at B2 6.1 The origins of life on Earth.

Using the fossil record

The fossil record helps us to understand how much organisms have changed since life developed on Earth. However, this understanding is often limited. Only small bits of skeletons or little bits of shells have been found. Luckily we have a very complete fossil record for a few animals, including the horse. These relatively complete fossil records can show us how some organisms have changed and developed over time.

Fossils also show us that not all animals have changed very much. For example, fossil sharks from millions of years ago look very like modern sharks. They evolved early into a form that was almost perfectly adapted for their environment and their way of life. Their environment has not changed much for millions of years so sharks have also remained the same.

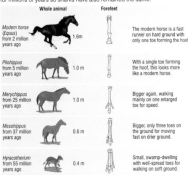

	Whole animal		Forefeet	
Modern horse (Equus) from 2 million years ago		1.6m		The modern horse is a fast runner on hard ground with only one toe forming the hoof.
Pliohippus from 5 million years ago		1.0 m		With a single toe forming the hoof, this looks more like a modern horse.
Merychippus from 25 million years ago		1.0 m		Bigger again, walking mainly on one enlarged toe for speed.
Mesohippus from 37 million years ago		0.6 m		Bigger, only three toes on the ground for moving fast on drier ground.
Hyracotherium from 55 million years ago		0.4 m		Small, swamp-dwelling with well-spread toes for walking on soft ground.

Figure 1 The evolutionary history of the horse based on the fossil record

Extinction

Throughout the history of life on Earth, scientists estimate that about 4 billion different species have existed. Yet only a few million species of living organisms are alive today. The rest have become extinct. **Extinction** is the permanent loss of all the members of a species.

As conditions change, new species evolve that are better suited to survive the new conditions. The older species that cannot cope with the changes gradually die out. This is because they are not able to compete so well for food and other resources. This is how evolution takes place and the number of species on Earth slowly changes. Some of the species that have become extinct are lost forever or only exist in the fossil record. Others have left living relatives.

a What is extinction?
b How many species of living organisms are thought to have existed on Earth over the years?

There are many different causes of extinction. They always involve a change in the environment such as new **predators**, new diseases or new, more successful competitors.

The gradual change of the climate over millions of years has also caused changes in the species that are adapted for a particular area. This is still happening today.

Organisms that cause extinction

Living organisms can change an environment and cause extinction in several different ways:

- New predators can wipe out unsuspecting prey animals very quickly. This is because the prey animals do not have adaptations to avoid them. New predators may evolve, or an existing species might simply move into new territory. Sometimes this can be due to human intervention. People accidentally brought the brown tree snake from Australia to the island of Guam after World War II. This caused the rapid extinction of many bird species on Guam. They were being eaten by the snakes. The birds had no time to evolve a defence against this new predator.

- New diseases (caused by microorganisms) can bring a species to the point of extinction. They are most likely to cause extinctions on islands, where the whole population of an animal or plant are close together. The Australian Tasmanian devil is one example of this. These rare animals are dying from a new form of infectious cancer. It attacks and kills them very quickly.

- Finally, one species can cause another to become extinct by successful competition. New mutations can give one type of organism a real advantage over another. Sometimes new species are introduced into an environment by mistake. This means that a new, more successful competitor can take over from the original animal or plant and make it extinct. In Australia, the introduction of rabbits has caused severe problems. They eat so much and breed so fast that the other native Australian animals are dying out because they cannot compete.

Summary questions

1 Copy and complete using the words below:

climate competitors diseases Earth environment extinction predators species

.... is the permanent loss of all the members of a .... from the .... It may be caused by new .... , new .... or new, successful .... It can also be caused by changes in the .... or the ....

2 Look at the evolution of the horse shown in Figure 1. Explain how the fossil evidence of the legs helps us to understand what the animals were like and how they lived.

3 Explain how each of the following situations might cause a species of animal or plant to become extinct.
  a Mouse Island has a rare species of black-tailed mice. They are preyed on by hawks and owls, but there are no mammals that eat them. A new family bring their pregnant pet cat to the island.
  b English primroses have quite small leaves. Several people bring home packets of seeds from a European primrose, which has bigger leaves and flowers very early in the spring.

?? Did you know ...?

The Scottish island of North Uist has a similar problem to Guam. Hedgehogs were brought to the island to combat the problem of garden slugs. Unfortunately, the hedgehogs bred rapidly and are eating the eggs and chicks of the many rare sea birds that breed on the island. Now people are trying to kill or remove the hedgehogs to save the birds.

Study tip

Always mention a *change* when you suggest reasons for extinction.

Key points

- We can learn from fossils how much or how little organisms have changed as life has developed on Earth.

- Extinction may be caused by new predators, new diseases or new, more successful competitors.

Further teaching suggestions

Missing links

- Show pictures of the skeleton and reconstructions of *Archaeopteryx* and ask students whether they think it is a bird or a reptile. List the bird-like features and the reptilian features separately. Then consider the features of modern birds which are like reptiles. Discuss 'missing links' or 'transitional species' and their importance in the fossil record.

What if humans become extinct...?

- Ask the students what they think would happen if humans suddenly became extinct. Get them to think of reasons why this might happen. They could discuss this in small groups and then bring all the ideas together.

Fossil fraud

- Students can carry out an internet search for information about fake fossils and the difficulties of establishing that a specimen is genuine. This could include finding out about how fossils are dated.

'Piltdown Man' and other hoaxes

- Tell the story of 'Piltdown Man' and the two skulls that were first announced in 1912 and finally proved to be forgeries in 1953. Get students to consider how such forgeries could be made. Mention other 'mistakes' or misidentifications, such as 'Nebraska Man' and 'Archaeoraptor'.

Answers to in-text questions

a The permanent loss of all the members of a species from the face of the Earth.

b About 4 billion.

Summary answers

1 extinction, species, Earth, predators/competitors, competitors/predators, diseases, environment/climate, climate/environment

2 It shows us how tall they were, what their feet were like, what their jaws and teeth were like and the basic body shape. This in turn tells us how they might have lived, how fast they moved, what they ate; it also allows us to compare them to modern horses.

3 a The cat has kittens, the kittens breed and soon there are lots of cats. Cats catch black-tailed mice easily, the mice numbers fall until there are not enough to breed and mice become extinct. Knock-on effect on owls and hawks as part of their diet has gone – which in turn will affect other prey animals.
  b European primroses will make more food and have bigger leaves – however, set seeds which will germinate sooner will be too much competition for the English primrose and eventually it could become extinct.

B2 6.3

More about extinction

Specification link-up: Biology B2.8

- Extinction may be caused by:
  - changes to the environment over geological time
  - new predators
  - new diseases
  - new, more successful competitors. [B2.8.1 e)]

Learning objectives

Students should learn:

- that environmental changes over geological time can cause extinction
- that mass extinctions of the past may have been caused by single catastrophic events.

Learning outcomes

Most students should be able to:

- explain what is meant by extinction
- describe some environmental changes that may have caused extinction
- suggest ways in which the extinction of the dinosaurs occurred.

Some students should also be able to:

- evaluate the theories for the extinction of the dinosaurs.

Lesson structure

Starters

Dead as a dodo – Search the internet for a picture of a dodo. Ask students to make a list, in rough, of as many types of extinct animal as they can in three minutes. Check who has the largest number and get the student to read the list. Ask others in the class to check and add. This leads into a discussion of what extinction means. *(5 minutes)*

What causes extinction? – Get the students to discuss in pairs or small groups the reasons why some species become extinct. Support students by giving prompts to help them identify ways in which animals may become extinct. Extend students by getting them to speculate on future causes of extinction and how they might be discussing this topic in 500 000 years time. *(10 minutes)*

Main

- Visit, for example, www.thedayaftertomorrowmovie.com to find information about global climatic changes. Highlight changes in temperature such as ice ages. Link, if possible, with the geological time scale discussed in B6.1 The origins of life on Earth and the evolution of different groups of organisms. Discuss the impact of these changes on the creatures around at the time. This can link up with the ideas of competition, survival of the fittest and natural selection.

- Much has been made of global warming altering our climate and the times at which plants flower, changing patterns of migration and growing different crops in different parts of the world. Ask: 'If our climate became warmer or colder, what animals and plants would be affected in Britain?'

- Show a video clip from the film *Deep Impact* of a simulated comet strike on Earth (search the web for 'Deep Impact trailer'). Make a model, using a light sensor attached to a data logger and a glass or plastic container containing some fine dust. Shine a light through and measure intensity before and after shaking up. Discuss the effects of the lack of light on life on Earth.

- Get the students to carry out an empathy exercise, imagining what it would have been like for the creatures living at the time of a comet strike or a global winter (if these theories are correct). Get them to write some creative prose or poetry to get across what it must have felt like being plunged into semi-darkness for months or years.

Support

- Initiate a class discussion on alteration of the climate. Then ask students to draw a picture to represent the kinds of crops which might be grown and the types of animals that might be farmed in the UK if the climate became hotter.

Extend

- Ask students to come up with a way of evaluating the relative strengths and weaknesses of opposing ideas on the way in which mass extinctions came about. You could hold a discussion on peer review and the importance of public scrutiny of research published in scientific journals.

Plenaries

Greatest impact – Write up the words 'Climate change', 'Meteorite', 'Predators', 'Disease' and 'Competition', or use the cards from 'The extinction game'. Ask students to rank the words in order of importance. Choose some to explain their choices. *(5 minutes)*

Mass extinction storyboard – Establish the different theories of why there were mass extinctions at the end of the age of the dinosaurs. Get the students, in pairs or small groups, to come up with an illustrated storyboard to guide production of a film, telling students their age about the different theories. Support students by showing them an example. Extend students by getting them to add a theory of their own. These students should provide more imaginative and complex responses than supported students. *(10 minutes)*

B2 6.3 — More about extinction

Learning objectives

- How does environmental change over long time scales affect living organisms?
- What caused the mass extinctions of the past?

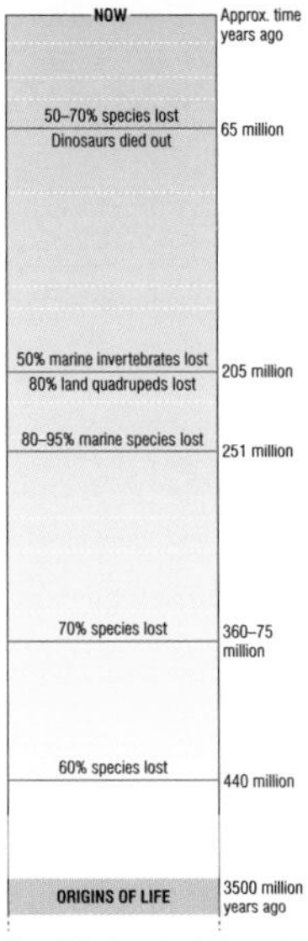

It isn't just changes in living organisms that bring about extinctions. The biggest influences on survival are changes in the environment.

Environmental changes

Throughout history, the climate and environment of the Earth has been changing. At times the Earth has been very hot. At other times, temperatures have fallen and the Earth has been in the grip of an Ice Age. These changes take place over millions and even billions of years.

Organisms that do well in the heat of a tropical climate won't do well in the icy conditions of an Ice Age. Many of them will become extinct through lack of food or being too cold to breed. However, species that cope well in cold climates will evolve and thrive by natural selection.

Changes to the climate or the environment have been the main cause of extinction throughout history. There have been five occasions during the history of the Earth when big climate changes have led to extinction on an enormous scale (see Figure 2).

Figure 1 The dinosaurs ruled the Earth for millions of years, but when the whole environment changed, they could not adapt and most of them died out. Mammals, which could control their own body temperature, had an advantage and became dominant.

a Why are Ice Ages often linked to extinctions?

Extinction on a large scale

Fossil evidence shows that at times there have been mass extinctions on a global scale. During these events many (or even most) of the species on Earth die out. This usually happens over a relatively short time period of several million years. Huge numbers of species disappear from the fossil record.

The evidence suggests that a single catastrophic event is often the cause of these mass extinctions. This could be a massive volcanic eruption or the collision of giant asteroids with the surface of the Earth.

b What is a mass extinction?

Figure 2 columns:

	Approx. time years ago
NOW	
50–70% species lost Dinosaurs died out	65 million
50% marine invertebrates lost 80% land quadrupeds lost	205 million
80–95% marine species lost	251 million
70% species lost	360–75 million
60% species lost	440 million
ORIGINS OF LIFE	3500 million years ago

Figure 2 The five main extinction events so far in the evolutionary history of the Earth

What destroyed the dinosaurs?

The most recent mass extinction was when the dinosaurs became extinct around 65 million years ago. In 2010 an international team of scientists published a review of all the evidence put together over the last 20 years. They agreed that around 65 million years ago a giant asteroid collided with the Earth in Chicxulub in Mexico.

We can see a huge crater (180 km in diameter) there. Scientists have identified a layer of rock formed from crater debris in countries across the world. The further you move away from the crater, the thinner the layer of crater debris in the rock. Also, deep below the crater, scientists found lots of a mineral only formed when a rock is hit with a massive force such as an asteroid strike.

The asteroid impact would have caused huge fires, earthquakes, landslides and tsunamis. Enormous amounts of material would have been blasted into the atmosphere. The accepted theory is that the dust in the atmosphere made everywhere almost dark. Plants struggled to survive and the drop in temperatures caused a global winter. Between 50–70% of all living species, including the dinosaurs, became extinct.

No sooner had this work been published than a group of UK scientists published different ideas and evidence. They suggest that the extinction of the dinosaurs started sooner (137 million years ago) and was much slower than previously thought.

Their idea is that the melting of the sea ice (caused by global warming) flooded the seas and oceans with very cold water. A drop in the sea temperature of about 9 °C triggered the mass extinction. Their evidence is based on an unexpected change in fossils and minerals that they found in areas of Norway.

As you can see, building up a valid, evidence-based history of events so long ago is not easy to do. Events can always be interpreted in different ways.

Figure 3 This layer of debris from the asteroid crater appears in rocks that are 65 million years old – the time the dinosaurs died out

links

For more information about the way people are changing the environment and bringing about extinction, see B3 chapter 4 How humans can affect the environment.

Study tip

Remember that the time scales in forming new species and mass extinctions are huge.

Try to develop an understanding of time in millions and billions of years.

Summary questions

1 **a** Give four causes of extinction in species of living organisms.
 b Give two possible causes of mass extinction events.

2 Why do you think extinction is an important part of evolution?

3 **a** Summarise the evidence for a giant asteroid impact as the cause of the mass extinction event that resulted in the death of the dinosaurs.
 b Explain why scientists think that low light levels and low temperatures would have followed a massive asteroid strike. Why would these have caused mass extinctions?

Key points

- Extinction can be caused by environmental change over geological time.
- Mass extinctions may be caused by single catastrophic events such as volcanoes or asteroid strikes.

Further teaching suggestions

Is extinction still happening?

- Discuss present environmental changes and ask students how they think these changes may affect the extinction of some species. How may such extinctions be prevented?

The stupidity of the dodos ...

- Search the internet for 'Ice age Dodo' and mention how the film portrays them as being very stupid. Discuss how stupid the real birds were. Ask: 'What can you deduce from their appearance? Could they run fast?' A video on the extinction of the dodo is available from Channel 4 as part of the series *Extinct* (0870 1234 344): could be shown in addition. Draw out reasons as to why they may have appeared stupid to invading humans.

The quagga

- The quagga, a relative of the zebra, became extinct in the 1880s. In the 1990s, attempts were started to 'revive' the species. An internet search can be made to find out about how this works.

Answers to in-text questions

a Many species of plants and animals are not adapted to deal with the very cold conditions, lack of food, etc. and so die out.

b When many different species all become extinct over the same relatively short period of time.

Summary answers

1 **a** Any four sensible suggestions, e.g. new predators, new diseases, new, more successful competitors, environmental changes such as global warming, more rainfall, etc.
 b Any sensible suggestions, e.g. massive volcanic eruptions, collision of giant asteroids with the Earth.

2 Because without extinction unsuccessful species would not die out. There would be too much competition for resources. New species would find it difficult to evolve. Any thoughtful point.

3 **a** Evidence for giant asteroid strike – crater, layer of rock debris, mineral formed when massive force hits rocks. The age of the rocks suggest this happened immediately before the mass extinction of dinosaurs.
 b An asteroid impact would have blasted huge amounts of dust and debris into the atmosphere. It would have triggered huge fires, earthquakes, landslides that would generate smoke and dust. This would have greatly reduced the levels of light reaching the Earth. In turn, this would have stopped plants growing and caused very low temperatures. This global winter would have caused the extinction of up to 70% of all the species on the Earth, including the dinosaurs because of the lack of food and an inability to keep warm, etc.

B2 6.4

Isolation and the evolution of new species

Learning objectives

Students should learn:

- that new species arise as a result of isolation
- that new species arise as a result of genetic variation and natural selection [HT only]
- that populations can be geographically isolated. [HT only]

Learning outcomes

Most students should be able to:

- describe the ways in which new species arise
- explain how some populations become isolated.

Some students should also be able to:

- explain that in isolated populations, alleles are selected which increase successful breeding [HT only]
- explain that speciation results when the isolated population becomes so different that interbreeding cannot take place. [HT only]

Answers to in-text questions

a The separation of two populations by geographical features.
b An organism which has evolved in one place only in geographical isolation.

Support

- Give students sets of diagrams to cut up, order in the correct sequence and stick into their books for each of the mechanisms of isolation. These should be checked for accuracy before sticking down.

Extend

- Get students to imagine a future global disaster where humans have been wiped out. Bearing in mind where our success as a species has come from, speculate as to how evolution may eventually fill the niche that we have up until now so dominantly occupied. Students could watch a clip from 'Planet of the Apes' as an introduction to this activity.

Specification link-up: Biology B2.8

- New species arise as a result of:
  - isolation – two populations of a species become separated, e.g. geographically
  - genetic variation: each population has a wide range of alleles that control their characteristics [HT only]
  - natural selection – in each population, the alleles that control the characteristics which help the organism to survive are selected [HT only]
  - speciation – the populations become so different that successful interbreeding is no longer possible. [B2.8.1 f)] [HT only]

Lesson structure

Starters

Aussies only, please! – Get the students to make a list of animals that only exist in Australia. Have some photographs ready to project of the obvious ones but also quite a few other ones. Draw out that there are large numbers of species that exist in Australia and nowhere else. Ask the students to think of why this might be and to summarise their ideas in a sentence to be read out to the class. *(5 minutes)*

What we know so far... – Get the students to put down their own ideas on how they would define a species and how new species might arise. Give a strict, short time limit and don't allow discussion at this stage. Collect responses on the board as to the ideas that are pre-existent within the class and encourage discussion of these to see which have the most currency. Support students by providing some suggestions or a list to choose from to help them to get started. Extend students by getting them to provide suggestions that are quite sophisticated. *(10 minutes)*

Main

- **What is a species?** – It is important that students have an understanding of the term 'species' from the beginning of this topic, so a brief review of the characteristics of the taxon may be needed.

- One way to get across the idea of an ecological niche is to show a picture of an architectural niche, such as a slot in a wall where a statue might be placed. A niche is probably best looked at as an opportunity to make a living. Ask the students to think of ways in which people make a living – where do they get what they need to survive? Extend this idea to animals and plants – what opportunities do they have to make a living? Get the students to list some of these (plants making their own food, herbivores eating plants, carnivores eating animals, parasites, decomposers, etc.). Get specific with some extreme examples. Tell them about the Hawaiian cleaner wrasse, *Labroides phthirophagus* (search the internet for details). Get the students to realise that a mass extinction would open up lots of niches (and habitats) previously occupied by other species. These other species would otherwise have competed successfully, had they not become extinct. The openings given by the mass extinction provided opportunities for making a living that were rapidly filled by evolution driven by natural selection.

- Use PowerPoint and exposition to get across the idea of separation leading to evolution of differences that eventually prevent interbreeding between the separated populations. Use video footage, if available, and examples from real life, such as the species of freshwater fish (*Salvelinus sp.*) in the lakes of Switzerland, Scandinavia and Great Britain. Almost every lake has a different form due to the barriers between them.

Plenaries

Just the job! – Show the students pairs of examples of convergent evolution, e.g. sharp teeth in a variety of carnivores, tiger and thylacine, ostrich and dodo, basking shark and filter feeding whales, etc. Ask the students to set down reasons why such separate species could finish up with such similar features, link this to speciation [HT only] as the mechanism for change. *(5 minutes)*

Lost world – Using the Bosavi Crater expedition to Papua New Guinea as a stimulus, get the students to imagine that they have encountered a hidden valley within an isolated mountain range where species have been geographically isolated for millions of years. What sort of creatures might you encounter? Support students by providing them with some suggestions. You could show them a clip from *Valley of the Dinosaurs* or *The Land That Time Forgot*. Extend students by getting them to produce a wide range of examples, imaginatively constructed from an analysis of different ecological areas that could theoretically be occupied by the descendants of other species that have evolved to fit them. *(10 minutes)*

Old and new species

B2 6.4

Isolation and the evolution of new species

Learning objectives

- How do new species arise?
- How do populations become isolated?
- Do new species always form at the same rate?
- How does speciation take place in an isolated population? [H]

?? Did you know ...?

Sometimes the organisms are separated by environmental isolation. This is when the climate changes in one area where an organism lives but not in others. For example, if the climate becomes warmer in one area plants will flower at a different time of year. The breeding times of the plants and the animals linked with them will change and new species emerge.

After a mass extinction, scientists have noticed that huge numbers of new species appear in the fossil record. This is evolution in action. Natural selection takes place and new organisms adapted to the different conditions evolve. But evolution is happening all the time. There is a natural cycle of new species appearing and others becoming extinct.

Isolation and evolution

You have already learnt about the role of genetic variation and natural selection in evolution. Any population of living organisms contains genetic variety. If one population becomes isolated from another, the conditions they are living in are likely to be different. This means that different characteristics will be selected for. The two populations might change so much over time that they cannot interbreed successfully. Then a new species evolves.

How do populations become isolated?

The most common way is by **geographical isolation**. This is when two populations become physically isolated by a geographical feature. This might be a new mountain range, a new river or an area of land becoming an island.

There are some well-known examples of this. Australia separated from the other continents over 5 million years ago. That's when the Australian populations of marsupial mammals that carry their babies in pouches became geographically isolated.

As a result of natural selection, many different species of marsupials evolved. Organisms as varied as kangaroos and koala bears appeared. Across the rest of the world, competition resulted in the evolution of other mammals with more efficient reproductive systems. In Australia, marsupials remain dominant.

a What is geographical isolation?

Organisms in isolation

Organisms on islands are geographically isolated from the rest of the world. The closely related but very different species on the Galapagos Islands helped Darwin form his ideas about evolution.

When a species evolves in isolation and is found in only one place in the world, it is said to be endemic to that area. An area where scientists are finding many new endemic species is Borneo. It is one of the largest islands in the world. Borneo still contains huge areas of tropical rainforest.

Between 1994 and 2006 scientists discovered over 400 new species in the Borneo rainforest. There are more than 25 species of mammals found only on the island. All of these organisms have evolved through geographical isolation.

Figure 1 Both the marsupial koala and the eucalyptus tree have evolved in geographical isolation in Australia

Speciation [k]

Any population will contain natural genetic variety. This means it will contain a wide range of alleles controlling its characteristics, that result from sexual reproduction and mutation. In each population, the alleles which are selected will control characteristics which help the organism to survive and breed successfully. This is natural selection. Sometimes part of a population becomes isolated with new environmental conditions. Alleles for characteristics that enable organisms to survive and breed successfully in the new conditions will be selected. These are likely to be different from the alleles that gave success in the original environment. As a result of the selection of these different alleles, the characteristic features of the isolated organisms will change. Eventually they can no longer interbreed with the original organisms and a new species forms. This is known as speciation.

This is what has happened on the island of Borneo, in Australia and on the Galapagos Islands. If conditions in these isolated places are changed or the habitat is lost, the species that have evolved to survive within it could easily become extinct.

b What is an endemic organism?

Geographical isolation may involve very large areas like Borneo or very small regions. Mount Bosavi is the crater of an extinct volcano in Papua New Guinea. It is only 4 km wide and the walls of the crater are 1 km high. The animals and plants trapped within the crater have evolved in different ways to those outside.

Very few people have been inside the crater. During a 3-week expedition in 2009 scientists discovered around 40 new species. These included mammals, fish, birds, reptiles, amphibians, insects and plants. All of these species are the result of natural selection caused by the specialised environment of the isolated crater. They include an enormous 82 cm long rat that weighs 1.5 kg!

Figure 2 Orang-utans like these are just one example of the many endemic species that have evolved in isolation in Borneo

Figure 3 Mount Bosavi in Papua New Guinea – a small, geographically isolated environment where many new species have evolved

Key points

- New species arise when two populations become isolated.
- Populations become isolated when they are separated geographically, e.g. on islands.
- There are natural cycles linked to environmental change when species form and when species die out.
- In an isolated population alleles are selected that increase successful breeding in the new environment. [H]
- Speciation takes place when an isolated population becomes so different from the original population that successful interbreeding can no long take place. [H]

Summary questions

1 Copy and complete using the words below:

geographically   interbreeding   populations   evolution   species   selection

When two .... become .... isolated .... may take place. Natural .... in each area means the populations become so different that successful .... can no longer take place. New .... have evolved.

2 **a** How might populations become isolated?

b Why does this isolation lead to the evolution of new species?

3 Explain how genetic variation and natural selection result in the formation of new species in isolated populations. [H]

Further teaching suggestions

Geographical isolation animation

- Based on common diagrammatic ways of showing geographical isolation resulting in new species, get the students to create animated versions of the diagrams. They could show an original population being split in two by a barrier. The evolutionary pressures will be different on each side resulting in some characteristics being more favoured in one section of the population than the other. This should eventually result in two very different populations that cannot interbreed. Encourage the students to use imagination and humour in their animations.

The Red Queen hypothesis – is it true?

- The theory accounting for the rate at which speciation occurs was called the Red Queen hypothesis. New research on speciation from the University of Reading suggests that random events rather than natural selection are responsible for the formation of new species. Students could find out more about the hypothesis and Professor Mark Pagel's new theory.

Summary answers

1 populations, geographically, evolution, selection, interbreeding, species

2 **a** Geographically by the formation of mountains, rivers, continents breaking apart, etc.

Environmentally – climate change in one area and not another or different types of change in different areas.

b Natural selection means organisms best suited to a particular environment will be most likely to survive and breed. So in two different environments, different features will be selected for and the organisms will become more and more different until they cannot interbreed and new species have evolved.

3 All populations have natural genetic variation due to sexual reproduction and mutation. This results in a wide variety of alleles in the population. If part of the population becomes isolated and conditions are different from the original population, different alleles are likely to give an advantage. These alleles will be selected for, as the organisms which have them will be most likely to survive and reproduce successfully in the new environment. As a result the characteristics of the organism will change until eventually they can no longer interbreed with the original population and a new species has evolved.

Summary answers

1 a The remains of organisms from many years ago, often found in rocks. They can be formed in a number of different ways.

b **Fossil X:** The dinosaur dies and falls to the ground and the flesh rots away, leaving the skeleton. This is covered with sand, soil or clay before it is damaged. Protected under layers of soil and rocks for millions of years, the skeleton becomes mineralised and turns to rock. Eventually it comes to the surface as a result of earth movements and erosion.

Fossil Y: The animal died in conditions where decay could not take place. In this case, it was frozen immediately after death and preserved.

c Evidence of species which are now extinct, can be used to show links to modern species and relationships between different fossil species. Bone fossils show anatomical structures of organisms, size, etc. whilst ice fossils show appearance of animals in life, colours, can show food, etc. and give DNA for comparison with modern specimens. Limitations – not many fossils found; fossil record often incomplete; rarely find complete skeleton; skeletal fossils do not show what organisms actually looked like; few soft bodied fossils; few complete evolutionary sequences; most fossils do not yield DNA, etc. Any sensible points.

d Earliest organisms all soft bodied – do not form fossils so little or no fossil evidence of the earliest life forms.

2 a The loss of all members of a species in an area or on the Earth.

b Species extinction is the loss of an entire species. Mass extinction the loss of a large percentage of all the species alive on the Earth over a relatively short period of time.

c Evidence in the fossil record of huge number of species disappearing.

d Any two theories, e.g. asteroid strike, volcanic eruption, global temperature change due to carbon dioxide levels, etc. with examples of relevant evidence.

e Importance – they have lead to the evolution of many new species adapted to the new conditions to fill the available niches and so moved the development of life forward.

3 a Rhino/rhinoceros.

b Got bigger – size of skull increased a lot as measured by scale so whole animal must have got bigger as well. Animals became more armoured, so became more aggressive; ate more – jaws and teeth became a lot bigger and if the animals got larger would need to take in more food to support the body. Head carriage changed considerably – did the animal begin to charge opponents/enemies as head carriage dropped? Any other sensible points.

c Limited evidence as only have heads here. Don't have complete sequence to modern day etc. plus any valid points.

d Ideally whole body, certainly legs, pelvis, etc. to see how they moved, see what happened to the feet, see how tall they were, to see where they lived, etc. Fossil faeces to analyse diet. Ice fossil to see exactly what they looked like, what they ate, etc. Any sensible points.

Summary questions *k*

1 Look at Figure 1 and answer the questions that follow.

Fossil X

Fossil Y

Figure 1

a What is a fossil?

b Explain fully how fossil X and fossil Y were formed.

c How can fossils like these be used as evidence for the development of life on Earth and what are their limitations?

d Why are fossils of little use in helping us understand how life on Earth began?

2 a What is extinction?

b How does mass extinction differ from species extinction?

c What is the evidence for the occurrence of mass extinctions throughout the history of life on Earth?

d Suggest at least two theories about the possible causes of mass extinctions and explain the sort of evidence that is used to support these ideas.

e What important part have mass extinctions played in the evolution of life on Earth and why?

3

20 cm   20 cm

Figure 2

a This sequence of skulls comes from the fossil reco of a group of animals known as perissodactyls. Suggest a possible living relative of these animals.

b How do you think these organisms changed as the evolved, based on the evidence of the diagram ab

c What are the limitations of this type of evidence?

d What other fossil remains would you want to see to understand more about the lives of these extinct organisms?

4 How does evolution take place?

5 Describe how evolution takes place in terms of speciation. Explain the roles of isolation and genetic variation in the process of speciation. Use as many examples and as much evidence as you can in your answer.

---

4 Students should demonstrate understanding of the importance of natural selection and changes in the environment as the driver of evolution. Answer should explain how changes in factors such as new predators etc. or new conditions mean some species die out and others evolve. Could include the idea of big changes and mass extinctions producing lots of new niches and organisms evolving to fill them. Look for good explanations and varied examples.

5 As answer to Question 4, but here the student should focus on the role of isolation – geographical or otherwise – as a reason for speciation to take place. Students should describe how organisms are unable to interbreed, natural genetic variety and how particular mutations become advantageous in isolated situations, leading to the formation of new species through natural selection. Look for good explanations and varied examples.

Practice questions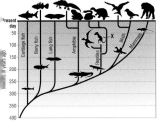

The diagram shows a timeline for the evolution of some groups of animals. The earliest forms of the animals shown below the line for **Present day** are extinct.

Use information from the diagram to answer these questions.

a Name the **four** groups of animals that developed legs.
(1)

b Which group of animals shown in the diagram evolved first? (1)

c The animal labelled **X** has been extinct for over 50 million years.

How do scientists know that it once lived? (1)

d Copy and complete the sentence by choosing the correct words from below.

diseases enzymes hormones plants predators rocks

Animals may become extinct because of new .... and new .... (2)
AQA, 2003

2 a What is meant by the term 'extinction'? (2)

b The bar charts show the population of the world from the 17th to the 20th century and the number of animal extinctions that have taken place over the same period.

Use the information in the bar charts to answer the questions.

i What was the world population in the 19th century? (1)

ii How many animals became extinct in the 18th century? (1)

iii What is the relationship between the population of humans and the number of animal extinctions? (2)

c Between 1900 and 1960 (20th century) 64 animals became extinct.

i How many animals became extinct from 1960–2000?
Show your working. (2)

ii Suggest a reason for the difference in numbers between the beginning and the end of the 20th century. (2)

3 The diagram shows how the number of groups of animals has changed during the history of life on Earth.

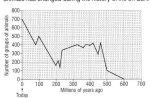

a i How long ago did the first living animals appear on Earth? Give your answer in millions of years. (1)

ii How long did it take for the number of groups to rise to 400? Give your answer in millions of years. (1)

b i Calculate the proportion of groups that disappeared between 100 million years and 80 million years ago. Show your working. (2)

ii Give **two** reasons why some groups of animals disappeared during the history of life on Earth (2)
AQA, 2008

4 In this question you will be assessed on using good English, organising information clearly and using specialist terms where appropriate.

Describe how new species may arise by isolation. [H] (6)

211

Kerboodle resources Ⓚ

Resources available for this chapter on Kerboodle are:

- Chapter map: Old and new species
- Support: History of the Earth time line (B2 6.1)
- Bump up your grade: Dead as a dodo (B2 6.2)
- WebQuest: What happened to the dinosaurs? (B2 6.3)
- Extension: A Madagascan mystery (B2 6.4)
- Interactive activity: How organisms change through time
- Revision podcast: Old and new species
- Test yourself: Old and new species
- On your marks: Old and new species
- Practice questions: Old and new species
- Answers to practice questions: Old and new species

Practice answers

1	a	amphibia reptile birds mammals	*(1 mark)*
	b	cartilage fish	*(1 mark)*
	c	from fossils	*(1 mark)*
	d	diseases/predators	*(2 marks)*

2 a **All** members of a species **die out**. *(2 marks)*

 b i 900 million (must have the units) *(1 mark)*
   ii 11 *(1 mark)*
   iii As the human population rises the number of extinctions rises. *(2 marks)*

 c i 4 [*if answer incorrect then 68-64 (1 mark)*] *(2 marks)*
   ii E.g. at the beginning of the century people using more land for housing etc.
   Loss of habitat; Industrialisation; Pollution
   E.g. at the end of the century more protected species (idea of) conservation of habitats/reintroduction. *(2 marks)*

3 a i 600 *(1 mark)*
   ii 135–140 millions of years *(1 mark)*

 b i 1/5 **or** 100/500 **or** 20%
   correct working shown but arithmetic error gains 1 mark *(2 marks)*
   ii any **two** from:
   - environmental change
   - new competitor
   - new disease
   - changing environmental conditions
   - new predator. *(2 marks)*

4 There is a clear, balanced and detailed explanation of speciation starting with isolation and ending with the inability to interbreed. The answer shows almost faultless spelling, punctuation and grammar. It is coherent and in an organised, logical sequence. It contains a range of appropriate or relevant specialist terms used accurately. *(5–6 marks)*

There is some attempt to explain speciation which shows an understanding of isolation. There are some errors in spelling, punctuation and grammar. The answer has some structure and organisation. The use of specialist terms has been attempted, but not always accurately. *(3–4 marks)*

There is a brief description of speciation. The spelling, punctuation and grammar are very weak. The answer is poorly organised with almost no specialist terms and/or their use demonstrating a general lack of understanding of their meaning. *(1–2 marks)*

No relevant content. *(0 marks)*

Examples of biology points made in the response:

- two populations of a species may become separated/idea of geographical separation
- populations have a wide range of alleles (allow genes)
- this leads to variation (of characteristics) in the population
- some characteristics may be beneficial
- organisms survive to breed
- if the populations stay separate/idea that separation may be for a long time
- they become too different
- can no longer interbreed.

Practice answers

1 a i gene – chromosome – nucleus – cell *(1 mark)*
ii controls the activity of the cell *(1 mark)*

b i absorbs light *(1 mark)*
ii oxygen *(1 mark)*

2 Fertilisation – A, Meiosis – C, Mitosis – B. *(3 marks)*

3 a i Stomach (*allow other correct organ which is part of the digestive tract*) *(1 mark)*
ii Epithelial *(1 mark)*

b Food materials are soluble. They diffuse from a region of high concentration (in the intestine) to a region of low concentration (in the blood) *(4 marks)*

4 a i 21.5–22 °C *and* 27–27.5 °C *(1 mark)*
ii ideas of
limiting factor/shortage of light/carbon dioxide/water/chlorophyll (*allow 1 for 'maximum/optimum rate of enzyme activity if no reference to limiting factors*) (*ignore denaturation*) *(2 marks)*

b 21.5–22 °C
(*allow **first** figure from answer to **i** so that no 'double-penalty but only if this first answer is 20 or greater*)
Because this is the maximum rate of photosynthesis. It is at its highest and fastest
(*but related to flat part of curve*)
It is the most economical heating temperature (*cheapest related to heating*)
(*must relate to the temperature the candidate has given*) *(3 marks)*

5 a i any **two** from:
• structural components
• hormones/named hormone
• Antibodies (*allow antigens*) *(2 marks)*
ii catalyst/speeds up a chemical reaction *(1 mark)*

b protein changes shape/denatures *(2 marks)*

c i amino acids *(1 mark)*
ii Genes code for a particular combination (of amino acids/answer from **b**) *(1 mark)*

6 a i muscles (*allow liver*) *(1 mark)*
ii (Normally) glycogen is turned to glucose and glucose is needed for the release of energy. *(2 marks)*

b i female parent – Gg, male parent – Gg
gametes correctly derived from parents
offspring correctly derived from gametes *(4 marks)*
ii $\frac{3}{4}$ or 3 out of 4 (*allow 3 : 1 or 75%, do not allow 1 : 3*) *(1 mark)*

7 There is a clear and detailed description of the changes which take place during exercise to ensure that the muscles receive enough oxygen and an explanation of anaerobic respiration. The answer shows almost faultless spelling, punctuation and grammar. It is coherent and in an organised, logical sequence. It contains a range of appropriate or relevant specialist terms used accurately. *(5–6 marks)*

There is a description of the changes which take place during exercise to ensure that the muscles receive enough oxygen and some explanation of anaerobic respiration. There are some errors in spelling, punctuation and grammar. The answer has some structure and organisation. The use of specialist terms has been attempted, but not always accurately. *(3–4 marks)*

1 a i Put the following structures into the correct order from the smallest to the largest. (1)
cell   chromosome   gene   nucleus
smallest   largest
....
ii What is the function of the nucleus? (1)
b Plant cells contain chloroplasts.
i What is the role of chloroplasts in photosynthesis? (1)
ii Name the gas produced in photosynthesis. (1)

2 The diagrams show three processes.
Match the correct letter to the process.

Process	Letter
Fertilisation	
Meiosis	
Mitosis	

A   B   C

(3)

3 The diagram shows two villi in the small intestine of a healthy person.
The small intestine is an organ in the digestive system.
a i Name another organ in the digestive system. (1)
ii Name tissue X. (1)
b The villi are surrounded by digested food materials which must enter the blood capillaries.
Explain how these materials enter the blood. (4)

X
Blood capillary

4 The graph shows the effect of temperature on photosynthesis.
a i Between which temperatures is the rate of photosynthesis fastest?
.... and .... °C (1)
ii Suggest why the rate of photosynthesis stays the same between these two temperatures. (2)
b A greenhouse owner wants to grow lettuces as quickly and cheaply as possible in winter.
At what temperature should he keep his greenhouse in order to grow the lettuces as quickly and cheaply as possible? .... °C
Explain your answer. (3)

Rate of photosynthesis (arbitrary units) / Temperature (°C)

212

Study tip
When reading graphs
(see Q4)
Do not be put off by the term 'arbitrary units' just look at the numbers. Sometimes examiners use this term to avoid writing very complex numbers or unit names.

Study tip
Photosynthesis questions often ask about limiting factors.
If raising the temperature does not increase the rate of photosynthesis any further, some other factor must be preventing this. Ask yourself 'What do plants need for photosynthesis?'

There is a brief description of some of the changes which take place during exercise to ensure that the muscles receive enough oxygen and reference to why anaerobic respiration occurs. The spelling, punctuation and grammar are very weak. The answer is poorly organised with almost no specialist terms and/or their use demonstrating a general lack of understanding of their meaning. *(1–2 marks)*

No relevant content. *(0 marks)*

Examples of biology points used in the response:
• increased breathing rate
• increased depth of breathing
• increased heart rate/increased blood flow to muscles
• (if too little oxygen) anaerobic respiration
• production of lactic acid
• ref to oxygen debt. *(6 marks)*

The picture shows a model of a protein.

Some proteins are enzymes but proteins also have other functions.

a **i** Give two other functions of proteins.

1 ....

2 .... (2)

ii What is the function of an enzyme? (1)

b This protein is normally found in neutral conditions. What would happen to the protein if it was placed in acid conditions? (2)

c When the model protein is put together the scientists use smaller molecules to make the specific shape.

i Choose the correct answer to complete the sentence.

amino acids   fatty acids   lactic acid

The smaller molecules used to make the model protein are .... (1)

ii Cells are able to put the smaller molecules together in the correct order.

Explain how the cell does this. (1)

6 Some cattle are affected by an inherited condition called glycogen storage disease.

a **i** Where is glycogen stored? (1)

ii Cattle with this disease become tired easily.

Explain why. (2)

b Glycogen storage disease can be inherited by a calf whose parents do not have the disease.

i Use the symbols G and g and a genetic diagram to explain how this is possible. (4)

ii If the same parents have another calf, what is the probability that it will not have glycogen storage disease? (1)

7 *In this question you will be assessed on using good English, organising information clearly and using specialist terms where appropriate.*

Describe the changes which take place in the human body during exercise to ensure that the muscles receive enough oxygen and what happens if oxygen is in short supply. (6)

Study tip

Q7 requires a description in a logical order. Think about your answer before writing. Make a brief list of the key words and number them in the correct sequence. Rehearse your answer in your head and change the numbers if necessary. Now write your answer using the numbered words as a guide.

Do not forget to cross out any notes which are not intended for marking.

Commentary

Photosynthesis questions often require an understanding of **limiting factors**. More able candidates usually have little difficulty in recognising what may be limiting the rate but weaker candidates often miss the point. Practising with computer models can help to develop an understanding of limiting factors.

Study tip

Use flash cards to link structure and function for plant and animal organs. Make sure that your students know the word but also recognise the organ on a diagram.

Sticking post-it note labels on themselves can be a fun way to learn the positions of the major organs.

B3 1.1

Osmosis

Learning objectives

Students should learn:

- that water often moves across boundaries by osmosis and why it is important
- that osmosis is the diffusion of water through a partially permeable membrane from a dilute to a more concentrated solution
- that differences in concentrations of solutes inside and outside cells cause water to move by osmosis.

Learning outcomes

Most students should be able to:

- define osmosis
- distinguish between diffusion and osmosis
- carry out an experiment to find out about the process of osmosis
- explain the results of experiments in terms of osmotic movement of water.

Some students should also be able to:

- explain the importance of osmosis in plants and animals.

Answers to in-text questions

a In diffusion all the particles move freely along concentration gradients. In osmosis only water molecules move across a partially permeable membrane from an area of high concentration of water to an area of low concentration of water.

b If the cell makes water during chemical reactions and the cytoplasm becomes too dilute, water moves out of the cell by osmosis. If the cell uses up water in chemical reactions the cytoplasm can become too concentrated, water moves in by osmosis to restore the balance.

Support

- Carry out a stop-motion of a plant wilting and being rehydrated using Intel play microscopes (the kit pot plastic ones). Explain using a football and a pump.

Extend

- Get students to investigate the effect of partial drowning. What effect would it have on the water balance in the body?

Specification link-up: Biology B3.1

- Dissolved substances move by diffusion and by active transport. *[B3.1.1 a]*
- Water often moves across boundaries by osmosis. Osmosis is the diffusion of water from a dilute to a more concentrated solution through a partially permeable membrane that allows the passage of water molecules. *[B3.1.1 b]*
- Differences in the concentrations of the solutions inside and outside a cell cause water to move into or out of the cell by osmosis. *[B3.1.1 c]*

  Controlled Assessment: B4.5 Analyse and interpret primary and secondary data. *[B4.5.4 a]*

Lesson structure

Starters

Bouncy castle – Show a picture of a bouncy castle. Has anyone got younger brothers or sisters who love these? How do they stay upright? Why don't they burst? What would happen if they were made out of elastic rubber like a thicker version of balloons? Draw out the idea of a balance of air going in, air coming out and pressure on a non-elastic skin providing support. Link with osmosis in plants providing support for plant tissues. *(5 minutes)*

What happens to the chips – Show the students a bag of chips. Ask who is going to the chip shop tonight. At what time? Explain that there is always a rush on at about six o'clock, so the owners prepare the chips in advance and keep them in water. Ask, 'What effect does the water have on the chips?' Support students by giving them some suggestions from which to choose. Draw out some ideas from the class. Extend students by asking them to suggest ways of testing these ideas. *(10 minutes)*

Main

- Modelling osmosis in cells (see 'Practical support'). The results from the model cells can be used to illustrate the principles of osmosis. Ask students to interpret each one in terms of the diffusion of water and sucrose molecules and the effect of the partially permeable membrane. Students may find it easier to understand osmosis if it is explained in terms of the diffusion of water molecules from where they are in high concentration (i.e. in a dilute solution) to where there is a lower concentration (i.e. a more concentrated solution). Diagrams help.

- Investigating osmosis in potato tissue (see 'Practical support').

- There are variations on the above which can be tried. Some students could measure changes in dimensions (i.e. length or volume) and others could measure changes in mass. Are the results similar? Which do they consider to be the most accurate?

- **Setting up an osmometer** – A simple osmometer can be made using a length of Visking tubing, tied securely at one end, filled with a concentrated sugar solution. (For quick results use syrup or treacle only slightly diluted) and then a capillary tube tied securely in the top. The whole apparatus is held in place by a clamp and stand and lowered into a beaker of water. The level of sucrose in the capillary tube is measured at the start and then again at regular intervals (5 minutes). A graph can be plotted of the distance moved by the sucrose against time.

Plenaries

Follow up to 'What happens to the chips?' – If the demonstrations were set up at the beginning of the experiment, they can be looked at. What has happened to the chips? They can be measured, their texture assessed and the results discussed. Support students by asking them whether their chosen suggestions were correct. Students can be extended by asking them to calculate percentage change in dimensions. *(5 minutes)*

Bank account osmosis – who is most in the red? – Select three students. Tell one they are overdrawn by £10. Tell another they are overdrawn by £20 and the third by £30. Give them each 2p. Tell them that they have to give it to anyone who has less money than they have (i.e. is more overdrawn than them). The money should go from the £10 overdrawn to the £20 overdrawn and finish up with the £30 overdrawn. Explain that it is the same with osmosis. The coins represent water, which always goes to the most negative of any pair of cells in contact. *(10 minutes)*

Practical support

⚙ Investigating osmosis
Equipment and materials required
Lengths of dialysis (Visking) tubing for each group of students, molar sucrose solution which can be diluted to the concentrations required, beakers, string, small measuring cylinders or pipettes to fill the tubes, glass tubes.

Details
Use the dialysis (Visking) tubing to make model cells. Lengths of tubing, about 10 cm long, should be wetted thoroughly and one end of each tied firmly with string. Fill the tubing bags with a concentrated sugar solution (molar sucrose) and tie the open ends firmly with string. These Visking tubing bags represent cells and can be immersed in beakers of water, less concentrated and more concentrated sugar solutions.

Investigating osmosis in potato tissue
Equipment and materials required
Fairly large potatoes, cork borers to make cylinders of tissue, knives and tiles to cut chips, molar sucrose, boiling tubes and racks, rulers and balances, tissues or paper towels to dry potato discs or slices.

Details
Chips or discs of potato tissue can be immersed in different concentrations of salt or sugar solutions, left for a period of time and then their change in mass or dimensions measured. Such experiments offer opportunities for the introduction of 'How Science Works' concepts and can be used as whole investigations. The change in mass or length can be plotted against the concentration of the solution and the solution which results in the least change is considered to be equivalent to the concentration of the cell sap of the potato.

Safety: Take care with sharp implements.

Exchange of materials

B3 1.1 | Osmosis Ⓚ

Learning objectives
- What is osmosis?
- How is osmosis different from diffusion?
- Why is osmosis so important?

Diffusion takes place when particles can spread freely from one place to another. However, the solutions inside cells are separated from those outside by the cell membrane. This membrane does not let all types of particles through. Membranes which only let some types of particles through are called partially permeable.

Osmosis Ⓚ
Partially permeable cell membranes let water move across them. Remember that a *dilute* solution of sugar contains a *high* concentration of water (the solvent). It has a *low* concentration of sugar (the solute). A **concentrated** sugar solution contains a relatively *low* concentration of water and a *high* concentration of sugar.

The cytoplasm of a cell is made up of chemicals dissolved in water inside a partially permeable bag of cell membrane. The cytoplasm contains a fairly concentrated solution of salts and sugars. Water moves from a high concentration of water molecules (in a dilute solution) to a less concentrated solution of water molecules (in a concentrated solution) across the membrane of the cell.

This special type of diffusion, where only water moves across a partially permeable membrane, is called osmosis.

a What is the difference between diffusion and osmosis?

Study tip
Remember, diffusion refers to movement of any particles from a region of high concentration to a region of low concentration.
Osmosis only refers to movement of water molecules.

Practical

Investigating osmosis
You can make model cells using bags made of partially permeable membrane (see Figure 1). You can see what happens to them if the concentrations of the solutions inside or outside the 'cell' change.

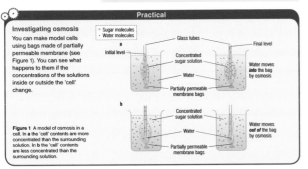

- ○ Sugar molecules
- • Water molecules

a
Initial level — Concentrated sugar solution — Water — Partially permeable membrane bags — Glass tubes — Final level — Water moves *into* the bag by osmosis

b
Concentrated sugar solution — Water — Partially permeable membrane bags — Water moves *out of* the bag by osmosis

Figure 1 A model of osmosis in a cell. In a the 'cell' contents are more concentrated than the surrounding solution. In b the 'cell' contents are less concentrated than the surrounding solution.

The concentration inside your cells needs to stay the same for them to work properly. However, the concentration of the solutions outside your cells may be very different to the concentration inside them. This can cause water to move into or out of the cells by osmosis.

Osmosis in animals
If a cell uses up water in its chemical reactions, the cytoplasm becomes more concentrated. More water immediately moves in by osmosis. If the cytoplasm becomes too dilute because more water is made in chemical reactions, water leaves the cell by osmosis. So osmosis restores the balance in both cases.

However, osmosis can also cause big problems in animal cells. If the solution outside the cell is more dilute than the cell contents, water will move into the cell by osmosis. The cell will swell and may burst.

If the solution outside the cell is more concentrated than the cell contents, water will move out of the cell by osmosis. The cytoplasm will become too concentrated and the cell will shrivel up. Then it can no longer survive. Once you understand the effect osmosis can have on cells, the importance of maintaining constant internal conditions becomes clear.

b How does osmosis help maintain body cells at a specific concentration?

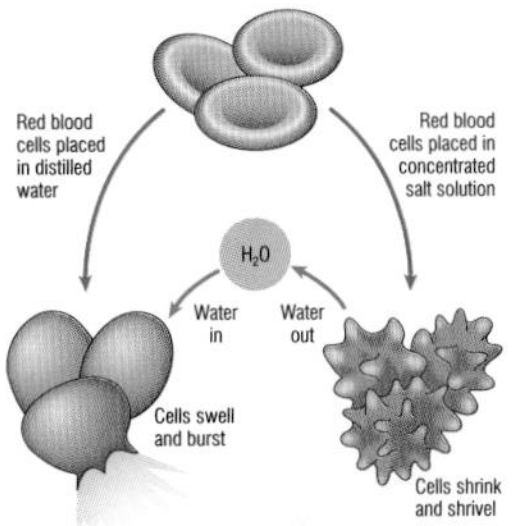

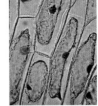

Red blood cells placed in distilled water — Red blood cells placed in concentrated salt solution — H₂O — Water in — Water out — Cells swell and burst — Cells shrink and shrivel

Figure 2 Osmosis can destroy your red blood cells, so it is important to keep your body fluids at the right concentration

Osmosis in plants Ⓚ
Plants rely on osmosis to support their stems and leaves. Water moves into plant cells by osmosis. This causes the vacuole to swell and press the cytoplasm against the plant cell walls. The pressure builds up until no more water can physically enter the cell. This makes the cell hard and rigid.

This swollen state keeps the leaves and stems of the plant rigid and firm. So plants need the fluid surrounding the cells to always have a higher concentration of water (to be a more dilute solution of chemicals) than the cytoplasm of the cells. This keeps water moving by osmosis in the right direction. If the solution surrounding the plant cells is more concentrated than the cell contents, water will leave the cells by osmosis. The cells will not support the plant tissues. Osmosis is important in all living organisms.

Figure 3 Plant cells in a concentrated sugar solution

Summary questions
1 Define the following words: diffusion, osmosis, partially permeable membrane.
2 a Explain, using a diagram, what has happened to the plant cells in Figure 3.
  b Explain, using a diagram, what would happen to these cells if you put them in distilled water.
3 Animals that live in fresh water have a constant problem with their water balance. The single-celled organism called *Amoeba* has a special vacuole in its cell. It fills with water and then moves to the outside of the cell and bursts. A new vacuole starts forming straight away. Explain in terms of osmosis why the *Amoeba* needs one of these vacuoles.

Key points
- Osmosis is a special case of diffusion.
- Osmosis is the diffusion/movement of water from a dilute to a more concentrated solution through a partially permeable membrane that allows water to pass through.
- Differences in the concentrations of solutions inside and outside a cell cause water to move into or out of the cell by osmosis.

214 / 215

Further teaching suggestions

Shelled eggs
- The effect of different concentrations of liquid on shelled eggs can be observed.

Measuring changes in mass
- Design an investigation to measure the mass change of potato when placed in a series of molarities of sucrose solution.

Summary answers

1 Diffusion – the net movement of particles of dissolved substances or gases from an area of high concentration to an area of low concentration.
Osmosis – the net movement of water from a high water concentration (dilute solution) to a low water concentration (concentrated solution) through a partially permeable membrane.
Partially permeable membrane – a membrane which lets some particles through but not others.

2 a The concentration of the solution outside the plant cells is higher than the concentration of the solution of the cell contents, so water moves out of the cells by diffusion so the cytoplasm shrinks as water is lost.

  b The solution outside the cell is more dilute than the solution inside the cell, so water moves into the cell by osmosis, swelling the cytoplasm and vacuoles so the cell contents press against the cell wall.

3 The cytoplasm of *Amoeba* contains a lower concentration of water particles than the water in which the organism lives. The cell membrane is partially permeable, so water constantly moves into *Amoeba* from its surroundings by osmosis. If this continued without stopping, the organism would burst. Water can be moved into the vacuole by active transport, and then the vacuole moved to the outside of the cell using energy as well.

B3 1.2

Active transport

Learning objectives

Students should learn:

- that active transport is the absorption of substances against a concentration gradient
- that energy from respiration is needed to carry out active transport
- that active transport enables cells to take up ions from very dilute solutions
- that sugars and ions can pass through cell membranes.

Learning outcomes

Most students should be able to:

- describe how active transport occurs
- state examples of active transport in plants and animals
- explain the importance of active transport to plants and animals.

Some students should also be able to:

- explain in detail how active transport across a cell membrane takes place.

Support

- Use a short piece of hosepipe with a perforated section where it passes a large card labelled 'kidney'. Pour a mixture of salt and sugar into the tube. Catch the salt and sugar as it comes out and put it back into another hole in the hose pipe that comes after the perforations. Explain that we need to reabsorb some substances even when there are more of them on the inside than on the outside and that this takes energy.

Extend

- Get students to do internet research on the number of ATP molecules produced during respiration of a glucose molecule. Relate this to the energy required to take in a molecule of glucose by active transport. If needed, set up a 'Scavenger Hunt'-style series of URLs with the data needed on them.

Specification link-up: Biology B3.1

- Substances are sometimes absorbed against a concentration gradient. This requires the use of energy from respiration. The process is called active transport. Active transport enables cells to absorb ions from very dilute solutions. [B3.1.1 g)]

Lesson structure

Starters

'Hungry hippos' game – Remind students of this game, where they have to grab marbles from a central arena using hippo-shaped scoops. The marbles caught end up in the traps. Use this as an analogy to describe taking molecules from an area of low concentration to an area of high concentration. *(5 minutes)*

Quick quiz – Give the students ten short questions on slips of paper, on osmosis and diffusion to recap work done so far. Support students by supplying them with the answers and getting them to match the answer to the correct question. Extend students by giving them the answers and getting them to write the questions. *(10 minutes)*

Main

- If easily available, show some animations on active transport. Note: It is very difficult to explain how active transport works without referring to carrier proteins and pumps in the membranes.

- Prepare a PowerPoint presentation on the need for certain mineral ions for healthy growth, (nitrate, magnesium and phosphate) the presence of these ions in the soil solution and the cell sap, and the way that plants accumulate ions against the concentration gradient.

- A useful example of the need for energy in respiration is to describe a hydroponics system, where solutions are aerated to provide oxygen for the respiration of the roots.

- Show photographs of marine vertebrates and discuss the problems of the salt in their diets and how they get rid of it. There is some information on the internet, especially from the RSPB website. www.rspb.org.uk

- To get across the idea of energy being needed, use a revolving door analogy. If something valuable is on the far side (students to decide what it is!), then it is worthwhile keeping on giving the door a good hard shove, even if you have got plenty inside already.

Plenary

Where in the body? – Give the students a blank body diagram each and get them to draw on where active transport will take place. Support students by providing them with strips of paper or labels with the names of body parts on them. Get them to place the labels for body parts where active transport takes place on to their blank diagrams. Extend students by getting them to explain why active transport occurs and what is being actively transported. Annotate with reasons. Examine in pairs. *(10 minutes)*

Answers to in-text questions

a Active transport moves things against a concentration gradient, using energy.

b Mitochondria are the sites of cellular respiration that produce the energy needed for active transport. So cells where lots of active transport take place need lots of mitochondria.

Further teaching suggestions

Cystic fibrosis and membrane structure
- Students could investigate the cause of cystic fibrosis, finding out about the mutation that involves a protein involved in active transport.

Energy needed
- Discuss the energy requirements of active transport. Link to respiration, and discuss the rate of uptake of ions linked to the rate of respiration using the graph in the Student Book.

Lots of mitochondria!
- Get students to suggest cells and tissues that are 'active' and contain many mitochondria. (Liver, kidney, muscle cells are examples and can be linked with active uptake. Link this with the Plenary 'Where in the body?').

Exchange of materials

B3 1.2 — Active transport ⓚ

Learning objectives
- What is active transport?
- Why is active transport so important?

Cells need to move substances in and out. Water often moves across the cell boundaries by osmosis. Dissolved substances also need to move in and out of cells. There are two main ways in which this happens. Substances move by diffusion, along a concentration gradient. This must be in the right direction to be useful to the cells. However, sometimes the substances needed by a cell have to be moved against a concentration gradient, or across a partially permeable membrane. This needs a special process called active transport.

Moving substances by active transport

Active transport allows cells to move substances from an area of low concentration to an area of high concentration. This movement is *against* the concentration gradient. As a result, cells can absorb ions from very dilute solutions. It also enables them to move substances, such as sugars and ions, from one place to another through the cell membranes.

a How does active transport differ from diffusion and osmosis?

It takes energy for the active transport system to carry a molecule across the membrane and then return to its original position (see Figure 1). The energy for active transport comes from cellular respiration. Scientists have shown in a number of different cells that the rate of respiration and the rate of active transport are closely linked (see Figure 2).

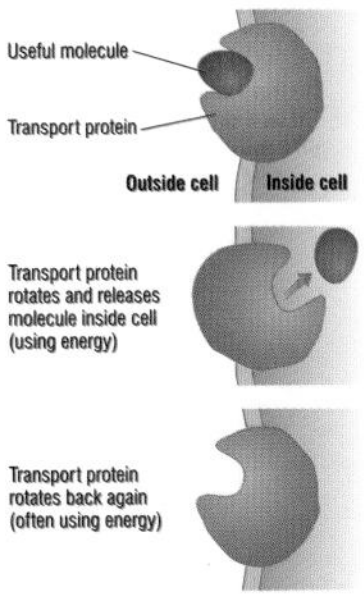

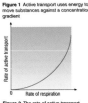

Useful molecule
Transport protein
Outside cell | **Inside cell**

Transport protein rotates and releases molecule inside cell (using energy)

Transport protein rotates back again (often using energy)

Figure 1 Active transport uses energy to move substances against a concentration gradient

Figure 2 The rate of active transport depends on the rate of respiration

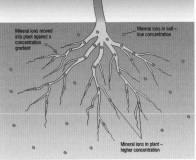

Mineral ions moved into plant against a concentration gradient

Mineral ions in soil – low concentration

Mineral ions in plant – higher concentration

Figure 3 Plants use energy from respiration in active transport to move mineral ions from the soil into the roots against a concentration gradient

In other words, if a cell is making lots of energy, it can carry out lots of active transport. Examples include root hair cells and the cells lining your gut. Cells involved in a lot of active transport usually have lots of mitochondria to provide the energy they need.

b Why do cells that carry out a lot of active transport have lots of mitochondria?

The importance of active transport

Active transport is widely used in cells. There are some situations where it is particularly important. For example, the mineral ions in the soil are usually found in very dilute solutions. These solutions are more dilute than the solution within the plant cells. By using active transport, plants can absorb these mineral ions, even though it is against a concentration gradient (see Figure 3).

Sugar such as glucose is always actively absorbed out of your gut and kidney tubules into your blood. This is often done against a large concentration gradient.

Figure 4 Crocodiles have special salt glands in their tongues. These remove excess salt from the body against the concentration gradient by active transport. That's why crocodiles can live in estuaries and even the sea.

Study tip

Remember, active transport requires energy. Particles are moved from a region of low concentration *against* the concentration gradient.

??? Did you know …?

People with cystic fibrosis (see B2 5.6 Inherited conditions in humans) have thick, sticky mucus in their lungs, gut and reproductive systems. This is the result of a mutation affecting a protein involved in the active transport system of the mucus-producing cells.

Summary questions

1 Copy and complete using the words below:
concentration transport osmosis against mitochondria diffusion energy
.... and .... depend on a .... gradient in the right direction to work. Substances are moved .... a concentration gradient by active ...., which uses .... produced by ....

2 Explain how active transport works in a cell.

3 Diffusion and osmosis do not need energy. Why is energy needed for active transport and where does it come from?

4 Why is active transport so important to:
  a marine birds such as albatrosses, which have special salt glands producing very salty liquid?
  b plants?

Key points
- Substances are sometimes absorbed against a concentration gradient by active transport.
- Active transport uses energy from respiration.
- Cells can absorb ions from very dilute solutions, and actively absorb substances such as sugar and salt against a concentration gradient using active transport.

216 | 217

Summary answers

1 diffusion/osmosis, osmosis/diffusion, concentration, against, transport, energy, respiration

2 A transport protein or system in the membrane is usually used. The substrate molecule binds to the transport protein in the membrane. This moves across the membrane carrying the substance to the other side. The substrate is released and the carrier molecule returns to its original position. This all uses energy.

3 Diffusion and osmosis are passive physical processes. When substances needed by your body have to be moved against a concentration gradient, or across a partially permeable membrane, the cell uses a transport system across the membrane. Energy is needed to move the transport protein across the membrane and back. This energy is produced by respiration in the mitochondria.

4 **a** They need to get rid of the excess salt from the salt water in the sea and they use active transport to secrete the salt against a concentration gradient into special salt glands that remove it from the body.

b Plants need to move mineral ions from the soil into their roots. Mineral ions are much more concentrated in the cytoplasm of plant cells than in soil water, so they have to be moved against a concentration gradient. This involves active transport and the use of energy from cellular respiration.

B3 1.3

The sports drink dilemma

Learning objectives

Students should learn:

- that sweat containing water and mineral ions is lost during exercise and can affect the concentration of the body fluids
- that water and mineral ions need to be replaced to avoid dehydration
- that sports drinks are claimed by the manufacturers to help the body replace used energy and replace water and mineral ions lost during sweating
- there are cheaper and equally effective alternatives to branded sports drinks.

Learning outcomes

Most students should be able to:

- explain that the water and mineral ions lost by sweating during exercise need to be replaced to avoid dehydration
- describe the composition of sports drinks
- describe how sports drinks restore the concentration of the body fluids
- evaluate the claims made by the manufacturers of sports drinks.

Some students should also be able to:

- assess the value of using sports drinks or alternatives after different levels of exercise.

Support

- Give students a set of yes/no tick lists for a comparative pair of drinks, one of which is a sports drink and one a standard soft drink. Read through the labels/adverts for these, displaying them clearly and, stopping at appropriate points, prompt responses from the students in order to finish up with a set of comparison sheets.

Extend

- Get students to use the internet, to find out the standards of proof which would be needed and accepted in order to back up and legitimise any claim of enhanced performance due to the use of a sports drink.

Specification link-up: Biology B3.1

- Most soft drinks contain water, sugar and ions. [B3.1.1 d)]
- Sports drinks contain sugars to replace the sugar used in energy release during the activity. They also contain water and ions to replace the water and ions lost during sweating. [B3.1.1 e)]
- If water and ions are not replaced, the ion / water balance of the body is disturbed and the cells do not work as efficiently. [B3.1.1 f)]
- Evaluate the claims of manufacturers about sports drinks. [B3.1]

Lesson structure

Starters

Sweating it out – Show a picture of a very sweaty face. Ask if students can remember the last time they were so hot that sweat was running down their face. Take examples. Ask if anyone has had sweat running into their eyes and what this feels like. Draw out that it is irritating because of the salt in your sweat. Ask where the salt has come from and draw out any consequences of losing salt from the body. *(5 minutes)*

Half-time! – Show photographs or video of footballers or rugby players at half-time taking drinks. Get the students to discuss with a friend what they would recommend the coach to put in the drinks bottles and why. Support students by handing out some clue cards to assist in forming and recording their opinions. Extend students by asking them how they would go about finding out the correct quantities of ingredients to put into the drinks. *(10 minutes)*

Main

- When analysing sports drinks, give the students a photocopied range of labels from different drinks, some of them should be sports drinks and some of them normal soft drinks (non-branded) as being beneficial for sports and some fruit juices. Get the students to analyse the contents of the drinks, drawing up some comparative bar charts so as to visualise the differences easily. Have different groups report their findings and discuss among the class.

- Take a sports drink and heat it slowly for a long time so as to evaporate off the water from it. Take the solid left and place a weighed sample of it in a deflagrating spoon. Use it to heat a sample of water. Students can record the increase in temperature and relate this to the energy content. If available, video footage of the use of a bomb calorimeter would help here to get across the idea that the energy content can be calculated.

- Get the students to look in close detail at advertisements for sports drinks. Draw out the claims that are being made and look to see if there is any evidence given to back these up. This activity can be extended by getting the students to carry out internet searches for sports drinks advertisements. They can investigate the claims found within them, becoming aware of the importance of key 'get-out' phrases such as 'up to...' Compare the constituents of sports drinks with those of a can of cola or other soft drink.

- Discuss the morality of using performance-enhancing substances in sport. In particular, discuss where the students think the line should be drawn with sports drinks. As a discussion prompt, get them to imagine that a sports drink has been developed which actually does significantly increase performance. What would the moral and ethical issues be in response to this?

Plenaries

Sauna safety – Show a picture of a sauna and or steam bath. Ask the students to imagine a scenario where a person takes repeated prolonged saunas in order to lose weight after each session (use jockeys and boxers as examples). Write them a note to warn them of the dangers they face and give guidance on how to avoid the dangers of dehydration and salt loss. Support students by giving them a list of key terms and phrases to choose from. Extend students by asking them to research the safe levels to which the human body can be dehydrated. *(5 minutes)*

DIY sports drink – Using the information in the Student Book, come up with a recommendation memo to junior athletes as to what they could effectively use as sports drink, and support this with reasons. Students should make it clear and informative, but fun. *(10 minutes)*

Further teaching suggestions

Do sports drinks have an effect on heart rates?

- Set up a heart monitor attached to a data logger and a digital projector. Give a number of students a range of soft drinks and sports drinks. Record their heart rates before, during and after partaking of the drinks. Analyse the results and see if there is a perceived effect. Study the statistical tests that would have to be employed to validate the results.

Answers to in-text questions

a You sweat to keep cool and sweat contains water and mineral ions such as salt (sodium chloride). The more you sweat the more water and mineral ions you lose.

b A drink which claims to improve your performance and help you recover faster from exercise. They contain water, sugar and ions along with colours and flavours.

B3 1.3   The sports drink dilemma ⓚ

Learning objectives

- How do sports drinks differ from ordinary soft drinks?
- Do sports drinks live up to their claims?

People love soft drinks. In the UK we spend £8–9 billion every year on them. Most of these soft drinks contain mainly water. Colouring, flavouring and some sugar or sweeteners are added, along with tiny amounts of mineral ions. Sometimes carbon dioxide gas is added for fizz.

Professional athletes and people who just enjoy sport often buy special sports drinks. They think these help their performance and recovery after exercise. Nearly £250 million worth of sports drinks were used last year.

What happens when you exercise?

When you exercise you release energy by respiration to make your muscles contract and move your body, using up sugar. You also sweat to keep your body temperature stable. Sweat contains water and mineral ions. The more you sweat, the more water and mineral ions you lose. This can affect the concentration of your body fluids. If the body fluids become concentrated, water will leave your cells by osmosis. The cells will become **dehydrated**.

If the water and mineral ions you lose in sweating are not replaced, the mineral ion/water balance of your body will be disturbed. Then your cells will not work as efficiently as usual. To keep exercising at your best, you need to replace the sugar used in respiration and the water and mineral ions lost through sweating. This also applies to recovering properly after exercise. Here is where manufacturers of sports drinks claim to help.

a How do you lose water and mineral ions when you exercise?

What is a sports drink?

A sports drink is mainly water. It also contains sugar (often glucose). It contains more mineral ions than most normal soft drinks. It also has colourings and flavourings added to make it pleasant to drink. Most sports drinks claim to aid hydration of the tissues, help replace lost energy and replace lost electrolytes (the mineral ions you lose when you sweat). But how good are they at doing this?

b What is a sports drink?

Figure 1 The runners in the London marathon certainly use plenty of sports drinks

⚙ How Science Works

Evaluating sports drinks

Sports drinks are usually more expensive than normal soft drinks. There is plenty of evidence to show that sports drinks do what they claim. They contain lots of water so they dilute the body fluids. This allows water to move back into the cells and **rehydrate** them by osmosis. They contain salt, which raises your ion levels, so ions move back into your cells by diffusion. They raise the blood sugar levels so sugar moves back into your cells by diffusion and active transport.

However, sports drinks are expensive. Are they worth the money? There is a lot of evidence which shows that using sports drinks, particularly for normal short-term exercise rather than endurance sports such as marathon running, is not needed. Jeanette Crosland is consultant nutritionist to the British Olympic team. She has examined a lot of evidence and says 'Isotonic sports drinks are not really necessary in activities lasting less than 1 hour, when plain water will suffice'.

So, simply drinking tap water will keep your cells **hydrated**. Ordinary orange squash will replace the sugar. If you make dilute orange squash and add a pinch of salt it will replace the most important mineral ions. This gives you a 'sports' drink as effective as most commercial products. Evidence is also building that milk drinks are one of the most effective ways of rehydrating your cells and replacing the sugars and salts used during exercise. Milk provides your muscles with extra protein and gives you vitamins as well.

Figure 2 Sports drinks are a growing market as more and more people try to improve their performance

Table 1 Data on sports drinks compared to milky drinks from the *Journal of the International Society of Sports Nutrition*

Nutrient value	250 cm³ skimmed milk (0.1% fat)	250 cm³ semi-skimmed chocolate milk (2% fat)	250 cm³ sports drink 1	250 cm³ sports drink 2
Energy (kJ)	90	189	52	53
Protein (g)	9	8	0	0
Carbohydrate (g)	13	27	15	15
Sodium ions (mg)	133	159	115	211
Potassium ions (mg)	431	446	31	95

Summary questions

1 Copy and complete using the words below:

salt respiration energy water ions exercise

When you _____ you release energy from _____ in your muscles. You lose _____ and _____ such as salt in your sweat as you cool down. You need to replace the _____ as well as the _____ and water you have lost through sweat.

2 **a** How do sports drinks differ from ordinary soft drinks?

b Some people claim that drinking an ordinary soft drink during exercise is as effective as a sports drink. How could you investigate that claim?

3 **a** How would you display the data given in Table 1? Explain your answer.

b What do you think are the advantages and disadvantages of using water, orange squash or milk drinks over special sports drinks, both from the data given here and your wider knowledge?

Key points

- Most soft drinks contain water, sugar and mineral ions.
- Sports drinks contain sugars to replace the sugar used in energy release during activity. They also contain water and ions to replace the water and mineral ions lost during sweating.
- Evidence suggests that for normal levels of exercise water is at least as effective as a sports drink.

Summary answers

1 exercise, respiration, water, ions, energy, salt

2 **a** They contain more mineral ions (salt) and sometimes more sugar than ordinary drinks.

b Any sensible suggestions for evaluating the relative effectiveness of an ordinary soft drink and a sports drink – many research projects give drinks and then measure time to exhaustion or similar.

3 **a** Any sensible suggestion. Bar chart if using the categoric data of different drinks on the same chart.

b **Water:** free, very effective at hydrating, doesn't need special storage. Nothing more needed for normal levels of exercise as don't lose excessive minerals or use excessive amounts of energy. Any other sensible point.

Orange squash: when dilute, very effective at rehydrating and supplies some sugar to provide extra energy. More expensive than water but still cheap, can add a pinch of salt to provide mineral ions, no special storage needed. Any other sensible point.

Milk advantages: cheaper, contains protein for your muscles, chocolate milk contains more energy per volume than most sports drinks, contains more sodium ions than one of the sports drinks, contains more vitamins, any other sensible point.

Milk disadvantages: skimmed milk – slightly less sodium, both contain fat, some people don't like taste of milk, may need to be kept in the fridge.

Sports drink advantages: refreshing, more carbohydrate for energy than skimmed milk, the sports drink has more sodium ions than the milk drinks, packaged for use.

Sports drink disadvantages: expensive, very little difference in carbohydrate levels with skimmed milk and much less than chocolate milk, artificial colours and flavours, no vitamins, no protein for muscles. Any other sensible points.

B3 1.4

Exchanging materials – the lungs

Learning objectives

Students should learn:

- that many organ systems are specialised for exchanging materials
- that exchange surfaces in humans and other organisms are adapted to maximise effectiveness
- that the lungs are especially adapted for the exchange of gases
- that the alveoli provide a large surface area over which gases can readily diffuse into and out of the blood.

Learning outcomes

Most students should be able to:

- describe the features of exchange surfaces that make them effective
- describe the function of the alveoli
- explain how the alveoli are adapted for the efficient exchange of gases.

Some students should also be able to:

- evaluate the importance of adaptations which give increased surface area to the effectiveness of gas exchange.

Answers to in-text questions

a Because the SA : V ratio gets smaller, so substances can no longer reach the inner cells of the organism by diffusion.

b It is covered in tiny buds to increase the surface area and has a rich blood supply.

c Gas exchange – oxygen into the blood, carbon dioxide out of the blood.

Support

- Reinforce the main vocabulary via the use of flashcards with the word on the front and the definition on the back. Get the students to work in pairs to test each other.

Extend

- Ask students to research oxygen transmissibility in contact lenses. Which factors are important? Are there similarities/differences between the conditions in the lungs and in the eyes?

Specification link-up: Biology B3.1

- Many organ systems are specialised for exchanging materials. The effectiveness of an exchange surface is increased by:
  - having a large surface area.
  - being thin, to provide a short diffusion path.
  - (in animals) having an efficient blood supply.
  - (in animals, for gaseous exchange) being ventilated. *[B3.1.1 h)]*
- Gas and solute exchange surfaces in humans and other organisms are adapted to maximise effectiveness. *[B3.1.1 i)]*
- The size and complexity of an organism increases the difficulty of exchanging materials. *[B3.1.1 j)]*
- In humans:
  - the surface area of the lungs is increased by the alveoli. *[B3.1.1 k)]*

Lesson structure

Starters

Looking at blood vessels – Students to get a partner to look closely as they pull down their own lower lip as far as they comfortably can (care with body fluids). Get them to observe the blood vessels that lie just below the skin. Ask: 'Can you see two different colours? Which and why?' They then reciprocate with the partner. (**Safety:** wash hands before and after.) *(5 minutes)*

Exchange surfaces – Show a series of pictures of a variety of living organisms (suggest protoctistans, seaweeds, worms, molluscs, etc. – need some obvious ones and some more obscure) and ask the students to write down where gas exchange takes place. Support students by giving them a list of locations (body surface, gills, lungs, etc.) as prompts. Extend students by giving them more of the obscure examples and getting them to give more details of how the exchanges take place. *(10 minutes)*

Main

- Prepare and show the students a PowerPoint presentation of the processes involved in gas exchange. This should include details from a wide variety of animals. If the 'Exchange surfaces' Starter is used, this could be a follow-up. It may be helpful to create a worksheet of questions for students to answer after watching the presentation.
- Demonstrate what is meant by a concentration gradient (see 'Demonstration support').
- To take a closer look at alveoli – either, mount some lung tissue from the sheep or pig's lungs looked at earlier, or show students prepared slides of lung tissue. Get them to comment on the blood supply and the proximity of the capillaries to the air sacs. If there are red blood cells on the slides, then it is possible to emphasise the thin nature of the alveolar wall and the short diffusion paths for the gases.

Plenaries

'Like a fish out of water!' – Ask a student to describe what this phrase means to them. Discuss with the class. Show a video of a fish floundering around on land or ask any student who goes fishing to describe what happens and why. *(5 minutes)*

O_2 in, CO_2 out – Give students cards to hold (or pin on badges on hats) that represent the parts of the respiratory system. Let one student represent 'oxygen' and get them to pass down the system and eventually into the blood and to the cells, where they join with a student labelled 'carbon'. They both come back up and out as 'CO_2'. Get the students involved so that they describe what is happening at each stage. Support students by walking them through the process. Extend students by asking them to work collectively to write information cards for what happens at each stage. *(10 minutes)*

Demonstration support

Concentration gradients

Equipment and materials required

Visking tubing, potassium manganate(VII) solution, large beakers.

Details

Demonstrate what is meant by a concentration gradient by using two pieces of Visking tubing, one filled with relatively concentrated potassium manganate(VII) solution and the other one with a visibly more dilute solution. Place both of them simultaneously into large beakers of water either on top of an OHP projector (care not to spill on the electrics!) or use a flexicam or similar. Get the students to observe the different rates of diffusion by noting the different rates at which the purple colour spreads into the surrounding water. Ask the students what they think would happen to the rate when the difference between the concentrations inside and outside the tubing became smaller and ask how they could prevent this? Draw parallels with what happens at gas exchange surfaces.

Safety: CLEAPSS Hazcard 81 Potassium manganate(VII) – oxidising/harmful. Will stain skin.

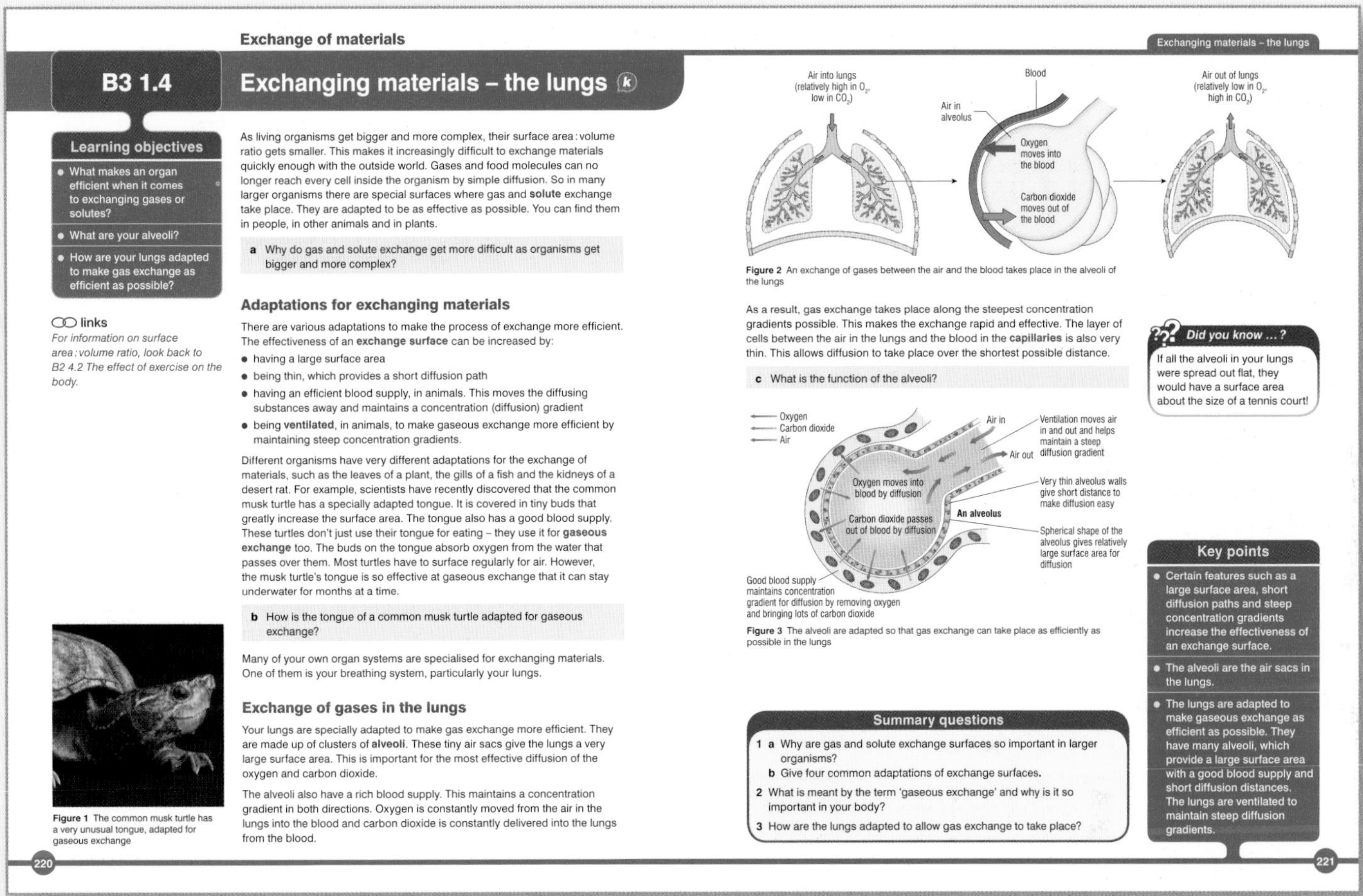

Exchange of materials

Exchanging materials – the lungs

B3 1.4 Exchanging materials – the lungs

Learning objectives

- What makes an organ efficient when it comes to exchanging gases or solutes?
- What are your alveoli?
- How are your lungs adapted to make gas exchange as efficient as possible?

links

For information on surface area : volume ratio, look back to B2 4.2 The effect of exercise on the body.

As living organisms get bigger and more complex, their surface area : volume ratio gets smaller. This makes it increasingly difficult to exchange materials quickly enough with the outside world. Gases and food molecules can no longer reach every cell inside the organism by simple diffusion. So in many larger organisms there are special surfaces where gas and **solute** exchange take place. They are adapted to be as effective as possible. You can find them in people, in other animals and in plants.

a Why do gas and solute exchange get more difficult as organisms get bigger and more complex?

Adaptations for exchanging materials

There are various adaptations to make the process of exchange more efficient. The effectiveness of an **exchange surface** can be increased by:

- having a large surface area
- being thin, which provides a short diffusion path
- having an efficient blood supply, in animals. This moves the diffusing substances away and maintains a concentration (diffusion) gradient
- being **ventilated**, in animals, to make gaseous exchange more efficient by maintaining steep concentration gradients.

Different organisms have very different adaptations for the exchange of materials, such as the leaves of a plant, the gills of a fish and the kidneys of a desert rat. For example, scientists have recently discovered that the common musk turtle has a specially adapted tongue. It is covered in tiny buds that greatly increase the surface area. The tongue also has a good blood supply. These turtles don't just use their tongue for eating – they use it for **gaseous exchange** too. The buds on the tongue absorb oxygen from the water that passes over them. Most turtles have to surface regularly for air. However, the musk turtle's tongue is so effective at gaseous exchange that it can stay underwater for months at a time.

b How is the tongue of a common musk turtle adapted for gaseous exchange?

Many of your own organ systems are specialised for exchanging materials. One of them is your breathing system, particularly your lungs.

Figure 1 The common musk turtle has a very unusual tongue, adapted for gaseous exchange

Exchange of gases in the lungs

Your lungs are specially adapted to make gas exchange more efficient. They are made up of clusters of **alveoli**. These tiny air sacs give the lungs a very large surface area. This is important for the most effective diffusion of the oxygen and carbon dioxide.

The alveoli also have a rich blood supply. This maintains a concentration gradient in both directions. Oxygen is constantly moved from the air in the lungs into the blood and carbon dioxide is constantly delivered into the lungs from the blood.

Air into lungs (relatively high in O_2, low in CO_2)
Air in alveolus
Blood
Oxygen moves into the blood
Carbon dioxide moves out of the blood
Air out of lungs (relatively low in O_2, high in CO_2)

Figure 2 An exchange of gases between the air and the blood takes place in the alveoli of the lungs

As a result, gas exchange takes place along the steepest concentration gradients possible. This makes the exchange rapid and effective. The layer of cells between the air in the lungs and the blood in the **capillaries** is also very thin. This allows diffusion to take place over the shortest possible distance.

c What is the function of the alveoli?

Did you know … ?

If all the alveoli in your lungs were spread out flat, they would have a surface area about the size of a tennis court!

Oxygen
Carbon dioxide
Air
Air in
Air out
Ventilation moves air in and out and helps maintain a steep diffusion gradient
Oxygen moves into blood by diffusion
Carbon dioxide passes out of blood by diffusion
Very thin alveolus walls give short distance to make diffusion easy
An alveolus
Spherical shape of the alveolus gives relatively large surface area for diffusion
Good blood supply maintains concentration gradient for diffusion by removing oxygen and bringing lots of carbon dioxide

Figure 3 The alveoli are adapted so that gas exchange can take place as efficiently as possible in the lungs

Summary questions

1 a Why are gas and solute exchange surfaces so important in larger organisms?
b Give four common adaptations of exchange surfaces.
2 What is meant by the term 'gaseous exchange' and why is it so important in your body?
3 How are the lungs adapted to allow gas exchange to take place?

Key points

- Certain features such as a large surface area, short diffusion paths and steep concentration gradients increase the effectiveness of an exchange surface.
- The alveoli are the air sacs in the lungs.
- The lungs are adapted to make gaseous exchange as efficient as possible. They have many alveoli, which provide a large surface area with a good blood supply and short diffusion distances. The lungs are ventilated to maintain steep diffusion gradients.

220 221

Further teaching suggestions

Simulations of gas exchange at the alveoli

- Use a digital teaching tool to display and interact with simulations of gas exchange at the alveoli.

Summary answers

1 a As organisms get bigger and more complex, the gas and solute exchange with the environment gets more difficult. The SA : V ratio decreases and diffusion distances get too big. Exchange surfaces increase the surface area again.

b Having a large SA, being thin so you have a short diffusion path, an efficient blood supply in animals, a ventilation system for gas exchange and moist to allow gasses to dissolve.

2 Gaseous exchange is the exchange of the gases oxygen and carbon dioxide in the lungs. This is vital because oxygen is needed by the cells for cellular respiration to provide energy, while carbon dioxide is a poisonous waste product which must not be allowed to build up.

3 The lung tissue is arranged into clusters of alveoli (tiny air sacs), which give ideal conditions for rapid gas exchange by diffusion. They have a very large SA and a rich blood supply so that a concentration gradient is maintained. Oxygen is constantly removed into the blood and more carbon dioxide is constantly delivered to the lungs. This makes sure that gas exchange can take place along the steepest concentration gradients possible, so that it occurs rapidly and effectively. The walls between the air in the lungs and the blood in the capillaries are also very thin, so that diffusion takes place over the shortest possible distance. The membranes are kept moist to allow the gases to dissolve and pass through the membranes.

B3 1.5

Ventilating the lungs

Learning objectives

Students should learn:

- that the lungs are located in the thorax, protected by the ribcage and separated from the abdomen by the diaphragm
- that air is taken into the body so that oxygen from the air can diffuse into the bloodstream and carbon dioxide can diffuse out
- that the movement of air into and out of the lungs is called ventilation and is achieved by movements of the ribcage and the diaphragm.

Learning outcomes

Most students should be able to:

- describe the structure of the lungs and the breathing process
- explain how movements of the ribcage and the diaphragm bring about changes in volume and pressure in the thorax.

Some students should also be able to:

- distinguish between the effects of the two sets of intercostal muscles.

Answers to in-text questions

a Movement of air in and out of the lungs.

b The chest, where the lungs and heart are found; the upper part of the body.

c The intercostals muscles between the ribs and the diaphragm muscles.

Support

- Get students to make a large cut-out-and-stick model of the thorax.

Extend

- Ask students to produce an 'I'll guess that organ' competition using minimal clues to guess the part of the respiratory system chosen. Spelling clues such as initial letters not allowed. Get them to write the clues down and count the letters. The winner produces the smallest successful clue.

Specification link-up: Biology B3.1

- The lungs are in the upper part of the body (thorax), protected by the ribcage and separated from the lower part of the body (abdomen) by the diaphragm. *[B3.1.2 a)]*
- The breathing system takes air into and out of the body so that oxygen from the air can diffuse into the bloodstream and carbon dioxide can diffuse out of the bloodstream into the air. *[B3.1.2 b)]*
- To make air move into the lungs the ribcage moves out and up and the diaphragm becomes flatter. These changes are reversed to make air move out of the lungs. The movement of air into and out of the lungs is known as ventilation. *[B3.1.2 c)]*
- Evaluate the development and use of artificial aids to breathing, including the use of artificial ventilators. *[B3.1]*

   Controlled Assessment: B4.3 Collect primary and secondary data. *[B4.3.1 a)]*

Lesson structure

Starters

How did that happen? Ask the students to take a deep breath, hold it, then let it out. Get them to write down then discuss their understanding of the mechanisms of ventilation. Support students by prompting. Extend students by encouraging them to provide a more detailed scientific response. *(5 minutes)*

Coughing your lungs out – What if someone did actually cough their lungs inside out? What would it look like when the structures were inverted? Ask the students to describe the structures they would see. *(10 minutes)*

Main

- Using a bell jar, a sheet of rubber and two balloons, it is possible to make a working model of the thorax. The bell jar represents the thorax; the sheet of rubber is tied firmly around the base and represents the diaphragm; the two balloons, representing the lungs, are attached to the two branches of a Y-shaped glass tube, which is inserted through the cork at the top of the bell jar. When the 'diaphragm' is pulled downwards, the 'lungs' should inflate. Get the students to describe and explain what is happening. Ask: 'In what ways does this differ from a human thorax?'
- Use a syringe with your finger on top to demonstrate how increasing the volume of a container decreases the pressure within it and that if it is open to the atmosphere then air will be drawn in due to being at a higher pressure on the outside than on the inside. Draw a parallel with vacuum cleaners.
- Obtain the lungs and trachea of a sheep or pig from a local butcher (find one where they slaughter their own or can get them for you when given notice). Create a worksheet for students so that they can fill in details of colour, texture, size and what happens when air is introduced into the trachea via a hose. When attaching a hose (or bellows) to the trachea, make sure the joint is airtight. **Safety**: Wash hands. Do not use your mouth to blow into the lungs. Use a cycle pump or foot pump to inflate the lungs. Keep the lungs in a large plastic bag to contain aerosols. CLEAPSS leaflet P5S64.
- Following the exercise above, show the students some (uncooked) spare ribs – a rack of ribs if possible. Observe the muscles and the cartilage and link with how they are arranged in the thorax. This introduces the idea that there are muscles controlling the movements of the ribcage. Show them the internal intercostal and the external intercostal muscles.
- You may wish to carry out an analysis of inhaled and exhaled air (see 'Practical support').

Plenaries

Breathing through your chest – Show the students a suitable picture of a chest wound such as a stab. Relate a true anecdote of a student who was climbing spiked railings and fell on them, piercing his ribcage but not his lungs. When he looked at the wound it was frothing and as he tried to breathe in, air was going into the wound. When he tried to breathe out air was bubbling out of it. Ask the students to explain why this would happen. Relate that the student solved the problem by holding a credit or debit card to the wound tightly until medical help arrived. Ask why this would work. *(5 minutes)*

Air flow – Get students to build up a flow chart of how air passes into the respiratory system and out again, naming the structures and processes involved. This will be useful as a revision aid. Support students by providing them with the stages which they should put in the correct order. Extend students by asking them to annotate their flow charts with the pressure and volume changes and include more details. *(10 minutes)*

Practical support

Comparing air breathed out and air breathed in

Equipment and materials required

Two boiling tubes, two 2-hole bungs, two short delivery tubes (90° bend), two long delivery tubes (90° bend), one boiling tube rack, limewater, CO_2 indicator, eye protection.

Details

For the experiment illustrated in the Student Book, you will need sets of apparatus made up as shown. If students are using this apparatus, they should be supervised. As an alternative to limewater,

hydrogencarbonate indicator could be used. It will be cherry red when in equilibrium with atmospheric air, but turns yellow as carbon dioxide is bubbled through it.

A more sophisticated experiment using a J-tube to analyse the oxygen and carbon dioxide content of inhaled and exhaled air is described in B3 3.1, Controlling internal conditions. The results of this more sophisticated experiment could be compared with the table for this lesson given in the Student Book.

Safety: Eye protection. CLEAPSS Hazcard 18 Limewater – irritant. CLEAPSS Recipe Card 34 Hydrogencarbonate indicator.

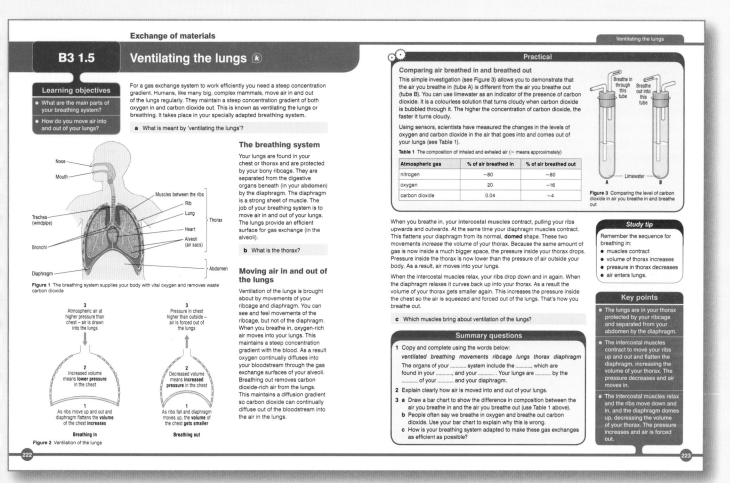

Further teaching suggestions

Alveoli under the microscope

- If this activity was not carried out in the previous spread, either mount some lung tissue from the sheep or pig's lungs looked at earlier, or show students prepared slides of lung tissue. Get them to comment on the blood supply and the proximity of the capillaries to the air sacs. If there are red blood cells on the slides, then it is possible to emphasise the thin nature of the alveolar wall and the short diffusion paths for the gases.

CPR

- Get the students to think about how you can breathe for someone who is unconscious and not breathing. Link to PSHE. Show clips from *Casualty* or a similar TV programme. Get someone in to demonstrate on the model used when learning cardiopulmonary resuscitation (do not attempt to try it out on a real person!).

Summary answers

1 breathing, lungs, thorax, diaphragm, ventilated movements, ribcage

2 Intercostal muscles contract to move your ribs up and out and diaphragm muscles contract to flatten the diaphragm, so the volume of your thorax increases, the pressure decreases and air moves in. Intercostal muscles relax and the ribs move down and in and the diaphragm relaxes and domes up so the volume of your thorax decreases. The pressure increases and air is forced out.

3 a Well-drawn bar chart.

 b Bar chart shows that we breathe in air which is mainly nitrogen with oxygen and a tiny bit of carbon dioxide. The air we breathe out has less oxygen and more carbon dioxide. So we take oxygen out of the air into the blood and pass carbon dioxide out of the blood into the air and change the composition of the air. BUT we only breathe in oxygen and only breathe out carbon dioxide.

 c Good ventilation system – breathing – to maintain a good concentration gradient; large SA; good blood supply; small diffusion distances – alveoli.

B3 1.6

Artificial breathing aids

Learning objectives

Students should learn:

- what happens if the surface area of the gas exchange surface in the lungs is reduced or you can't use your muscles to ventilate your lungs
- whether a machine can breathe for you
- how effective artificial lungs are.

Learning outcomes

Most students should be able to:

- explain what happens if the surface area of the gas exchange surface in the lungs is reduced or you can't use your muscles to ventilate your lungs
- describe how a machine can breathe for you
- evaluate, in a simple way, the relative benefits of different types of artificial lung.

Some students should also be able to:

- explain and evaluate the above in more detail.

Specification link-up: Biology B3.1

- Evaluate the development and use of artificial aids to breathing, including the use of artificial ventilators. *[B3.1]*

Lesson structure

Starters

Smoking monkey – Show the students a picture of a smoking monkey toy from the last century. Ask them to speculate how the toy could make the model monkey draw air into itself. Ask: Would it be possible to make a machine that would do the breathing for you? How might it work? Discuss. Support students by providing prompts. Extend students by encouraging them to provide reasoned and informative responses. *(5 minutes)*

Whales and Spaceships – In the Bible, a man called Jonah is swallowed by a whale and lives inside it for three days and three nights before emerging unharmed. Suppose that Jonah held his breath while the whale dived to the bottom of the sea. Ask: What would happen to Jonah's ribcage? Suppose that Jonah, on emerging from the whale, had been picked up by a passing spaceship and dumped out above the atmosphere. Again he holds his breath. What would happen now, with no pressure at all on his ribcage? Get the students to write down and share responses. Link in to methods of artificial breathing. *(10 minutes)*

Main

- Use exposition, video and internet images to illustrate the narrative of the Student Book and discuss each of the points as they arise. If an interactive whiteboard is available, use this to assemble ideas for use in a further activity to construct a mind map.

- Get the students to make a concise set of notes on the topic in bullet-point form.

- You might take advantage of a practical opportunity here by measuring lung volume (see 'Practical support'). If the results from a number of volunteers are collected, the variations in lung volume can be discussed. Are these variations related to size? Level of fitness? How much variation is there within the group?

- Using the information in the text (students could be extended by carrying out their own research), either in small groups or individually, produce a mind map showing the different types of artificial breathing apparatus, their functions and relative advantages and disadvantages. If this is done in groups, photocopy the end product and give one to each member.

Plenaries

Mind-map share – Pass the mind map produced earlier on in the lesson around other students. Get them to add various extra pieces to it if they see any omissions. *(5 minutes)*

Lung programming role-play – Split the class into groups of three. One person should play the role of a computer programmer, another a doctor and the third a patient with defective breathing. Discuss the requirements of a computer program which would respond to the patient's needs for breathing at different rates at different times. (Discourage any conversations which stray into inappropriate territory.) Support students by giving them suggested activities to work out. Extend students by encouraging them to be creative in their suggestions. *(10 minutes.)*

Support

- Give students slips of paper with the key words and ask them to complete the sentences in the first summary question.

Extend

- Get students to research the system of breathing used during a heart-lung transplant operation.

Practical support

Measuring lung volume

Equipment and materials required
5-litre translucent plastic bottle, water, glass trough, rubber tubing.

Details
Explain that for a positive pressure ventilation system, it is very important that the volume of air introduced does not exceed the volume of the lungs themselves or there will be trouble! Have an empty, clean 5-litre translucent plastic bottle, clearly marked every half-litre from the bottom to the neck. Markings should be upside down so as to be readable when the bottle is inverted. Fill the bottle with water and invert it over water in a glass trough with 1 cm or more depth in the bottom. Ensure that the capacity of the trough more than exceeds that of the bottle plus the water in the bottom of the trough. Place the end of a rubber tube under the neck of the bottle (a beehive shelf may help). Ask a volunteer to take a deep breath and then exhale slowly and completely. Read off the volume of air in the bottle and refill it for the next volunteer.

Safety: Use replaceable mouthpieces or wash the tube in sanitising fluid then rinse before reuse.

How Science Works — Exchange of materials — Artificial breathing aids

B3 1.6 — Artificial breathing aids

Learning objectives
- What happens if the surface area of the gas exchange surface in the lungs is reduced, or you can't use your muscles to ventilate your lungs?
- Can a machine breathe for you?
- How good are artificial lungs?

There are many different reasons why people sometimes struggle to breathe and get enough oxygen into their lungs. For example:
- The tubes leading to the lungs may be very narrow so less air gets through them.
- The structure of the alveoli can break down. This results in a few big air sacs that have a smaller surface area for gas exchange than healthy alveoli.
- Some people are paralysed in an accident or by disease so they can't breathe.

There are a number of artificial aids for supporting or taking over breathing that have saved countless lives. They work in two main ways – negative pressure and positive pressure.

a Why might someone need an artificial breathing aid?

The 'iron lung' – negative pressure
Polio is a disease that can leave people paralysed and unable to breathe. To keep polio sufferers alive until their bodies recovered, an external negative-pressure ventilator was developed. This was commonly known as the iron lung. Nowadays we are all vaccinated against polio and it has almost been wiped out worldwide.

The patient lay in a metal cylinder with their head sticking out and a tight seal around the neck. Air was pumped out of the chamber, lowering the pressure inside to form a vacuum. As a result, the chest wall of the patient moved up. This increased the volume and decreased the pressure inside the chest. So air from the outside was drawn into the lungs, just like normal breathing.

The vacuum then switched off automatically and air moved back into the chamber, increasing the pressure. The ribs moved down, lowering the volume and increasing the pressure inside the thorax. This forced air out of the lungs.

Figure 1 Without a negative pressure iron lung to ventilate its lungs this baby would have died

A more modern version, the 'shell', is a mini-cylinder that fits just around the chest so it is much easier for the patient to use. It was used mainly with paralysed patients. However, negative pressure ventilation is not used much anymore. It has been overtaken by positive pressure systems.

b What is an iron lung?

Positive pressure breathing
A positive pressure ventilator forces a carefully measured 'breath' of air into your lungs under a positive pressure. It's a bit like blowing up a balloon. Once the lungs have been inflated the air pressure stops. The lungs then deflate as the ribs move down again, forcing the air back out of the lungs.

Positive pressure ventilation can be used in patients with many different problems. It can be given using a simple face mask or by a tube going into the trachea. Positive pressure bag ventilators are held and squeezed by doctors or nurses in emergency treatments. They are very simple and temporary but can save lives. Full-scale positive pressure ventilating machines can keep patients alive through major surgery. They can help people who are paralysed to survive for years.

One of the big benefits of positive pressure ventilation is that patients do not have to be placed inside an iron lung machine. The equipment can be used at home and the patient can even move about. Another benefit is that patients can have some control over the machine. Modern systems can link a ventilator with computer systems, which help patients manage their own breathing much more easily.

Figure 2 Using a positive pressure bag ventilator

Activity

Artificial aids to breathing
Use the content of this page and your own research to help you put together a presentation evaluating three different types of artificial aids to breathing. There are long-term machines and short-term solutions, systems used in surgery and systems that can be used at home. Decide which you are interested in and evaluate:
a how they work
b how effective they are at replacing the normal breathing system of the patient
c the advantages and disadvantages of each system.

Summary questions
1 Copy and complete using the words below:
   negative breathing positive body aids breathe
   Artificial .... take over or help out a patient when their own .... is struggling or they cannot .... Older machines used external .... pressure but most modern machines use a .... pressure system.
2 a Explain the difference between the way an external negative pressure aid to breathing works and an internal positive pressure aid to breathing works.
   b Which is most similar to the natural pattern of breathing of the body?

Key points
- Different types of artificial breathing aids have been developed over the years to help people when their lungs or breathing systems don't function properly.
- The different methods have advantages and disadvantages.

224 / 225

Further teaching suggestions

Student Book activity
- Carry out the activity suggested in the Student Book. This can be done as an individual project or in groups and a presentation made to the rest of the class.

Wearing a shell respirator
- Get the students to imagine what it must be like to be fitted with a shell respirator. Ask them to write a short paragraph as to how their lives would be restricted. If some are read out, this could lead to a discussion on the advantages and disadvantages of artificial breathing aids.

Answers to in-text questions
a Anything which affects their ability to get air into and out of the lungs, e.g. narrowed tubes, damaged alveolar structure, paralysis which affects the muscles between the ribs and diaphragm.
b An artificial ventilation machine, where the whole body of the patient is put in the machine. It relies on negative pressure.

Summary answers

1 breathing, aids, body, breathe, negative, positive
2 a External negative pressure – lower the pressure outside the body which expands the chest, lowering pressure inside the lungs and so causing air to move in from the outside. When external pressure returns, the chest falls back down, reducing volume, increasing pressure and causing air to be squeezed out.

   Positive pressure – positive pressure used to force air/oxygen into the lungs, when pressure stops, ribs fall down, reducing volume, increasing pressure and squeezing air out of the lungs.
  b Negative pressure – the volume of the chest increases and pressure falls drawing air in as in normal breathing, followed by falling ribs, decreasing volume and increasing pressure as in a normal situation.

B3 1.7

Exchange in the gut

Learning objectives

Students should learn:

- that the villi increase the surface area of the small intestine
- that the villi have an extensive network of capillaries to absorb the products of digestion
- that the products of digestion are absorbed by diffusion and active transport.

Learning outcomes

Most students should be able to:

- describe the adaptations of the small intestine that increases the efficiency of absorption
- describe the structure of a villus.

Some students should also be able to:

- explain in detail how food is moved from the gut into the blood by active transport as well as diffusion.

Support

- Get students to make a model ileum by sticking towelling to the inside of a wide-bore, flexible, plastic pipe (or pink rain-jacket sleeve) and then invert it. Place wicks into the model and lead them to the pipes, symbolising the blood supply.

Extend

- Get students to use geometry to work out the surface area to volume ratio of a 10 cm length of smooth tube, one with a hundred villi per cm² and one with one hundred microvilli per villus. Each villus is 2 mm in length and 0.2 mm in diameter. Each microvillus is 100 microns in length and 10 microns in diameter. For ease of calculation, they can assume perfect cylinders. They then use the formula $\pi r^2 D$ for surface area, where $\pi = 3.14$, t = radius of villus or microvillus and D = length of villus or microvillus.

Specification link-up: Biology B3.1

- In humans: …
  - the surface area of the small intestine is increased by villi. [B3.1.1 k)]
- The villi provide a large surface area, with an extensive network of capillaries, to absorb the products of digestion by diffusion and active transport. [B3.1.1 l)]

Lesson structure

Starters

Getting through the gut wall – Make block models with the names of some large food molecules, such as starch and proteins, out of similar building bricks. Use stickers on the front of the block models to spell the name of the big molecule. Use smaller stickers on the backs of the individual bricks with the name(s) of the individual smaller molecules which go to make up the big molecule. Use plastic knives, representing enzymes to cut them up. A mixture of the large molecules and the smaller ones is placed into a Christmas tree net, or similar large mesh bag. Ask: 'Which ones go through?' (5 minutes)

Efficient absorption – Spill some water on purpose next to a student (avoiding them and any of their possessions). Give them a piece of cloth with poor absorbent qualities (e.g. a piece of nylon) and ask them to clean it up. Do the same next to another student, but give them a fluffy towel to dry it up with. Draw out in discussion as to why the towel is so much better than the nylon. Support students by giving them some clues and prompts. Extend students by getting them to explain what is happening in terms of SA (surface area) and permeability. Link this to the digestive system. (10 minutes)

Main

- There are some good scanning electron micrographs, but other prepared sections may be difficult to interpret, unless accompanied by a diagram.
- Allow time for students to view sections of a small intestine for themselves and to note the capillary network. It is possible to present the small intestine as having two important functions: it provides a large SA (surface area) for the completion of digestion, as well as for the absorption of the products of digestion.
- Provide diagrams or use the Student Book to help the students identify the structures in both the ileum and the villi.
- There are several websites where it is possible to download endoscope pictures of the small intestine. A video sequence could be shown to students separately. Search the Internet for 'video endoscopy'.
- The importance of the digestion of large, insoluble molecules into smaller, soluble ones can be demonstrated by using Visking, or dialysis tubing to model the gut.
- These experiments have already been described in B2 3.3 Enzymes in digestion. Several different experiments were described and it could be appropriate here to set up any that were not done.
- Students could be asked to design an experiment to show the need for the digestion of large molecules, such as starch, into smaller insoluble sugars that could pass through the gut wall. They could then use their previous knowledge to help them.

Plenaries

How big are your intestines? – Go to the gym or a large outdoor space and mark out an area of 2000 m², or tell the students the equivalent area in football pitches if it is not feasible to find a large space. Describe this as being the SA (surface area) of your intestines when fully spread out. Ask: 'How can this be?' Back in the laboratory, give each group of students a ball of string and a small matchbox. Run a competition to see which group can get the longest piece of string inside the matchbox. Link this with the length of the small intestine in the abdominal cavity. (5 minutes)

A bacon sandwich: my story – Describe the fate of a bacon sandwich from eating it to the defecation of the remains. Draw out what happens to all the parts, the bread, the butter and the bacon. Support students by using writing frames and giving support material if needed. Extend students by getting them to include details of exactly where the breakdown and absorption takes place. This could be started in class and students finish it off for homework. (10 minutes)

Further teaching suggestions

Importance of a good blood supply

- Carry out a modelling exercise where some students are designated as being villi. They give soluble food tokens to students representing the blood. These students take the food tokens to the liver (another student) who counts them per minute. Carry this out in single file slowly, then multiples as fast as possible. Draw out the importance of a good blood supply to the villi.

Homework

- Students to finish off the story of the bacon sandwich (see 'Plenaries').

Exchange of materials

B3 1.7 Exchange in the gut

Learning objectives

- What are the adaptations in your small intestine that allow you to absorb food efficiently?
- Why are your villi so important?

links

For information on glucose, amino acids, fatty acids and glycerol, look back to B2 3.3 Enzymes in digestion.

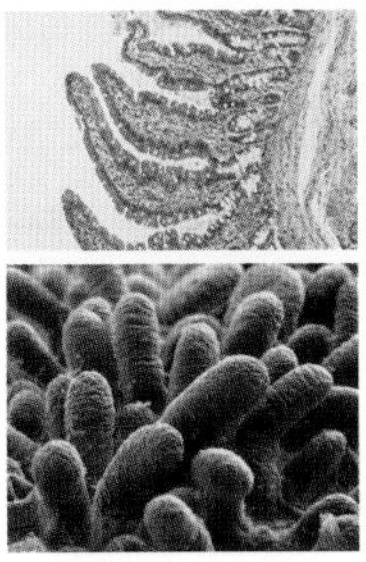

Figure 1 The villi of the small intestine increase the surface area available for diffusion many times so we can absorb enough digested food to survive

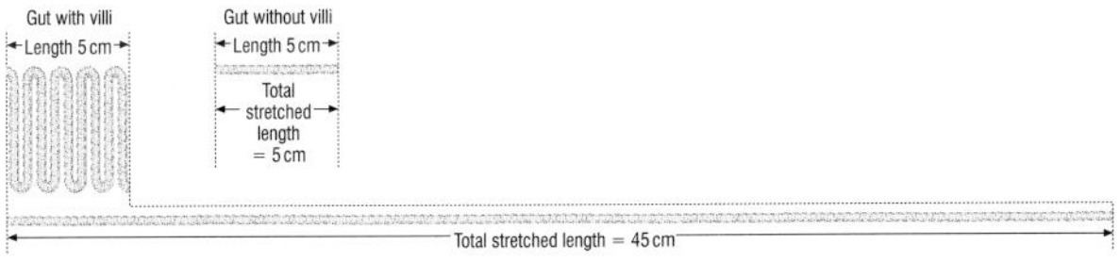

The food you eat is broken down in your gut. Food molecules get turned into simple sugars, such as glucose, amino acids, fatty acids and glycerol. Your body cells need these products of digestion to provide fuel for respiration and the building blocks for growth and repair. A successful exchange surface is very important.

Absorption in the small intestine

For the digested food molecules to reach your cells they must move from inside your small intestine into your bloodstream. They do this by a combination of diffusion and active transport.

a Why must the products of digestion get into your bloodstream?

The digested food molecules are small enough to pass freely through the walls of the small intestine into the blood vessels. They move in this direction because there is a very high concentration of food molecules in the gut and a much lower concentration in the blood. They move into the blood down a steep concentration gradient.

The lining of the small intestine is folded into thousands of tiny finger-like projections known as villi (singular: villus). These greatly increase the uptake of digested food by diffusion (see Figure 1). Only a certain number of digested food molecules can diffuse over a given surface area of gut lining at any one time. Increasing the surface area means there is more room for diffusion to take place (see Figure 2).

Each individual villus is itself covered in many microscopic microvilli. This increases the surface area available for diffusion even more.

b What is a villus?

Like the alveoli of the lungs, the lining of the small intestine has an excellent blood supply. This carries away the digested food molecules as soon as they have diffused from one side to the other. So a steep concentration gradient is maintained all the time, from the inside of the intestine to the blood (see Figure 3). This in turn makes sure diffusion is as rapid and efficient as possible down the concentration gradient.

c Why is it so important that the villi have a rich blood supply?

Figure 2 The effect of folding on the available surface for exchange

Active transport in the small intestine

Diffusion isn't the only way in which dissolved products of digestion move from the gut into the blood. As the time since your last meal gets longer you can have more dissolved food molecules in your blood than in your digestive system. Glucose and other dissolved food molecules are then moved from the small intestine into the blood by active transport. The digested food molecules have to move against the concentration gradient. This makes sure that none of the digested food is wasted and lost in your faeces.

Did you know … ?

Although your gut is only around 7 metres long and a few centimetres wide, the way it is folded into your body along with the villi and microvilli give you a surface area for the absorption of digested products of 200–300 m²!

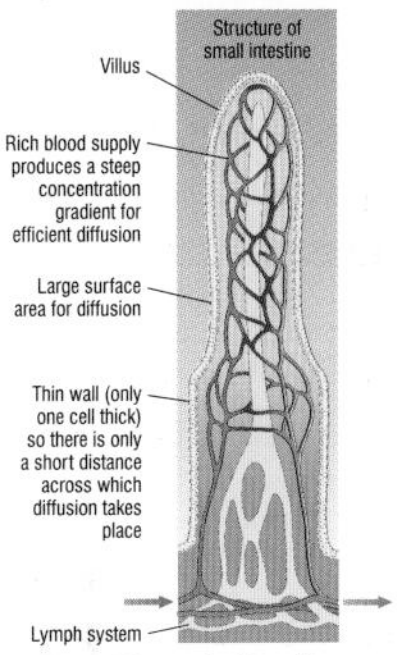

Structure of small intestine

Villus

Rich blood supply produces a steep concentration gradient for efficient diffusion

Large surface area for diffusion

Thin wall (only one cell thick) so there is only a short distance across which diffusion takes place

Lymph system

Figure 3 Thousands of finger-like projections in the wall of the small intestine – the villi – make it possible for all the digested food molecules to be transferred from your small intestine into your blood by diffusion and active transport

Summary questions

1 In the following sentences, match each beginning (A, B, C or D) to its correct ending (1 to 4).

A	Food needs to be broken down into small soluble molecules …	1	… by diffusion and active transport.
B	The villi are …	2	… carry away the digested food to the cells and maintain a steep concentration gradient.
C	Food molecules move from the small intestine into the bloodstream …	3	… so diffusion across the gut lining can take place.
D	The small intestine has a rich blood supply to …	4	… finger-like projections in the lining of the small intestine which increase the surface area for diffusion.

2 Explain why a folded gut wall can absorb more nutrients than a flat one.

3 Coeliac disease is caused by gluten, a protein found in wheat, oats and rye. The villi become flattened and the lining of the small intestine becomes damaged.
   a Why do you think people with untreated coeliac disease are often quite thin?
   b If someone with coeliac disease stops eating any food containing gluten, they will gradually gain weight and no longer suffer malnutrition. Suggest why this might be.

Key points

- The villi in the small intestine provide a large surface area with an extensive network of blood capillaries.
- This makes villi well adapted to absorb the products of digestion by diffusion and active transport.

Answers to in-text questions

a So that the soluble products can be carried to the cells of the body where they will be used.

b A tiny finger-like projection of the lining of the small intestine which increases the surface area for the absorption of digested products.

c To absorb and carry dissolved food molecules to the cells of the body; to maintain a concentration gradient.

Summary answers

1 A 3, B 4, C 1, D 2

2 A folded gut wall has a much larger SA (surface area) over which nutrients can be absorbed.

3 **a** Because they have flattened villi, so much smaller SA (surface area) is available for absorption of digested food; so much less food is absorbed; they don't get enough glucose and other nutrients and so lose weight and tend to be thin.

   b Someone with coeliac disease is affected by gluten. The villi are flattened and SA (surface area) for absorption of digested food products is lost. Without gluten in the diet, the gut can recover and the villi will reappear. Then the body can absorb nutrients properly from the gut and so gain weight etc.

B3 1.8

Exchange in plants

Learning objectives

Students should learn:

- that carbon dioxide enters the leaf cells by diffusion through stomata
- that most of the water and mineral ions are absorbed by root hair cells
- that the root hairs increase the surface area of the roots and the flattened shape and internal air spaces increase the surface area of the leaves.

Learning outcomes

Most students should be able to:

- describe how leaves are adapted for gaseous exchange
- describe how roots are adapted for the efficient uptake of water and mineral ions.

Some students should also be able to:

- explain why plants do not need carbon dioxide from the air continuously
- apply the principles of exchange surfaces to exchange mechanisms in plants.

Answers to in-text questions

a The flattened shape of a leaf increases the surface area for diffusion; thin leaves have shorter distances for the carbon dioxide to diffuse from the outside air to the active photosynthesising cells; the many air spaces allow carbon dioxide to come into contact with lots of cells speeding up diffusion. Many pores (stomata) on the lower leaf surface allow more diffusion into the air spaces inside.

b The leaves only photosynthesise in the light.

Support

- Use a modification of the Starter 'Round leaves v. flat leaves'. Give each student a block of modelling clay and see who can make the largest, thinnest leaf. Give them a jumbled sentence to complete on why a large surface area is an adaptation.

Extend

- Get students to investigate the root systems of plants growing in different environments to see how they are adapted for the efficient uptake of water and mineral ions. They can compare root systems of some desert plants and dune plants with typical flowering plants.

Specification link-up: Biology B3.1

- In plants:
  - carbon dioxide enters leaves by diffusion
  - most of the water and mineral ions are absorbed by roots. [B3.1.3 a)]
- The surface area of the roots is increased by root hairs and the surface area of leaves is increased by the flattened shape and internal air spaces. [B3.1.3 b)]
- Plants have stomata to obtain carbon dioxide from the atmosphere and to remove oxygen produced in respiration. [B3.1.3 c)]

Lesson structure

Starters

Revising leaf structure – Give each student a blank diagram of the external structure of a leaf, and a diagram of a transverse section through a leaf with the different tissues drawn in but not labelled. Support students by giving them a list of the names of the parts with which to label the diagrams. Extend students by asking them to add the functions as annotations to the labels. *(5 minutes)*

Round leaves v. flat leaves – Give each student a cube of modelling clay and measure its volume and then to make a round thick leaf shape with it. Measure the SA (surface area) by placing on graph paper and drawing round it. Then ask them to flatten the leaf and make it as thin as possible. Measure the new SA and work out the SA : V of both leaves. Relate this increase in SA to the greater efficiency of gas exchange. *(10 minutes)*

Main

- Observe the stomata using nail varnish (see 'Practical support'). Having made 'peels' of the lower epidermis of the leaf, the students could investigate the upper epidermis, comparing the numbers of stomata on each side. Ask: 'Are they the same? Which surface has the greater number?'

- The density of the stomata can be determined. The area of the leaf can be found by drawing around it on graph paper and counting the number of squares. Using a calibrated eye piece graticule in the eyepiece of the microscope, the number of stomata in a field of view of known area can be counted and hence the total number of stomata on the leaf or the number per cm^2 can be calculated.

- Give each student a leaf (could be the one they will use to make a nail varnish peel) and project a transverse section through a leaf showing all the cells. You will need a good section that shows a distinct palisade layer and a definitely spongy mesophyll with large air spaces. Get the students to write down all the features that they think are adaptations enabling efficient gaseous exchange, both externally and internally. Gather the information together and make a list on the board.

- Look at stomata on some fresh leaves (privet is good).

- Use binocular microscopes to observe the root hairs on young cress seedlings. If cress seeds are sown on damp filter paper in Petri dishes, they will germinate and the roots will grow in a few days. Provided that the atmosphere in the dish is kept moist, it should be possible to see the root hairs with a microscope. Use prepared slides of longitudinal sections through young roots to show root hairs and, if possible, carry out measurements. Find out how far the root hair region extends. Ask: 'Can you see young root hairs developing or older root hairs breaking down?'

Plenaries

Transplant – Get students to explain why it is important to keep a ball of soil around seedlings or bedding plants when you plant them out. Ask: 'Why do young trees come from the nursery with their roots in a ball of soil?' *(5 minutes)*

What was your journey like? – In small groups, students should write a conversation between a water molecule, a carbon dioxide molecule and a mineral ion as they meet in a leaf. They should describe their journeys to get there (as people go on about roads and journeys as small talk at parties) and ponder their fate. Support students by giving them support material and using writing frames. Extend students by encouraging them to include more detail and consideration of concentration gradients. *(10 minutes)*

Practical support

Looking at stomata

Equipment and materials required
Fresh privet leaves, clear nail varnish, paintbrushes, forceps, microscope slides and cover slips, microscopes.

Details
Apply a thin layer of clear nail varnish to the lower surface of the leaf. Allow the nail varnish to dry and then carefully peel it off using forceps. Place the 'peel' in a drop of water on a microscope slide and cover it with a cover slip. Look at the slide using the low power of the microscope. The stomata should be visible, but use the high power of the microscope to see the more detailed structure, including the guard cells.

Safety: Nail varnish is flammable and the vapour is harmful.

Exchange of materials

Exchange in plants

B3 1.8   Exchange in plants

Learning objectives
- How are the leaves of plants adapted for gaseous exchange?
- How are roots adapted for the efficient uptake of water and mineral ions?

links
Fore information on photosynthesis, look back to B2 2.1 Photosynthesis.

Surface area = 22 units²

(Leaf shape simplified to a square!)

Surface area
Top only = 49 units²
Top and bottom = 98 units²

Figure 1 The wide, flat shape of most leaves greatly increases the surface area for collecting light and exchanging gases, compared with more cylindrical leaves

Animals aren't the only living organisms that need to exchange materials. Plants rely heavily on diffusion to get the carbon dioxide they need for photosynthesis. They use osmosis to take water from the soil and active transport to obtain mineral ions from the soil. Plants have adaptations that make these exchanges as efficient as possible.

Gas exchange in plants

Plants need carbon dioxide and water for photosynthesis to take place. They get the carbon dioxide they need by diffusion through their leaves. The flattened shape of the leaves increases the surface area for diffusion. Most plants have thin leaves. This means the distance the carbon dioxide has to diffuse from the outside air to the photosynthesising cells is kept as short as possible.

What's more, leaves have many air spaces in their structure. These allow carbon dioxide to come into contact with lots of cells and give a large surface area for diffusion.

a How are leaves adapted for efficient diffusion of carbon dioxide?

However, there is a problem. Leaf cells constantly lose water by **evaporation**. If carbon dioxide could diffuse freely in and out of the leaves, water vapour would also be lost very quickly. Then the leaves – and the plant – would die.

The leaf cells do not need carbon dioxide all the time. When it is dark, they don't need carbon dioxide because they are not photosynthesising. Sometimes light is a limiting factor on the rate of photosynthesis. Then the carbon dioxide produced by respiration can be used for photosynthesis. But on bright, warm, sunny days a lot of carbon dioxide needs to come into the leaves by diffusion.

Leaves are adapted to allow carbon dioxide in only when it is needed. They are covered with a waxy **cuticle**. This is a waterproof and gasproof layer.

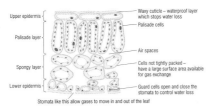

Upper epidermis — Waxy cuticle – waterproof layer which stops water loss
Palisade cells
Palisade layer
Air spaces
Spongy layer — Cells not tightly packed – have a large surface area available for gas exchange
Lower epidermis — Guard cells open and close the stomata to control water loss
Stomata like this allow gases to move in and out of the leaf

Figure 2 This cross section of a leaf shows the arrangement of the cells inside, with plenty of air spaces and short diffusion distances, means that the carbon dioxide needed for photosynthesis reaches the cells as efficiently as possible

All over the leaf surface are small openings known as stomata. The stomata can be opened when the plant needs to allow air into the leaves. Carbon dioxide from the atmosphere diffuses into the air spaces and then into the cells along a concentration gradient. At the same time oxygen produced by photosynthesis is removed from the leaf by diffusion into the surrounding air. This maintains a concentration gradient for oxygen from the cells into the air spaces of the leaf. The stomata can be closed the rest of the time to limit the loss of water. The opening and closing of the stomata is controlled by the **guard cells**. Water is also lost from the leaves by diffusion when the stomata are open.

b Why don't leaves need carbon dioxide all the time?

Open stomata   Closed stomata

Figure 3 Guards cells open and close the stomata to control the carbon dioxide going into the leaf and water vapour leaving it

Uptake of water and mineral ions in plants

Plant roots are adapted to take water and mineral ions from the soil as efficiently as possible. The roots themselves are thin, divided tubes with a large surface area. The cells on the outside of the roots near the growing tips have special adaptations that increase the surface area. These **root hair cells** have tiny projections from the cells which push out between the soil particles.

Water moves into the root hair cells by osmosis across the partially permeable root cell membrane. It then has only a short distance to move across the root to the xylem, where it is moved up and around the plant.

Plant roots are also adapted to take in mineral ions using active transport. They have plenty of mitochondria to supply the energy they need. They also have all the advantages of a large surface area and the short pathways needed for the movement of water.

links
For information on stomata, look back to B1 4.3 Adaptation in plants.

Did you know ...?
Root hairs have an amazing effect – a 1 m² area of lawn grass has 350m² of root surface area!

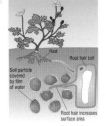

Root
Root hair cell
Soil particle covered by film of water
Root hair increases surface area

Figure 4 Many small roots, and the presence of microscopic root hairs on the individual root cells, increase diffusion of substances from the soil into the plant

links
For information on xylem, look back to B2 1.5 Tissues and organs.

Key points
- Plants have stomata that allow them to obtain carbon dioxide from the atmosphere.
- Carbon dioxide enters the leaf by diffusion. Leaves have a flat, thin shape and internal air spaces to increase the surface area available for diffusion.
- Most of the water and mineral ions needed by a plant are absorbed by the root hair cells, which increase the surface area of the roots.

Summary questions

1   **a** What are stomata?
    b Describe their role in the plant.
    c How are they controlled?

2   **a** How are plant roots adapted for the absorption of water and mineral ions?
    b How do the adaptations of plants for the exchange of materials compare with human adaptations in the lungs and the gut?

228   229

Further teaching suggestions

Observing water loss from plants
- As transpiration is the topic of the next spread, it could be beneficial to set up an experiment to observe water loss from plants. A potted plant can be set up with its aerial parts enclosed in a plastic bag. A piece of cobalt chloride paper can be placed inside the plastic bag. Alternatively, water the plant well, enclose the pot containing the roots in a plastic bag and then weigh the plant. Check the weight at the beginning of the next lesson. Avoid skin contact with cobalt chloride papers.

Summary answers

1   **a** Stomata are small openings all over the leaf surface.
    b The stomata open during daylight allowing air into the leaves so that carbon dioxide enters the cells for photosynthesis, but they close the rest of the time to control the loss of water.
    c The opening and closing of the stomata is controlled by the guard cells.

2   **a** Plant roots are thin, divided structures with a large SA. The cells on the outside of the roots near the growing tips also have extensions, called root hairs, which increase the SA for the uptake of substances from the soil. These tiny projections from the cells push out between the soil particles. The membranes of the root hair cells also have microvilli that increase the SA for diffusion and osmosis even more. The water then has only a short distance to move across the root to the xylem, where it is moved up and around the plant. Plant roots are also adapted to take in mineral ions using active transport. They have plenty of mitochondria to supply the energy they need, as well as all the advantages of the large SA and short pathways needed for the movement of water as well.
    b The adaptations are very similar: large SA, and small distances to travel. Plants are not always as effective as animals at maintaining concentration gradients through active circulation, but they have plenty of active transport systems to help them.

B3 1.9 Transpiration

Learning objectives

Students should learn:

- that water is lost through the leaf by evaporation through the stomata on the leaves of a plant
- that the rate of transpiration is more rapid in hot, dry and windy conditions
- that when plants lose water faster than it is replaced, the stomata can close to prevent further wilting.

Learning outcomes

Most students should be able to:

- explain why transpiration occurs
- describe the effect of environmental conditions on transpiration
- explain how water loss may be controlled.

Some students should also be able to:

- explain how to compromise between the need for carbon dioxide and water loss.

Answers to in-text questions

a The transpiration stream is constant movement of water molecules through the xylem, from the roots to the leaves, where it evaporates out through the stomata.

b Sunny, hot, dry, windy.

Support

- Use preprinted tables and graphs with the axes already drawn to carry out a mass–loss experiment with two plants, one exposed to moving warm air e.g. from a hairdryer. This can be done on a large scale using two spring balances at the front or individually (with assistance if available). Remember to cover the pots of the plants with polythene bags, or to make sure there is no water evaporating from anywhere except the aerial parts of the plants.

Extend

- Get students to consider:
  - What would limit the height to which water can travel up a tree trunk?
  - How would you estimate the leaf SA (surface area) of a whole tree?
  - How could you investigate the effect of humidity on the transpiration rate?

Specification link-up: Biology B3.1

- Plants mainly lose water vapour from their leaves. Most of the loss of water vapour takes place through the stomata.
  - evaporation is more rapid in hot, dry and windy conditions
  - if plants lose water faster than it is replaced by the roots, the stomata can close to prevent wilting. *[B3.1.3 d)]*
- The size of stomata is controlled by guard cells, which surround them. *[B3.1.3 e)]*
- Analyse and evaluate the conditions that affect water loss in plants. *[B3.1]*
  Controlled Assessment: B4.1 Plan practical ways to develop and test candidates' own scientific ideas. *[B4.1.1 a) b)]*; B4.3 Collect primary and secondary data. *[B4.3.1 a), B4.3.2 b) c)]*

Lesson structure

Starters

What has been happening to our plant? – Using the potted plant set up at the end of the previous topic, look at the results (observe the cobalt chloride paper if used or check the weight of the plant with its pot covered in the plastic bag) and ask students to write a sentence explaining what has caused the changes. Support students by prompting. Extend students by encouraging them to provide a detailed explanation. *(5 minutes)*

How does water get to the top of trees? – Ask the question then work in groups, with students to write down their ideas on large sheets of paper. Share results. *(10 minutes)*

Main

- You can model transpiration by placing a wick through a drinking straw and clip the wick to a small piece of card with blotting paper attached to it, to imitate a leaf. Place the imitation leaf into a boiling tube containing dyed water. The water will travel up the wick and evaporate from the blotting paper.
- To cover investigative aspects of 'How Science Works', the variables, such as leaf size, temperature and wind speed, can be altered and the rate of transpiration can be ascertained by weight loss under these different conditions.
- This exercise lends itself to group work. One group could investigate leaf size, another, the effects of temperature, etc. They need to report back at the end of the session.
- Potometers measure the rate of water uptake, which is linked with the rate at which water evaporates from the leaf surface. The best plant material to use is a woody twig, which can be firmly attached to the tubing. It is important that there are no bubbles in the system and that the whole apparatus is watertight.
- Once set up, it needs to be left to allow the plant to settle down after the handling. Introduction of air bubble enables measurements of the water uptake to be made. Either the distance travelled by the bubble in a set time or the time taken for the bubble to travel a set distance can be measured.
- Discuss reliability and precision of measurements ('How Science Works'). Repetitions are necessary to calculate a mean rate under each set of conditions.
- This exercise can be used to develop many 'How Science Works' concepts: predictions can be made, hypotheses formulated, measurements taken and the results plotted. It provides a good opportunity to concentrate on developing areas of relative weakness with individuals in the group.

Plenaries

Sequencing session – Make cards of the stages in the process of transpiration from water uptake in the soil to evaporation from the leaf cells. Get students to put these into the correct order. This makes an excellent summary for a revision card. *(5 minutes)*

Graph interpretation – Give students a graph of the transpiration rate of a plant over 24 hours. Break it into sections labelled with letters. The students have to explain why the rate changes at different times of day. Support students by providing them with the reasons for the changes and they have to link these to the letters on the graph. Extend students by encouraging them to think of as many different reasons as they can for each section, as there could be different explanations for some sections. Check all explanations at the end of the session. *(10 minutes)*

Practical support

Evidence for transpiration

Equipment and materials required

One potometer per group, preferably set up with the shoot inserted, electric fan to create air movements, bench lamps to provide light, hairdryer to provide warmer temperature (but it will create air movement as well), petroleum jelly to block stomata.

Details

It is important that there are no bubbles in the system and that the whole apparatus is watertight. Once set up, it needs to be left to allow the plant to settle down after the handling. Introduction of an air bubble enables measurements of the water uptake to be made. Either the distance travelled by the bubble in a set time or the time taken for the bubble to travel a set distance can be measured.

The electric fan will **increase the air movements**, the bench lamps will allow **the effect of light** to be investigated and the hairdryer allows the **effect of temperature** to be investigated. The **effect of changing the leaf area** can also be investigated, either by removing some of the leaves or by blocking the stomata with petroleum jelly. It is possible to calculate the uptake per unit area by measuring the total area of the leaves.

Safety: Take care with electrical equipment.

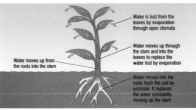

Further teaching suggestions

Emphasis on diffusion gradients

- Students need to be sure that they understand that transpiration is a consequence of gaseous exchange in land plants. The conditions that cause a rapid rate of transpiration are those that favour the evaporation of water, i.e. increase in temperature, decrease in humidity and increase in air movements. Students might find it helpful to consider the diffusion gradients involved.

Summary answers

1 a Transpiration is the loss of water vapour from the surface of plant leaves through the stomata.

b Water evaporates from the surface of the leaves. As this water evaporates, water is pulled up through the xylem to take its place. This constant moving of water molecules through the xylem from the roots to the leaves is known as the 'transpiration stream'.

2 a The waxy cuticle and the guard cells reduce the loss of water vapour.

b Reduces water loss a little, as it would not cover all the stomata. Not a big effect as most stomata are on the underside of the leaves.

c Greatly reduce the loss of water from the leaf, as most of the stomata would be covered and therefore little evaporation would take place. In turn, the rate of water uptake would be very much reduced.

d The rate of transpiration would increase because the rapid air movement across the leaf would increase the rate of evaporation of water and so increase the uptake of water as well.

e The uptake of water from the cut end of the plant stem.

3 a Transpire rapidly as stomata exposed directly to light and heat from the Sun.

b Not a problem as they live in water, so never a shortage to bring up from the roots.

Summary answers

1 a

Diffusion	Osmosis	Active transport
The net movement of particles from an area of high concentration to an area of lower concentration.	The net movement of water from a high concentration of water molecules to a lower concentration (dilute to more concentrated solution) across a partially permeable membrane.	The movement of a substance from a low concentration to a higher concentration, or across a partially permeable membrane.
Takes place because of the random movements of the particles of a gas or of a substance in solution in water.	Although all the particles are moving randomly, only the water molecules can pass through the partially permeable membrane.	Involves transport or carrier proteins which carry specific substances across a membrane.
Takes place along a concentration gradient.	Takes place along a concentration gradient of water molecules.	Takes place against a concentration gradient.
No energy from the cell is involved.	No energy from the cell is involved.	Uses energy from cellular respiration.

Diffusion is relatively uncontrolled so can cause problems for the cell. Osmosis is vital for many processes, including keeping plants upright, but it can cause problems if the concentrations inside and outside a cell are different. Water may enter or leave the cell in an uncontrolled way. Active transport is vital for moving substances around a cell or an organism against concentration gradients, but it can be poisoned. If active transport fails, the cell will not be able to function.

b Any sensible description of an investigation into the effect of temperature on osmosis showing awareness of good practical technique. The expectation should be that osmosis would happen faster – an increase in temperature increases the rate of movement of the particles and so diffusion along the concentration gradient occurs faster, whether or not through a partially permeable membrane.

2 a A full strength sports drink: blood sodium concentration increases approximately 2 full units.
Half strength sports drink: Blood sodium concentration increases just over 1.5 units.
Water: blood sodium concentration increases by about 0.5 units.

b Drinking the sports drink raises the blood sodium levels at a time when they could be going down because of sodium lost in sweat – so helping to maintain homeostasis and keep blood sodium levels up. Half strength does a similar thing but is less effective. Water has little or no effect on blood sodium levels over the race.

c You want to maintain stable body systems. Drinking water maintains the blood sodium levels with little change, which is ideal. Sports drinks increase sodium levels which increases thirst. Better off with water.

d Limitations due to small size of sample; research carried out by at least one person with vested interest; don't

Summary questions 🔑

1 a Produce a table to compare diffusion, osmosis and active transport. Write a brief explanation of the advantages and disadvantages of all three processes in cells.

b Josh thinks that an increase in temperature would increase the rate of osmosis. Abi isn't so sure. Plan and describe an investigation that you could carry out to see if temperature has any effect on the rate of osmosis. Explain the results you would expect to get and why.

2 This graph was produced by someone who was involved in the development of a particular brand of sports drink. It shows the blood sodium ion concentrations of groups of marathon runners. Seven drank full-strength sports drink, eight drank half-strength sports drink and six drank plain water.

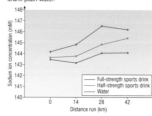

a Describe what has happened to the blood sodium levels of each group of runners.

b How could you use this evidence to support the idea that drinking a sports drink while exercising is a good idea?

c How could you use this evidence to support the idea that sports drinks are not really necessary and are a waste of money?

d What are the limitations of this research from the data you have been given and how could you improve the repeatability, reproducibility and validity of the results?

3 a How are the lungs adapted to allow the exchange of oxygen and carbon dioxide between the air and the blood?

b Explain what the experiment shown below tells us about inhaled and exhaled air.

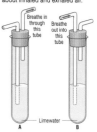

4 Some people stop breathing in their sleep, which disturbs them and can be dangerous. A nasal intermittent positive pressure ventilation system forces air into their lungs under pressure at regular intervals through a small facial mask they wear all night. The air enters the lungs, expanding the chest and is then squeezed out again as the chest falls.

a Explain how this differs from normal breathing.

b Explain the advantages of a system like this over an iron lung.

5 Compare the adaptations of plant leaves for the exchange of carbon dioxide, oxygen and water vapour with the adaptations of the roots for the absorption of water and mineral ions.

know age and sex of the runners etc. – any thoughtful point. Would need to see investigation repeated with much bigger numbers of runners; age and sex known; in different racing conditions; different fitness levels etc.

3 a The alveoli provide a very large SA (surface area) with thin walls and a rich blood supply.

b There is more carbon dioxide in exhaled air as the limewater goes milky/cloudy far more quickly than inhaled air drawn through the solution.

4 a Normal breathing – ribs move up and out and diaphragm flattens so volume increases and pressure decreases; so air moves in from the outside. Lungs then deflate as ribs move down passively and the diaphragm domes up reducing the chest volume and increasing the pressure within it.
The ventilator system relies on positive pressure from the outside; forcing air into the lungs. Then the passive falling of the ribs to increase pressure inside the chest and force air out again.

b Smaller, can be used at home; doesn't involve encasing the whole body in the machine; can be used whenever needed – any other sensible points.

5 Plant leaf: large SA (surface area) for diffusion; thin so small distances for diffusion; stomata allowing gases in and out; guard cells to control size of stomata so controlling diffusion; large internal SA; moist internal surfaces for diffusion.

Plant root: root hair cells and microvilli give huge SA for osmosis and diffusion; small distances for diffusion; moist internal surfaces for diffusion. All these are similar to the leaf, but active transport needed for uptake of mineral ions against the concentration gradient.

End of chapter questions

ractice questions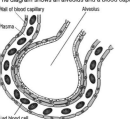

uring marathon races, athletes are advised to drink
ports drinks.

hoose the correct words from the list below to complete
he sentences.

lcohol fat ions protein starch sugar water

While running the athletes sweat.

he sports drink replaces the .... and .... lost in
weat.

he drinks are also a source of energy because they
ontain ....
(3)

he diagram shows an alveolus and a blood capillary.

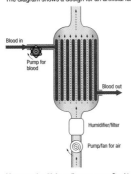

Vall of blood capillary
Alveolus
Plasma

ed blood cell

he alveolus and the blood capillary are gas exchange
urfaces.

i Where in the body would these structures be
found? (1)

ii Give **two** features visible in the diagram that allow
efficient gas exchange to take place. (2)

i Name the gas that moves from the alveolus into the
blood. (1)

ii Choose the correct word to complete the sentence.

diffusion osmosis ventilation

Gases are drawn into the alveolus by the process
of .... (1)

iii Describe **two** changes that take place in the body
to draw gases into the alveolus. (2)

3 Substances move in and out of plants.
List A shows some processes.
List B shows descriptions for these processes.
Match each process with its correct description.

List A	List B
active transport	how water is lost through stomata
osmosis	enables root cells to absorb ions from very dilute soil water
	transport of sugar through the plant
evaporation	movement of water from cell to cell

(3)

4 *In this question you will be assessed on using good English, organising information clearly and using specialist terms where appropriate.*

The diagram shows a design for an artificial lung.

Blood in

Pump for
blood

Blood out

Humidifier/filter

Pump/fan for air

Many people with lung disease are confined to a
wheelchair or are unable to do much exercise. Scientists
hope that a portable artificial lung, the size of a spectacle
case, can be developed. This device might replace the
need for lung transplants and allow patients to live a
normal life.

When scientists design an artificial lung, what features of
a normal lung must they copy? Suggest the advantages
of the artificial lung compared with a lung transplant. (6)

233

Practice answers

1 water and ions; *(either order)*; sugar (3 marks)

2 a i lung   **ii** any **two** from: large surface area;
(1 mark)   thin (walls): good blood supply (2 marks)

   b i oxygen   **ii** ventilation (2 marks)
     iii Any **two** from: rib muscles contract; diaphragm
contracts/flattens; ribcage moves out/up (2 marks)

3 Active transport – enables root cells to absorb ions from very
dilute soil water.
Osmosis – movement of water from cell to cell.
Evaporation – how water is lost through stomata. (3 marks)

4 Marks awarded for this answer will be determined by the Quality
of Written Communication (QWC) as well as the standard of the
scientific response.

There is a clear description of most of the features of a normal
lung which must be copied and at least two advantages of
the artificial lung. The answer shows almost faultless spelling,
punctuation and grammar. It is coherent and in an organised,
logical sequence. It contains a range of appropriate or
relevant specialist terms used accurately. (5–6 marks)

There is a description of at least three features of a normal
lung which must be copied and at least one advantage of the
artificial lung. There are some errors in spelling, punctuation
and grammar. The answer has some structure and
organisation. The use of specialist terms has been attempted,
but not always accurately. (3–4 marks)

There is a description of at least two features of the lung
which must be copied and at least one advantage of the
artificial lung. The spelling, punctuation and grammar are
very weak. The answer is poorly organised with almost no
specialist terms and/or their use demonstrating a general
lack of understanding of their meaning. (1–2 marks)

No relevant content. (0 marks)

Examples of biology points made in the response:
- large surface area
- thin membranes
- ventilation/described
- no operation needed
- no need for (immunosuppressant) drugs
- reference to ethics involved with transplants.
- method of removing carbon dioxide
- method of filtering the air going in
- no need for tissue matching
- few lungs become available

Practical suggestions

Practicals	AQA	k	📖	⚙
Use sensors e.g spirometers, to measure air flow and lung volume.	✓		✓	
Investigating potato slices and different concentrations of liquid in terms of mass gain and mass loss.	✓		✓	
Investigating the relationship between concentrations of sugar solution and change in length of potato strips.	✓		✓	
Placing shelled eggs in different concentrations of liquid to observe the effect.	✓		✓	
Placing slices of fresh beetroot in different concentrations of liquid to observe the effect, and then taking thin slices to observe the cells.	✓	✓	✓	✓
Observing guard cells and stomata using nail varnish.	✓		✓	
Observing water loss from plants by placing in a plastic bag with cobalt chloride paper.	✓		✓	✓
Design an investigation to measure the mass change of potato when placed in a series of molarities of sucrose solution.	✓		✓	

Kerboodle resources   k

Resources available for this chapter on Kerboodle are:
- Chapter map: Exchange of materials
- Data handling skills: Osmosis in potatoes (B3 1.1)
- Practical: Investigating osmosis in beetroot (B3 1.1)
- How Science Works: Investigating osmosis in beetroot (B3 1.1)
- Support: Which way does the flow go? (B3 1.1)
- Animation: Active transport (B3 1.2)
- WebQuest: Sports drinks (B3 1.3)
- Bump up your grade: In or out? (B3 1.4)
- Animation: Ventilation and gaseous exchange (B3 1.5)
- Maths skills: Calculating leaf surface area (B3 1.8)
- Support: Stomata (B3 1.8)
- Animation: Transpiration (B3 1.9)
- How Science Works: What factors affect how quickly a plant takes up water? (B3 1.9)
- Interactive activity: Exchange of materials
- Revision podcast: Exchange of materials
- Test yourself: Exchange of materials
- On your marks: Exchange of materials
- Practice questions: Exchange of materials
- Answers to practice questions: Exchange of materials

B3 2.1

The circulatory system and the heart

Learning objectives

Students should learn:

- there are two separate circulation systems
- that the heart pumps blood to the organs via the arteries and the blood returns to the heart in the veins
- that in the organs, materials needed by the cells pass out of the blood and materials produced by the cells pass into the blood.

Learning outcomes

Most students should be able to:

- describe double circulation in humans
- describe the action of the heart and the functions of the different blood vessels associated with it.

Some students should also be able to:

- explain the benefits of a double circulation.

Specification link-up: Biology B3.2

- The circulatory system transports substances around the body. *[B3.2.1 a)]*
- The heart is an organ and pumps blood around the body. Much of the wall of the heart is made from muscle tissue. *[B3.2.1 b)]*
- There are four main chambers (right and left atria and ventricles) of the heart. *[B3.2.1 c)]*
- Blood enters the atria of the heart. The atria contract and force blood into the ventricles. The ventricles contract and force blood out of the heart. Valves in the heart ensure that blood flows in the correct direction. Blood flows from the heart to the organs through the arteries and returns through the veins. There are two separate circulation systems, one for the lungs and one for all other organs of the body. *[B3.2.1 d)]*

Lesson structure

Starters

A circular route? – The human blood system can be compared with a circular bus route. Ask students to carry out their own comparison and work out the equivalents for the heart, the blood cells, the blood vessels and the substances carried by the blood. Gather ideas together and discuss. *(5 minutes)*

Who needs a heart? – Show students a range of animals from different phylum (as wide a range as possible to include very simple protoctistans to vertebrates). Ask 'Who needs a heart and why?' Draw out the need for an internal circulatory system and some means of pumping blood around the body. Link with increase in complexity and surface area (SA) to volume ratios. Support students by prompting. Extend students by encouraging them to provide more reasoned and detailed responses. *(10 minutes)*

Main

- Show the students an interactive heart animation – you should be able to find one on the internet. Answer questions and talk through the workings of the heart. There is much information on such animations and it could be beneficial to students to spend some time on it.

- Obtain complete sheep's hearts (or pigs') from a butcher (you will need to order these as they are usually trimmed before being sold). Ideally, have one heart per group of students. It could be useful to create a worksheet for students listing things to look for and suggesting that they make sketches of the different valves. You could include a drawing of the external appearance of the heart, to help the students locate the different blood vessels, including the coronary artery, as real hearts look very different from textbook diagrams. (See 'Practical support'.)

- If it is possible to have at least one heart with associated lungs, students can see the links with the lungs and trace the pulmonary circulation. It can also be used in the Plenary later to 'Feel the vessels'.

- It is also useful to have a model heart (the sort that comes apart to expose the internal structure) available for reference.

Support

- Give students a model heart and allow them to take it apart and fit it together again. (See 'Practical support' box.)

Extend

- Get students to research the circulatory systems of other vertebrates. Fish are mentioned in the 'Further teaching suggestions', but amphibians and reptiles are interesting cases. Relate their circulatory systems to their way of life, with particular reference to the heart structure.

Plenaries

Feel the blood vessels – From the dissection of the heart and lungs of a sheep or a pig, cut out a section of aorta and a section of vena cava. Allow students to place their fingers inside to feel the elasticity of the tissues (disposable gloves recommended or very thorough washing afterwards). Students will also appreciate the thickness of the walls and the difference in diameter of the lumen of each. This can act as an introduction to the differences between arteries and veins discussed in the next spread. *(5 minutes)*

Name the parts – Create blank diagrams of the heart and associated vessels for students. Get them to label the four main chambers and associated blood vessels. Support students by giving them the list of labels which they must put on to the correct structures. Extend students by asking them to indicate the passage of blood through the heart and whether it is oxygenated or deoxygenated. *(10 minutes)*

Practical support

Dissecting a sheep's heart

Equipment and materials required
One heart per group of students; scissors; mounted needles; dissecting board, gloves, eye protection.

Details
A fresh sheep's heart is a suitable size. Remove any connective tissue attached to the heart. Identify the vena cava on the top of the heart. Cut through the wall of this with a pair of scissors to expose the right atrium. Remove any congealed blood inside the chamber. Comment on the thin wall and the hole at the bottom leading to the right ventricle. Cut through the wall of this and follow it down as it curves around the heart. Comment on the tendons stopping the valve from turning inside out. Show the muscular right ventricle wall and using a seeker or your finger show where it exits through the pulmonary artery. Cut up through this to expose the semilunar valves. These can be lifted up with a seeker to show their structure. Repeat the procedure with the left atrium and ventricle, emphasising the thicker left ventricle wall and establishing the reason for this. Finally cut up through the aorta, emphasise the thickness and elasticity. Lift the semilunar valves and with a seeker, identify the coronary artery running back into the heart muscle itself.

Safety: Wash hands if handling animal material. Take care with sharp instrument, allowing one person at a time to do the cutting. Wear gloves and eye protection. Consider religious and moral objections.

Transporting materials

B3 2.1 — The circulatory system and the heart

Learning objectives
- What is your circulatory system?
- How does your heart work?

You are made up of billions of cells and most of them are far from a direct source of food or oxygen. A **transport system** is vital to supply the needs of your body cells and remove the waste material they produce. This is the function of your **blood circulation system**. It has three parts – the pipes (**blood vessels**), the pump (the **heart**) and the liquid (the **blood**).

a What are the main parts of your circulatory system?

A double circulation

You have two transport systems, called a **double circulation**. One carries blood from your heart to your lungs and back. This allows oxygen and carbon dioxide to be exchanged with the air in the lungs. The other carries blood around the rest of your body and back again to the heart.

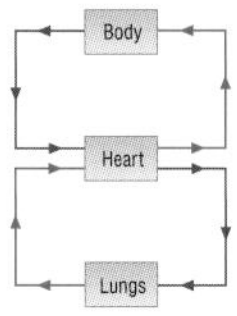

A double circulation like this is vital in warm-blooded, active animals like humans. It makes our circulatory system very efficient. Fully **oxygenated** blood returns to the heart from the lungs. This blood can then be sent off to different parts of the body at high pressure. So more areas of your body can receive fully oxygenated blood quickly.

In your circulatory system **arteries** carry blood away from your heart to the organs of the body. Blood returns to your heart in the **veins**.

b Why do we need a blood circulation system?

Figure 1 The two separate circulation systems supply the lungs and the rest of the body

[Diagram: Body — Heart — Lungs]

The heart as a pump

Your heart is the organ that pumps blood around your body. It is made up of two pumps (for the double circulation) that beat together about 70 times each minute. The walls of your heart are almost entirely muscle. This muscle is supplied with oxygen by the **coronary arteries**.

c What do your coronary arteries do?

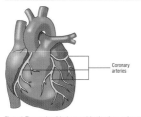

Figure 2 The muscles of the heart work hard so they need a good supply of oxygen and glucose. This is supplied by the blood in the coronary arteries.

The structure of the human heart is perfectly adapted for pumping blood to your lungs and your body. The two sides of the heart fill and empty at the same time. This gives a strong, coordinated heart beat.

Blood enters the top chambers of your heart (the **atria**). The blood coming into the right atrium from the **vena cava** is **deoxygenated** blood from your body. The blood coming into the left atrium in the **pulmonary vein** is oxygenated blood from your lungs. The atria contract together and force blood down into the **ventricles**. Valves close to stop the blood flowing backwards out of the heart.

- The ventricles contract and force blood out of the heart.
- The right ventricle forces deoxygenated blood to the lungs in the **pulmonary artery**.
- The left ventricle pumps oxygenated blood around the body in a big artery called the **aorta**.

As the blood is pumped into these two big vessels, valves close to make sure the blood flows in the right direction.

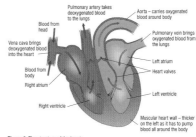

Figure 3 The structure of the heart

Did you know ...?
The noise of the heartbeat that you can hear through a stethoscope is actually the sound of the valves of the heart closing to prevent the blood from flowing backwards.

Study tip
Remember:
- The heart has **four** chambers.
- Ventricles pump blood *out of* the heart.

Summary questions

1 Copy and complete using the words below:
 heart oxygen organ circulatory body glucose pumps
 Your .... system transports substances such as ...., carbon dioxide and .... around the body.
 Your .... is a muscular .... that .... blood around the ....

2 Make a flowchart showing the route of a unit of blood as it passes through the heart and the lungs.

3 Blood in the arteries is usually bright red because it is full of oxygen. This is not true of the arteries leading from the heart to the lungs. Why not?

Key points
- The circulation system consists of the blood vessels, the heart and the blood.
- Human beings have a double circulation.
- The heart is an organ that pumps blood around the body.
- The valves make sure blood flows in the right direction through the heart.

234 / 235

Further teaching suggestions

Efficiency of the double circulation
- A useful comparison can be made between the single circulation in a fish (mentioned in the previous chapter) and the double circulation in mammals. This can be illustrated with simple diagrams. Students can discuss the advantages of keeping oxygenated and deoxygenated blood separate, the differences in pressure of blood going to lungs and that needed to pump blood to the rest of the body.

Homework
- There are some good opportunities here for students to make a set of revision cards about the heart, the blood vessels and the circulatory system.

Answers to in-text questions
a Blood vessels, heart, blood.

b To transport substances like oxygen, glucose and carbon dioxide around our bodies.

c Carry oxygen and glucose to the heart muscle.

Summary answers

1 circulatory, oxygen/glucose, glucose/oxygen, heart, organ, pumps, body

2 Vena cava, right atrium, atrium contracts, blood through valve, right ventricle, ventricle contracts, blood out through valves into pulmonary artery, to lungs where blood is oxygenated, back to heart through pulmonary vein, through valve into left atrium, left atrium contracts, blood through valve into left ventricle, left ventricle contracts, blood through valve into aorta, round body.

3 Blood carried from heart to lungs is deoxygenated blood from the body, so it is dark (purply) red until it picks up oxygen again in the lungs. It is called an artery because it carries blood leaving the heart.

B3 2.2

Keeping the blood flowing

Learning objectives

Students should learn:

- that there are three main types of blood vessels: arteries, veins and capillaries
- that substances needed by cells pass out of the blood and substances produced by the cells pass into the blood through the walls of the capillaries
- that stents can be inserted if the blood vessels become blocked and damaged valves can be replaced by artificial ones.

Learning outcomes

Most students should be able to:

- describe the three main types of blood vessels
- describe how capillaries form the link between arteries and veins
- explain how substances needed by cells pass out of the capillaries and how substances produced by the cells pass into the capillaries
- describe the problems associated with leaky valves and narrow blood vessels and how they can be treated.

Some students should also be able to:

- evaluate in detail the methods used to repair leaky valves and blocked blood vessels.

Support

- Get students to make models of the blood vessels from thin and thick-walled tubing. Capillaries can be made from plasticine discs rolled out to make very small tubes. Match the models with the names of the vessels.

Extend

- Get students to research the ideas of Galen (try the BBC history website). What might lead the ancients to these ideas? Also research William Harvey. How were his ideas different? How well were they accepted? What should we conclude about the permanence of scientific knowledge?

Specification link-up: Biology B3.2

- Arteries have thick walls containing muscle and elastic fibres. Veins have thinner walls and often have valves to prevent back-flow of blood. *[B3.2.1 e)]*
- If arteries begin to narrow and restrict blood flow, stents are used to keep them open. *[B3.2.1 f)]*
- In the organs, blood flows through very narrow, thin walled blood vessels called capillaries. Substances needed by the cells in body tissues pass out of the blood, and substances produced by the cells pass into the blood, through the walls of the capillaries. *[B3.2.1 g)]*
- Evaluate the use of artificial … heart valves. *[B3.2]*
- Evaluate the use of stents. *[B3.2]*

Lesson structure

Starters

Capillary loops – Smear clove oil on the cuticle of a finger or a thumb and then observe through a microscope with top illumination. Alternatively, look at photographs or videos of developing chick embryos. Ask: 'How does the blood circulate?' *(5 minutes)*

The heart of the problem – Project a diagram of the heart or use a model and ask students: What can go wrong with the heart? Support students by prompting them to think about the different parts of the heart. Extend students by encouraging them to refer to the heart muscle, coronary arteries, valves and blockages. They may also refer to congenital defects in babies. *(10 minutes)*

Main

- Students can practise finding their own and each other's pulse (see 'Practical support').
- Although the detailed structure of arteries and veins is not required, consider the differences in structure and function of the different blood vessels. Project slides of sections through arteries and veins to show students the differences in the structure of the walls. Allow them to make sketches and notes on the different layers.
- Emphasise the links between the blood vessels: arteries → arterioles → capillaries → venules → veins. Introduce the terms 'arteriole' and 'venule' or equivalent to the more able students. Create a worksheet for students so they can build up a table of differences between arteries and veins.
- You could link this with 'What goes where?' and describe what is taken up from the plasma at the capillary level. There are videos that show exchange of materials at the capillaries.
- Prepare an exposition or PowerPoint presentation on blood pressure. Show how blood pressure is measured. If possible, have a sphygmomanometer to show students, or a video of blood pressure readings being taken. You could show/demonstrate other types of blood pressure monitors, such as sensors, to the students. Explain what causes blood pressure, why it is important and why it varies during the day.

Plenaries

Mnemonics and acronyms – Get students to think up phrases, acronyms or jingles to help them remember what the different blood vessels do. For example, 'Arteries away!' could help to remind students that arteries carry blood away from the heart. Begin in class and continue for homework. *(5 minutes)*

Blood vessel quiz – Prepare ten questions about the functions of the different blood vessels and the nature of the blood transported in them. Get the students to write down their answers. Support students by making the questions simple and providing a list of choices for them. Extend students by asking more difficult questions and expecting them to give more detailed answers. *(10 minutes)*

Answers to in-text questions

a Only the capillaries have the thin walls needed to enable substances to diffuse across them into and out of the blood.

b A metal mesh used to hold open a narrowed or partly blocked artery.

Practical support

Blood flow

Equipment and materials required
Stopwatches or stop clocks if the pulse rate is to be measured.

Details
Working in pairs, students can find each other's pulse at the wrist (radial pulse) and on the side of the neck (carotid pulse).

- Ask: 'Is it easy to find? Why is the middle finger of the hand used on the wrist and not the thumb?'

Discuss what is happening and why the pulse can be felt. Students could be told of the other points (front ankle, posterior-tibial and femoral) and possibly try out the ankle ones.

- Ask: 'What information does the pulse give?'

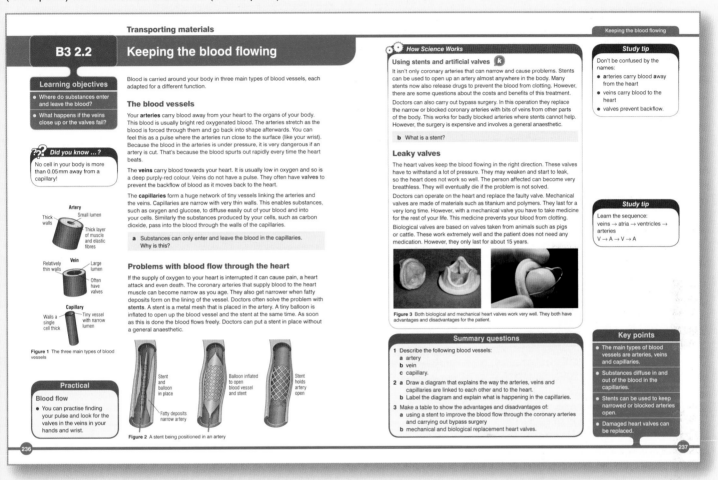

Transporting materials

B3 2.2   Keeping the blood flowing

Learning objectives
- Where do substances enter and leave the blood?
- What happens if the veins close up or the valves fail?

Blood is carried around your body in three main types of blood vessels, each adapted for a different function.

The blood vessels

Your **arteries** carry blood away from your heart to the organs of your body. This blood is usually bright red oxygenated blood. The arteries stretch as the blood is forced through them and go back into shape afterwards. You can feel this as a pulse where the arteries run close to the surface (like your wrist). Because the blood in the arteries is under pressure, it is very dangerous if an artery is cut. That's because the blood spurts out rapidly every time the heart beats.

The **veins** carry blood towards your heart. It is usually low in oxygen and so is a deep purply-red colour. Veins do not have a pulse. They often have **valves** to prevent the backflow of blood as it moves back to the heart.

The **capillaries** form a huge network of tiny vessels linking the arteries and the veins. Capillaries are narrow with very thin walls. This enables substances, such as oxygen and glucose, to diffuse easily out of your blood and into your cells. Similarly the substances produced by your cells, such as carbon dioxide, pass into the blood through the walls of the capillaries.

a Substances can only enter and leave the blood in the capillaries. Why is this?

Problems with blood flow through the heart

If the supply of oxygen to your heart is interrupted it can cause pain, a heart attack and even death. The coronary arteries that supply blood to the heart muscle can become narrow as you age. They also get narrower when fatty deposits form on the lining of the vessel. Doctors often solve the problem with stents. A stent is a metal mesh that is placed in the artery. A tiny balloon is inflated to open up the blood vessel and the stent at the same time. As soon as this is done the blood flows freely. Doctors can put a stent in place without a general anaesthetic.

??? Did you know ...?
No cell in your body is more than 0.05 mm from a capillary!

Figure 1 The three main types of blood vessels

- Artery — Thick walls, Small lumen, Thick layer of muscle and elastic fibres
- Vein — Relatively thin walls, Large lumen, Often have valves
- Capillary — Walls a single cell thick, Tiny vessel with narrow lumen

Practical

Blood flow
- You can practise finding your pulse and look for the valves in the veins in your hands and wrist.

Figure 2 A stent being positioned in an artery
- Stent and balloon in place
- Balloon inflated to open blood vessel and stent
- Stent holds artery open
- Fatty deposits narrow artery

How Science Works
Using stents and artificial valves

It isn't only coronary arteries that can narrow and cause problems. Stents can be used to open up an artery almost anywhere in the body. Many stents now also release drugs to prevent the blood from clotting. However, there are some questions about the costs and benefits of this treatment.

Doctors can also carry out bypass surgery. In this operation they replace the narrow or blocked coronary arteries with bits of veins from other parts of the body. This works for badly blocked arteries where stents cannot help. However, the surgery is expensive and involves a general anaesthetic.

b What is a stent?

Leaky valves

The heart valves keep the blood flowing in the right direction. These valves have to withstand a lot of pressure. They may weaken and start to leak, so the heart does not work so well. The person affected can become very breathless. They will eventually die if the problem is not solved.

Doctors can operate on the heart and replace the faulty valve. Mechanical valves are made of materials such as titanium and polymers. They last for a very long time. However, with a mechanical valve you have to take medicine for the rest of your life. This medicine prevents your blood from clotting.

Biological valves are based on valves taken from animals such as pigs or cattle. These work extremely well and the patient does not need any medication. However, they only last for about 15 years.

Figure 3 Both biological and mechanical heart valves work very well. They both have advantages and disadvantages for the patient.

Summary questions

1 Describe the following blood vessels:
 a artery
 b vein
 c capillary.

2 a Draw a diagram that explains the way the arteries, veins and capillaries are linked to each other and to the heart.
 b Label the diagram and explain what is happening in the capillaries.

3 Make a table to show the advantages and disadvantages of:
 a using a stent to improve the blood flow through the coronary arteries and carrying out bypass surgery
 b mechanical and biological replacement heart valves.

Study tip
Don't be confused by the names:
- arteries carry blood away from the heart
- veins carry blood to the heart
- valves prevent backflow.

Study tip
Learn the sequence:
veins → atria → ventricles → arteries
V → A → V → A

Key points
- The main types of blood vessels are arteries, veins and capillaries.
- Substances diffuse in and out of the blood in the capillaries.
- Stents can be used to keep narrowed or blocked arteries open.
- Damaged heart valves can be replaced.

Further teaching suggestions

Valves in veins
- It may be useful to demonstrate how the valves in veins prevent the backflow of blood. This can be done using the 'athletic' arm/prominent vein. Use a temporary tourniquet made from a tie or a Bunsen tube around the biceps. Pump the muscles by repeatedly clenching and relaxing the fist. Slap the arm to make the veins stand out prominently. Run a finger or a ruler gently up the arm and show that the blood will flow easily that way. Gently run a finger down the arm against the flow and notice that the valves stick out prominently. Do not keep the tourniquet on for long and do not over-pressurise the valves when inducing attempted back flow.

Summary answers

1 a Artery – blood vessel that carries blood away from the heart; has pulse from blood forced through them from the heart beat; have a small lumen and thick walls of muscle and elastic fibres.

 b Vein – blood vessel that carries blood towards the heart; no pulse; valves to keep blood flowing in the right direction; large lumen; relatively thin walls.

 c Capillary– very tiny vessel with narrow lumen and walls one cell thick so ideal for diffusion of substances in and out.

2 a Make sure students show the capillary network between arteries and veins and link the arteries and veins to the heart.

 b [These should be labelled: heart, lungs, artery to lungs, capillaries in lungs, vein to heart, artery to body, capillaries in organs of the body, vein to heart.]

In capillaries – oxygen and dissolved food substances diffuse into the cells and waste products such as carbon dioxide diffuse out of the cells into the blood.

3 a **Stent advantages:** No anaesthetic, relatively cheap, effective. **Stent disadvantages:** Can't open the most blocked or narrowed arteries.
 Bypass advantages: very effective against severe blockages. **Bypass disadvantages:** needs general anaesthetic, more expensive.

 b **Mechanical valve advantages:** Lasts a very long time, works well. **Mechanical valve disadvantages:** Need to take medication to prevent clotting for the rest of life, open-heart surgery.
 Biological valve advantages: Works extremely well, no medication needed. **Biological valve disadvantages:** Has to be replaced after about 15 years.

B3 2.3

Transport in the blood

Learning objectives

Students should learn:

- that blood is a tissue and consists of a fluid called plasma in which red blood cells, white blood cells and platelets are suspended
- that red blood cells contain a red pigment called haemoglobin, which transports oxygen
- that oxygen (in the lungs) combines with haemoglobin to form oxyhaemoglobin
- that blood plasma transports useful substances to the cells and removes waste products as the blood passes through the capillaries of the organs.

Learning outcomes

Most students should be able to:

- describe the composition of the blood
- describe the structure of red blood cells and their role in the blood
- describe how oxygen is transported from the lungs to the other body organs by haemoglobin
- describe the structure and functions of the white blood cells and the platelets
- describe the functions of the blood plasma in the transport of substances around the body.

Some students should also be able to:

- explain how red blood cells are adapted to carry out their function
- describe the reversible reaction between haemoglobin and oxygen.

Support

- Play a game of floor dominoes with A4 cards, each with a part of the blood and a function.

Extend

- Get students to do a calculation exercise. They could work out approximately how many red blood cells there are in the blood of an average-sized person (an average-sized person has about 5 litres of blood). This could be continued to calculate the number of molecules of haemoglobin and the number of molecules of oxygen capable of being taken up.

Specification link-up: Biology B3.2

- Blood is a tissue and consists of a fluid called plasma in which red/white blood cells, and platelets are suspended. *[B3.2.2 a)]*
- Blood plasma transports:
  - carbon dioxide from the organs to the lungs
  - soluble products of digestion from the small intestine to other organs
  - urea from the liver to the kidneys *[B3.2.2 b)]*
- Red blood cells transport oxygen from the lungs to the organs. Red blood cells have no nucleus. They are packed with a red pigment called haemoglobin. In the lungs haemoglobin combines with oxygen to form oxyhaemoglobin. In other organs oxyhaemoglobin splits up into haemoglobin and oxygen *[B3.2.2 c)]*
- White blood cells have a nucleus. They form part of the body's defence system against microorganisms. *[B3.2.2 d)]*
- Platelets are small fragments of cells. They have no nucleus. Platelets help blood to clot at the site of a wound. *[B3.2.2 e)]*

  Controlled Assessment: B4.3: Collect primary and secondary data. *[B4.3.2 c) d) e)]*; B4.4: Select and process primary and secondary data. *[B4.4.1 a) b)]*, *[B4.4.2 c)]*

Lesson structure

Starter

What do we know about blood? – Working in small groups, allow students 3 minutes to write down as many facts as they can about the blood, its composition and functions. Select one group to read out their list, writing up correct points on the board. Go on to other groups, adding more facts to the list until all students have contributed. Support students by prompting. Extend students by getting them to build up comprehensive lists. *(10 minutes)*

Main

- Using prepared slides of blood films, get students to identify the cells. You could create a worksheet showing the different types of cell and then ask them to find and draw as many as they can find on their slides.
- It could be interesting for each student, or group of students, to do a count of the numbers of the different cells in a field of view. Individual counts could be collated and some idea of the relative numbers/proportions of the different types could be achieved.
- If calibrated eyepiece graticules are available, students could measure the diameter of the different cells. (This relates to: 'How Science Works': making measurements.)
- Link the measurements with the diameter of capillaries and review the structure of lung tissue to highlight the close proximity of the red blood cells to the alveoli in the lungs for gaseous exchange.
- Demonstrate blood clotting (see 'Demonstration support').
- Discuss the affinity of haemoglobin for oxygen. Remind students of what happens when they cut themselves [the blood is always bright red].
- Then consider plasma. Plasma of the blood carries a large number of solutes, some of which are needed by cells and others that are waste products. Build up a list of these solutes and, using a large diagram of the human body with the major organs drawn in, consider what is removed and added to the plasma as it passes through the various organs.

Plenary

'Ten questions' – Write out slips of paper each with one of the following on them: a part of the blood; a part of the heart; a blood vessel; a substance carried by the blood. Choose a student to pick out a slip and then allow the rest of the class to ask ten questions to see if they can guess what it is. Support students by restricting the slips to one topic, such as the heart, and allow them to prepare for the questions that they are likely to be asked. Extend students by giving a wide range of parts etc., so that it is more difficult to guess in ten questions. *(10 minutes)*

Demonstration support

Blood clotting

Equipment and materials required
Pig's blood (from an abattoir), sodium citrate or another anti-coagulant.

Details
Obtain some pig's blood and use sodium citrate, or other anti-coagulant, to prevent clotting. Bubble some oxygen through this blood. Observe the colour changes and ask students to explain what is happening.

Safety: Handle pig's blood carefully and hygienically. Be aware of religious sensitivities. Wash hands after use.

B3 2.3 Transport in the blood

Learning objectives
- What is blood made up of?
- How are red blood cells adapted to carry oxygen around your body?

Your blood is a tissue that consists of a fluid called plasma. Plasma carries red blood cells, white blood cells and platelets suspended in it. It also carries many dissolved substances around your body. The average person has between 4.7 and 5.0 litres of blood.

a What types of cells are suspended in the plasma?

The blood plasma as a transport medium

Your blood plasma is a yellow liquid. The red colour of your blood comes from the red blood cells. The plasma transports all of your blood cells and some other things around your body. Carbon dioxide produced in the organs of the body is carried back to the lungs in the plasma.

Similarly, urea is carried to your kidneys in the plasma. Urea is a waste product formed in your liver from the breakdown of proteins. In the kidneys the urea is removed from your blood to form urine.

All the small, soluble products of digestion pass into the blood from your small intestine. These food molecules are carried in the plasma around your body to the other organs and individual cells.

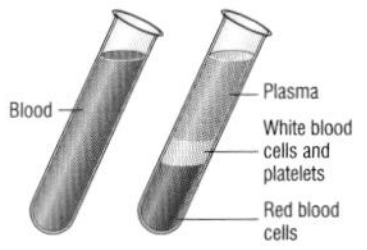

b What is transported in your blood plasma?

Red blood cells

The red blood cells pick up oxygen from your lungs. They carry the oxygen to the tissues and cells where it is needed. These blood cells have adaptations that make them very efficient at their job:

- They have a very unusual shape – they are **biconcave discs**. That means they are concave (pushed in) on both sides. This gives them an increased surface area to volume ratio over which the diffusion of oxygen can take place.

Figure 1 The main components of blood
- Blood
- Plasma
- White blood cells and platelets
- Red blood cells

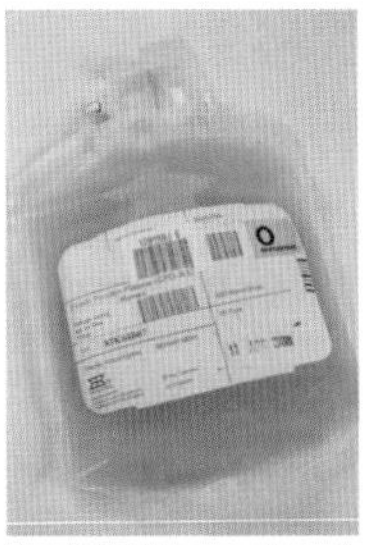

Figure 2 Blood plasma is a yellow liquid that transports everything you need – and need to get rid of – around your body

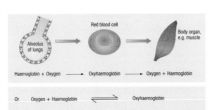

Red blood cell

Alveolus of lungs → Red blood cell → Body organ, e.g. muscle

Haemoglobin + Oxygen → Oxyhaemoglobin → Oxygen + Haemoglobin

Or   Oxygen + Haemoglobin ⇌ Oxyhaemoglobin

Figure 3 The reversible reaction between oxygen and haemoglobin makes life as we know it possible by carrying oxygen to all the places where it is needed

- They are packed full of a special red **pigment** called **haemoglobin** that can carry oxygen.
- They do not have a nucleus. This makes more space to pack in molecules of haemoglobin.

In a high concentration of oxygen, haemoglobin reacts with oxygen to form bright red **oxyhaemoglobin**. In other organs where the concentration of oxygen is lower, the oxyhaemoglobin splits up. It forms purply-red haemoglobin and oxygen, which diffuses into the cells where it is needed.

White blood cells

White blood cells are much bigger than the red cells and there are fewer of them. They have a nucleus and form part of the body's defence system against harmful microorganisms. Some white blood cells form antibodies against microorganisms. Others digest invading bacteria and viruses.

Platelets are small fragments of cells that have no nucleus. They are very important in helping the blood to clot at the site of a wound. They help produce a network of protein threads. The threads then capture lots of red blood cells and more platelets to form a jelly-like clot. This stops you bleeding to death. The clot dries and hardens to form a scab. The scab protects the new skin as it grows and stops bacteria getting into your body through the wound.

Red blood cell   Platelets   White blood cell

Figure 4 Red blood cells, white blood cells and platelets are suspended in the plasma to make up our blood

Did you know ... ?
One red blood cell contains about 250 million molecules of haemoglobin, which allow it to carry 1000 million molecules of oxygen!

Did you know ... ?
There are more red blood cells than any other type of blood cell in your body – about 5 million in each cubic millimetre of your blood.

Key points
- Your blood plasma transports dissolved food molecules, carbon dioxide and urea and has the blood cells suspended in it.
- Your red blood cells carry oxygen from your lungs to the organs of the body.
- Red blood cells are adapted to carry oxygen by being biconcave, giving them a bigger surface area, by containing haemoglobin and by having no nucleus so more haemoglobin can fit in.
- White blood cells are part of the defence system of the body.
- Platelets are cell fragments involved in the clotting of the blood.

Summary questions

1 Copy and complete using the words below:
transported glucose red blood cells urea blood lungs plasma oxygen
Substances are .... around your body in your .... Dissolved food molecules such as .... and waste substances such as .... are carried in the ...., while .... is carried from the .... to the cells by your ....

2 **a** Why is it not accurate to describe the blood as a red liquid?
 b What actually makes the blood red?
 c Give three important functions of blood plasma.

3 Explain the main ways in which the blood helps you to avoid infection, including a description of the parts of the blood involved.

Further teaching suggestions

Other vertebrate blood
- Mammalian blood is different from other vertebrate blood. Show slides of bird, fish, amphibian and reptile blood and get students to list the differences. Get them to think about how bloodstains may be identified and the forensic implications of this. For interest, show pictures of a horseshoe crab and comment that they do not have haemoglobin, so their blood is not red. They have hemocyanin instead which contains copper, so their blood is blue.

Effects of smoking
- This could be a good opportunity to consider the effects of smoking on the carriage of oxygen in the blood and carbon monoxide poisoning.

Answers to in-text questions

a Red blood cells, white blood cells, platelets (actually cell fragments).

b Carbon dioxide, urea, dissolved soluble products of digestion such as glucose.

Summary answers

1 transported, blood, glucose, urea, plasma, oxygen, lungs, red blood cells

2 **a** Blood plasma is a yellow liquid with cells suspended in it.
 b Red blood cells.
 c Three of: transports waste products, digested food, carbon dioxide, blood cells, hormones.

3 White blood cells form antibodies and actively digest microorganisms.
 Platelets help with clotting which keeps the microorganisms out.

B3 2.4

Artificial or real?

Learning objectives

Students should learn:

- that modern developments in research have resulted in the production and use of artificial blood and blood products
- that perfluorocarbons (PFCs) can transport dissolved gases around the body
- that artificial hearts have been developed that can take over the function of a diseased heart until a suitable donor organ becomes available.

Learning outcomes

Most students should be able to:

- describe what is meant by 'artificial blood'
- describe the properties of perfluorocarbons
- describe the way in which an artificial heart works
- interpret data relating to the differences between artificial and normal blood.

Some students should also be able to:

- evaluate in detail the use of artificial blood and artificial hearts.

Support

- Supply students with the components (images and text) to produce a poster in support of giving blood.

Extend

- Get students to find out more about blood groups and what is meant by agglutination.

Specification link-up: Biology B3.2

- Evaluate data on the production and use of artificial blood products. *[B3.2]*
- Evaluate the use of artificial hearts … . *[B3.2]*

Lesson structure

Starters

Android blood – Show a video clip of an android (a good one would be the section from the 1979 Ridley Scott film *Alien* where the reanimated head of the android 'Ash' warns the crew about the alien. He is covered in white-coloured artificial blood). Discuss what features artificial blood should have in order for it to work successfully in a human. *(5 minutes)*

Can I be a blood donor? – Blood donors must be over 17 years old. Working in small groups, get students to think of reasons why a person should not donate blood. Give them a time limit and then collate the reasons. Support students by prompting them or giving them suggestions which they have to think about. Extend students by asking them to group their reasons into categories such as age, past medical history, recent exposure to infection, travel overseas, etc. and give examples. *(10 minutes)*

Main

- Start with the need to match blood for transfusions. Explain to students about blood groups and how they are inherited. This can be done quite simply using A, B and O notation and explaining that there are three different alleles but we inherit two alleles, one from each parent. It will be necessary to explain that A and B are dominant and O is recessive. A simple table of who can receive blood from whom and donate blood to whom would illustrate the point made in the text.

- Using the data in Figure 1, discuss with students the different types of artificial blood and the advantages and disadvantages of using it. Compare the different ways in which blood or blood products are used in emergencies.

- Get the students to design a poster or produce an information leaflet encouraging people to become blood donors. The poster activity can be done individually, but the production of an information leaflet can be a group project. Whichever is undertaken, students may need to carry out some research into why blood is needed, how much is needed and why it is important for people to come forward as donors. As recommended in the Student Book, the NHS Blood and Transplant Service website is a valuable source of information, both about blood donation and also about transplants.

- It is suggested in the Student Book that students make a presentation on heart transplants and the use of artificial hearts. Groups of students could research different aspects of the topic and then present their findings to the rest of the class. Suggested areas for investigation could include the work of Dr Christiaan Barnard, reasons why transplants are performed, how a transplant is performed, problems associated with transplants and survival rates. They will need some time to research the different aspects: lesson time and homework time could be used.

Plenaries

Bloody anagrams – Give the students' anagrams of words associated with the blood. Support them by using simple terms. Extend students by leaving out the vowels and then asking them to write definitions of the words. *(5 minutes)*

Developing perfect artificial blood – Considering all the difficulties with artificial blood, get students to suggest how the effectiveness of artificial blood should be assessed. Have a brainstorming session as to how the perfect artificial blood might be developed. *(10 minutes)*

Activity 1

Artificial blood

1 Data show that PFCs contain more dissolved oxygen than plasma does, and the more concentrated the PFC, the more oxygen is dissolved. This shows that artificial blood products have the potential for carrying substantial amounts of oxygen, which could be useful when whole blood is not available.

2 Look for good use of data on artificial blood products and on the need for blood etc, along with clear presentation skills.

Activity 2

The story of heart transplants and artificial hearts

Look for evidence of thorough research, good presentation and an understanding of the benefits and limitations of artificial hearts in transplantation.

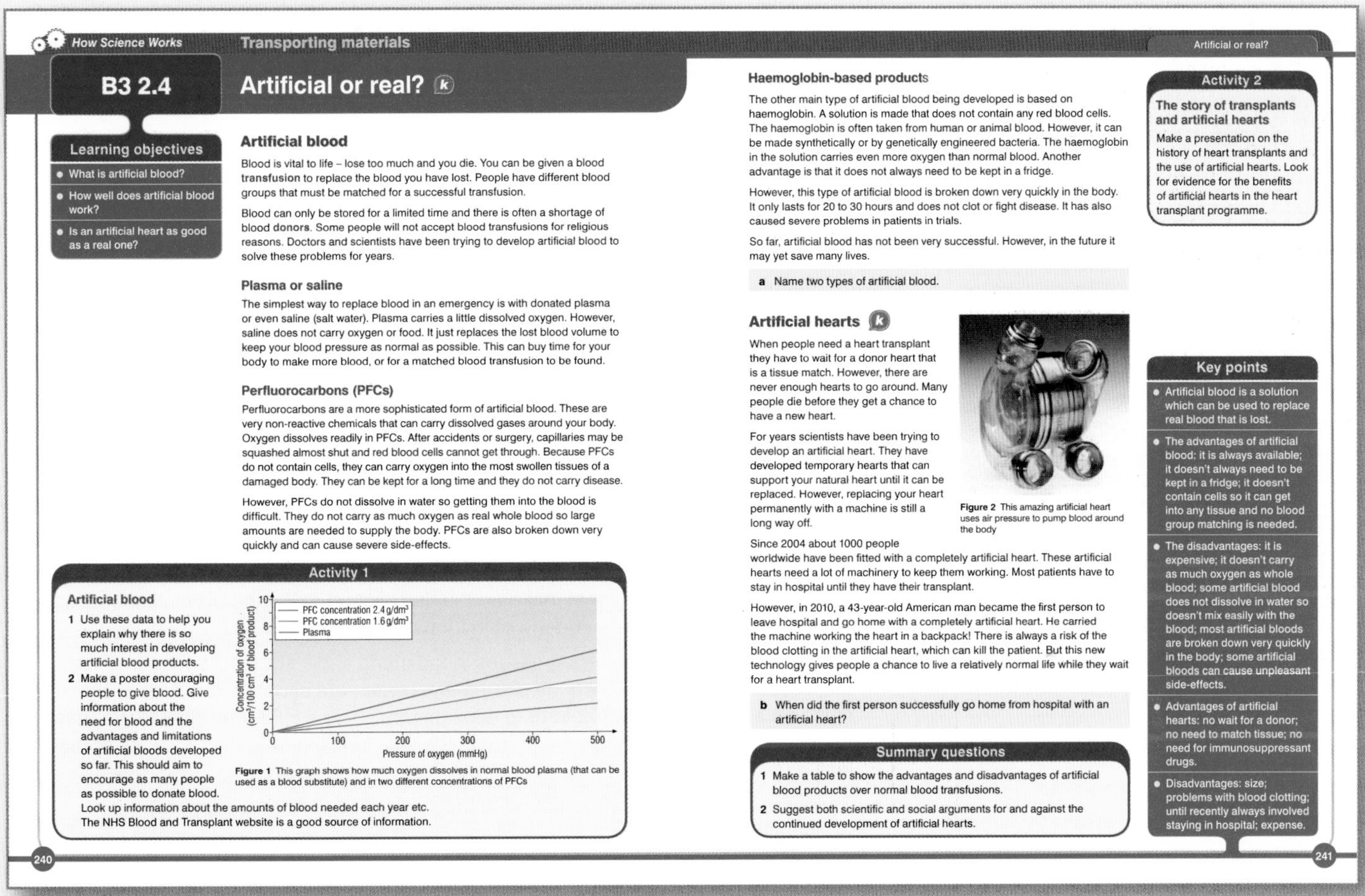

How Science Works — Transporting materials

Artificial or real?

B3 2.4   Artificial or real? (k)

Learning objectives
- What is artificial blood?
- How well does artificial blood work?
- Is an artificial heart as good as a real one?

Artificial blood

Blood is vital to life – lose too much and you die. You can be given a blood transfusion to replace the blood you have lost. People have different blood groups that must be matched for a successful transfusion.

Blood can only be stored for a limited time and there is often a shortage of blood donors. Some people will not accept blood transfusions for religious reasons. Doctors and scientists have been trying to develop artificial blood to solve these problems for years.

Plasma or saline

The simplest way to replace blood in an emergency is with donated plasma or even saline (salt water). Plasma carries a little dissolved oxygen. However, saline does not carry oxygen or food. It just replaces the lost blood volume to keep your blood pressure as normal as possible. This can buy time for your body to make more blood, or for a matched blood transfusion to be found.

Perfluorocarbons (PFCs)

Perfluorocarbons are a more sophisticated form of artificial blood. These are very non-reactive chemicals that can carry dissolved gases around your body. Oxygen dissolves readily in PFCs. After accidents or surgery, capillaries may be squashed almost shut and red blood cells cannot get through. Because PFCs do not contain cells, they can carry oxygen into the most swollen tissues of a damaged body. They can be kept for a long time and they do not carry disease.

However, PFCs do not dissolve in water so getting them into the blood is difficult. They do not carry as much oxygen as real whole blood so large amounts are needed to supply the body. PFCs are also broken down very quickly and can cause severe side-effects.

Activity 1

Artificial blood

1 Use these data to help you explain why there is so much interest in developing artificial blood products.

2 Make a poster encouraging people to give blood. Give information about the need for blood and the advantages and limitations of artificial bloods developed so far. This should aim to encourage as many people as possible to donate blood. Look up information about the amounts of blood needed each year etc. The NHS Blood and Transplant website is a good source of information.

Figure 1 This graph shows how much oxygen dissolves in normal blood plasma (that can be used as a blood substitute) and in two different concentrations of PFCs

Haemoglobin-based products

The other main type of artificial blood being developed is based on haemoglobin. A solution is made that does not contain any red blood cells. The haemoglobin is often taken from human or animal blood. However, it can be made synthetically or by genetically engineered bacteria. The haemoglobin in the solution carries even more oxygen than normal blood. Another advantage is that it does not always need to be kept in a fridge.

However, this type of artificial blood is broken down very quickly in the body. It only lasts for 20 to 30 hours and does not clot or fight disease. It has also caused severe problems in patients in trials.

So far, artificial blood has not been very successful. However, in the future it may yet save many lives.

a Name two types of artificial blood.

Artificial hearts (k)

When people need a heart transplant they have to wait for a donor heart that is a tissue match. However, there are never enough hearts to go around. Many people die before they get a chance to have a new heart.

For years scientists have been trying to develop an artificial heart. They have developed temporary hearts that can support your natural heart until it can be replaced. However, replacing your heart permanently with a machine is still a long way off.

Figure 2 This amazing artificial heart uses air pressure to pump blood around the body

Since 2004 about 1000 people worldwide have been fitted with a completely artificial heart. These artificial hearts need a lot of machinery to keep them working. Most patients have to stay in hospital until they have their transplant.

However, in 2010, a 43-year-old American man became the first person to leave hospital and go home with a completely artificial heart. He carried the machine working the heart in a backpack! There is always a risk of the blood clotting in the artificial heart, which can kill the patient. But this new technology gives people a chance to live a relatively normal life while they wait for a heart transplant.

b When did the first person successfully go home from hospital with an artificial heart?

Activity 2

The story of transplants and artificial hearts

Make a presentation on the history of heart transplants and the use of artificial hearts. Look for evidence for the benefits of artificial hearts in the heart transplant programme.

Key points

- Artificial blood is a solution which can be used to replace real blood that is lost.
- The advantages of artificial blood: it is always available; it doesn't always need to be kept in a fridge; it doesn't contain cells so it can get into any tissue and no blood group matching is needed.
- The disadvantages: it is expensive; it doesn't carry as much oxygen as whole blood; some artificial blood does not dissolve in water so doesn't mix easily with the blood; most artificial bloods are broken down very quickly in the body; some artificial bloods can cause unpleasant side-effects.
- Advantages of artificial hearts: no wait for a donor; no need to match tissue; no need for immunosuppressant drugs.
- Disadvantages: size; problems with blood clotting; until recently always involved staying in hospital; expense.

Summary questions

1 Make a table to show the advantages and disadvantages of artificial blood products over normal blood transfusions.

2 Suggest both scientific and social arguments for and against the continued development of artificial hearts.

240 | 241

Further teaching suggestions

Blood please!
- Students could carry out a survey to find out what people think about donating blood and their reasons for doing it or avoiding it.

Thanks!
- Students could write a letter thanking a blood donor for their services and saying how they benefited from the transfusion they received.

Answers to in-text questions

a Perfluorocarbons (PFCs), haemoglobin-based products.

b 2010.

Summary answers

1 **Advantages to include:** cheap, easily available, don't depend on donors, good carriage of oxygen (better than plasma or saline), no risk of disease, don't always need refrigeration, long shelf life, less religious objections, any other valid points.

Disadvantages to include: cause side effects, difficult to get into system, may rely on blood products anyway, broken down rapidly in the body, don't carry dissolved food, don't clot blood, don't offer defence against disease, any other valid points.

2 Look for well-argued points backed by evidence where possible.

B3 2.5

Transport systems in plants

Learning objectives

Students should learn:

- that flowering plants have separate transport systems
- that xylem tissue transports water and mineral ions from the roots to the stem and leaves
- that phloem tissue carries dissolved sugars from the leaves to the rest of the plant, including the growing regions and the storage organs.

Learning outcomes

Most students should be able to:

- state the tissues which make up the transport systems in plants
- describe which materials are moved in the phloem and the xylem.

Some students should also be able to:

- explain the importance of the transport systems in plants.

Specification link-up: Biology B3.2

- Flowering plants have separate transport systems:
  - xylem tissue transports water and mineral ions from the roots to the stem and leaves.
  - the movement of water from the roots through the xylem and out of the leaves is called the transpiration stream.
  - phloem tissue carries dissolved sugars from the leaves to the rest of the plant, including the growing regions and the storage organs. [B3.2.3 a)]

Lesson structure

Starters

Maple syrup – Show the students a bottle of maple syrup. Ask if anyone knows how maple syrup is made. Search the internet for a video clip of GardenGirlTV 'How to make maple syrup' (miss the introduction). Comment on this. Discuss the sticky liquid that drops from lime trees onto your car if you park underneath one. Link to phloem. *(5 minutes)*

Where am I going? – Give students a list of substances that are moved around plants [water, named ions, dissolved sugars] and get them to say where they are coming from and where they are going. Support students by giving them a list of options from which to choose for each one. Extend students by asking them to give the uses to which the substances are put when they have reached their destination. *(10 minutes)*

Main

- Produce an exposition or PowerPoint presentation on transport tissues in plants. Use prepared and stained transverse sections and longitudinal sections of the stem of an herbaceous plant to show the arrangement of the phloem and the xylem. Create worksheets and blank diagrams for the students to complete and label. Emphasise the tubular nature of the cells that make up the tissues and make the distinction between the xylem as a dead tissue and the phloem as a living tissue.

- Having introduced the transport tissues in the stem, show students sections of leaves and roots, pointing out where the phloem and xylem are situated. If possible, show students a leaf skeleton or hold up a thin leaf and shine a light through it to emphasise the complex network of vascular tissue in the leaf. Link this with the functions of the leaf.

- Then you could investigate transport in the xylem (see 'Practical support').

- Show students transverse sections through woody tissue from a tree. Have some sawn off slices of branches or tree trunks showing annual rings and the bark still on the outside. Explain that new vascular tissues are produced every year by the cambium just below the bark. The xylem tissue increases as the tree grows, but the phloem gets squashed and so there is only a narrow band of phloem just below the bark. Explain that damaging the bark or cutting a ring of bark away can remove the phloem and prevent the transport of sugars from the leaves to the roots. Explain that gnawing animals, such as squirrels and deer, can destroy trees.

Plenaries

Diagram labelling – Have prepared a number of appropriate keywords (xylem, phloem, vascular bundles, root, leaf etc.) on laminated flashcards (font size 100 is about right). Put sticky-tac or similar on the back. Project images of unlabelled diagrams of the vascular tissue in plants onto a board and get volunteers to attach the labels to the correct parts. Support students by using transverse sections only. Extend students by showing several different versions of the diagrams and include longitudinal sections. *(5 minutes)*

Crossword clues. Ask the students to produce clues for a crossword to summarise the learning in the lesson. Get them to write them onto slips of paper then hand them to the teacher. Read a few out, getting students to respond. Use selected clues to produce a crossword in either electronic or hard copy form, which can be used as a starter for the next lesson. *(10 minutes)*

Support

- Give students an outline of a transverse section of a tree trunk, or a sawn-off section, and get them to work out how old it is by counting the annual growth rings.

Extend

- Get students to find out the different types of cells that make up the xylem and phloem.

Practical support

Transport in the xylem

Equipment and materials required:
Leaf stalks of celery; small beakers; water coloured with eosin or red ink; rulers; stopwatches or stop clock; knives for cutting sections.

Details
This investigation can be carried out using leaf stalks of celery. The leaf stalks can be placed in a beaker of water containing a red dye,

such as eosin, or red ink. As the water is taken up, the dye stains the walls of the xylem cells. If sections of the leaf stalk are cut, it is possible to see that the red dye is confined to the xylem tissue.

It is possible to measure the flow rate by measuring how far the red dye has extended up the leaf stalk at timed intervals. A calculation of the rate of flow per unit time can then be made. It is preferable to use whole celery leaves for this activity, rather than leaf stalks only.

Safety: Care when handling knives.

B3 2.5   Transport systems in plants (k)

Learning objectives
- What substances are transported in plants?
- How does transport in the xylem and the phloem differ?

links
For information on phloem, look back to B2 1.5 Tissues and organs.

Plants make sugar by photosynthesis in the leaves and other green parts. This sugar is needed all over the plant. Similarly, water and mineral ions move into the plant from the soil through the roots, but they are needed by every cell of the plant. Plants have two separate transport systems to move substances around their bodies.

Phloem – moving food

The phloem transports the sugars made by photosynthesis from the leaves to the rest of the plant. This includes the growing areas of the stems and roots. Here the sugars are needed for making new plant cells. Food is also transported to the storage organs where it is needed to provide an energy store for the winter. Phloem is a living tissue.

Greenfly and other aphids are plant pests. They stick their sharp mouthparts right into the phloem and feed on the sugary fluid. If too many of them attack a plant they can kill it by taking all of the food.

Figure 1 Aphids take the liquid full of dissolved sugars directly from the phloem

Xylem – moving water and mineral ions

The xylem is the other transport tissue in plants. It carries water and mineral ions from the soil around the plant. Mature xylem cells are dead. In woody plants like trees, the xylem makes up the bulk of the wood and the phloem is found in a ring just underneath the bark. This makes young trees in particular very vulnerable to damage by animals. That's because if a complete ring of bark is eaten, transport in the phloem stops. Then the tree will die.

links
For information on xylem, look back to B2 1.5 Tissues and organs.

a Which plant transport tissue is living?
b What is transported in the xylem?

Why is transport so important?

It is very important to move the food made by photosynthesis around the plant. All the cells need sugars for respiration as well as to provide materials for growth. The movement of water and mineral ions from the roots is equally important. The mineral ions are needed for the production of proteins and other molecules within the cells.

The water is needed for several reasons. One is for photosynthesis, where carbon dioxide and water are combined to make sugar. Another is that water is needed to hold the plant upright. When a cell has plenty of water inside it the vacuole presses the cytoplasm against the cell walls. This pressure of the cytoplasm against the cell walls gives support for young plants and for the structure of the leaves. For young plants and soft-stemmed plants – although not trees – this is the main method of support.

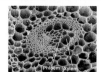

Figure 2 The phloem and xylem are arranged in vascular bundles in the stem

Figure 3 A simple way of demonstrating that water moves up the xylem

Study tip
Don't confuse xylem and phloem:
- For **phloem** think 'food' (sugar) transport.
- For **xylem** think 'transports water'.

Summary questions

1 Copy and complete using the words below:
xylem phloem two water sugars roots leaves plant
Plants have .... transport systems. The .... transports .... and mineral ions from the .... to the stems and leaves. The .... transports dissolved .... from the .... to the rest of the ....

2 **a** Why does a plant need a transport system?
  b Explain why a constant supply of sugar and water are so important to the cells of a plant.

3 A local woodland trust has set up a scheme to put protective plastic covers around the trunks of young trees. Some local residents are objecting to this, saying it spoils the look of the woodland. Write a letter to your local paper explaining exactly why this protection is necessary.

Key points
- Flowering plants have separate transport systems.
- Xylem tissue transports water and mineral ions from the roots to the stems and leaves.
- Phloem tissue transports dissolved sugars from the leaves to the rest of the plant, including the growing regions and storage organs.

Further teaching suggestions

Observing the passage of water
- Observe the passage of water through an entire plant using a Busy Lizzie, or other plant with a transparent stem. Stand the plant in a beaker of water containing a red dye for about 24 hours and then observe where the dye is inside it. If it is not entirely clear where the dye has gone, cut sections of the plant and look at them with a hand lens or binocular microscope.

Observing venation
- Water containing dyes can be used to show the veins in the petals of pale-coloured flowers. Stain the stems of the flowers in the coloured solution for a few days and then observe the petals.

Artificial phloem and xylem
- Investigate the content of artificial phloem and xylem and the appropriate tests which can be used to do this.

Summary answers

1 two, xylem, water, roots, phloem, sugars, leaves, plant

2 **a** To move food made in the leaves to the rest of the plant and to transport water and mineral ions taken from the soil to the rest of the plant.
  b All the cells need dissolved sugar for cellular respiration and also as the basis for making new plant material. Water is needed for photosynthesis to make sugar, and also to keep the cells rigid to support the plant.

3 Look for a well-written and argued letter which should explain why the transport tissues are important in plants and that they are found in the outer layer of the plant stem, so that if they are nibbled round by deer or rabbits, the young trees will die which is a waste of money and also means the woodland will not be maintained. Any other sensible points.

Answers to in-text questions
a Phloem.
b Water (and mineral ions).

Summary answers

1 a If there is a 'hole in the heart', then oxygenated and deoxygenated blood is no longer kept separate. The oxygenated and deoxygenated blood mix and so the level of oxygen in the blood going around the body is not as high as it should be. This explains the blue colour and the lack of energy. If surgeons close up the hole, then the heart works perfectly normally and the two types of blood no longer mix.

b The heart muscle itself becomes starved of oxygen and so cannot work properly. This is why the chest pain develops. If the blockage is not treated, the heart muscle can be damaged in a heart attack.

2 a After giving blood, the athlete will not perform as well. There is less blood available to carry oxygen and food to the muscles as they exercise. (The lack of oxygen is particularly noticeable because the blood volume is made up quickly but it takes longer to produce the new red blood cells).

b Iron is needed for the formation of haemoglobin; the red pigment in red blood cells that carries oxygen around the body. So if there is a lack of iron in the diet, there will be less haemoglobin, a lack of oxygen, resulting in a lack of energy and a tired feeling (anaemia).

3 a The shape of the red blood cells gives maximum SA (surface area) for oxygen to enter by diffusion. The red blood cells contain lots of haemoglobin to maximise the carriage of oxygen.

b **i** 35 and 90+

ii 15 and 70

iii In the lungs, the partial pressure of oxygen will be high and so a high percentage of the haemoglobin will become saturated with oxygen.

iv In the tissues, the concentration of carbon dioxide will be higher and so the haemoglobin will become less saturated with oxygen, giving up the oxygen to the tissues.

v The data suggests that haemoglobin-based artificial blood would be effective as the figures for oxygen saturation are made on haemoglobin rather than red blood cells.

4 a A stent is a metal framework which is inserted into a blocked vein to dilate it and restore normal blood flow. The stent holds the blood vessel open.

b Stenting appears more successful on the data presented, based on numbers of heart attacks, deaths and strokes that patients suffered in the first year after the procedure.

c Any sensible points e.g. were the procedures done on patients with similar levels of disease or was bypass surgery carried out on the sickest patients; numbers of patients in study, results from other studies, etc.

5 a

Artery	Vein
Carry blood away from the heart	Carry blood towards the heart
Usually carry bright red oxygenated blood	Usually carry purply red deoxygenated blood
Stretch as blood forced through them and then go back to shape – felt as a pulse	No pulse Valves to prevent back-flow of blood
Blood under pressure	Blood at relatively low pressure
Thick muscle and elastic tissue walls	Relatively thin walls
Any other sensible points	Any other sensible points

Summary questions

1 Here are descriptions of two heart problems. In each case use what you know about the heart and the circulatory system to explain the problems caused by the condition.

a Sometimes babies are born with a 'hole in the heart' – there is a gap in the central dividing wall of the heart. They may look blue in colour and have very little energy.

b The coronary arteries supplying blood to the heart muscle itself may become clogged with fatty material. The person affected may get chest pain when they exercise or even have a heart attack.

2 In each of the following examples, explain the effect on the blood and what this will mean to the person involved:

a an athlete running a race after acting as a blood donor and giving blood

b someone who eats a diet low in iron.

3 a How are the red blood cells adapted for the carriage of oxygen?

b The graph shows the effect of an increased carbon dioxide concentration on the way haemoglobin carries oxygen.

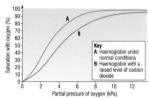

Figure 1 Graph to show the effect of carbon dioxide concentration on the reaction between haemoglobin and oxygen

i What is the percentage saturation of haemoglobin under normal conditions when the partial pressure of oxygen is 2 and 6?

ii What is the percentage saturation of haemoglobin when the partial pressure of oxygen is 2 and 6 and the concentration of carbon dioxide is raised?

iii What does this tell you about events in the blood capillaries in the lungs?

iv How does the concentration of carbon dioxide in the tissues affect gaseous exchange between the cells and the blood?

v Why do these data suggest that haemoglobin-based oxygen-carrying artificial blood would be effective?

4 If a patient has a blocked blood vessel, doctors may be able to open up the blocked vessels with a stent or replace the clogged up blood vessels with bits of heal blood vessels taken from other parts of the patient's body.

Figure 2 shows you the results of these procedures in one group of patients after one year.

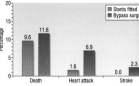

Figure 2 Results after 1 year

a What is a stent and how does it work?

b Which technique does the evidence suggest is the most successful for treating blocked coronary arteries? Explain your answer.

c What additional information would you need to deci whether this evidence was repeatable, reproducible and valid?

5 Arteries, veins, xylem and phloem are all transport vessels in living organisms.

a Make a table to compare arteries and veins.

b Make a table to compare xylem and phloem tissue

c Comment on the two different systems.

b

Xylem	Phloem
Dead tissue	Living tissue
Transports water and mineral ions from the soil to the rest of the plant	Transports sugars from the leaves around the plants
Any sensible points	Any sensible points

c The arteries and veins both contain blood. The blood is moved around the system by the pumping of the heart. The blood vessels are connected by the capillaries. All the tissue is living.

Xylem and phloem contain different solutes. Liquid moved by physical forces e.g. transpiration, evaporation. No pumping mechanism. Vessels not connected.

Any other relevant points.

End of chapter questions

Practice questions

a Platelets are found in the blood plasma. Some sick people need platelets as part of their treatment.

What is the function of platelets? (1)

b Some people donate whole blood, but the National Blood Service also needs platelet donations.

Read the facts about blood donation and platelet donation in the table below.

Use information from the table and your own knowledge to answer the questions.

i The National Blood Service needs more platelet donors.
Why? (1)

ii Give **two** reasons why doctors prefer platelet donation for seriously ill patients who require platelets. (2)

iii Give **one** disadvantage of platelet donation for the National Blood Service. (1)

iv Blood platelet donors choose to donate because they know the benefits to patients but there *are* disadvantages to donating platelets instead of whole blood.
Give **two** disadvantages for the donor of platelets. (2)

v Give **one** advantage to the donor for platelet donation over whole blood donation. (1)

2 The photograph shows a red blood cell in part of a blood clot. The fibres labelled **X** are produced in the early stages of the clotting process.

a Suggest how the fibres labelled **X** help in blood-clot formation. (1)

b The average diameter of a real red blood cell is 0.008 millimetres.
On the photograph, the diameter of the red blood cell is 100 millimetres.
Use the formula to calculate the magnification of the photograph.
diameter on photograph = real diameter × magnification
Magnification = (2)

c Some blood capillaries have an internal diameter of approximately 0.01 millimetres.

i Use information given in part **b** to explain why only one red blood cell at a time can pass through a capillary. (2)

ii Explain the advantages of red blood cells passing through a capillary one at a time. (2)

	Blood donation	Platelet donation
ge of donors	17+	17+
umber of possible donations per year	2–3	8–12
iet before donating	normal diet	a few days of low fat food, no aspirin or other 'blood-thinning drugs'
olume removed	470 cm³ blood	400–600 cm³ of straw coloured liquid
me to test blood before donation	time for confidential questionnaire plus a few minutes for a finger-prick test to find out haemoglobin levels	often a previous blood donor; extra blood tests take about 8 weeks to check platelet levels
sual time to donate	10 minutes to donate blood plus resting time; about 1 hour in total	90 minutes to donate platelets plus resting time; about 2 hours in total
me for blood to get back to normal	about 16 weeks	a few days
eeping time	depends on treatment – blood is separated into different parts such as red cells or plasma; some is frozen	5 days
umber of people to benefit from a ingle donation	blood is often split into components, including platelets; 3–7 people may benefit	three adults or up to 12 children
enefit to person receiving platelets	may require platelets from several donors	platelets received from one donor

245

Practice answers

1 a Platelets are needed for blood clotting. *(1 mark)*

b **i** Platelets only last 5 days. *Allow answers relating to more patients*. *(1 mark)*

ii only one donor needed;
less risk of infection *(2 marks)*

iii It takes 8 weeks to get results of donor blood tests. *(1 mark)*

iv restricted diet before donating/description;
time spent (to donate platelets) *(2 marks)*

v blood returns to normal quicker *(1 mark)*

2 a hold <u>cells</u> together or prevent flow of <u>cells</u> or trap <u>cells</u> *(1 mark)*

b 12 500 *(2 marks)*
if correct answer, ignore working/lack of working
$\frac{100}{0.008}$ *for 1 mark*
ignore any units

c **i** size RBC approximately same size capillary **or**
no room for more than one cell **or**
<u>only</u> one can fit **or**
RBC is <u>too</u> big
allow use of numbers
do not accept capillaries are narrow *(2 marks)*

ii more oxygen released (to tissues) **or**
more oxygen taken up (from lungs)
and any **two** from:
- slows flow or more time available
- shorter distance (for exchange) or close to cells/capillary wall
- more SA (surface area) exposed *(2 marks)*

Kerboodle resources

Resources available for this chapter on Kerboodle are:
- Chapter map: Transporting materials
- Extension: Stent advice (B3 2.2)
- Bump up your grade: The blood (B3 2.3)
- WebQuest: Artificial blood (B3 2.4)
- How Science Works: Which one should I have? (B3 2.4)
- Maths skills: Cells under a microscope (B3 2.5)
- Interactive activity: Transporting materials
- Revision podcast: Transporting materials
- Test yourself: Transporting materials
- On your marks: Transporting materials
- Practice questions: Transporting materials
- Answers to practice questions: Transporting materials

Practical suggestions

Practicals	AQA	k	📖	⚙
Dissection of the heart.	✓		✓	
Use software simulations of the work of the heart and blood vessels.	✓		✓	
Observation of arteries and veins from slides.	✓		✓	
Observation of blood smears.	✓		✓	
Observation of valves in veins preventing backflow of blood using the 'athletic' arm/ prominent vein.	✓		✓	
Investigate flow rate in xylem using celery, which can include calculation of flow rate.	✓		✓	
Investigate the content of artificial phloem and xylem given knowledge of the appropriate tests.	✓		✓	
Plan an investigation using a podometer to measure the effect of temperature or wind speed on the transpiration rate.	✓		✓	
Use sensors to measure blood pressure before, during and after exercise.	✓		✓	

B3 3.1

Controlling internal conditions

Learning objectives

Students should learn:

- that the internal conditions of the body need to be controlled
- that waste products have to be removed from the body
- how carbon dioxide and urea are removed
- that the water and ion balance and the temperature and blood sugar levels must be maintained at a steady level.

Learning outcomes

Most students should be able to:

- define the term 'homeostasis' and list the internal conditions of the body that are controlled
- explain why carbon dioxide and urea need to be removed from the body
- describe how carbon dioxide is removed from the body via the lungs
- describe the role of the kidneys in removing urea and controlling the water and ion content of the body.

Some students should also be able to:

- explain the complexity of homeostasis.

Support

- Give students a blank diagram with a body outline on it in the centre and four arrows coming from appropriate places. Get them to put the labels 'Urine', 'Faeces', 'Sweat' and 'CO$_2$ in breath' in the correct places.

Extend

- Ask students to hold their breath for 30 seconds (risk assessment for individuals). They can feel the desire to breathe building, due to the CO$_2$ building up. Ask: 'Does the feeling go when you breathe in? Why is this? Where might the sensors be that tell you that you have too much CO$_2$ in you? How can you tell?' This can link to the first activity in the Main part of the lesson.

Specification link-up: Biology B3.3

- Waste products that have to be removed from the body include:
  - carbon dioxide, produced by respiration and removed via the lungs when we breathe out
  - urea, produced in the liver by the breakdown of amino acids and removed by the kidneys in the urine, which is temporarily stored in the bladder. *[B3.3.1 a)]*
- If the water or ion content of the body is wrong, too much water may move into or out of the cells and damage them. Water and ions enter the body when we eat and drink. *[B3.3.1 b)]*

  Controlled Assessment: B4.3 Collect primary and secondary data. *[B4.3.2 b) c) f)]*; B4.4 Select and process primary and secondary data. *[B4.4.1 a) b)]*

Lesson structure

Starters

Keeping warm or staying cool – Show the Student Book photos of obviously different climatic conditions. Ask: 'What will the people's core temperature be like?' Students should predict, respond and discuss. *(5 minutes)*

What's in a word? – Write the word 'homeostasis' in large letters on the board and ask students if they can find any clues in the word which indicate its meaning. Support students by prompting (perhaps to distinguish 'homeo' from 'homo' and getting 'stasis' to link to 'static'). Extend students by encouraging them to find some clues and be able to come up with similar words and a definition of homeostasis. Discuss all the internal conditions that need to be maintained the same. *(10 minutes)*

Main

- Show the students some hydrogencarbonate indicator. It should be cherry red when it is in equilibrium with the air. If a little dilute acid is added it turns yellow, if alkali is added it will go purple. Get a volunteer to blow into a tube of indicator through a straw. Ask: 'What does this show about the effect of CO$_2$ on the indicator and therefore the pH of CO$_2$ in solution?' Use this for students to speculate on the effect of the accumulation of CO$_2$ in the cells of the body.

- Carry out an analysis of inspired and expired air. This is best done as a demonstration before the whole class. The sample of air is drawn into a capillary tube (called a J-tube, it consists of a syringe attached to a capillary tube bent into a square J-shape) and its volume *a* is recorded. Potassium hydroxide solution is then drawn into the tube to absorb the carbon dioxide. The volume will decrease. The new volume *b* is noted. The potassium hydroxide solution is almost all expelled. A reagent that absorbs oxygen (pyrogallol) is then drawn into the tube, causing the volume to decrease, and the new volume *c* noted.

  Safety: CLEAPSS Hazcard 12 Pyrogallol – harmful. Recipe card 64. CLEAPSS Hazcard 91 Potassium hydroxide – corrosive. Wear eye protection (chemical splashproof). The percentage of CO$_2$ in the air is given by the expression:
  $\frac{(a - b)}{a} \times 100$. The percentage of O$_2$ in the air is given by the expression:
  $\frac{(b - c)}{a} \times 100$.

- A sample of expired air can be obtained by immersing a boiling tube in a trough of water, raising it to a vertical position keeping the open end under water and then exhaling into it through a bent straw or capillary tube. The analysis of this sample of exhaled air can then be tested as above and the percentages compared. You could get a volunteer (student) to give you a sample of expired air.

- The samples need to be jiggled around in the J-tube so that the absorption of the gases takes place. Three samples should be measured and a mean taken. The samples need to be at room temperature before their volume is measured. (This relates to: 'How Science Works': repeatability, accuracy and precision of data.)

Plenaries

Urea or urine? – Ask students to compose a sentence using both words in order to emphasise the difference and the connection between the two words. *(5 minutes)*

Facts and figures – Produce some facts and figures from this spread (4%, 0.04%, kidneys, urea, etc.) and ask students to write a sentence about the relevance of each to the current topic. Support students by giving them a list of sentences which they need to match with the relevant fact. Extend students by asking them to link their sentences so that they have a convenient revision summary. *(10 minutes)*

Further teaching suggestions

Spirometer
- Have a spirometer for the students to look at and show how it can be used. (This relates to 'How Science Works': making measurements.) Use a volunteer student to demonstrate the use of the spirometer. Care needed and risk assessment required. Students could discuss how the tracings can be used to measure lung volume and the effect of exercise on breathing. See CLEAPSS handbook section 14.5.

pH inside cells
- Remind students of the experiment to find the optimum pH at which catalase works inside cells (B2 3.1 'Proteins, catalysts

and enzymes'). If it was not done, then a demonstration emphasises the need for the elimination of carbon dioxide to keep the conditions inside cells neutral so that enzymes, such as catalase, can work most efficiently.

Homeostasis in the long-distance runner
- There are articles about marathon running on The Physiological Society website that could be read out and discussed. (See www.physoc.org.)

B3 3.1 Controlling internal conditions

Learning objectives
- What body conditions need to be controlled?
- How do you get rid of the waste products from your cells?

links
For information on homeostasis, look back to B1 2.5 Controlling conditions.

For your body to work properly the conditions surrounding your millions of cells must stay as constant as possible. On the other hand, almost everything you do tends to change things. For example:
- as you move you produce energy that warms the body
- as you respire you produce waste
- when you digest food you take millions of molecules into your body.

Yet somehow you keep your internal conditions constant within a very narrow range. How do you manage this? The answer is through homeostasis. Many of the functions in your body help to keep your internal environment as constant as possible. Now you are going to find out more about some of them.

a What is homeostasis?

Figure 1 Whatever you choose to do in life, the conditions inside your body will stay more or less exactly the same

Removing waste products

No matter what you are doing, the cells of your body are constantly producing waste products. These are products of the chemical reactions that take place in the cells. The more extreme the conditions you put yourself in, the more waste products your cells make.

There are two main poisonous waste products – carbon dioxide and urea. They cause major problems for your body if their levels are allowed to build up.

Carbon dioxide

Carbon dioxide is produced during respiration. Every cell in your body respires, and so every cell produces carbon dioxide. It is vital that you remove this carbon dioxide because dissolved carbon dioxide produces an acidic solution. This would affect the working of all the enzymes in your cells.

The carbon dioxide moves out of the cells into your blood. Your bloodstream carries it back to your lungs. Almost all of the carbon dioxide is removed from your body via your lungs when you breathe out. The air you breathe in contains only 0.04% carbon dioxide. However, the air you breathe out contains about 4% carbon dioxide.

b How do you remove carbon dioxide from your body?

Study tip
Don't confuse *urea* and *urine*. Urea is made in the liver; urine is produced by the kidney. Urine contains urea.

Urea
The other main waste product of your body is urea.

When you eat more protein than you need, or when body tissues are worn out, the extra protein has to be broken down. Amino acids cannot be used as fuel for your body. Your liver removes the amino group and converts it into urea.

The rest of the amino acid molecule can then be used in respiration or to make other molecules. The urea passes from the liver cells into your blood.

Urea is poisonous and if the levels build up in your blood it will cause a lot of damage. Fortunately the urea is filtered out of your blood by your kidneys. It is then passed out of your body in your urine, along with any excess water and salt.

c Where is urea made?

Maintaining body balance

Water and ions enter your body when you eat or drink. The water and ion content of your body are carefully controlled, preventing damage to your cells. Water is lost through breathing, through sweating and in urine. The ions are lost in sweat and urine.

If the concentrations of your body fluids change, water will move into or out of your cells by osmosis. This could damage or destroy the cells. You saw this when you looked at the importance of keeping hydrated when you exercise. So water balance is vital.

It is also very important to control your body temperature. If it goes too high or too low it can be fatal. Finally, it is very important to control the levels of sugar in your blood. The amount of sugar coming into your body and the energy needed by your cells are always changing and a balance must always be maintained. So homeostasis plays a very important role in your body.

Figure 2 The average person produces up to 900 litres of urine a year!

links
For information on osmosis, look back to B3 1.1 Osmosis.

For information on keeping hydrated, look back to B3 1.3 The sports drink dilemma.

For information on body temperature, see B3 3.5 Controlling body temperature.

For information on controlling glucose levels, see B3 3.7 Controlling blood glucose.

Summary questions

1 Copy and complete using the words below:
blood   carbon dioxide   constant   controlled   environment   enzymes   homeostasis   sugar   temperature   urea   water

The internal .... of your body is kept relatively .... by a whole range of processes that together are known as .... Waste products such as .... and .... have to be removed from your .... all the time. The .... and ion concentration in your blood are constantly .... and so is your blood .... level. Your body .... is kept within a narrow range so your .... work effectively.

2 There are two main waste products that have to be removed from the human body – carbon dioxide and urea. For each waste product, describe:
   a how it is formed
   b why it has to be removed
   c where it is removed from the body.

3 Draw a spider diagram with the word 'homeostasis' in the centre and make as many links in the diagram as you can. Label the links made.

Key points
- The internal conditions of your body have to be controlled to maintain a constant internal environment. These include your body temperature, your water and ion balance and your blood sugar levels.
- Carbon dioxide is produced during respiration and leaves the body via the lungs when you breathe out.
- Urea is produced by your liver as excess amino acids are broken down, and is removed by your kidneys in the urine.

246 / 247

Answers to in-text questions

a The maintenance of a constant internal environment.

b From the cells in the body, it is carried in the blood to the lungs and then breathed out in the air from the lungs.

c In the liver.

Summary answers

1 environment, constant, homeostasis, carbon dioxide, urea, blood, water, controlled, sugar, temperature, enzymes

2 **a** **Carbon dioxide:** formed during aerobic respiration
   glucose + oxygen → energy + carbon dioxide + water
   Urea: excess amino acids from protein/worn out tissues
   amino group removed from amino acids and converted to urea in the liver.
   b Both are poisonous to the cells/damage the body.
   c Carbon dioxide removed in the lungs.
   Urea removed by the kidneys.

3 Look for as many accurate points and connections as possible.

B3 3.2

The human kidney

Learning objectives

Students should learn:

- that urine, containing urea, excess mineral ions and water, is removed from the body by the kidneys
- that sugar, mineral ions and water needed by the body are reabsorbed into the blood as it passes through the kidneys.

Learning outcomes

Most students should be able to:

- describe how the kidneys produce urine
- describe that the kidneys remove urea and regulate the water content of the body.

Some students should also be able to:

- explain the role of the kidney in homeostasis
- explain in detail that sugar and dissolved ions may be actively absorbed against a concentration gradient in the kidney tubules.

Support

- Make a model kidney out of chicken wire. Pass coloured beads into it – blue ones for water, yellow ones for urea, white ones for mineral ions and small sweets for glucose. Include some big red and white balls that cannot get out as blood cells. Arrange a collecting bowl underneath and get students to put the beads and sweets that escape into two tubes, a red one labelled 'back into the blood', the other labelled 'to the bladder and out' with a picture of a toilet on it.

Extend

- Get students to look at kidney structure in more detail, examining prepared slides and trying to identify the parts of the nephron, such as glomeruli, loop of Henle and the cells of the tubules.

Specification link-up: Biology B3.3

- A healthy kidney produces urine by:
  - first filtering the blood
  - reabsorbing all the sugar
  - reabsorbing the dissolved ions needed by the body
  - reabsorbing as much water as the body needs
  - releasing urea, excess ions and water as urine. [B3.3.1 c)]

  Controlled Assessment: B4.5 Analyse and interpret primary and secondary data. [B4.5.3 a)]; [B4.5.4 a) b)]

Lesson structure

Starters

Do you know where your kidneys are? – Ask students to place their hands on their bodies to indicate where they think their kidneys are. Inspect to see who can get it right. Discuss the protection they have and link with why boxers wear wide belts. *(5 minutes)*

'Kidney trouble' – Show a clip from *The Simpsons* (season 10, episode 8, 'Homer Simpson in: "Kidney Trouble"') where Homer doesn't let Abe get out of the car to urinate and his kidneys explode! Discuss the anatomy behind this. Create and project a blank (unlabelled) diagram of the human urino-genital system and ask students to label the parts. Support students by providing a list of labels. Extend students by asking them to suggest a function for each of the parts they label. *(10 minutes)*

Main

- Look at some statistics of the volume of blood filtered each day, the reabsorption of glucose and amino acids and the way in which the kidney controls the water and ion content of the blood.

- You could carry out a kidney dissection (see 'Practical support').

- Encourage the students to use their sense of smell during the dissection. The function of the kidneys in the production of urine will be deeply embedded by association!

- You could also look at the effect of drinking on urine production. This investigation can either be presented to the students as collected data, or they could carry it out themselves at home. The idea is to find out what effect drinking a large volume of water has on the volume and colour of the urine.

- The person carrying out the investigation should empty their bladder as completely as possible. After 15 minutes, they should urinate again into a measuring cylinder, record the volume produced and retain a small sample in a sealed specimen tube. A litre of water should then be drunk. After 15 minutes, the person should urinate, record the volume produced and retain a further sample in a specimen tube. The volume of urine produced at 15-minute intervals should be recorded and a sample taken for as long as possible. Wash hands and equipment at home.

- No extra liquid should be drunk during the experiment. The volume of urine produced can be plotted against time and the colour recorded at the different intervals.

- A slight variation of the above could be to suggest to the students that they design an experiment to investigate the effect of drinking a large quantity of water on the production of urine. They could then be given some figures to plot and colours to comment on. (This relates to: 'How Science Works': relationships between variables.) Ask: 'How could the samples be tested to see if glucose or amino acids were present?'

Plenaries

Rate of flow – To observe what the flow rate through the kidneys looks like, set a flow rate of 1200 cm^3 per minute (20 cm^3 per second) through a hose from a container by adjusting a clamp. *(5 minutes)*

Why do peanuts make you thirsty? – Get the students to write a note for the back of a packet of peanuts explaining why they can make you thirsty. They should aim for exactly 20 words; or if they are using computers – give them a text box of fixed size that they must fill. Support students by giving them some words to be included in the note. Extend students by suggesting they include some more detailed scientific information – perhaps with regard to the benefits of keeping body fluids constant. *(10 minutes)*

Practical support

Kidney dissection

Equipment and materials required
Obtain some fresh lamb's or pig's kidneys with the fat and vessels attached. (These usually need to be ordered specially from the butcher.)

Details
Direct students to work in pairs or small groups. You could provide a worksheet or talk them through the observations and dissection.

It is worth looking at the outside to see the blood vessels and to point out that the fat surrounding the kidney is all the protection they have. Using a scalpel, the kidney should be sliced horizontally, so that the cortex, medulla and the ureters can be seen. Students should identify the renal artery, the renal vein, the ureter and the collecting area (pelvis) for the urine. The cortex and the medulla can be distinguished by their difference in colour. Ask: 'Why is the outer part (the cortex) darker red than the inner part (the medulla)?'

Safety: Take care with sharp scalpels. Wash hands after the experiment.

Keeping internal conditions constant

B3 3.2 The human kidney

Learning objectives
- Why are your kidneys so important?
- How do your kidneys work?

Your kidneys are one of the main organs that help to maintain homeostasis. They keep the conditions inside your body as constant as possible.

What are the functions of your kidney?

Your kidneys are very important in your body for homeostasis. They are involved in excretion – the removal of waste products. For example, you produce urea in your liver when you break down excess amino acids. Urea is poisonous, but your kidneys **filter** it out of your blood. Then you get rid of it in your urine, which is produced constantly by your kidneys and stored temporarily in your **bladder**.

a What is urea?

Your kidneys are also vital in the water balance of your body. You gain water when you drink and eat. You lose water constantly from your lungs. The water evaporates into the air in your lungs and is breathed out. Whenever you exercise or get hot you sweat more and lose more water.

So how do your kidneys balance all these changes? If you are short of water your kidneys conserve it. You produce very little urine and most of the water is saved for use in your body. If you drink too much water then your kidneys produce lots of urine to get rid of the excess.

The ion concentration of your body is very important. You take in mineral ions with your food. The amount you take in varies. Sometimes you take in very little.

Did you know ...?
All the blood in your body passes through your kidneys about once every 5 minutes. Your kidneys filter about 180 litres of water out of your blood during the day. About 99% of it is returned straight back into your blood. So on average you produce about 1800 ml of urine a day. Urine trickles into your bladder where it is stored. When the bladder is full you will feel the need to empty it.

Study tip
Remember that kidneys *filter* water and soluble substances then *reabsorb* useful substances such as sugar and ions. Large molecules such as protein cannot be filtered.

Figure 1 The kidney is a very important organ of homeostasis. It controls the balance of water and mineral ions in the body and gets rid of urea.

Labels on Figure 1:
- Diaphragm
- Main artery (aorta)
- Left kidney
- Renal artery – brings blood containing urea and other substances in solution to the kidney
- Renal vein – carries blood away from the kidney, after urea and other substances have been removed from the blood
- The liver produces urea
- Main vein (vena cava)
- Right kidney
- Ureter – tube through which urine passes from the kidney to the bladder
- Ring of muscle which controls the opening and closing of the bladder
- The bladder stores urine
- Urethra – tube through which urine passes to the outside of your body

However, if you eat processed food which is high in salt, you take in a lot of mineral ions. Some are lost through your skin when you sweat. Again, your kidneys are most important in keeping a mineral ion balance. They remove excess mineral ions (particularly sodium and chloride ions from salt). These are passed out in the urine.

b Why do your kidneys work hard after you have eaten a lot of processed food?

How do your kidneys work?

Your kidneys filter your blood. Then they take back (**reabsorb**) everything your body needs. They have a rich blood supply. Sugar (glucose), amino acids, mineral ions, urea and water all move out of your blood into the kidney tubules. They move by diffusion along a concentration gradient. The blood cells and large molecules such as proteins are left behind. They are too big to pass through the membrane of the tubule.

All of the sugar is reabsorbed back into the blood by active transport. However, the amount of water and dissolved mineral ions that are reabsorbed varies. It depends on what is needed by your body. This is known as **selective reabsorption**. The amount of water reabsorbed into the blood is controlled by a very sensitive feedback mechanism.

Urea is lost in your urine. However, some of it leaves the kidney tubules and moves back into your blood. The urea moves back into the blood by diffusion along a concentration gradient.

What does urine contain?

Your urine contains the waste urea along with excess mineral ions and water not needed by your body. The exact quantities vary depending on what you have taken in and given out. For example, on a hot day if you drink little and exercise a lot you will produce very little urine. This will be concentrated and relatively dark yellow. On a cool day if you drink a lot of liquid and do very little you will produce a lot of dilute, almost colourless urine.

Water, glucose, urea and salt are all colourless, but your urine is yellow. This is the result of **urobilins**, yellow pigments that come from the breakdown of haemoglobin in your liver. They are excreted by your kidneys in the urine along with everything else, making it yellow.

Figure 2 These data show how your kidneys respond when you drink a lot. They show the volume of urine produced and the concentration of salt in the urine after a student drank a large volume of water.

Graph labels: Volume of urine / Normal / Time after drinking (mins) / 30 60 90 120 150; Concentration of salt in urine / Normal / Time after drinking (mins) / 30 60 90 120 150

Summary questions
1 a What do the kidneys do in your body?
  b How do the kidneys carry out their job?
2 Explain how your kidneys would maintain the water and mineral balance of your blood on:
  a a cool day when you stayed inside and drank lots of cups of tea
  b a hot sports day when you ran three races and had forgotten your drink bottle.

Key points
- The kidneys are important for excretion and homeostasis.
- A healthy kidney produces urine by filtering the blood. It then reabsorbs all of the sugar, plus any mineral ions and water needed by your body.
- Excess mineral ions and water, along with urea, are removed in the urine.

Further teaching suggestions

The effect of different activities on the volume and content of the urine
- Predict and explain how each of the following activities might alter the volume and composition of the urine: eating a Mars bar, running a marathon, drinking two pints of lager, eating two packets of crisps.

Answers to in-text questions
a Urea is a waste product from the breakdown of amino acids/ proteins in the liver.

b Processed food often contains a lot of salt. Excess salt is removed from the blood by the kidneys and excreted in the urine.

Summary answers

1 a filter out urea; balance the water and salt level of your blood

  b They filter the blood – sugar, mineral ions, amino acids, urea and water are filtered out of the blood into the kidney tubule and then selectively reabsorbed as the liquid travels along the tubule. All of the sugar is taken back into the blood but the amounts of mineral ions and water vary with the needs of the body. Some urea returns to the blood along a concentration gradient.

2 a Your blood would become diluted. The kidneys would retain all but the excess salt and lose a lot of water, so you would produce a lot of very dilute urine.

  b Your kidneys would conserve both salt (because you are losing it in sweat) and water, so you would produce small quantities of very concentrated urine.

B3 3.3 Dialysis – an artificial kidney

Learning objectives

Students should learn:

- that kidney failure can be treated by dialysis
- that dialysis removes the urea from the blood
- that dialysis restores the concentrations of dissolved substances in the blood to normal levels.

Learning outcomes

Most students should be able to:

- describe how dialysis is used to treat kidney failure
- explain why dialysis needs to be carried out at regular intervals
- describe what happens during kidney dialysis
- list some of the advantages and disadvantages of kidney dialysis.

Some students should also be able to:

- give a detailed explanation of kidney dialysis in terms of diffusion and concentration gradients
- evaluate the pros and cons of dialysis treatment.

Specification link-up: Biology B3.3

- People who suffer from kidney failure may be treated either by using a kidney dialysis machine or by having a healthy kidney transplanted. [B3.3.1 d)]
- Treatment by dialysis restores the concentrations of dissolved substances in the blood to normal levels and has to be carried out at regular intervals. [B3.3.1 e)]
- In a dialysis machine a person's blood flows between partially permeable membranes. The dialysis fluid contains the same concentration of useful substances as the blood. This ensures that glucose and useful mineral ions are not lost. Urea passes out from the blood into the dialysis fluid. [B3.3.1 f)]

Lesson structure

Starters

Why do we have kidneys? Get the students to write down their own existing ideas on what kidneys do. Discuss as a class and draw together the collective findings. *(5 minutes)*

Dialysis: what we know so far – Create and show a PowerPoint review of dialysis. Students could complete a set of questions following viewing and discussion. Support students by allowing them to complete the answers to the questions during the review. Extend students by making the questions more searching. *(10 minutes)*

Main

- Show a short video or project pictures of a kidney patient undergoing dialysis. Discuss what is happening. Search the internet for 'Video kidney dialysis'.

- If students have not done any practical work using dialysis tubing, then it could be helpful to set up a demonstration or allow them to carry out some simple experiments to show that small molecules, such as glucose, pass through the tubing while larger molecules do not. Experiments such as the model gut (see B3 1.7 Exchange in the gut) or the use of tubing to show water uptake and loss in cells could be used.

- Use an animation to show dialysis and kidney machines. There is some good information on the School Science and Nephron Information Centre websites which includes images, animations and questions.

- You could create student worksheets to focus on the issues and provide the students with the facts. This is a good opportunity to point out the differences between dialysis and the normal functioning of the kidney.

- A brief talk from a nurse experienced in dialysis, or from a person who undergoes regular dialysis, followed by a question and answer session, could be of benefit.

- There are links here with the question of transplants and also some careers information. You could combine a talk on dialysis with some discussion of transplants (see next spread).

Plenaries

Virtual dialysis – If not used as a Starter or in the main part of the lesson, show the virtual dialysis clip from the Nephron Information Centre (www.nephron.com). *(5 minutes)*

Leaflet on dialysis – In groups, students can produce a leaflet for kidney patients explaining what dialysis is and how it works. Use word processing or desktop publishing software, if available. Support students by asking them to design a poster and provide them with sentences to include. Extend students by asking them to include helpful, annotated diagrams. *(10 minutes)*

Support

- Use a loop of cellulose acetate tubing filled with a mixture of red particles that will not pass through (fine sand to represent red blood cells), and some yellow dye such as fluorescein (representing waste products) that will pass through. Observe the fluoroscein exiting the tube and relate this to the process in the kidney.

Extend

- Following a scavenger hunt through a series of linked websites (on a school intranet, through Word document links or using software such as Quia) to complete a table summarising the differences and similarities between haemo-dialysis and peritoneal dialysis.

Further teaching suggestions

Role play I

- Students to write a monologue or script for a video diary presentation of what it feels like to be a kidney patient and have to undergo dialysis on a regular basis. This could be set as a homework exercise and then some selected to be read out in class.

Role play II

- Students can take the roles of patient, doctor and family member in making decisions about the treatment of kidney failure. In particular, they should discuss the advantages and disadvantages of dialysis. Open up the discussion to the other students.

What should I eat?

- Patients undergoing dialysis have to be careful about their diet. Ask: 'What recommendations would you make to a patient? Why does the quantity of protein eaten need to be controlled? And why should salt and fluid intake make a difference? Suppose you were diagnosed with renal failure, what foods would you miss most?

What stays in and what comes out?

- It could be helpful in understanding the way in which haemo-dialysis works to build up a diagram of the concentrations of substances either side of the dialysing membrane. The concentration gradients in the dialysate are adjusted so that they are the same as in the blood. Students can then consider the differences in concentration and be very clear about what comes out and what stays.

Reproduced textbook pages 250–251: B3 3.3 Dialysis – an artificial kidney

---

Answers to in-text questions

a If the kidneys fail, there is a build-up of toxins such as urea and salt in the blood, which can change the internal environment and can cause death due to water moving in or out of cells or poisoning due to urea.

b Diffusion.

Summary answers

1 Blood out of artery → through pump → blood thinners added to prevent clotting → blood passes through dialysis membranes and excess salt and urea are removed → clean blood into bubble trap → blood returns to vein in an arm.

2 a People with kidney failure cannot remove excess salt or get rid of the urea produced by the breakdown of excess amino acids.

   b The excess salt and urea are removed during the process of dialysis.

3 a There is no urea, so a steep concentration gradient exists from the blood to the dialysis fluid.
   Normal plasma levels of salt, glucose etc. are present, so there is no net loss or gain due to diffusion.

   b To help maintain concentration gradients for diffusion.

B3 3.4

Kidney transplants

Learning objectives

Students should learn:

- that a kidney transplant involves the replacement of a diseased kidney by a healthy one from a donor
- that precautions need to be taken to prevent the rejection of the transplanted kidney by the immune system
- that there are advantages and disadvantages of kidney transplants.

Learning outcomes

Most students should be able to:

- describe how a diseased kidney is replaced by a healthy one
- explain the problems of rejection by the immune system
- list the ways in which rejection is prevented
- list the advantages and disadvantages of having a kidney transplant.

Some students should also be able to:

- evaluate in detail the advantages and disadvantages of treating kidney failure by dialysis or kidney transplant
- explain the issues of rejection and the advantages of close tissue matches for success.

Answer to in-text question

a If the donor and the recipient are identical twins, they will have the same antigens.

Support

- Get students to complete a concept map of the pros and cons of transplants and dialysis. Use prompts if needed, such as initial letters, colour coding of key words and the places they go on the map.

Extend

- Get students to draw up arguments for and against the use of xenotransplants. If necessary, do a preliminary trawl of the internet for information on xenotransplants (transplants between species).

Specification link-up: Biology B3.3

- In kidney transplants, a diseased kidney is replaced with a healthy one from a donor. However, the donor kidney may be rejected by the immune system unless precautions are taken. [B3.3.1 g)]
- Antigens are proteins on the surface of cells. The recipient's antibodies may attack the antigens on the donor organ as they do not recognise them as part of the recipient's body. [B3.3.1 h)]
- To prevent rejection of the transplanted kidney:
    - a donor kidney with a 'tissue-type' similar to that of the recipient is used
    - the recipient is treated with drugs that suppress the immune system. [B3.3.1 i)]
- Evaluate the advantages and disadvantages of treating kidney failure by dialysis or kidney transplant.

    Controlled Assessment: B4.5 Analyse and interpret primary and secondary data. [B4.5.1a) b)], [B4.5.4 b) c)]

Lesson structure

Starters

The importance of kidneys – Discuss how you would feel if you had to go into surgery to have a defective kidney removed and the wrong kidney was removed by accident (state that this has actually happened in the past). Talk over the importance of kidneys and what could go wrong. Support students by providing prompts and suggestions. Extend students by getting them to give full explanations of the problems. *(5 minutes)*

'Kidney trouble' – Show a clip from *The Simpsons* (season 10, episode 8, 'Homer Simpson in: "Kidney Trouble"'), where Homer first runs away from giving Grandpa a kidney transplant then is conned into doing so but plans to get one off Bart. *(10 minutes)*

Main

- Pictures and more detailed information are available on kidney transplants from websites. The Nephron Information Centre has information that could be helpful.
- You could create a worksheet for students to keep a tally of pros and cons as the presentation proceeds.
- Show a video of a kidney transplant operation. (Search the internet for 'Video kidney transplant'.)
- Draw up a table of the pros and cons of kidney transplants. Expand this to compare transplants with dialysis.
- Using information from the internet about the relative costs of the two procedures, students could work out the difference in cost to the NHS of a patient on dialysis for 20 years and a patient who has two kidney transplants in 20 years. (This relates to: 'How Science Works': the ethical and social issues of using science and technology, and making decisions.)

Plenaries

A bit of me once belonged to someone else – Discuss how it would feel to have an organ donated to you from someone else. Ask: 'Would it matter which organ it was?' Watch excerpts or give a plot summary and discuss the 1946 film *The Beast with Five Fingers,* directed by Robert Florey. For a real life situation, discuss Chris Hallam, the first person to have an arm transplant. He eventually asked for it to be removed. BBC News website has the story and pictures. *(5 minutes)*

Kidney 'Snakes and Ladders' – Draw up a series of statements for a 'Snakes and Ladders' game of kidney problems. Include the benefits and difficulties associated with both transplants and dialysis. Discuss in class and make a game for homework. Support students by giving them statements so they can decide which ones are Snakes and which are Ladders. Extend students by evaluating the benefits and difficulties and by deciding how long each Snake and Ladder should be. *(10 minutes)*

Further teaching suggestions

Design a poster
- Students could design a poster to encourage people to carry donor cards or encourage kidney donation.

Organ donation
- Discuss donor cards. Issue some to have a look at. Get students to write down their feelings about organ donation in preparation for a debate on the topic. 'Should organ donation be assumed unless you actively opt out?' Further preparation for this could be a homework task, to write a speech in favour of the motion and one against the motion.

Finding kidney donors
- Draw up a list of sources of kidneys for transplantation. Ask: 'Why is there such a shortage? How would you set about campaigning for more donors?' This exercise could draw together some of the issues raised in other suggested activities.

Kidneys for sale
- Debate whether or not people should be able to sell their kidneys if they want to. Students could research the scale of this and the legal issues involved. The Sunday Mirror website has some good material on this and there are sites where information can be gathered.

B3 3.4 Kidney transplants ⓚ

Learning objectives
- What is a kidney transplant?
- How can we stop the body rejecting a transplanted kidney?

Diseased kidneys can be replaced in a kidney transplant using a single healthy kidney from a donor. The donor kidney is joined to the blood vessels in the groin of the patient (the recipient). If all goes well, it will function normally to clean and balance the blood. One kidney can balance your blood chemistry and remove your waste urea for a lifetime.

The rejection problem

The main problem with transplanting a kidney is that the new kidney comes from a different person. The antigens (proteins on the cell surface) of the donor organ will be different to those of the recipient (person who needs the new kidney). There is a risk that the antibodies of the immune system of the recipient will attack the antigens on the donor organ. This results in rejection and destruction of the donated kidney.

a There is one situation where there is no risk of a new kidney being rejected. What do you think that might be?

There are a number of ways of reducing the risk of rejection. The match between the antigens of the donor and the recipient is made as close as possible. For example, we can use a donor kidney with a 'tissue type' very similar to the recipient (from people with the same blood group).

The recipient is given drugs to suppress their immune response (immunosuppressant drugs) for the rest of their lives. This helps to prevent the rejection of their new organ. Immunosuppressant drugs are improving all the time. Nowadays the need for a really close tissue match is getting less important.

⚭ links
For information on antigens, look back to B1 1.9 Immunity.

The disadvantage of taking immunosuppressant drugs is that they prevent the patients from dealing effectively with infectious diseases. They have to take great care if they become ill in any way. However, most people feel this is a small price to pay for a new, working kidney.

Transplanted organs don't last forever. The average transplanted kidney works for around 9 years although some last much longer. Once the organ starts to fail the patient has to return to dialysis. Then they have to wait until another suitable kidney is found.

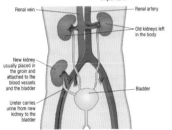

Renal vein — Renal artery
— Old kidneys left in the body
New kidney usually placed in the groin and attached to the blood vessels and the bladder
— Bladder
Ureter carries urine from new kidney to the bladder

Figure 1 A donor kidney takes over the functions of failed kidneys, which are usually left in place

⚛ How Science Works

Dialysis v. transplants

The great advantage of receiving a kidney transplant is that you are free from the restrictions which come with regular dialysis sessions. You can also eat what you want. An almost completely normal life is the dream of everyone waiting for a kidney transplant.

The disadvantages are mainly to do with the risk of rejection. You have to take medicine every day of your life in case the kidney is rejected. You also need regular check-ups to see if your body has started to reject the new organ. However, the biggest disadvantage is that you may never get the chance of a transplant at all.

Dialysis is much more readily available than donor organs, so it is there whenever kidneys fail. It enables you to lead a relatively normal life. However, you are tied to a special diet and regular sessions on the machine. Long term dialysis is much more expensive than a transplant.

Finding the donors

The main source of kidneys is from people who die suddenly. The deaths are often from road accidents or from strokes and heart attacks. In the UK, organs can be taken from people if they carry an organ donor card or are on the online donor register. Alternatively, a relative of someone who has died suddenly can give their consent.

There are never enough donor kidneys to go around. Many of us do not register as donors. What's more, as cars become safer, fewer people die in traffic accidents. This is very good news, but it means there are fewer potential donors. At any one time there are thousands of people having kidney dialysis. Most would love to have a kidney transplant but never get the opportunity. In 2008–9, 2497 people in the UK had kidney transplants. However, by the end of 2009 there were still almost 7000 people on dialysis waiting for a kidney.

Some scientists are working on xenotransplantation, producing genetically engineered pigs with organs that could be used for human transplants. Other scientists hope that stem cell research will produce a way of growing new kidneys on demand, so no one dies waiting for a suitable organ to become available.

Figure 2 This young woman has been given a new lease of life by a kidney transplant. A lack of donors means not everyone who suffers from kidney failure is so lucky. For more information on kidney treatment, see B3 3.6 Treatment and temperature issues.

Figure 3 This graph shows how the gap between people needing a kidney and available organs is getting bigger in the US. The same pattern is seen in most other countries, including the UK.

Graph legend:
— Registered kidney candidates
— Kidney transplant operations
(Number (thousands) 0–90; Year 1990–2005; 83,146; 16,829)

⚭ links
For information on stem cell research, look back to B2 5.3 Stem cells.

Summary questions

1 How does someone with a kidney transplant overcome the problems of kidney failure?

2 Sometimes a live donor – usually a close family member – will donate a kidney. These transplants have a higher rate of success than normal transplants from dead, unrelated donors.
  a Suggest two reasons why live transplants from a close family member have a higher success rate than normal transplants.
  b Why do you think that live donor transplants are relatively rare?

3 Produce a table to compare the advantages and disadvantages of treating kidney failure with dialysis or with a kidney transplant. Which treatment do you think is preferable and why?

Key points
- In a kidney transplant, diseased or damaged kidneys are replaced with a healthy kidney from a donor.
- To try and prevent rejection of the donor kidney, the tissue types of the donor and the recipient are matched as closely as possible. Immunosuppressant drugs are also used.

Summary answers

1 The transplanted kidney takes on the functions of the failed kidneys, balances the blood chemistry and gets rid of urea.

2 a Live organs have no tissue damage; family donors are a close tissue match.
  b Taking organs from a living healthy person can threaten their health. It is a big step to take.

3

Dialysis	Transplant
Machines available	Need donor, often not available
No problem with tissue matching	Need tissue match
Twice a week at least, for life	Surgery every ten years or more
Expensive long term	After surgery, relatively low cost of medicine
Always have to watch diet, spend time on dialysis machine, etc.	Can lead relatively normal life

[Preferable treatment personal choice, but must be justified by rational argument.]

B3 3.5

Controlling body temperature

Learning objectives

Students should learn:

- that the internal temperature of the body is monitored and controlled by the thermoregulatory centre in the brain
- that this centre receives information from the blood and from temperature receptors in the skin
- that if the core temperature fluctuates, responses are made so that the body is kept at optimum temperature.

Learning outcomes

Most students should be able to:

- describe how the body monitors body temperature
- describe the responses made by the body if the core temperature is too high
- describe the responses made by the body if the core temperature drops too low.

Some students should also be able to:

- explain how the blood vessels supplying the capillaries in the skin control body temperature. [HT only]

Support

- Remind the students of 'Goldilocks and the three bears', especially regarding porridge temperature. Produce a sheet with two boxes on one side with 'Too hot' in one and 'Too cold' in the other. Have another saying 'Just right!' and have the instruction 'Do nothing!' Opposite these, describe activities (e.g. put on more clothes, stamp feet and blow on hands) and physical responses (e.g. goosebumps, sweating). Students should link the boxes with lines.

Extend

- Get students to consider cold-blooded animals that cannot control their body temperatures. They can write out and illustrate a 'User's guide for an ectothermic body', giving warnings and suggestions.

Specification link-up: Biology B3.3

- Sweating helps to cool the body. More water is lost when it is hot, and more water has to be taken as drink or in food to balance this loss. *[B3.3.2 a)]*
- Body temperature is monitored and controlled by the thermoregulatory centre in the brain. This centre has receptors sensitive to the temperature of the blood flowing through the brain. *[B3.3.2 b)]*
- Also temperature receptors in the skin send impulses to the thermoregulatory centre, giving information about skin temperature. *[B3.3.2 c)]*
- If the core body temperature is too high:
  - blood vessels supplying the skin capillaries dilate so that more blood flows through the capillaries and more heat is lost
  - sweat glands release more sweat which cools the body as it evaporates. **[HT only]** *[B3.3.2 d)]*
- If the core body temperature is too low:
  - blood vessels supplying the skin capillaries constrict to reduce the flow of blood through the capillaries
  - muscles may 'shiver' – their contraction needs respiration, which releases some energy to warm the body. **[HT only]** *[B3.3.2 e)]*

Controlled Assessment: B4.3 Collect primary and secondary data. *[B4.3.2 c) d) f)]*; B4.4 Select and process primary and secondary data. *[B4.4.1 a) b)]*, *[B4.4.2 a) b) c)]*

Lesson structure

Starters

Same temperature? – Using forehead thermometers, get the students to take their own temperatures. Collect up results and find a mean for the group. Ask: 'Why are they all about the same? How much variation is there?' How much of this is due to variation in students' temperature and how much is due to variation in the resolution of the thermometers? How could you tell the difference? (This relates to 'How Science Works': consider the reliability of data.) *(5 minutes)*

Can you tell the temperature? – Have several containers of water at different temperatures. Students are to guess the temperatures. Support students by giving them cards with the temperatures on and ask them to place the cards in front of the correct containers. Extend students by giving them one actual temperature and letting them try to guess the rest. Ask: 'How easy is it? How accurate can you be?' Discuss why you need to be aware of whether you are hot or cold. It could be dangerous to become too hot or too cold. *(10 minutes)*

Main

- Consider the difference between core and skin temperature. Students can work in groups or these experiments could be done as a class demonstration (see 'Practical support').
- To cover aspects of 'How Science Works', the information gathered and the best way to present it can be discussed by the students. Ask: 'What conclusions can be drawn? Does it tell us about the thermoreceptors in the skin? Could we use this information to devise a method of measuring the heat loss from the human body?'
- Describe the changes that can take place in the diameter of the blood vessels supplying the skin capillaries and relate these changes to changes in the core body temperature. Also explain evaporation of water through sweating, which leads to cooling, followed by shivering. Shivering then leads to warming, as the action of the muscles releases heat energy. These are needed for the Higher Tier examination. Foundation Tier students should understand that the skin looks red when we are hot due to increased blood flow to the skin but do not need to know about the dilation and constriction of blood vessels supplying the capillaries.

Plenaries

'Quick quiz – Ask questions on the contents of the lesson. Support students by asking straightforward questions. Extend students by giving them more complex questions and expecting them to provide more relevant detail in their answers. *(5 minutes)*

Thermostat principles – Show students a heater connected into a circuit with a bimetallic strip, or other thermostatic device, arranged so that when it drops to a given temperature, the heater switches on. When the temperature rises, the heater switches off. Run through several cycles and ask the students to draw parallels with the human body. *(10 minutes)*

Practical support

Body temperature

Equipment and materials required

Thermometers, temperature probes, masking tape, duvet filling, data loggers, cold water, bowls.

Details

Ask for volunteers (risk assessment needed) to sit with one hand in very cold water. Monitor the core temperature and skin temperature of the other hand of the volunteer using temperature sensors and data loggers. Ask: 'What happens?'

A modification or extension of this can be done comparing energy loss from an insulated and non-insulated hand. Attach a temperature probe to each hand of a volunteer with masking tape, checking that the skin temperatures on both hands are identical. Insulate one hand fully with duvet filling, taping it and ensuring that it is of an even thickness all round. Allow time for equilibration, then record the skin temperatures of each hand and the core temperature. Change the environmental conditions (cooler temperatures, air movements) and repeat the temperature measurements.

Safety: If clinical thermometers are used, it is advisable to use separate thermometers for each student. Disinfect after use.

Keeping internal conditions constant

| **B3 3.5** | **Controlling body temperature** 🔑 |

Learning objectives

- How does your body monitor its temperature?
- How does your body stop you getting too hot?
- How does your body keep you warm?

Figure 1 People in different parts of the world live in conditions of extreme heat and extreme cold and still maintain a constant internal body temperature

Study tip

Remember that the thermoregulatory centre is in the brain and it monitors the temperature of the blood.

Wherever you go and whatever you do, your body temperature needs to stay around 37 °C. This is the temperature at which your enzymes work best. Your skin temperature can vary enormously without problems. It is the temperature deep inside your body, known as the core body temperature, which must be kept stable.

At only a few degrees above or below normal body temperature your enzymes don't function properly. All sorts of things can affect your internal body temperature, including:

- energy produced in your muscles during exercise
- fevers caused by disease
- the external temperature rising or falling.

Basic temperature control

You can change your clothing, light a fire, and turn on the heating or air-conditioning to help control your body temperature. However, it is your internal control mechanisms that are most important.

a Why is control of your body temperature so important?

Control of your core body temperature relies on the **thermoregulatory centre** in your brain. This centre contains receptors that are sensitive to temperature changes. They monitor the temperature of the blood flowing through the brain itself.

Extra information comes from the temperature receptors in the skin. These send impulses to the thermoregulatory centre, giving information about the skin temperature. The receptors are so sensitive they can detect a difference in temperature of as little as 0.5 °C!

If your temperature starts to go up, your sweat glands release more sweat, which cools the body down. Sweating also makes you lose water and mineral ions. Therefore you need to take in more drink to replace the water and ions you have lost.

Your skin also looks redder as more blood flows through it, cooling you down. If your temperature starts to go down you will look pale as less blood flows through your skin. This means you lose less energy.

Cooling the body down

If you get too hot, your enzymes denature and can no longer catalyse the reactions in your cells. When your core body temperature begins to rise, impulses are sent from the thermoregulatory centre to the body so more energy is released:

- The blood vessels that supply your skin capillaries dilate (open wider). This lets more blood flow through the capillaries. Your skin flushes, so you lose more energy by radiation.
- Your rate of sweating goes up. This extra sweat cools your body down as it evaporates. In humid weather when the sweat does not evaporate it is much harder to keep cool.

Reducing energy loss

It is just as dangerous for your core temperature to drop as it is for it to rise. If you get very cold, the rate of the enzyme-controlled reactions in your cells falls too low. You don't release enough energy and your cells begin to die. If your core body temperature starts to fall, impulses are sent from your thermoregulatory centre to the body to conserve and even release more energy:

- The blood vessels that supply your skin capillaries constrict (close up) to reduce the flow of blood through the capillaries. This reduces the energy released by radiation through the surface of the skin.
- Sweat production is reduced. Less sweat evaporates so less energy is released.
- You may shiver – your muscles contract and relax rapidly. These muscle contractions need lots of respiration, which releases more energy. This raises your body temperature. As you warm up, the shivering stops.

b Why is a fall in your core body temperature so dangerous?

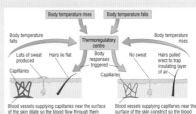

Figure 2 Changes in your core body temperature set off automatic responses to oppose the changes and maintain a steady internal environment

Practical

Body temperature

Use a temperature sensor and datalogger to record your skin and core body temperature on one hand as you plunge the other into icy water.

- Explain your observations.

Figure 3 A student using a temperature sensor and data logger

Key points

- Your body temperature is monitored and controlled by the thermoregulatory centre in your brain.
- Your body temperature must be kept at the level at which enzymes work best.
- Your body responds to cool you down or warm you up if your core body temperature changes.
- The blood vessels that supply the capillaries in the skin dilate and constrict to control the blood flow to the surface. **[H]**
- Energy is released through the evaporation of sweat from the surface of the skin to cool the body down. **[H]**
- Shivering involves contraction of the muscles that produces energy from respiration to warm the body. **[H]**

Summary questions

1 Copy and complete using the words below:
red sweating water rise skin temperature energy
If you exercise hard your body .... will start to .... Your skin goes .... and your rate of .... increases so you lose more .... through your .... Your temperature returns to normal and you need to drink .... to replace the water you have lost through sweating.

2 **a** Why is it so important to maintain a body temperature of about 37 °C?
b Explain the role of:
i the thermoregulatory centre in the brain, and
ii the temperature sensors in the skin in maintaining a constant core body temperature.

3 Explain how the body responds to both an increase and a decrease in core temperature to return its temperature to normal levels. **[H]**

Further teaching suggestions

The effect of evaporation on temperature

- Use alcohol evaporating from thermometers to show the effect of evaporation on temperature. (No naked flames).

Does the human body temperature fluctuate much?

- Suggest to students that they monitor their own body temperature over a period of 48 hours. If the results are plotted, it can be seen that the temperature does fluctuate. Ask: 'Can it be accounted for?' If it is not possible for students to do this themselves, project a graph and get students to discuss the variations.

Heat detection

- In pairs, one student closes their eyes, while the other brings the palm of their hand close to the other person's cheek. The one with eyes closed says when they can feel the heat. They estimate the distance and then swap roles.

Answers to in-text questions

a If the temperature becomes too hot or too cold, it affects the action of the enzymes in the body.

b The rate of the enzyme-controlled reactions slows down and not enough energy is released in the cells.

Summary answers

1 temperature, rise, red, sweating, energy, skin, drink, water

2 **a** This is the temperature at which enzymes work best.
b **i** The thermoregulatory centre in the brain is sensitive to the temperature of the blood flowing through it. It also receives information about the skin temperature from receptors in the skin and coordinates the body responses to keep the core temperature at 37°C.
ii Temperature sensors in the skin send impulses to the thermoregulatory centre in the brain giving information about the temperature of the skin and the things it touches. This is important for maintaining the core temperature because if the external surroundings and the skin are cold, the body will tend to conserve heat to keep the core temperature up, and vice versa.

3 Look for: If core temperature increases, to lower body temperature – blood vessels supplying capillaries in skin dilate – more blood in capillaries so more heat is lost. More sweat produced by sweat glands which cools the body as it evaporates. If core temperature decreases, to raise body temperature – blood vessels supplying blood to skin capillaries constrict – less blood transported to surface of skin so less heat is lost. Shivering occurs by rapid muscle movement which needs respiration – releasing heat energy.

B3 3.6

Treatment and temperature issues

Learning objectives

Students should learn:

- that there are different issues associated with the treatment of kidney failure
- that people can die from the effects of too much heat [HT only]
- that loss of heat from the body can cause hypothermia. [HT only]

Learning outcomes

Most students should be able to:

- evaluate the different issues associated with the treatment of kidney failure
- describe the effects of too much heat on the body [HT only]
- describe the signs of hypothermia. [HT only]

Some students should also be able to:

- explain the effects of heat stroke and hypothermia. [HT only]

Support

- Provide the students with a simple worksheet to fill in for the temperature homeostatic mechanisms with the keywords and numerical values given at the base of the page.

Extend

- Ask students to investigate the critical temperature ranges of a number of different organisms, particularly those that live in climatic conditions that pose challenges.

Specification link-up: Biology B3.3

- If the core body temperature is too high:
  - blood vessels supplying the skin capillaries dilate so that more blood flows through the capillaries and more heat is lost
  - sweat glands release more sweat which cools the body as it evaporates. **[HT only]** *[B3.3.2 d)]*
- If the core body temperature is too low:
  - blood vessels supplying the skin capillaries constrict to reduce the flow of blood through the capillaries
  - muscles may 'shiver' – their contraction needs respiration, which releases some energy to warm the body. **[HT only]** *[B3.3.2 e)]*
- Evaluate the advantages and disadvantages of treating kidney failure by dialysis or kidney transplant. *[B3.3]*

Lesson structure

Starters

Visualisation – Show the students a projected image or sheet of paper with 30 800 dots on it. Explain that each one represents a pound. Produce a pound coin to emphasise this. Explain that this is the cost each year of providing dialysis for **one** person. Show another projected image or sheet of paper with 6920 dots on it. Explain that each one represents a patient who needs a kidney transplant but has not got one in the last year. Get students to try to imagine a pile of coins that would represent 30 800 times 6920 (£213 136 000). Show the students a sheet with a million dots on it as a reference (construction advice available via various internet pages). Explain that this cost can be hugely reduced by transplants. Discuss. *(5 minutes)*

Dogs die in hot cars – Show the students a bumper sticker to this effect. Ask the students to think of why this is the case and to write their thoughts down. Ask the students why the dogs would not die if they were out in the open i.e. which natural mechanisms would protect them from overheating. Again ask them to write their thoughts down. Read out examples. Support students by providing guidance. Extend students by getting them to produce more coherent and well-argued ideas. *(10 minutes)*

Main

- There are several suggestions for activities associated with organ donation in the 'Further teaching suggestions' on B3 3.4 Kidney transplants.
- As suggested in the Student Book, students could write a paragraph explaining their own point of view and then design a poster, leaflet or webpage supporting kidney donation and asking for people to sign up as donors. Choose a target audience and make the appeal relevant to that age group.

Higher Tier only:

- Go on to deal with hypothermia. This could be tackled by considering warnings to New Year's Eve revellers! Show some stills or video of a New Year's Eve party. Draw out that many people will have been drinking and will not want to drive home. The weather at that time of year can be very cold indeed. Wearing inappropriate clothing might compound this. Ask the students to produce a leaflet to be handed out prior to New Year's Eve in order to warn people of the dangers of getting hypothermia, its causes and symptoms.
- Then deal with issues of the body overheating. Take the skin temperature of a volunteer. Ask them to do some vigorous exercise (preferably out of sight of the rest of the group to avoid distraction. Avoid excessive exercise). While they are away exercising, go over causes of heat stroke and the processes involved. Take the student's temperature when they come back in. Talk over the dangers associated with dancing vigorously while not drinking enough water.
- Get the students to draw out a simple flow chart showing the relationship between temperature and homeostatic feedback activity to regulate the temperature and keep it constant. Get them to add arrows off to 'hypothermia' and to 'heat stroke', which result if the feedback actions are not taken or are not sufficiently effective. Get the students to attach numerical values to their flow chart. Peer assess the outcomes.

- You can also relate the issues to climate change. As suggested in the Student Book, students could write articles for a lifestyle magazine on the topics listed. Variations could include writing for different groups, such as parents or older people, with advice on how to cope.

Plenaries

Splat the temp – Write a number of temperatures on a board. Include the key temperatures discussed in the text. Choose two students and give each one a different-coloured fly swat. Ask a question to which one of the temperature values is the answer. The students have to splat their fly swat on top of the correct number and hold it there. The first one there wins. Support students by reducing the number of options and adjusting the question difficulty. Extend students by giving more difficult questions and more cryptic clues. *(5 minutes)*

Kidney Interactives – Use an interactive Java script tool, such as those provided by Quia at www.quia.com. Create a series of interactive exercises based on the keywords associated with the 'kidneys' section of this unit. It should be possible to make a set of flashcards, a word search, a pairs game and a memory game all within a couple of minutes. If laptops or a computer room are available, these can be used to make this an individual plenary. If not, the exercises can be projected and completed as a class. *(10 minutes)*

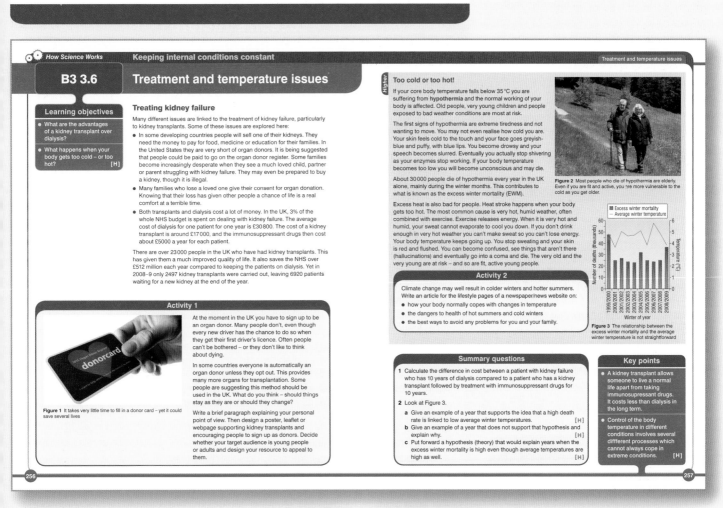

Further teaching suggestions

Where does a new kidney go?
- Show images of how a kidney transplant is carried out including details of where the new kidney is placed. Students should research reasons why it is not placed where the original kidneys are, and should find out reasons why the damaged or diseased kidneys are not normally removed.

Class temperatures
- Take the temperatures of all the members of the class. Show through this that there is a range of normal temperatures. Draw out that various factors can affect body temperature besides exercise – illness for example and in women (the time of the month) during their menstrual cycle.

Summary answers

1 Over a 10-year period the saving, if someone has a kidney transplant rather than relying on regular dialysis is around £241 000.

2 a 2008/9.
  b 2000/1, 2005/6.
  c Although the average winter temperature is high, there could have been spells or even days when temperatures were really low, which affects people and causes a surge in deaths even though the overall average for that year is relatively high.

B3 3.7

Controlling blood glucose

Learning objectives

Students should learn:

- that the pancreas monitors and controls the level of glucose in the blood
- how the pancreas functions to control the blood glucose concentration
- that diabetes is caused by a lack of insulin from the pancreas.

Learning outcomes

Most students should be able to:

- state that the pancreas monitors and controls blood glucose concentration
- describe the symptoms and causes of diabetes
- describe how diabetes can be treated.

Some students should also be able to:

- explain how the blood glucose concentration is monitored and controlled
- explain the causes of diabetes and how it is treated.

Answers to in-text questions

a Blood transports glucose to the cells where it is needed for cellular respiration.

b Insulin (glucagon not wrong but Higher Tier only and not covered at this point in the spread, so unlikely to be offered as an answer).

c Insulin is needed to enable glucose to enter the cells. If there is no insulin, the cells are deprived of fuel and therefore do not make enough energy in cellular respiration so the person feels tired etc.

Support

- Give students a large, clear and not-too-complex word search for the key words. The students should be provided with the definitions to the words and then cross them off as they find them.

Extend

- Ask students to produce a series of Word documents showing the feedback mechanism involving insulin and glucagon, glycogen and glucose, blood glucose levels too high, too low and normal. Link these together with hyperlinks so that they form the appropriate loops.

Specification link-up: Biology B3.3

- The blood glucose concentration of the body is monitored and controlled by the pancreas. The pancreas produces the hormone insulin, which allows the glucose to move from the blood into the cells. *[B3.3.3 a)]*
- A second hormone, glucagon, is produced in the pancreas when blood glucose levels fall. This causes glycogen to be converted into glucose and be released into the blood. **[HT only]** *[B3.3.3 b)]*
- Type 1 diabetes is a disease in which a person's blood glucose concentration may rise to a high level because the pancreas does not produce enough of the hormone insulin. *[B3.3.3 c)]*
- Type 1 diabetes may be controlled by careful attention to diet, exercise, and by injecting insulin. *[B3.3.3 d)]*

Controlled Assessment: B4.3 Collect primary and secondary data. *[B4.3.2 c) d) e)]*

Lesson structure

Starters

Blood glucose levels – Discuss the sweet-eating habits of younger brothers and sisters. Ask: 'Who eats the most at one go? Does eating a lot of sweets have an effect on their behaviour?' Talk about the blood glucose levels, the effect of increasing these dramatically and speculate as to how the body copes. *(5 minutes)*

How is diabetes diagnosed? – Discuss the symptoms of the disease and why they occur. Ask: 'What simple test could indicate that someone is suffering from diabetes? What is a glucose tolerance test and how can it be interpreted?' Students to analyse blood glucose graphs for non-diabetic people and for those with diabetes. Support students by prompting. Extend students by getting them to analyse the blood glucose graphs unaided. *(10 minutes)*

Main

- Show an animation on the control of the blood glucose levels by the pancreas – search the internet for 'abpi for schools'. This could include diagrams/photos of pancreas tissue showing the islets of Langerhans, alpha cells and beta cells. A feedback diagram can be built up showing how the control is achieved. Create worksheets for students and allow time to complete these during the lesson. Foundation Tier students only need reference to insulin: Higher Tier students also need to understand the action of glucagon.

- There is plenty of information about diabetes available from the doctor, from textbooks and on the internet (e.g. www.diabetes.org.uk). Students could be given the opportunity to follow up an aspect of the condition. For example, students could investigate:
  - the causes of diabetes, including type 1 and type 2
  - what happens if a diabetic has insufficient glucose in the blood, i.e. is hypoglycaemic
  - the treatment of diabetes, from the use of insulin from animals to the present-day use of genetically engineered insulin
  - the possibility of islet cell transplantation techniques
  - the importance of diet for a diabetic
  - the role of the diabetic nurse in your local GP practice.

  For each of these suggestions, students could compile a report to be presented to the class. They could be given homework time for research and writing their reports.

- Demonstrate Clinistix testing – test fake urine as suggested in B2 3.6 High-tech enzymes (Tinkle test). Compare this with the way in which blood is tested now. Students could be given 'mystery' samples of fake urine to test. It could be appropriate to point out that before the invention of Clinistix, urine samples were tested with Benedict's solution. Compare a Clinistix reading with a Benedict's test on the same sample. (This relates to: 'How Science Works': aspects of sensitivity/resolution and accuracy of testing.)

Plenaries

Why diabetes mellitus? – Discuss the origins of the word 'mellitus', with its link to honey. Tell students that many years ago doctors would taste their patient's urine to check it for sweetness. Some students may have heard of the other condition known as 'diabetes insipidus', where copious quantities of urine are produced and the patient is always thirsty. *(5 minutes)*

Spelling bee – Ask for volunteers to spell key words from this topic. Once a student has spelt a word correctly, they can choose another student to give a definition. Support students by giving them simple key words. Extend students by giving them more complex terms, imposing a time limit and asking them for a definition of each word. This could reinforce the differences between 'glucose', 'glucagon' and 'glycogen', which are frequently muddled by students. *(10 minutes)*

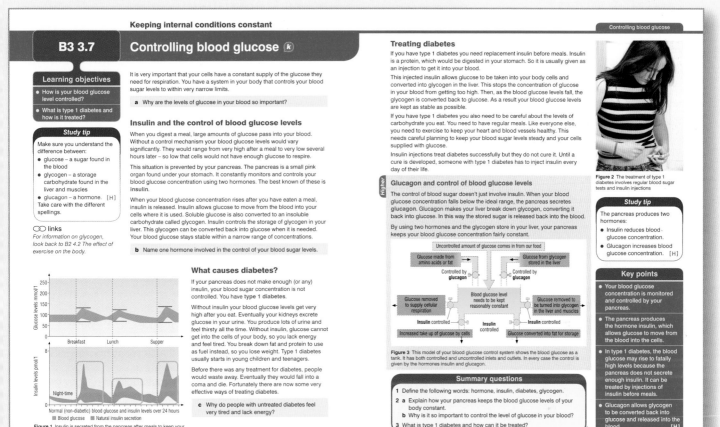

Keeping internal conditions constant

B3 3.7 — Controlling blood glucose ⓚ

Learning objectives
- How is your blood glucose level controlled?
- What is type 1 diabetes and how is it treated?

Study tip
Make sure you understand the difference between:
- glucose – a sugar found in the blood
- glycogen – a storage carbohydrate found in the liver and muscles
- glucagon – a hormone. [H]
Take care with the different spellings.

∞ links
For information on glycogen, look back to B2 4.2 The effect of exercise on the body.

It is very important that your cells have a constant supply of the glucose they need for respiration. You have a system in your body that controls your blood sugar levels to within very narrow limits.

a Why are the levels of glucose in your blood so important?

Insulin and the control of blood glucose levels

When you digest a meal, large amounts of glucose pass into your blood. Without a control mechanism your blood glucose levels would vary significantly. They would range from very high after a meal to very low several hours later – so low that cells would not have enough glucose to respire.

This situation is prevented by your pancreas. The pancreas is a small pink organ found under your stomach. It constantly monitors and controls your blood glucose concentration using two hormones. The best known of these is **insulin**.

When your blood glucose concentration rises after you have eaten a meal, insulin is released. Insulin allows glucose to move from the blood into your cells where it is used. Soluble glucose is also converted to an insoluble carbohydrate called glycogen. Insulin controls the storage of glycogen in your liver. This glycogen can be converted back into glucose when it is needed. Your blood glucose stays stable within a narrow range of concentrations.

b Name one hormone involved in the control of your blood sugar levels.

What causes diabetes?

If your pancreas does not make enough (or any) insulin, your blood sugar concentration is not controlled. You have **type 1 diabetes**.

Without insulin your blood glucose levels get very high after you eat. Eventually your kidneys excrete glucose in your urine. You produce lots of urine and feel thirsty all the time. Without insulin, glucose cannot get into the cells of your body, so you lack energy and feel tired. You break down fat and protein to use as fuel instead, so you lose weight. Type 1 diabetes usually starts in young children and teenagers.

Before there was any treatment for diabetes, people would waste away. Eventually they would fall into a coma and die. Fortunately there are now some very effective ways of treating diabetes.

c Why do people with untreated diabetes feel very tired and lack energy?

Figure 1 Insulin is secreted from the pancreas after meals to keep your blood glucose stable within narrow limits

Treating diabetes

If you have type 1 diabetes you need replacement insulin before meals. Insulin is a protein, which would be digested in your stomach. So it is usually given as an injection to get it into your blood.

This injected insulin allows glucose to be taken into your body cells and converted into glycogen in the liver. This stops the concentration of glucose in your blood from getting too high. Then, as the blood glucose levels fall, the glycogen is converted back to glucose. As a result your blood glucose levels are kept as stable as possible.

If you have type 1 diabetes you also need to be careful about the levels of carbohydrate you eat. You need to have regular meals. Like everyone else, you need to exercise to keep your heart and blood vessels healthy. This needs careful planning to keep your blood sugar levels steady and your cells supplied with glucose.

Insulin injections treat diabetes successfully but they do not cure it. Until a cure is developed, someone with type 1 diabetes has to inject insulin every day of their life.

Figure 2 The treatment of type 1 diabetes involves regular blood sugar tests and insulin injections

Glucagon and control of blood glucose levels

The control of blood sugar doesn't just involve insulin. When your blood glucose concentration falls below the ideal range, the pancreas secretes glucagon. Glucagon makes your liver break down glycogen, converting it back into glucose. In this way the stored sugar is released back into the blood.

By using two hormones and the glycogen store in your liver, your pancreas keeps your blood glucose concentration fairly constant.

Figure 3 This model of your blood glucose control system shows the blood glucose as a tank. It has both controlled and uncontrolled inlets and outlets. In every case the control is given by the hormones insulin and glucagon.

Study tip
The pancreas produces two hormones:
- Insulin reduces blood glucose concentration.
- Glucagon increases blood glucose concentration. [H]

Key points
- Your blood glucose concentration is monitored and controlled by your pancreas.
- The pancreas produces the hormone insulin, which allows glucose to move from the blood into the cells.
- In type 1 diabetes, the blood glucose may rise to fatally high levels because the pancreas does not secrete enough insulin. It can be treated by injections of insulin before meals.
- Glucagon allows glycogen to be converted back into glucose and released into the blood. [H]

Summary questions

1 Define the following words: hormone, insulin, diabetes, glycogen.

2 **a** Explain how your pancreas keeps the blood glucose levels of your body constant.
b Why is it so important to control the level of glucose in your blood?

3 What is type 1 diabetes and how can it be treated?

Further teaching suggestions

Diabetic diets or get the balance right
- Students could research diabetic diets. There has been a great deal of interest in the Glycaemic Index of foods and how this can help people to maintain a weight loss. Students could design menus suitable for people with mild forms of diabetes and research foods that are said to be for diabetics. Ask: 'What is used instead of sugar? Are these sensible recommendations for people who wish to lose weight?'

Summary answers

1 Hormone: a chemical message carried in the blood which causes a change in the body.

Insulin: a hormone made in the pancreas which causes glucose to pass from the blood into the cells where it is needed for energy.

Diabetes: a condition when the pancreas cannot make enough insulin to control the blood sugar.

Glycogen: an insoluble carbohydrate stored in the liver.

2 **a** Blood glucose levels go up above the ideal range. This is detected by the pancreas, which then secretes insulin. Insulin causes the liver to convert glucose to glycogen and causes glucose to move out of the blood into the cells of the body, thus lowering blood glucose levels. When the blood sugar level falls, glucose is released back into the blood.

If the blood glucose level drops below the ideal range, this is detected by the pancreas. The pancreas secretes glucagon, which causes the liver to convert glycogen into glucose, which increases the blood glucose level.

b Glucose needed for cells of body for respiration which releases energy for everything. Too much or too little glucose in the blood causes problems.

3 Diabetes is a condition where the pancreas does not make enough or any insulin. It can be treated by injections of insulin to help control blood glucose levels. The intake of carbohydrate needs to be carefully controlled. (New possibilities are pancreas cell transplants or embryonic stem cells.)

Treating difabetes

Learning objectives

Students should learn:

- that the treatment of diabetes has developed over the years
- that there are difficulties associated with the development of new treatments for diabetes.

Learning outcomes

Most students should be able to:

- describe the work of Banting and Best in the discovery of insulin
- understand that human insulin can be produced from genetically engineered bacteria
- list some of the ways in which diabetes may be cured and discuss them.

Some students should also be able to:

- evaluate in detail the different methods available for the treatment and cure of diabetes.

Support

- Provide students with a tick-list understanding sheet regarding the two types of diabetes studied. Give the students some clues to help them to complete the sheet.

Extend

- Get students to write an article, commenting on the problem of diabetes and suggesting alternative mechanisms or improvements to the system of blood sugar regulation that would overcome the current problems faced by sufferers.

Specification link-up: Biology B3.3

- Evaluate modern methods of treating diabetes. *[B3.3]*

Lesson structure

Starters

Card game – Students should be given cards that show a stage in the processing of sugar by the body. They are to play the cards one time and should explain the relevance of the word to the concepts covered so far under the topic of homeostasis. Look for key important points where misunderstanding could lead to life-threatening consequences. *(5 minutes)*

Diabetes – what we know so far…. Students should break into groups of about three and each group be given an A3 sheet of paper. Given a short time limit, (according to class but less than five minutes should be OK – use an internet countdown timer) they are to write out the word 'Diabetes' in the centre of the sheet and annotate the rest as their knowledge allows. Peer assess by getting groups to swap over sheets on conclusion. Support students by providing clues and prompts. Extend students by encouraging them to provide more sophisticated answers. *(10 minutes)*

Main

- Prepare an exposition or PowerPoint presentation on the work of Banting and Best on the discovery of insulin. Introduce the work of Frederick Sanger on discovering the chemical structure of insulin.
- Discuss the production of insulin from genetically modified bacteria. If suitable, outline the steps that need to be taken to introduce the genes into the bacteria. Discuss the benefits of this type of insulin over that which was previously used by diabetics.
- Get the students to produce a summary of the treatment that is available for these type 2 diabetic patients. Link it with the health benefits that will arise from an increase in general activity and exercise levels. Allow them to illustrate this and develop it for presentation in any way which will be stimulating for a target audience of their peers.
- Review pancreas transplants and the use of stem cells in the treatment and cure of type 1 diabetes. Make careful reference to the complex moral and ethical implications of the uses of stem cells from embryos. Ensure that the students realise the ethical benefits of using stem cells from adults.

Plenaries

How do we know it works? – Get students to imagine that they were in charge of the development of anti-diabetes treatments for the UK. They have a limited budget and have to decide which treatments they will fund. Which criteria would they select and why? Read out suitable student answers. *(5 minutes)*

Dog death letters – Get students to write posthumous 'thank you' letters to the dogs that involuntarily gave their lives in the study of the disease. Thank them and explain to them the importance of their sacrifice and the medical advances for the human race that the study they were involved in led to. Support students by giving them suggestions of words and phrases to use. Extend students by encouraging them to use their empathy and imagination. *(10 minutes)*

Activity

Student responses should include a summary of the main ethical points such as: Banting and Best: use of dogs would not be acceptable today. Is it justified by the benefits?

- Animal insulin: giving people insulin that didn't match human insulin. Was it fair to depend on the meat market?
- Human insulin produced by bacteria: genetic engineering and ethics of inserting human DNA into bacteria.
- Transplanting pancreases: not enough to go round, risky operation.
- Transplanting pancreatic cells: unsuccessful so far, not enough to go round.
- Embryonic stem cells: ethics of using human embryos, adult stem cells, genetic manipulation again.
- Lifestyle changes for type 2 diabetes: ethics of telling people how they should behave.

Further teaching suggestions

Rope bar charts

- Lay a rope down on the ground. Place a placard stating 'Agree!' at one end of the rope and another saying 'Disagree' at the other. The teacher is to read out various statements concerning the topic of the lesson, couched in appropriate language. The students are to line themselves up according to their opinions and be willing to defend them when challenged.

Ode to Bacteria

- Read an ode as an example of the form, e.g. 'Ode to a Nightingale' by Keats. Have the students create an 'Ode to Bacteria' praising their general usefulness to mankind (as well as the problems they create) and then get the students through interaction with the text and discussion with each other to evaluate and extend each other's odes. Use bacterial cells in research into diabetes as an example.

Why do people get type 2 diabetes?

- Students to carry out some research into what factors contribute to people suffering from this form of diabetes. (It can be caused by factors other than those given in the Student Book). Ask them if a better understanding of the causes could help in the future – either in diagnosis or in treatment?

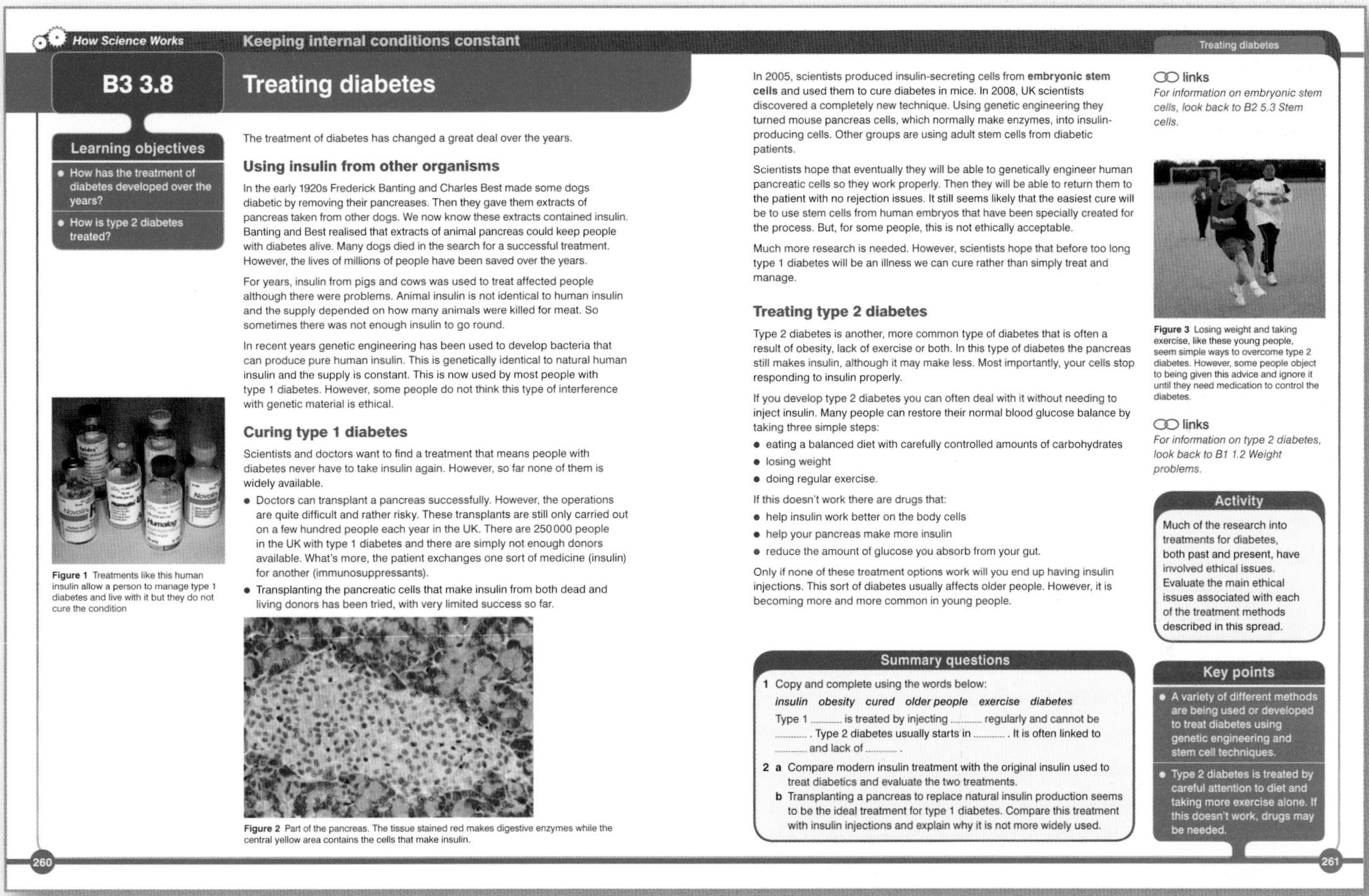

How Science Works Keeping internal conditions constant

B3 3.8 Treating diabetes

Learning objectives

- How has the treatment of diabetes developed over the years?
- How is type 2 diabetes treated?

The treatment of diabetes has changed a great deal over the years.

Using insulin from other organisms

In the early 1920s Frederick Banting and Charles Best made some dogs diabetic by removing their pancreases. Then they gave them extracts of pancreas taken from other dogs. We now know these extracts contained insulin. Banting and Best realised that extracts of animal pancreas could keep people with diabetes alive. Many dogs died in the search for a successful treatment. However, the lives of millions of people have been saved over the years.

For years, insulin from pigs and cows was used to treat affected people although there were problems. Animal insulin is not identical to human insulin and the supply depended on how many animals were killed for meat. So sometimes there was not enough insulin to go round.

In recent years genetic engineering has been used to develop bacteria that can produce pure human insulin. This is genetically identical to natural human insulin and the supply is constant. This is now used by most people with type 1 diabetes. However, some people do not think this type of interference with genetic material is ethical.

Curing type 1 diabetes

Scientists and doctors want to find a treatment that means people with diabetes never have to take insulin again. However, so far none of them is widely available.

- Doctors can transplant a pancreas successfully. However, the operations are quite difficult and rather risky. These transplants are still only carried out on a few hundred people each year in the UK. There are 250 000 people in the UK with type 1 diabetes and there are simply not enough donors available. What's more, the patient exchanges one sort of medicine (insulin) for another (immunosuppressants).
- Transplanting the pancreatic cells that make insulin from both dead and living donors has been tried, with very limited success so far.

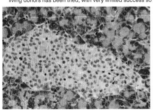

Figure 1 Treatments like this human insulin allow a person to manage type 1 diabetes and live with it but they do not cure the condition

Figure 2 Part of the pancreas. The tissue stained red makes digestive enzymes while the central yellow area contains the cells that make insulin.

In 2005, scientists produced insulin-secreting cells from **embryonic stem cells** and used them to cure diabetes in mice. In 2008, UK scientists discovered a completely new technique. Using genetic engineering they turned mouse pancreas cells, which normally make enzymes, into insulin-producing cells. Other groups are using adult stem cells from diabetic patients.

Scientists hope that eventually they will be able to genetically engineer human pancreatic cells so they work properly. Then they will be able to return them to the patient with no rejection issues. It still seems likely that the easiest cure will be to use stem cells from human embryos that have been specially created for the process. But, for some people, this is not ethically acceptable.

Much more research is needed. However, scientists hope that before too long type 1 diabetes will be an illness we can cure rather than simply treat and manage.

Treating type 2 diabetes

Type 2 diabetes is another, more common type of diabetes that is often a result of obesity, lack of exercise or both. In this type of diabetes the pancreas still makes insulin, although it may make less. Most importantly, your cells stop responding to insulin properly.

If you develop type 2 diabetes you can often deal with it without needing to inject insulin. Many people can restore their normal blood glucose balance by taking three simple steps:

- eating a balanced diet with carefully controlled amounts of carbohydrates
- losing weight
- doing regular exercise.

If this doesn't work there are drugs that:

- help insulin work better on the body cells
- help your pancreas make more insulin
- reduce the amount of glucose you absorb from your gut.

Only if none of these treatment options work will you end up having insulin injections. This sort of diabetes usually affects older people. However, it is becoming more and more common in young people.

links

For information on embryonic stem cells, look back to B2 5.3 Stem cells.

Figure 3 Losing weight and taking exercise, like these young people, seem simple ways to overcome type 2 diabetes. However, some people object to being given this advice and ignore it until they need medication to control the diabetes.

links

For information on type 2 diabetes, look back to B1 1.2 Weight problems.

Activity

Much of the research into treatments for diabetes, both past and present, have involved ethical issues. Evaluate the main ethical issues associated with each of the treatment methods described in this spread.

Summary questions

1 Copy and complete using the words below:
   insulin obesity cured older people exercise diabetes
   Type 1 .... is treated by injecting .... regularly and cannot be .... Type 2 diabetes usually starts in .... It is often linked to .... and lack of ....

2 **a** Compare modern insulin treatment with the original insulin used to treat diabetics and evaluate the two treatments.
   b Transplanting a pancreas to replace natural insulin production seems to be the ideal treatment for type 1 diabetes. Compare this treatment with insulin injections and explain why it is not more widely used.

Key points

- A variety of different methods are being used or developed to treat diabetes using genetic engineering and stem cell techniques.
- Type 2 diabetes is treated by careful attention to diet and taking more exercise alone. If this doesn't work, drugs may be needed.

260   261

Summary answers

1 diabetes, insulin, cured, older people, obesity, exercise

2 **a** Original – from pancreases of cattle and pigs used for meat; no control over quantities as used what was available from slaughterhouses; not exactly the same chemically.

   Modern – produced by genetically modified bacteria; exact quantity and quality control; exactly the same as naturally occurring human insulin.

   Genetically modified insulin is better as it is a match for the natural hormone and both quantity and quality of the product can be controlled to give better glucose control.

b Insulin treatment widely available; patient deals with it themselves; relatively cheap, etc.

   Pancreatic transplant is a good idea but complex surgery; high risk; expensive; patients have to be on immunosuppressant drugs for the rest of their lives; needs repeating eventually; not enough donors. These are the reasons why it is not more widely used.

Summary answers

1 a Diagram to show feedback – something goes up, receptor picks it up, chemical released to bring levels back down and the same idea if level drops. Annotations to show student understands principles of maintaining more-or-less constant levels.

b For cells to work properly they need to be at the right temperature (so enzymes work optimally); they need to be surrounded by the correct concentration of water and mineral ions in the blood so osmosis doesn't cause problems; they need glucose to provide energy and they need waste products to be removed as build up can change pH or poison systems. This is why the body systems must be controlled within fairly narrow limits.

2 a The range for the Kt/V test was 1.1 to 1.24 Kt/V.

b Pattern shows a gradual increase until May, then the pattern dropped to a constant level from June to August.

c They both show a similar pattern. Some students might notice that the URR remains below an acceptable level for one extra month.

d No. It is most likely to be by association.

e 5 months.

f Increases the reliability of the results.

g Economic issues related to kidney dialysis: cost of machines, cost of staffing and cost of loss of lifestyle. Any thoughtful point.

h Social issues related to kidney dialysis: when money is limited, who will be allowed to benefit from kidney dialysis and who will be left to die? Any thoughtful point.

3 a Deaths increased – gradually at first then by a lot.

b Around 25 °C.

c When very hot (often humid) so sweat doesn't evaporate to cool people down; people lose a lot of water by sweating so become dehydrated and therefore can't sweat and cool down; exercise in heat generates heat in muscles; body can't get rid of it by sweating, etc.; any sensible points.

4 a They go up.

b Between about 60–120 milligrams per litre.

c Between about 50–310 milligrams per litre.

d Insulin injections keep blood sugar levels within a reasonable range; prevent loss of blood sugar in the urine; allow cells to take up glucose etc.; Limitations – can't keep blood sugar within the narrow range of natural insulin control.

e Carbohydrates broken down into glucose (blood sugar), so the more carbohydrate-rich food eaten, the higher the blood sugar levels will climb and the harder it is for the insulin injections to maintain safe and healthy levels of blood sugar.

Summary questions

1 a Draw and annotate a diagram explaining the basic principles of homeostasis.

b Write a paragraph explaining why control of the conditions inside your body is so important.

2 A patient with kidney failure has dialysis three times a week. Every month the blood is checked to ensure that the machine is working properly. The blood is tested for its urea content (URR test), which should be above 64%. Also the amount of blood being filtered compared with the amount of fluid in the body (Kt/V test) should be more than 1.1.

Look at this chart and answer the questions below.

Test	Target	Jan	Feb	Mar	April	May	June	July	Aug
Kt/V	≥1.2	1.1	1.15	1.2	1.23	1.24	1.2	1.2	1.2
URR	≥65	60	62	64	65	66	65	65	65

a What was the range for the Kt/V test?

b What was the pattern for the Kt/V test?

c How do the Kt/V test results compare to those for the URR test?

d Can you say that there is a causal link between the two sets of test results?

e For how many months were both tests satisfactory?

f Urologists say that the two tests really measure the same thing. Why then is it a good idea to do both tests?

g What are the economic issues related to kidney dialysis?

h What are the social issues related to kidney dialysis?

3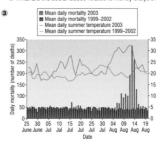

Mean daily mortality 2003
Mean daily mortality 1999–2002
Mean daily summer temperature 2003
Mean daily summer temperature 1999–2002

In August 2003 a heat wave hit Europe. The graph sh the effect it had on the number of deaths in Paris.

a What effect did the Paris heat wave have on death the city?

b From the data, what temperature begins to have a effect on the death rate?

c Explain why more people die when conditions are hot.

4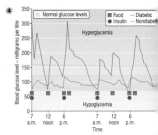

The graph shows the blood glucose levels of a non-diabetic person and someone with type 1 diabetes managed with regular insulin injections. They both e the same times. Use this graph to help you answer th questions below:

a What happens to the blood glucose levels in both individuals after eating?

b What is the range of blood glucose concentration the normal subject?

c What is the range of blood glucose concentration the person with diabetes?

d The graph shows the effect of regular insulin inject on the blood glucose level of someone with diabe Why are the insulin injections so important to their health and wellbeing? What does this data sugges are the limitations of insulin injections?

e People with diabetes have to monitor the amount o carbohydrate in their diet. Explain why.

Kerboodle resources

Resources available for this chapter on Kerboodle are:

- Chapter map: Keeping internal conditions constant
- Practical: Modelling kidney dialysis (B3 3.3)
- Viewpoints: Are you registered? (B3 3.4)
- WebQuest: Kidney transplants (B3 3.4)
- Extension: Transplant versus dialysis (B3 3.4)
- Video: Body temperature (B3 3.5)
- Bump up your grade: Body temperature (B3 3.5)
- How Science Works: Sweat-beater: Fake or real? (B3 3.5)
- Simulation: Control of blood glucose levels (B3 3.7)
- Interactive activity: Homeostasis
- Revision podcast: Keeping internal conditions constant
- Test yourself: Keeping internal conditions constant
- On your marks: Keeping internal conditions constant
- Practice questions: Keeping internal conditions constant
- Answers to practice questions: Keeping internal conditions constant

ractice questions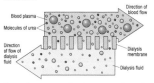

a The human body must keep internal conditions constant.

List A shows some conditions.

List B shows some monitoring or control centres.

Match each condition with its correct monitoring or control centre. (3)

List A		List B
blood glucose level		kidneys
body temperature		pancreas
blood water content		thermoregulatory centre
		skin

b Choose the correct words from the list below to complete the sentence.

amino fatty kidney lactic liver lung pancreas

Urea is produced in the .... by the breakdown of
.... acids. (2)

a Which **two** of the following substances are found in the urine of a healthy person?

glucose   mineral ions   proteins   water (2)

b A person with kidney disease can be treated by dialysis.
The diagram shows how dialysis works.
The circles represent molecules of different substances.

Choose the correct word or phrase to complete each sentence.

i During dialysis, urea moves out of the .... (1)
  blood cells   blood plasma   dialysis fluid

ii During dialysis, urea moves into the .... (1)
  blood cells   blood plasma   dialysis fluid

iii Urea moves by the process of .... (1)
  diffusion   digestion   transpiration

iv To allow the movement of urea, the dialysis membrane is .... (1)
  impermeable   partially permeable   thick

v The urea can pass through the membrane because the urea molecules are .... (1)
  large   round   small

c For most patients, a kidney transplant is better than continued dialysis treatment.

Choose the correct phrase to complete the sentence.

One major problem with a kidney transplant is that .... (1)

  drug treatment is needed to suppress the immune system

  hospital visits are needed three times a week

  yearly costs are higher than for dialysis

AQA, 2002

3 When a person has a kidney transplant, the donor kidney must be matched to their tissue type.

Choose the correct words from the list below to complete the sentences.

*antibodies antiseptics aspirin immunosuppressants
protein   urea*

On the surface of the kidney cells are antigens.

Antigens are made of ....

The antigens may be attacked by the person's ....

To prevent the attack on the donor kidney the person is given drugs called .... (3)

4 When a person gets too cold, the organs cannot function properly. Below 35 °C the person could die. Alcohol causes blood vessels to stay dilated.

A person found collapsed on a cold mountain should not be given an alcoholic drink. Explain why. [H] (4)

5 *In this question you will be assessed on using good English, organising information clearly and using specialist terms where appropriate.*

A person with type 1 diabetes cannot produce enough of the hormone insulin.

Some diabetics use an insulin pump that is attached to the body. They can increase or decrease the amount of insulin which is injected, depending on their lifestyle.

Describe how insulin controls blood glucose levels and explain why a diabetic may need to change their insulin levels at certain times. (6)

263

Practical suggestions

Practicals	AQA	k	📖	⚙
Plan an investigation to measure the cooling effect of sweating.	✓		✓	
Demonstrate blood testing (using meters).	✓		✓	
Test urine from diabetic and non-diabetic people using Clinistix.	✓		✓	
Disect and make observations of a kidney.	✓		✓	
Use surface-temperature sensors to monitor skin temperature in different conditions.	✓		✓	
Design a model kidney dialysis machine using Visking tubing as the filter.	✓	✓	✓	

Practice answers

1 a
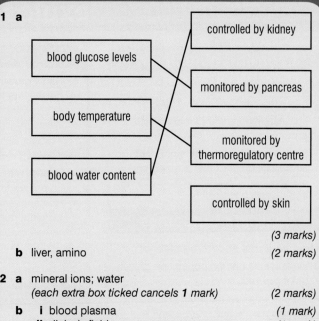

(3 marks)

b liver, amino (2 marks)

2 a mineral ions; water
  (each extra box ticked cancels 1 mark) (2 marks)

b i blood plasma (1 mark)
  ii dialysis fluid (1 mark)
  iii diffusion (1 mark)
  iv partially permeable (1 mark)
  v small (1 mark)

c drug treatment is needed to suppress the immune system (1 mark)

3 protein; antibodies; immunosuppressants (3 marks)

4 skin blood vessels dilate(d)
more heat lost (through skin)
by radiation
core temperature falls even further (4 marks)

5 There is a clear and detailed description of the role of insulin and the answer should show a clear understanding of how at least one lifestyle change can alter the amount of insulin pumped. The answer shows almost faultless spelling, punctuation and grammar. It is coherent and in an organised, logical sequence. It contains a range of appropriate or relevant specialist terms used accurately. (5–6 marks)

There is a description of the role of insulin and at least one reference to a lifestyle change which can alter the amount of insulin pumped. There are some errors in spelling, punctuation and grammar. The answer has some structure and organisation. The use of specialist terms has been attempted, but not always accurately. (3–4 marks)

There is an attempt to describe the role of insulin or to explain a lifestyle change which alters the amount of insulin to be pumped but little clarity and detail. The spelling, punctuation and grammar are very weak. The answer is poorly organised with almost no specialist terms and/or their use demonstrating a general lack of understanding of their meaning. (1–2 marks)

No relevant content. (0 marks)

Examples of biology points made in the response:
Description of role of insulin
● when blood sugar/glucose is raised
● pancreas secretes (more) insulin
● liver and muscles take in glucose
● blood sugar levels decrease.

Explanation of why diabetics might change insulin levels
● before a large meal – increase levels
● when undertaking exercise – decrease levels.

B3 4.1

The effects of the population explosion

Learning objectives

Students should learn:

- that rapid growth in the human population means that more waste is produced
- that humans reduce the amount of land available for other animals and plants by building, farming, quarrying and dumping waste.

Learning outcomes

Most students should be able to:

- explain how human population growth has occurred
- explain why raw materials are rapidly being used up and more waste is being produced
- describe the effects of population growth on land and resources.

Some students should also be able to:

- analyse and interpret scientific data concerning human population growth and environmental issues.

Specification link-up: Biology B3.4

- Rapid growth in the human population and an increase in the standard of living means that increasingly more waste is produced. Unless waste is properly handled, more pollution will be caused. *[B3.4.1 a)]*
- Waste may pollute:
  - water, with sewage, fertiliser or toxic chemicals
  - air, with smoke and gases such as sulfur dioxide, which contributes to acid rain
  - land, with toxic chemicals such as pesticides and herbicides, which may be washed from the land into waterways. *[B3.4.1 b)]*
- Humans reduce the amount of land available for other animals and plants by building, quarrying, farming and dumping waste. *[B3.4.1 c)]*

Lesson structure

Starters

How many people in the world? – Hold a brief competition to guess how many people are alive on Earth today. The students should write their estimates on cards and all stand up, holding up their estimates in front of them. Count alternately upwards and downwards towards the actual number, telling students to sit down as their answers are discounted. *(5 minutes)*

What sort of problems do we have if we go to music festivals? – Show a picture of masses of people at a festival like Glastonbury. Show some figures to illustrate how the festival has grown over the years (you can search the internet) Ask: 'What are the problems? How do we cope with the basic needs of living?' Support students by prompting them to think of their basic requirements. Extend students by getting them to draw comparisons with refugee camps and also to consider long-term effects on the environment. Draw comparisons with the human population on the whole of the planet. *(10 minutes)*

Main

- Consider how many babies will be born during this lesson. The figure is about 240 babies per minute. The point can be very pertinently made by keeping a running total on a board at the front, with a student adding to the total every 5 minutes (about 1200 every 5 minutes).

- As an alternative, project an internet-based global human population tool such as Worldometer www.worldometers.info. This can run throughout the lesson with notes of the numbers being taken every few minutes.

- Supply or project a partially completed graph of population numbers, and ask students to suggest what will happen over the next few hundred years if population growth continues as it is today. It might be interesting to compare world population with projected numbers for the developed world, Europe or the UK.

- This topic lends itself well to research projects. The class could split up into small groups, each group taking one aspect and prepare a report for the rest of the class. The topics could include 'pollution', 'use of resources', 'wildlife', 'quarrying', 'housing and roads', 'waste disposal', etc.

- Each group would need to be given a brief for their research project and access to suitable resources. A library box on each topic would be helpful. Probably some homework time could be allocated to this for the research, and the reports given in class, together with worksheets, so that students could make notes on the topics that other students researched.

Support

- Give students a picture of a very crowded room and ask them to imagine what could happen if all the people they knew come to live in their house. Ask: 'What problems would there be?' They could fill in a list or be shown pictures to act as visual prompts.

Extend

- Ask students to analyse why people in the developing world have such large families. They could write an article suggesting how to get round this problem.

Plenaries

Spaceship Earth analogy – Project a spaceship picture and draw out the 'Spaceship Earth analogy' – we have broken into the storeroom, the life-support system is failing and breeding is occurring quickly on finite resources. Ask the students to compose a radio message from the spaceship, asking for help or advice from anyone out there. Support students by getting them to fill in the blanks in a pre-prepared message. Extend students by asking them to be more specific about the type of help they think will be needed. *(5 minutes)*

Baby counter – Look at the count started at the beginning of the lesson. Create and show a PowerPoint presentation of real baby photographs very rapidly. If you give each one a name, then this emphasises what is really happening and that it will have an impact on them and their children in the future. If you have the resources, it could be good to vary the ethnic origin and names of the children in proportion to the increases in world population. Discuss what it is that balances this rapid increase in the population of the world. *(10 minutes)*

How humans can affect the environment

B3 4.1

The effects of the population explosion

Learning objective

- What effect is the growth in human population having on the Earth and its resources?

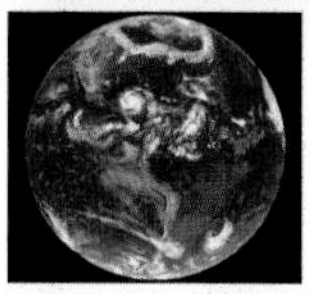

Humans have been on Earth for less than a million years. Yet our activity has changed the balance of nature on the planet enormously. Several of the changes we have made seem to be driving many other species to extinction. Some people worry that we may even be threatening our own survival.

Human population growth

For many thousands of years people lived on the Earth in quite small numbers. There were only a few hundred million of us. We were scattered all over the world, and the effects of our activity were usually small and local. Any changes could easily be absorbed by the environment where we lived.

However, in the past 200 years or so the human population has grown very quickly. By 2010 the human population was almost 7 billion people, and it is still growing.

If the population of any other species of animal or plant suddenly increased like this, nature would tend to restore the balance. Predators, lack of food, build-up of waste products or diseases would reduce the population again. But we have discovered how to grow more food than we could ever gather from the wild. We can cure or prevent many killer diseases. We have no natural predators. This helps to explain why the human population has grown so fast.

In many parts of the world our standard of living has also improved enormously. In the UK, we use vast amounts of electricity and fuel to provide energy for our homes and places of work. We use fossil fuels like oil to produce this electricity. We also use oil and oil-based fuels to move about in cars, planes, trains and boats at high speed and to make materials like plastics. We have more than enough to eat and if we are ill we can often be made better.

a Approximately how many people were living on the Earth in 2010?

The effect on land and resources

The increase in the numbers of people has had a big effect on our environment. All these billions of people need land to live on. More and more land is used for the building of houses, shops, industrial sites and roads. Some of these building projects destroy the habitats of other living organisms.

We use billions of acres of land around the world for farming. Wherever people farm, the natural animal and plant populations are destroyed.

In quarrying, we dig up great areas of land for the resources it holds, such as rocks and metal ores. This also reduces the land available for other organisms.

b How do people reduce the amount of land available for other animals and plants?

The huge human population drains the resources of the Earth. Raw materials are rapidly being used up. This includes non-renewable energy resources such as oil and natural gas. Also, once metal ores are processed they cannot be replaced.

Figure 1 The Earth – as the human population grows, our impact on the planet gets bigger every day

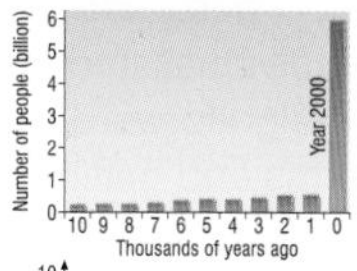

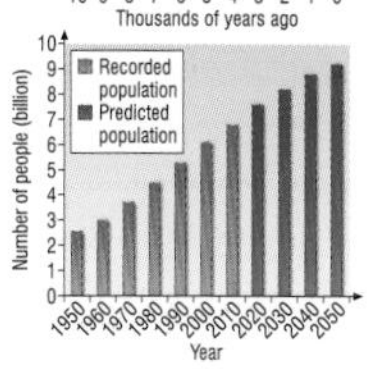

Figure 2 This record of human population growth shows the massive increase during the past 60 years – and predicts more to come

?? Did you know …?

Current UN predictions suggest that the world population will soar to 244 billion by 2150 and 134 trillion by 2300!

Managing waste

The growing human population also means vastly increased amounts of waste. This includes human bodily waste and the rubbish from packaging, uneaten food and disposable goods. The dumping of this waste is another way in which we reduce the amount of land available for any other life apart from scavengers.

There has also been an increase in manufacturing and industry to produce the goods we want. This in turn has led to industrial waste.

The waste we produce presents us with some very difficult problems. If it is not handled properly it can cause serious pollution. Our water may be polluted by sewage, by fertilisers from farms and by toxic chemicals from industry. The air we breathe may be polluted with smoke and poisonous gases such as sulfur dioxide.

The land itself can be polluted with toxic chemicals from farming such as pesticides and herbicides. It can also be contaminated with industrial waste, such as heavy metals. These chemicals in turn can be washed from the land into waterways.

If our ever-growing population continues to affect the ecology of the Earth, everyone will pay the price.

c What substances commonly pollute:
 i water
 ii air
 iii land?

Figure 3 In the UK alone hundreds of thousands of new houses and miles of new road systems are continuously being built. Every time we clear land like this, the homes of countless animals and plants are destroyed.

Study tip

Look for examples in the media of how humans pollute the environment and methods of controlling the pollution. These can be useful to refer to.

Summary questions

1 Copy and complete these sentences using the words below:
 diseases farming food increase population predators treat 200
 The human .... has increased dramatically in the past .... years. Better .... methods mean we have more .... We can .... and prevent many .... We have no natural .... All this has allowed the numbers of humans to ....

2 **a** List examples of how the standard of living has increased over the past 100 years?
 b Give three examples of resources that humans are using up.

3 Write a paragraph clearly explaining how the ever-increasing human population causes pollution in a number of different ways.

Key points

- The human population is growing rapidly and the standard of living is increasing.
- More waste is being produced. If it is not handled properly it can pollute the water, the air and the land.
- The activities of humans reduce the amount of land available for other animals and plants.
- Raw materials, including non-renewable resources, are being used up rapidly.

Further teaching suggestions

The effects of an increased standard of living
- Students could consider how an increase in the standard of living in the developed world has contributed to population growth and a decrease in resources.

Answers to in-text questions

a 6.8 billion.
b By building houses and roads, by farming, by quarrying and by dumping waste.
c **i** Water: excess nutrients from sewage and fertilisers from farms and by toxic chemicals from industry.
 ii Air: Carbon dioxide from the burning of fossil fuels, smoke and poisonous gases such as sulfur dioxide.
 iii Land: toxic chemicals from farming such as pesticides and herbicides, industrial waste, such as heavy metals.

Summary answers

1 population, two hundred, farming, food, treat, diseases, predators, increase

2 **a** Any sensible suggestions, e.g. use of electricity for lighting, heating, TV etc.; use of fossil fuels for transport (cars, planes etc.); plastics.
 b Any three suitable suggestions, such as fossil fuels, wood, land, metals, etc.

3 Look for clarity of explanation without copying the Student Book. Points covered should include:
 - Growing human population increases the amount of waste: bodily waste and the rubbish from packaging, uneaten food and disposable goods.
 - The dumping of waste produced by the ever-expanding human population makes large areas of land unavailable for other life.
 - Driving cars etc. leads to gases from exhausts.
 - Farming leads to the use of pesticides and fertiliser sprays that cause pollution.

Land and water pollution

Learning objectives

Students should learn:

- that more waste is being produced which may pollute water with sewage, fertilisers or toxic chemicals
- that land can be polluted with toxic chemicals that can be washed into water.

Learning outcomes

Most students should be able to:

- describe how pesticides and herbicides can pollute the land
- understand the need for the proper treatment of sewage
- describe what happens when water is polluted by fertilisers.

Some students should also be able to:

- assess the impact of land and water pollution on the environment.

Support

- Give students the stages in the treatment of sewage which they have to put in order. If these are on slips of paper, the students can stick them into their notebooks.

Extend

- Ask students to find out more about bioaccumulation and biomagnifications using the internet. They could produce a poster explaining the terms and giving more examples.

Specification link-up: Biology B3.4

- Waste may pollute:
  - water, with sewage, fertiliser or toxic chemicals …
  - land, with toxic chemicals such as pesticides and herbicides, which may be washed from the land into waterways. *[B3.4.1 b)]*

Controlled Assessment: B4.3 Collect primary and secondary data. *[B4.3.2 a) b) c) e) f)]*; B4.4 Select and process primary and secondary data. *[B4.4.1 a) b)]*, *[B4.4.2 a) b) c)]*; B4.5 Analyse and interpret primary and secondary data. *[B4.5.4 a) b) c)]*

Lesson structure
Starters

You don't know what you've got 'til it's gone – Play some suitable sections from the Joni Mitchell song 'Big Yellow Taxi'. Give the students a copy of the lyrics. Ask them to comment on any sections that they identify with or which touch them in any way. The song was written in Hawaii in response to the parking lots, which blight the natural beauty of some areas. *(5 minutes)*

Word meanings. Show the students flashcards with the words 'pesticide', 'herbicide', 'pollution', 'sewage', 'eutrophication', 'toxic' and 'fertilisers' on. Ask for individual student responses to these words. Support students by giving them the more straightforward terms (pollution, sewage, pesticide). Extend students by giving them all the terms and getting them to think about definitions, especially of the more straightforward ones. *(10 minutes)*

Main

- Consider what happens to our waste. Build up a list of waste materials from households and sort out what is biodegradable, what is recyclable and what needs to be treated to avoid polluting the land. Draw out the need for proper treatment of sewage. Contrast what happened to human waste before sewage treatment was introduced and the link with the spread of infectious diseases. Show pictures of sewage treatment plants and draw up a flow chart to summarise what happens to sewage. If possible, and convenient, organise a trip to a sewage treatment plant. As an alternative, get students to find out what happens to the sewage in their area.

- Students could discuss the positive and negative aspects of farming and produce one poster depicting the benefits of farming and another to show farming as damaging to the environment. This could be done in groups, making use of ICT and the posters displayed for further class discussion.

- Provide an exposition or PowerPoint presentation on DDT – its successful use as an insecticide, worldwide use and subsequent ban, as it was discovered to accumulate in food chains and also in the fatty tissue of humans. The BBC website has a comprehensive article on DDT, why it was banned and its present uses.

- The effect of additional nitrates and phosphates on the growth of water plants, such as duckweed (*Lemna sp.*) or algae, can be demonstrated by setting up the following experiment using different concentrations of a commercial fertiliser (see 'Demonstration support').

- The data collected can be used to plot graphs showing the number of leaves produced at each concentration over time. Students can link this experiment to the effect of fertiliser run-off on the vegetation in streams and ponds. This experiment introduces many 'How Science Works' concepts.

Plenaries

Keywords matching activity – Using a digital utility such as Hot Potatoes (http://hotpot.uvic.ca/) create a set of keywords and a set of definitions. The students have to match these to each other. *(5 minutes)*

Every label tells a story – Show the students the labels from a number of herbicides and pesticides (label information is freely available from the internet. Get them to draw from the labels any information they see as relevant regarding the safety of use of these products. Support sudents by giving them simplified versions of the labels or asking them for very specific, easily located data. Extend students by setting them more difficult and demanding tasks related to the labels. *(10 minutes)*

Demonstration support

The effect of additional nitrates and phosphates on the growth of water plants

Equipment and materials required
Small beakers; tap/pond water; *Lemna* plants; commercial fertiliser (Baby Bio).

Details
Fill five small beakers with water from the same source (tap water or pond water) and add different concentrations of the fertiliser to four of the beakers, leaving one untreated as the control. Refer to the manufacturer's instructions to decide on the concentrations to use. Mark the beakers with the concentration used. Mix thoroughly and place ten duckweed plants in each beaker. Count and record the number of leaves on the plants in each beaker. Place all the beakers in the same conditions of light and temperature. Record the total numbers of leaves on the plants at weekly intervals.

One set of beakers could be started about 3 weeks beforehand, so that some results are available in the lesson. Students could continue to monitor these, together with those set up during the lesson.

Safety: Care when handling the fertiliser.

B3 4.2 Land and water pollution

Learning objectives
- How do people pollute the land?
- How do people pollute the water?

As the human population grows, more waste is produced. If it is not handled carefully, it may pollute the land, the water or the air.

Polluting the land

People pollute the land in many different ways. The more people there are, the more bodily waste and waste water from our homes (sewage) is produced. If the human waste is not treated properly, the soil becomes polluted with unpleasant chemicals and gut parasites. In the developed world people produce huge amounts of household waste and hazardous (dangerous) industrial waste. The household waste goes into landfill sites, which take up a lot of room and destroy natural habitats. Toxic chemicals also spread from the waste into the soil.

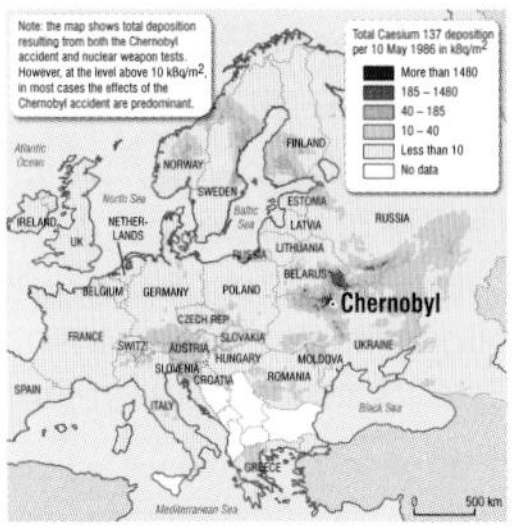

Toxic chemicals are also a problem in industrial waste. They can poison the soil for miles around. For example, after the Chernobyl nuclear accident in 1986 the soil was contaminated thousands of miles away from the original accident. Almost 30 years on, sheep from some farms in North Wales still cannot be sold for food because the radioactivity levels are too high.

a What is human bodily waste mixed with waste water known as?

Land can also be polluted as a side effect of farming. Weeds compete with crop plants for light, water and mineral ions. Animal and fungal pests attack crops and eat them. Farmers increasingly use chemicals to protect their crops. Weedkillers (or herbicides) kill weeds but leave the crop unharmed. Pesticides kill the insects that might otherwise attack and destroy the crop. The problem is that these chemicals are poisons. When they are sprayed onto crops they also get into the soil. From there they can be washed out into streams and rivers (see next page). They can also become part of food chains. The toxins get into organisms that feed on the plants or live in the soil. This can lead to dangerous levels of poisons building up in the top predators (see Figure 3).

Figure 1 The accident at Chernobyl nuclear power plant polluted the land a long way away

Figure 2 Welsh sheep

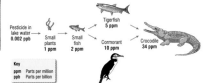
Pesticide in lake water 0.002 ppb → Small plants 1 ppm → Small fish 2 ppm → Tigerfish 5 ppm → Cormorant 10 ppm → Crocodile 34 ppm

Key
ppm   Parts per million
ppb   Parts per billion

Figure 3 The feeding relationships between different organisms can lead to dangerous levels of toxins building up in the top predators

Polluting the water

A growing human population means a growing need for food. Farmers add fertilisers to the soil to make sure it stays **fertile** year after year. The minerals in these fertilisers, particularly the nitrates, are easily washed from the soil into local streams, ponds and rivers. Untreated sewage that is washed into waterways or pumped out into the sea also causes high levels of nitrates in the water.

The nitrates and other minerals fertilise the water plants, which grow rapidly. Some plants die naturally. Others die because there is so much competition for light. There is a big increase in microorganisms feeding on the dead plants. These microorganisms use up a lot of oxygen. This increase in decomposers leads to a fall in oxygen levels dissolved in the water. This means there isn't enough oxygen to support some of the fish and other animals living in it. They die – and are decomposed by yet more microorganisms. This uses up even more oxygen.

Eventually, the oxygen levels in the water fall so low that all aquatic animals die, and the pond or stream becomes 'dead'. This is called **eutrophication**.

b Name a mineral in fertilisers and sewage that causes eutrophication.

Toxic chemicals such as pesticides and herbicides or poisonous chemicals from landfill sites can also be washed into waterways. These chemicals can have the same effect on aquatic food webs as they do to life on land. The largest carnivorous fish die or fail to breed because of the build up of toxic chemicals in their bodies.

In many countries, including the UK, there are now strict controls on the use of chemicals on farms. The same applies to the treatment of sewage and to landfill sites, to help avoid these problems arising.

Pollution levels in water can be measured in many different ways. Oxygen and pH levels are measured using instruments. The water can be analysed to show the levels of polluting chemicals such as pesticides or industrial waste. Bioindicators – species which can only be found in very clean or very polluted water – are also used to monitor pollution levels in our waterways.

Figure 4 This stream may look green and healthy but all the animal life it once supported is dead as a result of eutrophication

Study tip
Don't get herbicides and pesticides mixed up! Remember: herbicides are used to kill weed plants while pesticides kill insect pests.

Summary questions
1 Copy and complete these sentences using the words below:
   water chemicals air waste pollute land population
   As the human .... grows, more .... is produced. Unless this is properly handled it may .... the ...., the water or the .... Toxic .... are often washed from the land into the ....
2 Farming can cause pollution of both the land and the water. Explain how this pollution comes about, and how they are linked.

Key points
- Toxic chemicals such as pesticides and herbicides can pollute the land.
- If sewage is not properly handled and treated it can pollute the water.
- Fertilisers and toxic chemicals can be washed from the land into the water and pollute it.

Further teaching suggestions

The effect of leaf litter on the oxygen content of pond water
- An experiment can be set up to find out what effect decaying matter has on the oxygen content of pond water. Leaf litter, or other waste such as dung, can be weighed out, placed in a beaker, water added and then a number of small aquatic invertebrates (*Daphnia*) introduced. The oxygen content of the water in the beaker can be measured with a probe and the numbers of live animals in a known volume of the water recorded daily.

Eutrophication poem
- After studying the topic of eutrophication, ask the students to create a poem to illustrate the problems of eutrophication. Support students by giving them a list of key words and phrases that might be included.

Summary answers

1 population, waste, pollute, land/air, air/land, chemicals, water

2 Pollution of the land – pesticides and herbicides sprayed to reduce pest damage and overcrowding of crops soak into the soil and pollute it – can become part of food webs and damage predators.

   Pollution of the water – pesticides and herbicides sprayed as above, and fertilisers added to the soil to improve crop yields, can be washed out of the soil into waterways by rain. Toxic chemicals can kill water organisms through food webs. Nitrates from fertilisers cause eutrophication – excess plant growth, needing many microorganisms to decompose the plants, using up oxygen in water so fish and other animals die from lack of oxygen. This adds to the problem – more death, more decay etc.

Answers to in-text questions
a Sewage.
b Nitrates.

B3 4.3

Air pollution

Learning objectives

Students should learn:

- that air can be polluted with smoke and gases, such as sulfur dioxide, which contributes to acid rain
- that acid rain may damage trees
- that plants and animals cannot survive if the water in rivers and lakes becomes too acidic
- that tiny solid particles polluting the air can cause global dimming.

Learning outcomes

Most students should be able to:

- describe how acid rain is formed
- describe some of the effects of acid rain on living organisms
- explain how air pollution can result in global dimming.

Some students should also be able to:

- analyse and interpret scientific data concerning the effects of acid rain.

Answers to in-text questions

a Oil, coal, natural gas.

b Sulfur dioxide and nitrogen oxides.

c The acid kills the leaves, so the trees cannot make food. If it soaks into the soil, it can kill the roots.

Support

- Ask students to imagine what it would be like if the clouds rained vinegar! Give them a picture of a giant vinegar pot shaking over the roofs of a town. Ask: 'What would happen to the animals and plants? How could the rain be like vinegar?' Show them the results of 'Demonstration of combustion and the production of acid gases' and compare with the colour change if vinegar is tested.

Extend

- Get students to research sulfur in proteins and make a link with the amino acid cysteine, as a component of proteins in plants and animals. This in turn links with the sulfur released when fossil fuels are burned.

Specification link-up: Biology B3.4

- Waste may pollute:
  - …air, with smoke and gases such as sulfur dioxide, which contributes to acid rain. *[B3.4.1 b)]*
- Analyse and interpret scientific data concerning environmental issues. *[B3.4]*

  Controlled Assessment: B4.1 Plan practical ways to develop and test candidates' own scientific ideas. *[B4.1.1 a) b)]*; B4.3 Collect primary and secondary data. *[B4.3.1 a)]*, *[B4.3.2 a) to f)]*; B4.4 Select and process primary and secondary data. *[B4.4.1 a) b)]*, *[B4.4.2 a) b) c)]*

Lesson structure

Starters

Demonstration of combustion and the production of acid gases – Wearing eye protection, set fire to a bunch of matches inside a gas jar using a fuse (be careful!). Have some hydrogencarbonate indicator (or universal indicator) in the bottom of the jar. Shake the jar after the ignition and ask the students to observe the colour change. *(5 minutes)*

The acid test – If it is raining, send a student out to collect a sample of rainwater. If it is not raining, then use a sample collected earlier. Revise the pH scale and then test the rainwater with pH paper. They could also test tap water, some more acid things and some alkaline liquids so that the colour change is obvious. Support students by getting them to record the results of these tests as colours on a bar chart. Extend students by getting them to compare the pH of rainwater with that of local pond water. They could also explain why rainwater is likely to be acid. *(10 minutes)*

Main

- Consider the effect of acid rain on seedlings (see 'Practical support'). This practical can either be set up as a class demonstration or the students could set up their own experiment, working in groups. The investigation introduces 'How Science Works' concepts: predictions can be made, observations recorded and conclusions drawn.

- An alternative to the experiment suggested above would be to investigate the effect of acid rain on the germination of cress seedlings (see 'Practical support'). Make daily observations and count the number of seeds that germinate in each dish. Calculate the percentage germination and display the results graphically. Again, this exercise could be used to introduce 'How Science Works' concepts.

- Demonstrate the gases produced by fossil fuels by burning some coal or other sulfurous fuel (see 'Practical support').

- This demonstration can be linked to a survey of the fumes emitted by generating power using fossil fuels, the introduction of 'cleaner' petrol, etc. Some research on the components of the waste gases would benefit any discussions on the links between burning fossil fuels and acid rain. Students could be provided with some facts and figures available from chemistry textbooks or the internet.

- The People's Century series (from PBS) has some good material on acid rain, its sources and effects.

Plenaries

Acid lake effects – Acid rain causes the water in freshwater lakes to become acidic. Ask students to suggest what effects a change in pH might have on life in freshwater, to include the effects on insects, insect larvae, water plants and all stages of fish development. *(5 minutes)*

Air pollution – Search the internet for images of 'smog' and show students the effects of air pollution. Read a description of what it was like to be in a 'pea souper'. Ask students to write a time travelling 'Thank you' letter to the people responsible for the Clean Air Act, making our cities more pleasant places. Support students by giving them some phrases to incorporate into a letter. Extend students by encouraging them to include references to health, wildlife, buildings and the environment generally. *(10 minutes)*

Practical support

Investigate the effect of acid rain on seedlings

Equipment and materials required

Three or four trays or pots of cress seedlings, 1 M HCl, 0. 1 M HCl and 0.5 M HCl.

Details

For each investigation, you will need three or four trays or pots of cress seedlings, all at the same stage of growth. One set should be sprayed with water, one with 0.1 M HCl and one with 0.5 M HCl. If desired, a fourth set could be sprayed with 1.0 M HCl. The pots should be kept in the same place and observed after a few days.

Safety: Care when handling acid; wear eye protection. CLEAPSS Hazcard 47A Hydrochloric acid – corrosive.

Investigate the effect of acid rain on the germination of cress seedlings

Equipment and materials required

Three Petri dishes, 3 filter paper circles, water, 0.1 M HCl, 0.5 M HCl or 1.0 M HCl, 50 cress seeds.

Details

This is an alternative to the above experiment. Moisten the filter paper of one dish with water, another with 0.1 M HCl and a third with either 0.5 or 1.0 M HCl. Sow 50 cress seeds into each Petri dish, cover and keep in the same conditions. Make daily observations and count the number of seeds that germinate in each dish. Calculate the percentage germination and display the results graphically.

Safety: Ensure eye protection is worn. Take care with acid. CLEAPSS Hazcard 47A Hydrochloric acid – corrosive.

Showing the the gases produced by fossil fuels

Equipment and materials required

Coal or other sulfurous fuel, deflagrating spoon or vacuum pump and thistle funnel.

Details

Burn some coal or other sulfurous fuel using a deflagrating spoon, in a gas jar with an indicator in the bottom (shake and see the colour change). Or capture the gas emitted by drawing it into a thistle funnel attached to a vacuum pump. If a bubble trap of indicator is included, or a pH sensor attached to a data logger is arranged to display through a projector, then students can see the effect on pH.

Safety: Do the experiment in a fume cupboard. Wear eye protection.

How humans can affect the environment

B3 4.3 Air pollution

Learning objectives
- How is acid rain formed?
- What are the effects of acid rain on living organisms?

When the air you breathe is polluted, no one escapes the effects. A major source of air pollution is burning fossil fuels. As the human population grows and living standards increase we are using more oil, coal and natural gas. We also burn huge amounts of petrol, diesel and aviation (aeroplane) fuel made from oil. Fossil fuels are a non-renewable resource – eventually they will all be used up.

a Name three fossil fuels.

The formation of acid rain

When fossil fuels are burned, carbon dioxide is released into the atmosphere as a waste product. In addition, fossil fuels often contain sulfur impurities. These react with oxygen when they burn to form sulfur dioxide gas. At high temperatures, for example in car engines, nitrogen oxides are also released into the atmosphere.

Sulfur dioxide and nitrogen oxides can cause serious breathing problems for people if the concentrations get too high.

The sulfur dioxide and nitrogen oxides also dissolve in rainwater and react with oxygen in the air to form dilute sulfuric acid and nitric acid. This produces acid rain, which has been measured with a pH of 2.0 – more acidic than vinegar!

b What are the main gases involved in the formation of acid rain?

The effects of acid rain

Acid rain directly damages the environment. If it falls onto trees it may kill the leaves and, as it soaks into the soil, it can destroy the roots as well. Whole ecosystems can be destroyed.

Acid rain also has an indirect effect on our environment. As acid rain falls into lakes, rivers and streams the water in them becomes slightly acidic. If the concentration of acid gets too high, plants and animals can no longer survive. Many lakes and streams have become 'dead' – no longer able to support life.

c How does acid rain kill trees?

Acid rain is difficult to control. It is formed by pollution from factories. It also comes from the cars and other vehicles we use every day. The worst effects of acid rain are often not felt by the country that produced the pollution (see Figure 2). The sulfur dioxide and nitrogen oxides are carried high in the air by the winds. As a result, it is often relatively 'clean' countries that get the acid rain from their dirtier neighbours. Their own clean air goes on to benefit someone else.

The UK and other countries have worked hard to stop their vehicles, factories and power stations producing the polluting gases. They have introduced measures to reduce the levels of sulfur dioxide and nitrogen oxides in the air. Low-sulfur petrol and diesel are now used in vehicles. More and more cars are fitted with catalytic converters. Once hot, these remove the acidic nitrogen oxides before they are released into the air. There are strict rules about the levels of sulfur dioxide and nitrogen oxides in the exhaust fumes of new cars.

Figure 1 In some parts of Europe and America, large areas of woodland are dying as a result of acid rain

In the UK we have introduced cleaner, low-sulfur fuels such as gas in power stations and started generating more electricity from nuclear power. We have also put systems in power station chimneys to clean the flue gases before they are released into the atmosphere.

As a result, the levels of sulfur dioxide in the air, and of acid rain, have fallen steadily over the past 40 years. Many European countries have done the same (see Figure 3). Unfortunately there are still many countries around the world that do not have controls in place.

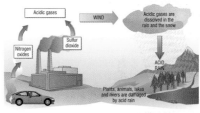

Figure 2 Air pollution in one place can cause acid rain – and serious pollution problems – somewhere else entirely, even in another country

Global dimming

One form of air pollution involves an increase in the number of tiny solid particles in the air. The sulfur products from the burning of fossil fuels are part of this problem. So is smoke from any type of burning. These particles reflect sunlight so less light hits the surface of the Earth. This causes a dimming effect. Global dimming could lead to a cooling of the temperatures at the surface of the Earth.

In Europe, where sulfur emissions and smoke are being controlled, dimming is being reversed. In many developing countries, dimming continues to get worse as air pollution grows.

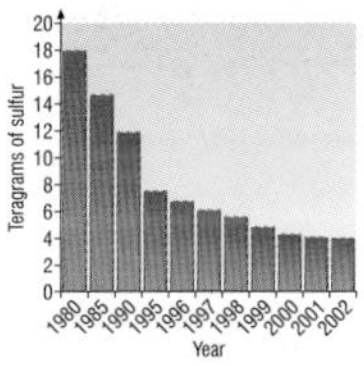

Figure 3 Bar chart to show the reductions in sulfur emissions made by European countries in recent years

Summary questions

1 Copy and complete using the words below:

acid rain carbon dioxide fossil nitric nitrogen oxides sulfur sulfuric

When .... fuels are burned, the pollutant gases ...., ... dioxide and .... are released into the atmosphere. The sulfur dioxide and nitrogen oxides dissolve in rainwater and react with oxygen to form dilute .... acid and .... acid. This is known as ....

2 **a** Explain how pollution from cars and factories burning fossil fuels pollute:
   i   the air
   ii the water
   iii the land.
   b In order to get rid of acid rain it is important that all countries in an area control their production of sulfur dioxide and nitrogen oxides. Explain why this is.

3 **a** What is global dimming?
   b From Figure 3, what was the percentage reduction in sulfur emissions in Europe between 1980 and 2002?
   c Dimming has been reversed over Europe between 1980 and the present day. Suggest an explanation for this.

Key points
- When we burn fossil fuels, carbon dioxide is released into the atmosphere.
- Sulfur dioxide and nitrogen oxides can be released when fossil fuels are burnt. These gases dissolve in rainwater and make it more acidic.
- Acid rain may damage trees directly. It can make lakes and rivers too acidic so plants and animals cannot live in them.
- Air pollution can cause global dimming as tiny solid particles in the air reflect away the sunlight.

268   269

Summary answers

1 fossil, carbon dioxide, sulfur, nitrogen oxides, sulfuric, nitric, acid rain

2 **a**
   i Sulfur dioxide, carbon dioxide and nitrogen oxides are produced from impurities when fossil fuels are burned. These cause air pollution.
   ii Sulfur dioxide and nitrogen oxides in the air dissolve in the rain and fall to the ground. The water runs into streams, rivers, etc. and lowers the pH, making them more acidic.
   iii Acid rain falls on the ground, soaks in and causes it to be acidic.
   b The sulfur dioxide and nitrogen oxides produced by burning fossil fuels are carried high in the air by the prevailing winds. They can be blown hundreds of miles before they dissolve in rain and are carried to the ground. So every country needs to control emissions from the burning of fossil fuels to prevent any country being affected by acid rain.

3 **a** Global dimming is the reduction in light reaching the surface of the Earth because light is reflected away by the build up of pollution particles in the air (from sulfur compounds and smoke particles).
   b $\frac{14}{18} \times 100 = 78\%$.
   c Europe has controlled air pollution as seen by reduction in sulfur emissions; smoke will be controlled at the same time; this reduces the number of particles in the air reflecting the light and so reverses dimming effect of air pollution.

B3 4.4

Deforestation and peat destruction

Learning objectives

Students should learn:

- that large-scale deforestation affects atmospheric carbon dioxide directly and methane levels indirectly
- that loss of forest leads to reduction in biodiversity
- that the destruction of peat bogs and other areas of peat releases carbon dioxide into the atmosphere.

Learning outcomes

Most students should be able to:

- define deforestation
- describe the ways in which deforestation affects carbon dioxide and methane levels in the atmosphere
- describe the impact of deforestation on biodiversity
- explain why the use of peat-free compost should be encouraged.

Some students should also be able to:

- explain in detail the effects and consequences of deforestation.

Answers to in-text questions

a Deforestation is the cutting down of large areas of forest and burning or removing the trees. There is no replacement planting.

b Rice growing in paddy fields and cattle reared to produce cheap beef.

Support

- Provide students with a true/false tick list of statements relating to the content of the unit. The difficulty of this can be adjusted to match the ability of the individual students.

Extend

- Ask students to search for the website of 'Recycle Now' and within that site search for why we should use peat-free compost. Get the students to produce a précis of the website in as concise and pithy a way possible. Peer-mark the results, awarding points for clarity, accuracy and humour.

Specification link-up: Biology B3.4

- Large-scale deforestation in tropical areas, for timber … . *[B3.4.2 a)]*
- Deforestation leads to reduction in biodiversity. *[B3.4.2 b)]*
- Deforestation has occurred so that … . *[B3.4.2 c)]*
- The destruction of peat bogs and other areas of peat … . *[B3.4.2 d)]*
- Analyse and interpret scientific data concerning environmental issues. *[B3.4]*

  Controlled Assessment: B4.1 Plan practical ways to develop and test candidates' own scientific ideas. *[B4.1.1 a) b) c)]*; B4.3 Collect primary and secondary data. *[B4.3.1 a)]*, *[B4.3.2 a) to f)]*; B4.5 Analyse and interpret primary and secondary data. *[B4.5.4 a) c) d)]*; B4.6 Use of scientific models and evidence to develop hypotheses, arguments and explanations. *[B4.6.1a)]*

Lesson structure

Starters

Why is deforestation such a bad thing? – Show a picture of deforestation. Ask students for reasons why it is considered a bad thing. Compile a list on the board. Ask: 'Are there any benefits – or, more importantly, who benefits?' *(5 minutes)*

For peat's sake – Show the students a dried, cut block of peat or find a lumpy bit in a commercial bag of peat-based compost. Ask the students to look closely at it. Speculate as to what it consists of and how it arose. Mount a portion in water on a microscope slide and view under microscope. Support students by giving a series of short sentences to sequence. Extend students by asking them to speculate as to how one might find the age of the organic matter in the peat. *(10 minutes)*

Main

- Ask why cows produce so much methane. Ask: 'Are they the only animals to produce this gas?'

- Get students to search the internet for 'world deforestation rates' (a good site is www.mongabay.com). Guide students to find the approximate current rate of primary forest loss. In 2005, this was about 6.0 million hectares per year. Find out the area of your school site and calculate firstly how many school-sites' worth of forest would be cut down every year. [Hint: divide 6×10^6 by the area of your school site in hectares]. Then, work out how long in hours it would take to clear your school site at the rate given above [the area of your school site divided by 6×10^6 multiplied by the number of hours in a year].

- Using a funnel attached to a Bunsen hose attached to a gas tap and bubble mix, produce a pile of foam bubbles. These can be set on fire. **Safety:** CLEAPSS Hazcard 45A Methane – extremely flammable. Explain that it is mostly methane. Show pictures of cows grazing on land cleared by deforestation. Explain that the global demand for beef burgers has led to an increase in cows and therefore in methane. As methane is 33 times more potent a greenhouse gas than carbon dioxide, then this may contribute significantly to global warming.

- Develop the notion of biodiversity by looking at various areas of the school grounds. Ask the students to select areas that have low biodiversity, such as the school playing field, and areas that have high biodiversity, such as the school gardens/wild areas etc. A species list will help. For more able students, it may be appropriate to introduce the concept of an index of biodiversity such as Simpsons index.

- Students could design their own experiments to investigate the different alternatives to peat-based compost (see 'Practical support').

Plenaries

Pete Boggs? – Show some photographs of 'bog bodies' – sacrificial victims whose corpses have not rotted due to the acidic nature of the peat. Relate that the idea of placating the spirits that live underwater lives in our society through the habit of throwing coins into water in public places. Explain that in ancient times they would throw in that which was of most value to them, i.e. their children. *(5 minutes)*

Cows, rice and methane – Get the students to summarise the information linking cows, rice and methane in the form of a mind map using the information in the Student Book and from the lesson, together with their own research. Support students by providing them with statements that they can link together. Extend students by getting them to produce comprehensive maps, including the effects of an increase in methane levels on the environment. *(10 minutes)*

Further teaching suggestions

Make some compost
● Consult the website of Garden Organic and follow advice given. This is a good opportunity to engage the students in a school-wide composting project. Provide bins in the staffroom, common rooms, kitchens and tech rooms. Develop a team of volunteers to empty these into compost bins and clean them. Use the compost in the school grounds.

Practical support

What sort of compost?

Equipment and materials required
Different types of compost (peat-based, peat-free, etc.), 9 cm-diameter pots, seedlings (tomato or equivalent).

Details
Students could design their own experiments to investigate the different alternatives to peat-based compost: bark, garden waste, coconut fibre. Set up trials growing plants using the different alternatives. Suggest they use seedlings in 9 cm diameter pots. This uses 'How Science Works' concepts of fair testing.

Safety: Wash hands after contact with peat or soil.

How humans can affect the environment

B3 4.4   **Deforestation and peat destruction** ⓚ

Learning objectives
● What is deforestation?
● Why does loss of biodiversity matter?
● What is the link between cows and methane?
● What is the effect of destroying peat bogs?

As the world population grows we need more land, more food and more fuel. One solution to this has been to cut down huge areas of forests. The loss of our forests may have many long-term effects on the environment and ecology of the Earth.

The effects of deforestation
All around the world, large-scale deforestation is taking place for timber and to clear the land for farming. When the land is to be used for farming, the trees are often felled and burned in what is known as 'slash-and-burn' clearance. The wood isn't used, it is just burned. The land produced is only fertile for a short time, after which more forest is destroyed. No trees are planted to replace those cut down.

Deforestation increases the amount of carbon dioxide released into the atmosphere. Burning the trees leads to an increase in carbon dioxide levels from combustion. The dead vegetation left behind decays. It is attacked by decomposing microorganisms, which release more carbon dioxide.

Normally, trees and other plants use carbon dioxide in photosynthesis. They take it from the air and it gets locked up for years in plant material like wood. So when we destroy trees we lose a vital carbon dioxide 'sink'. Dead trees don't take carbon dioxide out of the atmosphere. In fact they add to the carbon dioxide levels as they are burned or decay.

a What is deforestation?

Figure 1 Tropical rainforests are being destroyed by slash-and-burn clearance to provide cheap food for countries like ours

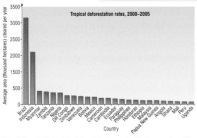
Tropical deforestation rates, 2000–2005
Average area (thousand hectares) cleared per year
Country

Figure 2 The rate of deforestation is devastating. For an animal like the orang-utan, which eats around 300 different plant species, losing the forest habitat is driving the species to extinction

Loss of biodiversity
Tropical rainforests contain more diversity of living organisms than any other land environment. When we lose these forests, we also lose biodiversity as many species of animals and plants die out. Many of these species have not yet been identified or studied. We could be destroying sources of new medicines or food for the future.

Deforestation is taking place at a tremendous rate. In Brazil alone an area about a quarter the size of England is lost each year. When the forests are cleared, they are often replaced by a monoculture (single species) such as oil palms. This process also greatly reduces biodiversity.

Cows, rice and methane
It isn't just carbon dioxide levels that are increasing in the atmosphere as a result of deforestation.

Much of the deforested land is used to produce food for the ever-increasing world population. One of these foods is rice. As rice grows in swampy conditions, known as paddy fields, methane is released. Methane is another gas that affects global warming.

Another food – and another source of methane – is from cattle. Cows produce methane during their digestive processes and release it at regular intervals. In recent years the number of cattle raised to produce cheap meat for fast food, such as burgers, has grown enormously. So the levels of methane are rising. Many of these cattle are raised on farms created by deforestation.

b Where does the methane that is building up in the atmosphere come from?

Peat bog destruction
Peat bogs are another resource that is being widely destroyed. Peat bogs form over thousands of years, usually in marshy areas. They are made of plant material that cannot decay completely because the conditions are very acidic and lack oxygen. Peat acts as a massive carbon store.

Peat can be burned as a fuel and is also widely used by gardeners because it helps to improve the properties of the soil. When peat is burned or used in gardens, carbon dioxide is released into the atmosphere and the carbon store is lost. Peat is formed very slowly so it is being destroyed faster than it is made. In the UK, the government is trying to persuade gardeners to use alternative 'peat-free' composts to reduce carbon dioxide emissions. Compost can be made from bark, from garden waste, from coconut husks and other sources – the problem is persuading gardeners to use them.

Figure 3 Peat-free compost effectively replaces peat-based compost – protecting peat bogs and reducing carbon dioxide emissions

Study tip
Remember that trees, plants in peat bogs and algae in the sea all use carbon dioxide for photosynthesis. Carbon compounds are then 'locked up' in these plants.

Summary questions
1 Define the following words:
  deforestation slash-and-burn biodiversity peat
2 Give three reasons why deforestation increases the amount of carbon dioxide in the atmosphere.
3 a Why are the numbers of:
    i rice fields and cattle in the world increasing
    ii peat bogs in the world decreasing?
  b Why is this cause for concern?

Key points
● Deforestation is the destruction or removal of areas of forest or woodland.
● Large-scale deforestation has led to an increase in the amount of carbon dioxide released into the atmosphere (from burning and the actions of microorganisms). It has also reduced the rate at which carbon dioxide is removed from the air by plants.
● More rice fields and cattle have led to increased levels of methane in the atmosphere because rice and cattle both produce methane as they grow.
● The destruction of peat bogs releases carbon dioxide into the atmosphere.

270 | 271

Summary answers

1 Deforestation: the cutting down of large areas of forest.
Slash-and-burn: cutting down trees and then burning the whole area.
Biodiversity: the range of different species or living organisms in a area.
Peat: substance made when plants decompose slowly and incompletely in an acidic, low oxygen environment.

2 Carbon dioxide produced by burning of trees; carbon dioxide produced by decomposition; less carbon dioxide removed from atmosphere by growing plants.

3 a i Rice fields are increasing because there is a population explosion; rice is the staple diet for many people, so more rice is needed.
Cattle are increasing because there is a demand for cheap beef to supply burgers. Increased standards of living also means a greater demand for animal products generally.
  ii Peat bogs decreasing as peat is used as a fuel and for compost for gardeners.
  b Rice and cows lead to increased levels of methane in the atmosphere. Methane is a greenhouse gas. Loss of peat bog leads to increase in carbon dioxide levels as peat is burnt or used as compost.

B3 4.5

Global warming

Learning objectives

Students should learn:

- that increasing levels of carbon dioxide and methane contribute to global warming
- that an increase in the Earth's temperature may cause changes in the climate
- that an increase in temperature may also reduce biodiversity and cause changes in the distribution of species.

Learning outcomes

Most students should be able to:

- explain what is meant by 'the greenhouse effect'
- describe how increasing levels of carbon dioxide and methane contribute to global warming
- describe some of the consequences of global warming.

Some students should also be able to:

- evaluate the impact of the greenhouse effect on conditions on the Earth.

Support

- Visit the school greenhouse or one locally (e.g. at a garden centre) and measure the temperature inside and outside. This could be done using a datalogger with a pair of probes, one placed inside the classroom and one placed outside.

Extend

- Ask students to predict how a mini greenhouse would respond when full of CO_2. Get a numerical prediction and try it out.

Specification link-up: Biology B3.4

- Levels of carbon dioxide and methane in the atmosphere are increasing and contribute to 'global warming'. An increase in the Earth's temperature of only a few degrees Celsius:
  - may cause big changes in the Earth's climate
  - may cause a rise in sea level
  - may reduce biodiversity
  - may cause changes in migration patterns, e.g. in birds
  - may result in changes in the distribution of species. [B3.4.3 a)]
- Carbon dioxide can be sequestered in oceans, lakes and ponds and this is an important factor in removing carbon dioxide from the atmosphere. [B3.4.3 b)]

Lesson structure

Starters

Changes in the world's climate – Find pictures of a beach and a desert on the internet and show these to students. Discuss the possible complications of a change in the climate. *(5 minutes)*

Changes in CO_2 levels – Get students to think about activities which release carbon dioxide into the atmosphere and activities which remove carbon dioxide. Compile a list on the board. Ask: 'Why are carbon dioxide levels increasing? Why is the number of plants decreasing?' Support students by prompting them to suggest the activities and give answers to the questions. Extend students by encouraging them to make the links and relate the discussion to climate change. *(10 minutes)*

Main

- Demonstrations to show the effects of melting ice at the North and South poles (see 'Demonstration support'). Both demonstrations can be extrapolated to a global level and explained in terms of the effects of melting ice at both poles.

- Link the suggestion above with reference to specific places, such as holiday destinations (e.g. Maldives) and the UK. Project a map of the UK after potential global warming sea-level rises. The Green Party produced a map 'The British Isle,' as part of their 2005 election materials. Discuss which parts of the British Isles might disappear. Who might have to move? What would happen to East Anglia and the Fens? Would it affect where you live? What effect might it have on food production?

- Set up a mini-greenhouse with temperature sensors inside and out, connected to data loggers. Ask the students to predict the differences in temperature readings with reasons and then investigate practically using an infrared lamp.

- To see and discuss graphs showing climate change, search the BBC website, www.bbc.co.uk, for 'climate change'.

Plenaries

Re-radiation – Expose a piece of black paper to sunlight or an infrared lamp for a few minutes. Ask a student to close their eyes and hold the paper close to their cheek. They should be able to tell you which cheek you held the paper close to. Ask students to explain and discuss the concept of re-radiation in terms of global warming. *(5 minutes)*

Key terms crossword – Supply the students with clues for the key words and terms used. Support students by using very simple clues or by putting in initial letters for clues which students are finding difficult. Extend students by asking them to compose cryptic clues for the terms. *(10 minutes)*

Demonstration support

Will melting the North Pole ice caps raise the sea level?

Equipment and materials required
Beaker, ice cubes, chute.

Details
Take a beaker three-quarters full of water, mark the level on the side of the beaker. Place an ice cube in the beaker and leave it at room temperature during the lesson. By the end of an hour, the ice cube should have melted. The new level of the water in the beaker should be marked. Is there any difference in the levels?

At the same time, a similar set of experiments can be arranged with a pile of ice cubes lined up on a chute leading into a beaker. As one melts, another falls into the water. Both these demonstrations can be extrapolated to a global level and explained in terms of the effects of melting ice at both poles.

Safety: No special precautions.

How humans can affect the environment

Global warming

B3 4.5 Global warming ⓚ

Learning objectives
● What is global warming?
● How will global warming affect life on Earth?

Many scientists are very worried that the climate of the Earth is getting warmer. This is often called global warming.

Changing conditions

For millions of years there has been a natural balance in the levels of carbon dioxide in the atmosphere. The carbon dioxide released by living things into the atmosphere from respiration has been matched by the amount removed. Carbon dioxide is removed by plants for photosynthesis and huge amounts are dissolved in the oceans, lakes and rivers. We say that the carbon dioxide is **sequestered** in plants and water, or that plants and water act as carbon dioxide sinks.

As a result, carbon dioxide levels in the air stayed about the same for a long period. However now, as a result of human activities, the levels of carbon dioxide are increasing. Unfortunately, the numbers of plants available to absorb it are decreasing. The speed of these changes means that the natural sinks cannot cope. So the levels of carbon dioxide in the atmosphere are building up. At the same time, the levels of methane are increasing too.

a Give two reasons for the observed increase in atmospheric carbon dioxide levels.

The greenhouse effect

Energy from the Sun reaches the Earth and much of it is radiated back out into space. However, gases such as carbon dioxide and methane absorb some of this energy so it can't escape. As a result, the Earth and its surrounding atmosphere are kept warm and ideal for life. Because carbon dioxide and methane act like a greenhouse around the Earth they are known as greenhouse gases. The way they keep the surface of the Earth warm is known as the greenhouse effect and it is vital for life on Earth.

b Name two greenhouse gases.

links
For information on photosynthesis, look back to B2 2.1 Photosynthesis.

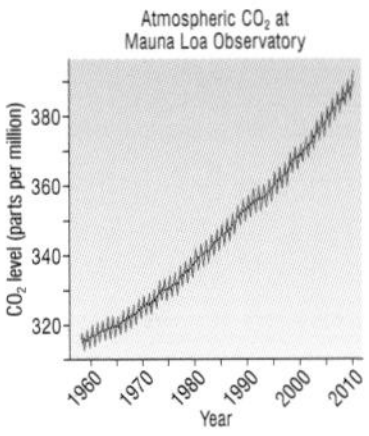

Figure 1 The atmospheric carbon dioxide readings for this graph are taken monthly on a mountain-top in Hawaii. There is a clear upward trend, which shows no sign of slowing down.

Figure 2 The greenhouse effect – vital for life on Earth

Global warming

However, as the levels of carbon dioxide and methane go up, the greenhouse effect is increasing. There are more greenhouse gases in the atmosphere to trap the energy of the Sun and the temperature at the Earth's surface is going up. The change is very small – only about 0.55°C from the 1970s to the present day. This is not much – but an increase of only a few degrees Celsius may cause:

● **big changes in the Earth's climate:** As the climate changes due to global warming, many scientists think that we will see an increase in severe and unpredictable weather conditions. Some people think the very high winds and extensive flooding seen around the world in the 21st century are early examples of the effects of global warming.
● **a rise in sea levels:** If the Earth warms up, the ice caps at the north and south poles and many glaciers will melt. This will cause sea levels to rise. There is evidence that this is already happening. It will mean more flooding for low-lying shores and eventually parts of countries, or even whole countries, may disappear beneath the seas.
● **reduced biodiversity:** As the climate changes, many organisms will be unable to survive and will become extinct, e.g. the loss of polar bears as the ice melts.
● **changes in migration patterns:** As climates become colder or hotter, and the seasons change, the migration patterns of birds, insects and mammals may change.
● **changes in distribution:** Some animals may extend their range as climate change makes conditions more favourable. Others may find their range shrinks. Some will disappear completely from an area or a country.

What's more, as sea temperatures rise less carbon dioxide can be held in the water, which makes the problem worse. Global warming is a big problem for us all.

Figure 3 Puffin populations in Northern Scotland failed to rear their chicks because a rise in sea temperatures reduced the numbers of small fish that puffins feed on. They may need to move to new breeding sites if they are to survive.

Summary questions

1 Copy and complete these sentences using the words below:
climate carbon dioxide temperature atmosphere biodiversity methane global warming
.... and .... levels in the .... are increasing and contributing to .... An increase in .... of only a few degrees could cause .... change and affect ....

2 **a** Use the data in Figure 1 to produce a bar chart showing the maximum recorded level of carbon dioxide in the atmosphere every tenth year from 1970 to the year 2010.
b Explain the trend you can see on your chart.
c Describe and explain the greenhouse effect. How might it affect the conditions on Earth?

3 Research one possible result of global warming and write a report, giving examples of organisms that have been or might be affected.

Key points
● Increasing levels of carbon dioxide and methane in the atmosphere give an increased greenhouse effect, leading to global warming – an increase in the temperature of the surface of the Earth.
● Global warming may cause a number of changes including climate change, a rise in sea level, loss of biodiversity and changes in migration patterns and distribution of species.

Further teaching suggestions

What effect will global warming have on our crops?
● Ask students to think about the crops that are grown in this country and then consider what effect a change of climate could have on the kinds of crops we could grow. What could still be grown? What might we be able to grow more of? How might the cultivation of crops change?

The great climate debate
● Is the climate changing? Are carbon dioxide levels increasing? Have the figures been manipulated? How far back should we go in trying to determine trends in climate change? Who should we believe? Students could discuss this in the light of controversy surrounding whether or not the data have been reported accurately.

Answers to in-text questions
a Deforestation so less removed, burning fossil fuels produces carbon dioxide.
b Any two of: carbon dioxide, methane, water vapour.

Summary answers

1 carbon dioxide/methane, methane/carbon dioxide, atmosphere, global warming, temperature, climate, biodiversity

2 **a** Look for an accurately drawn bar chart from the figures given, correctly labelled axes, neat columns etc.
b Levels of carbon dioxide have risen steadily since 1970 as a result of deforestation, burning fossil fuels, etc.
c The Sun's energy heats the Earth. Much of this is reflected back into space but some is absorbed by greenhouse gases which re-radiate it back. Therefore the Earth's surface is kept warm enough for life. Increased levels of greenhouse gases leads to excess warming. This could result in climate change such as more extreme weather events. Melting of polar ice caps may also increase sea levels and flood low-lying land.

3 Look for accurate information and good examples.

B3 4.6

Biofuels

Learning objectives

Students should learn:

- that biofuels can be made from natural products by anaerobic fermentation
- that there are advantages and disadvantages in using ethanol-based biofuels.

Learning outcomes

Most students should be able to:

- describe how yeast can produce ethanol for fuel
- describe the advantages and disadvantages of using ethanol-based fuels
- describe how second-generation biofuels are being developed.

Some students should also be able to:

- interpret economic and environmental data relating to the production of fuels by fermentation and their uses.

Support

- Play a simplified form of the 'Pass the briquette' game. Form groups of three and pass a charcoal briquette around. One student to be labelled 'CO_2 in the air', another 'sugar in plants' and a third 'alcohol in fuel'. Students have to pass the briquette from one to another stating what happens at each exchange (photosynthesis, distillation, combustion). Have prompt cards ready if they are needed, and repeat the cycling until they are familiar with it.

Extend

- Get students to research the possibility of obtaining fuel from fast-growing trees and plants. Ask: 'Which species of plants are already planted as "fast growing"? What would be needed for the plant material to be quickly and economically converted into biofuel?'

Specification link-up: Biology B3.4

- Biofuels can be made from natural products by fermentation … . *[B3.4.3 c)]*
- Analyse and interpret scientific data concerning environmental issues. *[B3.4]*

Lesson structure

Starters

Biofuels – Show the students a clip from *The Simpsons*, (season 4, episode 16 'Duffless'), where Homer has given up drinking for a month and is thinking about drinking biofuel, filling up his car on a 'one for you, one for me' basis. Discuss biofuels. *(5 minutes)*

Energy in alcohol – Set fire to some alcohol [a small amount – risk assess first] in a (glass!) evaporating basin. Pour a small amount into a film can and ignite when it has evaporated using a piezo spark gun. [Care where you point the lid! Try it out first.] A version of the gas-powered rocket from RSC '100 classic chemistry demonstrations' using alcohol instead of gas will also do. [Care to ensure all the alcohol has evaporated – follow safety instructions.] Support students by asking them where the energy in the alcohol comes from. Extend students by getting them to look into the Research Octane Number (RON) of ethanol as compared to standard unleaded petrol. Draw conclusions on the amount of fuel needed for the same amount of travel. *(10 minutes)*

Main

- Remind students of the process of the alcoholic fermentation of glucose by yeasts and write up the equation.

- List the sources of the sugars (sugar cane juice, bagasse and molasses in warmer countries; sugar beet and maize in colder ones) and the processes involved.

- Discuss gasohol and what it consists of. Ask: 'Is gasohol more environmentally friendly?' Draw out from the students the economic implications of producing alcohol for fuel. Link with their knowledge of the countries involved. Ask: 'Why is gasohol successful in Brazil? Why has it not been produced in the UK?'

- Prepare a PowerPoint presentation on biofuels, to include reference to fermentation processes, production of gasohol and the use of vegetable oils, such as coconut oil, palm and castor oil, sunflower oil and rapeseed oil.

- Present the students with a series of questions. Ask: 'Would the design of cars need to change? What sort of quantities would need to be produced to satisfy demand? Would agriculture need to change? How much do you think it would cost? Would it be the same for all countries?'

- Lead a discussion on the environmental considerations. Put this into the context of carbon emissions and compare with the combustion of fossil fuels.

- If students have access to computers, they could research this aspect and present their findings. For the contrasting points of view, there are several websites you and they could try, such as www.worldlandtrust.org, www.treepower.org, and www.ecocentre.org.uk.

Plenaries

True or false? – Give students 10 statements about biofuels and their origin. They hold up 'True' or 'False' cards for each one. *(5 minutes)*

Flow chart for Fuel? – Ask the students to create a flow chart for the production of ethanol-based fuel. Support students by providing pre-prepared stages on cards which they put into the correct order. Extend students by giving more details of the individual stages and processes involved. *(10 minutes)*

Further teaching suggestions

Use gasohol!

- In groups, write a TV advert for gasohol. Make sure the environmental benefits are flagged up, as well as some 'science'. If facilities are available, take the best script, get the students to perform it, record it digitally and show the rest of the class.

The carbon-neutral car?

- As a variation on the suggestion above, students to script a presentation about ethanol-based fuel on a *Top Gear*-type programme. This could take the form of a contest between

using ethanol-based fuel and conventional petrol or diesel. Use the format of the programme to generate some interest as well as presenting the facts.

Debate the issue

- Students could hold a debate on the subject of whether the government should fund the development of engines that run on ethanol-based fuels. Each student could write a short speech in favour of the proposal and one arguing the case against it. (This relates to: 'How Science Works': societal issues.)

How humans can affect the environment

Biofuels

B3 4.6 Biofuels

Learning objectives

- How can yeast produce fuel for your car?
- What is the environmental impact of biofuels?

CD links
For information on ethanol, look back to B2 1.2 Bacteria and yeast.

CD links
For information on deforestation, look back to B3 4.4 Deforestation and peat destruction.

Figure 1 In tropical regions plants grow fast, an important factor when they are grown for fuel

Everyone needs fuel of some sort but there is only a finite amount of fossil fuels to use. Around the world, we all need other, renewable forms of fuel. The production of **biofuels** has become increasingly important in both the developing and the developed world.

Biofuels are made from natural products by fermentation using yeast or bacteria. There are two main types of biofuels – ethanol-based fuels and **biogas**.

Ethanol-based fuels

Some of the land that is deforested is used for crops that grow very fast. The crops can then be used to produce biofuels. Sugarcane grows about 4 to 5 metres in a year and maize (sweetcorn) is another fast grower. The sugar-rich products from cane and maize are fermented anaerobically with yeast. The products are ethanol and carbon dioxide. You can extract the ethanol by **distillation**, and then use it in cars as a fuel.

Car engines need special modification to be able to use pure ethanol as a fuel, but it is not a major job. Many cars can run on a mixture of petrol and ethanol without any problems at all.

a Why are sugarcane and maize used as crops for the production of ethanol?

The advantages and disadvantages of ethanol as a fuel

In many ways ethanol is an ideal fuel. It is efficient and it does not produce toxic gases when you burn it. It is much less polluting than conventional fuels, which produce carbon monoxide, sulfur dioxide and nitrogen oxides. In addition, you can mix ethanol with conventional petrol to make a fuel known as gasohol, which reduces pollution levels considerably.

Using ethanol as a fuel is known as a **carbon neutral** process. This means that in theory there is no overall increase in carbon dioxide in the atmosphere when you burn ethanol. The original plants remove carbon dioxide from the air during photosynthesis. When you burn the ethanol, you simply return the same amount of carbon dioxide into the atmosphere.

The biggest difficulty with using plant-based fuels for our cars is that it takes a lot of plant material to produce the ethanol. As a result, the use of ethanol as a fuel has largely been limited to countries with enough space and a suitable climate to grow lots of plant material as fast as possible. Scientists are attempting to find ways of producing economically viable quantities of ethanol from plants that grow fast and well in Europe. They have tried pine trees and beet but have not yet been very successful. Now they are looking at fast-growing grasses.

b What is meant by the term 'carbon neutral'?

Figure 2 Increasing demand for gasohol in the US has lead to increasing production of ethanol from maize, as this data clearly shows

The latest biofuels

People around the world are worried about environmental problems such as global warming linked to burning fossil fuels. Interest in clean alternatives such as ethanol is soaring.

The main problem is finding enough ethanol. If Europeans added 5% ethanol to their fuel it would contribute to some reduction in Europe's carbon dioxide emissions. However, we would need 7.5 billion litres of ethanol a year, which would use a lot of plants.

The main methods of ethanol production use the edible parts of plants and leave large quantities of unused plant material. Many people are concerned about using plants for fuel that could feed hungry people. The aim is to make ethanol production work ethically and financially in the long term. To do this we need to find a way to use the waste, cellulose-rich biomass rather than the edible parts of plants.

The latest biofuel technologies use bacteria, enzymes and steam or chemical treatments to break down the cellulose in biomass. They use straw and woodchips as raw materials. The end-products of this breakdown are sugars. These can be respired by yeast to make more ethanol. We don't know exactly what the future will hold, but it seems likely that ethanol-based fuel will be part of it.

Summary questions

1 Make a table to summarise the advantages and disadvantages of ethanol as a fuel for cars.

2 Use the data in Figure 2 to help you answer the following questions:
   a What was the increase in ethanol production from maize in the USA between:
   i 1980 and 1990
   ii 1990 and 2000
   iii 2000 and 2007?
   b Graphs showing worldwide production of fuel ethanol follow a similar pattern. Explain what this suggests about the use of ethanol as a fuel.

Study tip

Be clear about the advantages and disadvantages of using land for growing 'biofuel crops'.

Figure 3 The latest biofuel plants like Longannet in Fife make ethanol from waste biomass

Key points

- Some land has been deforested so that crops can be grown, from which biofuels based on ethanol can be produced.
- Biofuels can be made from natural products using fermentation by yeast.

274 | 275

Answers to in-text questions

a They are fast-growing and contain a lot of sugar that can be fermented.

b There is no overall increase in the levels of carbon dioxide in the air as a result of the industry in question.

Summary answers

1

Advantages	Disadvantages
Efficient	Expensive to produce
Produces little pollution when it burns	Needs huge amount of plant material
Carbon dioxide neutral	Leaves large amounts of cellulose waste
Can be mixed with conventional fuel	Pure ethanol – cars need to be adapted but mixtures (gasohol) can be used in normal cars

2 **a** **i** 725 million gallons.
   ii 730 million gallons.
   iii 4850 million gallons.

b Use of ethanol as a fuel grew steadily through the 1980s and 1990s but has increased dramatically in the first 7 years of the 21st century. Any other points giving suggested reasons can be credited.

B3 4.7

Biogas

Specification link-up: Biology B3.4

- ... Biogas, mainly methane, can be produced by anaerobic fermentation of a wide range of plant products or waste material containing carbohydrates. *[B3.4.3 c)]*
- Evaluate the use of biogas generators. *[B3.4]*

Learning objectives

Students should learn:

- that biogas, mainly consisting of methane, can be produced by the anaerobic fermentation of waste materials containing carbohydrates
- that when biogas is burnt it can provide energy for domestic and industrial use
- that different designs of biogas generators are suitable for different circumstances.

Learning outcomes

Most students should be able to:

- describe the nature of biogas
- explain how biogas is produced in a generator.

Some students should also be able to:

- evaluate the advantages and disadvantages of given designs of biogas generator.

Lesson structure

Starters

Gas power – Show the students a photograph of a gas-powered bus as used during the Second World War. Show a video clip from *Dad's Army*, season 3, episode 1 'The Armoured Might of Lance Corporal Jones', where Corporal Jones' van has been converted to run off gas. Explain that sometimes the gas came from fermented chicken dung. Lead into a discussion of fermenters. *(5 minutes)*

Will o' the Wisp – Discuss the folk tales associated with 'Will o' the Wisp'. Give students a sheet of some of the tales (see website) and some DARTs (Directed Activities Related to Text), such as sequencing a mixed set of paragraphs, highlighting the real explanation sections from the folk tale sections. Try to create a 'Will o' the Wisp' effect by bubbling methane through water and igniting the bubbles as they surface. A tiny amount of detergent helps this process. [Risk assess and try out first.] **Safety:** use eye protection. Extend students by asking them to draw out the symbol equation for the reaction. Support students by differentiating the content of the sequenced sentence sections. *(10 minutes)*

Main

- Project a diagram of a biogas generator on to the board and describe the parts.
- The fixed-dome biogas generator and the domestic generator are fairly simple, but the biogas plant designed for use on farms can be used to power an engine that generates electricity. A flow chart would help students to understand the two stages of the process.
- Discuss the types of material that can be used and what happens to them.
- Additional information from alternative-technology websites could be researched.
- The composition of biogas is given in the Student Book. Ask: 'But where do the components come from?' List the materials that can be used, such as plant material and faeces, and what they are made up of. Most of the material contains carbohydrate.
- Give the students a simplified version (flow chart) of the stages, so that they can see how the breakdown occurs.
- The first stage of the process is the breakdown of the carbohydrates, proteins and lipids into simple sugars, amino acids and fatty acids and glycerol by aerobic bacteria.
- The second stage involves bacteria that convert the sugars and other compounds into ethanoic and other acids, with some carbon dioxide and hydrogen produced. This stage occurs as the oxygen levels are decreasing.
- The third stage occurs only in anaerobic conditions and bacteria convert the acids into methane.
- Annotate the flow chart to give the temperature conditions needed.

Plenaries

Word search – Students to design a word search using words from this topic and the previous ones. They write definitions for the words and, if necessary, finish for homework. These can be swapped around between the students at a later date and used for revision purposes. *(5 minutes)*

The right generator for the job – Project pictures of different types of biogas generator (to include domestic, farm and industrial if possible) on to the board and get students to say where they could be used and give their reasons why. Support students by giving them a list to choose from. Extend students by asking them to think about how governments can influence the development and uptake of new technology and write an advisory note as to how to encourage uptake of biofuel generators. *(10 minutes)*

Support

- Make cards showing dung coming from a cow, dung being placed in a fermenter, bubbles of gas coming from the mixture and a flame coming from the end of a gas pipe attached to the fermenter. Make caption cards to go with these, either complete, with initial letters or vowels depending on difficulty level.

Extend

- Get students to investigate in more detail the process through which faeces and urine can be broken down to methane. They could draw up a flow chart showing the three stages, putting in the names of the different groups of bacteria, their substrates and their products.

Further teaching suggestions

No more fossil fuels!

- Get students to imagine a time in the relatively near future when all the fossil fuels are used up. Discuss how biogas could replace fossil fuels. Students could compose a leaflet from their local council to householders, telling them about the organic refuse collection service and how to exchange your full waste containers for bottles of compressed methane. Ask: 'What modifications would need to be made in the home?'

Use of biogas in the UK

- Students to do some internet research. Set up a scavenger-hunt-style trail of URLs for the students to follow and give them a Word framework to fill in. Investigate landfill sites and the use of the gases.

B3 4.7   Biogas ⓚ

Learning objectives
- What is biogas?
- How is biogas produced?

Biogas is a biofuel that is becoming more and more important. Biogas is produced naturally in sewers and rubbish dumps. Today, it is becoming increasingly used as a fuel around the world.

What is biogas?

Biogas is a flammable mixture of gases. It is formed when bacteria break down plant material or the waste products of animals in anaerobic conditions. Biogas is mainly methane but the composition of the mixture varies. It depends on what is put into the generator and which bacteria are present (Table 1).

Table 1 Components of biogas

Component	Percentage in the mixture by volume
methane	50–80
carbon dioxide	15–45
water vapour	5
other gases including: hydrogen hydrogen sulfide	 0–1 0–3

a What is the main component of biogas?

??? Did you know ...?

In the days before electricity, biogas was taken from the London sewers and used as fuel for the gas lamps that lit the streets.

Figure 1 Biogas generators have made an enormous difference to many families and communities by producing cheap and readily available fuel

Biogas generators

Around the world, millions of tonnes of faeces and urine are made by animals like cows, pigs, sheep and chickens. We produce our fair share of waste materials too! Also, in many places, plant material grows very rapidly. Both the plant material and the animal waste contain carbohydrates. They make up a potentially enormous energy resource – but how can we use it?

When bacteria decompose waste material in anaerobic conditions they produce methane. Methane is a flammable gas that can be used as a fuel for heating and cooking. We can also use it to produce electricity or as a fuel for vehicles.

The bacteria involved in biogas production work best at a temperature of around 30 °C. So biogas generators tend to work best in hot countries. However, the process releases energy (the reactions are **exothermic**). This means that if you put some energy in at the beginning to start things off, and have your generator well insulated to prevent energy loss, biogas generators will work anywhere.

b What is an exothermic reaction?

IN
- Dung from people and animals
- Farm waste
- Garden rubbish

OUT
- Methane for cooking, heating or refrigeration

OUT
- Slurry, which can be used as a fertiliser

Figure 2 Biogas generators take in body waste or plants, and biogas and useful fertilisers come out at the other end

💡 How Science Works

Scaling up the process

At the moment most biogas generators around the world operate on a relatively small scale. They supply the energy needs of one family, a farm or at most a village.

What you put into your small generator has a big effect on what comes out. There are well over 7 million biogas units in China. These produce as much energy as 22 million tonnes of coal. Waste vegetables, animal dung and human waste are the main raw materials. These Chinese generators produce excellent fertiliser but relatively low-quality biogas.

In India, there are religious and social taboos against using human waste in biogas generators. As a result only cattle and buffalo dung is put into the generators. This produces very high quality biogas, but much less fertiliser.

The sizes and design of biogas generators will depend on local conditions. Many generators are sunk into the ground, which provides very good insulation. Others are built above ground, and are easier and cheaper to build. However, this offers less insulation so low night-time temperatures can cause problems.

Many countries are now looking at biogas generators and experimenting with using them on a larger scale. The waste material we produce from sugar factories, sewage farms and rubbish tips can be used to produce biogas. However, in the UK we have been relatively slow at starting to use biogas generators but a number of projects are now in place.

Vast herds of dairy cattle, containing several thousand cows, produce large amounts of slurry. This can be used to produce biogas which in turn can be used to generate electricity. This is already done in the US, Saudi Arabia and other countries, and may soon be set up in the UK.

Biogas could well be an important fuel of the future for all of us. It would help us to get rid of much of the waste we produce as well as providing a clean and renewable energy supply.

Figure 3 This commercial biogas plant in Texas uses the slurry from 10 000 cows as well as other agricultural waste as its raw material

Study tip

Do not be put off by unfamiliar diagrams of biogas generators in the examination. Remember, they all function in a similar way:
- anaerobic fermentation of waste carbohydrate, by microorganisms, to produce methane.

Summary questions

1 Explain simply what biogas is and how it can be made.
2 Some types of biogas generators are set up with a large amount of plant material like straw and a starter mixture of bacteria, and left to produce gas. These batch digesters produce biogas very efficiently. Once gas generation begins to drop, the generator is emptied and cleaned out and the process starts again.
  a Using a generator like this, how could you be sure of a continuous supply of gas for cooking?
  b What are the advantages and disadvantages of a batch-type digester over the types shown in Figure 2, where dung and plant waste is fed in continuously?

Key points

- Biogas – mainly methane – can be produced by anaerobic fermentation of a wide range of plant products and waste materials that contain carbohydrates.
- Biogas generators can be small, to supply a single family, or large, to deal with the sewage from an entire city.

276   277

Answers to in-text questions

a Methane

b One in which energy is released.

Summary answers

1 Biogas is a biofuel and is mainly methane with varying amounts of carbon dioxide, water and other gases. It is made by bacteria anaerobically breaking down plant and animal waste material that contains carbohydrates.

2 **a** More than one generator is needed. As one is being cleaned out, another is producing gas.

   b A batch-type digester will use plant material rather than the waste needed for the other types shown. In some places animal waste may be in short supply, or there may be religious or hygiene objections to using waste, yet the batch digester can still be used to produce biogas.

B3 4.8

Making food production efficient

Specification link-up: Biology B3.4

- At each stage in a food chain, less material and less energy are contained in the biomass of the organisms. This means that the efficiency of food production can be improved by reducing the number of stages in food chains. *[B3.4.4 a)]*
- The efficiency of food production can also be improved by restricting energy loss from food animals by limiting their movement and by controlling the temperature of their surroundings. *[B3.4.4 b)]*

Learning objectives

Students should learn:

- that at each stage in a food chain, less material and less energy are contained in the biomass of the organisms
- that the efficiency of food production can be improved by reducing the number of stages in food chains
- that the efficiency of food production can also be improved by restricting energy losses from food animals.

Learning outcomes

Most students should be able to:

- describe food chains associated with food production
- explain that reducing the number of stages in the food chains makes food production more efficient
- describe ways in which energy losses by animals can be reduced.

Some students should also be able to:

- compare the costs and benefits of intensive farming with those of free-range farming.

Lesson structure

Starters

The great taste test – If it is allowed (use a home economics room), and under controlled conditions (check for allergies etc.), provide small samples of burgers/sausages made with meat and meat substitutes. Ask for volunteers to feel and smell the samples (blindfold them first) to see if they can distinguish those products made from meat and those from meat substitutes. Discuss the results and look at what the substitutes are made from. *(5 minutes)*

How many food chains in my lunch? – Show the contents of three typical lunch boxes, but vary the main component. For example, one could have a cheese or egg sandwich, another pork pie or sausage roll and the third a portion of pasta salad. Ask the students to work out the food chains. Ask: 'Which has the fewest stages?' Support students by providing the stages jumbled up and get them to sort them into the correct chains. Extend students by asking them to work out which is the most efficient in terms of energy. *(10 minutes)*

Main

- Show photographs of factory farming – include reference to battery hens, intensive rearing of pigs, veal calves and fish. There are a number of websites with down-loadable pictures and videos, but most of them are aimed at vegetarians and some have a biased view. Try to stick to the facts, so that students can debate the issues later. Emphasise the way in which controlling temperature and limiting movement reduces energy losses. Encourage students to keep a balanced view.

- Students could write a short speech in support of the intensive rearing of chickens and one against. Each speech should include scientific facts and advantages as well as disadvantages. In the lesson, hold a debate, but students to draw lots, as to which side to support, i.e. which of their speeches to read out. In this way, they appreciate that they need to have a balanced view.

- In the suggestion above, the issue of the intensive rearing of chickens has been chosen, but you may wish to broaden the topic to include intensive rearing of any animals. Students may need homework time to prepare their speeches.

- Invite any vegetarians in the class to give a presentation about their diet. If there are none, then invite a member of staff or the person responsible for home economics to give a presentation. This exercise is about eating more plant food rather than the ethical issues, so the emphasis is on the types of food they eat and the variety. Try to make it as scientific as possible, students identifying where their essential nutrients are coming from. If possible, suggest they bring in recipes or samples of food. This makes a good link with food and nutrition/home economics. If the laboratory is not a suitable place for trying out foods, then perhaps the use of the home economics room can be negotiated.

- Following the exercise above, some discussion on the nature of proteins from plants could be appropriate. The concept of essential amino acids and fatty acids (without necessarily naming them) could be introduced. The different types of vegetarian (vegans, ovolacto- and pesco-vegetarians) could be researched, described and the balance of their diets discussed.

- Link with reference to staple foods, which are based mainly on vegetables, in the developing countries of the world.

- Display the constituents of a meal, or the packaging from produce, making sure that some of it has come from other countries. Get the students to work out the food miles involved. Discuss the efficiency of this and why it is done.

Answers to in-text questions

a Any sensible choices.

b Because as little of the biomass produced by plants as possible would be wasted as there are less steps in the food chain.

Support

- Get students to make a collage of items to include in a balanced lunch that does not include any meat. They could use pictures, packets and wrappers to make it colourful.

Extend

- Ask students to research the different types of vegetarianism and to suggest how each type gets the right type of proteins, vitamins and minerals without eating meat.

Plenaries

Eat less meat – Students to write down five ways in which they could change their own diets to eat less meat protein without eating less protein. Choose some to read out. *(5 minutes)*

Food chains – loss at each stage? Ask the students to draw out a simple food chain. Ask them to think about each level and how the energy that was passed from the previous level can be lost without being passed on to the next level. Support students by giving clue sheets for energy-loss mechanisms. Extend students by giving factual data on respiration rates and food intake and energy content. *(10 minutes)*

How humans can affect the environment

B3 4.8   Making food production efficient

Learning objectives
- Why do short food chains make food production more efficient?
- How can we manage food production to reduce energy losses?

links

For information on pyramids of biomass, look back to B1 5.1 Pyramids of biomass.

Figure 1 Reducing the number of stages in food chains could dramatically increase the efficiency of our food production. Eating less meat would mean more food for everyone.

links

For information on energy losses between trophic levels, look back to B1 5.2 Energy transfers.

Pyramids of biomass show us that the organisms at each successive stage of a food chain contain less material and therefore less energy. This has major implications for the way we produce food.

Food chains in food production

In the developed world much of our diet consists of meat or other animal products such as eggs, cheese and milk. The cows, goats, pigs and sheep that we use to produce our food eat plants. By the time it reaches us, much of the energy from the plant has been used up.

In some cases we even feed animals to animals. Ground up fish, for example, is often part of commercial pig and chicken feed. This means we have put another extra stage into the food chain. It goes from plant to fish, fish to pig, pig to people, making it even less efficient.

a Name three animals that we use for food.

There is a limited amount of the Earth's surface that we can use to grow food. The most energy-efficient way to use this food is to grow plants and eat them directly. If we only ate plants, then in theory there would be plenty of food for everyone on the Earth. Biomass produced by plants would be used to feed people and produce human biomass.

However, every extra stage we introduce results in less energy getting to us at the end of the chain. An example is feeding plants to animals before we eat the food ourselves. In turn this means less food to go around the human population.

b Why would there be more food for everyone if we all ate only plants?

Artificially managed food production **k**

As you saw in B1 5.2, animals don't turn all of the food they eat into new animal. Some of the food can't be digested and is lost as waste. Energy is also used in moving around and maintaining a constant body temperature.

Farmers apply these ideas to food production to make it more efficient. People want meat, eggs and milk – but they want them as cheaply as possible. So farmers want to get the maximum possible increase in biomass from animals without feeding them extra food. There are two ways of doing this:

- Limiting the movement of food animals: then they don't use much energy in moving their muscles and so have more biomass available from their food for growth.
- Controlling the temperature of their surroundings: then the animals will not have to use much energy keeping warm or cooling down. Again, this leaves more biomass spare for growth.

Controlling these factors means keeping the animals inside with restricted space to move, and a constant ideal temperature. This is what happens in the massive poultry rearing sheds where the majority of the chickens that we eat are produced.

Birds kept in these sheds can be ready to eat in a matter of weeks. They always have plenty of food but there is not much room to move. There is a risk of disease spreading quickly through the animals as they are so close together. They need constant monitoring, which costs money, but they can be sold for meat very quickly. Animals reared in this way can appear more like factory products than farm animals. That's why these intensive methods are sometimes referred to as factory farming.

Intensive farming methods are used because there has been a steady increase in demand for cheap meat and animal products. This is the only way farmers can meet these demands from consumers.

On the other hand, these animals live very unnatural and restricted lives. In comparison, birds reared outside grow more slowly but have a better quality of life. It takes more space, the weather can be a problem and it is a slower process but there is no heating or lighting to pay for.

More people are now aware of how our cheap meat and eggs are produced. As a result there has been a backlash against the conditions in which intensively reared animals live. Increasingly, intensive systems are being developed with far greater awareness of animal welfare issues. Contented animals gain biomass more quickly than stressed ones, so everyone benefits.

Food miles

Another aspect of efficiency in food production is how far the food travels. Food produced around the world can travel thousands of miles to reach your plate. This uses fuel, which increases the amount of carbon dioxide in the atmosphere. People are more aware of these 'food miles' now and many people try to buy meat, fruit and vegetables which have been grown relatively locally.

Figure 2 Intensively reared chickens versus free-range chickens

?? Did you know ...?

The biggest herd of dairy cows in the world is in Saudi Arabia, where 37 000 cows are all kept inside water-cooled buildings.

Study tip

Be clear about the ways in which the efficiency of food production can be improved to meet the needs of a growing human population. Make sure you are aware of the advantages and disadvantages of each method.

Key points

- Biomass and energy are reduced at each stage of a food chain. The efficiency of food production is improved by reducing the number of stages in our food chains.
- If you stop animals moving about and keep them warm, they waste less energy, making food production more efficient.

Summary questions

1 Copy and complete using the words below:
movement food chain biomass material temperature energy efficiency
At each stage in a .... less .... and less .... are contained in the .... of the organisms. Farmers improve the .... of food production by limiting .... and controlling the ....

2 Why are animals prevented from moving much and kept indoors in intensive farming?

3 a What are the advantages and disadvantages for a farmer of rearing animals intensively?
b What are the advantages and disadvantages of less intensive rearing methods?

278 / 279

Further teaching suggestions

What goes into animal feed?
- Cattle and sheep have a low protein conversion efficiency (PCE), because their natural diet is so high in carbohydrates that they have to digest and convert it into proteins. Pigs and poultry have a higher PCE and can be fed diets containing more protein. Students need to investigate the feeding of pigs and poultry in intensive systems in relation to the number of stages in the food chain.

How yellow is my yolk – or is battery best?
- It is often said that the best, most nutritious eggs have the brightest yellow yolks. Students could find out if this is true. Hard-boil an egg from each of the following sources: a battery farm, a deep litter or barn system and free range. Remove the shells, slice the eggs and compare the colour of the yolks (no tasting). Ask: 'Is there a difference? If so, can you work out why?'

Summary answers

1 food chain, material/energy, energy/material, biomass, efficiency, movement, temperature

2 Movement uses energy, so the less the animals move, the more energy is available for conversion into biomass. Animals that are kept indoors can have their temperatures controlled, so they don't use energy generating extra heat if temperatures fall, or sweating to lose heat if temperatures get too hot. Again this maximises the conversion of food to biomass.

3 a **Advantages:** Work indoors, animals grow faster so can be sold sooner and next lot started off.
Disadvantages: He has to heat animal houses, light animal houses, build animal houses and animals may be stressed, higher feed bills.

b **Advantages:** Animals reared more naturally (more contented?), animals healthier so lower vets bills, no heating/lighting bills, lower feed bills.
Disadvantages: Have to deal with the weather, animals grow more slowly, need land.

B3 4.9 Sustainable food production

Learning objectives

Students should learn:

- that there is a demand for increased food production as the human population increases
- that it is important to manage the oceans in order to conserve fish stocks
- that the production of mycoprotein is an example of sustainable food production.

Learning outcomes

Most students should be able to:

- explain the need for increased food production
- describe ways in which fish stocks can be maintained
- describe the production of mycoprotein.

Some students should also be able to:

- assess the success of conservation methods in maintaining fish stocks.

Support

- Encourage the development of school gardens especially those designed to produce fresh vegetables on a daily basis by students throughout the year. Examples would include sequential sowing of salad crops, soft fruit varieties which crop in different seasons etc.

Extend

- Ask students to design a biosphere food sustainability unit for a deep space mission. All the organisms must relate to each other in a way which will ensure that the conditions necessary for human life will be maintained. Searching the internet for a clip from the film *Silent Running* showing biodomes of this nature may be helpful.

Specification link-up: Biology B3.4

- Fish stocks in the oceans are declining. It is important to maintain fish stocks at a level where breeding continues or certain species may disappear altogether in some areas. Net size and fishing quotas play an important role in conservation of fish stocks. *[B3.4.4 c)]*
- The fungus Fusarium is useful for producing mycoprotein, a protein-rich food suitable for vegetarians. The fungus is grown on glucose syrup, in aerobic conditions, and the biomass is harvested and purified. *[B3.4.4 d)]*

Lesson structure

Starters

Tiger tail and chips, please! – Show an image of a tiger tail. Suppose that tiger tail was on the menu at your local restaurant. How would you respond? What if what was on the menu was an accepted part of social eating in your country? Would that make a difference? How would you respond personally? Discuss in pairs, then as a class. *(5 minutes)*

Born this lesson – If this was not done previously, project, from the internet, a live count of the estimated world population (www.worldometers.info). Have a student write down a start figure at the beginning of the lesson. Run a clock for a minute and make a note of the rate at which the number is growing. Carry out some simple maths to find growth per hour and per day. Discuss this in terms of global food production. Support students by giving them framework sheets for the maths. Extend students by getting them to estimate rate of growth per year and ask whether the growth will be linear, and if not why not? *(10 minutes)*

Main

- Search the internet for mycoprotein for information about the production of Quorn. Look for diagrams and flow charts showing the steps in production, together with information about the nutritional content.
- A worksheet could be created for students, so that they can build up a resource for themselves, which encompasses the manufacturing process and the nutritional benefits.
- Using meat sausages and Quorn sausages on cocktail sticks, students could carry out a survey amongst the students of a different year group to determine whether they can distinguish between the meat and the Quorn (use a home economics room for tasting). Announce the results on posters around the school.
- Quorn is not the only example of a food stuff produced by microorganisms. Other examples include 'Pruteen', 'Pekilo', spirulina and 'Toprina G'. Students could research one of these products and find out the organism used, the substrates it grows on, the product and what it is used for. Ask: 'What are the major disadvantages of single cell proteins? Why is it not more widely used?'
- Students could consider the consequences of a government decision that the eating of animals should be banned and that the nation should eat more protein from microorganisms. Ask: 'What would it mean to the farming industry? How much would it cost? What would be the long-term consequences?'
- Use PowerPoint and exposition to go over ways in which fish stocks can be conserved e.g. net size, quotas of catches, closed seasons, non-fished areas, reduced number of boats licensed, reduced number of days at sea, etc.

Plenaries

Fishy tales – Ask students to write a note from a concerned parent fish regarding her thousands of offspring and the likelihood or otherwise that they will come to attain her ripe old age. Differentiation by outcome – extension level students will produce imaginative and extended prose. Support level students may produce much more limited offerings. *(5 minutes)*

Mycoprotein advert – Ask the students to produce a short commercial advert for mycoprotein. This could be in any medium – art, cartoon, video, PowerPoint, wav file, etc. Peer assess the results and produce constructive commentary on which parts went well and ways to improve the advert. *(10 minutes)*

Further teaching suggestions

Compose a limerick ...

- Students to produce a limerick by completing the following 'A man who ate nothing but Quorn ... '. Students to work in groups and then read out the results.

Sushied to death

- Give the students computer access and ask them to research the plight of the blue fin tuna which is highly in demand as an edible fish despite being increasingly endangered due to overfishing. Have the students discuss this and draw out some ideas on how the practice could be curtailed.

Answers to in-text questions

a An enforced limit to the number, type and size of fish a fisherman can catch.

b Every 5 hours.

How humans can affect the environment

B3 4.9

Sustainable food production

Learning objectives

- What is sustainable food production?
- Can we use fungi to make sustainable food?

As the human population keeps increasing, we are becoming more aware of the need for sustainable food production. This means producing food in ways that can continue for many years. It involves maintaining the health of the soil so that plant crops grow well year after year. It also involves taking care of the fish stocks in our oceans so they do not run out.

Figure 1 Many scientists think that only a complete fishing ban can save the bluefin tuna. It has been overfished almost to extinction in spite of net size control and fishing quotas.

Managing the oceans

People have fished for food throughout human history. However, in the past 60 years or so commercial fishing fleets of large factory ships have built up. These are capable of taking huge quantities of fish on a regular basis. The result of this uncontrolled overfishing is that stocks of edible fish are falling. In some areas, such as the North Sea, they are becoming dangerously low. That's because almost all of the breeding fish have been caught.

It is important to maintain fish stocks at a level where breeding continues successfully. Otherwise certain species, such as cod and bluefin tuna, may disappear completely in some areas (Figure 1). People have been warning about the problems of overfishing for years. Numbers of some fish are so low they could disappear altogether. Finally, serious restrictions on fishing are being put in place.

Ways in which we can conserve fish populations include controlling the size of the holes in the nets. Then only the biggest fish are caught. There can also be bans on fishing in the breeding season and very strict quotas imposed on fishermen. This means they have a strictly enforced limit on the amount and type of fish they are allowed to catch.

Only with protection like this will we be able to conserve the fish stocks. Then we will be able to fish them sustainably for years to come.

a What is a fishing quota?

Mycoprotein production

Almost 30 years ago a completely new food based on fungi was developed. It is known as mycoprotein, which means 'protein from fungus'. It is produced using the fungus *Fusarium*. This grows and reproduces rapidly on a relatively cheap sugar syrup (made from waste starch) in large specialised containers called fermenters. *Fusarium* needs aerobic conditions to grow successfully. In optimum conditions it can double its mass every five hours! Because the fungi use cheap food and reproduce rapidly this is a very sustainable food source.

The fermenter is designed to react to changes, keeping the conditions as stable as possible (Figure 2). This means we can get the maximum yield. The fermenters have:

- an air supply to provide oxygen for respiration of the fungi
- a stirrer to keep the microorganisms in suspension. This maintains an even temperature and makes sure that oxygen and food are evenly spread throughout the mixture
- a water-cooled jacket, which removes the excess energy released by the respiring fungi. Any rise in temperature is used to heat the water, which is constantly removed and replaced with more cold water
- measuring instruments that constantly monitor factors such as the pH and temperature so that changes can be made if necessary.

b How quickly can *Fusarium* double its mass when conditions are right?

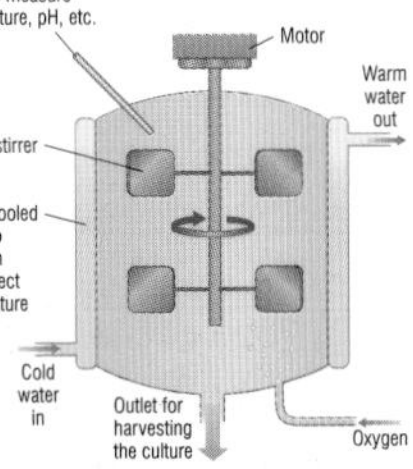

The fungal biomass is harvested and purified. Then it is dried and processed to make mycoprotein. This is a pale yellow solid with a faint taste of mushrooms. On its own it has very little flavour.

However, mycoprotein is given a range of textures and flavours to make it similar to many familiar foods (Figure 3). It is a high-protein, low-fat meat substitute. The protein content of mycoprotein is similar to that of prime beef. So it is used by vegetarians and people who want to reduce the fat in their diet.

When mycoprotein was first developed people thought a world food shortage was on its way. They were looking for new ways to make protein cheaply and efficiently. The food shortage never happened, but the fungus-based food continued. It is versatile, high in protein and fibre, low in fat and calories and very sustainable, so is widely used in the developed world.

Probe to measure temperature, pH, etc.

Motor

Warm water out

Paddle stirrer

Water-cooled jacket to maintain the correct temperature

Cold water in

Outlet for harvesting the culture

Oxygen

Figure 2 Conditions inside the fermenters used to culture microorganisms such as *Fusarium* are kept as stable as possible

Figure 3 Mycoprotein can be made to look like meat, chicken, fish or burgers. It is very versatile.

Study tip

Make sure you understand the meaning of 'sustainable food production'. Humans need food now but also need to plan for feeding the next generation.

Summary questions

1 Copy and complete these sentences using the words below:
species declining conserve disappear stocks breeding
Fish .... in the oceans are .... It is important to .... fish stocks at a level where .... continues or certain .... may .... completely.

2 **a** How has the fishing industry reached crisis point?
  b How can fish stocks be protected?
  c Why do you think these measures were not put in place a long time ago?

3 Mycoprotein is an example of sustainable food production. Explain how it is similar to and how it differs from intensive farming.

Key points

- Sustainable food production means producing food in a way which can continue for many years.
- It is important to control net size and impose fishing quotas to conserve fish stocks, so breeding continues and the decline in numbers is halted.
- The fungus *Fusarium* is grown on sugar syrup in aerobic conditions to produce mycoprotein foods.

280

281

Summary answers

1 stocks, declining , conserve, breeding, species, disappear

2 a Development of large commercial fleets and huge factory ships have overfished the seas.

  b Methods include controlling the size of the holes in the nets so only the largest fish are caught, banning fishing during the breeding season and strict catch quotas.

  c Because people earn a living from fishing and didn't want to lose their income, no-one believed it would happen; sea is big and seemed as if supply of fish is endless; any sensible points.

3 Similar: the fermenter like the enclosed shed or barn; the temperature is regulated and food supply (glucose) maintained to give the organism (*Fusarium*) the optimum conditions for maximum growth as fast as possible; cost of maintaining conditions outweighed by increase in production.

  Differs: fungus not an animal so conditions cause no stress – in fact ideal conditions; pH not monitored and maintained in farming; no free-range alternative.

Learning objectives

Students should learn:

- that humans can affect the global environment
- that the need for food and water can upset ecosystems
- that the repeatability, reproducibility and validity of environmental data should be evaluated before conclusions are drawn.

Learning outcomes

Most students should be able to:

- understand that humans can affect the environment locally and globally
- describe ways in which maintaining the supply of food and water for humans can affect ecosystems
- evaluate the methods used to collect data used as evidence for environmental change.

Some students should also be able to:

- evaluate the positive and negative effects of managing food production
- recognise that practical solutions for human needs may require compromises.

Support

- Provide students with discussion packs showing environmental impacts of various kinds along with simple comment cards. They should match the card to the picture.

Extend

- Get students to look at a food production system in detail and evaluate it in terms of the positive and negative effects that it has, introducing the concept of cost/benefit analysis.

Specification link-up: Biology B3.4

- Evaluate methods used to collect environmental data and consider their validity and reliability as evidence for environmental change. [B3.4]
- Evaluate the methods being used to feed and provide water to an increasing human population, both in terms of short term and long term effects. [B3.4]
- Evaluate the positive and negative effects of managing food production and distribution, and be able to recognise that practical solutions for human needs may require compromise between competing priorities. [B3.4]

Lesson structure

Starters

Photo response – Show the students a short series of photographs chosen so that they show a range of environments from pristine beautiful wilderness through farmland to industrial complexes. Include some that show human intervention in nature in a good light, such as gardens etc. Do not comment on the photographs as you project them nor let the students comment, but they can write down responses if they like. Show the series again, this time taking comments from the students and using their responses alone to build up a picture of how they are thinking about human interactions with the environment. *(5 minutes)*

Humanless Earth! – Ask the students to imagine that all humans caught a very contagious fatal disease and that the species was wiped out in a very short space of time. How would the Earth be different? Get the students to list the changes that would take place. Support students by giving some prompts in order to remind them of the effects humans have on the environment. Extend students by asking them to postulate as to the evolutionary future of the Earth under such circumstances? Would another super-dominant intelligent species arise? What might they look like and what might their fate be? *(10 minutes)*

Main

- Following on from one of the Starters, draw out the current level of student understanding of the concepts and vocabulary covered by this unit. Use examples and illustrations to deepen the students' understanding of the topic.
- Ask the students to write out a brief summary of the points previously made and then to swap and peer mark these, giving commentary on what went well and also how their summary could be improved.
- Consider the environmental impact of a dam and reservoir. As suggested in the Student Book, find out information about the building of a dam and reservoir. What effect did it have on the local population and on the local environment? What are the benefits and problems of the project? There are several examples of reservoir-building in the UK and there may be one local to the school which students could research.
- Ask students 'What can we do to make a difference?' Make a list of the environmental problems that have been raised in this chapter, such as greenhouse gases, global warming, food and water supplies. Get the students, working in groups, to research these issues and produce web pages for the school. They could suggest ways in which individuals and groups can conserve resources and change attitudes.

Plenaries

What a wonderful world! – Ask the students to imagine what the world would be like if all of the food and environmental problems had been solved at some time in the distant future. What would this world be like? What features would it have? Briefly discuss this in small groups then feed back to the whole class. Play the Louis Armstrong song of the same name as the title as background music. *(5 minutes)*

Feed me! – Ask the students to write an outline plan for a story for small children about an infant who demands to be fed all the time, with disastrous consequences for the poor parents and for the surrounding environment. Familiarise the students with the style of these stories, (repetition, patterns, short sentences, etc.) in advance. Read out some examples on completion. Support students by giving them a series of pictures to add comments to and a list of comments to choose from. Extend students by getting them to make the story rhyme. *(10 minutes)*

Further teaching suggestions

Keeping records
- Discuss with students the importance of monitoring climatic factors over a long period of time. Discuss the value of taking daily temperature readings. What can these show? Are there are other climatic factors that can be easily recorded and which might provide evidence for climate change?

Weather or climate?
- Discuss the difference between weather and climate with the students. It could be useful to refer to different climatic zones and the kind of weather associated with each. What is meant by 'weather patterns' and how may extreme weather patterns give an indication of climate change?

 *How Science Works* — How humans can affect the environment

B3 4.10 — Environmental issues

Learning objectives
- How do we affect the global environment?
- What sort of data have we got about environmental issues?
- How strong is the evidence for environmental change?

Figure 1 When the Aswan dam was built in Egypt, 60 000 people lost their homes as Lake Nasser was formed

Activity 1
Find out about the environmental impact of a single dam and reservoir. Then make a list of all the benefits and problems caused by that single project and decide if you think the dam was a good idea.

⌒⌒ links
For information on hard evidence for the build-up of greenhouse gases, look back to B3 4.5 Global warming.

Food and water – a vicious circle?

As the world population grows, we need ever more food and water. However, the way in which we get that food and water can affect the environment both locally and globally. You have already seen how food production can affect the environment. One example is deforestation. Others are the growth of crops, such as rice, and the rearing of livestock, such as cattle. These last two increase the production of the greenhouse gas methane.

Yet people need water as much as food. It isn't just people either – crops and animals also need water. One way of supplying water is to build a dam. A dam creates a reservoir, which can be used as a source of clean water for drinking and irrigating crops. Unfortunately there can be many environmental problems as a result:

- Dams destroy river ecosystems, particularly below the dam, where the rivers may be lost completely. This can cause huge areas to dry out.
- Flood plains with their fertile soil disappear, so people can no longer grow the crops they need.
- Environments are destroyed as the reservoir forms and animals, plants and people lose their homes (Figure 1).
- Reservoirs act as breeding grounds for the mosquitoes that carry diseases such as malaria.
- Dams and reservoirs may even add to methane in the atmosphere as eutrophication can occur.

How can we be sure?

The build-up of greenhouse gases cannot be denied, because there is hard evidence for it. The great majority of scientists now think the evidence shows that global warming is at least partly linked to human activities such as the burning of fossil fuels and deforestation, but not everyone agrees.

Some extreme weather patterns have been recorded in recent years. Yet throughout history there is evidence of other, equally violent, weather patterns. These occurred long before fossil fuels were used so heavily and deforestation was happening. Also, weather is not the same as climate. Weather can change from day to day but climate is the weather in an area over a long period of time.

How valid, reproducible and repeatable are the data on which the ideas are based? Scientists measure the daily temperatures in many different places. They also look at how the temperature of the Earth has changed over time (Figure 2). They collect many different types of evidence. For example, they use cores of ice that are thousands of years old (Figure 3), the rings in the trunks of trees and the type of pollen found in peat bogs.

Much of the evidence is published in well-respected journals, but there are some controversies. In 2009, it emerged that some scientists in the UK had hidden data that showed that global temperatures were falling slightly rather than rising. The scientists support the idea that human activities are causing global warming and did not want to publish data which might challenge that idea.

The evidence continues to be collected. At the moment, most people and governments are convinced we need to change the way we live if we are to reduce the damage that global warming might do.

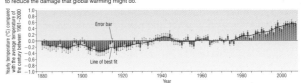

Figure 2 This graph shows how global surface temperatures have varied from the 1901–2000 mean over 130 years. These data are widely regarded as very reproducible and repeatable.

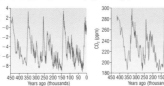

Figure 3 These graphs show data from the Vostok ice cores in Antarctica, giving evidence about temperature, carbon dioxide and dust levels over 420 000 years

Activity 2
Problems like greenhouse gas emissions, global warming and the management of food and water supplies for the world population can seem overwhelming. However, you can make a difference by the choices you make in everyday life.
- Research material on environmental problems.
- Carefully evaluate the evidence you find.
- Develop some web pages to be used by your school on environmental issues.
- Suggest ways in which individuals as well as governments can conserve resources and change attitudes.

Summary questions
1 Develop a spider diagram or flowchart to show how building a dam to produce water for people to drink can damage the environment.
2 Summarise the evidence shown on the graphs in Figures 2 and 3. Explain what they appear to show and how these data might be used as evidence for a human influence on global warming. What other data might you need to help confirm that conclusion?

Study tip
Media reports on environmental issues can be very confusing. If you are going to quote any, make sure that it is backed up by scientific evidence and not just an opinion.

Key points
- Methods used to produce food and water for people can have short- and long-term effects on the environment.
- There are a lot of data on environmental change. The validity, reproducibility and repeatability of all data must be evaluated before conclusions can be drawn.

282 / 283

Summary answers

1 Whatever your students produce will be personal to them and will reflect how they see priorities but all should include building a dam, providing clean water, reducing water-borne diseases, changing the water flow of local rivers/streams, flooding so loss of habitat for wildlife, loss of homes for people, creation of new habitats which can be positive and negative (e.g. malaria mosquito).

2 Figure 2 shows a general pattern that before the late 1930s, the mean global temperature each year was below the average for the century. And that from the late 1970s the mean global temperature has been above the average for the century. This data certainly suggests that global warming is taking place.

Figure 3 shows that there have been spikes in carbon dioxide, dust and temperature levels through the millennia. It shows that raised carbon dioxide levels are usually associated with raised mean temperature levels. That raised dust levels are usually associated with lower mean temperatures. This confirms our models of global warming and global dimming. We currently have raised carbon dioxide and raised temperature which ties in with data from Figure 2. Any other sensible suggestions.

Summary answers

1 a Building houses; shops, industrial sites and roads, for farming; for waste disposal; any other sensible suggestion.

b People need places to live; to buy food; to produce things they need; transport systems to move people and goods; to grow food; to get rid of waste and rubbish; any sensible suggestions

c Any two sensible suggestions, e.g.: recycle rubbish; build fewer houses; more flats which use up less land; use public transport so fewer roads needed, etc.

2 a Cars and factories produce sulfur dioxide and nitrogen oxides → up into the atmosphere → carried along by winds → dissolve in rain → fall as acid rain on land and in water.

b i 18 Tg per year **ii** As appropriate **iii** 4 Tg per year

c Sulfur dioxide emissions have fallen steadily and levelled out at a greatly reduced level. There are strict rules about the levels of sulfur dioxide and nitrogen oxides in the exhaust fumes of new cars – catalytic converters remove sulfur dioxide. Cleaner, low-sulfur fuels are used in cars and power stations. More electricity is generated from gas and nuclear power. Systems are used in power station chimneys that clean the flue gases.

3 a In summer months, plants photosynthesising a lot and growing fast take a lot of carbon dioxide out of the atmosphere. In winter, in all temperate regions, plants die back and trees lose their leaves so, much less photosynthesis takes place, so carbon dioxide levels rise.

b We can see the difference it makes when plants are actively photosynthesising in the summer, so we need plants there. If plants were not there to photosynthesise, imagine how carbon dioxide levels would build up, so it is vital to prevent deforestation.

c More people; more cars and factories means more CO_2; more deforestation means less uptake of CO_2; more paddy fields to grow rice to feed people means more methane; more cows to produce cheap beef also producing methane. These greenhouse gases could change the Earth's climate, producing more extreme weather events and altering rainfall and temperatures in different ways in different parts of the world. Any other sensible point.

d All sensible suggestions e.g. ice core data, measuring temperature at the surface of the Earth, monitoring weather patterns, tree rings, peat bog cores, etc. Most valid, repeatable and reproducible – data that can be checked and confirmed against other measures; data presented by groups without a bias; any sensible suggestions recognising that some data is more valid, repeatable and reproducible than others.

4 a The quality of biogas produced could be improved by changing the mix of bacteria in the fermenter and by changing the mix of waste put into the fermenter.

b **Reasons for could include:** could be done on a small scale; at a local level in schools or hospitals which produce a lot of waste; would be ecologically sound; could save money; could be done in villages and by farmers as well; bigger fermenters could be used at municipal tips.

Reasons against might include: smell; public health and hygiene issues; difficulty in collecting vegetable and food waste; many areas do not have animals; objections to the use of human waste.

Summary questions *k*

1 a List the main ways in which humans reduce the amount of land available for other living things.

b Explain why each of these land uses is necessary.

c Suggest ways in which two of these different types of land use might be reduced.

2 a Draw a flowchart showing acid rain formation.

b Look at Figure 3 in B3 4.3 Air pollution.

  i What was the level of sulfur emissions in 1980?

  ii What was the approximate level of sulfur in the air in the year that you were born? (Make sure you give your birth year.)

  iii What was the level of sulfur emissions in 2002?

c What do these data tell you about trends in the levels of sulfur emissions since 1980. Suggest explanations for the trends you have observed.

3 In Figure 1 in B3 4.5 Global warming, you can see clearly annual variations in the levels of carbon dioxide recorded each year. These fluctuations are thought to be due to seasonal changes in the way plants are growing and photosynthesising through the year.

a Explain how changes in plant growth and rate of photosynthesis might affect carbon dioxide levels.

b How could you use the evidence of this data to argue against deforestation?

c How is the ever-increasing human population affecting the build-up of greenhouse gases?

d What type of evidence is used to investigate the effect of this build-up of greenhouse gases on the climate of the Earth? Which types of evidence are most valid, repeatable and reproducible?

4 a Suggest ways in which people might improve the quality of biogas produced in their generators.

b Suggest reasons for and against the use of biogas generators and biogas in the UK.

5 Write a letter to your local authority, explaining why you think they should look into the idea of running all their vehicles – buses, emergency vehicles, etc. – on ethanol or gasohol. Explain the potential value of ethanol in helping to prevent the greenhouse effect and global warming.

6 Chicks grown for food arrive in the broiler house as 1-day-old chicks. They are slaughtered at 42 days of age when their mass is about 2 kg. The temperature, amount of food and water, and light levels are careful[ly] controlled. About 20 000 chickens are reared togethe[r] one house. The table below shows their average mas[s]

Age (days)	1	7	14	21	28	35
Mass (g)	36	141	404	795	1180	1657	1[...]

a Plot a graph to show the average growth rate (gai[n] mass) per chicken.

b Explain why the temperature is so carefully contro[lled] in the broiler house.

c Explain why so many birds are reared together in [a] relatively small area.

d Why are birds for eating reared like this?

e Draw a second line to show how you would expec[t] chicken reared outside in a free-range system to g[ain] in mass, and explain the difference.

7 Human cells cannot make some of the amino acids t[hat] we need. We must obtain these amino acids from ou[r] diet.

The table shows the amounts of four of these amino acids present in mycoprotein, in beef and in wheat.

Name of amino acid	Amount of amino acid per 100 g in mg			Daily amo[unt] needed [by] 70 kg hu[man] in m[g]
	Mycoprotein	Beef	Wheat	
lysine	910	1600	300	840
methionine	230	500	220	910
phenylalanine	540	60	680	980
threonine	610	840	370	490

A diet book states that mycoprotein is the best sourc[e of] amino acids for the human diet.

Evaluate this statement. It may help to calculate the percentage of the daily amount of each amino acid f[or] in the different foods. If there is obviously more than 100%, simply state that.

---

5 This letter would need to show a clear understanding of the science issues both in the production of ethanol and gasohol and also with respect to the greenhouse effect and global warming.

6 a [Marks for graph plotting, correct scale, labelled axes, axes correct way round, accurate points, suitable line through points.]

b Chickens use less energy maintaining their body temperature, so have more energy for growth.

c To make sure that they move as little as possible. Energy is used up in movement; less movement means more energy for growth and helps to maintain temperature.

d So that they grow as fast as possible to a weight when they can be eaten and another set of chickens start up; economic reasons.

e The line should be below the first line. Chickens outside use energy moving around and keeping warm or cool, so convert less biomass from their food for growth.

7 Mycoprotein has more than 100% of the lysine and threonine that we need. It has 25% of the methionine and 55% of the phenylalanine.
Beef also has more than 100% of the lysine and threonine that we need. It has 55% of the methionine but only 6% of the phenylalanine.
Wheat has less than 100% of all the amino acids.

Based on this analysis mycoprotein is the best source of protein for the human diet and the statement is correct. It has closest to 100%+ of these four amino acids. However, this is only out of the three food stuffs analysed, and only relates to the four amino acids given so it is not a complete analysis.

ractice questions

The diagram shows how the manure from a cow can be ecycled.

Choose the correct word to complete the sentences.

 i The gas used for cooking is .... (1)

   carbon dioxide   methane   nitrogen

 ii The gas released into the atmosphere is .... (1)

   carbon dioxide   methane   nitrogen

 iii The gas absorbed by the plants is .... (1)

   carbon dioxide   methane   nitrogen

 i Name the biological process that occurs in the biogas generator. (1)

 ii Name the organisms that are active in the biogas generator. (1)

 The biogas generator is built underground. Suggest two reasons for this. (2)

2 Humans need food, water and shelter. Large areas of land must be cleared to grow food or to build houses. Sometimes valleys are flooded in order to store water in reservoirs.

 a Land is usually cleared by cutting trees down. Give **two** disadvantages to the environment of removing trees. (2)

 b The cleared land may be used for rearing cattle or growing rice.
   i Name the **two** gases which increase in the atmosphere due to these activities. (2)
   ii Choose the correct answer to complete the sentence.
   These gases may contribute to .... (1)
   global warming   food production   deforestation

 c Water in reservoirs can sometimes be polluted by human farming activities. Explain how. (2)

3 *In this question you will be assesed on using good English, organising information clearly and using specialist terms where appropriate.*

 Producing food efficiently to feed an increasing human population is a challenge for farmers.

 Describe how farmers increase the efficiency of food production.

 You should refer to food chains and reducing energy loss in your answer. (6)

Kerboodle resources

Resources available for this chapter on Kerboodle are:

- Chapter map: How humans can affect the environment
- Bump up your grade: Deforestation mind map (B3 4.4)
- Extension: Just the facts (B3 4.5)
- Practical: Building a simple biogas generator (B3 4.7)
- Viewpoints: Chicken out (B3 4.8)
- Support: Chicken out (B3 4.8)
- Extension: Trouble at sea (B3 4.9)
- Interactive activity: How humans can affect the environment
- Revision podcast: How humans can affect the environment
- Test yourself: How humans can affect the environment
- On your marks: How humans can affect the environment
- Practice questions: How humans can affect the environment
- Answers to practice questions: How humans can affect the environment

---

Practical suggestions

Practicals	AQA	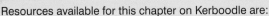		
Build a simple biogas generator to collect methane and demonstrate how the methane can be burned as a fuel.	✓	✓		
Investigate and design a way of measuring the gas output of a biogas generator and compare the amount of gas produced by different materials.	✓	✓		

Practice answers

1 a i methane (1 mark)
     ii carbon dioxide (1 mark)
     iii carbon dioxide (1 mark)

  b i fermentation/anaerobic respiration/anaerobic digestion/anaerobic decomposition (1 mark)
     ii microorganisms/bacteria/decomposing bacteria/ correctly named (1 mark)

  c Any **two** from:
    keeps it warm/maintains suitable temperature/
    allows manure to drain down/
    reference to unsightly above ground/takes up space
    on the field (2 marks)

2 a Increase of carbon dioxide (in atmosphere);
    decrease in biodiversity (2 marks)
    allow impact on soil stability/increased risk of flooding

  b i carbon dioxide;
       methane (2 marks)
     ii global warming (1 mark)

  c pesticides/herbicides/other named chemical/toxic chemical;
    may be washed from the land into the water (2 marks)

3 There is a clear, detailed answer which includes a description of energy loss through the food chain and methods of reducing energy loss in farm animals. The answer shows almost faultless spelling, punctuation and grammar. It is coherent and in an organised, logical sequence. It contains a range of appropriate or relevant specialist terms used accurately. (5–6 marks)

There is a description which includes a description of energy loss through the food chain and methods of reducing energy loss in farm animals. There are some errors in spelling, punctuation and grammar. The answer has some structure and organisation. The use of specialist terms has been attempted, but not always accurately. (3–4 marks)

There is a brief description of energy loss through the food chain and an attempt to describe methods of reducing energy loss in animals, which has little clarity and detail. The spelling, punctuation and grammar are very weak. The answer is poorly organised with almost no specialist terms and/or their use demonstrating a general lack of understanding of their meaning. (1–2 marks)

No relevant content. (0 marks)

Examples of biology points made in the response:

- plants capture solar energy
- some energy from plants is not transferred to herbivores
- description of why e.g. roots may not be eaten
- herbivores do not transfer all the energy into growth
- the more stages in a food chain – the more energy is 'lost'
- growing plant crops is more efficient
- farm animals/mammals/chickens move to find food
- use energy to maintain temperature/keep warm
- farmers restrict animal movements
- farmers keep animals warm.

Allow one reference to other methods of food production e.g. mycoprotein if in context of reducing energy losses.

Practice answers

1 blood is filtered; glucose is reabsorbed;
platelets are released; blood clots;
blood gets hot; skin looks red *(3 marks)*

2 a decrease *(1 mark)*

b increase *(1 mark)*

c increase *(1 mark)*

d decrease *(1 mark)*

e decrease *(1 mark)*

f stay the same *(1 mark)*

3 a xylem *(1 mark)*

b phloem *(1 mark)*

c root *(1 mark)*

4 a Any **two** from:
small fish could still grow;
small fish will not have a chance to breed;
fish stocks will decline *(2 marks)*

b less energy lost;
which could be used to let chickens grow more/produce
more eggs *(2 marks)*

c Any **one** of:
reduces biodiversity/loss of habitat;
less carbon locked up in wood;
increases carbon dioxide in the air/increases greenhouse
effect/may cause global warming *(1 mark)*

5 a i methane; *(1 mark)*
apply list principle;
allow symbols

ii <u>anaerobic</u> respiration/(anaerobic) fermentation
ignore decay/decomposition etc. *(1 mark)*

b i Any **two** from:
● manure disposed of
● gains fertiliser (for crops)
● gets (free) fuel **or** cheap supply of energy
  or (free) cooking/heating/lighting
  (allow converse
  allow not using wood/trees)
● can sell crops at higher price *(2 marks)*

ii <u>in the UK</u>
allow converse arguments for Sri Lanka;
lower temperature
or
not enough heat;
ignore other factor(s);
process is slower
or
enzyme action slower;
ignore references to efficiency/'bacteria working' *(2 marks)*

6 a sucrose → smaller (molecules)
or it gives simple sugars/glucose/fructose
(products) can be absorbed/taken in *(2 marks)*
if answer refers to digestion, assume reference is to
products

b i only small increase in yield at 25%
or not much difference in yield at 25%
extra cost/less economic if using 25% fungus
(2 marks)

ii Any sensible suggestion plus explanation e.g.:
● increased oxygen → increased respiration rate
(suggestion)
● less substrate available for making enzyme/toxic
product made
(explanation)
or
● more respiration occurs which releases
heat *(2 marks)*
must mention heat or temperature

Practice questions

1 Changes occur in the human body.
List A shows some causes.
List B shows some effects.
Match each cause with its correct effect.

List A	List B
blood is filtered	blood clots
platelets are released	glucose is reabsorbed
blood gets hot	skin looks red
	heart rate decreases

(3)

2 Choose the correct word or phrase to complete each sentence.
decrease   increase   stay the same
a When plant cells are transferred from warm water into cool water the rate of
diffusion will .... (1)
b When a human gets hot the rate of sweating will .... (1)
c When humans sweat a lot the concentration of their urine will .... (1)
d When humans lie down to rest their rate of breathing will .... (1)
e When insulin is released into the blood the level of blood sugar will .... (1)
f Dialysis fluid contains sugar and ions so that the concentration in the blood will
.... (1)

3 Flowering plants have transport systems.
Complete the following sentences.
a The tissue which transports water in a plant is .... (1)
b The tissue which transports sugar in a plant is .... (1)
c The organ which absorbs water from the soil is a .... (1)

4 Humans need food.
a Fishermen are not allowed to use nets that catch very small fish.
Explain why. (2)
b Some farmers keep their chickens in sheds.
Explain why. (2)
c Some people object to cutting down trees to clear land for food crops.
Give a reason why. (1)

5 Read the passage below about biogas production in Sri Lanka, which is a country with
a much warmer climate than the UK.

Mr Ratnayake is a farmer. Using nothing more than cow dung, he has enough power to cook and
provide heat and light for his home without using a single piece of wood. He collects the manure from
his cows in their cattle shed. He then mixes the manure with water and leaves it to ferment in a large
concrete pit. The gas produced is collected in a simple storage tank and is piped into his house for use.
The dried manure left after this biogas is generated is richer than ordinary manure. It makes a good
organic fertiliser for Mr Ratnayake's crops. He can then sell his crops at a higher price as they are
organic produce.

http://www.i-sis.org.uk

286

a i   What is the fuel gas present in biogas?   (1)
   ii   Name the process that produces biogas.   (1)
b i   Give **two** ways in which Mr Ratnayake benefits from making biogas as described
       in the passage.   (2)
   ii This design of biogas generator works well in Sri Lanka. It would not work so
       well in the UK. Explain why.   (2)
                                                                        AQA, 2009

Microorganisms are often used in the industrial production of useful substances.
The fungus, *Penicillium chrysogenum*, can be used to make an enzyme that digests the
sugar sucrose. When it is growing in a medium containing sucrose, the fungus releases
this enzyme into the surrounding solution.

a Explain why it is useful to the fungus to release the enzyme into the surrounding
   solution.   (2)
b Before setting up an industrial fermenter, laboratory-scale investigations are carried
   out to find the best conditions to use.
   A manufacturer investigated the effect of changing several factors on the amount of
   enzyme produced by the fungus. The results are shown in the table.

Condition	Concentration of enzyme produced in arbitrary units		
	24 hours	72 hours	120 hours
Amount of fungus added as %			
1	9.0	28.8	44.4
5	7.2	54.0	60.0
25	6.0	66.0	62.4
Aeration rate in arbitrary units			
0.5	9.0	36.0	45.8
1.0	7.2	54.0	60.0
2.0	10.8	43.2	52.8
Sucrose concentration at start as %			
4	7.2	54.0	60.0
8	3.0	29.7	48.3
12	0	54.0	21.6

The manufacturer decided to use the following conditions:

*   amount of fungus = 5%
*   aeration rate = 1.0 arbitrary units
*   time = 72 hours.

Suggest an explanation for each of the following.

i   The manufacturer decided to add 5% fungus rather than 25%.   (2)
ii The concentration of enzyme produced at an aeration rate of 2.0 arbitrary units
    was less than the concentration at an aeration rate of 1.0 arbitrary units.   (2)
                                                                        AQA, 2006

Commentary

Percentages can prove difficult – advise candidates that the answer will usually be less than 100% and they should always show their working.

Notes